POLITICAL SCIENCE
RESEARCH METHODS

POLITICAL SCIENCE
RESEARCH METHODS

SEVENTH EDITION

Janet Buttolph Johnson
University of Delaware

H. T. Reynolds
University of Delaware

Los Angeles | London | New Delhi
Singapore | Washington DC

Los Angeles | London | New Delhi
Singapore | Washington DC

FOR INFORMATION:

CQ Press
An Imprint of SAGE Publications, Inc.
2455 Teller Road
Thousand Oaks, California 91320
E-mail: order@sagepub.com

SAGE Publications Ltd.
1 Oliver's Yard
55 City Road
London, EC1Y 1SP
United Kingdom

SAGE Publications India Pvt. Ltd.
B 1/I 1 Mohan Cooperative Industrial Area
Mathura Road, New Delhi 110 044
India

SAGE Publications Asia-Pacific Pte. Ltd.
33 Pekin Street #02-01
Far East Square
Singapore 048763

Acquisitions Editor: Charisse Kiino
Production Editor: Sarah Fell
Copy Editor: Paula Fleming
Typesetter: C&M Digitals (P) Ltd.
Cover Designer: Kimberly Glyder Design
Marketing Manager: Chris O'Brien

Printed in the United States of America

Library of Congress Cataloging-in-Publication Data

Johnson, Janet Buttolph
Political science research methods/Janet Buttolph Johnson, H. T. Reynolds. — 7th ed.

p. cm.
Includes index.

ISBN 978-1-60871-689-0 (pbk.: alk. paper)

1. Political science—Research—Methodology. I. Reynolds, H. T. (Henry T.) II. Title.

JA71.J55 2011
320.072—dc23   2011038951

This book is printed on acid-free paper.

12 13 14 15 10 9 8 7 6 5 4 3 2

To the instructors and students
who have used this book over the years
J. B. J.

To my friends and family
H. T. R.

Brief Table of Contents

Contents

Tables, Figures, and Features

TABLES

FIGURES

HELPFUL HINTS

Chapter 2

Chapter 3

Chapter 5

Chapter 6

Chapter 13

Preface

The first question a student is likely to ask is, "I'm interested in government and politics. Why do I have to study research design, question wording, document analysis, and statistics?" Our goal in *Political Science Research Methods* is to address this question by demonstrating that with a modicum of effort, undergraduates can analyze many seemingly complicated political issues and controversies in ways that go far beyond accounts in the popular press and the political arena.

Political Science Research Methods, now in its seventh edition, continues to hold true to the three primary objectives that have guided us since the book's inception. Our first objective is to illustrate important aspects of the research process and to demonstrate that political scientists can produce worthwhile knowledge about significant political phenomena using the methods we describe in this book. To show this as vividly as possible, we begin again with several case studies of political science research drawn from different areas of the discipline that address key issues and controversies in the study of politics. We also made changes to fulfill our other two objectives: (1) to give readers the tools necessary to conduct their own empirical research projects and evaluate others' research and (2) to help students with limited mathematical backgrounds understand the statistical calculations that are part of social science research. Though we are increasingly concentrating on what various procedures can (and cannot) tell us about the real world, we've tried to separate computational details from the narrative (many equations have been placed in "How It's Done" boxes). The book also makes an effort to encourage students to understand and think about the practical and theoretical implications of statistical results. Because statistics often intimidates students, we strive to present the information as gently as possible. To this end, we have significantly reworked several chapters to provide more intuitive introductions to some of the field's most important methods. We hope that by meeting these goals, this book will continue to satisfy the needs of our undergraduate and graduate students as they embark on their studies in the field.

STRUCTURE AND ORGANIZATION OF THE BOOK

Because research methods may overwhelm some students at first, we have gone to some length (in the first chapter especially but throughout the book) to stress that seemingly esoteric topics can be relevant to the understanding of current events. This book is organized to show that research starts with ideas and then follows a series of logical steps. Chapter 1 introduces the case studies that are integrated into our discussion of the research process in the subsequent chapters. We chose these cases, which form the backbone of the book, to demonstrate a wide range of research topics within the discipline of political science: American politics, public administration, international relations, comparative politics, and public policy. We refer to these cases throughout the book to demonstrate the issues, choices, decisions, and obstacles that political scientists typically confront while doing research. We want to show what takes place behind the scenes in the production of research, and the best way to do this is to refer to actual articles. The advantage to this approach, which we feel has been borne out by the book's success over the years, is that it helps students relate substance to methods. For this edition, we updated and extended the example on income inequality and redistribution in Organisation for Economic Co-operation and Development (OECD) countries to include research into the causes of income inequality in the United States. This topic still links nicely to the example on voter turnout, which has also been updated. The example of control of the bureaucracy now mentions research on the role of interest groups in congressional oversight of agency decisions. Our discussion of research into human rights abuse tracks the evolution of that topic. Finally, we changed the example concerning public opinion about US military involvement in foreign affairs; we refer to recent research on public responses to alternative ways of framing the debate over whether the United States should continue prosecution of the Iraq war.

Chapter 2 examines the definition of scientific research and the development of empirical political science. We discuss the role of theory in the research process and review some of the debates in modern and contemporary political science. In response to adopter input, chapter 3 now focuses on the task of helping students to identify and refine appropriate research topics. For adopters who plan to have their students conduct independent research projects, it makes sense for this topic to occur earlier in the discussion of the research process. This chapter now contains an extended discussion of how to write a literature review. Chapters 4 and 5 address the building blocks of social scientific research: hypotheses, core concepts, variables, and measurements. Chapter 6 covers research design with an expanded discussion of small-N studies and includes a handy table that summarizes and compares the features of alternative research designs. Chapter 7, on sampling, precedes the chapters on data collection, based on the reasoning that sampling is not used solely by those conducting survey research but also by those using other data collection methods. It is also important background information for anyone interested in public policy and current events.

Chapters 8 through 10 discuss data collection, with an emphasis on the research methods that political scientists frequently employ and that students are likely to find useful in conducting or evaluating empirical research. We consider the principles of ethical research and the role of human subject review boards and note the ethical issues related to methods of data collection. We examine observation in Chapter 8 and document analysis and the use of aggregate data in chapter 9; the latter now includes an extended example of research based on content analysis. Chapter 10, on survey research, includes a discussion of questionnaire design and tips for face-to-face interviewing. In chapters 9 and 10, we include updated and Web-based sources of aggregate statistics and survey questions and data.

Chapters 11 through 14 focus on data analysis: How do we interpret data and present them to others? For this edition, we broke the introductory statistics chapter in two: one chapter for description, one for statistical inference. All four chapters contain updated examples and discussions. These are supplemented by a host of new figures and tables designed to illustrate the various techniques in as friendly and intuitive a way possible. We also strengthened the discussion of tests of statistical significance. Our goals are to make the logic of the tests more comprehensible and to stress the differences among statistical, theoretical, and practical significance. Chapter 14 includes material on logistic regression, an increasingly important statistical tool in social research. In all of this, we attempted to be as rigorous as possible without overwhelming readers with theoretical fine points or computational details. The content is still accessible to anyone with a basic understanding of high school algebra. Our goal, as always, is to provide an intuitive understanding of these sometimes intimidating topics without distorting the concepts or misleading our readers.

Finally, in chapter 15, we present a new research report, using a published journal article that investigates whether satisfaction with life is greater for citizens of countries with larger public sectors or for those who live in countries where the market plays a larger role. This research example ties in well with the research on income inequality used throughout the book to illustrate the research process. As in the past, this article is annotated, although we have changed the format so that students can see more clearly where in the article the authors address key aspects of the research process. We strongly suggest that instructors who assign a research paper have their students consult the example in this chapter and use it to pattern their own writing.

In addition to the "How It's Done" feature, the "Helpful Hints" boxes, highlighted by the light bulb icon, continue to give students practical tips. There are several new ones in this edition, particularly in the later chapters, where they're most needed. Each chapter has updated suggested reading lists and lists of terms introduced. A glossary at the end of the book, with more than 250 definitions, lists important terms and provides a convenient study guide.

COMPANION WEBSITE: STUDENT AND INSTRUCTOR RESOURCES

Jason D. Mycoff, a colleague at University of Delaware, is the brains behind the material on the book's companion Web site (http://psrm.cqpress.com/). Students will find useful chapter summaries to help review and study for exams, a set of multiple-choice and true/false quiz questions, flashcards with all of the key terms from the book for self-testing, and a set of annotated Web links to help with further research.

Instructors should click on "Instructor's Resources" to register and then access a wealth of teaching materials: a test bank with over 350 multiple-choice, fill-in-the-blank, and long-answer style questions; a set of 250 PowerPoint lecture slides covering key topics in each of the chapters; and all of the tables and figures from the book in .jpg and PowerPoint format for use in lectures.

ACCOMPANYING WORKBOOK

In addition to updating all of the Web site materials, Jason Mycoff has substantially revised the accompanying workbook, *Working with Political Science Research Methods, Third Edition,* providing many new exercises while retaining the ones we feel worked well in the previous edition. Based on user feedback, he looked for opportunities to add more open-ended, complex questions. Each workbook chapter briefly reviews key concepts covered by the corresponding chapter in the text. Students and instructors will find data sets and other documents and materials used in the workbook exercises at http://psrm.cqpress.com/. The data sets, available on a variety of platforms, may also be used for additional exercises and test items developed by instructors. Instructors may want to add on to the data sets or have their students do so as part of a research project. A solutions manual for adopters of the workbook is also available online at http://psrm.cqpress.com/.

In closing, we would like to make a comment on statistical software. Instructors remain divided over the extent to which computers should be part of an introductory research course and what particular programs to require. We believe many members of the discipline are wedded to a suite of programs such as SPSS. Others prefer that students take a more hands-on approach and use handheld and online statistical calculators. These tools offer step-by-step control, interactive data analysis, enriched graphics, and simulation tools, as well as the familiar statistical routines. We strongly encourage instructors and students to begin exploring the many other online statistical resources such as SDA, ICPSR, American Factfinder, Rice Virtual Statistics Lab, and Vassarstats. These systems have become so powerful and easy to use that they may obviate the need for expensive software packages and laboratories.[1]

---

[1] Virtually all of the computations were performed with R, a statistical programming environment. Although perhaps too difficult for many undergraduates, R is assuming a greater prominence in political science, and we encourage instructors and students alike to explore this resource, which is totally in the public domain. The program and libraries, documentation, tutorials, books, and other instructional materials can be found on the R website: R Development Core Team (2011). *R: A language and environment for statistical computing.* R Foundation for Statistical Computing, Vienna, Austria. ISBN 3-900051-07-0, URL http://www.R-project.org/.

ACKNOWLEDGMENTS

We would like to thank our careful reviewers who helped us shape this new edition: Joseph Derdzinski, US Air Force Academy; Brandy Faulkner, Virginia Tech; Nick Jorgensen, University of Idaho; James Roberts, Towson University; David Sacko, US Air Force Academy; and Gina Woodall, Arizona State University. Each of these reviewers has helped make the seventh edition stronger than ever, and we are grateful for their assistance.

Jason Mycoff's contribution to the auxiliaries and his assumption of responsibility for the *Workbook* are greatly appreciated.

We would like to thank several people who have contributed to this edition: Paula Fleming, our copy editor; Sarah Fell, our production editor; and Catherine Getzie, managing editor. We are especially thankful for the continued support and patience of Charisse Kiino, our editor at CQ Press. A book with as many bells and whistles as this one needs many sets of eyes to watch over it. We are glad to have had so many good ones.

Janet Buttolph Johnson
H. T. Reynolds

INTRODUCTION

POLITICAL SCIENTISTS ARE INTERESTED in learning about and understanding a variety of important political phenomena.

Some of us are interested in the conditions that lead to stable and secure political regimes without civil unrest, rebellion, or government repression.

Another area of interest is the relationships and interactions between nations and how some nations exercise power over others.

Other political scientists are more interested in the relationship between the populace and public officials in democratic countries and, in particular, whether or not public opinion influences the policy decisions of public officials.

Still others are concerned with how particular political institutions function. Does Congress serve the interests of well-financed groups rather than of the general populace? Do judicial decisions depend upon the personal values of individual judges, the group dynamics of judicial groups, or the relative power of the litigants? To what extent can American presidents influence the actions of federal agencies? Does the use of nonprofit service organizations to deliver public services change government control of and accountability for those services? To what extent does race play a role in voter candidate preferences? How much do the policy outputs of states vary, and why?

These are just a very few examples of the types of questions political scientists investigate through their research.

This book is an introduction to the process and methods of using **empirical research**—research based on actual, "objective" observation of phenomena—to achieve scientific knowledge about political phenomena. Scientific knowledge, which is discussed in more detail in chapter 2, differs from other types of knowledge, such as intuition, common sense, superstition, or mystical knowledge.

application of principles

One difference stems from the way in which scientific knowledge is acquired. In conducting empirical research, researchers adhere to certain well-defined principles for collecting, analyzing, and evaluating information. **Political science,** then, is simply the application of these principles to the study of phenomena that are political in nature.

Students should learn about how political scientists conduct empirical research for three major reasons. First, citizens in contemporary American society are often called upon to evaluate arguments and research about political phenomena. Debates about the wisdom of the death penalty, for example, frequently hinge on whether or not it is an effective deterrent to crime, and debates about term limits for elected officials involve whether or not such limits increase the competitiveness of elections and the responsiveness of elected officials to the electorate. Similarly, evaluating current developments in the regulation of financial markets can be informed by research on what influences the behavior of regulatory agencies and their staff. In these and many other cases, thoughtful and concerned citizens find that they must evaluate the accuracy and adequacy of the theories and research of political (and other social) scientists.

A second reason is that an understanding of empirical research methods concepts is integrally related to students' assimilation and evaluation of knowledge in their coursework. An important result of understanding the scientific research process is that a student may begin to think more independently about concepts and theories presented in courses and readings. For example, a student might say, "That may be true under the given conditions, but I believe it won't remain true under the following conditions." Or, "If this theory is correct, I would expect to observe the following." Or, "Before I will accept that interpretation, I'd like to have this additional information." Students who can specify what information is needed and what relationships among phenomena must be observed in support of an idea are more likely to develop an understanding of the subjects they study.

A third, and related, reason for learning about political science research methods is that students often need to conduct research of their own, whether for a term paper in an introductory course on American government, a research project in an upper-level seminar, a senior thesis, or a series of assignments in a course devoted to learning empirical research methods. Familiarity with empirical research methods is generally a prerequisite to making this a profitable endeavor.

The prospect of learning empirical research methods is often intimidating to students. Sometimes students dislike this type of inquiry because it involves numbers and statistics. To understand research well, one must have a basic knowledge of statistics and how to use statistics in analyzing data and reporting research findings. However, the empirical research process that we describe here is first and foremost a way of thinking and a prescription for disciplined reasoning. Statistics will be introduced only after an understanding of the thought process involved in empirical research is established and then in a way that should be understandable to any student familiar with basic algebra.

Thus, the plan for this book is as follows:

Chapter 2 discusses what we mean by the scientific study of political phenomena. We also review the historical development of political science as a discipline and introduce alternative perspectives on what is the most appropriate approach to the study of political phenomena; not all political scientists agree that politics can be studied scientifically or that the results of such efforts have been as useful or inclusive of important political phenomena as critics wish.

In chapter 3, we address an aspect of the research process that often poses a significant challenge to students: finding an interesting and appropriate research topic and developing an clearly stated research question. Therefore, in this edition we show how to explore "the literature" and find out what political scientists and others have written about political phenomena in order to sharpen the focus of a research topic, a discussion that came later in previous editions. Chapter 3 focuses on investigating relationships among concepts and developing explanations for political phenomena. It also includes an example and discussion of how to write the literature review section of a research paper.

Chapter 4 builds on the discussion in chapter 3 by adding the "building blocks" of scientific research: defining complex concepts, hypotheses, variables, and units of analysis.

Chapter 5 addresses the challenge of developing valid and reliable measures of political phenomena. It also discusses how our choices about how we measure variables affect the statistics we may use later to analyze the data we collect.

Chapter 6 presents research designs, both experimental and nonexperimental. The strengths and weaknesses of research designs are discussed, particularly as they relate to causality. The concepts of internal validity and external validity are reviewed here as well.

Chapter 7 covers the logic and basic statistical features of sampling. Various types of samples, including probability and nonprobability samples, are described. Much of our information about political phenomena is based on samples, so an understanding of the strengths and limitation of sampling is important.

Chapter 8 is the first of three chapters discussing the major methods used by political scientists and other social scientists to collect data. This chapter reviews the main methods and the reasons for choosing one method over another. It concludes with a discussion of observation as a data collection method.

Chapter 9 focuses on the multitude of documents available for use by political scientists, ranging from media clips to diaries to written speeches to the vast body of data collected by government as well as private organizations. This chapter includes an extended discussion of a research example using content analysis.

Chapter 10 discusses interviewing and survey research or polling. It reviews various types of polls and their strengths and weaknesses, as well as the design of survey instruments.

Chapter 11 offers an extensive discussion of descriptive statistics and the analysis of single variables. We present a variety of graphical options useful in displaying data, as visual representations of data are often an extremely effective way to present information. Tips on recognizing and avoiding misleading uses of graphical displays are an essential part of this chapter.

In this edition, we decided to put our discussion of statistical inference into its own chapter. Thus, Chapter 12 is devoted to the concepts of statistical inference, hypothesis testing, and calculating estimates of population parameters. This chapter builds on the foundation established in the earlier chapter on sampling.

Chapter 13 then moves on to the analysis of bivariate data analysis—the investigation of the relationship between two variables.

Chapter 14 is the final statistics chapter. Here we explore statistical techniques used in the quest for explanation and demonstrating causality. These involve multivariate analysis, as the explanation of a political phenomenon rarely is based on simply one other factor or variable.

As in previous editions, we conclude with an annotated example of an actual, peer-reviewed research article. Chapter 15 contains a new example that allows students to see the discussion and application of many of the concepts and statistical procedures covered in earlier chapters.

Researchers conduct empirical research studies for two primary reasons. One reason is to accumulate knowledge that will apply to a particular problem in need of solution or to a condition in need of improvement. Research on the causes of crime, for example, may be useful in reducing crime rates, and research on the reasons for poverty may aid governments in devising successful income maintenance and social welfare policies. Such research is often referred to as **applied research** because it has a fairly direct, immediate application to a real-world situation.

empirical research
① to accumulate knowledge to apply to a problem
② satisfy curiosity about a subject

Researchers also conduct empirical research to satisfy their intellectual curiosity about a subject, regardless of whether the research will lead to changes in government policy or private behavior. Many political scientists, for example, study the decision-making processes of voters, not because they are interested in giving practical advice to political candidates but because they want to know if elections give the populace influence over the behavior of elected public officials. Such research is sometimes referred to as **pure, theoretical,** or **recreational research** to indicate that it is not concerned primarily with practical applications.[1]

Political scientists ordinarily report the results of their research in books or articles published in political science research journals (see chapter 3 for a discussion of how to find articles in these journals). Research reported in academic journals typically contains data and information from which to draw conclusions. It also undergoes peer review, a process by which other scholars evaluate the soundness of the research before it is published. Occasionally, however, political science research questions and analyses appear in newspapers and magazines, which have a wider audience. Such popularly presented investigations may use empirical political science methods and techniques as well.

In the remainder of this chapter, we describe several political science research projects that were designed to produce scientific knowledge about significant political phenomena. We refer to these examples throughout this book to illustrate many aspects of the research process. We present them in some detail now so that you will find the later discussions easier to understand. We do not expect you to master all the details at this time; rather, you should read these examples while keeping in mind that their purpose is to illustrate a variety of research topics and methods of investigation. They also show how decisions about aspects of the research process affect the conclusions that may be drawn about the phenomena under study. And they represent attempts by political scientists to acquire knowledge by building on the research of others to arrive at increasingly complete explanations of political behavior and processes.

RESEARCH ON WINNERS AND LOSERS IN POLITICS

In 1936 Harold Lasswell published *Politics: Who Gets What, When, How.*[2] Ever since, political scientists have liked this title because it succinctly states an important truth: politics is about winning and losing. No political system, not even a perfectly democratic one, can always be all things to all people. Inevitably, policies favor some and disadvantage others. So important is this observation that one of political science's main tasks is to discover precisely which individuals and groups benefit the most from political struggle and why.

Research into income inequality in the United States and other industrialized democracies is a prime example. Recent research has addressed the following questions:

- To what extent has income inequality increased over the past several decades?

- How should income be measured? As market income (income before taxes are taken out and before any government cash transfers to taxpayers) or as disposable income (income after taxes and transfers)? For individual or for household?

- What explains growth in income inequality in the United States since the 1970s?

- Why does the increase in inequality of income, both market and disposable, vary among industrialized democracies? In particular, why has the growth in income inequality in the United States been so much higher than in other industrialized democracies?

In a 2005 study, Lane Kenworthy and Jonas Pontusson analyzed trends in the distribution of gross market income—the distribution of income before taxes and government transfers—for affluent Organisation for Economic Co-operation and Development (OECD) countries using data from the Luxembourg Income Study.[3] Kenworthy and Pontusson were interested in whether inequality in market income had increased and to what extent government policies had responded to changes in market income inequality. In particular, they were interested in testing the median-voter model developed by Allan H. Meltzer and Scott F. Richard.[4]

According to the median-voter model, support for government redistributive spending depends on the distance between the income of the median voter and the average market income of all voters. The greater the average market income is in comparison to the median income, the greater the income inequality and, thus, the greater the demand from voters for government spending to reduce this gap. Countries with the greatest market inequalities should have more such government spending.

One way to test the median-voter model is to see whether changes in redistribution are related to changes in market inequality. One would expect that larger changes in market inequality would cause larger changes in redistribution if governments are responsive to the median voter. Kenworthy and Pontusson found this to be the case, although the United States, Germany, and the United Kingdom did not fit the pattern very well. In further analyses in which they looked at country-by-country responsiveness to market inequality over several decades, they found that most OECD countries are responsive to market income inequalities, although to varying degrees, and that the United States is the least responsive.

Perhaps, Kenworthy and Pontusson suggested, government responsiveness to market inequality is related to voter turnout. If one assumes that lower-income voters are less likely to turn out to vote than are higher-income voters, then one would expect that the lower the turnout, the less likely governments would be pressured to respond to income inequality. The median-voter model still would apply, but in countries with low voter turnout, the median voter would be less likely to represent lower-income households. Kenworthy and Pontusson used regression analysis and a scatterplot (you will learn about these in chapter 12), shown in figure 1–1, to show that the higher the voter turnout, the more responsive a country is to market income inequality. The results provide an explanation for why the United States is less responsive to changes in market inequality than are other nations: the United States has the lowest turnout rate among the nations included in the analysis.

These research findings are interesting in view of another body of research that we will consider shortly: the possibility that since the mid-1950s, the bottom classes in America have been increasingly dropping out of electoral politics.

More recently in 2010, an entire issue of the journal *Politics & Society* was devoted to the topic of income inequality. In the lead article, "Winner-Take-All

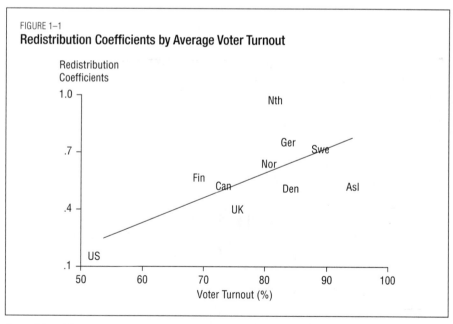

FIGURE 1–1
Redistribution Coefficients by Average Voter Turnout

Source: Adapted from figure 9 in Lane Kenworthy and Jonas Pontusson, "Rising Inequality and the Politics of Redistribution in Affluent Countries," *Perspectives on Politics* 3, no. 3 (2005): 462.

Note: Asl = Australia; Can = Canada; Den = Denmark; Fin = Finland; Ger = Germany; Nth = The Netherlands; Swe = Sweden; UK = United Kingdom; US = United States. Presidential elections for the United States; general parliamentary elections for the other countries. Redistribution data are for working-age households only.

Politics: Public Policy, Political Organization, and the Precipitous Rise of Top Incomes in the United States," Jacob S. Hacker and Paul Pierson took issue with much of the previous research on the causes of income inequality in the United States.[5] First, they dismissed economic accounts that attribute growth in inequality to "apolitical processes of economic change" for failing to explain differences among nations, as illustrated in figure 1–2. This figure shows that the top 1 percent's share of national income is the highest in the United States (16%) and that it increased the most, almost doubling, between the 1970s and 2000. Second, they attacked previous political analyses on three counts: for downplaying "the extreme concentration of income gains at the top of the income ladder" (figure 1–3 shows the gain in the top 1 percent's share of national pretax income from 1960 to 2007), for missing the important role of government policy in creating what they called a "winner-take-all" pattern, and for focusing on the median-voter model and electoral politics instead of important changes in the political organization of economic interests. They argued that the median-voter model and the extreme skew in income don't add up. Even accounting for lower turnout among lower income voters, the difference between the income of the median voter and the incomes at the very top is too big to argue that politicians are responding to the economic interests of the median voter.

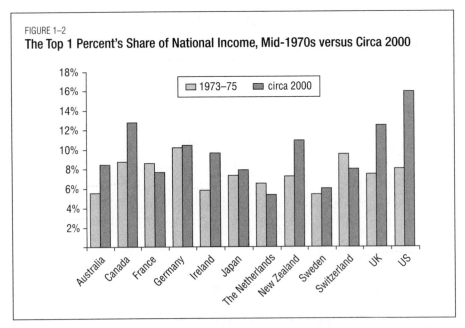

FIGURE 1–2

The Top 1 Percent's Share of National Income, Mid-1970s versus Circa 2000

Legend: 1973–75 | circa 2000

(Countries: Australia, Canada, France, Germany, Ireland, Japan, The Netherlands, New Zealand, Sweden, Switzerland, UK, US)

Source: Andrew Leigh, "How Closely Do Top Incomes Track Other Measures of Inequality?" *Economic Journal* 117, no. 524 (2007): 619–33, http://econrsss.anu.edu.au/~aleigh/pdf/TopIncomesPanel.xls, cited in Jacob S. Hacker and Paul Pierson, "Winner-Take-All Politics: Public Policy, Political Organization, and the Precipitous Rise of Top Incomes in the United States," *Politics & Society* 38, no. 2 (2010): fig. 2, p. 160. Copyright © 2010 Sage Publications. Reprinted by Permission of SAGE Publications.

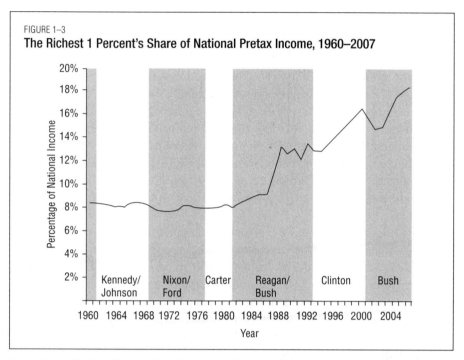

FIGURE 1–3

The Richest 1 Percent's Share of National Pretax Income, 1960–2007

Sources: Thomas Piketty and Emmanual Saez, "Income Inequality in the United States, 1913–1998," *Quarterly Journal of Economics* 118, no. 1 (2003): 1–39, and updated tables and figures for Piketty and Saez at http://elsa.berkeley.edu/~saez/ TabFig2007.xls, as cited in Jacob S. Hacker and Paul Pierson, "Winner-Take-All Politics: Public Policy, Political Organization, and the Precipitous Rise of Top Incomes in the United States," *Politics & Society* 38, no. 2 (2010): fig. 1, p. 156. Copyright © 2010 Sage Publications. Reprinted by Permission of SAGE Publications.

Note: Excluding capital gains.

Their explanation for the "precipitous rise" in top incomes in the United States rejects the median-voter model and instead focuses on the following features of American economic policy, politics, and policy change:

■ Government involvement in economic policy is "broad and deep" and includes more than decisions about tax policy and income transfer programs, which affect after-tax income. They argue that policies governing corporate structure and pay, the functioning of financial markets, and the framework of industrial relations have had much to do with pretax income (so-called market income).

■ Change in government policies affecting income distribution comes not only from new laws and policies but also from "policy drift," the failure to change existing policies when they no longer have their originally intended effects. Policy effects change due to shifting circumstances. "Drift" occurs when policy makers (1) recognize the change in effects and (2) are knowledgeable about viable alternatives yet fail to update policy. This happens because intense and attentive minority interests or a relatively few political actors are able to block reform of existing policies by exploiting the multiple veto points in the American policy-making process.

■ A shift in the balance of power of organized interests has occurred in the United States, with business interests becoming much better organized and more powerful since the 1970s and aligning predominantly with the Republican Party. They argue that lobbying and campaign contributions advantage high-income interests. Furthermore, the influence of lower- and moderate-income economic interests in elections and the ability of the Democratic Party to represent those interests are blunted by the alignment of moderate-income Christian conservatives with the Republican Party.

Thus, Hacker and Pierson's explanation identified numerous political factors that they argue are the true causes of "winner-take-all" income distribution in the United States. Subsequent articles in the same issue of *Politics & Society* examined the accuracy of Hacker and Pierson's data on income distribution, offered alternative viewpoints about the relative importance of various policy changes, discussed additional factors to consider in explaining the rapid growth in income inequality in the United States and the lack of public reaction, and suggested questions warranting further investigation.[6]

The point of this example is not to make a statement about the value of particular ideologies or parties. Instead, we want to stress that important questions—what could be more crucial than knowing who gets what from a political system?—can be answered systematically and objectively, even if tentatively, through careful thought and analysis. Moreover, we hope to show that the techniques used in these debates are not beyond the understanding of students of the social sciences.

WHO VOTES; WHO DOESN'T?

The previous example of research showed the importance of group power in determining political winners and losers. Political participation is a major factor: those individuals who make themselves heard in politics "do better" than do those who are apathetic. So a natural question is, Why do some people participate more than others?

A good place to start looking for the answer is with the decision to vote. Except for new research, which we review briefly later in this chapter, most political scientists accept two generalizations about voting in the United States. First, voting varies by socioeconomic class. Members of the lower classes participate less frequently than do more affluent and better-educated citizens. There is, in short, a "class gap" in turnout rates.[7] The second finding is that since the 1950s, a smaller and smaller proportion of the population has been going to the polls. Voting rates in federal elections have dropped more or less steadily, rebounding somewhat to 55 percent in 1992 but falling to a new low of less than 50 percent in 1996. Since then turnout has increased in presidential elections to 56.8 percent in 2008. The voting rate has been even lower in recent congressional or "off-year" elections and in the South.

The political scientist Walter Dean Burnham combined these findings into an argument that has come to be known as "selective class demobilization."[8] In a nutshell, Burnham's thesis is that the decline in turnout is especially pronounced among those in the lower and working classes; those with relatively little education and income; and those who work in manual, routine service, and unskilled occupations. Those higher up the ladder, so to speak, have voted at more or less the same rates since the 1950s. In Burnham's words, "The attrition rate among various working-class categories is more than three times as high as in the professional and technical category and well over twice as high as for the middle class as a whole."[9] In other words, for every upper-class nonvoter, there are now two or three lower-class nonvoters. It appeared to Burnham and others that the lower classes are effectively abandoning electoral politics. As a consequence, and in keeping with the research on winners and losers, it appears that political rewards may increasingly favor the middle and upper classes.

In the tradition of modern political science, Burnham supported his case by using hard empirical data—measured turnout rates for various social strata. (He relied heavily on census data and graphical and tabular displays to make his points.) But even more important, he supplied a theory that explains this apparent selective demobilization. He contended that political parties in America, never very strong to begin with, have become even weaker in the post–World War II years as a result of many factors, including the rise of candidate-centered campaigns and the increased use of primary elections in party nominations. The weakening of party organization has been especially pronounced in the Democratic Party.[10] The decline of parties places an especially onerous burden on the working and lower classes. Why? Because these groups, having less education and information about government, rely more heavily on cues and motivation supplied by political parties; without this guidance, these citizens lose their way in politics and frequently drop out.[11]

So selective class demobilization has a cause (the decline of parties) and a consequence (the loss of political influence). If true, Burnham's analysis would have enormous implications for the understanding of American politics. Stated bluntly, public policy will have an upper-class bias. Being so provocative, Burnham's thesis naturally sparked considerable comment and controversy, a fact that illustrates an important aspect of scientific research.

As discussed in chapter 2, science demands independent verification of findings. Conclusions such as Burnham's are not accepted at face value but must be verified by others working separately. In this case, additional research has produced mixed results. Some investigators agree with Burnham that the decline in turnout has been concentrated disproportionately among lower socioeconomic classes.[12] Some have investigated alternative explanations for a decline in turnout among lower socioeconomic classes. In research that has great relevance in light of the research mentioned earlier on income inequality, Frederick Solt investigated the "Schattschneider hypothesis," named after the political scientist E. E. Schattschneider.[13] Schattschneider suggested in 1960 that low participation and high-income voter bias are the result of economic inequality because as the rich grow richer relative to other citizens, they also grow better able to define the alternatives that are considered within the political system and exclude matters of importance to poor citizens.[14] Solt found that citizens of states with greater income inequality are less likely to vote in gubernatorial elections and that income inequality increases income bias in the electorate, thus providing empirical support for Schattschneider's hypothesis. But others, using alternative measures of class and other data sets, have come to a conclusion different from Burnham. Jan E. Leighley and Jonathan Nagler, for instance, found "that the class bias [in nonvoting] has not increased since 1964."[15]

Complicating matters further, recent research calls into question even the basic belief that voter turnout in general has been declining. These newer investigations say the apparent decrease in the rate of electoral participation stems from an artifact in how turnout is measured. The voting rate has typically been measured as the number of votes cast divided by the number of eligible voters. This procedure may seem straightforward, but a problem arises. How should the eligible voting population be defined? The Census Bureau uses the so-called voting-age population (VAP) as its measure of the eligible electorate. But, as Michael P. McDonald and Samuel L. Popkin maintained, this approach "includes people who are ineligible to vote, such as noncitizens, felons, and the mentally incompetent, and fails to include [Americans] living overseas but otherwise eligible."[16] They developed an alternative measure of the pool of legally eligible voters or voting-eligible population (VEP) and showed that when it is used in the denominator of voting-rate calculations, "nationally and outside the South there are virtually no identifiable turnout trends from 1972 onward, and within the South there is a clear trend of *increasing* turnout rates [emphasis added]."[17]

In a recent article, "Does Measurement Matter? The Case of VAP and VEP in Models of Voter Turnout in the United States," Thomas Holbrook and Brianne Heidbreder investigated the impact of using VAP or VEP on our understanding of the causes of variation in turnout among states.[18] Because states control numerous factors affecting the ease of voting (such as early voting, voting by absentee ballot, and variable registration deadlines), whether or not gubernatorial elections are held concurrently with federal elections, and whether ballots initiatives are allowed or not, studying voter turnout at the state level can tell us a lot about the relative importance of these factors and other determinants of turnout. Considerable variation exists among the states regarding voting restrictions placed on felons and the size of the noncitizen population. Therefore, the difference between VAP and VEP for some states could be significant. Using VAP as the measure of turnout could mask the impact of factors on the turnout of those voters actually eligible to vote. Holbrook and Heidbreder's analysis showed a strong correlation exists between VEP and VAP, but for some states the two measures do diverge. Furthermore, using VEP rather than VAP changes the extent to which per capita income, Hispanic population, and number of ballot initiatives are found to affect voter turnout: per capita income and ballot initiatives become more significant and Hispanic population less so when VEP is used.

Adjusting the VAP to exclude felons raises another series of questions investigated by political scientists: To what extent does the disenfranchisement of non-incarcerated offenders (a practice that in the United States results in the disenfranchisement of large numbers of citizens) alter the outcome of elections? Why is the United States alone among democratic countries in this regard? And what accounts for differences in restricting access to the ballot among the American states?[19]

Finally, here is another curious twist in research on voter turnout. Some investigators approach the study of political phenomena by building what are known as formal models. Modelers begin with a set of a priori assumptions and propositions and use logic to deduce further statements from them. In the case of voter turnout, the modeling approach begins with the assumption that citizens are rational, in the sense that they try to maximize their utility (the things that they value) at the least cost to themselves. So a potential voter will think about the personal benefits of going to the polls and weigh these against the costs of doing so (for example, taking the time to become informed, registering, and finding and driving to the polling place). Surprisingly, many models lead to the conclusion that a rational person—one who wants to maximize utility at least cost—will decide that voting is not worth the effort and simply abstain.[20] The reason for this conclusion: one single individual's participation has an exceedingly small probability of affecting the outcome of an election. So, according to the deduction, the small chance of bringing benefits by voting is easily outweighed by the costs, however low. Consequently, the formal model predicts that hardly anyone will vote. But in point of fact millions of Americans do vote, which seems to belie the model's conclusions. This situation, which has been called the "paradox of voting," has sparked an enormous amount of discussion and controversy since the 1950s.[21] One recent attempt to explain why citizens in a democracy vote, therefore, includes psychological or motivational variables in a model of voting.[22]

This is not the place to sort out all of the research related to voter turnout. Instead we have used studies of voter turnout to illustrate some features of research that are described in more detail in the following chapters, including the derivation of hypotheses from existing theory, measurement of concepts, and the use of objective standards to adjudicate among competing ideas. The major point, perhaps, is that if one's procedures are stated clearly, others can pick up the thread of analysis and independently investigate the problem. In this sense empirical political research is, like all science, a cumulative process. Usually no one person or group can discover a definitive answer to a complicated phenomenon like voting or nonvoting. Rather the answers come, if they do at all, from the gradual accumulation of findings from numerous investigators working independently of one another to validate or invalidate each other's claims. Finally, research on voter turnout shows the connections among empirical research, values, and public policy. People look at research to obtain useful knowledge about voter turnout rates as a whole or differences in voter turnout rates for different groups of potentially eligible voters. Those who believe that turnout rates should be higher may advocate changes in public policy to encourage voting.

REPRESSION OF HUMAN RIGHTS

As a result of improvements in the availability of data, public and scholarly interest focused on the human rights practices of governments has increased substantially over the past two decades. Several organizations (Amnesty International, the US Department of State, and Freedom House, for example) publish annual reports on the human rights performance of nations worldwide. More recently, information and news about human rights has become available on the Internet.

Researchers Wesley T. Milner, Stephen C. Poe, and David Leblang noted that much of this research has tried to explain cross-national variation in protection and enjoyment of three legally recognized human entitlements: security rights or personal integrity rights, which include the rights to be free from arbitrary or politically motivated torture, execution, and imprisonment; subsistence rights or basic human needs; and civil and political liberties, which include political and economic rights.[23] They also noted that there has been considerable discussion about the relationships among these rights, particularly whether these basic rights are distinct and necessary for the enjoyment of all other rights, or whether there are trade-offs between types of rights—that governments can provide more of one if they restrict another. Yet no single empirical study to date had examined the linkages among all three rights.

Milner, Poe, and Leblang enumerated a number of hypotheses about such linkages and engaged in exploratory data analyses to illustrate empirical linkages and trends.

- Fulfillment of basic human needs is expected to be strongly related to the realization of personal integrity rights. Previous research has shown that higher per capita gross national product (GNP) is strongly related to the achievement of subsistence rights. Other research has shown that higher GNP is strongly related to personal integrity rights. Therefore, one might expect the two types of rights to be directly and positively related. Why? Perhaps if the population is satisfied, there is less need for repression by elites. (Given our earlier discussion of income inequality, one might expect that the degree of income inequality in a country would affect this relationship. Per capita GNP does not reveal information about the distribution of income in a country.)

- The enjoyment of political liberties and that of personal integrity rights are expected to go together. After all, personal integrity abuses certainly deprive people of political liberties. Yet the rights are not one and the same. Political and civil liberties are most often associated with democracies. Democratic processes provide alternatives to violence for resolving conflict and allow voters to remove potentially abusive leaders from office before they have a chance to engage in repression. Furthermore, typical civil liberties such as freedom of speech, press, and assembly allow citizens to publicize any abuses committed by a regime and to advocate replacement of the regimes at election time.

- Subsistence rights and liberties are also expected to go together. Just as democracies place limits on personal integrity abuses, they can also be expected to yield to demands for the provision of basic human needs. Milner, Poe, and Leblang actually separated liberties into two dimensions: civil liberties and economic liberties. Insofar as economic liberties, such as private property rights, lead to economic growth and economic growth leads to the satisfaction of basic human needs, the relationship between subsistence rights and economic liberties is expected to be positive. However, some have argued that there might be a trade-off between political and economic rights and subsistence rights.[24]

Research into human rights illustrates the importance of accurate measurement of concepts, in this case the measurement of the various types of rights. We'll have more to say about this in chapter 5, but, as an example, Milner, Poe, and Leblang discussed two approaches to the measurement of personal integrity abuses. One is events based and relies on newspaper accounts. This poses a problem in that research typically uses Western newspapers, which may not report abuses systematically and without bias. Furthermore, especially closed regimes may prevent abuses from appearing in news reports. An alternative approach, the standards-based approach, involves coders reading various reports on governments' human rights practices and classifying countries according to a set of predetermined criteria. This approach, too, has its problems, but it is more likely to result in relatively accurate measures for comparison across nations.

Milner, Poe, and Leblang plotted trends in rights using line graphs. Graphs are an important feature of presenting research findings (discussed in chapter 11). Trends in personal integrity rights are reported in figure 1–4; higher scores on the Amnesty International (AI) Human Rights Index indicate greater realization of rights. In the graph, data are presented for the world, OECD countries, and non-OECD countries. Notice that personal integrity rights worsened between 1989 and 1992 among non-OECD countries; this period corresponds with the outbreak of ethnic conflicts in Eastern Europe. The researchers found that globally, the trends in democratic rights, physical quality of life, and economic freedoms had been positive since 1975.

After examining the trends for each type of right, the authors investigated the extent to which higher scores on one measure of rights are associated with higher scores on another measure of rights for each pair of the four rights for a

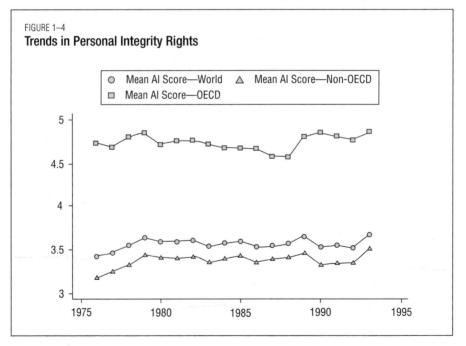

FIGURE 1–4
Trends in Personal Integrity Rights

Source: Wesley T. Milner, Stephen C. Poe and David Leblang, "Security Rights, Subsistence Rights, and Liberties: A Theoretical Survey of the Empirical Landscape," *Human Rights Quarterly* 21, no. 2 (1999): 431, figure 3. © 1999 The Johns Hopkins University Press. Reprinted with permission of The Johns Hopkins University Press.

sample of OECD and non-OECD countries. To do this, they used a statistical procedure called correlation. (We will show the actual table of correlation coefficients and explain them in chapter 12.) They found that countries with more democratic political institutions protect personal integrity rights more and have higher scores on measures of physical quality of life and economic rights than do less democratic countries.

A LOOK INTO JUDICIAL DECISION MAKING AND ITS EFFECTS

When the decisions of public officials clearly and visibly affect the lives of the populace, political scientists are interested in the process by which those decisions are reached. This is as true when the public officials are judges as when they are legislators or executives. As one legal scholar stated in his review of the development of empirical research on judicial decision making, "given the often critical role judges play in our constitutional, political, and social lives, it is axiomatic that we need to better understand how and why judges reach the decisions they do in the course of discharging their judicial roles."[25] The decision-making behavior of the nine justices of the US Supreme Court is especially intriguing because they are not elected officials, their deliberations are secret, they serve for life, and their decisions constrain other judges and public officials. As a result, political scientists have been curious for some time about how Supreme Court justices reach their decisions.

Researchers have approached the study of judicial decision making from several perspectives. Early studies investigated the influences of a judge's background (for example, as a prosecutor or defense attorney) and personal attributes such as race or gender. The results have been mixed, with little evidence to support the influence of these factors.[26] One school of thought concerning judicial decision making holds that decisions are shaped primarily by legal doctrine and precedent. Because most Supreme Court judges have spent many years rendering judicial decisions while serving on lower courts, and because judges in general are thought to respect the decisions made by previous courts, this approach posits that the decisions of Supreme Court justices depend on a search for, and discovery of, relevant legal precedent.

Another view of judicial decision making proposes that judges, like other politicians, make decisions in part based on personal political beliefs and values. Furthermore, because Supreme Court judges are not elected, serve for life, seldom seek any other office, and are not expected to justify their decisions to the public, they are in an ideal position to act in accord with their personal value systems.[27]

One of the obstacles to discovering the relationship between the personal attitudes of justices and the decisions handed down by the Court is the difficulty of measuring judicial attitudes. Supreme Court justices do not often consent to give interviews to researchers while they are on the bench, nor do they fill out attitudinal surveys. Their deliberations are secret, they seldom make public speeches during their terms, and their written publications consist mainly of their case decisions. Consequently, about all we can observe of the political attitudes of Supreme Court justices during their terms are the written decisions they offer, which are precisely what researchers are seeking to explain. Some researchers use political party and the appointing president as indicators of judicial attitudes, although these are less than satisfactory measures.

An inventive attempt to overcome this obstacle is contained within Jeffrey A. Segal and Albert D. Cover's article "Ideological Values and the Votes of U.S. Supreme Court Justices."[28] Segal and Cover decided that an appropriate way to measure the attitudes of judges, independent of the decisions they make, would be to analyze the editorial columns written about them in four major US daily newspapers after their nomination by the president but before their confirmation by the Senate. This data source, the researchers argued, provides a comparable measure of attitudes for all justices studied, independent of the judicial decisions rendered and free of systematic errors. Here, too, though, the researchers had to accept a measure that was not ideal, for the editorial columns reflected journalists' perceptions of judicial attitudes rather than the attitudes themselves.

Despite this limitation, the editorial columns did provide an independent measure of the attitudes of the eighteen Supreme Court justices who served between 1953 and 1987. Segal and Cover found a strong relationship between the justices' decisions on cases dealing with civil liberties and the justices' personal attitudes as evinced in editorial columns. Those justices who were perceived to be liberal *before* their term on the Supreme Court voted in a manner consistent with this perception once they got on the Court. Judicial attitudes, then, do seem to be an important component of judicial decision making.

Other researchers have investigated the influence of so-called extra-legal factors on the decisions of Supreme Court justices. Are there factors in addition to ideology but outside of legal precedent that influence judicial decision making? Do judges behave strategically to increase their prestige or influence vis-à-vis other judges and other branches of government?[29] Are they subject to influence by other judges and governmental actors? Among the possibilities are congressional influence (given the ability of Congress to pass legislation that overrides Court decisions and to initiate constitutional amendments, among other actions), presidential influence, and public opinion.[30]

The presidential election in 2000 brought into sharp relief for many Americans the importance of Supreme Court decisions to American politics. Some people felt that the high regard that Americans have for the Supreme Court brought closure to the highly contentious election and that support for the

Supreme Court as an institution helped people to accept its decision in *Bush v. Gore* (2000). Others argued that general support and respect for the Supreme Court was undermined among those disappointed by the decision. Interestingly, political scientist Valerie J. Hoekstra was already busy investigating the two general questions raised so vividly by the 2000 decision: (1) How does the content of Supreme Court decisions affect support for the Court? That is, does respect for the Court decline among people who disagree with a decision? (2) Do Supreme Court decisions have any effect on public opinion? In other words, does the public change its mind about public policy issues once the Supreme Court has spoken?[31]

Hoekstra's work demonstrates how the choice of a research design (the topic of chapter 6) affects a researcher's ability to answer research questions with confidence. Hoekstra noted that public opinion polls generally show that the Supreme Court enjoys higher and more stable levels of public support than Congress or presidents, but that stability of aggregate-level measures such as public opinion polls does not mean that the opinions of individuals have not changed.[32] She argued that a panel study, one in which the same individuals are interviewed before and after a Supreme Court decision, is best to examine how support for the Supreme Court changes and whether individuals change their views about an issue in response to the Court's decision on a case. She also argued that it is important to interview individuals who are aware of the case to be decided by the Court. One cannot expect a decision of the Supreme Court to influence how people feel about an issue if people are not aware of the decision. Most Supreme Court decisions do not have the national significance and high level of public awareness as did *Bush v. Gore.* Therefore, Hoekstra selected four cases and interviewed people in the communities from which the cases originated.

Hoekstra hypothesized that people who are more supportive of the Supreme Court are more likely to change their view of an issue in the direction of the Court's decision and that people who have strong opinions about an issue are less likely to change their views than are people whose opinions are not as strong. In two of the four cases, Hoekstra found that public opinion shifted in the direction of the Court's decision, but initial levels of support for the Court did not have an effect on the amount of change.[33] She did find that people who paid more attention to politics, and presumably were more aware of the issue, were more likely to change their opinion in the direction of the Court's decision.[34] Overall, she found limited support for the persuasive effect of Supreme Court decisions.

In terms of the effect of Supreme Court decisions on the public's support of the Court, Hoekstra found that people who were pleased with the Court's decision became more confident in and supportive of the Court, whereas those who were disappointed with the decision became less supportive. These changes were affected by how strongly a person felt about the issue: those who cared strongly about an issue tended to change their views of the Court more than those who did not care as much about the issue.[35]

INFLUENCING BUREAUCRACIES

Recent disasters—such as the deaths of twenty-nine miners in an explosion in the Upper Big Branch mine in Montcoal, West Virginia, on April 5, 2010, and the explosion of BP's Deepwater Horizon oil rig on April 20, 2010, which killed 11 workers, injured 17, and spilled an estimated 4.9 million barrels of crude oil into the Gulf of Mexico—tragically brought the performance of two federal bureaucracies into the limelight. In the case of the mining disaster, questions are being raised about whether the US Mine Safety and Health Administration effectively enforces mining regulations. In the case of the Deepwater Horizon explosion, the US Minerals Management Service is being criticized for being too closely aligned with the oil industry and for, among other things, insufficient scrutiny of oil spill response plans.

Political control of bureaucracy is an ongoing topic of discussion and investigation by political scientists. A variety of theories and beliefs about political influence on bureaucratic activities have ascended, only to be superseded by new theories and beliefs based on yet more research. Theories have evolved from the politics versus administration dichotomy, which strictly separates politics and administration and argues that the way to avoid problems such as political patronage and corruption in administration is to pursue professionalism and independence in administration, to the iron triangle (or capture) theory, which argues that administration and politics are inseparable and views agencies as responsive to a narrow range of advantaged and special interests assisted by a few strategically located members of Congress. This theory raises serious questions about democratic control of government agencies. A more recent theory, principal-agent theory, suggests that presidents and Congress (the principals) do have ways to control bureaucratic activities or agents. According to this theory, policy makers use rewards or sanctions to bring agency activities back in line when they stray too far from the policy preferences of elected politicians. Control mechanisms include budgeting, political appointments, structure and reorganization, personnel power, and oversight.[36]

Research shows that agency outputs vary with political changes. The emergence of a new presidential administration, the seating of new personnel on the courts, and change in the ideological stances of congressional oversight committees all influence agency outputs.[37] Research also indicates that presidents and Congress compete over the control of agencies and that agencies vary in the extent to which they are designed to be insulated from presidential control.[38]

Other research, however, presents evidence that bureaucratic values may be more influential than political control mechanisms.[39]

Richard L. Hall and Kristina C. Miler noted that Congress tries to compensate for the difficulty of overseeing agency decisions by designing procedural requirements to improve the visibility of decision making, openness to multiple points of view, and accountability (by including standing to sue, for example). Sometimes Congress will limit agency discretion specifically through statutes.[40] Yet questions remain about who influences agency decisions and by what means. Hall and Miler investigated the circumstances surrounding the decisions by members of Congress to intervene in agency decisions ex poste—that is, to decide whether to challenge, or defend in the face of a challenge, a particular agency rule—and the role that interest groups play in those decisions.

Oversight behaviors include writing a letter, submitting comments, giving a speech, introducing a bill, offering an appropriations rider, and challenging (or defending) an agency policy during a congressional oversight hearing. Such behaviors are costly to legislators; gathering issue-specific information consumes time and labor that could be spent on other priorities, and, as Hall and Miler explained, constituents may not notice and reward oversight activity. Oversight activity is easier for legislators serving on the relevant committees and subcommittees because they have more staff and issue-specific expertise.

Hall and Miler hypothesized that lobbyists "subsidize" legislative oversight by providing labor and information to legislators. Pursuing the subsidy perspective, they also hypothesized that lobbyists will target legislative allies, rather than trying to persuade uncertain legislators unfriendly to their position. To test their hypotheses, they used the case of the 1997 fight over the EPA's proposal to strengthen air quality standards for ground-level ozone and particulate matter. They interviewed six of eight principle lobbyists on the pro-regulation side and nine of fourteen on the antiregulation side. They asked lobbyists how many times they had contacted each member on the House Commerce Committee, which had oversight jurisdiction over the EPA. The number of contacts made by industry was about twice the number of contacts made by health and environmental coalition (HEC) lobbyists. The pattern of contacts is shown in figure 1–5. As expected according to the subsidy hypothesis, lobbyists focused their contacts on "friendly" legislators, those who were allied with their side of the issue.

The researchers also found that the more HEC groups lobbied pro-environment legislators, the more likely those legislators were to send comments to the EPA in support of the stricter regulations. Similarly, the more industry groups lobbied pro-industry legislators, the more likely those legislators were to send comments to the EPA critical of those regulations. Figure 1–6 shows the impact of lobbying

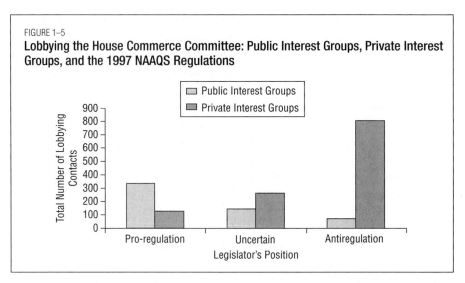

FIGURE 1–5

Lobbying the House Commerce Committee: Public Interest Groups, Private Interest Groups, and the 1997 NAAQS Regulations

Source: Richard L. Hall and Kristina C. Miler. "What Happens After the Alarm? Interest Group Subsidies to Legislative Overseers." *Journal of Politics* 70, no. 4 (2008): fig. 1, p. 997. Reproduced with the permission of Cambridge University Press.

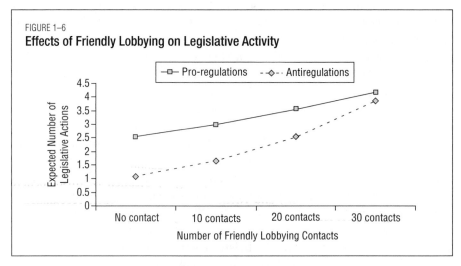

FIGURE 1–6

Effects of Friendly Lobbying on Legislative Activity

Source: Richard L. Hall and Kristina C. Miler. "What Happens After the Alarm? Interest Group Subsidies to Legislative Overseers." *Journal of Politics* 70, no. 4 (2008): fig. 2, p. 1002. Reproduced with the permission of Cambridge University Press.

contact on the number of comments made by friendly committee members. So, for example, a legislator who was contacted 30 times by industry lobbyists would make about 4 antiregulation comments, while a legislator who received no contact from industry lobbyists would make 2.5 comments. HEC-friendly legislators who received 30 contacts from HEC lobbyists made almost 4 comments, while those who received no contacts made an average of 1 comment.

Hall and Miler also investigated the possibility that campaign contributions played a role in the commenting behavior of committee members and found that they had little or no impact. The researchers concluded that lobbying targeted at friendly legislators was effective for both environmental and industry lobbyists. Lobbying targeted at friendly legislators who are subcommittee and committee leaders was especially effective. Industry lobbyists were at an advantage because they were able to contact legislators more (they contacted nine members more than thirty times, and some of them eighty times, while HEC lobbyists contacted only one member more than thirty times) and because industry-friendly legislators were full committee leaders. While this research looked at lobbying and oversight in only one case, it is a case involving highly technical issues that are difficult or costly for legislators to oversee and, therefore, a good case to use to test the subsidy theory of lobbying.

EFFECTS OF CAMPAIGN ADVERTISING ON VOTERS

Enormous sums of money are spent on campaign advertising by candidates vying for political office. Political scientists have long been interested in the effects of campaign advertising on voters. Some have argued that advertising has little effect due to the public's ability to screen out messages conflicting with their existing views. Others have suggested that campaign activity, including advertising, stimulates voter interest and increases turnout. Still others suggest that negative campaign advertising, particularly television advertisements, has harmful effects on the democratic process: negative campaign ads are thought to increase cynicism about politics and to cause the electorate to turn away from elections in disgust, a phenomenon called demobilization.

A 1994 study on so-called attack advertising by Stephen D. Ansolabehere, Shanto Iyengar, Adam Simon, and Nicholas Valentino is widely recognized as establishing support for the demobilization theory. Noting that "more often than not, candidates criticize, discredit, or belittle their opponents rather than providing their own ideas," the researchers hypothesized that, rather than stimulating voter turnout, such campaigns would depress turnout.[41]

Ansolabehere and colleagues devised a controlled experiment in which groups of prospective voters were exposed to one of three advertisement treatments: positive political advertisements, no political advertisements, or negative political advertisements. After taking into account other factors likely to affect a person's intention to vote, the researchers found that exposure to negative (as compared to positive) advertisements depressed intention to vote by 5 percent.

Recognizing that the size of the experimental effect—that is, how much impact advertising has on behavior—might not match the size of the real-world effect, the researchers also devised a strategy to measure the effect of negative advertising in real campaigns. They measured the tone of the campaigns in the thirty-four states that held a Senate election in 1992. They calculated the turnout rate and something called the "roll-off rate" for each Senate race. The roll-off rate measures the extent to which people who were sufficiently motivated to vote in the presidential election chose not to vote in the Senate race. The researchers found that both the turnout rate and the roll-off rate were affected by campaign tone. Turnout in states with a positive campaign tone was 4 percent higher than in states where the tone was negative. The difference in roll-off rates was 2.4 percent, with roll-off rates higher in those states with more negative campaign advertising. These results confirmed the team's earlier results and demonstrated that negative campaigns may in fact depress voter turnout.

Ansolabehere and his colleagues suggested that the decline in presidential and midterm voter turnout since 1960 may be due in part to the increasingly negative tone of national campaigns. They also raised some interesting questions, asking whether or not candidates should "be free to use advertising techniques that have the effect of reducing voter turnout" and whether or not "in the case of publicly financed presidential campaigns, [it is] . . . legitimate for candidates to use public funds in ways that are likely to discourage voting."[42]

Subsequent researchers have conducted studies using different approaches that qualify this finding. For example, Martin P. Wattenberg and Craig Leonard Brians investigated the contention that "the intent of most negative commercials is to convert votes by focusing on an issue for which the sponsoring candidate has credibility in handling but on which the opponent is weak."[43] Using survey or poll data from the 1992 and 1996 American presidential elections that allowed the identification of respondents who recalled seeing negative ads, positive ads, or no ads at all and the comparison of their turnout rates, Wattenberg and Brians found that negative ads did not depress turnout. In fact, for groups considered unlikely to vote (such as young people or those lacking a high school education), turnout rates were higher for those who recalled seeing either a positive or negative ad, compared to those who recalled no ad. For groups expected to have higher turnout rates, ad recall had only a slight effect on turnout rates. After taking into account a wide range of factors associated with turnout, the researchers found that recall of negative political ads was significantly associated with higher turnout rates in the 1992 elections. For the 1996 elections, they found that recall of ads, whether positive or negative, had no impact on turnout rates. They also concluded that recalling a negative ad did not have a depressing effect on a person's sense of political efficacy.

They suggested that the experimental findings of Ansolabehere and his colleagues do not hold up in the real world of elections. Recall, though, that those experimental findings were buttressed by the analysis of aggregate voting data in the 1992 Senate races. Wattenberg and Brians questioned these findings and pointed out that the election data used by Ansolabehere and his colleagues are different from the official 1992 election returns published by the Federal Election Commission (FEC).

As we noted earlier in the chapter, political science is an iterative or cumulative activity and often involves debates over measurement of variables. Ansolabehere and his colleagues responded to Wattenberg and Brians's study by noting that survey recall data are prone to inaccuracies: recall is a poor measure of actual exposure, and people who are likely to vote are more likely to recall seeing a political ad.[44] They analyzed the survey data for the 1992 and 1996 elections, making adjustments for exposure to campaign ads that Wattenberg and Brians did not. They used data measuring the volume of ads in the different senatorial elections, noting that higher-volume campaigns have disproportionately more negative ads. They also noted that the tone of campaigns becomes more negative as elections approach. Thus, respondents surveyed earlier in an election will have been exposed to less negative campaigning than those interviewed later in an election. Their analysis showed that recall of negative ads was significantly higher in states with higher levels of advertising and in the latter stages of the campaign and that intention to vote was lower in states with more television advertising and in the latter stages of campaigns. They therefore concluded that negative advertising has a negative impact on voter turnout. They also replicated their analyses of the Senate races using official FEC data (previously they had used data obtained directly from the election officers in each state) and concluded that, on average, turnout in positive campaigns is nearly 5 percentage points higher than turnout in negative campaigns.

One might think that in the fifteen-plus years since the early research investigating the demobilization hypothesis, that the topic would have run its course. Quite the contrary. In 2009 Richard R. Lau and Ivy Brown Rowner commented on the "explosion" of research on negative campaigning over the past two decades.[45] They reported that by the end of 2006, there were 110 books, chapters, dissertations, and articles on the effects of negative political advertisements or negative campaigns and many more exploring other aspects of negative campaigns. They also discussed some of the difficulties researchers face in investigating whether negative advertising mobilizes or demobilizes voters or whether or not negative campaigning is an effective campaign technique. First they pointed out that there is no real evidence that negative campaigning has increased despite increased attention and concern. Surprisingly, "it is only with the advent of 'ad detector' technology developed by the Campaign Media Analysis Group, which tracks satellite-based feeds of political advertisements, that we have been able to gather any solid evidence on how often different televised ads are shown

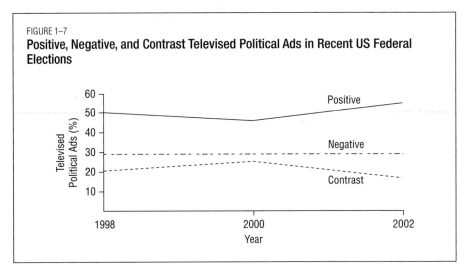

FIGURE 1–7

Positive, Negative, and Contrast Televised Political Ads in Recent US Federal Elections

Source: Richard R. Lau and Ivy Brown Rovner, "Negative Campaigning," *Annual Review of Political Science* 12 (2009): 285–306, fig. 1, p. C-1. Copyright 2009 by ANNUAL REVIEWS, INC. Reproduced with permission of ANNUAL REVIEWS, INC. in the format Textbook and Other book via Copyright Clearance Center.

in different media markets."[46] Indeed, they presented data that show, at least at the federal level, negative advertising has not increased (see figure 1–7). What does seem to have increased since 1980, the authors showed, is the number of stories in the news media about negative advertising—stories that often focus on the most outrageous examples.

Among the difficulties researchers face are reconciling their definitions of negative advertising with what the public considers to be fair or unfair attack ads; measuring negativity based only on the text of an ad rather than its accompanying visuals and music; measuring the impact of negative campaigning on the outcome of races when campaigns are most likely to go negative in closely contested races; measuring the tone of all campaign-related material (television ads, phone calls, campaign mail, and personal contacts); taking into account both tone (the proportion of negative ads) as well as volume (the total number of ads shown in a media market); determining the effect of negative ads on the outcome of a single race or type of race when in most cases multiple election contests are occurring simultaneously; and determining the effect of negative campaign ads on the political system as a whole when studying the amount of negative campaigning in a single race or type of race. In chapter 6 we discuss some ways to design research to investigate the effects of advertising on political behavior. We simply note for now that this issue will surely continue to preoccupy researchers and illustrates some of the complexities and excitement of the empirical study of politics, including the impact of technology on the practice of research.[47]

RESEARCH ON PUBLIC SUPPORT FOR US FOREIGN INVOLVEMENT

The ongoing wars in Iraq and Afghanistan highlight the relevance of research into public support for US military involvement in foreign affairs. Researchers have investigated a wide range of factors associated with public support for US military involvement. Some of these focus on attributes of individuals, including attitudes toward the use of military force and US involvement in world affairs in general, education, and knowledge of foreign affairs. Others focus on situational factors, such as the primary purpose or objective of US military involvement, the relative power of the United States vis-à-vis an adversary, the costs of involvement (particularly US military casualties), the extent of elite consensus over whether the United States should be involved, and multilateral support for involvement.[48] Let's take a look at one particularly relevant example that investigates the public's willingness to expend additional resources, both human and financial, in an ongoing war.

In an article titled "'Don't Let Them Die in Vain': Casualty Frames and Public Tolerance for Escalating Commitment in Iraq," William A. Boettcher III and Michael D. Cobb investigated the extent to which the public responds to rhetoric to the effect that the "sunk costs" or "sacrifices" made by the men and women killed in war must be redeemed through further conflict.[49] They pointed out that while there may be logical and rational reasons for continuing the fighting in Iraq, spent money and dead soldiers cannot be recovered by additional deaths and more spending. They noted that such a rhetorical argument (which they call "investment framing") appeals to a well-known and researched psychological bias called the "sunk-cost trap" in which "individuals pursue irrational and costly courses of action to redeem losses that cannot be recovered" or "throwing good money after bad."[50]

They set out to test whether or not "investment frames" increase the public's willingness to continue the war (defined as willingness to tolerate additional casualties and to spend more money) and whether or not it makes a difference if well-known figures with credibility make the argument. They also took into consideration if individuals felt the United States "did the right thing" by going to war or if they felt the United States "should have stayed out of Iraq." Thus, they hypothesized that "the casualty and spending tolerance of individuals supportive of the decision to go to war in Iraq will increase when exposed to investment frames, while the casualty and spending tolerance of individuals opposed to the decision to go to war in Iraq will be unaffected or decrease when exposed to investment frames."[51]

In a survey of 1,342 individuals of a representative sample of US households, respondents were given a battery of questions about Iraq. Then they were assigned to a control group or to one of several experimental groups in which the "investment framing" conditions were varied. In the unattributed investment frame condition, respondents read, "Some people say we need to stay and complete the mission in Iraq to honor the dead and make sure they did not die in vain." In two other conditions, the phrase "some people" was replaced with either "General Casey, the Commanding General in Iraq," or "Pat Robertson, founder of the Christian Coalition." A fourth, an alternative "consumer" frame, was attributed to Pope Benedict and discouraged respondents from honoring sunk costs by saying, "Staying will not bring them back and will only result in more loss of life."

While we cannot explore all of Boettcher and Cobb's results, they found that the investment frames had a positive impact on tolerance for additional casualties and spending among those who supported going to war in Iraq, with the unattributed frame having the most consistent impact. The investment frame attributed to General Casey had an especially negative impact on the tolerance of those opposed to going to war in the first place. The researchers surmised that respondents were discounting the investment argument because coming from this source, it was perceived as self-serving. Overall they concluded that investment frames are counterproductive unless targeted at sympathetic audiences.

Clearly, both citizens and politicians have quite a bit to learn from recent political science research on the conditions under which the public will support the use of military force and foreign policies advocated by national political leaders. It is exciting for researchers to investigate these issues and to pursue greater understanding of these and related questions.

CONCLUSION

Political scientists are continually adding to and revising our understanding of politics and government. As the several examples in this chapter illustrate, empirical research in political science is useful for satisfying intellectual curiosity and for evaluating real-world political conditions. New ways of designing investigations, the availability of new types of data, and new statistical techniques contribute to the ever-changing body of political science knowledge. Conducting empirical research is not a simple process, however. The information a researcher chooses to use, the method that he or she follows to investigate a research question, and the statistics used to report research findings may affect the conclusions drawn. For instance, some of these examples used sample surveys to measure important phenomena such as public opinion on a variety of public policy issues. Yet surveys are not always an accurate reflection of people's beliefs and attitudes. In addition, how a researcher measures the phenomena of interest can affect the conclusions reached. Finally, some researchers conducted experiments in which they were able to control the application of the experimental or test factor, whereas others compared naturally occurring cases in which the factors of interest varied.

Sometimes researchers are unable to measure political phenomena themselves and have to rely on information collected by others, particularly government agencies. Can we always find readily available data to investigate a topic? If not, do we choose a different topic or collect our own data? How do we collect data firsthand? When we are trying to measure cause and effect in the real world of politics, rather than in a carefully controlled laboratory setting, how can we be sure that we have identified all the factors that could affect the phenomena we are trying to explain? Finally, do research findings based on the study of particular people, agencies, courts, communities, or countries have general applications to all people, agencies, courts, communities, or countries? To develop answers to these questions, we need to understand the process of scientific research, the subject of this book.

Terms Introduced

Applied research. Research designed to produce knowledge useful in altering a real-world condition or situation.

Empirical research. Research based on actual, "objective" observation of phenomena.

Political science. The application of the methods of acquiring scientific knowledge to the study of political phenomena.

Pure, theoretical, or recreational research. Research designed to satisfy one's intellectual curiosity about some phenomenon.

Notes

1. *Recreational research* is a term used by W. Phillips Shively in *The Craft of Political Research*, 2nd ed. (Englewood Cliffs, N.J.: Prentice-Hall, 1980), chap. 1.

2. Harold Lasswell, *Politics: Who Gets What, When, How* (New York: Hittlesey House, 1936). A more recent statement of the idea is found in Benjamin I. Page, *Who Gets What from Government* (Berkeley: University of California Press, 1983).

3. Lane Kenworthy and Jonas Pontusson, "Rising Inequality and the Politics of Redistribution in Affluent Countries," *Perspectives on Politics* 3, no. 3 (2005): 449–71. Available at http://www.u.arizona.edu/~lkenwor/pop2005.pdf.

4. Allan H. Meltzer and Scott F. Richard, "A Rational Theory of the Size of Government," *Journal of Political Economy* 89, no. 5 (1981): 914–27.

5. Jacob S. Hacker and Paul Pierson, "Winner-Take-All Politics: Public Policy, Political Organization, and the Precipitous Rise of Top Incomes in the United States," *Politics & Society* 38, no. 2 (2010): 152–204.

6. See especially Andrea Brandolini, "Political Economy and the Mechanics of Politics," *Politics & Society* 38, no. 2 (2010): 212–26; and Lane Kenworthy, "Business Political Capacity and the Top-Heavy Rise in Income Inequality: How Large an Impact?" *Politics & Society* 38, no. 2 (2010): 255–65.

7. Thomas E. Patterson, *The Vanishing Voter* (New York: Vintage Books, 2003), 44–46.

8. Walter Dean Burnham, "The Turnout Problem," in A. James Richley, ed., *Elections American Style* (Washington, D.C.: Brookings Institution, 1987).

9. Ibid., 125.

10. Burnham wrote, "While no one doubts that the Republican party suffers from some internal divisions and even occasional bouts of selective abstention among its supporters . . . the GOP remains much closer to being a true party in the comparative sense than do today's Democrats" (ibid., 124). This remark is as true in the early twenty-first century as it was in the mid-1980s when Burnham wrote it.

11. Ibid., 123–24.

12. Stephen E. Bennett, "Left Behind: Exploring Declining Turnout among Noncollege Young Whites, 1964–1988," *Social Science Quarterly* 72, no. 2 (1991): 314–33; and Patterson, *The Vanishing Voter,* chap. 2.

13. Frederick Solt, "Does Economic Inequality Depress Electoral Participation? Testing the Schattschneider Hypothethis," *Political Behavior* 32, no. 1 (2010): 285–301.

14. E. E. Schattschneider, *The Semisovereign People: A Realist's View of Democracy in America* (New York: Holt, Reinhart, and Winston, 1960).

15. Jan E. Leighley and Jonathan Nagler, "Socioeconomic Class Bias in Turnout, 1964–1988: The Voters Remain the Same," *American Political Science Review* 86, no. 3 (1992): 734. Also see Ruy A. Teixeria, *Why Americans Don't Vote: Turnout Decline in the United States, 1960–1984* (Westport, Conn.: Greenwood, 1987).

16. Michael P. McDonald and Samuel L. Popkin, "The Myth of the Vanishing Voter," *American Political Science Review* 95, no. 4 (2001): 963. Available at http://elections.gmu.edu/APSR McDonald and_Popkin_2001.pdf.

17. Ibid., 968. Also see Michael P. McDonald, "On the Overreport Bias of the National Election Study Turnout Rate," *Political Analysis* 11, no. 2 (2003): 180–86.

18. Thomas Holbrook and Brianne Heidbreder, "Does Measurement Matter? The Case of VAP and VEP in Models of Voter Turnout in the United States," *State Politics & Policy Quarterly* 10, no. 2 (2010): 159–81.

19. Jeff Manza and Christopher Uggen, "Punishment and Democracy: Disenfranchisement of Nonincarcerated Felons in the United States," *Perspectives on Politics* 2, no. 3 (2004): 491–505. Available at http://www.soc.umn.edu/~ uggen/Manza_Uggen_POP_04.pdf.

20. One of the first to arrive at this conclusion was the economist Anthony Downs, whose seminal book *An Economic Theory of Democracy* (New York: Harper and Row, 1957) sparked a generation of research into the seeming irrationality of voting.

21. See Donald P. Green and Ian Shapiro, *The Pathologies of Rational Choice Theory: A Critique of Applications in the Social Sciences* (New Haven, Conn.: Yale University Press, 1994); and Jeffrey Friedman, ed., *The Rational Choice Controversy: Economic Models of Politics Reconsidered* (New Haven, Conn.: Yale University Press, 1996).

22. Joshua Harder and Jon A. Krosnick, "Why Do People Vote? A Psychological Analysis of the Causes of Voter Turnout," *Journal of Social Issues* 64, no. 3 (2008): 525–49.

23. Wesley T. Milner, Stephen C. Poe and David Leblang, "Security Rights, Subsistence Rights, and Liberties: A Theoretical Survey of the Empirical Landscape," *Human Rights Quarterly* 21, no.2 (1999): 403–43.

24. Ibid.

25. Michael Heise, "The Past, Present, and Future of Empirical Legal Scholarship: Judicial Decision Making and the New Empiricism," *University of Illinois Law Review* 2002, no. 4 (2002): 832. Available at http://illinoislawreview.org/wp-content/ilr-content/articles/2002/4/Heise.pdf.

26. Ibid., 834–35.

27. For an example of research that considers both precedent and values, see Youngsik Lim, "An Empirical Analysis of Supreme Court Justices' Decision Making," *Journal of Legal Studies* 29, no. 2 (2000): 721–52.

28. Jeffrey A. Segal and Albert D. Cover, "Ideological Values and the Votes of U.S. Supreme Court Justices," *American Political Science Review* 83, no. 2 (1989): 557–65.

29. For an example of an investigation of strategic considerations, see Forrest Maltzman and Paul J. Wahlbeck, "Strategic Policy Considerations and Voting Fluidity on the Burger Court," *American Political Science Review* 90, no. 3 (1996): 581–92.

30. See Thomas G. Hansford and David F. Damore, "Congressional Preferences, Perceptions of Threat, and Supreme Court Decision Making," *American Politics Quarterly* 28, no. 4 (2000): 490–510; and Jeff Yates and Andrew Whitford, "Presidential Power and the United States Supreme Court," *Political Research Quarterly* 51, no. 2 (1998): 539–50.

31. Valerie J. Hoekstra, *Public Reaction to Supreme Court Decisions* (New York: Cambridge University Press, 2003).

32. Ibid., 13.

33. Ibid., 113.

34. Ibid., 114.

35. Ibid., 137.

36. This discussion is based on B. Dan Wood and Richard W. Waterman, "The Dynamics of Political Control of the Bureaucracy," *American Political Science Review* 85, no. 3 (1991): 801–28.

37. Ibid.

38. David E. Lewis, *Presidents and the Politics of Agency Design: Political Insulation in the United States Government Bureaucracy, 1946–1997* (Stanford, Calif.: Stanford University Press, 2003).

39. See Kenneth J. Meier and Laurence J. O'Toole Jr., "Political Control versus Bureaucratic Values: Reframing the Debate," *Public Administration Review* 66, no. 2 (2006): 178–92; and Martha Wagner Weinberg, *Managing the State* (Cambridge, Mass.: MIT Press, 1977).

40. Richard C. Hall and Kristina Miller, "What Happens After the Alarm? Interest Group Subsidies to Legislative Overseers," *Journal of Politics* 70, no. 4 (2008): 990–1005.

41. Stephen D. Ansolabehere, Shanto Iyengar, Adam Simon, and Nicholas Valentino, "Does Attack Advertising Demobilize the Electorate?" *American Political Science Review* 88, no. 4 (1994): 829–38. Available at http://weber.ucsd.edu/~tkousser/Ansolabehere.pdf.

42. Ibid., 835.

43. Martin P. Wattenberg and Craig Leonard Brians, "Negative Campaign Advertising: Demobilizer or Mobilizer?" *American Political Science Review* 93, no. 4 (1999): 891. Available at http://weber.ucsd.edu/~tkousser/Wattenberg.pdf.

44. Stephen D. Ansolabehere, Shanto Iyengar, and Adam Simon, "Replicating Experiments Using Aggregate and Survey Data: The Case of Negative Advertising and Turnout," *American Political Science Review* 93, no. 4 (1999): 901–10.

45. Richard R. Lau and Ivy Brown Rovner, "Negative Campaigning," *Annual Review of Political Science* 12 (2009): 285–306.

46. Ibid., 287

47. For these and additional articles on the controversy, see the "Forum" section of the *American Political Science Review* 93, no. 4 (1999): 851–909.

48. For example, see Bruce Jentleson, "The Pretty Prudent Public: Post-Vietnam American Opinion on the Use of Military Force," *International Studies Quarterly* 36, no. 1 (1992): 49–74; Eric Larson, *Casualties and Consensus: The Historical Role of Casualties in Domestic Support for U.S. Military Operation* (Santa Monica, Calif.: RAND, 1996); Steven Kull, I. M. Destler, and Clay Ramsay, *The Foreign Policy Gap: How Policymakers Misread the Public* (Washington, D.C.: Center for Strategic and International Studies, 1997); Miroslav Nincic, "Domestic Costs, the U.S. Public, and the Isolationist Calculus," *International Studies Quarterly* 41, no. 4 (1997): 593–610; Richard K. Herrmann, Philip E. Tetlock, and Penny S. Visser,

"Mass Public Decisions to Go to War: A Cognitive-Interactionist Framework," *American Political Science Review* 93, no. 3 (1999): 553–74; and Bruce W. Jentleson and Rebecca L. Britton, "Still Pretty Prudent: Post–Cold War American Public Opinion on the Use of Military Force," *Journal of Conflict Resolution* 42, no. 4 (1998): 395–417.

49. William A. Boettcher and Michael D. Cobb, "'Don't Let Them Die in Vain': Casualty Frames and Public Tolerance for Escalating Commitment in Iraq," *Journal of Conflict Resolution* 53, no. 5 (2009): 677–97.

50. Ibid., 678.

51. Ibid., 683.

THE EMPIRICAL APPROACH TO POLITICAL SCIENCE

BEFORE DESCRIBING THE METHODS used in the research briefly summarized in chapter 1, we need to take an important detour and clarify *why* many political scientists prefer these tools and concepts over other ways of obtaining knowledge. Not everyone agrees that the so-called empirical approach is the best way to study government and politics. But it does seem to have a "privileged" place in the discipline, and we need to explore its philosophical basis. This takes us to the scientific method.

Of course, it is reasonable to wonder why we should bother with the philosophy of science. Why not just get to sampling, to questionnaires, to actual research techniques? Fair enough. We have, we believe, three very good reasons for this digression.

First, as noted, a "scientific" perspective now dominates the study of human institutions and behavior, and in order to understand and evaluate researchers' myriad findings, it helps to be familiar with the basic logic of the scientific method.

Second, science is not the only path to knowledge, and some scholars do not think it is entirely appropriate for the study of government and politics. Thus, we should recognize what a science of human affairs can and cannot tell us and be aware of alternative perspectives.

Third, and perhaps most important, popular political discourse usually contains a mix of facts and values. Making sense of current events requires the ability to sort out these elements to determine which can be accepted on logical or rational grounds and which must be taken on faith. Think for a moment about contemporary hot-button issues like climate change, evolution, gay marriage, the death penalty, and nuclear power. Participants in these debates make claims and counterclaims about reality. Although the science of the subjects may be complicated, even impenetrable to nonscientists, citizens can still make informed judgments if they understand the elements of scientific reasoning and the limits of its explanatory power.

To put some flesh on these ideas let's return to an example presented in chapter 1. Recall that we summarized a few articles about the effectiveness and effects of negative political advertisements. The editors of the *New York Times* had this to say about the 2010 American national election: "Times are tough, and Americans are understandably worried and angry. This year's campaign has only made things worse. Billions of dollars have been spent to destroy character rather than debate serious ideas."[1]

Let's look at two of the results of two studies about the negativity in campaigns:

1. "At least for the studies considered here, the experimental, survey, and aggregate data converge on the same conclusion: Negative advertising demobilizes voters."[2]

2. "At the very least, however, these data should put to rest any worries that negative campaigning in and of itself demobilizes the electorate. . . ."[3]

The first says negative campaign advertising discourages voting; the second claims it has no ill effects. Which of these opposing positions is right? How do we know it is right? What constitutes a compelling case for one side or the other? Answering these types of questions is the goal of *Political Science Research Methods.*

Look again at the two sentences. Clearly they differ, but do they have any characteristics in common? We point out two. First, they make assertions about the "real world" (that is, they state that bombarding the electorate with negative political ads does in fact result in either X or Y). Second, these assertions can actually be checked or verified against the "facts" of that real world. To find out who is right, a neutral person could presumably observe a series of campaigns and elections over a period of time to ascertain which claim fits the data. It may not be easy, but in principle an objective study could lead to a "truthful" answer.

Now contrast those statements with this assertion:

■ "Negative political advertising should be banned."

This is clearly a different kind of contention because it asserts that the world *should be* in a certain state, not that it actually is so. That is, it expresses an opinion, which can be accepted or not on the basis of one's values and beliefs but can't be proved right or wrong or "checked" against facts. How does one provide evidence for the assertion that attack ads should be banned? One could offer *reasons* for their elimination. But in the end, the truth of this attitude cannot be established in the same way that the truth of the first studies can.

Next, consider this statement:

■ "Negative political advertising should be banned because it harms democracy."

Here we have a compound argument that contains both an opinion ("should be banned") and an assertion of fact ("harms democracy"). The second part can (theoretically, anyway) be confirmed by looking at the actual effects of advertising on voting and citizenship. Yet the first part is still an opinion and isn't proved by any data. Suppose it is true that negative ads have demonstrably harmful effects, such as depressing voter turnout. One might still argue that this consequence is just the price of free speech and has to be tolerated.

Finally, think about this one:

■   "Negativity dispirits the soul of society. Candidates may prevail in elections by tearing down rather than uplifting, but they cannot then unite an angered citizenry." [4]

This statement is a bit ambiguous. Like the previous sentence, the author clearly expresses an opinion—he dislikes attack advertising—and the author expresses a supporting argument seemingly couched in terms that appear to be verifiable. Yet the language is so general and vague (e.g., "dispirits the soul of," "cannot . . . unite an angered citizenry") that establishing the statement's truth might in fact be impossible. We might call this a rhetorical proposition.[5] As we see shortly, some political scientists turn away from these sorts of declarations unless they are translated into a form amenable to systematic and objective study. Doing so too rigorously, however, risks distorting or missing the author's intention.

The approach described in this book attempts to identify claims that in principle can be verified, cast them into observational terms, and then see if data support them. Those that are value laden or rhetorical are set aside for philosophers and others to evaluate. Taking a scientific attitude toward research, we maintain, leads to a better understanding of politics, policy, and government—an understanding that citizens and policy makers can use to make informed rational choices.

Hence, the methods described in this book rest on what we call an empirical viewpoint, and its practitioners we lump into the category *empiricists*.[6] This label is rather broad, even crude, since modern political science includes an endless variety of methodologies. At heart, however, all of them are based on the idea that researchers can achieve an impartial understanding of human affairs, much as sciences strive for an objective knowledge of the natural world.

Although the empirical approach, broadly defined, has a dominant place in the discipline, we stress that it has its share of critics, and we certainly don't maintain that it is the only or even the best way to study political science. There is plenty of room, we believe, for normative theorists and political history. Nor do we believe that quantitative analysis is superior to qualitative studies. (In practice, most research contains a mix of both.) So in this chapter we briefly describe different points of view, ones that challenge the apparently privileged position of science in the study of political affairs. Again, these thinkers come in a variety of sizes and colors, so we simply classify them as *nonempiricists*.[7]

It is easy to wonder why all this theorizing is necessary when all you wanted to know is how to conduct and analyze a public opinion poll. Once more, we have a compelling answer: how one studies a subject greatly affects one's substantive conclusions. To demonstrate the point, we conclude the chapter by showing how empiricists and nonempiricists have answered the question, "Who governs the United States?"

CHARACTERISTICS OF SCIENTIFIC KNOWLEDGE

In our daily lives we "know" things in many different ways. We know, for example, that water boils at 212 degrees Fahrenheit and that human immunodeficiency virus (HIV) causes AIDS. We also may "know" that liberals are "weaker" on national defense than are conservatives or that democracy is "better" than dictatorship. In some cases, we know something because we believe what we read in the newspaper or hear on the radio. In other cases, we believe it because of personal experience or because it appears to be consistent with common sense or is what a trusted authority told us.

Modern political science, though, relies heavily on one kind of knowledge, knowledge obtained through objective observation, experimentation, and logical reasoning.[8] This way of knowing differs greatly from information derived from myth, intuition, faith, common sense, or authority. It has certain characteristics that these other types of knowledge do not completely share.[9] Scientists believe that their findings are based on objective, systematic observation and that their claims can and must in principle be verified or rejected by observation using a shared set of standards and procedures. The ultimate goal of science, which is not always attained, is to use verified results to construct causal theories that explain why phenomena behave the way they do.[10] Scientific knowledge exhibits several characteristics. First, a statement must be demonstrated by unbiased observation. A political scientist uses senses to observe and record phenomena—such as the number and type of political ads, the number of ballots cast in an election, and invasions of the territory of one nation by another—and then describes and explains the observations as accurately as possible.

Second, scientific knowledge depends on verification. That is, our acceptance or rejection of a statement regarding something "known" must be influenced by observation.[11] Thus, if we say that people in the upper classes have more political power than members of the lower strata, we must be able to provide tangible evidence to support this statement. The contention cannot be accepted simply because someone said so or our instinct tells us so. The empirical nature of scientific knowledge distinguishes it from mystical knowledge. In the latter case, only "true believers" are able to observe the phenomena that support their beliefs, and observations that would disprove their beliefs are impossible to specify. Knowledge derived from superstition and prejudice is usually not subjected to empirical verification either. Superstitious or prejudiced persons are likely to note only phenomena that reinforce their beliefs, while ignoring or dismissing those that do not. Thus, their knowledge is based on selective and biased experience and observation. Superstitious people are often fearful of empirically testing their superstitions and resist doing so.

Reconstructed Research

In this section and again later in the chapter, we list and describe various characteristics of scientific activity. These attributes can be thought of as ideals. Not every social scientific statement or procedure meets all the criteria of scientific study. Empirical research is not a matter of blindly following a predetermined, general set of instructions. And research results are almost always a bit messy and tentative. So you should not expect to find many examples of researchers following a recipe. Nor will you in your own studies always be able to follow a prescribed formula. Intuition, luck, and serendipity are sometimes necessary. What we present here is a reconstruction (or an abstraction) of the principles underlying the scientific research process. If you understand these principles, then political science research will be much easier to read about or undertake.

Some philosophers of science insist that a key characteristic of scientific claims is **falsifiability,** meaning the statements or hypotheses can in principle be rejected in the face of contravening empirical evidence. A claim not refutable by any conceivable observation or experiment is nonscientific. In this sense, the findings of science are usually considered tentative: they are "champions" only so long as competing ideas do not upend them. Indeed, the philosopher Karl Popper argued that scientists should think solely in terms of attempting to refute or falsify theories, not prove them.[12]

In any event, note that commonsense knowledge as well as knowledge derived from casual observation may be valid. Yet neither constitutes scientific knowledge until it has been empirically verified in a systematic and unbiased way.

In view of the importance of verification and falsification, scientists must always remain open to alterations and improvements of their research. To say that scientific knowledge is provisional does not mean that the evidence accumulated to date can be ignored or is worthless. It does mean, however, that future research could significantly alter what we currently believe. In a word, scientific knowledge is *tentative.* Often when people think of science and scientific knowledge, they think of scientific "laws." Even though political scientists strive to develop lawlike generalizations, they understand and accept the fact that such statements are subject to revision. In this sense science is self-corrective.

Sometimes efforts to investigate commonsense knowledge have surprising results. For example, given America's high levels of literacy, the emergence of mass communications, the development of modern transportation networks, and the steady expansion of voting rights for the last 200 years, we might assume that participation in national elections would be high and that it would increase as time goes by. But, as the example in chapter 1 suggested, neither of these conditions holds. Lots of evidence indicates that half or more of eligible Americans regularly skip voting and that the number doing so may be increasing despite all the economic and civic progress that has been made. In the studies described in chapter 1, the researchers subjected their claims and explanations to empirical verification. They observed phenomena, recorded instances of the occurrence (and nonoccurrence) of these phenomena, and looked for patterns that were consistent with their expectations. In other words, they accumulated a body of evidence that gave other social scientists a basis for further study.

Scientific knowledge is supposedly "value-free." Empiricism addresses what is, what might be in the future, and why. It does not typically address whether or not the existence of something is good or bad, although it may be useful in making these types of determinations. Political scientists use the words *normative* and *nonnormative* to express the distinction. Knowledge that is evaluative, value laden, and concerned with prescribing what ought to be is known as **normative knowledge.** Knowledge that is concerned not with evaluation or prescription but with factual or objective determinations is known as **nonnormative knowledge.** Most scientists would agree that science is (or should attempt to be) a nonnormative enterprise.

Types of Assertions

It is sometimes tricky to tell an empirical statement from a normative one. The key is to infer the author's intention: Is he or she asserting that something is simply the way it is, no matter what anyone's preference may be? Or is the person stating a preference or desire? Sometimes normative arguments contain auxiliary verbs, such as *should* or *ought,* which express an obligation or a desire. Empirical arguments, by contrast, often use variations of *to be* or direct verbs to convey the idea that "this is the way it really is in the world." Naturally, people occasionally believe that their values are matters of fact, but scientists must be careful to keep the types of claims separate. Finally people often state opinions (beliefs) as if they were a matter of fact in rhetorical sentences, as in "No tax hike ever created a job."

When reading research reports or (even more important) when following political discussions in the media, on the Internet, or on the campaign trail, try to keep in mind that statements that seem to be of the same type can be surprisingly different.

- Empirical: A verifiable assertion of "what is"
- Normative: An assertion of "what should be"

- Combination: A compound claim containing a mixture of at least two of the preceding types
- Rhetorical: A statement to the effect that "my belief is a fact"

This is not to say that empirical research operates in a valueless vacuum. A researcher's values and interests, which are indeed subjective, affect the selection of research topics, periods, populations, and the like. A criminologist, for example, may feel that crime is a serious problem and that long prison sentences deter would-be criminals. He or she may therefore advocate stiff mandatory sentences as a way to reduce crime. But the researcher should test that proposition in such a way that personal values and predilections do not bias the results of the study. And it is the responsibility of other social scientists to evaluate whether or not the research meets the criteria of empirical verification. Scientific principles and methods of observation thus help both researchers and those who must evaluate and use their findings. Note, however, that within the discipline of political science, as well as in other disciplines, the relationship between values and scientific research is frequently debated. We have more to say about this subject later in the chapter.

Even though political scientists may strive to minimize the impact of biases on their work, it is difficult, if not impossible, to achieve total objectivity. An additional characteristic of scientific knowledge helps to identify and weed out prejudices (inadvertent or otherwise) that may creep into research activities.[13] Scientific knowledge must be **transmissible**—that is, the methods used in making scientific discoveries must be made explicit so that others can analyze and replicate findings. The transmissibility of scientific knowledge suggests "science is a social activity in that it takes several scientists, analyzing and criticizing each other, to produce more reliable knowledge."[14] To accept results, people must know what data were collected and how they were analyzed. A clear description of research procedures allows this independent evaluation. It also permits other scientists to collect the same information and test the original propositions themselves. If researchers use the same procedures but do not replicate the original results, the results may be incorrect.

This idea leads to another characteristic of scientific knowledge: it is **cumulative**, in that both substantive findings and research techniques are built upon those of prior studies. As Isaac Newton famously observed of his own accomplishments, "I have stood on the shoulders of giants." He meant that the attainment of his revolutionary insights depended in part on the knowledge other scientists had generated in the previous decades and centuries.

Shortcomings in a research design often lead others to doubt the results, prompting them to devise their own tests. This would not be possible, however, if researchers did not specify their research strategy and methods. Such descriptions permit a better assessment of results and allow others to adjust their designs and measurements when pursuing further study. The results of these new studies can then be compared with the earlier results. This process produces an accumulated body of knowledge about the phenomenon in question.

This does not mean that scientific knowledge is accumulated only or primarily through the exact repetition of earlier studies. Often, research procedures are changed intentionally to see whether similar results are obtained under different conditions. Researchers investigating the effects of campaign advertising on turnout have followed precisely this path. Michael Franz and his colleagues listed several ways one can measure citizens' exposure to advertising: experimental manipulation, voters' recalls of ad exposure, the amount campaigns spend on advertisements, archival data, and others.[15] As one might expect, research using one measurement has led to different substantive claims than studies relying on different methods. A result is never totally accepted until it has been explored from different perspectives and generally confirmed. Franz's study, for instance, found that the pessimistic conclusions of previous research on the deleterious effects of negative advertising were not supported by its combination of survey (polling) data and independent indicators of the quantity and quality of what was actually aired:

> Employing our exposure measure across different years, different elections, and a number of different datasets, we found that campaign ads play a role in informing and mobilizing Americans. . . . We found only a single instance in which campaign ads have what could be seen as a negative effect on democratic citizenship.[16]

The lesson for scholars and citizens alike is that a scientific "discovery" or an assertion is never definitively accepted unless and until it has been demonstrated by independent research. The process of replication usually results not in the total dismissal of a claim but in its modification. For example, there has lately been much controversy about global warming and evolution. Thus, if someone makes the claim that "greenhouse gases are causing a rise in average global temperature," a responsible response is to ask how many (independently) conducted studies corroborate the assertion.

Another important characteristic of scientific knowledge is that it is general, or applicable to many rather than just a few cases. Advocates of the scientific method argue that knowledge that describes, explains, and predicts many phenomena or a set of similar occurrences is more valuable than knowledge that addresses a single phenomenon.[17] For example, the knowledge that states with easier voter registration systems have higher election turnout rates than do states with more difficult systems is preferable to the knowledge that Wisconsin has a higher turnout rate than does Alabama. Knowing that party affiliation strongly influences many voters' choices among candidates is more useful knowledge to someone seeking to understand elections than is the simple fact that John Doe, a Democrat, voted for a Democratic candidate for Congress in 2006. The knowledge that a state that has a safety inspection program has a lower automobile fatality rate than another state, which does not, is less useful information to a legislator considering the worth of mandatory inspection programs than is the knowledge that states that require automobile inspections experience lower average fatality rates than those that do not.

In short, the empirical approach strives for **empirical generalization,** statements that describe relationships between particular sets of facts.[18] For example, the assertion that positive campaigns lead to higher voter turnout than do those that engage in mudslinging and name-calling is intended to summarize a relationship that holds in different places and at different times.

Another characteristic of scientific knowledge is that it is **explanatory;** that is, it provides a systematic, empirically verified understanding of why a phenomenon occurs. In scientific discourse, the term *explanation* has various meanings, but when we say that knowledge is explanatory, we are saying that a conclusion can be derived (logically) from a set of general propositions and specific initial conditions. The general propositions assert that when things of type X occur, they will be followed by things of type Y. An initial condition might specify that X has in fact occurred. The observation of Y is then explained by the conjunction of the condition and the proposition. The goal of explanation is, sometimes, to account for a particular event—the demise of the Soviet Union, for example—but more often it is to explain general classes of phenomena such as wars or revolutions or voting behavior.

THE USES OF REPLICATION

When picking a research topic, keep in mind a basic premise of scientific investigation: independent verification. If you come across a claim based on research that you find interesting or provocative or contrary to common sense, you might attempt to replicate at least part of the study. Suppose, for example, that a newspaper reports that the public generally favors a certain policy, but you suspect that the results are misleading because of the way the questions were worded or the circumstances in which they were asked. You might be able to replicate the study using a different set of data and reach a different conclusion. In other words, don't hesitate to study a problem that has already been well researched.

Explanation, then, answers "why" and "how" questions. The questions may be specific (e.g., "Why did a particular event take place at a particular time?") or more general (e.g., "Why do upper-class people vote more regularly than, say, blue-collar workers?"). Observing and describing facts are, of course, important. But most political scientists want more than mere facts. They are usually interested in identifying the factors that account for or explain human behavior. Studies of turnout are valuable because they do more than simply describe particular election results; they offer an explanation of political behavior in general.

An especially important kind of explanation for science is that which asserts *causality* between two events or trends. A causal relation means that in some sense, the emergence or presence of one condition or event will always (or with high probability) bring about another. Causation implies more than that one thing follows another: instead, it means one *necessarily* follows the other. It is one thing to say that economic status is somehow related to level of political participation. It is quite another to assert that economics determines or causes behavior. Statements asserting cause and effect are generally considered more informative and perhaps useful than ones simply stating an unexplained connection exists. After all, there may be a relationship between the birthrate in countries and the size of their stork populations. But this connection is purely coincidental. We discuss causality in more detail in chapter 6.

In this vein, explanatory knowledge is also important because, by offering systematic, reasoned anticipation of future events, it can be predictive. Note that prediction based on explanation is not the same as forecasting or soothsaying or astrology, which do not rest on empirically verified explanations. An explanation gives scientific reasons or justifications—for why a certain outcome is to be expected. In fact, many scientists consider the ultimate test of an explanation to be its usefulness in prediction. Prediction is an extremely valuable type of knowledge, since it may be used to avoid undesirable and costly events and to achieve desired outcomes. Of course, whether or not a prediction is "useful" is a normative question. Consider, for example, a government that uses scientific research to predict the outbreak of popular unrest but uses the knowledge not to alleviate the underlying conditions but to suppress the discontented with force.

In political science, explanations rarely account for all the variation observed in attributes or behavior. So exactly how accurate, then, do scientific explanations have to be? Do they have to account for or predict phenomena 100 percent of the time? Most political scientists, like scientists in other disciplines, accept **probabilistic explanation,** in which it is not necessary to explain or predict a phenomenon with 100 percent accuracy.

At this point, we should acknowledge that many explanations and predictions in political science are weak or even false. Indeed some have so many counterinstances that they do not seem worthy of the designation *scientific,* and many critics rightfully point out that the social sciences have never come close to the rigor and precision of the natural sciences. For this reason, philosophers and methodologists maintain that social scientists cannot achieve the exactitude and precision of the natural sciences and that, instead, they should attempt not to explain behavior but to understand it.[19] Needless to say, we do not entirely agree with this view, but later in the chapter we acknowledge that this position has merits.

Scientists also recognize another characteristic of scientific knowledge: **parsimony,** or simplicity. Suppose, for instance, two researchers have developed explanations of why some people trust and follow authoritarian leaders. The first account mentions only the immediate personal social and economic situation of the individuals, whereas the second account accepts these factors but also adds deep-seated psychological states stemming from traumatic childhood experiences. And imagine that both provide equally compelling accounts and predictions of behavior. Yet, since the first relies on fewer explanatory factors than does the second, it will generally be the preferred explanation, all other things being equal. This is the principle of Ockham's razor, which might be summed up as "keep explanations as simple as possible."

THE IMPORTANCE OF THEORY

The accumulation of related explanations sometimes leads to the creation of a **theory**—that is, a body of statements that systematize knowledge of and explain phenomena. A theory about a subject such as war or voting or bureaucracy consists of several components: a set of "primitive" terms (words and concepts whose meanings are taken for granted); assumptions or axioms about some of

the subject matter; explicit definitions of key concepts; a commitment to a particular set of empirical tools such as survey research (that is, polling) or document analysis; and, most important, general, verifiable statements that explain the subject matter. Two crucial aspects of empirical theory are (1) that it leads to specific, testable predictions and (2) that the more observations there are to support these predictions, the more the theory is confirmed.

Example: Proximity Theory of Electoral Choice

To clarify some of these matters, let us take a quick look at an example. The "proximity theory of electoral choice" provides a concise explanation for why voters choose parties and candidates.[20] Superficially the theory may seem simplistic. Its simplicity can be deceiving, however, for it rests on many years of multidisciplinary research[21] and involves considerable sophisticated thinking.[22] But essentially the theory boils down to the assertion that people support parties and candidates who are "closest" to them on policy issues.

Take a particularly simple case. Suppose we consider the abortion debate. Positions on this issue might be arrayed along a single continuum running from, say, "Abortion should always be allowed" to "Abortion should never

---

KEEP TERMS STRAIGHT: *THEORY* VERSUS *FACT*

It's common to hear people say, "Evolution is a theory, not a fact," as if being a "theory" is grounds for doubt. Surprisingly perhaps, most scientists would reply, "So what if it is a theory?" And they would immediately add that evolution is a particular kind of theory, a *scientific* theory.* A scientific theory has, among other attributes, the property that its claims can be falsified by empirical observation and testing. The ideas and predictions of evolutionary theory have been repeatedly tested and confirmed by scientific methods and standards, and evolutionary theory today (it's sometimes called the "modern synthesis") rests on a solid body of confirmed evidence. So nearly every scientist accepts it as the more or less valid account of, say, human ancestry. But being verified is not the same as being "proved." So no, evolution is not a proven fact but a set of well-supported findings. Scientists will gladly abandon Darwinism if and when a better scientific explanation comes along.

If one relies on a different epistemology (or method for determining what is true), such as faith or the advice of trusted people, then the fact that evolutionary theory has the support of science may be beside the point. One might still doubt that humans and chimpanzees shared a common ancestor. In so doing one is using a different—not necessarily inferior—methodology for deciding what is true. But this method is *not* based on scientific principles.

---

*The biologist Richard Dawkins writes in *The Greatest Show on Earth* (New York: Free Press, 2009): "Evolution is a fact" (p. 8). Despite appearances to the contrary, Dawkins knows evolution is a theory and clearly illustrates how scientists use the word *theory* in a scientific context, where its meaning may differ from that of common usage

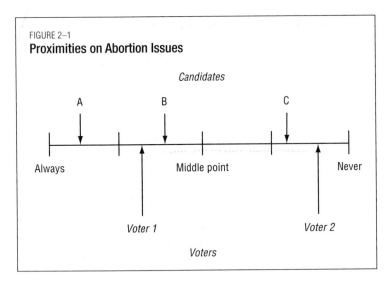

FIGURE 2–1
Proximities on Abortion Issues

Candidates

A   B   C

Always   Middle point   Never

Voter 1   Voter 2

Voters

be permitted" (see figure 2–1). Proximity theorists believe that both voters and candidates (or parties) can be placed or located on this scale and, consequently, that the distances or proximities between them (voters and candidates) can be compared. The theory's prediction is straightforward: an individual votes for the candidate to whom he or she lies closest on the continuum.

To expand a bit, theorists in this camp argue (1) that analysts using proper measurement techniques can position both issues and candidates on scales that show how "close" they are to each other and to other objects and (2) that voters vote for candidates who are closest (most proximate) to themselves on such scales. People choose nearby candidates out of their desire to maximize utility, or the value that results from one choice over another. Knowing this fact, candidates adjust their behavior to maximize the votes they receive. Adjusting behavior means not only taking or moving to positions as close as possible to those of the average or typical voter (the so-called median voter) but also, if and when necessary, obscuring one's true position (that is, following a strategy of ambiguity).[23] Figure 2–1, for instance, shows that Voter 1's position is closest to Candidate B's; therefore, Voter 1 would presumably vote for that candidate. Similarly Voter 2 would prefer Candidate C. Note also that Candidate A could attract Voter 1's support by moving closer to the middle, perhaps by campaigning on an "abortion-only-in-certain-circumstances" platform.

The proximity theory has many of the characteristics of an empirical theory. It explains why things happen as they do, and it offers specific and testable predictions. It is also an implicitly causal theory in that it hypothesizes that the desire to maximize utility "causes" voters to support specific candidates. It is general since it claims to apply to any election in any place at any time. As such, it provides a much more sweeping explanation of voting than a theory that uses time- and place-bounded terms such as "the 2006 gubernatorial election in Pennsylvania." In addition, it provides a parsimonious or relatively simple account of candidate choice. It does not invoke additional explanatory factors such as psychological or mental states, social class membership, or current economic conditions to describe the voting act. Most important, although the proximity theory rests on considerable formal (and abstract) economic and decision-making reasoning, it puts itself on the line by making specific empirical predictions.

As a theory, it incorporates or uses numerous primitive or undefined terms such as *issue, candidate,* and *utility.* These words and concepts may have well-accepted dictionary meanings, but the theory itself takes their common understanding for granted. When a theory is challenged, part of the dispute might involve slightly divergent interpretations of these terms. At the same time, the theory makes explicit various other assumptions. It assumes, among other things, that a researcher can place individuals on issue dimensions, that people occupy these positions for reasonably long time periods, that voters are rational in that they maximize utility, and that candidates have objective positions on these issues.[24] Moreover, by assumption, certain possibilities are not considered. The theory does not delve into the question of whether or not a person holds a "correct" position on the scale, given his or her objective interests. Finally, to test the proximity or spatial idea, researchers assume that one can assign individuals meaningful spatial positions by asking certain kinds of questions on surveys or polls.[25] This may be a perfectly reasonable assumption (we touch on that matter in chapter 10), but it is an assumption nevertheless.

Still, spatial modelers, as they are called, go to great lengths to define and explain key concepts. How *distance* is defined is a serious matter because different definitions can lead to different substantive conclusions.[26] And, as we noted earlier, the theory establishes clear hypotheses. Consider, for example, Voter 1 in figure 2–1. The theory predicts that this person will vote for Candidate B, not A or C, because that candidate is closest. Voter 2, on the other hand, is closest to C and will vote for that candidate. All of these predictions can be checked with appropriate survey data.

The Role of Assumptions

No theory rests entirely on "facts" because it invariably contains unproven or unexamined definitions and statements. These assumptions may be based on previous usage and research, but the theory does not address them directly, except possibly to acknowledge their existence. For example, a theory of war might assert that one nation will attack another one if conditions X, Y, and Z hold. In making this argument, however, the theory may use words and ideas (e.g., *aggression, nation-state, balance of power*) that go undefined, or it may assume that the best way to see if the conditions apply is to use certain historical documents. Hence, if the theory's main assertion—if conditions X, Y, and Z occur, an armed conflict follows—may fail to explain or predict the occurrence of a specific war because

1. the theory itself is just wrong;

2. one or more of its underlying concepts or assumptions is incorrect or ambiguous; or

3. both (1) and (2) are incorrect (the most likely case).

This characteristic means that scientific theories are provisional, that is, always subject to revision and change. In fact, according to the philosopher Thomas S. Kuhn, most "normal" activity in science involves checking the adequacy and implications of existing theories.[27] Thus, new observations, more accurate measurements, improved research design, and the testing of alternative explanations may reveal the limitations or empirical inadequacies of a theory. In this case, the theory will have to be modified or rejected.[28] One of the excitements of reading scholarly literature is to witness the battle of clashing theories.[29]

The Explanatory Range of Theories

Theories are sometimes described by their explanatory range, or the breadth of the phenomena they purport to explain. Usually one does not have a theory of "why Barack Obama won the 2008 presidential election." (It is, of course possible to find several theories that account for this particular outcome. But note that 2008 election results are an instance, or "token," of the kind of event with which these theories deal.) Instead, a good theory of electoral outcomes presumably pertains not only to the 2008 presidential contest but also to other elections in other times and places.

In the social sciences, so-called narrow-gauge or middle-range theories pertain to limited classes of events or behaviors, such as a theory of voting behavior or a theory about the role of revolution in political development.[30] Thus, a theory of voting may explain voter turnout by proposing factors that affect people's perceptions of the costs and benefits of voting: socioeconomic class, degree of partisanship, the ease of registration and voting laws, choices among candidates, availability of election news in the media, and so forth.[31] Global or broad-range theories, by contrast, claim to describe and account for an entire body of human behavior. Hence, we find theories of "international relations" or "the rise and fall of civilizations."[32] In short, theories play a prominent role in natural and social sciences because they provide general accounts of phenomena.[33] Other things being equal, the broader the range of the things to be explained, the more valuable the theory.

But theory builders must not forget the basic standards for judging scientific theories: Are assumptions and axioms clearly separated from substantive propositions and hypotheses? Can the claims be verified or falsified? Are they empirical, not normative? Do they provide general explanations and add to existing knowledge? Are their statements transmissible to others? Are they parsimonious?

OVERVIEW OF SCIENTIFIC RESEARCH

So what exactly is scientific research? In reality, no scientist in the field or laboratory adheres to a prescribed set of steps like someone following a script. Scientists rely not just on formal procedures but also on intuition, imagination, and even luck at times. Nevertheless, we may conceptualize what they do by identifying the underlying logic of their activities. Here is an idealization of a scientific research program.

Development of an Idea to Investigate or a Problem to Solve

A scientist gets topics from any number of sources, including literature about a subject, a general observation, an intuition (or hunch), the existence of conflicts or anomalies in reported research findings, and the implications of an established theory. For example, newspaper accounts suggest that evangelical Christians tend to support conservative candidates because of "moral values." Several research questions are raised by these accounts: Do evangelicals behave in politics differently than do other religious groups? Do evangelicals turn out to vote more in elections where there are distinct differences between candidates on moral issues than in elections where the differences are small?

Hypothesis Formation

After selecting a topic, an investigator tries to translate the idea or problem into a series of specific hypotheses. As we see in chapter 4, hypotheses are tentative statements that, if confirmed, show how and why one thing is related to another or why a condition comes into existence. These statements have to be worded unambiguously and in a way that their specific claims can be evaluated by commonly accepted procedures. After all, one of the requirements of science is for others to be able to independently corroborate a discovery. If assertions are not completely transparent, how can someone else verify them? In the preceding example, we might hypothesize that evangelical Christians are more likely than others to base their vote on candidates' positions on moral issues or that evangelical Christians are more likely than other voters to vote for conservative candidates.

Research

This is where the rubber meets the road: the essence of science comes in the empirical testing of hypotheses through the collection and analysis of data. In this example, we need to define in operational and understandable terms the concepts *moral values, conservative,* and *evangelical Christian.* We might, for instance, tentatively identify evangelicals as people who attend certain churches, moral values as attitudes toward abortion and gay marriage, and support for conservatives as voting for Republican candidates for state and national office. It would be possible (but not necessarily easy) to write a series of questions to be administered in a survey or a poll to elicit this information. If this operational hypothesis holds water, we would expect certain responses (for example, opposition to gay marriage) to be associated with certain behaviors (for example, voting for Republicans).

Decision

The logical next step is to see whether or not the observed results are consistent with the hypotheses. Though simple in principle, judging how well data support scientific hypotheses is usually not an easy matter. Suppose, for example, we find that 75 percent of evangelical Christians opposed gay marriage and 90 percent of these individuals voted for a Republican House candidate in 2006. So far, so good. But suppose, in addition, that 70 percent of nonevangelicals also oppose gay marriage and that more than 90 percent of these people also voted Republican in the same election. It appears that attitudes might be affecting voting, but the data do not necessarily establish a connection between religious preference and political behavior. Weighing quantitative or statistical evidence requires expertise, practice, and knowledge of the subject matter plus good judgment, and this skill is often difficult to teach. Still, chapters in this book are devoted to showing ways to make valid inferences about tenability of empirical hypotheses.

Modification and Extension

Depending on the outcome of the test, one can tentatively accept, abandon, or modify the hypothesis. If the results are favorable, it might be possible to derive new predictions to investigate. If, however, the data do not or only very weakly support the hypothesis, it will be necessary to modify or discard it. Let us stress here that negative results—that is, those that do not support a particular hypothesis—can still be interesting or helpful.[34] As we suggested earlier, some scholars, such as Popper, believe that science advances by disproving claims, not by accepting them. Consequently, a valuable contribution to science can come from disconfirming widely held beliefs, and the only way to do that is to replicate or reinvestigate the research upon which the beliefs rest. The key is not so much the result of a hypothesis test but how substantively important the hypothesis is to begin with.

In essence, the scientific method entails using quantitative or qualitative data to test specific propositions. But exactly how does one use evidence to establish a hypothesis? What kind of thinking is involved?

TYPES OF SCIENTIFIC REASONING: DEDUCTION AND INDUCTION

In some areas of science, such as mathematics, the proper application of logic guarantees the truthfulness of a proposition. This type of reasoning is called **deduction.** A valid deductive argument is one in which, if the premises are true, the conclusion must necessarily be true as well. The classic example is this syllogism:

All men are mortal.
Socrates is a man.

Socrates is mortal.

The conclusion (the sentence below the line) must be true if the premises (the statements above the line) are true. In this example, if all men are mortal and Socrates is a man, how could he *not* be mortal? Note that whether or not the premises are true is immaterial to the validity of the reasoning. In a valid deduction, it is the structure of the argument that counts: if the conditions ("All men . . .") are true and the argument is stated correctly, then the conclusion must be true.

As mentioned earlier, a common application of deductive reasoning is found in mathematics, in which theorems are deduced from a set of premises assumed to be or having been established as true. Deductive arguments find their way into political science, too. Social scientists have attempted to develop many axiomatic or deductive accounts of voting, group and coalition behavior, decision making, and the outbreak of war to name a few. For example, voters are supposed to be motivated to vote on the basis of the costs and benefits to them of the policies espoused by the candidates in an election. If this premise is true and large policy differences exist between candidates in an election, then turnout in the election will be high because voter motivation will be higher than it is in elections in which there are small policy differences.

A more common type of reasoning is **induction.** Induction refers to the process of drawing an inference from a set of premises and observations. This type of reasoning differs from deduction because the premises do not guarantee the conclusion but instead lend support to it. An inductive argument, in other words, does not rely on formal proof but rather gives us (more or less solid) reasons for believing in the conclusion's truthfulness. A common type of inductive argument in the social sciences is one that makes a generalization on the basis of a sample. An argument based on sampling, for instance, has the following general form:[35]

In a particular sample, *X* percent of As are Bs.

X percent of *all* As are Bs.

One might argue, for instance, that 75 (*X*) percent of those people in a sample of Americans who attend church more than once a week (A) think that the Bible is the literal word of God (B). Then, you would have some reason to believe (but would not have proved deductively) that in the population as a whole, 75 percent of frequent church attendees will regard the Bible as the actual word of God. This is, in effect, the kind of argumentation used by pollsters who want to make a generalization about a population based on the results of a sample. For us to accept the argument, we must have confidence in the sampling and analysis procedures. But even if we do, there is no assurance that the conclusion is true. It might seem probable or likely, but we have not demonstrated it conclusively.

DEDUCTION AND INDUCTION: THE CASE OF "THE PARADOX OF NOT VOTING"

Deduction and induction are not necessarily mutually exclusive activities. Some political scientists stress one or the other. Many pursue both strategies. But conclusions derived from one method may contradict results from another. Consider turnout in elections. Deductive models, which are logically consistent and valid, lead to conclusions that survey research, an inductive approach, do not support.

"Deductive models" of turnout produce these results:

Premise 1: Citizens are rational (i.e., they choose action A out of a set of possible actions that brings the highest satisfaction or utility U).

Premise 2: Utility U will be discounted (reduced) by the expected probability that the action A will in fact bring the reward or utility U.

Premise 3: Utility will also be discounted (reduced) by the costs of performing action A.

Premise 4: Citizen performs act A if and only if expected utility E(U) exceeds the costs of performing the action.

Condition 1: The probability that a citizen's vote making a difference in the outcome of an election is virtually nil.

Condition 2: Becoming informed and actually going to the polls are costly.

Conclusion: A rational citizen will *not* vote.

"Inductive studies" of turnout reach an opposite conclusion:

Assumption: Citizens are rational.

Hypothesis: Because they are rational, citizens will not vote (see text for reasons).

Make a series of observations:

Survey 1: A random sample of the voting age population in New England using unambiguous survey questions, accurate reporting, and careful analysis reveals that 4 out of 5 respondents report voting.

Survey 2: A random sample of the voting age population in the United States using unambiguous survey questions, accurate reporting, and careful analysis reveals that 3 out of 5 respondents report voting.

Survey *n:* Many additional national and regional samples using unambiguous survey questions, accurate reporting, and careful analysis.

Conclusion: The hypothesis is not confirmed.

REACTIONS TO THE EMPIRICAL APPROACH: PRACTICAL OBJECTIONS

The search for regularities in behavior assumes that people act consistently and in a predictable manner. Yet, because people are self-aware and (partly, at least) in control of their behavior, they can intentionally act in unpredictable or misleading ways. In fancy words, humans are introspective and forward looking. This problem is occasionally encountered among subjects "cooperating" in a research project. For example, a subject may figure out that he or she is part of an experiment to test a theory about how people behave when put in a difficult or stressful or confusing situation. The subject with this knowledge may then act in a way not predicted by, or in conflict with, the theory. Or the subject may try to confirm the researchers' hypothesis. Similarly, people may be reluctant or refuse to reveal what is really on their minds or what they have done in the past or would do in the future. In other words, our ability to accurately observe the attributes of people can at times be severely limited. It is, for instance, frequently difficult to measure and explain illegal or socially unacceptable behaviors such as drug use.[36]

Problems also arise because the concepts of interest to many political scientists are abstract or have many meanings or are value laden. Chapter 1 showed that an idea as seemingly straightforward as "the number of eligible voters" can present problems that affect our substantive conclusions about how civic minded Americans are. Or consider unemployment, another seemingly unambiguous concept. One common measure of unemployment takes into account only persons who are out of work but actively seeking employment. An argument may be made that such a measure greatly underestimates unemployment because it does not include those who are so discouraged by their failure to find a job that they are no longer actively seeking work. Finding an adequate definition of poverty can be just as difficult, because people live in different types of households and have available different kinds of support beyond just their observed income. What one scholar may feel constitutes poverty another may see as nothing more than acceptable hardship.

Furthermore, political scientists must face the fact that human behavior is complex, perhaps even more complex than the subject matter of other sciences (genes, subatomic particles, insects, and so on). Complexity has been a significant obstacle to the discovery of general theories that accurately explain and predict almost every kind of behavior. After all, developing a theory with broad applicability requires the identification and specification of innumerable variables and the linkages among them. Consequently, when a broad theory is proposed, it can be attacked on the grounds that it is too simple or that too many exceptions to it exist. Certainly to date no empirically verified generalizations in political science match the simplicity and explanatory power of Einstein's famous equation $E = mc^2$.[37]

There are other obstacles. The data needed to test explanations and theories may be extremely hard to obtain. Indeed, often the potentially most informative data are totally unavailable. People with the needed information, for example, may not want to release it for political or personal reasons. Pollsters, for instance, find refusal to answer certain questions, such as those designed to measure attitudes toward ethnic groups, to be a major problem in gauging public opinion. Similarly, some experiments require manipulation of people. But since humans are the subjects, the researchers must contend with ethical considerations that might preclude them from obtaining all the information they want. Asking certain questions can interfere with privacy rights, and exposing subjects to certain stimuli might put the participants at physical or emotional risk. Tempting someone to commit a crime, to take an obvious case, might tell a social scientist a lot about adherence to the law but would be unacceptable nevertheless.

Self-Reflection and Individuality

Like any other organisms, humans are aware of their surroundings. They have the additional ability to empathize with others and frequently attempt to read others' minds. As John Medearis put it, "human beings—individually, but especially jointly—are self-interpreting and reflective, capable of assigning meanings to their actions and revising these meanings recursively."[38] Observations of this sort led many social scientists and philosophers to question whether or not the scientific method can be applied to the study of something as intrinsically language based as politics. This doubt appears later in the chapter when we discuss interpretation versus explanation. In the meantime, let us point to a practical problem. Since humans are self-reflexive and empathetic creatures, they often anticipate a researcher's goals and adjust their actions accordingly (e.g., "The experimenter seems to dislike negative advertisements, so I'll be against them too, even though I don't care much one way or the other."). As we see in chapter 6, this tendency is sometimes called the "demand characteristics" of the experiment.)

When it comes to studying political behavior such as voting or decision making, another difficulty arises. Many experiments in science assume that the entities under investigation are for all intents and purposes identical and, hence, can be interchanged without fear of compromising the conclusion. An iron ion (Fe^+) from one source is as good as another from somewhere else (no matter where in the universe) when it comes to studying iron's reaction with oxygen. But can the same be said of humans? Consider a political scientist who wants to investigate the effects of negative advertising on attitudes. Suppose Jane and Mary are selected. We cannot assume that they will react to the experimental stimuli exactly the same way, even though they are the same age, are of the same political persuasion, are the same gender, are residents of the same city, attend the same college, and so forth.

Social scientists have to get around this problem by using groups or samples of individuals and then examining the *average* effect of the stimulus. Any generalization that results has the form: given subjects with characteristics A, B, . . . , X (the stimulus) *on average* affects Y (the response) by *approximately N* units. In other words, sometimes the basic units under the scientist's microscope can be considered pure, even if they are complex molecules, but not so in political science. The objects political scientists study are multifaceted and conscious beings with a volition of their own; thus, statements about them must necessarily be tentative, general, and time bound.

Finally, there is the inescapable subjectivity of politics. We provide an example that bedevils research into the studies of power. As we see at the end of the chapter, most political scientists would agree that, if a power elite or bloc exists, it should at a minimum make or heavily influence key policy decisions. The problem is how does one objectively identify "key" policies. Should the choice be left to the judgment of the researcher or knowledgeable/informed experts? Or are there concrete indicators or measures of importance. Suppose we want to class decision A as "important." On what grounds do we make the assignment? The number of people A affects? Its cost? The number of times it is mentioned in the press? Its length in legal codes? The number of times it is litigated? Any or all of these might be useful. But for a variety reasons none of these may capture the significance (or lack of significance) of a decision. Importance often comes from how people interpret or understand A, and understanding of this sort, many assert, lies beyond the scope of empirical sciences.[39]

All of these claims about the difficulty of studying political behavior scientifically may have merit. Yet they can be overstated. Consider, for example, that scientists studying natural phenomena encounter many of the same problems. Paleontologists must attempt to explain events that occurred millions or even billions of years ago. Astronomers and geologists cannot mount repeated experiments on most of the phenomena of greatest interest to them. They certainly cannot visit many of the places they study most intensively, like other planets or the center of the earth. And what can be more complex than organisms and their components, which consist of thousands of compounds and chemical interactions? Stated quite simply, it is in no way clear that severe practical problems distinguish political science from any of the other sciences.

Is Political Science Trivial or Irrelevant?

The empirical approach in political science, with its advent in earnest in the 1960s, seemed to bring with it all the accoutrements of rigorous natural sciences: equations and mathematical models, statistical analysis, instrumentation and quantification, computers and electronic databases, esoteric concepts (e.g., "multidimensional issue spaces"). Yet practically from the moment the empirical or scientific perspective arrived on the scene, doubters and skeptics appeared. Among other complaints, they pointed to the trivial nature of some of the "scientific" findings and applications. Common sense would have told us the same thing, they argued. Moreover, and far worse in some people's minds, the empirical approach with its emphasis on quantification seemed to become more and more irrelevant to a practical understanding of government, a concern that persists to this day:

> Academics have followed the architectonic path of turning the study of politics into a theoretical pursuit unconcerned with the needs of and far removed from the understanding of the ordinary citizen or political leader. No one reading the last dozen issues of the American Political Science Review would find much that would provide an answer to the most fundamental of all political questions: "What is to be done?"[40]

Of course, as we explained earlier, there is a difference between intuition and scientific knowledge. To build a solid base for further research and accumulation of scientific knowledge in politics, commonsense knowledge must be verified empirically and, as is frequently the case, discarded when wrong. Still, "scientism" left many political scientists dismayed.

A more serious criticism of the scientific study of politics is that it leads to a failure to focus enough scholarly research attention on important social issues and problems. Some critics contend that, in the effort to be scientific and precise, political science overlooks the moral and policy issues that make the discipline relevant to the real world. Studies rarely address the implications of research findings for important public policy choices or political reform. In other words, the quest for a scientific knowledge of politics has led to a focus on topics that are quantifiable and relatively easy to verify empirically but that are not related to significant, practical, and relevant societal concerns.[41] In the late 1960s and later in 2000, well-publicized "revolts" against hard-core empiricism took place. After all, to say "I'm only concerned with facts" may be to turn a blind eye to injustice.

These worries, plus deep philosophical doubts about the utility of the scientific method's applicability to the study of human behavior, led to the emergence of alternative or revisionist methodologies.

COMPETING STANCES

Before exploring alternative methodological perspectives, let us summarize the essential canons of the empirical method:

- Realism: There is a real world that exists independently of observers. (It's there even if we aren't there to see it.)

- Materialism: Only concrete and observable (if only indirectly) entities have causal efficacy.

- Regularity: Natural phenomena (human behavior and institutions) exhibit regularities and patterns that can be revealed by reason and observation.

- Verification and falsification: Statements about the world must be verified or falsified by experience or data. (Don't take anything on faith alone.)

- Irrelevance of preferences: To the maximum extent, one's values and biases should not affect the decision to reject or accept an empirical claim.

- Theory and causal explanation: The goal of science is to create general, verified explanatory theories (even laws).

As widely accepted and useful as science has become in modern times, serious philosophers and social scientists have challenged these premises. We cannot explain all of their objections here, but the essence of their argument is that certain aspects of human life are simply not amenable to systematic and objective analysis. More important, an uncritical faith in realism, objectivity, and material causality is unwarranted. We concentrate on two points:

1. Human actions cannot be explained scientifically but must be *interpreted* from the point of view of the actors. Meaning and understanding are the proper goals.

2. Social scientists have to realize that the world, far from having an independent existence, is partly *constructed* by observers themselves.

We next see how these beliefs lead to alternative approaches: interpretation and constructionism.

Interpretation

Some people question the empirical strategy, however, because the subject matter, human institutions and behavior, differs from material objects such as atoms or stars, and these differences raise all sorts of complexities. One indicator of the inapplicability is that progress in developing and testing contingent causal laws has been agonizingly slow.[42] Moreover, both the methods and the content of the discipline have not come close to the exactitude and elegant sophistication of sciences such as biology or physics, and, consequently, nowhere can we find empirical generalizations with the level of precision and confirmation enjoyed by, say, the theories of relativity and evolution.

Skeptics argue that there are good reasons for this outcome. Since politics inescapably involves actions—that is, behavior that is done for reasons—and not mere physical movement, analyzing it brings up challenges not encountered in the natural sciences. **Actions** are behavior done for a reason. Opponents of the empirical approach claim that scientific methods do not explain nearly as much about behavior as their practitioners think. The problem is that to understand human behavior, one must try to see the world the way individuals do. (Those who hold this belief are the interpretationists, whom we discuss in a moment.) And doing so requires empathy, or the ability to identify and in some sense experience the subjective moods or feelings or thoughts of those being studied. Instead of acting as outside, objective observers, we need to "see" how individuals themselves view their actions. Only by reaching this level of understanding can we hope to answer "why" questions such as "Why did John still vote in the last election even though he was bombarded by countless attack ads on television, the Internet, radio . . . everywhere he turned?" The answers require the interpretation of behavior, not its scientific explanation in terms of general laws. In short, **interpretation** means decoding verbal and physical actions, which is a much different task than proposing and testing hypotheses.

Given this way of looking at the research task, some social scientists advocated stressing the interpretation or empathetic understanding of actions and institutions. One of the earliest and best known proponent of this methodology was Clifford Geertz, an anthropologist, who felt that "man is an animal suspended in webs of significance he himself has spun. I take culture to be those webs, and the analysis of it to be therefore not an experimental science in search of law but an interpretive one in search of meaning."[43] As a simple example of the difference between empirical and interpretative approaches, take journalist James O'Toole's analysis of a close Pennsylvania US Senate election in 2010: "it's now a pretty close race, according to the polls and the body language of the campaigns."[44] Here he relies on both an empirical tool (polling) and intuition (the "body language of the campaign"). Those who closely follow electoral politics would perhaps agree that a minimum of interpretation and subjective analysis is always helpful.

Another way of looking at interpretation is to consider the concept of **social facts**. What exactly are things like political parties, elections, laws, and administrative regulations? In what sense are they real? They do not have same kind of material existence as atoms, bacteria, and mountains but have an entirely subjective existence *only* in the minds of people living in a particular culture. One philosopher remarks that "minds create institutions. There would be no money or marriage or private property without human minds to create these institutions."[45] How, then, should they be studied? The sociologist Emile Durkheim told his students to take them seriously: "the first and most basic rule [of social inquiry] is *to consider social facts as things.*"[46] And many political scientists almost instinctively adhere to that principle. Nonetheless the notion that much of what is studied is socially constructed raises some thorny epistemological issues.

Constructionism and Critical Theory

Most political scientists take reality pretty much as a given. That is, they posit that the objects they study—elections, wars, constitutions, government agencies—have an existence independent of observers and can be studied more or less objectively. But an alternative perspective, called the social construction of reality or **constructionism**,[47] casts doubt on this uncritical, perhaps blasé attitude. According to constructionism, humans do not simply discover knowledge of the real world through neutral processes, such as experimentation or unbiased observation, but rather *create* the reality they analyze. In other words, instead of knowing reality directly in its unvarnished or pure form, our perceptions, understandings, and beliefs about many "facts" stem largely, if not entirely, from human cultural and historical experiences and practices. We put *facts* in quotation marks to stress the constructionist belief that what people often assume to be pure facts are conditioned by the observers' perceptions, experiences, opinions, and similar mental states. This position is perhaps another way of saying, "Facts do not speak for themselves but are always interpreted or constructed by humans in specific historical times and settings."

One version of this position admits that entities (for example, molecules, planets) exist separately from anyone's thoughts about them, but it also insists that much of what people take for granted as being "real" or "true" of the world is built from learning and interaction with others and does not have an existence apart from human thought.[48] Consider the term *Democratic Party.* Instead of having an independent, material existence like an electron or a strand of DNA, a political party exists only because citizens behave as if it did exist. This means that two individuals who come from different social, historical, and cultural backgrounds may not comprehend and respond to the term in the same way. What is important in studying, say, individuals' responses to Democratic candidates is fathoming their personal beliefs and attitudes about the party.

Constructivists rely on an explanatory strategy that very nearly reverses the rationalist logic. They view choice not, as rationalists do, as an adequate or appropriate response of actors to objective conditions but as creative and novel action that makes the conditions of action what they are. The slogan "Anarchy is what states make of it" is a good summary of this line of thinking. Realist international relations theorists believe that nation-states inhabit an anarchical world or raw state of nature—no supranational power or world government keeps a lid on conflict. Hence, nation-states must act first and foremost to secure their territorial integrity or sovereignty. This position lies at the heart of the so called "realist" school of international relations. But for some constructivists, "anarchy" is not an objective state of nature. Rather, as one theorist put it, "anarchy is what states make of it."[49] Consequently, nations do not necessarily have to adopt specific security policies; rather, they are free to choose their responses, and it is in these responses one finds anarchy's true meaning.

As this example suggests, in constructivist thinking, social conduct is shaped not by the environment or a structure but by the way that environment is defined or interpreted by the actors under study. Two political scientists explain that

> *In short, constructivists want to show that important things happen in the world not because people react predictably to certain situations, but because people interpret actions and events in new, bold, and creative ways even when there is nothing in the logic of the situation that drives them to do so. That interpretation in turn, creates a new set of structures.*[50]

Constructionist thinking now plays a strong role in international relations theory, where a concept such as *anarchy* is not considered a "given and immutable" cause of the behavior of states (for example, their desire for security through power politics). Rather, concepts like this one have to be understood in terms of what actors (individuals, states) make of them.[51]

The constructionist viewpoint, which comes in innumerable varieties, challenges the idea of an objective epistemology, or theory of knowledge. Such ideas, however, are of a deeply methodological nature and raise deep philosophical issues that go well beyond the task of describing the empirical methods used in the discipline.[52] We thus acknowledge that the scientific study of politics is controversial but nevertheless maintain that the procedures we describe in the chapters that follow are widely accepted and can in many circumstances lead to valuable understandings of political processes and behavior. Moreover, they have greatly shaped the research agenda and teaching of the discipline, as can be seen by looking at the evolution of the field in the twentieth century.

The emergence and domination of the empirical perspective has also brought about renewed interest in normative philosophical questions of "what ought to be" rather than "what is."[53] Part of the discipline has become receptive to variations of **critical theory,** or the belief that a proper goal of social science is to critique and improve society (by making it more just and humane) rather than merely understand or explain what is going on. Critical theorists feel, in other words, that by simply analyzing a polity as it is amounts to a tacit endorsement of its institutions and the distribution of power. Contrary to the idea that science should be value-free, critical theorists argue that proposing and working for reforms are legitimate activities for the social sciences. They therefore analyze institutions, practices, ideologies, and beliefs not only for their surface characteristics but also for their "hidden meanings" and implications for behavior.

Take, for example, the statement "I'm just not interested in politics."[54] An empirical political scientist might take this simply as a cut-and-dried case of apathy. He or she might then look for variables (e.g., age, gender, ethnicity) associated with "not interested" responses on questionnaires. A critical theorist, by contrast, might ask, "Does this person really have *no* interest in current events? After all, isn't everyone affected by most political outcomes, like decisions about taxes, war and peace, and the environment, and thus in fact *have* an interest in politics? So, perhaps we have a case of, say, 'false consciousness,' and it is crucial to uncover the reasons for lack of awareness of one's 'real' stake in politics. Is the indifference a matter of choice, or does it stem from the (adverse) effects of the educational system, the mass media, modern campaigning, or some other source?"

Here is another case. An important challenge to research in political science (as well as in other social science disciplines, such as sociology) has come from feminist scholars. Among the criticisms raised is that "the nature of political action and the scope of political research have been defined in ways that, in particular, exclude *women as women* [emphasis added] from politics."[55] Accordingly, "what a feminist political science must do is develop a new vocabulary of politics so that it can express the specific and different ways in which women have wielded power, been in authority, practiced citizenship, and understood freedom."[56] Even short of arguing that political science concepts and theories have been developed from a male-only perspective, it is all too easy to point to examples of gender bias in political science research. Examples of such bias include failing to focus on policy issues of importance to women, assuming that findings apply to everyone when the population studied was predominantly male, and using biased wording in survey questions.[57]

A related complaint is that political science in the past ignored the needs, interests, and views of the poor, the lower class, and the powerless and served mainly to reinforce the belief that existing institutions were as good as they could be. Concerns about the proper scope and direction of political science have not abated, although nearly all researchers and teachers accept the need to balance the scientific approach with consideration of practical problems and moral issues.[58]

Let's wrap up our discussion so far before returning to the all-important question: What difference does all this philosophizing make? Table 2–1 lists some of the key differences between what we have been calling the empirical and nonempirical schools.

WHY METHODOLOGY MATTERS: "WHO GOVERNS?"

Steven B. Smith wrote that "From its very beginnings political science has been a complex discipline torn in conflicting directions."[59] It is fair to conclude, however that empiricism stands in the mainstream of the discipline. Yet, as noted, it has competitors. Why take these philosophical arguments seriously? Because frequently the different perspectives lead to sharply differing substantive conclusions.

TABLE 2–1
Methodological Locations in Political Science

	Nonempirical	Empirical
Goals	To understand behavior To interpret actions	Causal explanations and predictions of individual and institutional behaviors General theory and laws Information of practical use "Value-free" knowledge
Assumptions	Social facts (at least) are "constructed." Institutions are social creations. Objective observation not generally possible because our very senses are affected by culturally defined and imposed prior beliefs. Totally value-free research is impossible.	Realism (appearance and reality are the same). Independent, objective observation is possible. Behavior and, implicitly, institutions exhibit regularities. Claims about the real world must be verified. Attitudes (values, biases, beliefs) must not affect observation and analysis. There are no causeless effects.
Basic toolkit	Qualitative	Quantitative
Methods	Qualitative analysis (e.g., ethnography, content and document analysis, study of discourse) Case studies and comparisons	Case studies and comparisons Experiments and field experiments Mathematical models Surveys Statistical analysis of data Simulations
Objections	Observation is impressionistic, subjective, and nonsystematic. Knowledge is nontransmissible. Findings are tainted by investigator's values and biases.	Takes "politics out of political science." Concentration on formalism, quantitative measurement, and mathematical analysis leads to trivial and practically meaningless results.
Alleged biases	Conclusions are affected by political and social ideologies.	Inherently favors the status quo and existing power structures.

Source: This table is based partly on tables in Colin Hay, *Political Analysis: A Critical Introduction* (New York: Palgrave, 2002), chap. 1.

This point can be seen in the long-running battle over the "power elite model" of American government, a debate that continues to this day, as is illustrated by the vignette on business influence and inequality presented in chapter 1. Here we present a snippet of this complex problem. The research on business influence on economic policy[60] is just the latest in a long line of studies of political power in the United States. The goal of this work has been to answer a fundamental question: "Who governs?" Those in the empirical school want answers that can be empirically verified by evidence showing who exactly wields influence on whom and under what conditions. Those on what we have been calling the nonempirical side also want the truth, but they do not want to be mislead or deceived by a slavish adherence to methods that may not be able to discern the *actual* as opposed to manifest exercise of power. Moreover, in the tradition of the critical social sciences, they are not shy about condemning what they consider an unequal and unjust distribution of power.

Looking at how these sides have thought about who governs provides an opportunity to see how different methodologies may lead to very different, even diametrically opposite, substantive conclusions. For expository purposes, we concentrate on a narrow and early aspect of the debate. This is, of course, a very abbreviated and rough description of a subject crawling with complexities, nuances, and ideological stances.

In what were called "community power studies," sociologists attempted to answer the question, "Who governs?" by investigating decision making in towns and cities.[61] Conducted mostly by sociologists, this research found that business and political elites often ran local politics. In a famous (some political scientists might say "infamous") study, Floyd Hunter concluded that Regional City (Atlanta, Georgia) was effectively run by a small coterie of business and political insiders.[62] These notables exerted their influence in subtle, unobtrusive ways, but, contrary to democratic expectations, govern they did.

How did Hunter arrive at this conclusion? Using what became known as the reputational method, he asked respected Atlantans whom they considered the most influential people in their city. He then interviewed those named to find out whom they *thought* were the most important leaders and, in turn, interviewed them for suggestions. Hunter eventually had a list of names that appeared again and again. These individuals, he claimed, did in fact constitute a governing elite. In his words,

> In Regional City the men of power were located by finding persons in prominent positions in four groups that may be assumed to have power connections . . . business, government, civic associations, and "society" activities. From the recognized, or nominal, leaders of the groups . . . lists of persons presumed to have power in community affairs were obtained. Through a process of selection, utilizing a cross section of "judges" in determining leadership rank, and finally by a further process of self-selection, a rather long list of possible power leadership candidates was cut down to manageable size for the specific purpose of this study [emphasis added].[63]

Observing the national scene, the sociologist C. W. Mills also found that a relatively small and ideologically cohesive elite dominated the federal government. Calling it *the* power elite, Mills claimed a triumvirate of top corporate, military, and political leaders, acting in their self-interest, made most decisions of national significance: "the power elite is composed of men whose positions enable them to transcend the ordinary environments of ordinary men and women; they are in positions to make decisions having major consequences."[64]

Although Hunter, Mills and other "elite theorists" thought of themselves as hard-nosed social scientists, members of the growing empirical political science movement harbored doubts about the soundness of the methodology used to establish the existence of elites and soon began to criticize the results on the grounds that the power elite theorists had employed faulty methods. What was it in the research that troubled them? The greatest failures, detractors believed, were a reliance on unverified assumptions, faulty concept development, and misleading measurement techniques that violated the spirit of the growing reliance on empirical methodology. The research was too "traditional."

Traditional political science, which grew out of the study of law, institutions, and ethics, flourished until the early 1960s. It emphasized historical, legalistic, and institutional subjects.[65] The historical emphasis produced detailed descriptions of the developments leading to political events and practices. Legalism, in contrast, involved the study of constitutions and legal codes. And the concentration on institutions included studies of the powers and functions of political institutions such as legislatures, bureaucracies, and courts.

In general, traditional political science focused on formal governments and their legally defined powers. Legal and historical documents, including laws, constitutions, proclamations, and treaties, were studied to trace the development of international organizations and key concepts such as sovereignty, the state, federalism, and imperialism. Informal political processes—the exercise of informal power and the internal dynamics of institutions, for example—were frequently ignored. Most important, however, was the failure to formulate testable hypotheses and check them against data. Research was primarily descriptive rather than explanatory. Most practitioners did not feel a need to conduct research that had the characteristics of the so-called hard sciences, which were often deemed inapplicable to social behavior and institutions.

The newly arrived empiricists charged that the traditional school lacked rigor and generality and that, although theorists occasionally came up with intriguing and well-reasoned verbal theories, these discoveries were usually not subjected to empirical verification. For example, one power elite skeptic complained about the

> *tendency in current studies of community power . . . [to] to regard power as exercised covertly. . . . This often leads researchers to disbelieve their senses, and to substitute unfounded speculation for plain fact. There is often a puzzling disjunction between the conclusions of current studies of community power and the case material reported in them.* [66]

The earlier studies were also condemned for their alleged ideological biases.[67]

In contrast, political scientist Robert Dahl and his students offered a critique of the previous research that rested heavily on empirical or scientific thinking. Power, they said, is not a "thing" that comes in identifiable and measurable amounts. Moreover, no statement about power could be inferred from mere appearances or reputation. Simply because a group is widely acknowledged to be influential does not demonstrate that it actually makes any decisions. Nor can one infer power from mere possession of resources such as money, status, and "insider" connections; one has to show that these resources are actually put to work and that their possessor succeeds in getting his or her way in a series of conflicts. In addition, having power in one arena (e.g., mass transportation) does not necessarily imply power in another (e.g., education policy). Nelson Polsby, one of Dahl's students, argued as follows:

> One way—perhaps the only scientifically acceptable way—to resolve a dilemma in which empirical experience is contradicted by one's suspicions about what is happening behind the scenes is to let the behaviour of citizens decide, by observing behaviour directly, or by reconstructing it from interviews, newspapers, and documents. The point to be emphasized here, however, is the commonness of this dilemma in community studies.[68]

So how should power holders be identified? In a famous article, Dahl proposed an *empirical test* of the elite model.

1. Consider an actor: A. A may be, for example, a single individual, a collection of business leaders, an organization, or some other group. Whatever the case, its members must be *identifiable*. A can't be some mysterious and unseen clique, nor can its existence merely be assumed.
2. Identify opposing actors: B, C, . . . These may be average citizens, organizations, social or economic classes, etc. The key is that their goals conflict with A's on a given controversy. That is, the issue must be such that A either *wins or loses*.
3. Identify a set of conflicts—X, Y, Z . . .—that actually appear on the agenda and divide A from others.
4. Record the winners.
5. Infer a power elite if and only if A prevails over B, C, . . . on some large proportion of the decisions.[69]

Put bluntly: if you want to show that power is being wielded, you have to find situations of actual, observable conflict. If there is no fight, there are no winners or losers and, hence, no elite. Dahl, like any good scientist, demanded an empirical test of the ruling-elite hypothesis. It is not enough to guess that since corporations have access to seemingly unlimited cash, expertise, and organizational resources, they must be powerful. One has to see them use their muscles to get their way over their opponents in actual policy struggles.

When Dahl and others applied this reasoning to the study of power in America, they concluded that although citizens do not (and for practical reasons, cannot) govern directly, there is little evidence that a single unified group, a power elite, dominates decision making either in cities or in the nation's capital. They found instead that groups "win some, lose some." One implication is that business organizations, no matter how big or well funded, simply cannot structure economic policy to their own advantage. Corporations, banks, and other financial institutions, for instance, have to share power with other groups, such as labor unions, environmental groups, and citizen alliances. At most, an organization exerts influence in a relatively narrow policy area, such as banking or agriculture. Since there are so many power centers in American society, the power structure of the country is best described by the term *pluralism* and advocates of this viewpoint came to be known as *pluralists.* Many in political science came to regard pluralism as the only empirically grounded theory of governance because it had been carefully crafted to contain only measurable concepts and empirically verified propositions.

Yet, there was an immediate backlash to pluralism. Propelling much of the counterattack was the belief that pluralists had been badly misled by their strict empiricism. Peter Bachrach and Morton Baratz, two political scientists whom we place in the interpretationist camp, encouraged observers to look behind the manifest appearance of power as measured, say, in recorded town council votes. Instead, they suggested we try to get inside the heads of decision makers. It is essential, for example, to see how the participants in the policy-making process perceived the agenda (the choices before them). How much influence did the supposed decision makers really have in determining the range of alternatives? Did they consider or advance choices that never came to a vote or to a point of decision?

Dahl's scheme tells us to identify the specific set of available choices so we can see who wins. But suppose an alternative proposal, M, is kept *off* the list of items by A, who does not want it even voted on. A may not care much about X, Y, or Z one way or the other, but in no circumstances does A want M enacted. So A works behind the scenes or quietly manipulates the political process so that M never comes to the fore. Bachrach and Baratz called these "nondecisions" and argued it was necessary to factor them into any measurement of the distribution of power. This agenda-setting power is not necessarily picked up by an empirical analysis.[70] Using this standard, one might find a power elite where the pluralists saw none. Bachrach and Baratz put the matter this way:

> *Of course power is exercised when A participates in the making of decisions that affect B. But power is also exercised when A devotes his energies to creating or reinforcing social and political values and institutional*

*practices that limit the scope of the political process to public consider-
ation of only those issues which are comparatively innocuous to A. To the
extent that A succeeds in doing this, B is prevented, for all practical purposes, from bringing to the fore any issues that might in their resolution
be seriously detrimental to A's set of preferences.*[71]

Later Bachrach and Baratz, following the lead of the Italian Marxist sociologist Antonio Gamsci, expanded the concept of nondecisions into the notion of a
"mobilization" of bias: "the prevailing norms, precedents, myths, rituals, institutions and procedures" that dominate policy making.[72] They recommended that
an investigator into power structures analyze "the dominant values, the myths
and the established political procedures and rules of the game" and then

*make a careful inquiry into which persons or groups, if any, gain
from the existing bias and which, if any, are handicapped by it. Next,
he would investigate the dynamics of* nondecision *making; that is, he
would examine the extent to which and the manner in which the status quo oriented persons and groups influence those community values and those political institutions . . . which tend to limit the scope
of actual decision-making to "safe" issues. Finally, using his knowledge of the restrictive face of power as a foundation for analysis and
as a standard for distinguishing between "key" and "routine" political
decisions, the researcher would, after the manner of the pluralists,
analyze participation in decision making of concrete issues."*[73]

The difference in views about the distribution in power became a bone of
contention within the social sciences. The pluralist side demand testable propositions and solid data. When the power elite idea was subjected to these standards, it failed.[74] Pluralists believed American government is about as
democratic as can reasonably be expected. Their opponents, on the other hand,
chastised hard-core empiricists for being naïve about how power is wielded in
the United States. Bachrach and Baratz, along with most of the others, thought
of themselves as mainstream social scientists who accepted standard research
methods. But it is easy to see why the new advocates of rigorous, systematic,
formal, and quantitative analysis would interpret many of their arguments as
not only unverified but *unverifiable.* Consider this recent comment by sociologist William Domhoff:

*Dahl's [Dahl represents the "scientific" wing of political science] oper-
ationalization of power solely in terms of who wins and who loses in
the decisional arenas of government attempted to constrain the study
of power . . . to a power indicator that can seldom be used with any
confidence without access to historical archives and/or after-the-fact
revelations by participants or whistleblowers [emphasis added].*[75]

The argument is that pluralism has been tripped up by its demand for hard data and verification. As a result, it painted a too rosy picture of American democracy.

The key to understanding power is to know who, if anyone, controls, dominates, influences, and benefits from the dominant belief systems. Hacker and Pierson's study[76] found that the growth in economic inequality in the United States is caused by the growth in business political power:

> Explaining the remarkable rise of winner-take-all requires a true political economy—that is, a perspective that sees modern capitalism and modern electoral democracies as deeply interconnected. On the one side, government profoundly influences the economy through an extensive range of policies that shape and reshape markets. On the other side, economic actors—especially when capable of sustained collective action on behalf of shared material interests—have a massive and ongoing impact on how political authority is exercised.[77]

Bachrach and Baratz might amend that claim by saying, "This is no surprise. Want to know who governs? Find out who dominates the 'mobilization of bias'"[78]

Research on power structures is alive and well today.[79] The subject has grown considerably more complex, with some scholars concentrating on elites, others advocating a modified pluralism, and still others arguing that governments (states) do not simply get "taken over" or manipulated by self-interested outsiders but in fact have the ability and independence to act as the state managers see best.[80] Who is right and who is wrong is not the point here. Instead, we emphasize that whatever side you come down on will depend to a large degree on your faith in the adequacy of a science of politics and government.

POLITICAL SCIENCE TODAY: PEACEFUL COEXISTENCE?

During the growth of empirical political science and the reaction it produced, political scientists became extremely self-conscious about its methods and methodology. Innumerable journal articles and books debated the relative merits of attempting to study politics scientifically. Many of the debates became acrimonious, with the participants charging each other with misunderstanding and misstating each other's positions. Departments at many colleges and universities became bitterly divided between "quantitative" and "qualitative or traditional" methodologies. Being associated with one faction or the other could jeopardize someone's job or chances for tenure, and many scholars charged that the major journals in the field—the most important venues for getting published and advancing careers—were being "taken over" by methodological purists. (If you wanted to publish an article on Plato's philosophy of justice, for instance, you might be out of luck finding a leading journal that would publish the paper unless it had an empirical, preferably quantitative, slant.) Indeed, this level of discord would surprise those students who believe that scholarship is a calm, dispassionate activity.

Fortunately, although deep differences remain, a sort of cease-fire emerged, and methodological disputes are not as public or bitter as before. We might, then, think of the current era as eclectic, meaning that although the discipline continues to be divided by empiricism versus interpretative and constructionist schools, the sides seem to live in relative harmony.

Still, the empirical approach continues to have what its critics think is a privileged position in major universities and journals, and it certainly dominates certain subfields such as the study of electoral behavior, public opinion, decision making, and political economy. The research coming from this side is increasingly technical, especially in its use of mathematics, statistics, and formal modeling. Therefore, to read and understand modern political science literature, one needs a basic understanding of its tools and techniques. Supplying this knowledge is, of course, the point of *Political Science Research Methods.*

CONCLUSION

In this chapter we described the characteristics of scientific knowledge and the scientific method. We presented reasons why political scientists are attempting to become more scientific in their research and discussed some of the difficulties associated with empirical political science. We also touched on questions about the value of the scientific approach to the study of politics. Despite these difficulties and uncertainties, the empirical approach is widely embraced, and students of politics need to be familiar with it. In chapter 3 we begin to examine how to develop a strategy for investigating a general topic or question about some political phenomenon scientifically.

Terms Introduced

Actions. Human behavior done for a reason.

Constructionism. An approach to knowledge that asserts humans actually construct—through their social interactions and cultural and historical practices—many of the facts they take for granted as having an independent, objective, or material reality.

Critical theory. The philosophical stance that disciplines such as political science should assess society critically and seek to improve it, not merely study it objectively.

Cumulative. Characteristic of scientific knowledge; new substantive findings and research techniques are built upon those of previous studies.

Deduction. A process of reasoning from a theory to specific observations.

Empirical generalization. A statement that summarizes the relationship between individual facts and that communicates general knowledge.

Explanatory. Characteristic of scientific knowledge; signifying that a conclusion can be derived from a set of general propositions and specific initial considerations; providing a systematic, empirically verified understanding of why a phenomenon occurs as it does.

Falsifiability. A property of a statement or hypothesis such that it can (in principle, at least) be rejected in the face of contravening evidence.

Induction. A process of reasoning in which one draws an inference from a set of premises and observations; the premises of an inductive argument support its conclusion but do not prove it.

Interpretation. Philosophical approach to the study of human behavior that claims that one must understand the way individuals see their world in order to understand truly their behavior or actions; philosophical objection to the empirical approach to political science.

Nonnormative knowledge. Knowledge concerned not with evaluation or prescription but with factual or objective determinations.

Normative knowledge. Knowledge that is evaluative, value laden, and concerned with prescribing what ought to be.

Parsimony. The principle that among explanations or theories with equal degrees of confirmation, the simplest—the one based on the fewest assumptions and explanatory factors—is to be preferred; sometimes known as Ockham's razor.

Probabilistic explanation. An explanation that does not explain or predict events with 100 percent accuracy.

Social facts. Values and institutions that have a subjective existence in the minds of people living in a particular culture.

Theory. A statement or series of related statements that organize, explain, and predict phenomena.

Transmissible. Characteristic of scientific knowledge; indicates that the methods used in making scientific discoveries are made explicit so that others can analyze and replicate findings.

Suggested Readings

Box-Steffensmier, Janet, Henry Brady, and David Collier. *The Oxford Handbook of Political Methodology.* New York: Oxford University Press, 2008.

Eichler, Margrit. *Nonsexist Research Methods: A Practical Guide.* Boston: Allen and Unwin, 1987.

Elster, Jon. *Nuts and Bolts for the Social Sciences.* Cambridge: Cambridge University Press, 1990.

Hay, Colin. *Political Analysis: A Critical Introduction.* New York: Palgrave, 2002.

Hindmoor, Andrew. *Rational Choice.* New York: Palgrave Macmillian, 2006

Isaak, Alan C. *Scope and Methods of Political Science.* 4th ed. Homewood, Ill.: Dorsey, 1985.

Kuhn, Thomas. *The Structure of Scientific Revolutions.* 2nd ed. Chicago: University of Chicago Press, 1971.

Nielsen, Joyce McCarl, ed. *Feminist Research Methods: Exemplary Readings in the Social Sciences.* Boulder, Colo.: Westview, 1990.

Rosenberg, Alexander. *The Philosophy of Social Science.* 3rd ed. Boulder, Colo.: Westview, 2007.

Silver, Brian L. "I Believe." Chap. 2 in *The Ascent of Science.* New York: Oxford University Press, 1998.

Notes

1. "Vote" [editorial], *New York Times,* November 1, 2010, http://www.nytimes.com/2010/11/02/opinion/02tue1.html.

2. Stephen D. Ansolabehere, Shanto Iyengar, and Adam Simon, "Replicating Experiments Using Aggregate and Survey Data: The Case of Negative Advertising and Turnout," *American Political Science Review* 93, no. 4 (1999): 907.

3. Richard R. Lau and Gerald M. Pomper, "Effects of Negative Campaigning on Turnout in U.S. Senate Elections, 1988–1998," *Journal of Politics* 63, no. 3 (2001): 818.

4. James Leach, "Negative Political Ads Hurt the United States," *U.S. News & World Report,* October 6, 2008, http://politics.usnews.com/opinion/articles/2008/10/06/james-leach-negative-political-ads-hurt-the-united-states.html.

5. Our use of the descriptor *rhetorical* is not meant to be pejorative, nor do we assume that a rhetorical expression cannot be truthful. The kind of statements we have in mind often aim to appeal to or persuade one side of a debate.

6. In particular, we do not equate empirical with quantitative methods, although many political scientists do. John Medearis cites a study that "finds that more than half of 57 leading graduate political science programs she surveyed effectively define 'empirical' research as 'quantitative' research"; John Medearis, review of *Perestroika! The Raucous Rebellion in Political Science,* by Kristen Renwick Monroe, ed., *Perspectives on Politics* 4, no. 3 (2006): 576.

7. Those who follow the philosophy of social science, or epistemology, know that naming the sides in these methodological debates is virtually impossible. Someone we might label a *non-empiricist* might very well foreswear the tag. We are just attempting to sort out tendencies.

8. Careful readers will note that we are combining all sorts of activities under one label. Specialists in one method or another often call themselves different things to emphasize the kind of research they do. For instance, those who rely on deductive reasoning and do not spend much time observing the world often refer to themselves "formal modelers" or "rational choice theorists."

9. We hasten to add that there is not one, definitive definition or interpretation of *science* and the *scientific method.* Philosophers, scientists, and social scientists have argued long and hard about core ideas and propositions. Our listing of the characteristics of scientific knowledge, however, includes widely accepted attributes, even if other writers describe them in different terms.

10. Whether or not political science or any social science can find causal laws is very much a contentious issue in philosophy. See, for instance, Alexander Rosenberg, *The Philosophy of Social Science,* 3rd ed. (Boulder, Colo.: Westview, 2007).

11. Ibid., 107.

12. The most ardent proponent of the idea that science really amounts to an effort to falsify (not prove) hypotheses and theories is Karl Popper. See, for example, *The Logic of Scientific Discovery* (New York: Basic Books, 1959).

13. Alan C. Isaak, *Scope and Methods of Political Science,* 4th ed. (Homewood, Ill.: Dorsey, 1985), 30.

14. Ibid., 31.

15. Michael M. Franz, Paul B Freedman, Kenneth M. Goldstein, and Travis N. Ridout, *Campaign Advertising and American Democracy* (Philadelphia: Temple University Press, 2008), chap. 3.

16. Ibid., 138.

17. It may be tempting to think that historians are interested in describing and explaining only unique, one time events, such as the outbreak of a particular war. This is not the case, however. Many historians search for generalizations that account for several specific events. Some even claim to have discovered the "laws of history."

18. Isaak, *Scope and Methods,* 103.

19. These are the interpretationists mentioned earlier. See, for example, R. G. Collingwood, *The Idea of History* (Oxford, UK: Oxford University Press, 1946). For a good introduction to the distinction between understanding behavior and explaining it, see Martin Hollis, *The Philosophy of Social Science: An Introduction* (Cambridge: Cambridge University Press, 1994), chap. 7.

20. Many varieties of this theory exist, but they share the components presented here.

21. Anthony Downs, an economist, provided one of the first explications of the theory in *An Economic Theory of Democracy* (New York: Harper & Row, 1957). His ideas in turn flowed from earlier economic analyses. See, for example, Harold Hotelling, "Stability in Competition," *Economic Journal* 39, no. 153 (1929): 41–57, available at http://www.edegan.com/pdfs/Hotelling (1929)—Stability in competition.pdf.

22. See James Enelow and Melvin Hinch, *The Spatial Theory of Voting: An Introduction* (New York: Cambridge University Press, 1984).

23. Kenneth Shepsle, "The Strategy of Ambiguity: Uncertainty and Electoral Competition," *American Political Science Review* 66, no. 2 (1972): 555–68.

24. As an example, see Anders Westholm, "Distance versus Direction: The Illusory Defeat of the Proximity Theory of Electoral Choice," *American Political Science Review* 91, no. 4 (1997): 870.

25. Here is an example: "Please look at . . . the booklet. Some people believe that we should spend much less money for defense. Suppose these people are at one end of a scale, at point 1. Others feel that defense spending should be greatly increased. Suppose these people are at the other end, at point 7. And, of course, some other people have opinions somewhere in between, at points 2, 3, 4, 5 or 6." See *American National Election Study (ANES) 2004 Codebook* (2006), Available at the Survey Documentation and Analysis, University of California–Berkeley Web site: http://sda.berkeley.edu/D3/NES2004public/Doc/nes0.htm.

26. The conceptualization of distance and other matters related to the proximity theory are debated in Westholm, "Distance versus Direction," 865–73; and Stuart Elaine Macdonald, George Rabinowitz, and Ola Listhaug, "On Attempting to Rehabilitate the Proximity Model: Sometimes the Patient Just Can't Be Helped," *Journal of Politics* 60, no. 3(1998): 653–90.

27. Thomas S. Kuhn, *The Structure of Scientific Revolutions,* 2nd ed. (Chicago: University of Chicago Press, 1971).

28. Ibid.

29. The discussion of voter turnout presented in chapter 1 provides a clear and important example.

30. A good example is Theda Skocpol, *States and Social Revolutions: A Comparative Analysis of France, Russia and China* (New York: Cambridge University Press, 1979).

31. See Raymond E. Wolfinger and Steven J. Rosenstone, *Who Votes?* (New Haven, Conn.: Yale University Press, 1980).

32. An excellent example of the latter is Jared Diamond's study of the demise of the Mayan, Anasazi, and other societies. See his *Collapse: How Societies Choose to Fail or Succeed* (New York: Viking, 2005), especially part 2; and *Guns, Germs, and Steel: The Fates of Human Societies* (New York: Norton, 1999).

33. Isaak, *Scope and Methods,* 167.

34. An often remarked on characteristic of scholarly journals is that they tend to report mostly positive findings. An article that shows "X is related to Y" may be more likely to be accepted for publication than one that asserts "X is *not* related to Y." Whether or not a "negative result" makes a significant contribution to knowledge depends on the the importance of the original claim. Suppose that a team of psychologists found that "love and marriage" really do *not* "go together." That would be worth publishing.

35. Merrilee H. Salmon, *Introduction to Logic and Critical Thinking,* 2nd ed. (San Diego, Calif.: Harcourt Brace Jovanovich, 1989), 88–97.

36. Social scientists are aware of these pitfalls and try to design research protocols to avoid them. We discuss these topics in great detail in chapter 6, "Research Design."

37. For further discussion of complete and partial explanations, see Isaak, *Scope and Methods,* 143.

38. Medearis, review of *Perestroika!,* 577.

39. For an effort to objectively measure policy importance, see David Mayhew, *Divided We Govern: Party Control, Lawmaking, and Investigations, 1946–2002,* 2nd ed. (New Haven, Conn.: Yale University Press, 2005).

40. Stephen B. Smith, "Political Science and Political Philosophy: An Uneasy Relation," *PS: Political Science and Politics* 33, no. 2 (2000): 189. Or, "We proceed with a two-fold working hypothesis: (1) Academic political science has very little awareness of the knowledge about politics held by practitioners, and (2) Political science is increasingly limited to a highly abstract understanding of politics. . . . We subscribe . . . to the view that academics have limited understanding about the practical work of politics and governance. The academic understanding expressed in concepts, models, and theories is abstract and usually innocent of the nuances regularly experienced by practitioners"; see John R. Petrocik and Frederick T. Steeper, "The Politics Missed by Political Science," *The Forum* 8, no. 3 (2010): 1.

41. See Charles A. McCoy and John Playford, eds., *Apolitical Politics: A Critique of Behavioralism* (New York: Thomas Y. Crowell, 1967).

42. See Alexander Rosenberg, *The Philosophy of Social Science,* 3rd ed. (Boulder, Colo.: Westview, 2007).

43. Clifford Geertz, *The Interpretation of Cultures* (New York: Basic Books, 1973), 5; see also follow discussion on pages 6–7.

44. "Federal Spending Front and Center in Pa., Wash. Senate Races," *PBS NewsHour,* October 26, 2010, http://www.pbs.org/newshour/bb/politics/july-dec10/campaign_10–26.html.

45. Colin McGinn, "Is Just Thinking Enough?" review of *Making the Social World: The Structure of Human Civilization,* by John R. Searle, *New York Review of Books,* November 11, 2010, 58. Available at http://www.nybooks.com/articles/archives/2010/nov/11/just-thinking-enough/.

46. Emile Durkheim, *The Rules of Sociological Method and Selected Texts on Sociology and Method,* ed. Steven Lukes (New York: The Free Press, 1982), 60.

47. The term *constructionism* encompasses an enormous variety of philosophical perspectives, the description of which goes far beyond the purposes of this book. The seminal work that brought the ideas into sociology and from there into political science is Peter L. Berger and Thomas Luckmann, *The Social Construction of Reality* (New York: Doubleday, 1966). An excellent but challenging analysis of constructionism is Ian Hacking, *The Social Construction of What?* (Cambridge, Mass.: Harvard University Press, 1999). Equally important, members of this school have widely varying opinions about the place of empiricism in social research. Many constructivists feel their position is perfectly consistent with the scientific study of politics; others do not.

48. See John R. Searle, *The Construction of Social Reality* (New York: Free Press, 1995).

49. Alexander Wendt, "Anarchy Is What States Make of It: The Social Construction of Power Politics," *International Organization* 46, no. 2 (1992): 391–425.

50. David Dessler and John Owen, "Constructivism and the Problem of Explanation: A Review Article," *Perspectives on Politics* 3, no. 3 (2005): 598. Available at http://www.euce.gatech .edu/files/Dessler-and-Owen-Constructivism-and-the-Problem-of-Explanation.pdf.

51. Wendt, "Anarchy Is What States Make of It."

52. For an excellent collection of articles about the pros and cons of studying human behavior scientifically, see Michael Martin and Lee C. Anderson, eds., *Readings in the Philosophy of Social Science* (Cambridge, Mass.: MIT Press, 1996).

53. Isaak, *Scope and Methods,* 45.

54. This example is based on an article by Issac D. Balbus, "The Concept of Interest in Pluralist and Marxian Analysis," *Politics & Society* 1, no. 2 (1971): 151–77.

55. Kathleen B. Jones and Anna G. Jonasdottir, "Introduction: Gender as an Analytic Category in Political Science," in *The Political Interests of Gender,* ed. Kathleen B. Jones and Anna G. Jonasdottir (Beverly Hills, Calif.: Sage, 1988), 2.

56. Kathleen B. Jones, "Towards the Revision of Politics," in *The Political Interests of Gender,* ed. Kathleen B. Jones and Anna G. Jonasdottir (Beverly Hills, Calif.: Sage, 1988), 25.

57. Margrit Eichler, *Nonsexist Research Methods: A Practical Guide* (Boston: Allen and Unwin, 1987).

58. See the articles comprising "Political Science and Political Philosophy: A Symposium," *PS: Political Science and Politics* 33, no. 2 (2000): 189–97.

59. Smith, "Political Science and Political Philosophy," 189.

60. Jacob S. Hacker and Paul Pierson, "Winner-Take-All Politics: Public Policy, Political Organization, and the Precipitous Rise of Top Incomes in the United States," *Politics & Society* 38, no. 2 (2010): 152–204.

61. See, for example, Robert S. Lynd and Helen M. Lynd, *Middletown in Transition: A Study in Cultural Conflicts* (New York: Harcourt, Brace, 1937).

62. Floyd Hunter, *Community Power Structure: A Study of Decision Makers* (Chapel Hill: University of North Carolina Press, 1953).

63. Hunter, *Community Power Structure,* 11.

64. C. Wright Mills, *The Power Elite,* new ed. (New York: Oxford University Press, 2000), 3–4. Originally published 1956.

65. Isaak, *Scope and Methods,* 34–38.

66. Nelson W. Polsby, "Power in Middletown: Fact and Value in Community Research," *Canadian Journal of Economics and Political Science* 26, no. 4 (1960): 602.

67. One political scientist wrote of a community power studies of Muncie, Indiana, that "the Lynds [Robert and Helen Lynd, the investigators] put a great deal of emphasis on their theory of the power elite, for the existence of a power elite accommodates the Marxist necessity for conspiracy—the critical obstacle which blocks the realization of social justice. An obstacle is an obstacle only when it lies in somebody's path; hence the conspiracy theory of elite rule also presupposes class struggle. Once again, the Lynds maintain the Marxist position only with the greatest effort. They look for class struggle everywhere, and, failing to find it, insist on its incipience" (Polsby, "Power in Middletown," 595).

68. Polsby, "Power in Middletown," 603.

69. Robert A. Dahl, "Critique of the Ruling Elite Model," *American Political Science Review,* 52, no. 2 (1958): 466.

70. Pluralists demand that concepts be "measurable." But, Bachrach and Baratz noted: "The question is, however, how can one be certain in any given situation that the 'unmeasurable elements' are inconsequential, are not of decisive importance? Cast in slightly different terms, can a sound concept of power be predicated on the assumption that power is totally embodied and fully reflected in 'concrete decisions' or in activity bearing directly upon their making? We think not"; Peter Bachrach and Morton S. Baratz, "Two Faces of Power," *American Political Science Review,* 56, no. 4 (1962): 948. Available at http://www.columbia .edu/itc/sipa/U6800/readings-sm/bachrach.pdf.

71. Bachrach and Baratz, "Two Faces of Power," 948.

72. Bachrach and Baratz, "Two Faces of Power," 949.

73. Bachrach and Baratz, "Two Faces of Power," 952.

74. In later years, Dahl and other pluralists modified their theory by recognizing the unequal strength of groups and classes in the political arena. But they never accepted the idea that single, small cadre of power holders ran the show in Washington and elsewhere.

75. G. William Domhoff, "C. Wright Mills, Power Structure Research, and the Failures of Mainstream Political Science," *New Political Science* 29, no. 1 (2007): 99. Available at http://sociology.ucsc.edu/whorulesamerica/theory/mills_critique.html. Domhoff might very well not call himself a critical theorist or anything like it. His argument, however, illustrates many points raised by the nonempirical group.

76. Hacker and Pierson, incidentally, doubtlessly consider themselves to be empirical scientists.

77. Hacker and Pierson, "Winner-Take-All Politics," 196.

78. Peter Bachrach and Morton S. Baratz, "Power and Its Two Faces Revisited: A Reply to Geoffrey Debnam," *American Political Science Review* 69, no. 3 (1975): 900.

79. For a review of this research, see Clyde Barrow, *Critical Theories of the State* (Madison: The University of Wisconsin Press, 1993).

80. See, for example, Theda Skocpol, "Bringing the State Back In: Strategies of Analysis in Current Research," in *Bringing the State Back In,* ed. Peter B. Evans, Dietrich Rueschemeyer, and Theda Skocpol (New York: Cambridge University Press, 1985), 3–38.

BEGINNING THE RESEARCH PROCESS:

IDENTIFYING A RESEARCH TOPIC, DEVELOPING RESEARCH QUESTIONS, AND REVIEWING THE LITERATURE

MANY STUDENTS FIND CHOOSING AN APPROPRIATE RESEARCH topic to be a challenging part of the research process. In this chapter, therefore, we discuss general attributes of promising research topics, suggest some methods for discovering interesting topics and research questions, and provide guidelines for conducting a systematic review of the literature on a topic and tips on writing a literature review—an important component of all academic articles and research reports.

SPECIFYING THE RESEARCH QUESTION

One of the most important purposes of social scientific research is to answer questions about social phenomena. The research projects summarized in chapter 1, for example, attempt to answer questions about some important political attitudes or behaviors: Why is wealth distributed more equally among the population in some countries than in others? Why do some people vote in elections while others do not? Why do Supreme Court justices reach the decisions they do on the cases before them? Do Supreme Court decisions affect people's opinions on issues and people's support of the Supreme Court? Does economic growth lead to more democratic institutions and practices and fewer human rights abuses? Under what circumstances are people most likely to support US involvement in foreign affairs? How does the American public respond to different ways of framing arguments in favor of or in opposition to continued military operations in Iraq? Does it matter who presents the argument? Does negative campaign advertising have any impact on the electorate? How do interest groups influence the extent to which members of Congress engage in oversight of agency decisions? In each case, the researchers identified a political phenomenon that interested them and tried to answer questions about that phenomenon.

The phenomena investigated by political scientists are diverse and are limited only by whether they are significant (that is, would advance our understanding of politics and government), observable, and political. Political scientists attempt to answer questions about the political behavior of individuals (voters, citizens, residents of a particular area, Supreme Court justices, members of Congress, presidents), groups (political parties, interest groups, labor unions, international organizations), institutions (state legislatures, city councils, bureaucracies, district courts), and political jurisdictions (cities, states, nations).

Most students, when confronting a research project for the first time, do not have a well-formulated research question as their starting point. Some will start by saying, "I'm interested in X," where X may be the Supreme Court, media coverage of the war in Iraq, campaign finance policy, the response to Hurricane Katrina, or some other political phenomenon. Others may not have any specific interest or topic in mind at all. Thus, the first major task in a research effort often is to find a topic and to translate an interest in a general topic into a manageable research question or series of questions or propositions. Framing an engaging and appropriate research question will get a research project off to a good start by defining, and limiting, the scope of the investigation and determining what information has to be collected to answer the question. A poorly specified question inevitably leads to wasted time and energy. Any of the following questions would probably lead to a politically significant and informative research project:

- Why is voter turnout for local elections higher in some cities than in others?

- Why does the amount spent per pupil by school districts vary (within a state or among states)?

- Do small nations sign more multilateral treaties than large nations?

- Why did some members of Congress vote for the Restoring Financial Stability Act of 2010, whereas others opposed it?

- Does the legislative output of legislatures change after term limits have gone into effect?

- Why do some nations have cap-and-trade programs for carbon dioxide emissions while others do not?

- Do independents have more moderate views on major political issues than those who identify themselves as strong partisans?

A research project will get off on the wrong foot if the question that shapes it fails to address a political phenomenon, is unduly concerned with discrete facts, or is focused on reaching normative conclusions. Although the definition of *political phenomenon* is vague, it does not include the study of *all* human characteristics or behavior.

Research questions, if they dwell on discrete or narrow factual issues, may limit the significance of a research project. Although important, facts alone are not enough to yield scientific explanations. What is missing is a **relationship**—that is, the association, dependence, or covariance of the values of one variable with the values of another. Researchers are generally interested in how to advance and test generalizations relating one phenomenon to another. In the absence of such generalizations, factual knowledge of the type called for by the following research questions will be fundamentally limited in scope:

■ How many seats in the most recent state legislative elections in your state were uncontested (had only one contestant)?

■ How many states passed budgets last year that were more than 10 percent lower than the previous year's?

■ How many members of Congress had favorable environmental voting records in the last session of Congress?

■ How many trade disputes have been referred to the World Trade Organization (WTO) for resolution in the past five years?

■ What percentage of registered voters voted in the most recent US Senate elections?

■ How many cabinet members have been replaced in each of the past three presidential administrations?

■ How many speeches, press releases, and announcements were issued by the Obama administration in the first three months after the 2010 BP oil spill in the Gulf of Mexico?

Factual information, however, may lead a researcher to ask "why" questions. For example, if a researcher has information about the number of uncontested seats and notes that this number varies substantially from state to state, the research question, "Why are legislative elections competitive in some states and not in others?" forms the basis of an interesting research project. Alternatively, if one had data from just one state, one could investigate the question, "Why do some districts have competitive elections and not others?" This would involve identifying characteristics of districts and elections that might explain the difference.

Or someone might notice that the number of trade disputes referred to the WTO has varied from year to year. What explains this fluctuation? When collecting data on the number of disputes, the researcher might notice that the complaints originate in many different countries. It would be interesting then to find out how the disputes are resolved. Is there any pattern to their resolution in regard to which countries benefit or the principles and arguments underlying the decisions? Why?

Similarly, the environmental voting records of members of Congress differ. Why? Is political party a likely explanation? Is ideology? Or is some other factor responsible?

Sometimes important research contributions come from descriptive or factual research because the factual information being sought is difficult to obtain or, as we discuss in chapter 5, disagreement exists over which information or facts should be used to measure a concept. In this situation, a research effort will entail showing how different ways of measuring a concept have important consequences for establishing the facts. For example, how income inequality should be measured is certainly an important aspect of research on that topic.

Questions calling for normative conclusions also are inconsistent with the research methods discussed in this book. (Refer to chapter 2 for the distinction between normative and empirical statements.) For example, questions such as "Should the United States give preference in reconstruction contracts to those nations that supported going to war in Iraq?" or "Should a new federal agency be placed within the Executive Office of the President?" or "Should states give tax breaks to new businesses willing to locate within their borders?" are important and suitable for the attention of political scientists (indeed, for any citizen), but they are inappropriate as framed here. As written, they ask for a normative response, seeking an indication of what is good or of what should be done. Although scientific knowledge may be helpful in answering questions like these, it cannot provide the answers without regard for an individual's personal values or preferences. The answers to these questions involve what someone ultimately likes or dislikes, values or rejects.

Normative questions, however, may lead you to develop an empirical research question. For example, a student of one of the authors felt that Pennsylvania's method of selecting judges using partisan elections was not a good way to choose judges. To contribute to an informed discussion of this issue, she collected data on the amount of money raised and spent by judicial candidates, the amount of money spent per vote cast in judicial races compared with that spent in other state elections, and the voter turnout rate in judicial races as compared with other races. This information spoke to some of the arguments raised against partisan judicial elections, but she discovered that it was very difficult to collect empirical evidence to answer the interesting question of whether reliance on campaign contributions jeopardized the independence and impartiality of judges.

SOURCES OF IDEAS FOR RESEARCH TOPICS

Potential research topics about politics come from many sources. These sources may be classified as personal, nonscholarly, or scholarly. Personal sources include your own life experiences and political activities and those of your family and friends, as well as class readings, lectures, and discussions.

You can also look to nonscholarly sources for research topics, including print, broadcast, and Internet sources. Becoming aware of current or recent issues in public affairs will help you develop interesting research topics. You can start by reading a daily newspaper or issues of popular magazines that deal with government policies and politics. The Web site accompanying this book (http://psrm .cqpress.com/) offers many possibilities and lists of other Web sites. The best print sources include national newspapers and magazines featuring in-depth political coverage. First, consider reading major urban daily newspapers like the *New York Times* and the *Washington Post.* Daily newspapers provide the most up-to-date printed political news and discussions. In addition, look at weekly magazines like *Atlantic, Harper's,* the *Economist,* the *American Prospect, National Review,* the *New Republic,* the *New Yorker,* and the *Weekly Standard.* Most of these weeklies have a decidedly partisan leaning (either conservative or liberal, Republican or Democratic), but—and this is a key point—they contain serious discussions of domestic and foreign government and politics and are wonderful sources of ideas and claims to investigate.[1] Each of these sources also features online material, much of which is free.

An underappreciated source of potential research topics within these printed sources is the editorial and letters-to-the-editor pages. Although these pieces express opinions, the writers often support them with what they claim are empirical facts. Consider an editorial asserting that the "death penalty deters crime" and is therefore justified. It may be tricky, but you might test this claim by comparing the incidence of homicide in states with and without capital punishment. "Utah has the nation's most permissive gun laws, according to the Brady Campaign to Prevent Gun Violence, but it has one of the lowest murder rates in the country. California, with the strictest laws, has a homicide rate higher than the national average."[2] (Maybe California has gun laws because it has a crime problem; it's not likely the presence of such laws cause an increase/ excess of gun violence or that such laws are irrelevant. Maybe they prevent even more murders.)

Broadcast news sources can also inspire topical research projects. The best radio and television programs for this purpose are those that include long segments dedicated to political news, discussion, and debate. Radio programs with a civic or political focus featuring a variety of topics include National Public Radio's *Morning Edition* and *All Things Considered.* Your local public radio station may have a program devoted to local and regional public affairs such as *Radio Times,* a daily two-hour program emanating from Philadelphia's public radio station, WHYY. Numerous political talk shows, like the *Rush Limbaugh Show,* do not hesitate to make assertions about political matters that can be put to the empirical test. Television shows such as NBC's *Meet the Press,* CBS's *Face the Nation,*

CHECK POPULAR BELIEFS

Consider scouring the popular press or mass media—the sorts of newspapers and magazines read by average citizens—for statements that are widely believed and repeated but that you suspect might be misleading or downright wrong. If an argument pertains to an important issue, and if you can discredit it with empirical evidence, you might well make a potential, even if modest, contribution to the public's knowledge of current events.

ABC's *This Week,* Fox's *News Sunday,* PBS's *Charlie Rose Show* and the *News Hour with Jim Lehrer,* and investigative journalism programs like CBS's *60 Minutes* tend to feature long interviews with political actors.

Internet sources can include the print and broadcast sources discussed above, found through the publications' and broadcasts' sites on the Web. In addition to offering the same content that is printed or broadcast, many print and broadcast sources feature exclusive Internet material. An example is the *Washington Post*'s *White House Watch,* a daily blog focusing on the presidency. Other Internet sources include government, university, or organization Web sites; Web sites created by individuals; and political blogs. Blogs like *Daily Kos* or *InstaPundit* have become fixtures in the national political debate, raising topics or uncovering evidence that the traditional news media have not. Blogs, much like talk radio or magazines, often feature political discussion and debate from a particular ideological or partisan perspective.

Although personal and nonscholarly sources are good places to find potential research topics, surveying the scholarly literature will help you identify a topic relevant to the discipline. The scholarly literature includes books and articles written by political scientists and other academics or political practitioners. Such literature establishes which topics and questions are important to political scientists. Simply perusing the list of article titles of several issues of a journal can give you ideas for a topic. Here is a short list of some of the major political science publications, many (if not all) of which are available online:

*American Journal of Political Science—*Broad coverage of political science and public administration

*American Political Science Review—*The official journal of the American Political Science Association

DIFFERENTIATING SCHOLARLY FROM NONSCHOLARLY LITERATURE

You can differentiate scholarly works from nonscholarly ones by looking for a few characteristics. Most important, professional articles and books published in political science or other disciplines will often go through a peer-review process. The most common peer-review standard is that a journal or book editor sends an article or book manuscript submitted for publication to one or more scholars with expertise in the topical area of the article. The review is performed in a blind fashion; that is, the reviewers are not told the author's name to ensure that reviewers assess only the quality of the work. The editor relies on the peer reviewers' comments to suggest revisions of the work and assess whether or not the work makes a sufficient contribution to the literature to deserve publication. The peer-review process helps assure that the work published in scholarly journals and books is of the best possible quality and of the most value to the discipline. It also assures the reader that, although there still may be mistakes or invalid or unreliable claims, the article or book has been vetted by one or more experts on the topic.

Alternatively, some scholarly journals and books are reviewed only by the editorial staff. Although this method provides a check on the quality of the work, it is usually not as rigorous as a blind peer review. The type of review a journal or book publisher uses will typically be explained in the journal or on the journal or publisher's Web site.

In addition to a peer-review process, some other indicators can differentiate scholarly from nonscholarly work. Scholarly articles and books are usually written by academics, journalists, political actors, or other political practitioners, so looking for a description of the authors is the place to start. Scholarly books are published by both university presses and commercial presses for a professional audience rather than a general audience.[3] As such, the work will include complex analyses and be written with the assumption that the reader is familiar with the literature and method.

If you are still unsure about whether or not a particular work is scholarly, consult with a reference librarian or your instructor.

British Journal of Political Science—Although emphasizing a comparative perspective, this publication contains important research on American political institutions and behavior.

Comparative Politics—Begin here when looking for scholarly studies on all aspects of cross-national politics and government.

International Organization—Contains important articles on international relations. One of the leading journals in the field.

Journal of Conflict Resolution—A widely cited journal with articles on, among other topics, international relations, war and peace, and individual attitudes and behavior. Authors use a variety of methods and research designs.

Journal of Politics—Broad coverage of political science and public administration

Legislative Studies Quarterly—Articles about legislative organization and functioning and electoral behavior

Political Analysis—For students with a serious interest in methods and statistics. Articles frequently contain important substantive results.

Political Research Quarterly—Broad coverage of political science and public administration

Polity—Articles on American politics, comparative politics, international relations, and political philosophy

Social Science Quarterly—Articles on a wide range of topics in the social sciences

World Politics—Analytical and theoretical articles, review articles, and research notes in international relations, comparative politics, political theory, foreign policy, and modernization

In addition, research is frequently presented at professional conferences before it is published. If you want to be informed up-to-the-minute or if a research topic is quite new, it may be worthwhile to investigate papers given at professional conferences.

The *Index to Social Sciences and Humanities Proceedings* indexes published proceedings. However, the proceedings of the annual meetings of the American Political Science Association (APSA) and regional political science associations are not published. Summer issues of APSA's *PS* contain the preliminary program for the forthcoming annual meeting. The program lists authors and titles of papers. The *International Studies Newsletter* publishes preliminary programs for International Studies Association meetings. Copies of programs for other political science and related conferences (frequently announced in *PS*) may be obtained from the sponsoring organizations. Abstracts for some fields—for example, *Sociological Abstracts*—include papers presented at conferences. After promising papers presented at professional conferences have been located, copies of the papers can usually be obtained through online archives like APSA's *Proceedings*[4] or by writing to the authors directly. Although these unpublished articles represent the most up-to-date work in the discipline, care should be taken in relying on them as they have not yet been vetted by a peer-review process and may be less reliable than published work.

To guide you further in finding topics and searching for appropriate sources, this book's companion Web site lists additional professional journals as well as indexes and bibliographies, data banks, guides to political resources, and the like. A reference librarian will undoubtedly be able to provide additional information and guidance on particular library sources available.

Still another source of ideas for research papers is a textbook used in substantive courses, such as American politics, comparative politics, or international relations. These works can be particularly valuable for pointing out controversies within a field. For example, as the discussion of judicial behavior in chapter 1 of this textbook illustrated, political scientists argue about what underlies judges' decisions, political ideology, or adherence to legal precedent and principles. You might do a case study of a particular justice to see which side this person's rulings seem to support.

So far, we have talked about using a variety of sources, including the scholarly literature, to help you identify a research topic of interest to you in a general sense. We haven't yet indicated how you might search the literature (both scholarly and nonscholarly) once you have at least a general interest in a topic. Before we show you how to conduct a search of the literature, however, we want to talk about why every serious research project conducts what is called a **literature review** and why scholarly articles and books contain a section or a chapter in which the literature related to the topic is discussed.

WHY CONDUCT A LITERATURE REVIEW?

Most research topics are initially much too broad to be manageable. It would be virtually impossible to write something new on "international terrorism" or even "the causes of terrorism in the Middle East" without first knowing a great deal about the subject. Good research, therefore, involves reviewing previous work on the topic to motivate and sharpen a research question. Among the many reasons for doing so are (1) to see what has and has not been investigated, (2) to develop general explanations for observed variations in a behavior or a phenomenon, (3) to identify potential relationships between concepts and to identify researchable hypotheses, (4) to learn how others have defined and measured key concepts, (5) to identify data sources that other researchers have used, (6) to develop alternative research designs, and (7) to discover how a research project is related to the work of others. Let us examine some of these reasons more closely.

Often someone new to empirical research will start out by expressing only a general interest in a topic, such as terrorism or the effects of campaign advertising on public opinion and international relations, but the specific research question has yet to be formulated (for example, "What kinds of people become terrorists?" or "Do negative televised campaign advertisements sway voters?" or "Does the public support isolationism or internationalism?"). A review of previous research can help you sharpen a topic by identifying research questions that others have asked.

Alternatively, you may start with an overly specific research question such as "Do married people have different views on abortion policy than those who are single?" Reading the literature related to public opinion on abortion likely will reveal that your specific research question is one of many aimed at answering the more general research question: What are the characteristics or attributes of people who oppose abortion, and do they differ from those of supporters? This latter research question constitutes a topic, whereas the former is likely to be too narrow to sustain a research paper.

After reading the published work in an area, you may decide that previous reports do not adequately answer the question. Thus, you may design a research project to answer an old question in a new way. An investigation may replicate a study to confirm or challenge a hypothesis or expand our understanding of a concept. Replication is one of the cornerstones of scientific work. By testing the same hypothesis in different ways or confirming the results from previous research using the same data and methods, we increase our confidence that the results are correct. Replication can therefore help build consensus or identify topics that require further work.

At other times, research may begin with a hypothesis or with a desire to develop an explanation for a relationship that has already been observed. Here

---

How to Come Up with a Research Topic

- Pose a "how many" question. Where possible, collect data for more than one time (e.g., year, election) or for more than one case (e.g., more than one city, state, nation, primary election). Do any patterns emerge? What might explain these patterns?

- Is it difficult to find information to answer a question? Why? Could you make a meaningful contribution by collecting appropriate data?

- Do you think that the ways in which other researchers have measured what you are interested in are adequate? Are there any validity or reliability problems with the measures? (Measurement validity and reliability are discussed in chapter 5.)

- Find an assertion or statement in the popular press or a conclusion in a research article that you believe to be incorrect. Look for empirical evidence so that you can assess the statement or examine the evidence used by the author to see if any mistakes were made that could have affected the conclusion.

- Find two studies that reach conflicting conclusions. Try to explain or reconcile the conflict. Test conflicting explanations by applying them to different cases or data.

- Take a theory or general explanation for certain political behavior and apply it to a new situation.

Note: We wish to thank one of our anonymous reviewers for suggesting that we include tips for coming up with paper topics and for suggesting some of the tips listed here.

a literature review may reveal reports of similar observations made by others and may also help you develop general explanations for the relationship by identifying theories that explain the phenomenon of interest. Your research will be more valuable if you can provide a general explanation of the observed or hypothesized relationship rather than simply a report of the empirical verification of a relationship.

In addition to seeking theories that support the plausibility and increase the significance of a hypothesis, you should be alert for competing or alternative hypotheses. You may start with a hypothesis specifying a simple relationship between two variables. Since it is uncommon for one political phenomenon to be related to or caused by just one other factor or variable, it is important to look for other possible causes or correlates of the dependent variable. Data collection should include measurement of these other relevant variables so that, in subsequent data analysis, you may rule out competing explanations or at least indicate more clearly the nature of the relationship between the variables in the original hypothesis.

COLLECTING SOURCES FOR A LITERATURE REVIEW

After selecting a research topic using the sources described above, you must begin collecting sources for use in writing a literature review. Although personal and nonscholarly sources can be quite helpful in selecting a research topic, and a literature review can encompass virtually anything published on your topic, we strongly encourage you to become familiar with the scholarly literature. Relying on scholarly sources rather than nonscholarly ones will improve the quality of a literature review. In addition, as a practical concern, many instructors may not accept or give much credit for citations from nonscholarly sources unless their content constitutes part of your topic. After all, a literature review is supposed to establish the knowledge about a topic that has been attained and communicated according to professional or scientific principles.

Students commonly ask, "How many sources must I find to write my literature review?" The answer, unfortunately, is not straightforward. How many books and articles to include in a literature review depends on the purpose and scope of the project as well as available resources. If your project is focused largely on reporting the work of others, you will probably need to include more sources than if your project is focused mostly on your own analysis. Furthermore, a more complex topic, or a topic with a larger literature, may require a more

PYRAMID CITATIONS

Each time you find what appears to be a useful source, look at its list of notes and references. One article, for example, may cite two more potentially useful papers. Each of these, in turn, may point to two or more additional ones, and so on. Even if you start with a small list, you can quickly assemble a huge list of sources. Moreover, you increase your chances of covering all the relevant literature.

in-depth literature review than will a more straightforward topic or one with a smaller literature. Finally, consider how much time and effort you are willing to dedicate to collecting sources. Although we cannot provide a simple answer to the question of how many sources are necessary, we can explain how available time and effort could be best directed and used most efficiently.

Identifying the Relevant Scholarly Literature

It would be impossible for anyone to identify, let alone read and or write about, every book or article with relevance to any particular research project. With that caveat in mind, you can think of the first step in collecting sources—identifying the relevant literature—as limiting the search to only those books and articles with the most direct relevance to the research topic of interest. You can begin to narrow the field of potential sources in many ways. The first step is to search comprehensive **electronic databases**, such as Web of Science or Google Scholar, or databases that include links to full text articles, such as JSTOR. These databases allow you to quickly locate a large number of articles that investigate similar topics.

Web of Science is a particularly useful starting point for building a literature review because you can

- search the Social Sciences Citation Index database of social science journal articles generally, using a keyword search;
- search for articles written by a particular social scientist; or,
- perhaps most important for starting a literature review, you can search for all of the articles in the database that cite an article of interest and for articles that subsequently cited those articles.

Two quick examples highlight the value of these searches. First, suppose you are interested in understanding judicial behavior.

1. By typing the phrase *judicial behavior* into the "quick search" field, limiting the period to 1970–2011, and searching only the Social Sciences Citation Index, we found 447 articles. This is far too many articles to read.

2. You might want to refine your search further by limiting subject areas to law and political science and to the United States (a Countries/Territories option with a drop-down menu allows you to choose a country). Doing this reduced the number of items to 297. This is still a lot, but after reading through article abstracts in this larger topic, you might narrow the search to a particular kind of judicial behavior. For example, say that, after reading a few abstracts and articles, you found you were interested in the debate over judicial activism.

3. By entering the phrase *judicial activism* into the "search within these results" search field, we narrowed the search to only six articles. This is a manageable number of articles to examine.

4. You may find that not all of the articles are actually relevant to your topic, but if you find one article that is of direct relevance, you can use it to find more like it using the approach we describe next.

A second way to use the Web of Science is to begin with a single article instead of searching for topics.

1. Suppose that at the beginning of your search, you decided to search for articles related to an article you had already found—from your course syllabus, for example. Imagine that while reading Jeffrey A. Segal and Albert D. Cover's "Ideological Values and the Votes of U.S. Supreme Court Justices" (a brief discussion of the article is found in chapter 1), you found that the topic interested you and thought you might like to find out what else was written on it. Because you had discussed the article in class, and your professor had told you of the importance of the article in establishing our current understanding of judicial decision making, you decided that it was an important article to include in your literature review.

2. With this single article, you could use the Web of Science to quickly find other work in the literature investigating similar research questions. For example, by using an advanced search and selecting the Social Sciences Citation Index and the default of "all years," you could find Segal and Cover's article by searching for the authors' names and part of the article's title, as shown in figure 3–1. (Do not bother to restrict your search to the English language and to just articles, even though you know both of these items to be true in the case of the item you are searching for. The authors did this and the search came up empty. No search engine is perfect, and casting as wide a net as is reasonable can avoid searches that for some reason fail to find relevant items.)

3. Clicking on the underlined "1" will reveal the results from the search. Click on "view full text" or "AE Get Article" buttons to find the full text of the article if it is available through the library's database subscriptions, or click on the article title to find a wealth of information about the article. Figure 3–2 shows the full citation, which will be needed for the works cited or notes, the number of articles the article cited, and the number of articles that subsequently cited Segal and Cover's article.

4. Segal and Cover cited thirty-four references in their article; by clicking on "Cited References: 34," you will find all thirty-four references with electronic links to those references included in the Web of Science database. This feature makes it easy to review the base of knowledge that was in place before Segal and Cover's article.

5. As of this writing, Web of Science has identified 216 articles in its database that have cited Segal and Cover's article. By clicking on "Times Cited: 216," you can find a link to each of these articles. This is particularly important because once you find an essential reference like Segal and Cover's article—an article that most work in this literature includes as a reference—you can easily identify a large number of articles for your own literature review. In this example, we located 250 references to relevant books and articles in a matter of minutes. Notice that some of the articles that cite the Segal and Cover article are listed on the right-hand side of figure 3-2.

FIGURE 3–1

"Advanced" Search on Web of Science Database

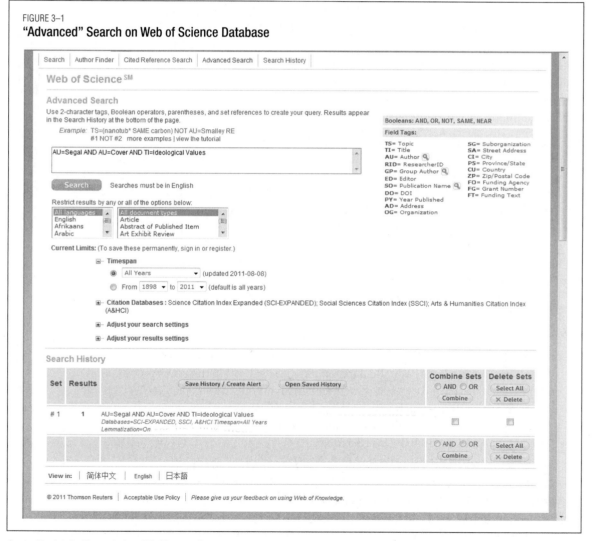

Source: Reprinted with permission of The Thomson Corporation.

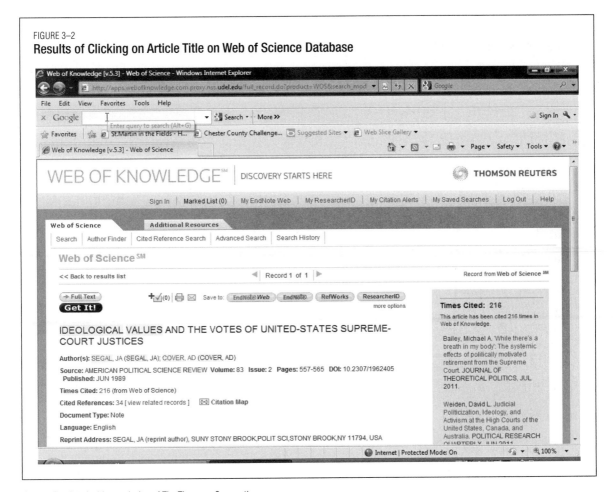

FIGURE 3–2
Results of Clicking on Article Title on Web of Science Database

Source: Reprinted with permission of The Thomson Corporation.

The larger lesson from this example is that once you find a relevant article, you can sharpen the direction of your search for relevant literature by examining the literature review and works cited in that article. Since the article is directly relevant to the research topic of interest, the sources used in the article will likely be related as well. By building a list of sources in this fashion, you can save a great deal of time and effort as well as collect sources with a greater certainty that you will not overlook important work.

Remember, however, that even though both of the above example strategies will help you find relevant articles quickly, articles without much relevance may also come up in a search. Two articles that share a common **search term** do not necessarily have much related content. Furthermore, one article's citing another does not necessarily mean that the two articles investigate the same topic or

FIGURE 3–3
"Advanced" Search on JSTOR

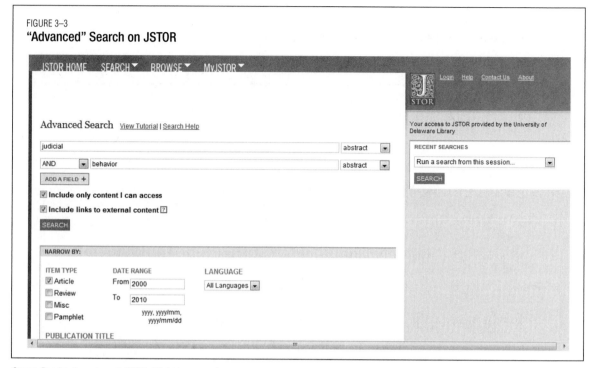

even that the more recent article mentions the older article in the text. Therefore, you should search for relevant literature using multiple search parameters and tools.

You could also search for articles on judicial behavior using a database like JSTOR, a comprehensive electronic archive of academic journals and publications. Although not every campus has access to it, and it does not include full-text articles from many important sources, JSTOR is widely available. Moreover, a description of how to search it illustrates guidelines for searching other databases.

FINDING A TERM ON A PAGE

Most Internet browsers have a "hot key" combination that allows you to search for a particular word or phrase on a displayed Web page. With Internet Explorer and Firefox, for example, use CTRL-F. Take advantage of this shortcut when viewing a massive document that has small text or lots of content.

Figure 3–3 shows the preparation of a JSTOR search for articles containing the phrase *judicial behavior*. Note the limitations on the search. Because a lot of work deals with judicial behavior, we hunted only for *articles* with the phrase in their abstracts. We also confined the search to the last decade (2000–2010). Finally, we limited our search to political science and law journals (not shown in figure 3–3), although many useful articles may be found in journals specializing in related disciplines such as economics or psychology.

The results of the search appear in Figure 3–4. For the particular criteria used, the database returned sixty-four articles. As previously mentioned, JSTOR provides the full text of some articles in the database. In other cases, it provides links to the full content of articles on external sites or to the abstract (which we discuss in greater detail in the next section) and the full citations. An advantage

FIGURE 3–4

Results of JSTOR Search for "Judicial Behavior"

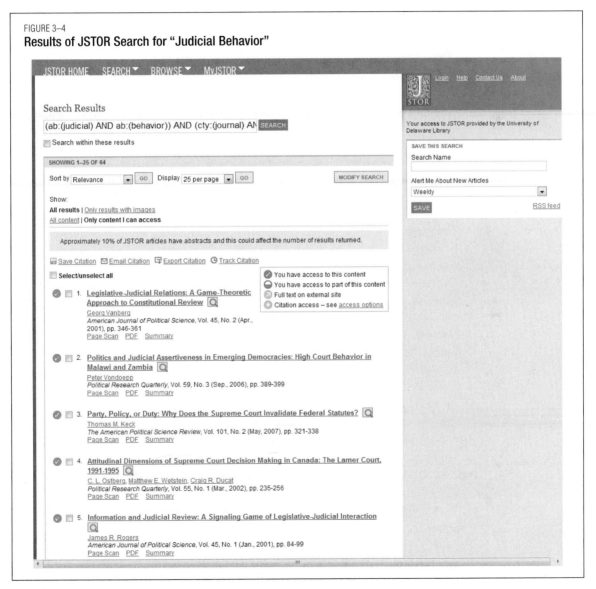

of finding articles via a full-text Web site like JSTOR is that you can save electronic copies of articles for review without incurring printing expenses. And similar to Web of Science, JSTOR has a feature that allows you to locate all of the articles in the JSTOR database that cite an article or all of the references in the Google Scholar database.

Identifying Useful Popular Sources

As most students use the Internet on a regular basis, you may be familiar with using it to look for articles and other sources of information on topics of interest. One of the benefits of the revolution in global communications is that it places an almost limitless supply of information literally at your fingertips. Scouring the Internet also allows you to find many kinds of documents and data that a traditional library search will not turn up or that are simply not available on many campuses. It is tempting to think that you need only to access a **search engine**, a computer program that systematically visits and searches Web pages, and type in a few search terms, or keywords. However powerful the facilities may be, the search process is not always simple.

Search engines such as Google or Yahoo! may be a good place to start if you are trying to see what sources are available on a topic and you are not looking for a specific reference. These search engines, however, can be quite indiscriminate in what they return and leave the user with pages of unsuitable or redundant findings. As an example, we used Google and Yahoo! to search for the phrase *judicial behavior*. A Yahoo! Advanced Web Search conducted on January 7, 2011, for the exact phrase *judicial behavior* for sites updated anytime and on any domain, and filtering out adult Web search results, yielded 21,700,000 hits. This is an overwhelming number. A Google Scholar search on *judicial behavior* restricted to articles between the years of 1995 and 2010 yielded 86,600 references. That is, of course, way too many to read.

Search programs often order the results by the frequency of appearance of search words in the title and in the text near the top of the page or by the regularity with which the page is visited. But these may not be the best criteria for your purposes. Use of the Internet clearly has drawbacks unless careful planning and thought have preceded the search. As with many of life's activities, the more time you spend searching for literature review materials, the easier it will become. Nevertheless, following a few practical guidelines will expedite the process.

- When first visiting a site, particularly one with search features, click the "help" button, which usually provides specific instructions for how to search that site.

- If possible, pyramid your search by going first to a political science page and, from there, looking for more specific sites.

- If you have a clear topic in mind, start with a specific Internet site, such as one sponsored by a research organization or university. Doing so will reduce the number of false hits.

- Open a simple word-processing program such as Notepad or WordPad. Highlight and copy selected text from a Web page to facilitate collecting information. Be sure to document the source of this material properly. This technique is especially helpful for copying complicated, long Internet addresses (URLs).

- On a complicated page with lots of text and images, use your browser's Find option to locate the word or phrase of interest.

- Take advantage of advanced search options. If possible, limit your search to specified periods, to certain types of articles, to particular authors or subjects, and to data formats.

- Check this book's Web site (http://psrm.cqpress.com/) for links to specific topics.

Most search engines and databases enable you to narrow a search to meet your specific needs. Usually you want to see only the documents that contain all the words—or even specific phrases, such as *international terrorism*—on a list. Advanced search features allow you to use connectors and modifiers to specify exactly what words or phrases should be included in the document and which ones should be excluded. If you enter the desired words without adding modifiers, in all likelihood the search engine will look for pages that contain any of the listed words but not necessarily all of them.

Although the Internet allows for a wide search of material, not all information found on the Internet is reliable. Virtually anyone or any group, no matter what its credentials, can create a Web site. The only way to know for sure that the information you are looking at is dependable is to be familiar with the site's sponsor. In general, sites presented by individuals, even those with impressive-looking titles and qualifications, may not have the credibility or scholarly standing that your literature review requires. In contrast, you can usually have confidence in sources cited in professional publications or by established authors or reputable organizations. Note, too, that even sources in the form of opinion can be dependable. Many associations that hold strong political or ideological positions nevertheless offer useful information that is worth citing. If in doubt about the reliability of a source, check with your instructor or adviser. He or she should be able to help you assess whether or not accessed information is usable.

Internet sources must be cited properly, partly because so much variation exists in the quality of these sources but also, and even more important, because academic standards dictate that proper citations be provided for any work consulted. In this way authors are fully credited for their data and ideas, and readers can check the accuracy of the information and the quality of a literature review.

At a minimum, the citation should include the author or creator of the page and the title of the article as well as the complete Internet address at which the article was found. If the information you retrieve is from a Web site is likely to have changed since you accessed it, as in the case of a crowdsourced encyclopedia article or a page that continuously posts up-to-date data, then you would add the date you accessed the site, perhaps in parentheses after the URL. Following is a generic format for citing a Web page in a bibliography:

Author [last name–first name or full organization name]. (Date of publication, if available). Web Page Title. Full Web address.

For example,

Stroupe, Kenneth S., Jr., & Larry J. Sabato. (2004). Politics: The Missing Link of Responsible Civic Education (CIRCLE working paper 18). http://www.civicyouth.org/PopUps/WorkingPapers/WP18Stroupe.pdf.

Organizing References

The first time you conduct a comprehensive literature search, the number of citations you discover may overwhelm you. Managing them systematically is often a challenge. It may help to put each relevant citation on a separate three-by-five-inch index card. If the citation proves to be useful, then complete bibliographic information can be entered later on the card in the format you will be using for your bibliography. These cards can be sorted according to various needs. This method preserves the fruits of a literature search in a form that will be useful to you, and it saves the step of writing the citation information onto a list and then transferring it to a card.

indicates that your information is from a report by Kenneth S. Stroupe Jr. and Larry J. Sabato and is available on a Web page administered by the Center for Information & Research on Civic Learning And Engagement (CIRCLE) that you accessed at http://www.civicyouth.org/PopUps/WorkingPapers/WP18Stroupe.pdf.

Citation style will depend on the standards set by your institution or instructor, but include at least enough detail to let a reader retrieve the page and verify information.

Reading the Literature

Once you have identified references for possible inclusion in a literature review, the next step is to figure out how the references fit together in a way that (1) explains the base of knowledge, or what we know about a topic from previous work, with respect to the research question and (2) establishes how the current project is going to build on that knowledge. The best way to understand the base of knowledge is to read the work that answers the central research questions and understand how each contributes to a comprehensive understanding of the important research questions. To read an entire literature would take far too much time, so it is wise to rely on shortcuts whenever available.

First, following the suggestions in the preceding section, take care in selecting references. Once references are identified and collected, you can rely on the abstract on the first page of most articles and the preface at the beginning of most books to serve as a short description of the organization and conclusions contained therein. A good abstract will include a great deal of important information about the contents of an article, including the research question, the theory and hypotheses, the data and methods used to test the hypotheses, and the results and conclusions. Most article abstracts are only 200 to 300 words long, so they offer an easy way to assess quickly whether an article is worth reading further. A good preface will include the same kind of information, but a book's length makes this summary much more cursory or general. A preface will also include more attention to organization of the chapters. Reading book reviews in scholarly journals is another way to learn quickly the value of a book to a given project. For most books, you can find a review that will relay the book's theoretical importance or help you understand how it fits in the context of the existing literature and what it adds to the base of knowledge—in addition to assessing the quality of the research.

Use of abstracts, prefaces, and book reviews will help narrow a list of references. This smaller list can then be culled for those references that are essential to motivating the current research project and those that add depth, range, or a unique perspective to the literature review. In addition, the first few pages of political science articles contain most of the description of the key components of the research project—the research question, theory and hypotheses, and data and methods—and include a literature review. The conclusion or discussion of findings will summarize the results and explain how they add to the base of knowledge. Students with limited time for reading articles should read the first few pages and the conclusion and then, if more information is needed, proceed to the rest of the article. Finally, although many political science articles include complex methods and tables, the text describing the results usually includes a more jargon-free description of the results that does not require an advanced understanding of statistics. The same time-saving tips can be applied to books by concentrating on a book's introduction and conclusion as well as selected relevant chapters, which you can identify in the table of contents.

Nonscholarly references like magazine or newspaper articles, or Web site content, generally are much shorter than references from the scholarly literature and require fewer shortcuts. These sources can typically be read quickly and in most cases do not provide an abstract.

WRITING A LITERATURE REVIEW

After you have identified the relevant literature and started reading the literature, it is time to begin crafting the literature review. In this section, we explain how you can integrate a collection of related materials into an effective literature review. Essential to this process is limiting the discussion of materials to the most relevant previous work and focusing the literature review on concepts and ideas rather than around individual books, articles, or authors. This is important because organizing the literature review in this way will make it easier to establish the base of knowledge and demonstrate how the current research project can extend or add to that knowledge—with a new perspective, new data, or a different method—by resolving conflicting results in the literature or by replicating, and thereby validating, previous research. When thinking about a literature review as motivating a research project in one of these ways, you will see that the literature review is an integral part of a research project and requires a great deal of attention to establish the direction of the project.

The key to organizing and writing an effective literature review is to focus on concepts, ideas, and methods shared across the literature. Many students are used to writing about multiple references with a focus on the individual references, discussing each collected reference in turn. For example, imagine that you have collected ten articles for a literature review. You might decide that the easiest way to organize a review that incorporates all ten articles would be to take the first article, perhaps selected because it was the most relevant, and summarize the most important parts of the article: the research question, theory, hypotheses, data, methods, and results. After summarizing the first article, you then move on to the second article and write a similar summary in the next paragraph, then the third, and so on, until all ten articles have been summarized. We call this approach to a literature review the "boxcar method" because such a review links the independent discussions of each article much like a series of boxcars on a train.

Although this may be the easiest method for including multiple references in a literature review, it is ineffective. It does not explain how the ten articles fit together to establish the base of knowledge to which the current project will add, nor does it establish how the current project will add to that knowledge. By tacking together independent discussions of articles, you will find it difficult to discuss common themes across references, conflicting results or conclusions, or questions left unanswered in the literature.

A more effective way to write a literature review is to focus on the concepts, ideas, and methods in the relevant literature. For example, imagine that you have the same ten articles from the previous example, but instead of discussing each independently, you begin by identifying the common themes across all ten articles. The first step might be to group the articles according to their research questions. It is likely that all ten articles address a similar broad topic but do not share exactly the same research questions. You can begin to establish the base of knowledge by identifying, for example, three common research questions among the ten articles (four articles answering question one, three articles answering question two, and three articles answering question three). These three research questions represent the three areas of study the previous literature has undertaken in building our understanding of the broader topical area. Beginning the literature review with a discussion of these three research questions, and citing the articles that use each, will be an effective start to defining the base of knowledge.

Next, you might regroup the articles based on the data or research designs used. Perhaps three of the articles used experiments and seven of the articles used case studies. Researchers commonly discuss in their literature reviews the different research designs used in the literature because, as explained in chapter 6, different approaches have advantages and disadvantages and will be better or worse for making certain kinds of conclusions.

In addition to differences in research design, each of the three experiments and seven case studies also likely used different data. Some of the case studies may have relied on personal interviews; others may have used participant-observation methods. Likewise, some of the experiments may have collected data from college students, and others may have collected data from the general population. Much as do differences in research designs, differences in the data might lead to different conclusions.

As a final example, you might sort the ten references by the results or conclusions. It is unlikely that all ten articles came to the same conclusion. In fact, results of at least one of the ten articles likely contradict the results of the others. Identifying commonalities and contradictions in the literature review allows a researcher to identify ideas that have been established through replication as accepted widely in the literature and areas of disagreement that are ripe for further clarification and explanation. Conflicting results can provide a wonderful motivating factor for new research and establish for the reader the importance and relevance of the current research project.

Compared to the boxcar method, the latter example describes a much more sophisticated literature review because it integrates previous research along conceptual and methodological lines and provides a more effective organization for the researcher to explain the base of knowledge and how the current project fits into that literature. As we noted earlier, the boxcar method may be attractive because it seems easier, but the integrated literature review will better inform the current research project and the reader—and, practically speaking, will earn a better grade for students.

A literature review is not all that different from a conventional research paper in which you write an essay about what is known about a topic. In both cases, the discussion needs to be organized around key themes, and it is your task as the reviewer to choose the important themes on which to focus. A literature review for an empirical research paper tends to focus more on methodological aspects of previous studies in addition to the substantive content of previous research.

ANATOMY OF A LITERATURE REVIEW

To demonstrate further how you might write a highly effective literature review, we include in figure 3–5 a literature review from an article discussed in chapter 1: "Does Attack Advertising Demobilize the Electorate?" by Stephen Ansolabehere, Shanto Iyengar, Adam Simon, and Nicholas Valentino. In this section, we dissect this literature review to highlight the value of integrating references by focusing on concepts and ideas rather than individual articles or books. This literature review begins with the first paragraph in the article and continues to page 2. As we will see, the authors do an excellent job of explaining previous work on the effect of campaign advertising on voters, explaining the received wisdom from this work, identifying the shortcomings of previous work, and explaining how this article will correct those shortcomings.

Note first that this is a scholarly article from a highly respected political science journal. The article is written following the style and citation guidelines for the *American Political Science Review* (*APSR*). *APSR* and many other journals use parenthetical notation to identify for the reader, at a glance, the names of the cited authors, the year of the cited publication, and a page number if relevant. The interested reader will find that the names and dates match a full citation in the works cited at the end of the literature review. Other journals may use a different citation style, such as endnotes or footnotes, but in all cases the author must provide citations acknowledging others' work and a full citation within the article. You should do the same, or your literature review will fail to give credit where credit is due and leave you open to charges of plagiarism.

In the first paragraph, the authors begin by identifying the conventional wisdom that "it is generally taken for granted that political campaigns boost citizens' involvement—their interest in the election, awareness of and information about current issues, and sense that individual opinions matter."[5] This sentence succinctly captures the essence of the received wisdom about the relationship between campaigns and voters and is followed by citations of those responsible for laying the early groundwork in developing this understanding. The second and third sentences extend the discussion of the conventional wisdom and cite two more recent studies that tested these ideas and found similar results.

The second paragraph explains that the authors question this conventional wisdom and cites various changes to the nature of campaigns since the 1940s—primarily the role of television. As in the first paragraph, after introducing a new idea in the literature review, the authors include parenthetical notes citing the work responsible for the idea. In this section, the authors cite four references for the role television has played and one reference that documents the increasing importance of paid political advertising to campaign operatives.

FIGURE 3–5
A Well-Constructed Literature Review

American Political Science Review   Vol.88, No. 4   December 1994

DOES ATTACK ADVERTISING DEMOBILIZE THE ELECTORATE?

STEPHEN ANSOLABEHERE *Massachusetts Institute of Technology*
SHANTO IYENGAR, ADAM SIMON, and
NICHOLAS VALENTINO *University of California, Los Angeles*

We address the effects of negative campaign advertising on turnout. Using a unique experimental design in which advertising tone is manipulated within the identical audiovisual context, we find that exposure to negative advertisements dropped intentions to vote by 5%. We then replicate this result through an aggregate-level analysis of turnout and campaign tone in the 1992 Senate elections. Finally, we show that the demobilizing effects of negative campaigns are accompanied by a weakened sense of political efficacy. Voters who watch negative advertisements become more cynical about the responsiveness of public officials and the electoral process.

It is generally taken for granted that political campaigns boost citizens' involvement—their interest in the election, awareness of and information about current issues, and sense that individual opinions matter. Since Lazarsfeld's pioneering work (Berelson, Lazarsfeld, and McPhee 1954; Lazarsfeld, Berelson, and Gaudet 1948), it has been thought that campaign activity in connection with recurring elections enables parties and candidates to mobilize their likely constituents and "recharge" their partisan sentiments. Voter turnout is thus considered to increase directly with "the level of political stimulation to which the electorate is subjected" (Campbell et al. 1966, 42; Patterson and Caldeira 1983).

The argument that campaigns are inherently "stimulating" experiences can be questioned on a variety of grounds. American campaigns have changed dramatically since the 1940s and 1950s (see Ansolabehere et al. 1993). It is generally accepted that television has undermined the traditional importance of party organizations, because it permits "direct" communication between candidates and the voters (see Bartels 1988; Polsby 1983; Wattenberg 1984, 1991). All forms of broadcasting, from network newscasts to talk show programs, have become potent tools in the hands of campaign operatives, consultants, and fund-raisers. In particular, paid political advertisements have become an essential form of campaign communication. In 1990, for example, candidates spent more on televised advertising than any other form of campaign communication (Ansolabehere and Gerber 1993).

We are now beginning to realize that the advent of television has also radically changed the nature and tone of campaign discourse. Today more than ever, the entire electoral process rewards candidates whose skills are rhetorical, rather than substantive (Jamieson 1992) and whose private lives and electoral viability, rather than party ties, policy positions, and governmental experience, can withstand media scrutiny (see Brady and Johnston 1987; Lichter, Amundson, and Noyes 1988; Sabato 1991). Campaigns have also turned increasingly hostile and ugly. More often than not, candidates criticize, discredit, or belittle their opponents rather than promoting their own ideas

and programs. In the 1988 and 1990 campaigns, a survey of campaign advertising carried out by the *National Journal* found that attack advertisements had become the norm rather than the exception (Hagstrom and Guskind 1988, 1992).

Given the considerable changes in electoral strategy and the emergence of negative advertising as a staple of contemporary campaigns, it is certainly time to question whether campaigns are bound to stimulate citizen involvement in the electoral process. To be sure, there has been no shortage of hand wringing and outrage over the depths to which candidates have sunk, the viciousness and stridency of their rhetoric, and the lack of any systematic accountability for the accuracy of the claims made by the candidates (see Bode 1992; Dionne 1991; Rosen and Taylor 1992). However, as noted by a recent Congressional Research Service survey, there is little evidence concerning the effects of attack advertising on voters and the electoral process (see Neale 1991).

A handful of studies have considered the relationship between campaign advertising and political participation, with inconsistent results. Garramone and her colleagues (1990) found that exposure to negative advertisements did not depress measures of political participation. This study, however, utilized student participants and the candidates featured in the advertisements were fictitious. In addition, participants watched the advertisements in a classroom setting. In contrast to this study, an experiment reported by Basil, Schooler, and Reeves (1991) found that negative advertisements reduced positive attitudes toward both candidates in the race, thereby indirectly reducing political involvement. This study, however, was not conducted during an ongoing campaign and utilized a tiny sample, and the participants could not vote for the target candidates. Finally, Thorson, Christ, and Caywood (1991) reported no differences in voting intention between college students exposed to positive and negative advertisements.

We assert that campaigns can be either mobilizing or demobilizing events, *depending upon the nature of the messages they generate.* Using an experimental design that manipulates advertising tone while holding all

(Continued)

FIGURE 3–5 (CONTINUED)

Attack Advertising and Demobilization   December 1994

other features of the advertisements constant, we demonstrate that exposure to attack advertising in and of itself significantly decreases voter engagement and participation. We then reproduce this result by demonstrating that turnout in the 1992 Senate campaigns was significantly reduced in states where the tone of the campaign was relatively negative. Finally, we address three possible explanations for the demobilizing effects of negative campaigns.

EXPERIMENTAL DESIGN

There is a vast literature, both correlational and experimental, concerning the effects of televised advertisements (though not specifically negative advertisements) on public opinion (for a detailed review, see Kosterman 1991). This literature, however, is plagued by significant methodological shortcomings. The limitations of the opinion survey as a basis for identifying the effects of mass communications have been well documented (see Bartels 1993; Hovland 1959). Most importantly, surveys cannot reliably assess exposure to campaign advertising. Nor is most of the existing experimental work fully valid. The typical experimental study, by relying on fictitious candidates as the "target" stimuli, becomes divorced from the real world of campaigns. Previous experimental studies thus shed little evidence on the interplay between voters' existing information and preferences and their reception of campaign advertisements. When experimental work has focused on real candidates and their advertisements, it is difficult to capture the effects of particular characteristics of advertising because the manipulation confounds several such characteristics (Ansolabehere and Iyengar 1991; Garramone 1985; Pfau and Kenski 1989). That is, a Clinton spot and Bush spot differ in any number of features (the accompanying visuals, background sound, the voice of the announcer, etc.) in addition to the content of the message. Thus there are many possible explanations for differences in voters' reactions to these spots.

To overcome the limitations of previous research, we developed a rigorous but realistic experimental design for assessing the effects of advertising tone or valence[1] on public opinion and voting. Our studies all took place during ongoing political campaigns (the 1990 California gubernatorial race, the 1992 California Senate races, and the 1993 Los Angeles mayoral race) and featured "real" candidates who were in fact advertising heavily on television and "real" voters (rather than college sophomores) who on election day would have to choose between the candidates whose advertisements they watched. Our experimental manipulations were professionally produced and could not (unless the viewer were a political consultant) be distinguished from the flurry of advertisements confronting the typical voter. In addition, our manipulation was unobtrusive; we embedded the experimental advertisement into a 15-minute local newscast.

The most-distinctive feature of our design is its ability to capture the casual effects of a particular feature of campaign advertisement—in this case, advertising tone or valence. The advertisements that we produced were identical in all respects but tone and the candidate sponsoring the advertisement. In the 1992 California Senate primaries, for example, viewers watched a 30-second advertisement that either promoted or attacked on the general trait of "integrity." The visuals featured a panoramic view of the Capitol Building, the camera then zooming in to a closeup of an unoccupied desk inside a Senate office. In the "positive" treatments (using the example of candidate Dianne Feinstein), the text read by the announcer was as follows:

> For over 200 years the United States Senate has shaped the future of America and the world. Today, California needs honesty, compassion, and a voice for all the people in the U.S. Senate. As mayor of San Francisco, Dianne Feinstein *proposed* new government ethics rules. She *rejected* large campaign contributions from special interests. And Dianne Feinstein *supported* tougher penalties on savings-and-loan crooks.
> California *needs* Dianne Feinstein in the U.S. Senate.

In the "negative" version of this Feinstein spot, the text was modified as follows:

> For over 200 years the United States Senate has shaped the future of America and the world. Today, California needs honesty, compassion, and a voice for all the people in the U.S. Senate. As state controller, Gray Davis *opposed* new government ethics rules. He *accepted* large campaign contributions from special interests. And Gray Davis *opposed* tougher penalties on savings-and-loan crooks.
> California *can't afford a politician* like Gray Davis in the U.S. Senate.

By holding the visual elements constant and by using the same announcer, we were able to limit differences between the conditions to differences in tone.[2] With appropriate modifications to the wording, the identical pair of advertisements was also shown on behalf of Feinstein's primary opponent, Controller Gray Davis, and for the various candidates contesting the other Senate primaries.

In short, our experimental manipulation enabled us to establish a much tighter degree of control over the tone of campaign advertising than had been possible in previous research. Since the advertisements watched by viewers were identical in all other respects and because we randomly assigned participants to experimental conditions, any differences between conditions may be attributed only to the tone of the political advertisement (see Rubin 1974).

The Campaign Context

Our experiments spanned a variety of campaigns, including the 1990 California gubernatorial election, both of the state's 1992 U.S. Senate races, and the 1993 mayoral election in Los Angeles. In the case of the senatorial campaigns, we examined three of the four primaries and both general election campaigns.

Source: Stephen Ansolabehere, Shanto Iyengar, Adam Simon, and Nicholas Valentino, "Does Attack Advertising Demobilize the Electorate?" *American Political Science Review* 88, no. 4 (Dec. 1994): 829–830. Copyright © 1994 American Political Science Association. Reprinted with the permission of Cambridge University Press.

The third paragraph discusses similar themes and cites work that examines the value of rhetorical skill and the ability to withstand media scrutiny during an election. Finally, the third paragraph explains that campaigns have become "increasingly hostile and ugly" and cites two references to establish the point. As you can see, the first three paragraphs of this literature review are organized around concepts and ideas that are essential to understanding the base of knowledge about the relationship between campaign advertising and voters.

An important aspect of the fourth and fifth paragraphs is that they transition from establishing that the nature of campaigns has changed since early work on the topic to establishing that some work has attempted to measure this new relationship. The authors cite "Neale 1991" when claiming that "there is little evidence concerning the effects of attack advertising on voters and the electoral process."[6] They also cite three studies that examined the same research question as Ansolabehere et al.: "Garramone and her colleagues (1990)"; "Basil, Schooler, and Reeves (1991)"; and "Thorson, Christ, and Caywood (1991)." According to the authors, the previous work was inconclusive because it found conflicting results. Garramone et al. found that negative advertising did not depress turnout; Basil, Schooler, and Reeves found that negative advertisements indirectly reduced political participation; and Thorson, Christ, and Caywood reported that negative advertisements had no effect on the intention of voting. With each citation, the authors also identify some of the problems in each research design that might lead to suspect results. Given these conflicting results, the authors propose in the sixth paragraph that they will attempt to provide clarity by improving upon previous work by correcting research design flaws.

The first new paragraph on the second page, under the "Experimental Design" heading, provides further detail about the flaws of previous work using two different approaches: survey research and experimental research. The authors first point the interested reader to another reference that has documented the literature on television advertising and public opinion, "Kosterman 1991." They then turn their attention to survey research and identify the main drawback of this approach: a lack of measurement of direct exposure to advertising, as documented by two cited references. Next, the authors discuss the flaws of previous experimental work, primarily issues of external validity, and point to three cited references. The following paragraph begins the description of this article's research design.

With this example, you can see that there is a logical order to the literature review: establish conventional wisdom, establish that the nature of politics has changed—while the conventional understanding has not, and identify flaws in previous research that can be corrected. Discussing the literature in this manner makes a convincing case to the reader that this research project will be an important addition to the literature because it will improve our understanding of a topic that until now has been misunderstood.

Also, by organizing the literature review in this way, the authors have found a clear motivation for designing their research project as they have. Throughout the literature review, the authors integrated twenty-nine references by focusing on the concepts, ideas, and methods that were shared across the literature.

Finally, the authors established that this is an important area of study (as others have an interest in writing in this area) and that our understanding is not complete (as there is disagreement through conflicting results and conclusions).

Although different literature reviews will vary in the organizational style they use, we recommend that students working on their own literature reviews try to follow this topical style of integrating references; it will make even a brief discussion, like the two pages in the Ansolabehere et al. article, very powerful.

CONCLUSION

No matter what the original purpose of your literature review, it should be thorough. In your research report, you should discuss the sources that provide explanations for the phenomenon you are studying and that support the plausibility of your hypotheses. You should also discuss how your research relates to other research and use the existing literature to document the significance of your research. You can look to the example in the previous section or to an example of a literature review contained in the research report in chapter 15. Another way to learn about the process is to read a few articles in any of the main political science journals that we listed earlier in this chapter and take some time to study the literature reviews carefully, looking for effective styles that would suit your own project.

Terms Introduced

Electronic databases. A collection of information (of any type) stored on an electromagnetic medium that can be accessed and examined by certain computer programs.

Literature review. A systematic examination and interpretation of the literature for the purpose of informing further work on a topic.

Relationship. The association, dependence, or covariance of the values of one variable with the values of another.

Search engine. A computer program that visits Web pages on the Internet and looks for those containing particular directories or words.

Search term. A word or phrase entered into a computer program (a search engine) that looks through Web pages on the Internet for those that contain the word or phrase.

Suggested Readings

Fink, Arlene. *Conducting Research Literature Reviews: From the Internet to Paper.* 3rd ed. Los Angeles: Sage, 2010.

Galvan, Jose L. *Writing Literature Reviews: A Guide for Students of the Social and Behavioral Sciences.* 4th ed. Glendale, Calif.: Pyrczak, 2009.

Pan, M. Ling. *Preparing Literature Reviews: Qualitative and Quantitative Approaches.* 3rd ed. Glendale, Calif.: Pyrczak, 2008.

David and Lorraine Cheng Library, William Patterson University. "Guide for Citing Electronic Information." http://ww2.wpunj.edu/library/citing.htm.

Notes

1. The *Political Science Research Methods* CD contains several text documents that illustrate this point and allow the reader to extract empirical and testable claims from verbal arguments.

2. Steve Chapman, "Restricting 2nd Amendment Isn't the Answer," *Real Clear Politics,* January 13, 2011, http://www.realclearpolitics.com/articles/2011/01/13/restricting_2nd_amendment _isnt_the_answer.html.

3. Larry P. Goodson, Bradford Dillman, and Anil Hira, "Ranking the Presses: Political Scientists' Evaluations of Publisher Quality," *PS: Political Science and Politics* 32, no. 2 (1999): 257–62. Available at http://webserver1.pugetsound.edu/facultypages/bdillman/ps.pdf.

4. See the American Political Science Association, "Conference Papers," http://www.apsanet .org/conferencepapers/.

5. Stephen Ansolabehere, Shanto Iyengar, Adam Simon, and Nicholas Valentino, "Does Attack Advertising Demobilize the Electorate?" *American Political Science Review* 88, no. 4 (1994): 829. Available at http://weber.ucsd.edu/~tkousser/Ansolabehere.pdf.

6. Ibid.

THE BUILDING BLOCKS OF SOCIAL SCIENTIFIC RESEARCH:

Hypotheses, Concepts, and Variables

IN CHAPTERS 1 AND 2, WE DISCUSSED what it means to acquire scientific knowledge and presented examples of political science research intended to produce this type of knowledge. In chapter 3, we discussed how to search for a topic and begin to pose an appropriate research question. In this chapter, we focus on taking the next steps beyond specifying the research question. These steps require us to (1) propose a suitable explanation for the phenomena under study, (2) formulate testable hypotheses, and (3) define the concepts identified in the hypotheses. Although we discuss these steps as if they occur in sequence, the actual order may vary. All the steps must be taken eventually, however, before a research project can be completed successfully. The sooner the issues and decisions involved in each of the steps are addressed, the sooner the other portions of the research project can be completed.

PROPOSING EXPLANATIONS

Once a researcher has developed a suitable research question or topic, the next step is to propose an explanation for the phenomenon the researcher is interested in understanding. Proposing an explanation involves identifying other phenomena that we think will help us account for the object of our research and then specifying how and why these two (or more) phenomena are related. Or, alternatively, we may identify a political phenomenon and want to know whether or not it has any impact on other political phenomena. Your literature review should have given you plenty of ideas about relationships between concepts.

In the examples referred to in chapter 1, the researchers proposed explanations for the political phenomena they were studying. Kenworthy and Pontusson investigated whether increases in market incomes lead to increases in government spending for redistributive programs.[1] Holbrook and Heidbreder investigated to what extent differences in per capita income, percent Hispanic population, the presence of ballot initiatives, and other factors accounted for variation in turnout among the states.[2] Milner, Poe and Leblang investigated to what extent three types of human rights (security, subsistence, and civil rights) tend to be found together or if a trade-off exists, with countries being able to afford more of some rights but less of others.[3] Hall and Miler wanted to know what accounted for differences in agency oversight activity among members of Congress.[4] And Stephen D. Ansolabehere and his colleagues thought that voter turnout would be affected by the tone of campaign advertising.[5]

To help clarify relationships between phenomena, political scientists refer to phenomena as variables and identify several types of variables. A phenomenon that we think will help us explain political characteristics or behavior is called an **independent variable.** Independent variables are the measurements of the phenomena that are thought to influence, affect, or cause some other phenomenon. A **dependent variable** is thought to be caused, to depend upon, or to be a function of an independent variable. Thus, if a researcher has hypothesized that acquiring more formal education will lead to increased income later on (in other words, that income may be explained by education), then years of formal education would be the independent variable, and income would be the dependent variable.

As the word *variable* connotes, we expect the value of the concepts we identify as variables to vary or change. A concept that does not change in value is called a constant and is not a suitable phenomenon to investigate as part of the research process we focus on in this book. Unfortunately, sometimes a concept is expected to vary and thus be suitable for inclusion in a research project, only for a researcher to discover later that the concept does not vary. For example, a student working on a survey to be distributed to her classmates wanted to see if students having served in the military or having a family member in the military had different attitudes toward the war in Iraq than did students without military service connections. She discovered that none of the students had any military service connections: having military service connections was a constant.

Proposed explanations for political phenomena are often more complicated than the simple identification of one independent variable that is thought to explain a dependent variable. More than one phenomenon is usually needed to account adequately for most political behavior. For example, suppose a researcher proposes the following relationship between state efforts to regulate pollution and the severity of potential harm from pollution: the higher the threat of pollution (independent variable), the greater the effort to regulate pollution (dependent variable). The insightful researcher would realize the possibility that another phenomenon, such as the wealth of a state, might also affect a state's regulatory effort. The proposed explanation for state regulatory effort, then, would involve an alternative variable (wealth) in addition to the original independent variable. As another example, remember from chapter 1 that Lane Kenworthy and Jonas Pontusson thought that larger changes in market inequality would cause larger changes in redistribution but that changes in redistribution would also be affected by turnout rates in national elections.[6] It is frequently desirable to compare the effect of each independent variable on the dependent variable. This is done by "controlling for" or holding constant one of the independent variables so that the effect of the other may be observed. This process is discussed in more detail in chapters 13 and 14.

Sometimes, in addition to explaining how independent variables are related to the dependent variable, researchers are able to propose explanations for how the independent variables are related to each other. In particular, we might want to determine which independent variables occur before other independent variables and indicate which ones have a more direct, as opposed to indirect, effect on the phenomenon we are trying to explain (the dependent variable). A variable that occurs prior to all other variables and that may affect other independent variables is called an **antecedent variable.** A variable that occurs closer in time to the dependent variable and is itself affected by other independent variables is called an **intervening variable.** The roles of antecedent and intervening variables in the explanation of the dependent variable differ significantly. Consider these examples.

Suppose a researcher hypothesizes that a person who favored national health insurance was more likely to have voted for Barack Obama in 2008 than was a person who did not favor such extensive coverage. In this case, the attitude toward national health insurance would be the independent variable and the presidential vote the dependent variable. The researcher might wonder what causes the attitude toward national health insurance and might propose that those people who have inadequate medical insurance are more apt to favor national health insurance. This new variable (adequacy of a person's present medical insurance) would then be an antecedent variable, since it comes before and affects (we think) the independent variable. Thinking about antecedent variables pushes our explanatory scheme further back in time and, we hope, will lead to a more complete understanding of a particular phenomenon (in this case, presidential voting). Notice how the independent variable in the original hypothesis (attitude toward national health insurance) becomes the dependent variable in the hypothesis involving the antecedent variable (adequacy of health insurance). Also notice that in this example, adequacy of health insurance is thought to exert an indirect effect on the dependent variable (presidential voting) via its impact on attitudes toward national health insurance.

Now consider a second example. Suppose a researcher hypothesizes that a voter's years of formal education affect her or his propensity to vote. In this case, education would be the independent variable and voter turnout the dependent variable. If the researcher then begins to consider what about education has this effect, he or she has begun to identify the intervening variables between education and turnout. For example, the researcher might hypothesize that formal education creates or causes a sense of civic duty, which in turn encourages voter turnout, or that formal education causes an ability to understand the different issue positions of the candidates, which in turn causes voter turnout. Intervening variables come between an independent variable and a dependent variable and help explain the process by which one influences the other.

Hacker and Pierson's explanation of "winner-take-all" economic outcomes focused on the increase in the political capacity of business interests in the United States since the 1970s.[7] This in turn led to new policies and failure to revise existing policies to respond to changing economic conditions, thus resulting in income inequality, especially at the very top. Lane Kenworthy argued that a more complete explanation would include additional factors such as shifts in perceptions of US economic strength; features of American political institutions; changes in technology, economic competition, and corporate governance; as well as other factors.[8]

Explanatory schemes that involve numerous independent, alternative, antecedent, and intervening variables can become quite complex. An **arrow diagram** is a handy device for presenting and keeping track of such complicated explanations. The arrow diagram specifies the phenomena of interest; indicates which variables are independent, alternative, antecedent, intervening, and dependent; and shows which variables are thought to affect which other ones. In figure 4–1 we present arrow diagrams for the two voting examples we just considered.

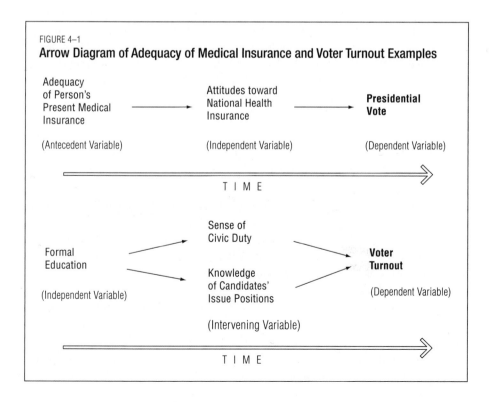

FIGURE 4–1
Arrow Diagram of Adequacy of Medical Insurance and Voter Turnout Examples

Adequacy of Person's Present Medical Insurance → Attitudes toward National Health Insurance → **Presidential Vote**

(Antecedent Variable) (Independent Variable) (Dependent Variable)

T I M E

Formal Education → Sense of Civic Duty / Knowledge of Candidates' Issue Positions → **Voter Turnout**

(Independent Variable) (Intervening Variable) (Dependent Variable)

T I M E

In both diagrams, the dependent variable is placed at the end of the time line, with the independent, alternative, intervening, and antecedent variables placed in their appropriate locations to indicate which ones come earlier and which later. Arrows indicate that one variable is thought to explain or be related to another; the direction of the arrow indicates which variable is independent and which is dependent in that proposed relationship.

Figure 4–2 shows two examples of arrow diagrams that have been proposed and tested by political scientists. Both diagrams are thought to explain presidential voting behavior. In the first diagram, the ultimate dependent variable, Vote, is thought to be explained by Candidate Evaluations and Party Identification. The Candidate Evaluations variable, in turn, is explained by the Issue Losses, Party Identification, and Perceived Candidate Personalities variables. These, in turn, are explained by other concepts in the diagram. The variables at the top of the diagram tend to be antecedent variables (the subscript t–1 denotes that these variables precede variables with subscript t, where t indicates time); the ones in the center tend to be intervening variables. Nine independent variables of one sort or another figure in the explanation of the vote.

The second diagram also has Vote as the ultimate dependent variable, which is explained directly by only one independent variable, Comparative Candidate Evaluations. The latter variable, in turn, is dependent upon six independent variables: Personal Qualities Evaluations, Comparative Policy Distances, Current Party Attachment, Region, Religion, and Partisan Voting History. In this diagram, sixteen variables figure, either indirectly or directly, in the explanation of the Vote variable, with the antecedent variables located around the perimeter of the diagram and the intervening variables closer to the center. Both of these diagrams clearly represent complicated and extensive attempts to explain a dependent variable.

Figure 4-3 shows arrow diagrams for explanations of the growth in top incomes. The top diagram indicates a simple three-step causal relationship. The lower diagram indicates that US political institutions and shifts in perceived American economic performance intervene between business political capacity and shifts in policy. Shifts in Republican Party political culture and strategy are shown as having a direct impact on shifts in policy. The model indicates that factors outside the political realm also contributed to concentration at the top. One can imagine that there would be some debate about how much change in these factors occurred independently of politics and policy.

Note that arrow diagrams show hypothesized causal relationships. A one-headed arrow connecting two variables is a shorthand way of expressing the proposition "X directly causes Y." If arrows do not directly link two variables, the variables may be associated or correlated, but the relationship is indirect, not causal. As we discuss in greater depth in chapter 6, when we assert X causes Y, we are in effect making three claims. One is that X and Y covary—a change in one

FIGURE 4–2
Two Causal Models of Vote Choice

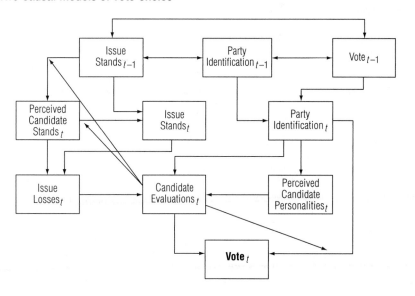

Source: Gregory B. Markus and Philip E. Converse, "A Dynamic Simultaneous Equation Model of Electoral Choice," *American Political Science Review* 73 (December 1979): 1059. Copyright © 1979 American Political Science Association. Reprinted with permission of Cambridge University Press.

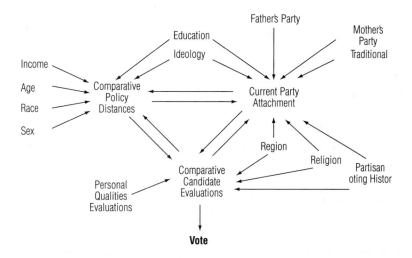

Source: Benjamin I. Page and Calvin C. Jones, "Reciprocal Effects of Policy Preferences, Party Loyalties and the Vote," *American Political Science Review* 73 (December 1979): 1083. Copyright © 1979 American Political Science Association. Reprinted with permission of Cambridge University Press.

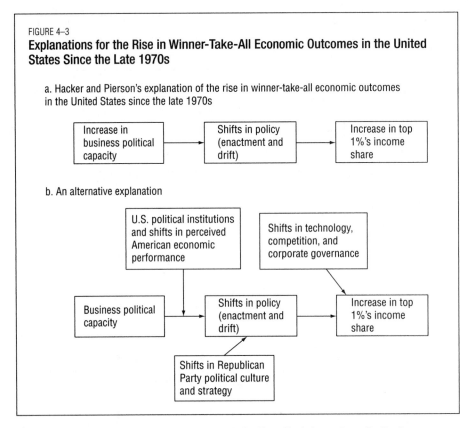

FIGURE 4–3

Explanations for the Rise in Winner-Take-All Economic Outcomes in the United States Since the Late 1970s

a. Hacker and Pierson's explanation of the rise in winner-take-all economic outcomes in the United States since the late 1970s

| Increase in business political capacity | → | Shifts in policy (enactment and drift) | → | Increase in top 1%'s income share |

b. An alternative explanation

Source: Lane Kenworthy, "Business Political Capacity and the Top-Heavy Rise in Income Inequality: How Large an Impact?" *Politics & Society* 38, no. 2 (2010): figs. 1 and 2, p. 256. Copyright © 2010 SAGE Publications. Reprinted by Permission of SAGE Publications.

variable is associated with a change in the other. Second, we are claiming that a change in the independent variable (*X*) *precedes* the change in the dependent variable (*Y*). Finally, we are stating that the covariation between *X* and *Y* is not simply a coincidence or spurious—that is, due to change in some other variable—but is direct.

We have discussed the first two steps in the research process—asking a question and then proposing an explanation—as occurring in this order, but quite often this is not the case. In chapter 2, we pointed out that researchers might start out with a theory and make deductions based on it. Thus researchers often start with an explanation and look for an appropriate research question that the theory might answer. Theory is an important aspect of explanation, for in order to be able to argue effectively that something causes something else, we need to be able to supply a reason or, to use words from the natural sciences, to identify the *mechanism* behind the relationship. This is the role of theory. For example, the theory of the median voter supplies a reason for changes in government policies.

FORMULATING HYPOTHESES

Thus far we have discussed two stages in the research process: identifying the research question and proposing explanations for the phenomena of interest. By this point, then, the researcher is ready to state what his or her hypotheses are. A **hypothesis** is an explicit statement that indicates how a researcher thinks the phenomena of interest are related. A hypothesis is a guess (but of an educated nature) that represents the proposed explanation for some phenomenon and that indicates how an independent variable is thought to affect, influence, or alter a dependent variable. Since hypotheses are proposed relationships, they may turn out to be incorrect.

Characteristics of Good Hypotheses

For a hypothesis to be tested adequately and persuasively, it must be stated properly. It is important to start a research project with a clearly stated hypothesis because it provides the foundation for subsequent decisions and steps in the research process. A poorly formulated hypothesis often indicates confusion about the relationship to be tested or can lead to mistakes that will limit the value or the meaning of any findings. Many students find it challenging to write a hypothesis that precisely states the relationship to be tested: it takes practice to write consistently well-worded hypotheses. A good hypothesis has six characteristics: (1) it is an empirical statement, (2) it is stated as a generality, (3) it is plausible, (4) it is specific, (5) it is stated in a manner that corresponds to the way in which the researcher intends to test it, and (6) it is testable. The following discussion of these six characteristics will alert students to some common mistakes to avoid.

EMPIRICAL STATEMENT.   First, hypotheses should be empirical statements. They should be educated guesses about relationships that exist in the real world, not statements about what ought to be true or about what a researcher believes should be the case. Consider someone who is interested in democracy. If the researcher hypothesizes that "Democracy is the best form of government," he or she has formulated a normative, nonempirical statement that cannot be tested. The statement communicates the preference of the researcher; it does not explain a phenomenon. By now, this researcher ought to have defined the central concept—in this case, democracy—and those concepts thought to be related to democracy (such as literacy, size of population, geographical isolation, and economic development). Therefore, to produce an acceptable hypothesis, the researcher ought to make an educated guess about the relationship between democracy and another of these concepts; for example, "Democracy is more likely to be found in countries with high literacy than in countries with low literacy." This hypothesis now proposes an explanation for a phenomenon that can be observed empirically. Or, one might think that democracy is preferable to other systems because it produces higher standards of living. We cannot prove that one thing is preferable to another, but we could certainly compare countries on numerous measures of well-being, such as health status. The conclusion might then be "Compared with people living under dictatorships, citizens of democracies have higher life expectancies." Whether the hypothesis is confirmed empirically is not necessarily related to whether the researcher thinks the phenomenon (in this case, democracy) is good or bad.

In some cases, empirical knowledge can be relevant for normative inquiry. Often, people reach normative conclusions based on their evaluation of empirical relationships. Someone might reason, for example, that negative campaign ads cause voters to become disgusted with politics and not vote in elections; one might further reason that because low turnout is bad, negative campaign ads are bad as well. The first part of the assertion is an empirical statement, which could be investigated using the techniques developed in this book, whereas the next two (low turnout and negative ads being bad) are normative statements.

Normative thinking is useful because it forces an individual to clarify his or her values and it encourages research on significant empirical questions. For example, a normative distaste for crime encourages empirical research on the causes of crime or on the effectiveness of particular sentencing policies. Consequently, the two modes of inquiry—normative and empirical—should be viewed as complementary rather than contradictory.

GENERALITY.   A second characteristic of a good hypothesis is generality. It should explain a general phenomenon rather than one particular occurrence of the phenomenon. For example, one might hypothesize that the cause of World War II was economic upheaval in Germany. If the hypothesis were confirmed, what would be the extent of our knowledge? We would know the cause of one war. This knowledge is valuable, but it would be more useful to know if economic upheaval *in general* causes wars. That knowledge would pertain to many occurrences of a phenomenon (in this case, many wars) rather than just to one occurrence. A more general hypothesis, then, might be "Countries experiencing economic upheaval are more likely to become involved in a war than are countries not experiencing economic upheaval." Knowledge about the causes of particular occurrences of a phenomenon could be helpful in formulating more general guesses about the relationships between concepts, but with a general hypothesis, we attempt to expand the scope of our knowledge beyond individual cases. Stating hypotheses in the plural form, rather than the singular, makes it clear that testing the hypothesis will involve more than one case.

The four hypotheses in the left column below are too narrow, whereas the four hypotheses in the right column are more general and more acceptable as research propositions:

Senator X voted for a bill because it is the president's bill and they are both Democrats.	Senators are more likely to vote for bills sponsored by the president if they belong to the same political party as the president.
The United States is a democracy because its population is affluent.	Countries with high levels of affluence are more likely to be democracies than countries with low levels of affluence.
The United States has more murders than other countries because so many people own guns there.	Countries with more guns per capita will experience more murders per capita than countries with fewer guns.
Joe is a liberal because his mother is one, too.	People tend to adopt political viewpoints similar to those of their parents.

PLAUSIBILITY.   A third characteristic of a good hypothesis is that it should be plausible. There should be some logical reason for thinking that it might be confirmed. Of course, since a hypothesis is a guess about a relationship, whether it will be confirmed cannot be known for certain. Any number of hypotheses could be thought of and tested, but many fewer are plausible ones. For example, if a researcher hypothesized that "people who eat dry cereal for breakfast are more likely to be liberal than are people who eat eggs," we would question his or her logic even though the form of the hypothesis may be perfectly acceptable. It is difficult to imagine why this hypothesis would be confirmed.

But how do we make sure that a hypothesis has a good chance of being confirmed? Sometimes the justification is provided by specific instances in which the hypothesis was supported (going from specific to general knowledge in the manner discussed in chapter 2—that is, using induction). For example, a researcher may have observed a particular election in which a hotly contested primary campaign damaged the eventual nominee's chances of winning the general election. The researcher may then hypothesize that "the more difficult it is for candidates to secure their party's nomination, the more poorly those candidates will do in the general election."

And, as we pointed out earlier in our discussion of proposing explanations, a hypothesis also may be justified through the process of deduction. A researcher may deduce from more general theories that a particular hypothesis is sensible. For example, there is a general psychological theory that frustration leads to aggression. Some political scientists have adapted this general theory to the study of political violence or civil unrest and have hypothesized that civil unrest occurs when a civilian population is frustrated. A population may feel frustrated when many people believe that they are economically or politically worse off than they should be, than they used to be, or than other people like themselves are. This feeling, as we now know, is called relative deprivation, and it has figured prominently in hypotheses seeking to explain civil unrest. In this way, the general frustration-aggression theory led to a more specialized, deduced hypothesis for the occurrence of civil unrest.

The need to formulate plausible hypotheses is one of the reasons why researchers conduct a literature review early in their research projects. Literature reviews can acquaint researchers with both general theories and specific hypotheses advanced by others. In either case, reading the literature on a subject can improve the chances that a hypothesis will be confirmed. There are no hard and fast rules to ensure plausibility, however. After all, people used to think that "germs cause diseases" was an implausible hypothesis and that "dirt may be turned into gold" was a plausible one.

SPECIFICITY. The fourth characteristic of a good hypothesis is that it is specific. The researcher should be able to state a **directional hypothesis**—that is, he or she should be able to specify the expected relationship between two or more variables. Following are examples of directional hypotheses that specify the nature of the relationship between concepts:

- Median family income is higher in urban counties than in rural counties.
- States that are characterized by a "moralistic" political culture will have higher levels of voter turnout than will states with an "individualistic" or "traditionalistic" political culture.

The first hypothesis indicates which relative values of median family income are related to which type or category of county. Similarly, the second hypothesis predicts a particular relationship between specific types of political culture (the independent variable) and voter turnout (the dependent variable).

The direction of the relationship between concepts is referred to as a **positive relationship** if the concepts are predicted to increase in size together or decrease in size together; that is, as X increases, so does Y, and as X decreases, so does Y. The following are examples of hypotheses that predict positive relationships:

- The more education a person has, the higher his or her income.
- As the percentage of a country's population that is literate increases, the country's political process becomes more democratic.
- The older people become, the more likely they are to be conservative.

- People who read the newspaper more are more informed about current events than are people who read the newspaper less.

- The lower a state's per capita income, the less money the state spends per pupil on education.

If, however, the researcher thinks that as one concept increases in size or amount, another one will decrease in size or amount, then a **negative relationship** is suggested, as in the following examples:

- Older people are less tolerant of social protest than are younger people.

- The more income a person has, the less concerned about mass transit the person will be.

- More affluent countries have less property crime than do poorer countries.

In addition, the concepts used in a hypothesis should be defined carefully. For example, a hypothesis that suggests "There is a relationship between personality and political attitudes" is far too ambiguous. What is meant by personality? Which political attitudes? A more specific reformulation of this hypothesis might be "The more self-esteem a person has, the less likely the person is to be an isolationist." Now personality has been narrowed to self-esteem, and the political attitude has been defined as isolationism, both more precise concepts, although not precise enough. Eventually even these two terms must be given more precise definitions when it comes to measuring them. (We return to the problem of measuring concepts in chapter 5.) As the concepts become more clearly defined, the researcher is better able to specify the direction of the hypothesized relationship.

Following are four examples of ambiguous hypotheses that have been made more specific:

How a person votes for president depends on the information he or she is exposed to.	The more information favoring candidate X a person is exposed to during a political campaign, the more likely that person is to vote for candidate X.
A country's geographical location matters for the type of political system it develops.	The more borders a country shares with other countries, the more likely that country is to have a nondemocratic political process.
A person's capabilities affect his or her political attitudes.	The more intelligent a person is, the more likely he or she is to support civil liberties.
Guns do not cause crime.	People who own guns are less likely to be the victims of crimes than are persons who do not own guns.

CORRESPONDENCE TO THE WAY IN WHICH THE RESEARCHER INTENDS TO TEST THE HYPOTHESIS. A fifth characteristic of a good hypothesis is that it is stated in a manner that corresponds to the way in which the researcher intends to test it—that is, it should be "consistent with the data."[9] For example, although the hypothesis "Higher levels of literacy are associated with higher levels of democracy," does state how the concepts are related, it does not indicate how the researcher plans to test the hypothesis. In contrast, the hypothesis "As the percentage of a country's population that is literate increases, the country's political process becomes more democratic" suggests that the researcher is proposing to use a time series design by measuring the literacy rate and the amount of democracy for a country or countries at several times to see if increases in democracy are associated with increases in literacy (that is, if changes in one concept lead to changes in another).

If, however, the researcher plans to test the hypothesis by measuring the literacy rates and levels of democracy for many countries at one point in time to see if those with higher literacy rates also have higher levels of democracy, it would be better to rephrase the hypothesis as "Countries with higher literacy rates tend to be more democratic than countries with lower literacy rates." This way of phrasing the hypothesis reflects that the researcher is planning to use a cross-sectional research design to compare the levels of democracy in countries with different literacy rates. This differs from comparing a country's level of democracy at more than one point in time to see if it changes in concert with changes in literacy.

TESTABILITY. Finally, a good hypothesis is testable. It must be possible and feasible to obtain data that will indicate whether the hypothesis is defensible. Hypotheses for which either confirming or disconfirming evidence is impossible to gather are not subject to testing and, hence, are unusable for empirical purposes.

Consider this example of a promising yet difficult-to-test hypothesis: "The more a child is supportive of political authorities, the less likely that child will be to engage in political dissent as an adult." This hypothesis is general, plausible, fairly specific, and empirical, but in its current form it cannot be tested because no data exist to verify the proposition. The hypothesis requires data that measure a set of attitudes for individuals when they are children and a set of behaviors when they are adults. Consequently, a frustrating practical barrier prevents the testing of an otherwise acceptable hypothesis. Students in one-semester college courses on research methods often run up against practical constraints. A semester is not usually long enough to collect and analyze data, and some data may be too expensive to acquire. In fact, many interesting hypotheses go untested simply because even professional researchers do not have the resources to collect the data necessary to test them.

Hypotheses stated in tautological form are also untestable. A **tautology** is a statement linking two concepts that mean essentially the same thing; for example, "The less support there is for a country's political institutions, the more tenuous the stability of that country's political system." This hypothesis would be difficult to disconfirm because the two concepts—support for political institutions and stability of a political system—are so similar. To conduct a fair test, one would have to measure independently—in different ways—the support for the political institutions and the stability of the political system.

In their study of government maltreatment of citizens, Steven C. Poe and C. Neal Tate defined human rights abuses as coercive activities (such as murder, torture, forced disappearance, and imprisonment of persons for their political views) designed to induce compliance.[10] Other researchers have included lack of democratic processes and poor economic conditions in their definitions of human rights abuses, but Poe and Tate did not include these concepts because they wanted to use democratic rights and economic conditions as independent variables explaining variation in human rights abuses by governments.

Many hypotheses, then, are not formulated in a way that permits an informative test of them with empirical research. Readers of empirical research in political science, as well as researchers themselves, should take care that research hypotheses are empirical, general, plausible, specific, consistent with the data, and testable. Hypotheses that do not share these characteristics are likely to cause difficulty for the researcher and reader alike and make a minimal contribution to scientific knowledge.

Specifying Units of Analysis

In addition to proposing a relationship between two or more variables, a hypothesis also specifies, or strongly implies, the types or levels of political actor to which the hypothesis is thought to apply. This is called the **unit of analysis** of the hypothesis, and it also must be selected thoughtfully. A clearly established unit of analysis structures and helps to organize the collection of data to measure variables of interest.

As noted in chapter 2, political scientists are interested in understanding the behavior or properties of all sorts of political actors (individuals, groups, states, government agencies, organizations, regions, nations) and events (elections, wars, conflicts). The particular type of actor whose political behavior is named in a hypothesis is the unit of analysis for the research project. In a legislative behavior study, for example, the individual members of the House of Representatives might be the units of analysis in the following hypothesis:

■ Members of the House who belong to the same party as the president are more likely to vote for legislation desired by the president than are members who belong to a different party.

In the following hypothesis, a city is the unit of analysis, since attributes of cities are being explored:

■ Northeastern cities are more likely to have mayors, while western cities have city managers.

Civil wars are the units of analysis in this hypothesis:

■ Civil wars that are halted by negotiated peace agreements are less likely to re-erupt than are those that cease due to the military superiority of one of the parties to the conflict.

Elections are the unit of analysis in this example:

■ Elections in which the contestants spend the same amount of money tend to be decided by closer margins of victory than elections in which one candidate spends a lot more than the other candidate(s).

Finally, consider this proposition:

■ The more affluent a country is, the more likely it is to have democratic political institutions.

Here the unit of analysis is the country. It is the measurement of national characteristics—affluence (the independent variable) and democratic political institutions (the dependent variable)—that is relevant to testing this hypothesis. In sum, the research hypothesis indicates the researcher's unit of analysis and the behavior or attributes that must be measured for that unit.

Cross-Level Analysis: Ecological Inference and Ecological Fallacy

Sometimes researchers conduct what is called **cross-level analysis**. In this type of analysis, researchers use data collected for one unit of analysis to make inferences about another unit of analysis. Christopher H. Achen and W. Phillips Shively pointed out that "for reasons of cost or availability, theories and descriptions referring to one level of aggregation are frequently testable only with data from another level."[11] A discrepancy between the unit of analysis specified in a hypothesis and the entities whose behavior is empirically observed can cause problems, however.

A frequent goal of cross-level analysis is to make an **ecological inference,** that is, to use aggregate data to study the behavior of individuals.[12] Data of many kinds are collected for school districts, voting districts, counties, states, nations, or other aggregates in order to make inferences about individuals. The relationships between schools' average test scores and the percentage of children receiving subsidized lunches, national poverty and child mortality rates, air pollution indexes and the incidence of disease in cities, and the severity of state criminal penalties and crime rates are examples of relationships explored using aggregate data. The underlying hypotheses of such studies are that children who receive subsidized lunches score lower on standardized tests, that poor children are more likely to die of childhood diseases, that individuals' health problems are due to their exposure to air pollutants, and that harsh penalties deter individuals from committing crimes. Yet, if a relationship is found between group indicators or characteristics, it does not necessarily mean that a relationship exists between the characteristics for individuals in the group. The use of information that shows a relationship for groups to infer that the same relationship exists for individuals when in fact there is no such relationship at the individual level is called an **ecological fallacy.**

Let's take a look at an example to see how an ecological fallacy might be committed as a result of failing to be clear about the unit of analysis. Suppose a researcher wants to test the hypothesis "Democrats are more likely to support a sales tax increase than are Republicans." Individuals are the unit of analysis in this hypothesis. If the researcher selects an election in which a sales tax increase was at issue and obtains the voting returns as well as data on the proportions of Democrats and Republicans in each election precinct, the data are aggregate data, not data on individual voters. If it is found that sales tax increases received more votes in precincts with a higher proportion of Democrats than in the precincts with a higher proportion of Republicans, the researcher might take this as evidence in support of the hypothesis. There is a fundamental problem with this conclusion, however. Unless a district is 100 percent Democratic or 100 percent Republican, the researcher cannot necessarily draw such a conclusion about the behavior of individuals from the behavior of election districts. It could be that support for a sales tax increase in a district with a high proportion of Democratic voters came mostly from non-Democrats and that most of the support for sales tax increase in the Republican districts came from Republicans. If this is the case, then the researcher would have committed an ecological fallacy. What was true at the aggregate level was not true at the individual level.

Let us take two hypothetical election precincts to illustrate how this fallacy could occur. Suppose we have Precinct 1, classified as a "Democratic" district, and Precinct 2, a "Republican" district. If the Democratic district voted 67 percent to 33 percent in favor of the sales tax increase, and the Republican district voted 53 percent to 47 percent in favor of the sales tax increase, we might be tempted to conclude that Democrats as individuals voted more heavily for the sales tax increase than did Republicans.

But imagine we peek inside each of the election precincts to see how individuals of different ethnicities behaved; that is, suppose we obtain information about individuals within the districts. The data in table 4–1 show that in the Democratic district, Democrats split 25–25 for the tax increase, Republicans voted 18–2 for it, and others voted 24–6 for it. This resulted in the 67–33 percent edge for the tax increase in Precinct 1. In the Republican district, Precinct 2, Democrats voted

TABLE 4–1
Voting by Democrats, Republicans, and Others for a Sales Tax Increase

Ethnicity	Number	Raw Vote		Percentage of Vote	
		Against Tax Increase	For Tax Increase	Against Tax Increase	For Tax Increase
Precinct 1					
Democrats	50	25	25	50.0	50.0
Republicans	20	2	18	10.0	90.0
Other	30	6	24	20.0	80.0
Total	100	33	67	33.0	67.0
Precinct 2					
Democrats	40	24	16	60.0	40.0
Republicans	50	20	30	40.0	60.0
Other	10	3	7	30.0	70.0
Total	100	47	53	47.0	53.0
Voting of Individuals					
Democrats	90	49	41	54.4	45.6
Republicans	70	22	48	31.4	68.6
Other	40	9	31	22.5	77.5
Total	200	80	120	40.0	60.0

Note: Hypothetical data.

16–24 against the tax increase, Republicans split 30–20 for it, and others voted 7–3 in favor. This resulted in the 53–47 percent margin for the sales tax increase in Precinct 2. When we compare the percentage of Democrats, Republicans, and others voting for the sales tax increase, the difference in the voting behavior of party identifiers becomes clearer. In both precincts, the percentage of Democrats voting for the sales tax increase was lower than that of the two other groups of voters. In Precinct 1, 50 percent of the Democrats voted for the sales tax increase, compared with 90 percent of the Republican voters and 80 percent of the others. In Precinct 2, only 40 percent of the Democrats voted for the sales tax increase, compared with 60 percent of the Republicans and 70 percent of the other voters. In other words, Republicans as individuals were more likely to have voted for the tax increase than were Democrats as individuals in both precincts. Knowing only the precinct-level totals gave the opposite impression. When the results for both districts are combined and broken down by party, we see that, overall, 68.6 percent of Republicans and 45.6 percent of Democrats voted for the sales tax increase.

In the research by Ansolabehere and his colleagues reported on in chapter 1, the tone of campaign advertising and the roll-off rates were measured in thirty-four Senate races, and states with races characterized by a negative tone had higher roll-off rates than states with positive campaigns.[13] The inference is that those individuals exposed to negative campaign ads are less likely to vote than are those exposed to positive campaign ads. But the researchers lacked data that showed the relationship between actual exposure to campaign ads of individuals and their voting behavior in the Senate elections. Remember, however, that the researchers examined and reported on individual-level data obtained from experiments, so they did not rely just on aggregate data to test their hypotheses about individuals.

Use of aggregate data to examine hypotheses that pertain to individuals may be unavoidable in some situations because individual-level data are lacking. Achen and Shively pointed out that before the development of survey research, aggregate data generally were the only data available and were used routinely by political scientists.[14] Several statistical methods have been developed to try to adjust inferences from aggregate-level data, although a discussion of these is beyond the scope of this book.[15]

Another mistake researchers sometimes make is to mix different units of analysis in the same hypothesis. "The more education a person has, the more democratic his or her country is" doesn't make much sense because it mixes the individual and country as units of analysis. However, though "The smaller a government agency, the happier its workers" concerns an attribute of an agency and an attribute of individuals, it does so in a way that makes sense. The size of the agency in which individuals work may be an important aspect of the context or environment in which the individual phenomenon occurs and may influence the individual attribute. In this case, the unit of analysis is clearly the individual, but a phenomenon that is experienced by many cases is used to explain the behavior of individuals, some of whom may well be identically situated.

In short, a researcher must be careful about the unit of analysis specified in a hypothesis and its correspondence with the unit measured. In general, a researcher should not mix units of analysis within a hypothesis.

DEFINING CONCEPTS

Political scientists are interested in why people or social groupings (organizations, political parties, legislatures, states, countries) behave in a certain way or have particular attributes or properties. The words that we choose to describe these behaviors or attributes are called *concepts*. Concepts should be accurate, precise, and informative. Clear definitions of the concepts of interest to us are important if we are to develop specific hypotheses and avoid tautologies. Clear definitions also are important so that the knowledge we acquire from testing our hypotheses is transmissible and empirical.

In our daily life, we use concepts frequently to name and describe features of our environment. For example, we describe some snakes as poisonous and others as nonpoisonous, some politicians as liberal and others as conservative, some friends as shy and others as extroverted. These attributes, or concepts, are useful to us because they help us observe and understand aspects of our environment, and they help us communicate with others.

Concepts also contribute to the identification and delineation of the scientific disciplines within which research is conducted. In fact, to a large extent a discipline maintains its identity because different researchers within it share a concern for the same concepts. Physics, for example, is concerned with the concepts of gravity and mass (among others); sociology, with social class and social mobility; psychology, with personality and deviance. By contrast, political science is concerned with concepts such as democracy, power, representation, justice, and equality. The boundaries of disciplines are not well defined or rigid, however. Political scientists, developmental psychologists, sociologists, and anthropologists all share an interest in how new members of a society are socialized into the norms and beliefs of that society, for example. Nonetheless, because a particular discipline has some minimal level of shared consensus concerning its significant concepts, researchers can usually communicate more readily with other researchers in the same discipline than with researchers in other disciplines.

A shared consensus over those concepts thought to be significant is related directly to the development of theories. Thus, a theory of politics will identify significant concepts and suggest why they are central to an understanding of political phenomena. Concepts are developed through a process by which some human group (tribe, nation, culture, profession) agrees to give a phenomenon or a property a particular name. The process is ongoing and somewhat arbitrary and does not ensure that all peoples everywhere will give the same phenomena the same names. In some areas of the United States, for example, a *soda* is a carbonated beverage, while in other areas it is a drink with ice cream in it. Likewise, the English language has only one word for *love*, whereas the Greeks have three words to distinguish among romantic love, familial love, and generalized feelings of affection.[16] Concepts disappear from a group's language when they are no longer needed, and new ones are invented as new phenomena are noticed that require names (for example, computer *programs* and *software*, *cultural imperialism*, and *hyperkinetic* behavior).

Some concepts—such as *car, chair,* and *vote*—are fairly precise because there is considerable agreement about their meaning. Others are more abstract and lend themselves to differing definitions—for example, *liberalism, crime, democracy, equal opportunity, human rights, social mobility,* and *alienation.* A similar concept is *orange.* Although there is considerable agreement about it (orange is not usually confused with purple), the agreement is less than total (whether a particular object is orange or red is not always clear).

Many interesting concepts that political scientists deal with are abstract and lack a completely precise, shared meaning. This hinders communication concerning research and creates uncertainty regarding the measurement of a phenomenon. Consequently, a researcher must explain what is meant by the concept so that a measurement strategy may be developed and so that those reading and evaluating the research can decide if the meaning accords with their own understanding of the term. Although some concepts that political scientists use—such as *amount of formal education, presidential vote,* and *amount of foreign trade*—are not particularly abstract, other concepts—such as *partisan realignment, political integration,* and *regime support*—are far more abstract and need more careful consideration and definition.

Suppose, for example, that a researcher is interested in the kinds of political systems that different countries have and, in particular, why some countries are more democratic than others. *Democracy* is consequently a key concept that needs definition and measurement. The word contains meaning for most of us; that is, we have some idea what is democratic and what is not. But once we begin thinking about the concept, we quickly realize that it is not as clear as we thought originally. In fact, a group of researchers wrote in 2011, "Perhaps no other concept is as central to policymakers and scholars. Yet, there is no consensus about how to conceptualize and measure regimes such that meaningful comparisons can be made through time and across countries."[17] To some, a country is democratic if it has "competing political parties, operating in free elections, with some reasonable level of popular participation in the process."[18] To others, a country is democratic only if legal guarantees protect free speech, the press, religion, and the like. To others, a country is democratic if the political leaders make decisions that are acceptable to the populace. And to still others, democracy implies equality of economic opportunity among the citizenry. If a country has all these attributes, it would be called a democracy by any of the criteria, and there would be no problem classifying the country. But if a country possesses only one of these attributes, its classification would be uncertain, since by some definitions it would be democratic but by others it would not be. Different definitions require different measurements and may result in different research findings. Hence, defining one's concepts is important, particularly when the concept is so abstract as to make shared agreement difficult.

Concept definitions have a direct impact on the quality of knowledge produced by research studies. Suppose, for example, that a researcher is interested in the connection between economic development and democracy, the working hypothesis being that countries with a high level of economic development will be more likely to have democratic forms of government. And suppose that there are two definitions of *economic development* and two definitions of *democracy* that might be used in the research. Finally, suppose that the researcher has data on twelve countries (A–L) included in the study. In table 4–2, we show that the definition selected for each concept has a direct bearing on how different countries are categorized on each attribute. By definition 1, countries A, B, C, D, E, and F are economically developed; however, by definition 2, countries A, B, C, G,

TABLE 4–2

Concept Development: The Relationship between Economic Development and Democracy

Is the country economically developed?

			By definition 1	
			Yes	No
	By definition 2	Yes	A,B,C	G,H,I
		No	D,E,F	J,K,L

Is the country a democracy?

			By definition 1	
			Yes	No
	By definition 2	Yes	D,E,F	J,K,L
		No	A,B,C	G,H,I

H, and I are. By definition 1, countries A, B, C, D, E, and F are democracies; by definition 2, countries D, E, F, J, K, and L are.

This is only the beginning of our troubles, however. When we look for a pattern involving the economic development and democracy of countries, we find that our answer depends mightily on how we have defined the two concepts. If we use the first definitions of the two concepts, we find that all economically developed countries are also democracies (A, B, C, D, E, F), which supports our hypothesis. If we use the first definition for economic development and the second for democracy (or vice versa), half of the economically developed nations are democracies and half are not. If we use the second definitions of both concepts, none of the economically developed countries is a democracy, whereas all of the undeveloped countries are (D, E, F, J, K, L). In other words, because of our inability to formulate a precise definition of the two concepts, and because the two definitions of each concept yield quite different categorizations of the twelve countries, our hypothesis could be either confirmed or disconfirmed by the data at hand. Our conceptual confusion has put us in a difficult position.

Consider another example. Suppose a researcher is interested in why some people are liberal and some are not. In this case we need to define what is meant by *liberal* so that those who are liberal can be identified. *Liberal* is a frequently used term, but it has many different meanings: one who favors change, one who favors redistributive income or social welfare policies, one who favors increased government spending and taxation, or one who opposes government interference in the political activities of its citizens. If a person possesses all these attributes, there is no problem deciding whether or not he or she is a liberal. A problem arises, however, when a person possesses some of these attributes but not others.

The examples here illustrate the elusive nature of concepts and the need to define them. The empirical researcher's responsibility to define terms is a necessary and challenging one. Unfortunately, many of the concepts used by political science researchers are abstract and require careful thought and extensive elaboration.

Researchers can clarify the concept definitions they use simply by making the meanings of key concepts explicit. This requires researchers to think carefully about the concepts used in their research and to share their meanings with others. Other researchers often challenge concept definitions, requiring researchers to elaborate upon and justify their meanings.

Another way in which researchers get help defining concepts is by reviewing and borrowing (possibly with modification) definitions developed by others in the field. For example, a researcher interested in the political attitudes and behavior of the American public would find the following definitions of key concepts in the existing literature:

- *Political participation:* "Those activities by private citizens that are more or less directly aimed at influencing the selection of government personnel and/or the actions they take"[19]

- *Political violence:* "All collective attacks within a political community against the political regime, its actors—including competing political groups as well as incumbents—or its policies"[20]

- *Political efficacy:* "The feeling that individual political action does have, or can have, an impact upon the political processes—that it is worthwhile to perform one's civic duties"[21]

- *Belief system:* "A configuration of ideas and attitudes in which the elements are bound together by some form of constraint or functional interdependence"[22]

Each of these concepts is somewhat vague and lacks complete shared agreement about its meaning. Furthermore, it is possible to raise questions about each of these concept definitions. Notice, for example, that the definition of *political participation* excludes the possibility that government employees (presumably "nonprivate" citizens) engage in political activities and that the definition of *political efficacy* excludes the impact of collective political action on political processes. Consequently, we may find these and other concept definitions inadequate and revise them to capture more accurately what we mean by the terms.

Over time, a discipline cannot proceed very far unless some minimal agreement is reached about the meanings of the concepts with which scientific research is concerned. Researchers must take care to think about the phenomena named in a research project and make explicit the meanings of any problematic concepts.

CONCLUSION

In this chapter, we discussed the beginning stages of a scientific research project. A research project must provide—to both the producer and the consumer of social scientific knowledge—the answers to these important questions: What phenomenon is the researcher trying to understand and explain? What explanation has the researcher proposed for the political behavior or attributes in question? What are the meanings of the concepts used in this explanation? What specific hypothesis relating two or more variables will be tested? What is the unit of analysis for the observations? If these questions are answered adequately, then the research will have a firm foundation.

Terms Introduced

Antecedent variable. An independent variable that precedes other independent variables in time.

Arrow diagram. A pictorial representation of a researcher's explanatory scheme.

Cross-level analysis. The use of data at one level of aggregation to make inferences at another level of aggregation.

Dependent variable. The phenomenon thought to be influenced, affected, or caused by some other phenomenon.

Directional hypothesis. A hypothesis that specifies the expected relationship between two or more variables.

Ecological fallacy. The fallacy of deducing a false relationship between the attributes or behavior of individuals based on observing that relationship for groups to which the individuals belong.

Ecological inference. The process of inferring a relationship between characteristics of individuals based on group or aggregate data.

Hypothesis. A tentative or provisional or unconfirmed statement that can (in principle) be verified.

Independent variable. The phenomenon thought to influence, affect, or cause some other phenomenon.

Intervening variable. A variable coming between an independent variable and a dependent variable in an explanatory scheme.

Negative relationship. A relationship in which the values of one variable increase as the values of another variable decrease.

Positive relationship. A relationship in which the values of one variable increase (or decrease) as the values of another variable increase (or decrease).

Tautology. A hypothesis in which the independent and dependent variables are identical, making it impossible to disconfirm.

Unit of analysis. The type of actor (individual, group, institution, nation) specified in a researcher's hypothesis.

Suggested Readings

Achen, Christopher H., and W. Phillips Shively. *Cross-Level Inference.* Chicago: University of Chicago Press, 1995.

King, Gary. *A Solution to the Ecological Inference Problem.* Princeton, N.J.: Princeton University Press, 1997.

King, Gary, Ori Rosen, and Martin A. Tanner, eds. *Ecological Inference: New Methodological Strategies.* Cambridge: Cambridge University Press, 2004.

Outhwaite, William, and Stephen P. Turner, eds. *The Sage Handbook of Social Science Methodology.* Los Angeles: Sage, 2007.

Notes

1. Lane Kenworthy and Jonas Pontusson, "Rising Inequality and the Politics of Redistribution in Affluent Countries," *Perspectives on Politics* 3, no. 3 (2005): 449–71. Available at http://www.u.arizona.edu/~lkenwor/pop2005.pdf.

2. Thomas Holbrook and Brianne Heidbreder, "Does Measurement Matter? The Case of VAP and VEP in Models of Voter Turnout in the United States," *State Politics & Policy Quarterly* 10, no. 2 (2010): 159–81.

3. Wesley T. Milner, Stephen C. Poe and David Leblang, "Security Rights, Subsistence Rights, and Liberties: A Theoretical Survey of the Empirical Landscape," *Human Rights Quarterly* 21, no. 2 (1999): 403–43.

4. Richard C. Hall and Kristina Miler, "What Happens After the Alarm? Interest Group Subsidies to Legislative Overseers," *Journal of Politics* 70, no. 4 (2008): 990–1005.

5. Stephen D. Ansolabehere, Shanto Iyengar, Adam Simon, and Nicholas Valentino, "Does Attack Advertising Demobilize the Electorate?" *American Political Science Review* 88, no. 4 (1994): 829–38. Available at http://weber.ucsd.edu/~tkousser/Ansolabehere.pdf.

6. Kenworthy and Pontusson, "Rising Inequality and the Politics of Redistribution."

7. Jacob S. Hacker and Paul Pierson, "Winner-Take-All Politics: Public Policy, Political Organization, and the Precipitous Rise of Top Incomes in the United States," *Politics & Society* 38, no. 2 (2010): 152–204.

8. Lane Kenworthy, "Business Political Capacity and the Top-Heavy Rise in Income Inequality: How Large an Impact?" *Politics & Society* 38, no. 2 (2010): 255–65.

9. This term is used by Susan Ann Kay in *Introduction to the Analysis of Political Data* (Englewood Cliffs, N.J.: Prentice Hall, 1991), 6.

10. Steven C. Poe and C. Neal Tate, "Repression of Human Rights to Personal Integrity in the 1980s: A Global Analysis," *American Political Science Review* 88, no. 4 (1994): 853–72.

11. Christopher H. Achen and W. Phillips Shively, *Cross-Level Inference* (Chicago: University of Chicago Press, 1995), 4.

12. Ibid.

13. Ansolabehere et al., "Does Attack Advertising Demobilize the Electorate?"

14. Achen and Shively, *Cross-Level Inference,* 5–10.

15. For example, see Gary King, *A Solution to the Ecological Inference Problem* (Princeton, N.J.: Princeton University Press, 1997); Achen and Shively, *Cross-Level Inference;* and Barry C. Burden and David C. Kimball, "Measuring Ticket Splitting," chap. 3 in *Why Americans Split Their Tickets: Campaigns, Competition, and Divided Government* (Ann Arbor: University of Michigan Press, 2002).

16. Kenneth R. Hoover, *The Elements of Social Scientific Thinking* (New York: St. Martin's, 1980), 18–19.

17. Michael Coppedge and John Gerring, "Conceptualizing and Measuring Democracy: A New Approach," *Perspectives on Politics* 9, no. 2 (2011): 247–67.

18. W. Phillips Shively, *The Craft of Political Research* (Englewood Cliffs, N.J.: Prentice Hall, 1980), 33.

19. Sidney Verba and Norman H. Nie, *Participation in America: Political Democracy and Social Equality* (New York: Harper and Row, 1972), 2.

20. Ted Robert Gurr, *Why Men Rebel* (Princeton, N.J.: Princeton University Press, 1970), 3–4.

21. Angus Campbell, Gerald Gurin, and Warren E. Miller, *The Voter Decides* (Evanston, Ill.: Row, Peterson, 1954), 187.

22. Philip E. Converse, "The Nature of Belief Systems in Mass Publics," in *Ideology and Discontent,* ed. David E. Apter (New York: Free Press, 1964), 207.

THE BUILDING BLOCKS OF SOCIAL SCIENTIFIC RESEARCH:

MEASUREMENT

IN THE PREVIOUS CHAPTERS, WE DISCUSSED the beginning stages of political science research projects: the choice of research topics, the formulation of scientific explanations, the development of testable hypotheses, and the definition of concepts. In this chapter, we take the next step toward testing empirically the hypotheses we have advanced. This entails understanding some issues involving the **measurement,** or systematic observation and representation by scores or numerals, of the variables we have decided to investigate.

In chapter 2, we said that scientific knowledge is based on empirical research. In this chapter, we confront the implications of this fact. If we are to test empirically the accuracy and utility of a scientific explanation for a political phenomenon, we will have to observe and measure the presence of the concepts we are using to understand that phenomenon. Furthermore, if this test is to be adequate, our measurements of the political phenomenon must be as accurate and precise as possible. The process of measurement is important because it provides the bridge between our proposed explanations and the empirical world they are supposed to explain. How researchers measure their concepts can have a significant impact on their findings; differences in measurement can lead to totally different conclusions.

Lane Kenworthy and Jonas Pontusson's investigation of income inequality in affluent countries illustrates well the impact on research findings of how a concept is measured.[1] One way to measure income distribution is to look at the earnings of full-time employed individuals and to compare the incomes of those at the top and the bottom of the earnings distribution. Kenworthy and Pontusson argued that it is more appropriate to compare the incomes of households than incomes of individuals. The unemployed are excluded from the calculations of individual earnings inequality, but households include the unemployed. Also, low-income workers disproportionately drop out of the employed labor force. Using working-age household income reflects changes in employment among household members. Kenworthy and Pontusson found that when individual income was used as a basis for measuring inequality, inequality had increased the most in the United States, New Zealand, and the United Kingdom, all liberal market economies. They further found that income inequality had increased significantly more in these countries than in Europe's social market economies and Japan. When household income was used, the data indicated that inequality had increased in all countries with the exception of the Netherlands.

Another example involves the measurement of turnout rates (discussed in chapter 1). Political scientists have investigated whether turnout rates in the United States have declined in recent decades.[2] The answer may depend on how the number of eligible voters is measured. Should it be the number of all citizens of voting age, or should this number be adjusted to take into account those who are not eligible to vote, or should the turnout rate be calculated using just the number of registered voters as the potential voting population?

The researchers discussed in chapter 1 measured a variety of political phenomena, some of which posed greater challenges than others. Milner, Poe, and Leblang wanted to measure three different types of human rights: personal integrity or security rights, subsistence rights, and civil and political rights. Each of these types of rights has multiple dimensions. For example, civil and political rights consist of both civil liberties, such as freedom of speech, as well as economic liberties, including private property rights. Jeffrey A. Segal and Albert D. Cover measured both the political ideologies and the written opinions of US Supreme Court justices in cases involving civil rights and liberties.[3] Valerie J. Hoekstra measured peoples' opinions about issues connected to Supreme Court cases and their opinions about the Court.[4] Richard L. Hall and Kristina Miler wanted to measure oversight activity by members of Congress, the number of times they were contacted by lobbyists, and whether members of Congress and lobbyists were pro-regulation or antiregulation.[5] And Stephen Ansolabehere, Shanto Iyengar, Adam Simon, and Nicholas Valentino measured the intention to vote reported by study participants to see if it was affected by exposure to negative campaign advertising.[6] In each case, some political behavior or attribute was measured so that a scientific explanation could be tested. All of these researchers made important choices regarding their measurements.

DEVISING MEASUREMENT STRATEGIES

As we pointed out in chapter 4, researchers must define the concepts they use in their hypotheses. They also must decide how to measure the presence, absence, or amount of these concepts in the real world. Political scientists refer to this process as providing an **operational definition** of their concepts—in other words, deciding what kinds of empirical observations should be made to measure the occurrence of an attribute or a behavior.

Let us return, for example, to the researcher trying to explain the existence of democracy in different nations. If the researcher were to hypothesize that higher rates of literacy make democracy more likely, then a definition of two concepts—literacy and democracy—would be necessary. The researcher could then develop a strategy, based on these two definitions, for measuring the existence and amount of both attributes in nations.

Suppose *literacy* was defined as "the completion of six years of formal education" and *democracy* was defined as "a system of government in which public officials are selected in competitive elections." These definitions would then be used to develop operational definitions of the two concepts. These operational definitions would indicate what should be observed empirically to measure both literacy and democracy, and they would indicate specifically what data should be collected to test the researcher's hypothesis. In this example, the operational definition of *literacy* might be "those nations in which at least 50 percent of the population has had six years of formal education, as indicated in a publication of the United Nations," and the operational definition of *democracy* might be "those countries in which the second-place finisher in elections for the chief executive office has received at least 25 percent of the vote at least once in the past eight years."

When a researcher specifies a concept's operational definition, the concept's precise meaning in a particular research study becomes clear. In the preceding example, we now know exactly what the researcher means by *literacy* and *democracy*. Since different people often mean different things by the same concept, operational definitions are especially important. Someone might argue that defining literacy in terms of formal education ignores the possibility that people who complete six years of formal education might still be unable to read or write well. Similarly, it might be argued that defining democracy in terms of competitive elections ignores other important features of democracy, such as freedom of expression and citizen involvement in government activity. In addition, the operational definition of *competitive elections* is clearly debatable. Is the "competitiveness" of elections based on the number of competing candidates, the size of the margin of victory, or the number of consecutive victories by a single party in a series of elections? Unfortunately, operational definitions are seldom absolutely correct or absolutely incorrect; rather, they are evaluated according to how well they correspond to the concepts they are meant to measure.

It is useful to think of arriving at the operational definition as being the last stage in the process of defining a concept precisely. We often begin with an abstract concept (such as democracy), then attempt to define it in a meaningful way, and finally decide in specific terms how we are going to measure it. At the end of this process, we hope to attain a definition that is sensible, close to our meaning of the concept, and exact in what it tells us about how to go about measuring the concept.

Let us consider another example: the researcher interested in why some individuals are more liberal than others. The concept of *liberalism* might be defined as "believing that government ought to pursue policies that provide benefits for the less well-off." The task then is to develop an operational definition that can be used to measure whether particular individuals are liberal or not. The following question from the General Social Survey might be used to operationalize the concept:

> *73A. Some people think that the government in Washington ought to reduce the income differences between the rich and the poor, perhaps by raising the taxes of wealthy families or by giving income assistance to the poor. Others think that the government should not concern itself with reducing this income difference between the rich and the poor.*
>
> *Here is a card with a scale from 1 to 7. Think of a score of 1 as meaning that the government ought to reduce the income differences between rich and poor, and a score of 7 as meaning that the government should not concern itself with reducing income differences. What score between 1 and 7 comes closest to the way you feel? (CIRCLE ONE)*[7]

An abstract concept, liberalism has now been given an operational definition that can be used to measure the concept for individuals. This definition is also related to the original definition of the concept, and it indicates precisely what observations need to be made. It is not, however, the only operational definition possible. Others might suggest that questions regarding affirmative action, school vouchers, the death penalty, welfare benefits, and pornography could be used to measure liberalism.

The important thing is to think carefully about the operational definition you choose and to try to ensure that the definition coincides closely with the meaning of the original concept. How a concept is operationalized affects how generalizations are made and interpreted. For example, general statements about liberals or conservatives apply to liberals or conservatives only as they have been operationally defined, in this case by this one question regarding government involvement in reducing income differences. As a consumer of research, you should familiarize yourself with the operational definitions used by researchers so that you are better able to interpret and generalize research results.

EXAMPLES OF POLITICAL MEASUREMENTS: GETTING TO OPERATIONALIZATION

Let us take a closer look at some operational definitions used by the political science researchers referred to in chapter 1 as well as some others. To measure the strength of a legislator's intervention in air pollution regulations proposed by the Environmental Protection Agency, Hall and Miler coded and counted the number of substantive comments made by legislators challenging or defending the agency's proposed air quality regulations during five oversight hearings held in Congress and during the public comment period.[8] Agencies are required to maintain a public docket that contains all the comments received during the comment period. Transcripts were available for each of the hearings. The researchers ended up with two variables: one was the number of supporting comments; the other was the number of comments in opposition to the proposed regulation. To measure constituency interests in each of the members' districts, they measured the number of manufacturing jobs in each district and created an index of air pollution based on district levels of PM 10 particulate matter and ground-level ozone (the pollutants addressed by the proposed regulations). Because Hall and Miler were interested in investigating whether lobbyists targeted their efforts toward members of Congress friendly toward the lobbyists' positions, they needed to measure the pro- or antienvironmental policy positions for each member of Congress, and this variable had to measure position *before* the oversight hearings and regulatory comment period. Fortunately for the researchers, the leaders of the health and environmental coalition had classified members in terms of their likely support for the rule prior to the lobbying period and were willing to share their ratings. These measures were based on legislators' previous voting record on health and environmental issues.

The research conducted by Segal and Cover on the behavior of US Supreme Court justices is a good example of an attempt to overcome a serious measurement problem to test a scientific hypothesis.[9] Recall that Segal and Cover were interested, as many others have been before them, in the extent to which the votes cast by Supreme Court justices were dependent on the justices' personal political attitudes. Measuring the justices' votes on the cases decided by the Supreme Court is no problem; the votes are public information. But measuring the personal political attitudes of judges, *independent of their votes,* is a problem (remember the discussion in chapter 4 on avoiding tautologies, or statements that link two concepts that mean essentially the same thing). Many of the judges whose behavior is of interest have died, and it is difficult to get living Supreme Court justices to reveal their political attitudes through personal interviews or questionnaires. Furthermore, one ideally would like a measure of attitudes that is comparable across many judges and that measures attitudes related to the cases decided by the Court.

Segal and Cover limited their inquiry to votes on civil liberties cases between 1953 and 1987, so they needed a measure of related political attitudes for the judges serving on the Supreme Court over that same period. They decided to infer the judges' attitudes from the newspaper editorials written about them in four major daily newspapers from the time each justice was appointed by the president until the justice's confirmation vote by the Senate. They selected the editorials appearing in two liberal papers and in two conservative papers. Trained analysts read the editorials and coded each paragraph for whether it asserted that a justice designate was liberal, moderate, or conservative (or if the paragraph was inapplicable) regarding "support for the rights of defendants in criminal cases, women and racial minorities in equality cases, and the individual against the government in privacy and First Amendment cases."[10]

Because of practical barriers to ideal measurement, then, Segal and Cover had to rely on an indirect measure of judicial attitudes *as perceived by four newspapers* rather than on a measure of the attitudes themselves. Although this approach *may* have resulted in flawed measures, it also permitted the test of an interesting and important hypothesis about the behavior of Supreme Court justices that had not been tested previously. Without such measurements, the hypothesis could not have been tested.

Next, let us consider research conducted by Bradley and his colleagues on the relationship between party control of government and the distribution and redistribution of wealth.[11] The researchers relied on the Luxembourg Income Study (LIS) database, which provides cross-national income data over time in OECD (Organisation for Economic Co-operation and Development) countries.[12] They decided, however, to make adjustments to published LIS data on income inequality. That data included pensioners. Because some countries make comprehensive provisions for retirees, retirees in these countries make little provision on their own for retirement. Thus, many of these people would be counted as "poor" before any government transfers. Including pensioners would inflate the pretransfer poverty level as well as the extent of income transfer for these countries. Therefore, Bradley and his colleagues limited their analysis to households with a head aged twenty-five to fifty-nine (thus excluding the student-age population as well) and calculated their own measures of income inequality from the LIS data. They argued that their data would measure redistribution across income groups, not life-cycle redistributions of income, such as transfers to students and retired persons. *Income* was defined as income from wages and salaries, self-employment income, property income, and private pension income. The researchers also made adjustments for household size using an equivalence scale, which adjusts the number of persons in a household to an equivalent number of adults. The equivalence scale takes into account the economies of scale resulting from sharing household expenses.

Researchers investigating the impact of exposure to negative campaign ads on elections use a variety of strategies to measure the tone of campaigns and campaign ads. Kim Fridkin Kahn and Patrick J. Kenney measured the tone of campaigns in US Senate elections three ways: one was based on a sample of TV commercials from candidates' campaigns, the second on a sample of newspaper articles selected from the largest-circulating newspaper in each state in which there was a Senate election, and the third on asking campaign managers to characterize the level of mudslinging in the campaigns. Each commercial was rated on a 3-point scale, and a negativity score, representing the proportion of negative to positive messages associated with each race, was computed. This negativity score was multiplied by the amount of money spent during the race, with the assumption that the more money spent, the more people were exposed to the tone of the ads.[13]

Martin P. Wattenberg and Craig Leonard Brians measured exposure by responses to a survey question that asked respondents if they recalled a campaign ad and whether or not it was negative or positive in tone.[14] Finally, Ansolabehere and his colleagues measured exposure to negative campaign ads in the 1990 Senate elections by accessing newspaper and magazine articles about the campaigns and determining how the tone of the campaigns was described in these articles.[15]

The cases discussed here are good examples of researchers' attempts to measure important political phenomena (behaviors or attributes) in the real world. Whether the phenomenon in question was judges' political attitudes, income inequality, the tone of campaign advertising, or the attitudes and behavior of legislators, the researchers devised measurement strategies that could detect and measure the presence and amount of the concept in question. These observations were then generally used as the basis for an empirical test of the researchers' hypotheses.

To be useful in providing scientific explanations for political behavior, measurements of political phenomena must correspond closely to the original meaning of a researcher's concepts. They must also provide the researcher with enough information to make valuable comparisons and contrasts. Hence, the quality of measurements is judged in regard to both their *accuracy* and their *precision*.

THE ACCURACY OF MEASUREMENTS

Because we are going to use our measurements to test whether or not our explanations for political phenomena are valid, those measurements must be as accurate as possible. Inaccurate measurements may lead to erroneous conclusions, since they will interfere with our ability to observe the actual relationship between two or more variables.

There are two major threats to the accuracy of measurements. Measures may be inaccurate because they are *unreliable* and/or because they are *invalid*.

Reliability

Reliability "concerns the extent to which an experiment, test, or any measuring procedure yields the same results on repeated trials. . . . The more consistent the results given by repeated measurements, the higher the reliability of the measuring procedure; conversely, the less consistent the results, the lower the reliability."[16]

Suppose, for example, you are given the responsibility of counting a stack of 1,000 paper ballots for some public office. The first time you count them, you obtain a particular result. But as you were counting the ballots, you might have been interrupted, two or more ballots might have stuck together, some might have been blown onto the floor, or you might have written down the totals incorrectly. As a precaution, then, you count them five more times and get four other people to count them once each as well. The similarity of the results of all ten counts would be an indication of the reliability of the measure.

Or suppose you design a series of questions to measure how cynical people are and ask a group of people those questions. If, a few days later, you ask the same questions of the same group of people, the correspondence between the two measures would indicate the reliability of that particular measure of cynicism (assuming that the amount of cynicism has not changed).

Similarly, suppose you wanted to test the hypothesis that the *New York Times* is more critical of the federal government than is the *Wall Street Journal.* This would require you to measure the level of criticism found in articles in the two papers. You would need to develop criteria or instructions for identifying or measuring criticism. The reliability of your measuring scheme could be assessed by having two people read all the articles, independently rate the level of criticism in them according to your instructions, and then compare their results. Reliability would be demonstrated if both people reached similar conclusions regarding the content of the articles in question.

The reliability of political science measures can be calculated in many different ways. We describe three methods here that are often associated with written test items or survey questions, but the ideas may be applied in other research contexts. The **test-retest method** involves applying the same "test" to the same observations after a period of time and then comparing the results of the different measurements. For example, if a series of questions measuring liberalism is asked of a group of respondents on two different days, a comparison of their scores at both times could be used as an indication of the reliability of the measure of liberalism. We frequently engage in test-retest behavior in our everyday lives. How often have you stepped on the bathroom scale twice in a matter of seconds?

The test-retest method of measuring reliability may be both difficult and problematic, since one must measure the phenomenon at two different points. It is possible that two different results may be obtained because what is being measured has changed, not because the measure is unreliable. For example, if your bathroom scale gives you two different weights within a few seconds, the scale is unreliable as your weight cannot have changed. However, if you weigh yourself once a week for a month and find that you get different results each time, is the scale unreliable, or has your weight changed between measurements? A further problem with the test-retest check for reliability is that the administration of the first measure may affect the second measure's results. For instance, the difference between SAT Reasoning Test scores the first and second times that individuals take the test may not be assumed to be a measure of the reliability of the test, since test takers might alter their behavior the second time as a result of taking the test the first time (e.g., they might learn from their first experience with the test).

The **alternative-form method** of measuring reliability also involves measuring the same attribute more than once, but it uses two different measures of the same concept rather than the same measure. For example, a researcher could devise two different sets of questions to measure the concept of liberalism, ask the same respondents questions at two different times using one set of questions the first time and the other set of questions the second time, and compare the respondents' scores. Using two different forms of the measure reduces the chance that the second scores are influenced by the first measure, but it still requires the phenomenon to be measured twice. Depending on the length of time between the two measurements, what is being measured may change.

The **split-halves method** of measuring reliability involves applying two measures of the same concept at the same time. The results of the two measures are then compared. This method avoids the problem that the concept being measured may change between measures. The split-halves method is often used when a multi-item measure can be split into two equivalent halves. For example, a researcher may devise a measure of liberalism consisting of the responses to ten questions on a public opinion survey. Half of these questions could be selected to represent one measure of liberalism, and the other half selected to represent a second measure of liberalism. If individual scores on the two measures of liberalism are similar, then the ten-item measure may be said to be reliable by the split-halves approach.

The test-retest, alternative-form, and split-halves methods provide a basis for calculating the similarity of results of two or more applications of the same or equivalent measures. The less consistent the results are, the less reliable the measure is. Political scientists take very seriously the reliability of the measures they use. Survey researchers are often concerned about the reliability of the answers they receive. For example, respondents' answers to survey questions often vary considerably when the instruments are given at two different times.[17] If respondents are not concentrating or taking the survey seriously, the answers they provide may as well have been pulled out of a hat.

Now, let us return to the example of measuring your weight using a home scale. If you weigh yourself on your home scale, then go to the gym and weigh yourself again there, and get the same number (alternative forms test of reliability), you may conclude that your home scale is reliable. But what if you get two different numbers? Assuming your weight has not changed, what is the problem? If you go back home immediately and step back on your home scale and find that it gives you a measurement that is different from the first it gave you, you could conclude that your scale has a faulty mechanism, is inconsistent, and therefore is unreliable. However, what if your bathroom scale gives you the same weight as the first time? It would appear to be reliable. Maybe the gym scale is unreliable. You could test this out by going back to the gym and reweighing yourself. If the gym scale gives a reading different from that it gave the first time, then it is unreliable. But, what if the gym scale gives consistent readings? Each scale appears to be reliable (the scales are not giving you different weights at random), but at least one of them is giving you a wrong measurement (that is, not giving you your correct weight). This is a problem of validity.

Validity

Essentially, a valid measure is one that measures what it is supposed to measure. Unlike reliability, which depends on whether repeated applications of the same or equivalent measures yield the same result, **validity** refers to the degree of correspondence between the measure and the concept it is thought to measure.

Let us consider first some examples of measures whose validity has been questioned. Suppose a researcher hypothesizes that the larger a city's police force is, the less crime that city will have. This requires the measurement of crime rates in different cities. Now also assume that some police departments systematically overrepresent the number of crimes in their cities to persuade public officials that crime is a serious problem and that the local police need more resources. Some police departments in other cities may systematically underreport crime to make their cities appear safe or because victims' reports of a particular type of crime are not taken seriously by the police (as has been known to happen in the case of rape and domestic violence). If the researcher relied on official, reported measures of crime, the measures would be invalid because they would not correspond closely to the actual amount of crime in some cities. Consider also that not all crimes are reported to the police. A more valid measure of crime might be "victimization" surveys, which ask respondents whether they have been a victim of a crime.

Many studies look into the factors that affect voter turnout and, thus, require an accurate measurement of voter turnout. One way of measuring voter turnout is to ask people if they voted in the last election. However, given the social desirability of voting in the United States, will all the people who did not vote in the previous election admit that to an interviewer? More people might say that they voted than actually did, resulting in an invalid measure of voter turnout. In fact, this is what usually happens. Voter surveys commonly overestimate turnout by several percentage points.[18]

A measure's validity is more difficult to demonstrate empirically than is its reliability because validity involves the relationship between the measurement of a concept and the actual presence or amount of the concept itself. Information regarding the correspondence is seldom abundant. Nonetheless, there are ways to evaluate the validity of any particular measure.

Face validity may be asserted (not empirically demonstrated) when the measurement instrument appears to measure the concept it is supposed to measure. To assess the face validity of a measure, we need to know the meaning of the concept being measured and whether the information being collected is "germane to that concept."[19] For example, suppose you want to measure an individual's political ideology, that is, whether someone is conservative, moderate, or liberal. It may be tempting to use an individual's responses to a question on party identification (assuming that all Democrats are liberal, Republicans conservative, and independents moderate). Yet, because some Democrats hold views that are considered to be conservative and some Republicans hold liberal ones, partisan identification does not correspond exactly to the concept of political ideology. Similarly, some observers have argued that the results of many standard IQ tests measure intelligence *and* exposure to middle-class white culture, thus making the test results a less valid measure of intelligence than might be assumed.

Consider now the concept of leadership power in US state legislatures. This concept has been measured using two different strategies. One is to enumerate the formal powers such as power over committee assignments, control of legislative processes, and control of legislative resources. This measure of leadership influence certainly has face validity. It is far from perfect, however, because it fails to take into account context such as the relative power of other political actors (e.g., governors) or informal sources of power (e.g., the personal skills of legislative leaders).

A second approach is to ask state legislators how powerful their legislative leaders are, thus measuring perceived power. Using this approach would likely capture the personal strengths of legislative leaders and could also measure their power relative to other political actors. This second approach also has face validity. The second approach is harder to use, however, because research that looks at changes in power over time would require that regular surveys be taken. It is much easier to measure the formal powers of legislative leaders for all fifty states on an annual basis.[20]

In general, measures lack face validity when there are good reasons to question the correspondence of the measure to the concept in question. In other words, assessing face validity is essentially a matter of judgment. If no consensus exists about the meaning of the concept to be measured, the face validity of the measure is bound to be problematic.

Content validity is similar to face validity but involves determining the full domain or meaning of a particular concept and then making sure that measures of all portions of this domain are included in the measurement technique. For example, suppose you wanted to design a measure of the extent to which a nation's political system is democratic. As noted earlier, *democracy* means many things to many people. Raymond D. Gastil constructed a measure of democracy that included two dimensions, political rights and civil liberties. His checklists for each dimension consisted of eleven items.[21] Similarly, a measure of leadership power constructed using both formal and perceived power approaches would have more content validity than a measure that used just one approach. Political scientists are often interested in concepts with multiple dimensions or complex domains and spend quite a bit of time discussing and justifying the content of their measures.

A third way to evaluate the validity of a measure is by empirically demonstrating **construct validity.** When a measure of a concept is related to a measure of another concept with which the original concept is thought to be related, **convergent construct validity** is demonstrated. In other words, a researcher may specify, on theoretical grounds, that two concepts ought to be related in a positive manner (say, political efficacy with political participation or education with income) or a negative manner (say, democracy and human rights abuses). The researcher then develops a measure of each of the concepts and examines the relationship between them. If the measures are positively or negatively correlated, then one measure has convergent validity for the other measure. In the case there is no relationship between the measures, then the theoretical relationship is in error, at least one of the measures is not an accurate representation of the concept, or the procedure used to test the relationship is faulty. The absence of a hypothesized relationship does not mean a measure is invalid, but the presence of a relationship gives some assurance of the measure's validity.

Discriminant construct validity involves two measures that theoretically are expected *not* to be related; thus, the correlation between them is expected to be low or weak. If the measures do not correlate with one another, then discriminate construct validity is demonstrated.

A good example of an attempt to demonstrate construct validity involves the Graduate Record Exam (GRE), a standardized test required for admission to most graduate schools. Since GRE test scores are supposed to measure a person's aptitude for graduate study, presumably construct validity could be demonstrated if the scores did, in fact, accurately predict the person's performance in graduate school. Controversy arose after a 1997 study found weak correlations between GRE scores and first-year performance in graduate school.[22] Over the years, Educational Testing Service (ETS) has tested the relationships between GRE scores and first-year graduate school grade point averages (GPAs) and has argued that GRE performance *is* a useful predictor of graduate school performance. For example, figure 5–1 shows several graphs from a report examining the predictive validity of GRE scores.[23] These graphs indicate that those who score higher on the GRE tend to get higher first-year GPAs in graduate school. The relationship is far from perfect. However, the strength of the correlation between first-year graduate GPA and GRE test scores is affected by the fact that persons with low GRE scores are generally

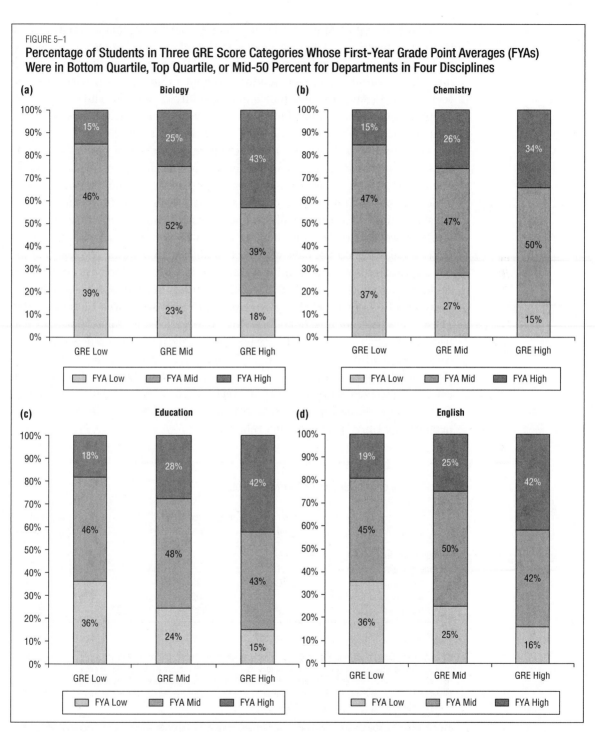

FIGURE 5–1

Percentage of Students in Three GRE Score Categories Whose First-Year Grade Point Averages (FYAs) Were in Bottom Quartile, Top Quartile, or Mid-50 Percent for Departments in Four Disciplines

Source: Brent Bridgeman, Nancy Burton, and Frederick Cline, "Understanding What the Numbers Mean: A Straightforward Approach to GRE Predictive Validity," ETS GRE Board Report No. 04–03, ETS RR–08–46, September 2008, figs. 1, 2, 3, and 4, pp. 10–11. Reprinted by permission of Educational Testing Service, the copyright owner.

not admitted to graduate school. Therefore, we lack performance measures for them. The people for whom we can test the relationship between scores and performance may be of similar ability and, therefore, less likely to exhibit meaningful variation in their graduate school performance. Hence, the test scores may in fact be valid indicators of ability and might show a stronger relationship to performance for a less selective sample of test takers (one that included people who were not admitted to graduate school).

Let us return to the question of measuring the power of legislative leaders because it provides a good example of the importance of construct validity. As we pointed out before, the perceived-influence approach to measuring power is more difficult to use than the formal-powers approach. Therefore, if the two measures are shown to have construct validity, operationalizing leadership power using the formal-powers approach by itself might be a valid way to measure the concept. If the two measures do not have construct validity, then it would be clear that the two approaches are not measuring the same thing. Thus, which measure is used could greatly affect the findings of research into the factors associated with the presence of strong leadership power or on the consequences of such power. These were the very questions raised by political scientist James Coleman Battista.[24] He constructed several measures of perceived leadership power and correlated them with a measure of formal power. The results, shown in table 5–1, show that the measure of formal power correlates only weakly with three measures of perceived power (which as expected, correlate well with each other.) Therefore, measures of perceived power and the measure of formal power do not demonstrate convergent construct validity.

TABLE 5–1
Correlations of Leadership Power Measures

	Formal power index	Avg. perceived power	% rating highest (all)	% rating highest (internal)
Formal power index	1			
Average perceived power	.186	1		
Prop. rating highest (all)	.086	.698*	1	
Prop. rating highest (internal)	.119	.702*	.684*	1
Combined power index	.915*	.558*	.338*	.375*

*$p < .05$

Note: We show here only the results for Battista's analysis when southern states are excluded. Because southern states have a history of little two-party competition but may have to contend with party factions, and the question asked respondents to rate the power of legislative leaders as *party* leaders, respondents were likely to give low perceived power ratings. Southern legislative leaders, however, may be strong *chamber* leaders, which is what is being measured in states with a history of two-party competition.

Source: James Coleman Battista, "Formal and Perceived Leadership Power in U.S. State Legislatures," *State Politics and Policy Quarterly* 11, no. 1 (2011): table 2, p. 209. Copyright © The Author 2011. Reprinted by Permission of SAGE Publications.

A fourth way to demonstrate validity is through **interitem association.** This is the type of validity test most often used by political scientists. It relies on the similarity of outcomes of more than one measure of a concept to demonstrate the validity of the entire measurement scheme. It is often preferable to use more than one item to measure a concept—reliance on just one measure is more prone to error or misclassification of a case.[25]

Let us return to the researcher who wants to develop a valid measure of liberalism. First, the researcher might measure people's attitudes toward (1) welfare, (2) military spending, (3) abortion, (4) Social Security benefit levels, (5) affirmative action, (6) a progressive income tax, (7) school vouchers, and (8) protection of the rights of the accused. Then the researcher could determine how the responses to each question relate to the responses to each of the other questions. The validity of the measurement scheme would be demonstrated if strong relationships existed among people's responses across the eight questions.

The results of such interitem association tests are often displayed in a **correlation matrix**. Such a display shows how strongly related each of the items in the measurement scheme is to all the other items. In the hypothetical data shown in table 5–2, we can see that people's responses to six of the eight measures were strongly related to each other, whereas responses to the questions on protection of the rights of the accused and school vouchers were not part of the general pattern. Thus, the researcher would probably conclude that the first six items all measure liberalism and that, taken together, they are a valid measurement of liberalism.

The figures in table 5–2 are product-moment correlations: numbers that can vary in value from −1.0 to +1.0 and that indicate the extent to which one variable is related to another. The closer the correlation is to ±1, the stronger the relationship; the closer the correlation is to 0.0, the weaker the relationship. The

TABLE 5–2

Interitem Association Validity Test of a Measure of Liberalism

	Welfare	Military Spending	Abortion	Social Security	Affirmative Action	Income Tax	School Vouchers	Rights of Accused
Welfare	x							
Military Spending	.56	x						
Abortion	.71	.60	x					
Social Security	.80	.51	.83	x				
Affirmative Action	.63	.38	.59	.69	x			
Income Tax	.48	.67	.75	.39	.51	x		
School Vouchers	.28	.08	.19	.03	.30	−.07	x	
Rights of Accused	−.01	.14	−.12	.10	.23	.18	.45	x

Note: Hypothetical data.

figures in the last two rows are considerably closer to 0.0 than are the other entries, indicating that people's answers to the questions about school vouchers and rights of the accused did not follow the same pattern as their answers to the other questions. Therefore, it looks like school vouchers and rights of the accused are not connected to the same concept of liberalism as measured by the other questions.

Content and face validity are difficult to assess when agreement is lacking on the meaning of a concept, and construct validity, which requires a well-developed theoretical perspective, usually yields a less-than-definitive result. The interitem association test requires multiple measures of the same concept. Although these validity "tests" provide important evidence, none of them is likely to support an unequivocal decision concerning the validity of particular measures.

Problems with Reliability and Validity in Political Science Measurement

Survey researchers often want to measure respondents' household income. Measurement of this basic variable illustrates the numerous threats to the reliability and validity of political science measures. The following is a question used in the 2004 American National Election Study (ANES):

> *Please look at the booklet and tell me the letter of the income group that includes the income of all members of your family living here in 2003 before taxes. This figure should include salaries, wages, pensions, dividends, interest, and all other income. Please tell me the letter of the income group that includes the income you had in 2003 before taxes.*

Respondents were given the following choices.

A. None or less than $2,999	P. $30,000–$34,999
B. $3,000–$4,999	Q. $35,000–$39,999
C. $5,000–$6,999	R. $40,000–$44,999
D. $7,000–$8,999	S. $45,000–$49,999
E. $9,000–$10,999	T. $50,000–$59,999
F. $11,000–$12,999	U. $60,000–$69,999
G. $13,000–$14,999	V. $70,000–$79,999
H. $15,000–$16,999	W. $80,000–$89,999
J. $17,000–$19,999	X. $90,000–$104,999
K. $20,000–$21,999	Y. $105,000—$119,000
M. $22,000–$24,999	Z. $120,000 and over
N. $25,000–$29,999	

Both the reliability and the validity of this method of measuring income are questionable. Threats to the reliability of the measure include the following:

- Respondents may not know how much money they make and therefore incorrectly guess their income.

- Respondents may not know how much money other family members make and guess incorrectly.

- Respondents may know how much they make but carelessly select the wrong categories.

- Interviewers may circle the wrong categories when listening to the selections of the respondents.

- Data entry personnel may touch the wrong numbers when entering the answers into the computer.

- Dishonest interviewers may incorrectly guess the income of a respondent who does not complete the interview.

- Respondents may not know which family members to include in the income total; some respondents may include only a few family members, while others may include even distant relations.

- Respondents whose income is on the border between two categories may not know which one to pick. Some may pick the higher category; others, the lower one.

Because of these measurement problems, if this measure were applied to the same people at two different times, we could expect the results to vary, resulting in inaccurate measures that are too high for some respondents and too low for others.

In addition to these threats to reliability, there are numerous threats to the validity of this measure:

- Respondents may have illegal income they do not want to reveal and therefore may systematically underestimate their income.

- Respondents may try to impress the interviewer, or themselves, by systematically overestimating their income.

- Respondents may systematically underestimate their before-tax income because they think of their take-home pay and underestimate how much money is being withheld from their paychecks.

Notice that this list of problems contains the word *systematically*. These problems are not simply caused by inconsistencies in measurements, with some being too high and others too low for unpredictable reasons.

This long list of problems with both the reliability and the validity of this fairly straightforward measure of a relatively concrete concept is worrisome.

Imagine how much more difficult it is to develop reliable and valid measures when the concept is abstract (for example, tolerance, environmental conscience, self-esteem, or liberalism) and the measurement scheme is more complicated.

The reliability and validity of the measures used by political scientists are seldom demonstrated to everyone's satisfaction. Most measures of political phenomena are neither completely invalid or valid nor thoroughly unreliable or reliable but, rather, are partly accurate. Therefore, researchers generally present the rationale and evidence available in support of their measures and attempt to persuade their audience that their measures are at least as accurate as alternative measures would be. Nonetheless, a skeptical stance on the part of the reader toward the reliability and validity of political science measures is often warranted.

Note, finally, that reliability and validity are not the same thing. A measure may be reliable without being valid. One may devise a series of questions to measure liberalism, for example, that yields the same result for the same people every time but that misidentifies individuals. A valid measure, however, will also be reliable: if it accurately measures the concept in question, then it will do so consistently across measurements. It is more important, then, to demonstrate validity than reliability, but reliability is usually more easily and precisely tested.

THE PRECISION OF MEASUREMENTS

Measurements should be not only accurate but also precise; that is, measurements should contain as much information as possible about the attribute or behavior being measured. The more precise our measures, the more complete and informative can be our test of the relationships between two or more variables.

Suppose, for example, that we wanted to measure the height of political candidates to see if taller candidates usually win elections. Height could be measured in many different ways. We could have two categories of the variable "height"—*tall* and *short*—and assign different candidates to the two categories based on whether they were of above-average or below-average height. Or we could compare the heights of candidates running for the same office and measure which candidate was the tallest, which the next tallest, and so on. Or we could take a tape measure and measure each candidate's height in inches and record that measure. The last method of measurement captures the most information about each candidate's height and is, therefore, the most precise measure of the attribute.

Levels of Measurement

When we consider the precision of our measurements, we refer to the **level of measurement.** The level of measurement involves the type of information that we think our measurements contain and the type of comparisons that can be made across a number of observations on the same variable. The level of measurement also refers to the claim we are willing to make when we assign numbers to our measurements.

There are four different levels of measurement: nominal, ordinal, interval, and ratio. Few concepts used in political science research inherently require a particular level of measurement, so the level used in any specific research project is a function of the imagination and resources of the researcher and the decisions made when the method of measuring each of the variables is developed.

A **nominal measurement** is involved whenever the values assigned to a variable represent only different categories or classifications for that variable. In such a case, no category is more or less than another category; they are simply different. For example, suppose we measure the religion of individuals by asking them to indicate whether they are Christian, Jewish, Muslim, or other. Since the four categories or values for the variable religion are simply different, the measurement is at a nominal level. Other common examples of nominal-level measures are gender, marital status, and state of residence. A nominal measure of partisan affiliation might have the following categories: Democrat, Republican, Green, Libertarian, other, and none. Numbers will be assigned to the categories when the data are coded for statistical analysis, but these numbers do not represent mathematical differences between the categories.

Nominal-level measures ought to consist of categories that are exhaustive and mutually exclusive; that is, the categories should include all the possibilities for the measure, and every observation should fit in one and only one category. For example, if we attempted to measure "types of political systems" with the categories democratic, socialist, authoritarian, undeveloped, traditional, capitalist, and monarchical, the categories would be neither exhaustive nor mutually exclusive. (In which one category would Japan, Great Britain, and India belong?) The difficulty of deciding the category into which many countries should be put would hinder the very measurement process the variable was intended to further. Notice that the categories of the measure of religion are exhaustive because of the "other" category as well as mutually exclusive (since presumably an individual cannot be of more than one religion). Researchers use "other" when they are unable to specify all alternatives, or when they expect very few of their observations to fall into the "other" category but want to provide an option for respondents who do not fall into one of the labeled categories (respondents may fail to complete surveys with questions that don't apply to them). If using "other" as a category, you should check your data to make sure that only a relatively few observations fall into it. Otherwise subsequent data analysis will not be very meaningful.

An **ordinal measurement** assumes observations can be compared in terms of having more or less of a particular attribute. For example, we could create an ordinal measure of formal education completed with the following categories: "eighth grade or less," "some high school," "high school graduate," "some college," and "college degree or more." Here we are concerned not with the exact difference between the categories of education but only with whether one category is more or less than another. When coding this variable, we would assign higher numbers to higher categories of education. The intervals between the numbers have no meaning; all that matters is that the higher numbers represent more of the attribute than do the lower numbers. An ordinal variable measuring partisan affiliation with the categories "strong Republican," "weak Republican," "neither leaning Republican nor Democrat," "weak Democrat," and "strong Democrat" could be assigned codes 1, 2, 3, 4, 5 or 1, 2, 5, 8, 9 or any other combination of numbers, as long as they were in ascending or descending order.

 Dichotomous nominal-level measures—that is, nominal-level variables with only two categories—are frequently treated as ordinal-level measures. For example, gender is a measure with two categories, male and female. One could interpret being male as being less female than a female. To give another example, a person who did not vote in the last election lacks, or has less of, the attribute of having voted than a person who did vote.

With an **interval measurement**, the intervals between the categories or values assigned to the observations do have meaning. The value of a particular observation is important not just in terms of whether it is larger or smaller than another value (as in ordinal measures) but also in terms of how much larger or smaller it is. For example, suppose we record the year in which certain events occurred. If we have three observations—1950, 1962, and 1977—we know that the event in 1950 occurred twelve years before the one in 1962 and twenty-seven years before the one in 1977. A one-unit change (the interval) all along this measurement is identical in meaning: the passage of one year's time.

Another characteristic of an interval level of measurement that distinguishes it from the next level of measurement (ratio) is that in the former case, the zero point is assigned arbitrarily and does not represent the absence of the attribute being measured. For example, many time and temperature scales have arbitrary zero points. Thus, the year 0 CE does not indicate the beginning of time—if this were true, there would be no BCE dates. Nor

DEBATING THE LEVEL OF MEASUREMENT

Suppose we ask individuals three questions designed to measure social trust, and we believe that individuals who answer all three questions a certain way have more social trust than persons who answer two of the questions a certain way, and these individuals have more social trust than individuals who answer one of the questions a certain way. We could assign a score of 3 to the first group, 2 to the second group, 1 to the third group, and 0 to those who did not answer any of the questions in a socially trusting manner. In this case, the higher the number, the more social trust an individual has.

What level of measurement is this variable? It might be considered to be ratio level, if one interprets the variable as simply the number of questions answered indicating social trust. But does a person who has a score of 0 have no social trust? Does a person with a score of 3 have three times as much social trust as a person with a score of 1? Perhaps then, the variable is an interval-level measure, if one is willing to assume that the difference in social trust between individuals with scores of 2 and 3 is the same as the difference between individuals with scores of 1 and 2. But what if the effect of answering more questions in the affirmative is not simply additive? In other words, perhaps a person who has a score of 3 has a lot more social trust than someone with a score of 2 and that this difference is more than the difference between individuals with scores of 1 and 2. In this case, then, the measure would be ordinal level, not interval level.

does 0°C indicate the absence of heat; rather, it indicates the temperature at which water freezes. For this reason, with interval-level measurements we cannot calculate ratios; that is, we cannot say that 60°F is twice as warm as 30°F.

The final level of measurement is a **ratio measurement.** This type of measurement involves the full mathematical properties of numbers. That is, the values of the categories order the categories tell something about the intervals between the categories and state precisely the relative amounts of the variable that the categories represent. If, for example, a researcher is willing to claim that an observation with ten units of a variable possesses exactly twice as much of that attribute as an observation with five units of that variable, then a ratio-level measurement exists. The key to making this assumption is that a value of zero on the variable actually represents the absence of that variable. Because ratio measures have a true zero point, it makes sense to say that one measurement is x times another. It makes sense to say a sixty-year-old person is twice the age of a thirty-year-old person ($60/30 = 2$), whereas it does not make sense to say that 60°C is twice as warm as 30°C.[26]

Political science researchers have measured many concepts at the ratio level. People's ages, unemployment rates, percentage of the vote for a particular candidate, and crime rates are all measures that contain a zero point and possess the full mathematical properties of the numbers used. However, more political science research has probably relied on nominal- and ordinal-level measures than on interval- or ratio-level measures. This has restricted the types of hypotheses and analysis techniques that political scientists have been willing and able to use.

Identifying the level of measurement of variables is important, since it affects the data analysis techniques that can be used and the conclusions that can be drawn about the relationships between variables. However, the decision is not always a straightforward one, and uncertainty and disagreement often exist among researchers concerning these decisions. Few phenomena inherently require one particular level of measurement. Often a phenomenon can be measured with any level of measurement, depending on the particular technique designed by the researcher and the claims the researcher is willing to make about the resulting measure.

Working with Precision: Too Little or Too Much

Researchers usually try to devise as high a level of measurement for their concepts as possible (nominal being the lowest level of measurement and ratio the highest). With a higher level of measurement, more advanced data analysis techniques can be used, and more precise statements can be made about the relationships between variables. Thus, researchers measuring attitudes or concepts with multiple operational definitions often construct a scale or an index from nominal-level measures that permits at least ordinal-level comparisons between observations. We discuss the construction of indexes and scales in greater detail in the following paragraphs.

It is easy to transform ratio-level information (e.g., age in number of years) into ordinal-level information (e.g., age groups). However, if you start with the ordinal-level measure, age groups, you will not have each person's actual age. If you decide you want to use a person's actual age, you will have to collect that data. Similarly, a researcher investigating the effect of campaign spending on election outcomes could use a ratio-level variable measuring how much each candidate spent on his or her campaign. This information could be used to construct a new variable indicating how much more one candidate spent than the other or simply whether or not a candidate spent more than his or her opponent. Candidate spending could also be grouped into ranges.

Nominal and ordinal variables with many categories or interval- and ratio-level measures using more decimal places are more precise than measures with fewer categories or decimal places, but sometimes the result may provide more information than can be used. Researchers frequently start out with ratio-level measures or with ordinal and nominal measures with quite a few categories but then collapse or combine the data to create groups or fewer categories. They do this so that they have enough cases in each category for statistical analysis or to make comparisons easier to follow. For example, one might want to present comparisons simply between Democrats and Republicans rather than presenting data broken down into categories of strong, moderate, and weak for each party.

It may seem contradictory now to point out that extremely precise measures also may create problems. For example, measures with many response possibilities take up space if they are questions on a written questionnaire or more time to explain if they are included in a telephone survey. Such questions may also confuse or tire survey respondents. A more serious problem is that they may lead to measurement error. Think about the possible responses to a question asking respondents to use a 100-point scale (called a thermometer scale) to indicate their support for or opposition to a political candidate, assuming that 50 is considered the neutral position and 0 is least favorable or "coldest" and 100 most favorable. Some respondents may not use the whole scale (to them, no candidate ever deserves more than an 80 or less than a 20), whereas others respondents may use the ends and the very middle of the scale and ignore the scores in between. We might predict that a person who gives a candidate a 100 is more likely to vote for that candidate than a person who gives the same candidate an 80, but in reality they may like the candidate pretty much the same way and would be equally likely to vote for the candidate. Another problem with overly precise measurements is that they may be unreliable. If asked to rate candidates on more than one occasion, respondents could vary the number that they choose, even if their opinion has not changed.

One last example illustrates how concerns about measurement error affected the measurement and operationalization of a concept. Poe and Tate defined human rights abuses to involve instances of state terrorism: murders, disappearances, and imprisonment.[27] They noted that there are two approaches to measuring repression of human rights: an events-based approach, which would involve counting the occurrences of these events and thus would be a ratio-level measure, and a standards-based approach, in which countries would be ranked on an ordinal scale based on the extent to which these events occur:

> 1. Countries [are] under a secure rule of law, people are not imprisoned for their views, and torture is rare or exceptional. . . . Political murders are extremely rare.

> 2. There is a limited amount of imprisonment for nonviolent political activity. However, few persons are affected, torture and beating are exceptional. . . . Political murder is rare.

> 3. There is extensive political imprisonment, or a recent history of such imprisonment. Execution or other political murders may be common. Unlimited detention, with or without trial, for political views is accepted.

> 4. The practices of [level 3] are expanded to larger numbers. Murders, disappearances are a common part of life. . . . In spite of its generality, on this level terror affects primarily those who interest themselves in politics or ideas.

> 5. The terrors [of level 4] have been expanded to the whole population. . . . The leaders of these societies place no limits on the means or thoroughness with which they pursue personal or ideological goals.[28]

Poe and Tate rejected the events-based approach on two grounds: (1) accurate data are not available, and (2) the count of one event may be affected by the occurrence of another event (e.g., the number of executions may be affected by the number of arrests).[29] They concluded that the events-based approach would not be a valid measure, even though superficially it would appear to be a more precise measure. They were able to check the reliability of their data using the standards-based method because they had reports for many countries from two sources: Amnesty International and the US State Department. Coders read the reports and assigned scores. In most cases, scores based on the two reports were highly correlated.[30]

MULTI-ITEM MEASURES

Many measures consist of a single item. For example, the measures of party identification, whether or not one party controls Congress, the percentage of the vote received by a candidate, how concerned about an issue a person is, the policy area of a judicial case, and age are all based on a single measure of each phenomenon in question. Often, however, researchers need to devise measures of more complicated phenomena that have more than one facet or dimension. For example, internationalism, political ideology, political knowledge, dispersion of political power, and the extent to which a person is politically active are complex phenomena or concepts that may be measured in many different ways.

In this situation, researchers often develop a measurement strategy that allows them to capture numerous aspects of a complex phenomenon while representing the existence of that phenomenon in particular cases with a single representative value. Usually this involves the construction of a multi-item index or scale representing the several dimensions of the phenomenon. These multi-item measures are useful because they enhance the accuracy of a measure, simplify a researcher's data by reducing them to a more manageable size, and increase the level of measurement of a phenomenon. In the remainder of this section, we describe several common types of indexes and scales.

Indexes

A **summation index** is a method of accumulating scores on individual items to form a composite measure of a complex phenomenon. An index is constructed by assigning a range of possible scores for a certain number of items, determining the score for each item for each observation, and then combining the scores for each observation across all the items. The resulting summary score is the representative measurement of the phenomenon.

A researcher interested in measuring how much freedom exists in different countries, for example, might construct an index of political freedom by devising a list of items germane to the concept, determining where individual countries score on each item, and then adding these scores to get a summary measure. In table 5–3, such a hypothetical index is used to measure the amount of freedom in countries A through E.

TABLE 5–3

Hypothetical Index for Measuring Freedom in Countries

	Country A	Country B	Country C	Country D	Country E
Does the country possess:					
Privately owned newspapers	1	0	0	0	1
Legal right to form political parties	1	1	0	0	0
Contested elections for significant public offices	1	1	0	0	0
Voting rights extended to most of the adult population	1	1	0	1	0
Limitations on government's ability to incarcerate citizens	1	0	0	0	1
Index Score	5	3	0	1	2

Note: Hypothetical data. The score is 1 if the answer is yes, 0 if no.

The index in table 5–3 is a simple, additive one; that is, each item counts equally toward the calculation of the index score, and the total score is the summation of the individual item scores. However, indexes may be constructed with more complicated aggregation procedures and by counting some items as more important than others. In the preceding example, a researcher might consider some indicators of freedom as more important than others and wish to have them contribute more to the calculation of the final index score. This could be done either by weighting (multiplying) some item scores by a number indicating their importance or by assigning a higher score than 1 to those attributes considered more important.

Indexes are often used with public opinion surveys to measure political attitudes. This is because attitudes are complex phenomena and we usually do not know enough about them to devise single-item measures. So we often ask several questions of people about a single attitude and aggregate the answers to represent the attitude. A researcher might measure attitudes toward abortion, for example, by asking respondents to choose one of five possible responses—strongly agree, agree, undecided, disagree, and strongly disagree—to the following three statements: (1) Abortions should be permitted in the first three months of pregnancy. (2) Abortions should be permitted if the woman's life is in danger. (3) Abortions should be permitted whenever a woman wants one.

An index of attitudes toward abortion could be computed by assigning numerical values to each response (such as 1 for *strongly agree,* 2 for *agree,* 3 for *undecided,* and so on) and then adding the values of a respondent's answers to these three questions. (The researcher would have to decide what to do when a respondent did not answer one or more of the questions.) The lowest possible score in this case would be a 3, indicating the most extreme pro-abortion attitude, and the highest possible score would be a 15, indicating the most extreme anti-abortion attitude. Scores in between would indicate varying degrees of approval of abortion.

Indexes are typically fairly simple ways of producing single representative scores of complicated phenomena such as political attitudes. They are probably more accurate than most single-item measures, but they may also be flawed in important ways. Aggregating scores across several items assumes, for example, that each item is equally important to the summary measure of the concept and that the items used faithfully encompass the domain of the concept. Although individual item scores can be weighted to change their contribution to the summary measure, the researcher often has little information upon which to base a weighting scheme.

Several standard indexes are often used in political science research. The FBI crime index, the Consumer Confidence Index, and the Consumer Price Index, for example, have been used by many researchers. Before using these or any other readily available index, you should familiarize yourself with its construction and be aware of any questions raised about its validity. Although simple summation indexes are generally more accurate than single-item measures of complicated phenomena, it is often unclear how valid they are or what level of measurement they represent. For example, is the index of freedom an ordinal-level measure, or could it be an interval-level or even a ratio-level measure? Another possible issue with indexes such as the Consumer Price Index is that what goes into its calculation can change over time.[31]

Scales

Although indexes are generally an improvement over single-item measures, their construction also contains an element of arbitrariness. Both the selection of particular items making up the index and the way in which the scores on individual items are aggregated are based on the researcher's judgment. Scales are also multi-item measures, but the selection and combination of items in them is accomplished more systematically than is usually the case for indexes. Over the years, several different

---

CREATING AN INDEX OF SPEAKERS' INSTITUTIONAL POWERS

Richard A. Clucas created an index of the institutional power of state house speakers by sorting powers into five general categories and assigning values to powers within those categories using the following scoring procedure:

■ Appointment power index

Speaker selects all chairs and party leaders = 5 points

Selects chairs and a majority of leaders = 4

Selects chairs; selects few or no leaders = 3

Shares powers to select chairs; selects few or no leaders = 2

Does not select chairs; selects few or no leaders = 1

■ Committee Power Index

Speaker assigns all members to committee; decides number of committees = 5.0

Assigns all members; shares power over number = 4.5

Assigns all members; does not decide number = 4.0

Assigns majority members; decides number = 3.5

Assigns majority members; shares power over number = 3.0

Assigns majority members; does not decide number = 2.5

Another actor has formal power over assignments, but the speaker shares in process, such as serving as a member of rules committee; decides committee number = 2.0

Shares in assignment process; shares power over number = 1.5

Shares in assignment process; does not decide number = 1.0

Not involved in either = 0.0

■ Resource Power Index

Campaign committee exists; speaker has control over legislative employees = 5.0

Committee exists; speaker does not control employees = 3.0

Committee does not exist; speaker controls employees = 1.0

Committee does not exist; speaker does not control employees = 0.0

■ Procedural Power Index: The index was created by first creating separate indices for the speaker's power over bill referral and floor procedures. The average of these scores was then used for the index.

■ Bill Referral Power Index

Speaker has complete control over bill referral = 5

Controls referral, but there are restrictions on its use = 4

Shares power over referral; no restrictions on use = 3

Shares power over referral; actions restricted = 2

Not involved in referral = 1

■ Floor Powers Index

Speaker prepares calendar, decides question, directs chamber = 5

Controls two of these floor powers = 4

Controls one of these floor powers = 3

Has no control over floor = 1

■ Tenure Power Index

No tenure limit = 5

Eight years = 4

Six years = 3

Four years = 2

Two years = 1

Clucas's overall index can range in value from 3 to 25. Each category has a maximum value of 5; thus, he is making the claim that full power in each category is of equal significance. He uses the index as if it were an interval-level measure, which means that a unit change in any power category is equivalent. These assumptions are reasonable but are certainly open to challenge.

Source: Richard A. Clucas, "Principle-Agent Theory and the Power of State House Speakers," *Legislative Studies Quarterly* 26, no. 2 (2001): 319–38; material taken from the appendix on pages 335 and 336.

kinds of multi-item scales have been used frequently in political science research. We discuss three of them: Likert scales, Guttman scales, and Mokken scales.

A **Likert scale** score is calculated from the scores obtained on individual items. Each item generally asks a respondent to indicate a degree of agreement or disagreement with the item, as with the abortion questions discussed earlier. A Likert scale differs from an index, however, in that once the scores on each of the items are obtained, only some of the items are selected for inclusion in the calculation of the final score. Those items that allow a researcher to distinguish most readily those scoring high on an attribute from those scoring low will be retained, and a new scale score will be calculated based only on those items.

For example, consider the researcher interested in measuring the liberalism of a group of respondents. Since definitions of *liberalism* vary, the researcher cannot be sure how many aspects of liberalism need to be measured. With Likert scaling, the researcher would begin with a large group of questions thought to express various aspects of liberalism with which respondents would be asked to agree or disagree. A provisional Likert scale for liberalism, then, might look like the one in table 5–4.

In practice, a set of questions like this would be scattered throughout a questionnaire so that respondents do not see them as related. Some of the questions might also be worded in the opposite way (that is, so an "agree" response is a conservative response) to ensure genuine answers.

TABLE 5–4
Provisional Likert Scale to Measure Concept of Liberalism

	Strongly Disagree (1)	Disagree (2)	Undecided (3)	Agree (4)	Strongly Agree (5)
The government should ensure that no one lives in poverty.	—	—	—	—	—
Military spending should be reduced.	—	—	—	—	—
It is more important to take care of people's needs than it is to balance the federal budget.	—	—	—	—	—
Social Security benefits should not be cut.	—	—	—	—	—
The government should spend money to improve housing and transportation in urban areas.	—	—	—	—	—
Wealthy people should pay taxes at a much higher rate than poor people.	—	—	—	—	—
Busing should be used to integrate public schools.	—	—	—	—	—
The rights of persons accused of a crime must be vigorously protected.	—	—	—	—	—

The respondents' answers to these eight questions would be summed to produce a provisional score. The scores in this case can range from 8 to 40. Then the responses of the most liberal and the most conservative people to each question would be compared; any questions with similar answers from the disparate respondents would be eliminated—such questions would not distinguish liberals from conservatives. A new summary scale score for all the respondents would be calculated from the questions that remained. A statistic called Cronbach's alpha, which measures internal consistency of the items in the scale and has a maximum value of 1.0, is used to determine which items to drop from the scale. The rule of thumb is that Cronbach's alpha should be 0.8 or above; items are dropped from the scale one at a time until this value is reached.[32]

Likert scales are improvements over multi-item indexes because the items that make up the multi-item measure are selected in part based on the respondents' behavior rather than on the researcher's judgment. Likert scales suffer two of the other defects of indexes, however. The researcher cannot be sure that all the dimensions of a concept have been measured, and the relative importance of each item is still determined arbitrarily.

The **Guttman scale** also uses a series of items to produce a scale score for respondents. Unlike the Likert scale, however, a Guttman scale presents respondents with a range of attitude choices that are increasingly difficult to agree with; that is, the items composing the scale range from those easy to agree with to those difficult to agree with. Respondents who agree with one of the "more difficult" attitude items will also generally agree with the "less difficult" ones. (Guttman scales have also been used to measure attributes other than attitudes. Their main application has been in the area of attitude research, however, so an example of that type is used here.)

Let us return to the researcher interested in measuring attitudes toward abortion. He or she might devise a series of items ranging from "easy to agree with" to "difficult to agree with." Such an approach might be represented by the following items:

Do you agree or disagree that abortions should be permitted:

1. *When the life of the woman is in danger*

2. *In the case of incest or rape*

3. *When the fetus appears to be unhealthy*

4. *When the father does not want to have a baby*

5. *When the woman cannot afford to have a baby*

6. *Whenever the woman wants one*

This array of items seems likely to result in responses consistent with Guttman scaling. A respondent agreeing with any one of the items is likely to also agree

TABLE 5–5
Guttman Scale of Attitudes toward Abortion

Respondent	Life of Woman	Incest or Rape	Unhealthy Fetus	Father	Afford	Anytime	No. of Agree Answers	Revised Scale Score
1	A	A	A	A	A	A	6	5
2	A	A	A	D	A	D	4	4
3	A	A	A	D	D	D	3	3
4	A	A	D	A	D	D	3	2
5	A	D	D	A	D	D	2	1
6	D	A	D	D	D	D	1	0

Note: Hypothetical data. A = Agree, D = Disagree.

with those items numbered lower than that one. This would result in the "stepwise" pattern of responses characteristic of a Guttman scale.

Suppose six respondents answered this series of questions, as shown in table 5–5. Generally speaking, the pattern of responses is as expected; those who agreed with the "most difficult" questions were also likely to agree with the "less difficult" ones. However, the responses of three people (2, 4, and 5) to the question about the father's preferences do not fit the pattern. Consequently, the question about the father does not seem to fit the pattern and would be removed from the scale. Once that has been done, the stepwise pattern becomes clear.

With real data, it is unlikely that every respondent would give answers that fit the pattern perfectly. For example, in table 5–5, respondent 6 gave an "agree" response to the question about incest or rape. This response is unexpected and does not fit the pattern. Therefore, we would be making an error if we assigned a scale score of 0 to respondent 6. When the data fit the scale pattern well (number of errors is small), researchers assume that the scale is an appropriate measure and that the respondent's "error" may be "corrected" (in this case, either the "agree" in the case of incest or rape or the "disagree" in the case of the life of the woman). There are standard procedures to follow to determine how to correct the data to make it conform to the scale pattern. We emphasize, however, that this is done only if the changes are few.

Guttman scales differ from Likert scales in that, in the former case, generally only one set of responses will yield a particular scale score. That is, to get a score of 3 on the abortion scale, a particular pattern of responses (or something very close to it) is necessary. In the case of a Likert scale, however, many different patterns of responses can yield the same scale score. A Guttman scale is also much more difficult to achieve than a Likert scale, since the items must have been ordered and be perceived by the respondents as representing increasingly more difficult responses reflecting the same attitude.

Both Likert and Guttman scales have shortcomings in their level of measurement. The level of measurement produced by Likert scales is, at best, ordinal (since we do not know the relative importance of each item and so cannot be sure that a 5 answer on one item is the same as a 5 answer on another), and the level of measurement produced by Guttman scales is usually assumed to be ordinal.

Another type of scaling procedure, called **Mokken scaling**, also analyzes responses to multiple items by respondents to see if, for each item, respondents can be ordered and if items can be ordered.[33] Mokken scaling was used by Saundra K. Schneider, William G. Jacoby, and Daniel C. Lewis to see if there was structure and coherence in public opinion regarding the distribution of responsibilities between the federal government and state and local governments.[34] Respondents were asked whether they thought state or local governments "should take the lead" rather than the national government for thirteen different policy areas. The scaling procedure allowed the researchers to see if a specific sequence of policies emerged while moving from one end of the scale to the other. One end of the scale would indicate maximal support for national policy activity, while the other end would indicate maximal support for subnational government policy responsibility.

The results of their analysis are shown in figure 5–2. The scale runs from 0 to 13, with 0 indicating that the national government should take the lead in all thirteen policy areas and a score of 13 indicating that the respondent believes that state and local governments should take the lead in all policy areas. A person at any scale score believes that the state and local should take the lead in all policy areas that fall below that score. Thus, a person with a score of 9 believes that the national government should take the lead in health care, equality for women, protecting the environment, and equal opportunity and that state and local governments should take the lead responsibility for natural disasters down to urban development. The bars in the figure correspond to the percentage of respondents who received a particular score. Thus, just slightly more than 5 percent of the respondents thought that state and local governments should take the lead in all policy areas, whereas only 1 percent of the respondents thought the national government should take the lead in all thirteen policy areas. Most respondents divided up the responsibilities. The authors concluded from their analysis that the public does have a rationale behind its preferences for the distribution of policy responsibilities between national versus state and local governments.

The procedures described so far for constructing multi-item measures are fairly straightforward. There are other advanced statistical techniques for summarizing or combining individual items or variables. For example, it is possible that several variables are related to some underlying concept. **Factor analysis** is a statistical technique that may be used to uncover patterns across measures. It is especially useful when a researcher has a large number of measures and when there is uncertainty about how the measures are interrelated.

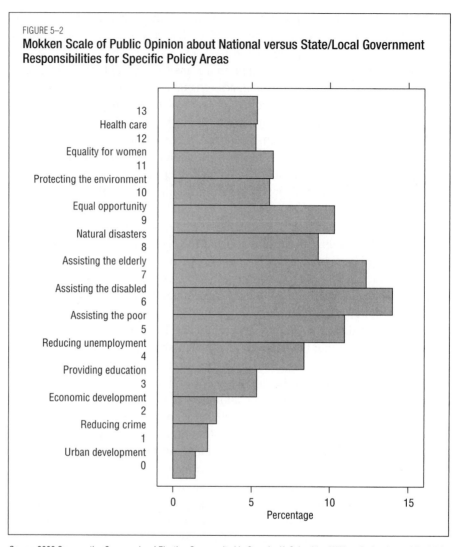

FIGURE 5–2

Mokken Scale of Public Opinion about National versus State/Local Government Responsibilities for Specific Policy Areas

Source: 2006 Comparative Congressional Election Survey, cited in Saundra K. Schneider, William G. Jacoby, and Daniel C. Lewis, "Public Opinion Toward Intergovernmental Policy Responsibilities," *Publius: The Journal of Federalism* 41, no. 1 (2011): fig. 3, p. 14. Reprinted by permission of Oxford University Press. © The Author 2010. Published by Oxford University Press on behalf of CSF Associates: Publius, Inc.

An example is the analysis by Daniel D. Dutcher, who conducted research on the attitudes of owners of streamside property toward the water quality improvement strategy of planting trees in a wide band (called riparian buffers) along the sides of streams.[35] He asked landowners to rate the importance of twelve items thought to affect the willingness of landowners to create and maintain riparian buffers. He wanted to know whether the attitudes could be grouped into distinct dimensions that could be used as summary variables instead of using each of the twelve items separately. Using factor analysis, he found that the items factored into three dimensions. These dimensions and the items included in each dimension are listed in table 5–5. The first dimension, which he labeled "maintaining property aesthetics," included items such as maintaining a view of the stream, neatness, and maintaining open space. A second dimension contained items related to concern over water quality. The third dimension related to protecting property against damage or loss.

Factor analysis is just one of many techniques developed to explore the dimensionality of measures and to construct multi-item scales. The readings listed at the end of this chapter include some resources for students who are especially interested in this aspect of variable measurement.

Through indexes and scales, researchers attempt to enhance both the accuracy and the precision of their measures. Although these multi-item measures have received most use in attitude research, they are often useful in other endeavors as well. Both indexes and scales require researchers to make decisions regarding the selection of individual items and the way in which the scores on those items will be combined to produce more useful measures of political phenomena.

TABLE 5–6

Items Measuring Landowner Attitudes toward Riparian Buffers on Their Streamside Property Sorted into Dimensions Using Factor Analysis

Maintaining Property Aesthetics

- Maintaining my view of the stream
- Maintaining the look of a pastoral or meadow stream
- Maintaining open space
- Wanting the neighbors to think that I'm doing my part to keep up the traditional look of the neighborhood

Contributing to Stream and Bay Quality

- Being confident that maintaining or creating a streamside forest on my property is necessary to protect the stream
- Contributing to the improvement of downstream areas, including the Chesapeake Bay
- Maintaining or improving stream-bank stability on my property

Protecting Property against Damage or Loss

- Keeping vegetation from encroaching on fields or fences
- Minimizing the potential for flood damage to lands or buildings
- Discouraging pests (deer, woodchucks, snakes, insects, etc.)
- Initial costs, maintenance costs, or loss of income

Source: Adapted from table 3.4 in Daniel D. Dutcher, "Landowner Perceptions of Protecting and Establishing Riparian Forests in Central Pennsylvania" (Ph.D. diss., Pennsylvania State University, May 2000), 64.

CONCLUSION

To a large extent, a research project is only as good as the measurements that are developed and used in it. Inaccurate measurements will interfere with the testing of scientific explanations for political phenomena and may lead to erroneous conclusions. Imprecise measurements will limit the extent of the comparisons that can be made between observations and the precision of the knowledge that results from empirical research.

Despite the importance of good measurement, political science researchers often find that their measurement schemes are of uncertain accuracy and precision. Abstract concepts are difficult to measure in a valid way, and the practical constraints of time and money often jeopardize the reliability and precision of measurements. The quality of a researcher's measurements makes an important contribution to the results of his or her empirical research and should not be lightly or routinely sacrificed.

Sometimes the accuracy of measurements may be enhanced through the use of multi-item measures. With indexes and scales, researchers select multiple indicators of a phenomenon, assign scores to each of these indicators, and combine those scores into a summary measure. Although these methods have been used most frequently in attitude research, they can also be used in other situations to improve the accuracy and precision of single-item measures.

 **Terms Introduced**

Alternative-form method. A method of calculating reliability by repeating different but equivalent measures at two or more points in time.

Construct validity. Validity demonstrated for a measure by showing that it is related to the measure of another concept.

Content validity. Validity demonstrated by ensuring that the full domain of a concept is measured.

Convergent construct validity. Validity demonstrated by showing that the measure of a concept is related to the measure of another, related concept.

Correlation matrix. A table showing the relationships among discrete measures.

Dichotomous variable. A nominal-level variable having only two categories that for certain analytical purposes can be treated as a quantitative variable.

Discriminant construct validity. Validity demonstrated by showing that the measure of a concept has a low correlation with the measure of another concept that is thought to be unrelated.

Face validity. Validity asserted by arguing that a measure corresponds closely to the concept it is designed to measure.

Factor analysis. A statistical technique useful in the construction of multi-item scales to measure abstract concepts.

Guttman scale. A multi-item measure in which respondents are presented with increasingly difficult measures of approval for an attitude.

Interitem association. A test of the extent to which the scores of several items, each thought to measure the same concept, are the same. Results are displayed in a correlation matrix.

Interval measurement. A measure for which a one-unit difference in scores is the same throughout the range of the measure.

Level of measurement. The extent or degree to which the values of variables can be compared and mathematically manipulated.

Likert scale. A multi-item measure in which the items are selected based on their ability to discriminate between those scoring high and those scoring low on the measure.

Measurement. The process by which phenomena are observed systematically and represented by scores or numerals.

Mokken scale. A type of scaling procedure that assesses the extent to which there is order in the responses of respondents to multiple items. Similar to Guttman scaling.

Nominal measurement. A measure for which different scores represent different, but not ordered, categories.

Operational definition. The rules by which a concept is measured and scores assigned.

Ordinal measurement. A measure for which the scores represent ordered categories that are not necessarily equidistant from each other.

Ratio measurement. A measure for which the scores possess the full mathematical properties of the numbers assigned.

Reliability. The extent to which a measure yields the same results on repeated trials.

Split-halves method. A method of calculating reliability by comparing the results of two equivalent measures made at the same time.

Summation index. A multi-item measure in which individual scores on a set of items are combined to form a summary measure.

Test-retest method. A method of calculating reliability by repeating the same measure at two or more points in time.

Validity. The correspondence between a measure and the concept it is supposed to measure.

Suggested Readings

DeVellis, Robert F. *Scale Development: Theory and Applications.* 2nd ed. Thousand Oaks, Calif.: Sage, 2003.

Kim, Jae-On, and Charles W. Mueller. *Introduction to Factor Analysis: What It Is and How to Do It*. A Sage University Paper: Quantitative Applications in the Social Sciences no. 07–013. Beverly Hills, Calif.: Sage, 1978.

Mertler, Craig A., and Rachel A. Vannatta. *Advanced and Multivariate Statistical Methods: Practical Application and Interpretation*. 3rd ed. Glendale, Calif.: Pyrczak, 2005.

Netemeyer, Richard G., William O. Bearden, and Subhash Sharma, *Scaling Procedures: Issues and Applications*. Thousand Oaks, Calif.: Sage, 2003.

Walford, Geoffrey, Eric Tucker, and Madhu Viswanathan. *The Sage Handbook of Measurement*. Los Angeles: Sage, 2010.

Notes

1. Lane Kenworthy and Jonas Pontusson, "Rising Inequality and the Politics of Redistribution in Affluent Countries," *Perspectives on Politics* 3, no. 3 (2005): 449–71, http://www.u.arizona.edu/~lkenwor/pop2005.pdf.

2. See Walter Dean Burnham, "The Turnout Problem," in *Elections American Style*, ed. A. James Reichley (Washington, D.C.: Brookings Institution, 1987), 97–133; Michael P. McDonald and Samuel L. Popkin, "The Myth of the Vanishing Voter," *American Political Science Review* 95, no. 4 (2001): 963–74, http://elections.gmu.edu/APSR%20McDonald%20and_Popkin_2001.pdf.

3. Jeffrey A. Segal and Albert D. Cover, "Ideological Values and the Votes of U.S. Supreme Court Justices," *American Political Science Review* 83, no. 2 (1989): 557–65, http://www.uic.edu/classes/pols/pols200mm/Segal89.pdf.

4. Valerie J. Hoekstra, *Public Reaction to Supreme Court Decisions* (New York: Cambridge University Press, 2003).

5. Richard C. Hall and Kristina Miler, "What Happens After the Alarm? Interest Group Subsidies to Legislative Overseers," *Journal of Politics* 70, no. 4 (2008): 990–1005.

6. Stephen Ansolabehere, Shanto Iyengar, Adam Simon, and Nicholas Valentino, "Does Attack Advertising Demobilize the Electorate?" *American Political Science Review* 88, no. 4 (1994): 829–38. Available at http://weber.ucsd.edu/~tkousser/Ansolabehere.pdf.

7. Question wording for the variable EQWLTH from GSS 1998 *Codebook,* http://www.thearda.com/Archive/Files/Codebooks/GSS1998_CB.asp.

8. Hall and Miler, "What Happens After the Alarm?"

9. Segal and Cover, "Ideological Values and the Votes of U.S. Supreme Court Justices."

10. Ibid., 559.

11. David Bradley, Evelyne Huber, Stephanie Moller, Francoise Nielsen, and John D. Stephens, "Distribution and Redistribution in Postindustrial Democracies," *World Politics* 55, no. 2 (2003): 193–228.

12. For information on the LIS database, see http://www.lisdatacenter.org/our-data/lis-database/.

13. Kim Fridkin Kahn and Patrick J. Kenney, "Do Negative Campaigns Mobilize or Suppress Turnout? Clarifying the Relationship between Negativity and Participation," *American Political Science Review* 93, no. 4 (1999): 877–89.

14. Martin P. Wattenberg and Craig Leonard Brians, "Negative Campaign Advertising: Demobilizer or Mobilizer?" *American Political Science Review* 93, no. 4 (1999): 891–99, http://weber.ucsd.edu/~tkousser/Wattenberg.pdf.

15. Ansolabehere, Iyengar, Simon, and Valentino, "Does Attack Advertising Demobilize the Electorate?"

16. Edward G. Carmines and Richard A. Zeller, *Reliability and Validity Assessment*, A Sage University Paper: Quantitative Applications in the Social Sciences no. 07–017 (Beverly Hills, Calif.: Sage, 1979).

17. Philip E. Converse, "The Nature of Belief Systems in Mass Publics," in *Ideology and Discontent*, ed. David E. Apter (New York: Free Press of Glencoe, 1964); Pauline Marie Vaillancourt, "Stability of Children's Survey Responses," *Public Opinion Quarterly* 37, no. 3 (1973): 373–87; J. Miller McPherson, Susan Welch, and Cal Clark, "The Stability and Reliability of Political Efficacy: Using Path Analysis to Test Alternative Models," *American Political Science Review* 71, no. 2 (1977): 509–21; and Philip E. Converse and Gregory B. Markus, "Plus ça change . . . : The New CPS Election Study Panel," *American Political Science Review* 73, no. 1 (1979): 32–49.

18. Raymond E. Wolfinger and Steven J. Rosenstone, appendix A in *Who Votes?* (New Haven, Conn.: Yale University Press, 1980).

19. Kenneth D. Bailey, *Methods of Social Research* (New York: Free Press, 1978), 58.

20. James Coleman Battista, "Formal and Perceived Leadership Power in U.S. State Legislatures," *State Politics & Policy Quarterly* 11, no. 1 (2011): 102–18. Available at http://spa.sagepub.com/content/11/1/102.full.pdf + html.

21. As discussed in Ross E. Burkhart and Michael S. Lewis-Beck, "Comparative Democracy: The Economic Development Thesis," *American Political Science Review* 88, no. 4 (1994): appendix A.

22. Robert J. Sternberg and Wendy M. Williams, "Does the Graduate Record Examination Predict Meaningful Success in the Graduate Training of Psychologists? A Case Study," *American Psychologist* 52, no. 6 (1997): 630–41.

23. Nancy W. Burton and Ming-Mei Wang, *Predicting Long-Term Success in Graduate School: A Collaborative Validity Study*, GRE Board Research Report no. 99–14R (Princeton, N.J.: Educational Testing Service, 2005).

24. Battista, "Formal and Perceived Leadership Power in U.S. State Legislatures."

25. Joseph A. Gliem and Rosemary R. Gliem, "Calculating, Interpreting, and Reporting Cronbach's Alpha Reliability Coefficient for Likert-Type Scales" (paper presented at 2003 Midwest Research to Practice Conference in Adult, Continuing and Community Education, Ohio State University, Columbus, 2003), https://scholarworks.iupui.edu/bitstream/handle/1805/344/Gliem + & + Gliem.pdf?sequence = 1.

26. The distinction between an interval-level and a ratio-level measure is not always clear, and some political science texts do not distinguish between them. Interval-level measures in political science are rather rare; ratio-level measures (money spent, age, number of children, years living in the same location, for example) are more common.

27. Steven C. Poe and C. Neal Tate, "Repression of Human Rights to Personal Integrity in the 1980s: A Global Analysis," *American Political Science Review* 88, no. 4 (1994): 853–900.

28. Ibid., 867.

29. Ibid., 868.

30. Ibid., 855.

31. Brett Arends, "Why You Can't Trust the Inflation Numbers," *Wall Street Journal*, January 26, 2011, http://online.wsj.com/article/SB10001424052748704013604576104351050317610.html.

32. Gliem and Gliem, "Calculating, Interpreting, and Reporting Cronbach's Alpha Reliability Coefficient for Likert-Type Scales."

33. Robert Jan Mokken, *A Theory and Procedure of Scale Analysis with Applications in Political Research* (The Hague, Neth.: Mouton, 1971). Mokken scaling is an example of a nonparametric item response theory (IRT) model. It differs from Guttman scaling in that it has a probabilistic interpretation whereas Guttman scaling does not. See Ate Dijktra, Girbe Buist, Peter Moorer, and Theo Dassen, "Construct Validity of the Nursing Care Dependency Scale," *Journal of Clinical Nursing* 8, no. 4 (1999): 380–88.

34. Saundra K. Schneider, William G. Jacoby, and Daniel C. Lewis, "Public Opinion Toward Intergovernmental Policy Responsibilities," *Publius: The Journal of Federalism* 41, no. 1 (2011): 1–30.

35. Daniel D. Dutcher, "Landowner Perceptions of Protecting and Establishing Riparian Forests in Central Pennsylvania" (PhD. diss., Pennsylvania State University, 2000).

RESEARCH DESIGN:

MAKING CAUSAL INFERENCES

HERE IS THE TRANSCRIPT OF A RUN-OF-THE-MILL campaign ad that aired in the 2010 Pennsylvania Democratic senatorial primary:

ANNOUNCER: Joe Sestak, Relieved of Duty in the Navy for creating a poor command climate.
(picture of Joe Sestak with headline, "Relieved of Duty" and "creating a poor command climate")

ANNOUNCER: Joe Sestak, the worst attendance of any Pennsylvania congressman.
(picture of Joe Sestak with text "Worst Attendance of any Pennsylvania Congressman")

ANNOUNCER: And near the bottom of the entire Congress.
(picture of Joe Sestak with text "Near the bottom of the entire Congress")

ANNOUNCER: Last year alone, Sestak missed 127 votes.
(Picture of desk with cobwebs and text "missed 127 votes")

ANNOUNCER: Sestak says missed votes weren't important, he went campaigning instead.
(picture of Pennsylvania with text "Missed votes weren't important")

ANNOUNCER: Say no to No Show Joe.[1]

As noted in chapters 1 and 2, some political scientists argue that negative advertisements of this sort demobilize the electorate.[2] Others think that they have few, if any, harmful effects and may in fact help mobilize and inform voters.[3]

Well, then, what are the effects of negative political advertisements? Do they discourage people from voting? Misinform them? Or does this sort of campaigning excite citizens by piquing their interest? The discussion in chapter 1 showed that this is an ongoing and lively issue in political science. Furthermore, we noted in chapters 2 and 4 that questions such as these can be stated in a testable or verifiable way. It is now time to think about *how* one might approach a problem of this sort. We require a plan or strategy for collecting and analyzing information in such a way that we can have confidence that our conclusions rest on solid evidence rather than on faulty reasoning or mere opinion.

A **research design** is a plan that shows how a researcher intends to study an empirical question. It indicates what specific theory or propositions will be tested, what the appropriate "units of analysis" (e.g., people, nations, states, organizations) are for the tests, what measurements or observations (that is, data) are needed, how all this information will be collected, and which analytical and statistical procedures will be used to examine the data. All the parts of a research design should work to the same end: drawing sound conclusions supported by observable evidence.

In this chapter, we discuss various types of designs along with their advantages and disadvantages. Just as important, we show how a poor research strategy can result in uninformative or misleading results. Poor planning may produce insignificant or erroneous conclusions, no matter how original and brilliant the investigator's ideas and hypotheses happen to be.

Many factors affect the choice of a design. One is the purpose of the investigation. Whether the research is intended to be exploratory, descriptive, or explanatory will most likely influence its design. The project's feasibility or practicality is another consideration. Some designs may be unethical, while others may be impossible to implement for lack of data or insufficient time and money. Researchers frequently must balance what is possible to accomplish against what would ideally be done to investigate a particular hypothesis. Consequently, many common designs entail unfortunate but necessary compromises, and thus the conclusions that may be drawn from them are more tentative and incomplete than anyone would like.

Research to test specific hypotheses (e.g., the more negative ads in a campaign, the less voter participation will be) attempt to

1. establish a relationship between two (or more) variables (e.g., exposure and turnout);

2. demonstrate that the results are generally true in the real world and not in just a particular context;

3. reveal whether one phenomenon precedes another in time; and

4. eliminate as many alternative explanations for the observed finding as possible.

In this chapter, we explain how various designs allow or do not allow researchers to accomplish these four objectives.

VERIFYING CAUSAL ASSERTIONS

Causal versus Spurious Relationships

Let us return to the question of the effects of campaign advertising on voting. A tentative hypothesis is that negative ads, repeated over and over, bore, frustrate, and even anger potential voters to the point that they think twice about going to the polls. Consequently, we might expect that the more citizens are subjected to commercials and advertisements that vilify candidates, the less inclined they will be to vote. Therefore, in a campaign flooded with negative ads, turnout will be lower than in one in which the candidates stick to the issues. We might even be tempted to make the stronger claim that negative political advertising *causes* a decline in participation.

How could we support such assertions? Just after an election, it might be possible to interview a sample of citizens, ask them if they had heard or been aware of attack ads, and then determine whether or not they had voted. We might even find a relationship or connection between exposure and turnout. Let's say, for instance, that all those who report viewing negative commercials tell us that they did *not* vote, whereas all those who were not aware of these ads cast ballots. We might summarize the hypothetical results in a simple table. Let X stand for whether or not people saw the campaign ads and Y for whether or not they voted. (We will see the reason for using these letters in a moment.) What this table symbolizes is a relationship or association between X and Y.

This strategy, frequently called opinion research, involves an investigator observing behavior indirectly by asking people questions about what they believe and how they act. Since we do not directly observe their actions, we can only take the respondents' word about whether or not they voted or saw attack ads.

What can we make of the findings in table 6–1? Yes, there is a relationship. It is sometimes called a correlation or perhaps, less formally, an association. Note that 100 percent of the people who said they were "exposed" also said they did not vote and vice versa for those who did not watch any ads. But does that mean that negative advertising causes a decline in turnout? After all, it is possible that those who missed the ads differ in other ways as well from those who saw them. Perhaps they have a higher level of education and *that* accounts for their higher turnout rate. Or maybe they had a

CAUSALITY VERSUS CORRELATION

The ability to tell the difference between causation and correlation is an essential skill for political scientists and interested citizens alike. Why? Because so many arguments about policy and politics contain statements that may or may not be legitimately or reasonably interpreted as causal.

In social science research as well as common parlance, a **correlation** is simply a statement that two things are systematically related. If you see one thing, chances are that you will see the other. But that's the extent of the information carried by a statement of correlation.

A *causal* declaration, by contrast, communicates much more. A change in the state of one thing brings about (in full or in part) a change in the state of another. This statement carries with it claims about time order and the elimination of alternative explanations for the observed relationship.

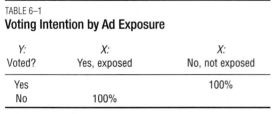

TABLE 6–1
Voting Intention by Ad Exposure

Y: Voted?	X: Yes, exposed	X: No, not exposed
Yes		100%
No	100%	

Note: Hypothetical data.

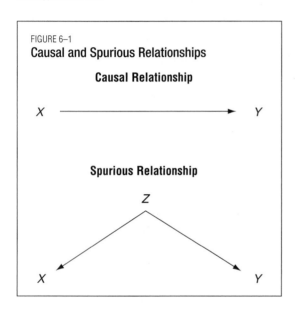

FIGURE 6–1
Causal and Spurious Relationships

Causal Relationship

$X \longrightarrow Y$

Spurious Relationship

Z

$X \qquad Y$

generally strong sense of civic duty and would always vote, no matter what the campaigns do or say.

At the same time, people with less education might watch a lot of television and *coincidentally* not bother voting in any election. If conditions of these sorts hold, we may observe a connection between advertisement exposure and turnout, but it would not be a *causal* relationship. And outlawing negative campaigning would not necessarily have any effect on turnout because the one does not cause the other. In this case, the association would be an example of what we call a *spurious,* or false, relationship.

A spurious relationship arises because two things, such as viewing negative ads and voting, are both affected by some third factor and thus appear to be related. Once this additional factor has been identified and controlled for, the original relationship weakens or disappears altogether. To take a trivial example, we might well find a positive relationship between the number of operations in hospitals and the number of patients who die in hospitals. But this doesn't mean that operations cause deaths. Rather, it is probably the case that people with serious illnesses or injuries need operations *and* because of their conditions are prone to die. Figure 6–1 illustrates causal and spurious relationships.[4]

Distinguishing real, causal relations from spurious ones is an important part of any scientific research. To explain phenomena, we must know how and why two things are connected, not simply that they are associated. Thus, one of the major goals in designing research is to come up with a way to make valid causal inferences. Ideally such a design does three things:

1. *Covariation:* It demonstrates that the alleged cause (call it *X*) does in fact covary with the supposed effect, *Y.* Our simple study of advertising and voting does this because, as we saw in table 6–1, viewing negative advertisements is connected to nonvoting, and not viewing the ads is associated with voting. Public opinion polls or surveys can relatively easily identify associations. To make a causal inference, however, more is needed.

2. *Time order:* The research must show that the cause preceded the effect: *X* must come before *Y* in time. After all, can an effect appear before its cause? In our survey of citizens, we might reasonably assume that the television

ads preceded the decision to vote or not. But note that however reasonable this assumption may be, we have not really demonstrated it empirically. And in other observational settings, it may be difficult, if not impossible, to tell whether *X* came before or after *Y*. Still, even if we can be confident of the time order, we have to demonstrate that a third condition holds.

3. *Elimination of possible alternative causes, sometimes termed "confounding factors":* The research must be conducted in such a way that all possible joint causes of *X* and *Y* have been eliminated. To be sure that negative television advertising directly depresses turnout, we need to rule out the possibility that the two are connected by some third factor, such as education or interest in politics.

Figure 6–2 shows the necessity for the third requirement. How do you interpret these so-called causal models or arrow diagrams? The first one (Causal Relationship) shows a "true" causal connection between *X* (ad exposure) and *Y* (voting). The arrow indicates causality: *X* causes *Y*. If this is the way the world really is, then attack advertisements have a direct link to nonvoting. The arrowhead indicates the direction of causality, because in this example *X* causes *Y* and not vice versa. In the second diagram (Spurious Relationship), by contrast, the *X* and *Y* are not directly related; there is no causal arrow between them. Yet an apparent association is produced by the action of a third factor, *Z*. Hence, the presence of the third factor, *Z* (education), creates the impression of a causal relationship between *X* and *Y*, but this impression is misleading, because once we take into account the third factor—in language we use later, "once we control for *Z*"—the original relationship weakens or disappears.

It might not being going too far to say that causal assertions are the life blood of political and policy discourse. Take just about any contentious subject. Its manifest argument may be about "we should . . ." statements. But underlying the argument, we guarantee, you will always find causal assertions (e.g., "We should limit greenhouse gas emissions because they cause an increase in global temperatures.").

Since virtually any potential relations of interest could be spurious,

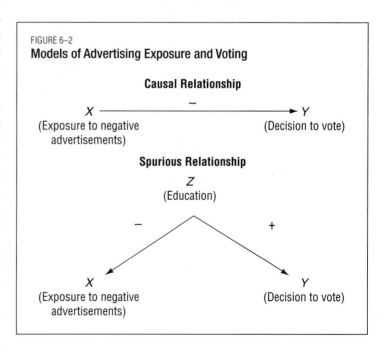

FIGURE 6–2
Models of Advertising Exposure and Voting

Causal Relationship

X ——————— − ——————→ *Y*
(Exposure to negative   (Decision to vote)
advertisements)

Spurious Relationship

Z
(Education)

−   +

X   *Y*
(Exposure to negative   (Decision to vote)
advertisements)

how do we make valid causal inferences? The answer leads to research design, because how we frame problems and plan their solutions greatly affects the confidence we can have in our results. Asking a group of people about what they have seen and heard in the media and relating their answers to their reported behavior is known in common parlance as "polling." A more formal term is *survey research*. This involves the direct or indirect collection of information from individuals by asking them questions, having them fill out forms, or other means. (We discuss survey research in chapter 10.) This approach is perhaps the most commonly used in the social sciences, and it is the one followed in the hypothetical example above. A difficulty with survey research, however, is that it is not the best way to make dependable causal inferences. For this reason, many social scientists think laboratory experiments lead to more valid conclusions.

The Classical Randomized Experiment

An **experiment** allows the researcher to control exposure to an experimental variable (often called a **test stimulus, test factor,** or independent variable), the assignment of subjects to different groups, and the observation or measurement of responses and behavior. As we will see, experimental designs theoretically allow researchers to make causal inferences with greater confidence in their dependability than do nonexperimental approaches, such as polling. Although most political scientists do conduct experiments[5]—recall Stephen Ansolabehere and colleagues' study of the effects of campaign advertising described in chapter 1[6]— most research in the field uses nonexperimental methods. This situation results partly from the nature of the phenomena of greatest interest to political science, such as who votes in actual elections rather than in experimental settings. Nevertheless, understanding experimental design is crucial for both students of political science and citizens because it provides an especially clear way to see what must done to validate or confirm or support a causal claim.

As we noted earlier, making a valid causal claim involves showing three things: covariation, time order, and the absence of confounding factors. In theory, an experiment can unambiguously accomplish all these objectives. How? Let's look at the following five basic characteristics of a **classical randomized experimental design:**[7]

1. The experimenter starts by establishing two groups: an **experimental group** (actually, there can be more than one), which receives or is exposed to an experimental treatment or test factor, and a **control group,** so called because its subjects do not undergo the experimental manipulation or receive the experimental treatment or test stimulus. So, for example, Ansolabehere and his colleagues had some citizens (the experimental group) watch a negative political ad and others (the control group) watch a nonpolitical commercial.

The investigators determined who watched the political ad and who watch the nonpolitical commercial; they did not rely on self-reports of viewership. This control over the two groups is directly analogous to a biologist exposing some laboratory animals to a chemical and leaving others alone.

2. Equally important, the researcher *randomly* assigns individuals to the groups. The subjects do not get to decide which group they join. Random assignment to groups is called **randomization,** and it means that membership is a matter of chance, not self-selection. Moreover, if we start with a pool of subjects, random assignment ensures that at the outset, both the experimental and control groups are virtually identical in all respects. They will, in other words, contain similar proportions, or averages, of females and males; liberals, moderates, conservatives, and nonpartisans; Republicans and Democrats; political activists and nonvoters; and so on. On average, the groups will not differ in any respect.[8] Randomization, as we will see, is what makes experiments such powerful tools for making causal inferences.

3. Third, the researcher "administers" the experimental treatment (the test factor); simply put, the experimenter determines when, where, and under what circumstances the experimental group is given the stimulus.

4. Fourth, in an experiment, the researcher establishes and measures a dependent variable—the response of interest—both before and after the stimulus is given. The measurements are often called pre- and postexperimental measures, and they indicate whether or not there has been an **experimental effect.** An experimental effect, as the term suggests, reflects differences between the two groups' responses to the test factor. *This effect measures the impact of the independent variable on the dependent variable and, consequently, is a main focus of experimental research.*

5. Finally, the environment of the experiment—that is, the time, location, and other physical aspects—is under the experimenter's direction. Such control means that he or she can control or exclude extraneous factors or influences other than the independent variable that might affect the dependent variable. If, for instance, both groups are studied at the same time of day, any differences between the control and experimental subjects cannot be attributed to temporal factors.

To see how these characteristics tie in with the requirements of causal inferences, let us conduct a hypothetical randomized experiment in order to see if negative political advertising depresses the intention to vote. This case is purely hypothetical, but it roughly resembles the research conducted by Ansolabehere and his associates. More to the point, it shows the inferential power of experiments. (The example will also show some of the weaknesses of this design.)

Our hypothesis states that exposure to negative television advertising will cause people to be less inclined to vote. Stated this way, the test factor, or experimental variable, is seeing a negative ad ("yes" or "no"), and the response is the stated intention to vote ("likely" or "not likely"). We recruit from somewhere a pool of subjects and randomly assign them to either an experimental (or treatment) group or a control group. It is crucial that we make the assignments randomly. We do not, for example, want to put mostly women in one group and men in the other, because if afterward we find a difference in propensity to vote, we would not be able to tell if it arose because of the advertisement or because of gender. We illustrate the procedure in figure 6–3.

Note that we draw subjects from some population, perhaps by advertising in a newspaper or giving extra credit in an American government class. This pool of subjects does not constitute a random sample of any population. After all, the subjects volunteered to participate; we did not randomly pick them. But, and here is the key, once we have a pool of individuals, we can *then* randomly assign them to the groups. Assume the first subject arrives at the test site. We could flip a coin and, depending on the result, assign him to the experimental group or to the control section. When the next person arrives, we flip the coin again and, based on just that result, send her to one or the other of the groups. If our pool consists of 100 potential subjects, our coin tossing should result in about 50 in each group.

Now suppose we administer a questionnaire to the members of both groups in which we ask about demographic characteristics (e.g., age, sex, family income, years of education, place of birth) and about political beliefs and opinions (e.g., party identification, attitude toward gun control, ideology, knowledge of politics). Of course, we would also ask about the dependent variable, the

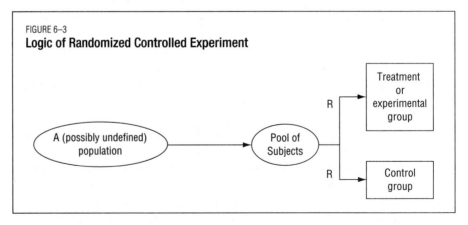

FIGURE 6–3
Logic of Randomized Controlled Experiment

Note: R = random assignment.

intention to vote. If we compare the groups' averages on the variables, we should find that they are about the same. The experimental group may consist of 45 percent males, be on average 33.5 years old, and generally (75 percent, say) not care much for liberals. But the control group should also reflect these characteristics and tendencies. There may be only 40 percent males and the average age may be 35.0 years, but the differences reflect only chance (or, as we see in chapter 7, "sampling error"). Of greatest importance, the proportions on the response variable, the intention to vote in the next election, should be approximately the same. Thus, at the beginning of the experiment, we have two nearly identical groups.

After the initial measurement of the dependent variable (the **pretest**), we start the experiment. To disguise our purpose, we tell the informants that we are interested in television news. Those assigned to the experimental treatment go to room 101, those in the control panel to room 106. Both groups now watch an identical fifteen-minute news broadcast. So far, both groups have been treated the same. If there are any differences between them, they are the result of happenstance.

Next, the first set of subjects sees a thirty-second negative political ad, which we have constructed to be as realistic as possible, while the others see a thirty-second commercial about hair conditioners, also as true to life as we can make it. The different treatment constitutes the experimental manipulation (seeing versus not seeing a negative political advertisement). After the commercials have aired, we show both groups another fifteen-minute news clip.

When the broadcast is over, we wrap up the experiment by administering parts of the first questionnaire again and measuring the likelihood of voting. This calculation gives us an indication of the size of the experimental variable's effect, if there is one. Hypothetical results from this experiment are shown in table 6-2.

Note, first, that both control and experimental subjects had about the same initial stated intention of voting (63 and 65 percent, respectively), as we would expect, because the participants had been randomized. But the posttest measurement shows quite a change for the experimental group: the percentage intending

TABLE 6-2
Results of Hypothetical Media Experiment

Group	Before Measure of Intention (percent intending to vote)	After Measure of Intention (percent intending to vote)
Experimental	65%	45%
Control	63%	62%
Hypothetical experimental data		

to vote has dropped from 65 to 45 percent. But the control group has changed hardly at all. The treatment effect on the experimental group is 60% − 40% = 20%, quite a reduction in civic-mindedness if it turns out to be valid in the general population (see the following discussion).

So we might conclude that the experimental factor did indeed cause a decline in intention to vote. How can we make this inference? In the first place, the experimental design satisfied all the conditions necessary for making such claims. In table 6–2, we show that the two variables, exposure to negative ads and intention to vote, covary; those who have seen a negative ad are much less likely to vote than are those who did not (45% versus 62%). We have also established the time order, since we explicitly determined the timing of the experimental treatment and the subsequent posttest measurement. Finally, and most convincing of all, we have been able to rule out any reasonable alternative explanation of the covariation, for our randomization and experimental manipulation ensured that the groups differed *only* because one received the treatment and the other did not. Since that was the only difference, the gap between the posttest percentages of the two groups could be attributed only to viewing the commercial.

The purpose of an experiment is to isolate and measure the effects of the independent variable on a response. Researchers want to be able to separate the effect of the independent variables from the effects of other factors that might also influence the dependent variable. Control over the random assignment of subjects to experimental and control groups is the key feature of experiments, because it helps them to "exclude," rule out, or control for the effects of factors that might create a spurious relationship.

The Power of Random Assignment

As we have stressed, the way researchers actually assign subjects to control and experimental groups is important. The best way is randomization, or assigning subjects to groups not according to one of their characteristics such as gender or age, under the assumption that extraneous factors will affect all groups equally and thus "cancel out." Random assignment is an especially attractive choice when it is not possible to specify possible extraneous factors in advance or when there are so many that assigning subjects to experimental and control groups in a manner that ensures the equal distribution of these factors is not possible.

Even given random assignment, extraneous factors may not be totally randomly distributed and, therefore, can affect the outcome of the experiment. This is especially likely if the number of subjects is small. Prudent researchers do not assume that all significant factors are randomly distributed just because the study design has randomized the study's participants. So, in addition to random assignment, investigators use pretests to see if the control and experimental groups are, in fact, equivalent with regard to those factors that are known to influence the outcome or suspected of doing so.

And, if researchers know ahead of time that certain features are related to differences in the dependent variable, they can use *matching* to control for them. This requires creating matched pairs of subjects who are as similar as possible and assigning one to the experimental group and the other to the control group. Thus, no one has to depend solely on randomization to eliminate or control for extraneous factors. One problem with matching is that when there are many factors to be controlled, it becomes difficult to match subjects on all relevant characteristics, and a larger pool of prospective subjects is required. A second problem is that the researcher may not know ahead of time all extraneous factors. To guard against bias in the assignment of pairs, each member of the matched pairs should be randomly assigned to the control and experimental groups.

One of the biggest obstacles to experimentation in social science research is the inability of researchers to control the assignment of subjects to experimental and control groups. Even though the point of conducting an experiment is to test whether a treatment or program has a beneficial effect, it is often practically, ethically, or politically difficult to assign subjects to a to different treatment and control groups. Suppose, for example, that one group was to receive a generous welfare package while another one got nothing. How long could such an experiment go on?

Internal Validity

If we look at causation in a particular way, statistical theory—and common sense—tell us that experiments properly conducted can lead to valid inferences about causality.[9] In this

Interpreting and Generalizing the Results of an Experiment

Most readers, we hope, have followed the logic of our arguments. But they must be flabbergasted at the unrealism of the hypothetical example we introduced and wonder how anyone could make a definitive statement about negative advertising based on these data, even if we had actually carried out this experiment on real people using real television commercials. Someone might exclaim, "This test is invalid!" It may be, but before jumping to that conclusion, we need to consider carefully and closely the term *validity*.

context, however, *validity* has a particular meaning, namely, that the manipulation of the experimental or independent variable itself, and not some other variable, *did in fact* bring about the observed effect on the dependent variable. Social scientists call this kind of validity "internal validity." **Internal validity** means that the research procedure demonstrated a true cause-and-effect relationship that was not created by spurious factors. Social scientists generally believe that the type of research design we have been discussing—a randomized controlled experiment—has strong internal validity. But it is not foolproof.

Several things can affect a research study's internal validity. As we have argued, the principle strength of experimental research is that the researcher has enough control over the environment to make sure that exposure to the experimental stimulus is the only significant difference between experimental and control groups. However, sometimes *history,* or events other than the experimental stimulus that occur between the pretest and posttest measurements of the dependent variable, will affect the dependent variable. For example, suppose that after being selected and assigned to a room, the experimental subjects happen to hear a radio program that undercuts their faith in the electoral process. Such a possibility might arise if there was a long lag between the first measurement of their attitudes and the start of the experiment

Another potential confounding influence is *maturation,* or a change in subjects over time that might produce differences between experimental and control groups. For example, subjects may become tired, confused, distracted, or bored during the course of an experiment. These changes may affect their reaction to the test stimulus and introduce an unanticipated effect on posttreatment scores.

The standard experimental research design involves measurement or observation, which is sometimes called testing. However, *test-subject interaction,* the process of measuring the dependent variable prior to the experimental stimulus, may itself affect the posttreatment scores of subjects. For example, simply asking individuals about politics on a pretest may alert them to the purposes of the experiment. And that, in turn, may cause them to behave in unanticipated ways. Similarly, suppose a researcher wanted to see if watching a presidential debate makes viewers better informed than nonviewers. If the researcher measures the political awareness of the experimental and control groups prior to the debate, he or she runs the risk of sensitizing the subjects to certain topics or issues and contributing to a more attentive audience than would otherwise be the case. Consequently, we would not know for sure whether any increase in awareness was due to the debate, the pretest, or a combination of both. Fortunately, some research designs have been developed to separate these various effects.

Selection bias can also lead to problems. Such bias can creep into a study if subjects are picked (intentionally or not) according to some criterion and not randomly. A common selection problem occurs when subjects volunteer to participate in a program. Volunteers may differ significantly from nonvolunteers; for example, they may be more compliant and eager to please, healthier, or more outgoing. Sometimes a person might be picked for participation in an experiment because of an extreme measurement (very high or very low) of the dependent variable. Extreme scores may not be stable; when measured again, they may move back toward average scores. Thus, changes in the dependent variable may be attributed erroneously to the experimental factor. This problem is called **statistical regression**.[10]

As we stressed, in assigning subjects to experimental and control groups, a researcher hopes that the two groups will be equivalent. If subjects selectively drop out of the study, experimental and control groups that were the same at the start may no longer be equivalent. Thus, **experimental mortality,** or the differential loss of participants from comparison groups, may raise doubts about whether the changes and variation in the dependent variable are due to manipulation of the independent variable.

Another possible problem comes from **demand characteristics,** or aspects of the research situation that cause participants to guess at the investigator's goals and adjust their behavior or opinions accordingly. You may remember from chapter 2 that the human ability to empathize and anticipate others' feelings and intentions (self-reflection) troubles some methodologists, who wonder if this trait doesn't make behavior inaccessible to scientific inquiry. Most political science experimenters don't think so, but they do realize that test subjects can interact with the experimental personnel and setting in subtle and occasionally unpredictable ways. It has been found that people often want to "help" or contribute to an investigator's goals by acting in ways that will support the main hypotheses.[11] Perhaps something about our experiment on political advertising tips off subjects that we, the researchers, expect to find that negative ads depress turnout, and perhaps they (even unconsciously) adjust their feelings in order to prove the proposition and hence please us. In this case, it is the desire to satisfy the researchers' objectives that affects the disposition to vote, not the commercials themselves. This is not a minor issue. You may have heard about "double-blind studies" in medical research. The goal of this kind of design is to disguise to both patients and attendants who is receiving a real experimental medicine and who is receiving a traditional medicine or placebo, thus reducing the possibility that demand characteristics affect the dependent variable.

In short, a lot of things can go wrong in even the most carefully planned experiment. Nevertheless, experimental research designs are better able to resist threats to internal validity than are other types of research designs. (In fact, they provide an ideal against which other research strategies may be compared.) Moreover, we discuss below some ways to mitigate these potential errors. Yet even if we devised the most rigorous laboratory experiment possible to test for media effects on political behavior, some readers still might not be convinced that we have found a cause-and-effect relationship that applies to the "real world." What they are concerned about, perhaps without being aware of the term, is externality validity.

External Validity

External validity, the extent to which the results of a study can be generalized across populations, times, and settings, is the touchstone for natural and social scientists alike. Gerber and Green explained:

> *When evaluating the external validity of political experiments, it is common to ask whether the stimulus used in the study resembles the stimuli of interest in the political world, whether the participants resemble the actors who are ordinarily confronted with these stimuli, whether the outcome measures resemble the actual political outcomes of theoretical or practical interest, and whether the context within which actors operate resembles the political context of interest.[12]*

In short, the findings of a study have "high" external validity if they hold for the world outside of the experimental situation; they have low validity if they only apply to the laboratory.

What sorts of things can compromise one's results? One possibility is that the effects may not be found using a different population. Refer again to figure 6–3, which showed that a pool of participants are selected from some population (of possibly unknown characteristics) and then assigned to one of two groups. But what if the population from which they have been drawn does not reflect any meaningful broader population? Suppose, for instance, we conducted an experiment on sophomores from a particular college. Results might be valid for second-year students attending that particular school but not for the public at large. Indeed, the conclusions might not apply to other classes at that or any other university. To take another example, findings from an experiment investigating the effects of live television coverage on legislators' behavior in state legislatures with fewer than 100 members may not be generalizable to larger state legislative bodies or to Congress. In general, if a study population is not representative of a larger population, the ability to generalize about the larger population will be limited.

OTHER RANDOMIZED EXPERIMENTS

Now that we have discussed the classical randomized experiment, let's consider some extensions of this approach. Each one represents a different attempt to retain experimental control over the experimental situation while at the same time dealing with threats to internal and external validity. Although you may not have an opportunity to employ these designs, knowledge of them will help you understand published research and determine whether the research design employed supports the author's conclusions.

Posttest Design

A simple variant, the **posttest design**, involves two groups and two variables, one independent and one dependent, as before. Likewise, subjects are randomly assigned to one or the other of two groups. One group, the experimental group, is exposed to a treatment or stimulus, and the other, the control group, is not or is given a placebo. Then the dependent variable is measured for each group. The difference between this and the classical randomized experiment is that there is no pretest, so one cannot be certain that at the outset the two groups (experimental and control) have the same average levels on all relevant variables (see figure 6–4).

Nonetheless, researchers using this design can justifiably make causal inferences because they know that the treatment occurred prior to measurement of

FIGURE 6–4
Simple Posttest Experiment

		Posttest
R Experimental Group	X	M_{exp}
R Control Group		$M_{control}$

X = Experimental manipulation
M = Measurements
R = Random assignment of subjects to groups

the dependent variable and that any difference between the two groups on the measure of the dependent variable is attributable to the difference in the treatment Why? This design still requires random assignment of subjects to the experimental and control groups and, therefore, assumes that extraneous factors have been controlled for. It also assumes that, prior to the application of the experimental stimulus, both groups were equivalent with respect to the dependent variable. If the assignment to experimental or control groups is truly random, and the size of the two groups is large, these are ordinarily safe assumptions. However, if the assignment to groups is not truly random or the sample size is small, or both, then posttreatment differences between the two groups may be the result of pretreatment differences and not the result of the independent variable. Because it is impossible with this design to tell how much of the posttreatment difference is simply a reflection of pretreatment differences, a classical experimental research design is considered to be a stronger design.

Repeated-Measurement Design

Naturally, when an experiment uses both a pretest and a posttest, the pretest comes before the experiment starts and the posttest afterward. But exactly how long before and how long afterward? Researchers seldom know for sure. Therefore, an experiment, called a **repeated-measurement design**, may contain several pretreatment and posttreatment measures, especially when researchers don't know exactly how quickly the effect of the independent variable should be observed or when the most reliable pretest measurement of the dependent variable should be taken. An example of a repeated-measurement experimental design would be an attempt to test the relationship between watching a presidential debate and support for the candidates. Suppose we started out by conducting a classical experiment, randomly assigning some people to a group that watches a debate and others to a group that does not watch the debate. On the pre- and posttests, we might measure the scores shown in table 6–3.

TABLE 6–3
Pre- and Posttest Scores in Non-Repeated-Measurement Experiment

	Predebate Support for Candidate X	Treatment	Postdebate Support for Candidate X
Experimental Group	60	Yes	50
Control Group	55	No	50

Note: Hypothetical data.

These scores seem to indicate that the control group was slightly less supportive of Candidate X before the debate (that is, the random assignment did not work perfectly) and that the debate led to a decline in support for Candidate X of 5 percent: $(60 - 50) - (55 - 50)$. Suppose, however, that we had the additional measures shown in table 6–4.

It appears now that support for Candidate X eroded throughout the period for both the experimental and control groups and that the rate of decline was consistently more rapid for the experimental group (that is, the two groups were not equivalent prior to the debate). Viewed from this perspective, it seems that the debate had no effect on the experimental group, since the rate of decline both before and after the debate was the same. Hence, the existence of multiple measures of the dependent variable, both before and after the introduction of the independent variable, would lead in this case to a more accurate conclusion regarding the effects of the independent variable.

Multiple-Group Design

To this point, we have discussed mainly research involving one experimental and one control group. In a **multiple-group design**, more than one experimental or control group are created so that different levels of the experimental variable can be compared. This is useful if the independent variable can assume several values or if the researcher wants to see the possible effects of manipulating the

TABLE 6–4
Pre- and Posttest Scores in Repeated-Measurement Experiment

	Pretest				Posttest		
	First	Second	Third	Treatment	First	Second	Third
Experimental Group	80	70	60	Yes	50	40	30
Control Group	65	60	55	No	50	45	0

Note: Hypothetical data

independent variable in several different ways. Multiple-group designs may involve a posttest only or both a pretest and a posttest. They may also include a time series component.

Here's an example. The proportion of respondents who return questionnaires in a mail survey is usually quite low. Consequently, investigators have attempted to increase response rates by including an incentive or token of appreciation inside the survey. Since incentives add to the cost of the survey, researchers want to know whether or not the incentives increase response rates and, if so, which incentives are most effective and cost-efficient. To test the effect of various incentives, we could use a multiple-group posttest design. If we wanted to test the effects of five treatments, we could randomly assign subjects to six groups. One group would receive no reward (the control group), whereas the other groups would each receive a different reward—for example, 25¢, 50¢, $1.00, a pen, or a key ring. Response rates (the posttreatment measure of the dependent variable) for the groups could then be compared. In table 6–5 we present a set of hypothetical results for such an experiment.

The experimental data indicate that rewards increase response rates and that monetary incentives have more effect than do token gifts. Furthermore, it seems that the dollar incentive is not cost-effective, since it did not yield a sufficiently greater response rate than the 50¢ reward to warrant the additional expense. Other experiments of this type could be conducted to compare the effects of other aspects of mail questionnaires, such as the use of prepaid versus promised monetary rewards or the inclusion or exclusion of a prestamped return envelope.

Randomized Field Experiments

As might be readily guessed, laboratory experiments, whatever their power for making causal inferences, cannot be used to study many, if not most, of the phenomena that interest political scientists. This is especially true for the study of public policies and programs. Imagine trying to discover whether or not a desegregation plan could ultimately lead to higher average test scores in school districts

TABLE 6–5
Mail Survey Incentive Experiment

(Random Assignment)	Treatment	Response Rate (percentage)
Experimental Group 1	25¢	45.0
Experimental Group 2	50¢	51.0
Experimental Group 3	$1.00	52.0
Experimental Group 4	pen	38.0
Experimental Group 5	key ring	37.0
Control Group	no reward	30.2

Note: Hypothetical data.

across the country. At a minimum you would need to randomly assign the integration schemes—the treatment—to a sample of school districts while using others as controls. That would be possible in theory but impossible in practice. How would you force districts to integrate? If you accept voluntary participation in place of random allocation, the voluntary districts might very well differ from those that won't accept the plan in unknown ways.

Nonetheless, the basic principles of experimental design can be taken into the field. A **field experiment** adopts the logic of randomization and variable manipulation by applying these techniques to naturally occurring situations and units.[13] Samples of individuals or aggregates of people (e.g., students in a city's school districts) are randomly chosen to receive a treatment (e.g., a new mathematics curriculum), while others receive another or are used as controls. Once the experiment has been concluded, the investigator can take posttest measurements to determine if the treatment had an effect. Let's look at an example.

Like others mentioned in this chapter, David Niven speculated about the effects of campaigning on electoral participation. He first noted that

> *various . . . studies inquire about intentions to vote, or candidate preferences, but none is equipped to measure actual [emphasis added] resulting behavior. . . . Regardless of the rigor of the researchers or the ingenious nature of their design, the laboratory remains a difficult setting in which to demonstrate the effect of negative advertising on the real world behavior of turning out to vote.*[14]

As a way around this inferential obstacle, he conducted an experiment on citizens of West Palm Beach, Florida:

> *Voters in the sample were randomly assigned to either the control group (700 voters who would not receive any mailings) or to one of seven experimental groups (which varied in the number of negative mailings each would receive). . . . Subjects receiving the treatment were randomly assigned to one of seven groups which received either one, two, or three negative ads. . . . After the ads were distributed and the election had occurred, official voting records were consulted to determine who cast a ballot in the election.*[15]

Niven found a positive effect: turnout among the residents receiving the negative mailings was a bit higher (32.4%) than among those in the treatment condition (26.6%).[16] Hence, Niven comes down on the side of those who feel negative advertising might have a beneficial impact on voters. (Incidentally, we see again the necessity of replication and verification in empirical political science.[17])

Another, perhaps more common application of randomized field experiments is found in policy evaluation studies. **Policy evaluation** (sometimes called "policy analysis") simply means objectively analyzing the economic, political, cultural, or social impacts of public policies.[18] Targets of these sorts of research projects span policy domains from housing to health care, transportation to education, crime prevention to recycling. (Occasionally governments mandate these efficacy studies to see if the taxpayers' dollars are having a genuine effect.)

A famous field experiment was the New Jersey Income Maintenance study, funded by the Office of Economic Opportunity, which was conducted from 1967 to 1971.[19] This effort was the forerunner of other large-scale social experiments designed to test the effects of new social programs. The experiment also provides insights into the difficulty of testing the effects of public policies on a large scale in a natural setting.

In 1965 Congress considered establishing a "negative income tax," which would provide a minimum, nontaxable allowance to all families and attempt to maintain work incentives by allowing the poor to keep a significant fraction of their earnings. For example, a family of four might be guaranteed an income of $5,000 and be allowed to keep 50 percent of all its earnings up to a break-even point, where it could choose to remain in the program or opt out. Critics of the proposal worried that a guaranteed minimum income would encourage people to reduce their work effort. Others expressed concern about whether families would spend their cash allowances for "beneficial" uses. There were numerous administrative questions as well. Because of these uncertainties, researchers designed the New Jersey income-maintenance experiment to test the consequences of a guaranteed minimum income system on actual recipients in a natural setting.[20]

A main goal was to find out if people who were guaranteed a minimum income would reduce their labor force participation. If so, what minimum level of income discouraged recipients from looking for and accepting jobs? Put differently, the research tested the "work-leisure hypothesis," which asserts that under certain conditions, a guaranteed income will diminish work effort.[21]

Combing survey research (see chapter 10) and the fundamental techniques of laboratory experiments, the investigators obtained a sample of about 1,300 low-income families in New Jersey and Pennsylvania who met various criteria, such as ethnicity and employment status. The families were randomly divided into experimental and control groups. Those in the experimental condition received varying levels of guaranteed income; depending on the treatment condition, any earnings from work above a certain level were subject to different tax rates.[22] Ideally, the researchers would have found a numerical ceiling beyond which people would prefer government assistance to a job.

The initial study seemed to confirm the hypothesis about the trade-off between leisure and work:

For the experimental group as a whole there was a slight reduction in work effort in comparison to the control families. Variations were noted for ethnicity and sex: for white male heads the effect was a small reduction (5–6%) in average hours worked; the unemployment of Spanish-speaking men increased; but black men increased their work effort slightly. A large decrease in labor force participation for wives occurred.[23]

The New Jersey Income Maintenance Experiment eventually turned into a series of evaluation studies in several states conducted over more than a decade. Despite the time and money that went into the studies, problems of administration and interpretation arose. There remained, for instance, the issue of external validity. Treatments must of necessity consist of discrete levels—in the New Jersey study, combinations of guarantee levels and tax rates—applied in specific locations at specific times. Inferring the effects of treatments not represented in the study requires assuming that the samples are representative. Internal validity also has to be carefully assessed. Since the research was carried out in naturalistic settings, it is possible that other factors—demand characteristics, experimental mortality, maturation, test-subject interaction, and so forth—affected the outcome variable (e.g., job seeking and holding) in conjunction with or despite the ostensible experimental factor.

NONRANDOMIZED DESIGNS: QUASI-EXPERIMENTS

Suppose we set up an experiment like the one exploring the effects of negative campaigns ads on intention to vote, but we do *not* randomly assign the students to the experimental and control groups. Instead, we use our judgment or, more likely, preexisting groups—perhaps two sections of Political Science 101. Suppose, for instance, both classes are taught in similar case-study rooms, but in one there is a monitor in front of every student, whereas the second has a single screen at the head of the room. We might decide that the treatment should be applied to the former room because students have monitors right in front of them and we can be sure that each person has a clear field of view. Those in the smaller, less equipped room will be seeing bland commercials and can make do with a single screen. Since we are going to measure intention to vote both before and after the experiment, we reason that under the circumstances, this plan provides a reasonable approximation of a classical experiment.

More realistically perhaps, units get picked for study because they have or are going to undergo some treatment. (Suppose we discovered that the two sections of Political Science 101 were to use different texts and Web materials in such a way that they could serve as rough approximations to our desired experimental and control groups.) Since their selection is totally independent of the investigator, he or she is merely an observer, albeit one who puts the data in a logically coherent form so they resemble experimental results. Consequently, although a quasi-experiment "looks" like a classical experiment, there is one key difference: no randomization. A **quasi-experimental design** contains treatment and control groups, but the experimenter does randomly assigned individual units to these groups. The effects, if any, of putative treatments have to be inferred without the help of strong internal validity. To compensate for the lack of randomization, experimenters turn to judgment, theory, common sense, and statistical and mathematical tools to rule out spurious or confounding causes. Any scientific activity requires some inference, but as one moves from randomized designs to quasi-experiments, inferences about causal effects demand more and more of the researcher's substantive knowledge and analytic skills.

Figure 6–5 applies a quasi-experimental design to our hypothetical experiment on the effects of campaign advertising. (For simplicity, assume all the students are eligible to vote.)

In the current example, we are not adhering to the standard protocol—neither the students nor the treatment have been randomized—so our inferences could well be misleading or wrong. Why? Because we cannot be assured that at the outset the two groups are homogenous (have the same average values on all background variables). Put aside the fact that the experimental settings differ: here, the study would be conducted in dissimilar classrooms taught by possibly different instructors, a setup that violates the assumption that the groups only differ with respect to the stimulus and not with regard to the experimental conditions. Consider instead that the members of the seminar section might on average be older (or younger) or have higher (or lower) GPAs or are more (or less) interested and knowledgeable about campaigns and elections. If we find an ostensible or apparent effect—ads reduce motivation to vote—it might be

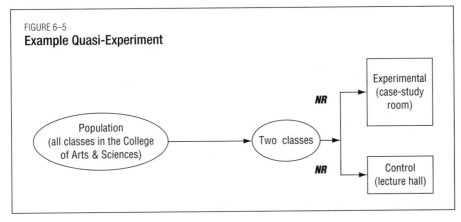

FIGURE 6–5
Example Quasi-Experiment

Note: NR = random assignment to group.

because the ads really do have an effect or because of the operation of some unmeasured or unobserved factor, or both. The problem is that we just don't know. The internal validity of an experiment is suspect.

What is to be done?

Because physically assigning groups or subjects to different treatments by randomization may be difficult or impossible, social scientists turn to observational and statistical methods. These, too, follow a pattern, but their missing ingredient is randomization. This fact makes causal inferences much more tenuous. Although it may be stretching things a bit, we might term any such study a quasi-experiment because the goal is the same—that is, to identify causal relationships—but it does not fulfill a key requirement of experimentation: random assignment of units or treatments.

The logic can be outlined this way:

- Let Y, the dependent "variable," stand for the phenomenon of interest, the *explanandum*, or "that which must be explained."

- Identify X—a "treatment" or independent variable with at least two values or states and possibly many more—that might causally affect Y.

- Look for covariation: Do values of X vary with different outcomes, or different values of Y?

- Observe the dynamics of the interaction: Did changes in X seem to precede changes in Y?

Look for and ensure that all other possible effects on Y have been taken into account. In terms of the trade, this procedure is called "controlling" or "holding constant" variables.

All methods considered in this section fit under this scheme. They look for X-Y relationships. Note that X and Y do not necessarily refer to numbers. Y, for example, might consist of two categories, "war occurred" and "war did not occur," or possibly three states (peace, tension but no armed conflict, armed conflict). But beyond just looking for a relationship, the analyst factors in variables or conditions that might also cause Y. How? By judgment, careful observation, application of previous research, common sense and logic, and—in some cases, where appropriate—by statistical adjustment. Throughout *Political Science Research Methods* we show how some of these techniques or methods actually work.

In our contrived example, we might have access to course rosters and the instructors' records and be able to measure the average class level, gender, major, and so forth. We hope that there would be no appreciable variation between groups on these indicators, thereby increasing our confidence that treatment did indeed have the hypothesized effect (see table 6–6).

TABLE 6–6
Results from Hypothetical Quasi-Experiment

	Before Measurements	Postmeasurements
Experimental (negative ads in case-study room)		
Percentage intending to vote	60	50
Percentage male	45	45
Percentage liberal arts majors	70	70
Percentage undeclared	40	40
Control (bland ads in lecture hall)		
Percentage intending to vote	55	52
Percentage male	50	50
Percentage liberal arts majors	65	65
Percentage undeclared	35	35

We see that at the start, both classes had roughly the same percentages on all the variables we were able to measure explicitly, including "intention to vote" in the next election. After the quasi-experiment, the dependent variable (Y) has decreased 10 points from 60 to 50 percent in the experimental group, while it had changed hardly at all among the control subjects (55 to 52 percent). As expected, the other variable averages have stayed the same. Consequently, we make two tentative conclusions: (1) the treatment (exposure to negative ads) is *associated with* a drop in voting, and (2) this decrease is *not* explained by changes in any other measured variables, which have remained at their same levels. So, for example, the drop in expected turnout in the experimental group is presumably not due to changes in major or gender, which are constant. That leaves among the measured factors only the exposure-nonexposure difference.

Naturally this is not a very compelling example. But it reveals the logic behind most empirical studies in political science, whether or not they are quantitative: they use judgment and explicit measurement and controls to rule out the possibility that the treatment-effect relationship is not spurious. Even if quasi-designs do not meet the standards of randomized experiments, they constantly lead to new knowledge.

NATURAL EXPERIMENTS

If you think about it, you can extend the idea of observing the effects of treatment and variables into the natural world. Suppose, to take a whimsical case, you wanted to study the effect of weather on voter turnout. It would be natural to collect (randomly even) a sample of voting districts. On election day, you would presumably record the final turnout and the temperature and precipitation readings (the values of the treatment). In addition, you could measure other aspects of the districts, such as average turnout over the last, say, five elections. Then, you could plot turnout against precipitation. If you find a relationship, you might be tempted to conclude that "bad weather depresses turnout." To bolster your argument, you would show that the other variables could not explain the association. Of course, someone could always object: "But what about a variable you didn't measure? What if it is causing the precipitation-turnout connection?" Here is where knowledge of the field comes in.[24] In any case, the experimental manipulation (rainfall) occurs naturally, and the investigator can only record the results.

In a more realistic example, professor of geography Jared Diamond employed a "natural experiment of borders" to explain why two countries sharing the same island and thus having roughly similar physical environments have drastically different standards of living. Diamond compared Haiti and Dominican Republic, which occupy the island of Hispaniola (see table 6–7). In essence, he treated the more or less artificial and arbitrary border between the countries as a kind of ongoing experimental treatment.[25] As Diamond explained, this kind of analysis

> examines the effects of drawing a border where previously there was none . . . or the effect of removing a border where previously there was one. . . . These comparisons can shed light on the effects of differing institutions and histories. They reduce the effects of other variables, either by comparison of the same geographic area before and after the creation or removal of the border, or by simultaneous comparison of two neighboring and geographically similar areas.[26]

Until the early twentieth century, Haiti was a far more populous and richer than its neighbor (but poor nonetheless). Then their fortunes reversed: Haiti remains one of the world's poorest countries, while its neighbor to the east has experienced a growing economy. The data in table 6–7 point to a few of the differences. Why the turnabout in status? Diamond cited several possible causative factors:

TABLE 6–7
Haiti and Dominican Republic Compared

Indicators of Well-being	Dominican Republic	Haiti
Life expectancy at birth (years)	72.4	61.0
Adult literacy rate (% ages 15 and above)	89.10	62.10
GDP per capita (USD)	6,706	1,155
Probability of not surviving to age 40 (%)	9.40	18.50

Source: Jared Diamond, "Intra-Island and Inter-Island Comparisons," in *Natural Experiments of History,* ed. Jared Diamond and James A. Robinson (Cambridge, Mass.: Belknap Press of Harvard University Press, 2010): 120–41.

- Precipitation and agriculture: The Dominican Republic receives most of the seasonal rainfall and hence has an agricultural advantage. Also, decades of deforestation in Haiti with attendant soil erosion eventually gave this country a disadvantage.[27]

- History: The colonial histories of the two countries differed in ways that helped produce the situation we see today. The French colonized the western (Haitian) part of the island, where they established a thriving timber and sugar export economy based on slave labor. The slaves won their freedom in the world's first and only successful slave revolt. But this success had unintended consequences. After violently driving the French out and killing most of the remaining white settlers in 1803, Haitians were suspicious of Europeans and became increasingly isolated. The Dominican Republic, by contrast, followed a more or less peaceful path to independence and early on established commercial relations with other countries. This experience led to a more open society that was not as adverse to innovation and outside ideas as its neighbor.

- Language: Dominicans adopted the language of the colonial power, Spanish. But as Diamond noted, "Haitian slaves, who came from many different African-language groups, developed for communication a Creole language of their own. . . . Today, about 90% of Haiti's population still speaks only Haitian Creole (a language spoken by virtually no one else in the world except emigrant Haitians). . . . [Consequently,] Haitians are linguistically isolated from the rest of the world."[28]

- Political leadership: The two nations entered the modern age under two vastly different political leadership styles. By the 1930s, both were governed by tyrannical dictatorships. The Dominican Republic's General Rafael Trujillo, who ruled from 1930 to 1961, governed with an iron fist but (mostly for personal aggrandizement) developed export industries, attracted foreign investment, preserved forests, and encouraged immigration. Consequently, the economy grew under the "evil" Trujillo and his successors to the point where it could sustain a middle class and nascent democratic institutions. The story in Haiti, though, turned out much differently. The secretive François ("Papa Doc") Duvalier, Haiti's ruler from 1957 to 1971, "had little interest in economic development, export industries, or logging . . . did not bring in foreign consultants, and allowed deforestation to continue."[29] Under his and his son's leadership, the country began to lag further and further behind the Dominican Republic.

In the language of experimentation, Haiti was "exposed" to one set of levels of the "treatments" (the Xs or explanatory factors); the Dominican Republic to

TABLE 6–8
Natural Experiment "Results"

	Environmental Variables		Cultural and Political Variables			Outcome
	Favorable climate (e.g., rainfall)	Fertile soil	History of slavery	"Universal" language	Leadership	"Successful" development
Dominican Republic	Yes	Yes	No	Yes	Yes	Yes
Haiti	No	No	Yes	No	No	No

Source: Based on Jared Diamond, "Intra-Island and Inter-Island Comparisons," in *Natural Experiments of History,* ed. Jared Diamond and James A. Robinson (Cambridge, Mass.: Belknap Press of Harvard University Press, 2010): 120–41.

another set. The "response" variable is, loosely, economic and political development (*Y*). *Successful* in this case means being higher on just about every imaginable indicator of well-being from freedom to food to health to democracy to life expectancy to political stability. Diamond hypothesized that the *X*s caused Y. Although the study did not explicitly present a formal analysis, the results can be represented schematically in a table (see table 6–8.) We have described the research as being a quasi- or natural experiment; the logic is actually the same as that of many comparative studies, a point we demonstrate shortly. [30]

INTERVENTION ANALYSIS

In one version of a nonexperimental time series design, called **intervention analysis** or "interrupted time series analysis," measurements of a dependent variable are taken both before and after the "introduction" of an independent variable. Here we speak figuratively: as with the other nonrandomized designs, the occurrence of the independent variable is *observed,* not literally introduced or administered. We could observe, for instance, the annual poverty rate both before and after the ascension of a leftist party to see if regime change makes any difference on living standards. The premeasurements allow a researcher to establish trends in the dependent variable that are presumably unaffected by the independent variable so that appropriate conclusions can be drawn about post-treatment measures. Refer to figure 6–6. Panel (a) shows an increase in a dependent variable over time. (Suppose it is the poverty rate in metropolitan areas.) At a specific moment or period, an intervention takes place (perhaps the enactment of a jobs-training program). But the trend line remains undisturbed: *Y* grows at the same rate before and after the "appearance" of the independent variable. In this case, the intervention did not interrupt or alter the trend. (We would conclude, for example, that the program did not affect the increase in poverty.) Now consider the second figure (b). It shows an increase in Y until the intervention occurs, at which point the growth in the trend begins to abate. In this instance, the introduction of the factor appears to have caused the trend to flatten (e.g., the advent of job training slowed the growth in poverty).

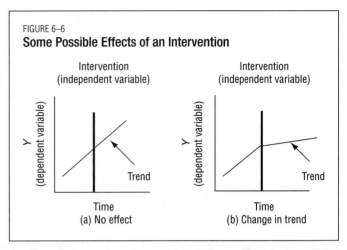

FIGURE 6–6
Some Possible Effects of an Intervention

For a perhaps more realistic example, let us return briefly to the case Hacker and Pierson made about the growth of business power and income inequality in the United States (see chapter 1).[31] Recall that the authors first documented an increase in the share of America's wealth going to the wealthiest individuals. Figure 6–7 shows, for instance, that the richest 5 percent of citizens received about 16.5 percent of aggregate income in 1967; that portion had grown to nearly 23 percent by 2009. Hacker and Pierson claimed that this phenomenon—the rich getting richer, leaving less for the middle and lower classes—does not result from mere economic change or happenstance but follows as a direct result of policy changes (e.g., tax rates and financial deregulation). They explained that

> Policy—both what government has done and what, as a result of
> drift, it has failed to do—has played an absolutely central role in the
> rise of winner-take-all economic outcomes. . . . Moreover, in the main
> areas where the role of government appears most significant, we see a
> consistent pattern: active, persistent, and consequential action on the
> part of organized interests that stood to gain from a transformation of
> government's role in the American economy. A winner-take-all poli-
> tics accompanied, and helped produce a winner-take-all economy.[32]

Hacker and Pierson dated the transformation from the mid-1980s, when the so-called conservative or Reagan "revolution" began. Policy shifts advantageous to the wealthy, however, have been sustained with the help of Democrats in the White House and Congress.[33] It is a stretch, but we could analyze the argument with an intervention analysis. Figure 6–7 shows the share of aggregate income going to the richest 5 percent of Americans each year from 1967 to 2009. (These data are called a "time series.") We see that this share remained at about 16 to 20 percent through the early part of the 1970s. Beginning in the late 1970s and accelerating when Ronald Reagan took office in 1980, the federal government began to cut taxes and roll back regulations of the finance industry. We might

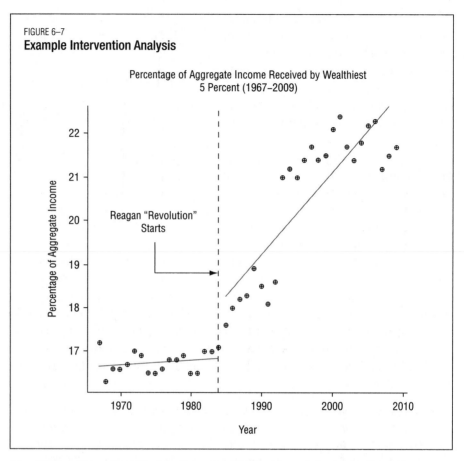

FIGURE 6–7
Example Intervention Analysis

Percentage of Aggregate Income Received by Wealthiest
5 Percent (1967–2009)

Source: US Census Bureau, *Current Population Survey: Annual Social and Economic Supplements; Historical Income Tables—Income Inequality,* table H-2: "Share of Aggregate Income Received by Each Fifth and Top 5 Percent of Households (All Races) 1967 to 2009. Available at http://www.census.gov/hhes/www/income/data/historical/inequality/index.html.

conceptualize this change as a policy "intervention." We see its "effects" in the jump in income going to the top group after about 1984, when Reagan was reelected to a second term; after climbing to above 20 percent, it has since stabilized. The straight lines—technically called "regression" lines—show that changes were relatively modest from 1967 to 1984 and then soared. There is, in statistical language, a shift in both the level (average) and slope (trend) in the series of income shares.

This analysis is, of course, vastly oversimplified. But it illustrates the quasi-experimental design and its pitfalls. We can imagine an omnipotent experimenter manipulating the policy regime to see what impact the change would have on incomes. The data from Hacker and Pierson's study suggest that increasing concentration of wealth had a cause, namely, the tax and other conservative policies pushed by the corporate and financial sectors. But notice our use of the weasel word *suggest*. The conclusion rests on an inference that no other factors were at work to produce the observed changes. Since no one randomized the years to control and experimental groups, we have no assurance that other unmeasured variables were at work. And Hacker and Pierson's critics argue that many other factors were surely in play. Yet, as we stress throughout the book, it is incumbent on the skeptics to identify those alternative causes and show how they, not growing business power, account for the results.

In closing this example, we point out that a "real" intervention analysis involves the application of statistical techniques to, among other things, ensure that the observed shifts in level and trend are not merely the result of chance fluctuations in the time series. A more realistic study would require measuring other variables and adjusting the data to remove the effects of random error.[34]

Before showing further designs, let us review what we have discussed regarding experimental designs. Table 6–9 compares the essential features of randomized and quasi-experiments. Randomized laboratory and field experiments enjoy a modest (and growing) place in political science's tool kit, most research relies on extensions of the quasi-experimental design. Besides logistical considerations, these approaches can lead to somewhat higher levels of external validity (realism). Still, as we have seen, *all* social and political research depends heavily on untested (sometimes unrecognized) assumptions and inferences.

TABLE 6–9
Randomized and Quasi-Experiments Compared

	Design Type	
	Classical Randomized Experiments	Quasi-Experiments
Assignment of subjects to treatment and control groups	Random	Nonrandom (judgment, self-selection, natural processes, history)
Treatment	Experimentally manipulated directly or by power of random assignment	Observation of occurrence, distribution, duration
Time order	Controlled by investigator	Inferred by investigator
Effects	Can potentially be classified as causal	Difficult to classify as causal without extra-experimental data
Internal validity*	High	Medium to low
External validity*	Low	Medium
Example designs	Randomized before-and-after design	Natural experiment
	Multiple-group design	Comparison
	Field experiment	Intervention analysis
	Policy evaluation study	Observational study (see table 6–10)

*For most designs.

OBSERVATIONAL STUDIES

One could reasonably apply the term **observational study** to describe quasi-experimental designs in which the researcher does not manipulate experimental variables or randomly assign subjects to treatments but instead merely *observes* causal sequences and covariations. A simple comparison, for example, could be recast as a thought experiment in which the effect of a supposed treatment is examined for two or more groups. Think of "political party system" (one party, two parties, and three parties) as an experimental factor whose effects on voting turnout are of interest. (The basic hypothesis might be that turnout as a percentage of eligible voters increases as a nation moves from a one-party structure to one having two or more competitive parties.) We cannot assign a country to a party-system type, but we can compare (observe) turnout in different party systems to determine if there is at least an association between treatment and effect. Using historical and socioeconomic data, we might conclude that aside from the treatment, the countries in our sample have approximately similar values on all our measured variables. Hence, if there are differences in turnout (in the predicted direction), we might infer that they are caused by type of party system. Critics, in turn, might object that we have not included all relevant historical and political factors, that the countries differ in fundamental ways other than the type of electoral system, and it is these unobserved, unmeasured variables that create the differences in turnout. (Of course, it is incumbent on the critic to specify these missing variables.) This is the sort of comparative analysis that students of political science are used to. Note, however, the underlying logic and how it differs from that of randomized studies.

We provide an overview of some the possibilities in table 6–10. When reading the table, it is important to note that many of the entries are only indicative of what can be done. Look, for example, at the row labeled "Surveys." A survey or poll can include anywhere from 100 to 5,000 (or more!) individuals, but polling fewer than 100 people is possible and not necessarily unsound. Furthermore, many research projects combine elements of different designs, as in a panel study with an intervention interpretation (see the following discussion). In the sections that follow, we discuss these designs in more detail.

Whatever the design, the purpose is always to collect information or data in order to test hypotheses, look for relationships among variables, and where possible make causal inferences. To compensate for the inferential shortcomings of the nonexperimental designs (especially the lack of random assignment), it is frequently necessary to achieve a rough approximation of randomization by statistical means. For instance, as demonstrated in later chapters, especially chapter 13, surveys can gather quantitative and qualitative data, which can then be mathematically manipulated to control for the effects of one or more extraneous variables while seeing how the main independent variable influences the dependent

TABLE 6–10
Some Observational and Statistical Designs

Design	Typical number of units or cases (N) *	Examples of units of analysis	Purpose	Examples
		Small-N Designs		
Single case (case study)	N = 1	Event, nation, group, county, individual . . .†	Provide a detailed explanation.	Study of French Revolution; study of House Ways and Means Committee, analytic biography
Comparative▼	2–20	Events, nations, groups, counties, individuals . . .	Compare two or several units in relative detail.	Comparison of French and Russian Revolutions; study of five Latin American countries; in-depth interviews with selected members of the British parliament
Focus group	10–20	Individuals	Often used in market research to probe reactions to stimuli such as commercials.	Test of campaign ad's effectiveness
		Cross-Sectional Designs		
Surveys (polls)▼	100–5,000	Individuals	A large number of people are measured on several variables to search for (possibly causal) relationships.	Study of voting and public opinion; awareness of campaign commercials
Aggregate data analysis▼	20–500	Aggregates:@ states, counties, cities, countries . . .	Variables are often averages or percents of geographical areas, but the goal is to search for (possibly causal) relationships.	Study of the death penalty and crime rates in different states; study of the relationship between union strength and welfare spending in developed countries
		Longitudinal (Time-Series) Designs		
Trend analysis▼	20–300	Aggregates, individuals, cohorts+, . . .	Measurements on same variables at different time periods to examine changes in levels.	Study of changing levels of trust in government; level of unemployment; and occurrence of civil strife in Europe, 1900–2000
Panel study▼	200–5,000	Individuals, households, cohorts	The same units are measured at different times to investigate relationships, changes in strength of relationships, and causality.	Study of changes in opinions toward prime minister of England

Notes:

▼May rely heavily on statistical analysis.

*These numbers are merely suggestive; some designs involve fewer or more cases.

@Data are usually summations or averages of aggregations of individuals (often in geographical areas), such as by median income in cities or counties.

+Individuals who experience the same event or experience or characteristics, such as a "birth cohort" (those people born in a specific year or period) or "event cohort" (e.g., those who first voted in 1972).

variable. A few of these designs are described here and in subsequent chapters. In reviewing them, we compare their features to the characteristics of ideal experiments mentioned earlier.

Small-*N* Designs

CASE STUDIES AND COMPARATIVE ANALYSIS.   In a **small-*N* design**, the researcher examines one or a few cases of a phenomenon in considerable detail, typically using several data collection methods, such as personal interviews, document analysis, and observation. When just one thing is under investigation, the design is often called a **case study design**; when two or more are involved, the term *comparative* or *comparative case study or analysis* is frequently used. The units of analysis or the subjects of the study can be people (e.g., prime ministers), events (e.g., outbreak of the Korean war), institutions (e.g., the US Senate), nations or alliances (e.g., NATO), decisions (e.g., the decision to invade Iraq), or policies (e.g., Clean Air Act). The point is that one or a few cases or instances are studied in depth. As the sociologist Theda Skocpol explained, these type of designs involve "too many variables and not enough cases,"[35] meaning that the investigator collects lots of data on one or a few units.

A small-*N* study may be used for exploratory, descriptive, or explanatory purposes. Exploratory case studies are sometimes conducted when little is known about a phenomenon. Researchers initially may observe only one or a few cases of that phenomenon, and careful observation of this small set of cases may suggest possible general explanations for the behavior or attributes that are observed. These explanations—in the form of hypotheses—can then be tested more systematically by observing more cases (see figure 6–8.) Carefully scrutinizing the origins of political unrest within a single country may suggest general explanations for dissent, or following a handful of incumbent representatives when they return to their districts may suggest hypotheses relating incumbent attributes, district settings, and incumbent-constituency relations.[36]

The purpose of a descriptive study may be to discover and describe what happened in a single or select few situations, thereby finding avenues for further research. Here, the emphasis is not on developing general explanations for what happened. Alternatively, in some situations a single case may provide a critical test of a theory.[37] Recall from chapter 2 that verification and falsification are crucial activities in science, so finding a single exception may cast doubt on a previously accepted proposition. Therefore, if you can find a well-documented instance in which a widely accepted or important proposition does not hold, you may make a significant contribution.

Finally, according to Robert K. Yin, case studies are most appropriately used to answer "how" or "why" questions.[38] These questions direct our attention toward *explaining* events. The strongest case studies start out with clearly identified theories that are expected to explain the events.

For years some scholars considered this approach a suspect or even inferior research strategy, partly because of its limited "sample sizes." Moreover, it might be thought that small-*N* designs are useless in causal analysis. But social scientists now recognize this type of design as a "distinctive form of empirical inquiry" and an important design for the development and evaluation of public policies as well as for developing explanations and testing theories of political phenomena.[39] Figure 6–8 illustrates some of these ideas.

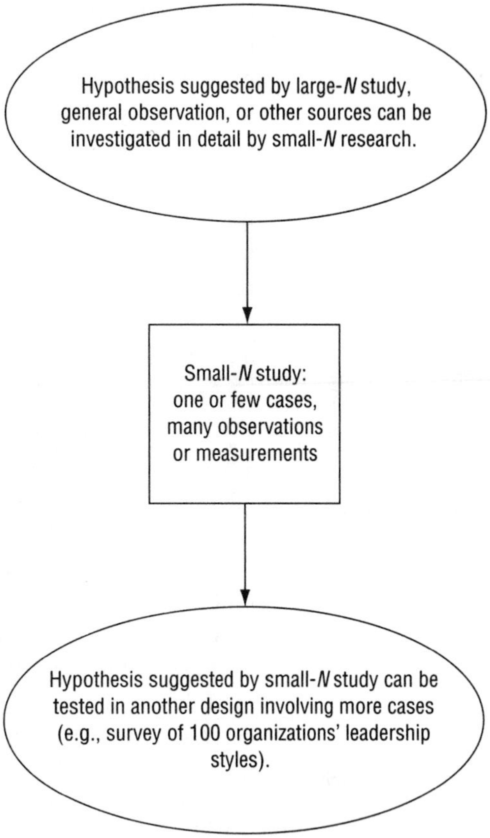

Proponents argue that a small-*N* design has some distinct advantages over experimental and cross-sectional designs for testing hypotheses under certain conditions. For example, a case study may be useful in assessing whether a statistical correlation between independent and dependent variables, discovered using a cross-sectional design with survey data (see the following discussion), is really causal.[40] By choosing a case in which the appropriate values of the independent and dependent variables are present, researchers can try to determine the timing of the introduction of the independent variable and how the independent variable actually caused the dependent variable. That is, they can learn whether there is an actual link between the variables and, therefore, can more likely offer an explanation for the statistical association. Benjamin Page and Robert Shapiro concluded their study of the statistical relationship between public opinion and public policy with numerous case studies.[41]

FIGURE 6–8
Small-*N* Designs and Hypothesis Investigation

Hypothesis suggested by large-*N* study, general observation, or other sources can be investigated in detail by small-*N* research.

Small-*N* study: one or few cases, many observations or measurements

Hypothesis suggested by small-*N* study can be tested in another design involving more cases (e.g., survey of 100 organizations' leadership styles).

These studies differ from experimental designs in that the researcher is able neither to assign subjects or cases to experimental and control groups nor to manipulate the independent variable. Furthermore, the researcher does not control the context or environment as in a laboratory experiment. Yet the careful selection of a case or cases can lead to the approximation of a quasi-experimental situation. For example, a historian or political scientist may choose cases with different values of an independent variable but with the same values for important control variables. Cases with similar environments can be chosen. Furthermore, lack of complete control over the environment or context of a phenomenon can be seen as useful. If it can be shown that a theory actually works and is applicable in a real situation, then the theory may more readily be accepted. This may be especially important, for example, in testing theories underlying public policies and public programs.

COMPARATIVE STUDY.   This kind of research may involve more than one case; such studies are often called *comparative case studies.* A comparative or multiple-case study is more likely to have explanatory power than a single case study because it provides the opportunity for replication; that is, it enables a researcher to test a single theory more than once. For some cases, similar results will be predicted; for others, different results will be predicted.[42] Multiple cases should not be thought of as a "sample," because cases are not chosen using a statistical procedure to form a "representative" sample from which the frequency of a particular phenomenon will be calculated and inferences about a larger population drawn. Rather, cases are chosen for the presence or absence of factors that a political theory has indicated are important.

As an example of the logic and layout of a comparative study and its potential utility in causal analysis, suppose a political scientist wanted to know why socialism never emerged as a major political force in the United States, especially compared to European nations like Great Britain, a situation that has intrigued innumerable scholars for the past one hundred years.[43] The most commonly cited "causes" of the failure of socialism to take root in America include, among others, "its relatively high levels of social equalitarianism, [enormous] economic productivity, and social mobility (particularly into elite strata), alongside the strength of religion, the weakness of the central state, the earlier timing of electoral democracy, ethnic and racial diversity, and . . . the absence of fixed social classes."[44] Imagine the researcher trying to sort out these possibilities by comparing France and the United States.

One strategy is to apply the *method of difference* as introduced by the English philosopher John Stuart Mill: "If an instance in which the phenomenon under investigation occurs, and an instance in which it does not occur, have every circumstance in common save one, that one occurring only in the former: the circumstance in which alone the two instances differ, is the effect, or cause, or a necessary part of the cause, of the phenomenon."[45] For example, our investigator would first identify a country in which the condition (socialism) is present in and one which it is not, and he or she would then look for similarities and differences in these antecedents. As the hypothetical data in table 6–11 suggest, it might be the case that in the nineteenth century, the United States and France shared similar experiences such as extensive industrialization and urbanization and that in both countries citizens spoke common languages (French and English), but they *differed* in that the French had a fixed and rigid social class system (including a landed aristocracy) whereas America did not. Since the two countries have parallel backgrounds except for their class structures, we may infer that this difference rather than the other factors explains why socialism has not had much influence on American politics.

TABLE 6–11
Mill's Method of Difference

Case (country)	Socialist movements?	Condition or Effect Antecedent 1 (industrialized)	Antecedent 2 (urbanized)	Antecedent 3 (common language)	Antecedent 4 (historically strong and fixed social classes)
United States	yes	yes	yes	yes	no
France	no	yes	yes	yes	yes

Needless to say, this comparison is woefully inadequate and simplistic. In fact, no real analysis would take exactly this form. Instead, the table is a "reconstruction" (see chapter 2) of the logic of comparison using this method. (Mill, by the way, introduced several other comparative methods, but knowing them is not essential for understanding gist of comparative analysis.[46]) If you were to attempt research of this sort, you have to consider many more factors and make difficult decisions about when an antecedent is or is not present. But the method of difference and similar designs underlies a great deal of political research.[47] By the way, note that one can interpret this approach as a natural experiment.

Despite case studies' potential to make important contributions to our understanding of political phenomena, there are some concerns about the knowledge they generate.[48] One potential problem is the "lack of rigor" in presenting evidence and the possibility for bias in using it. Typically, researchers sift through enormous quantities of detailed information about their cases. But how does one know all the important possible antecedents have been identified? Has something significant been omitted? Or the researcher may be the only one to have recorded certain behavior or phenomena. Still, the potential for bias of this sort is not limited to case studies.

Another frequently raised criticism of case studies is the problem of generalization. One response to this criticism is to use multiple case studies. In fact, as Yin pointed out, the same criticism can be leveled against a single experiment: scientific knowledge is usually based on multiple experiments rather than on a single experiment.[49] Yet people do not say that performing a single experiment is not worthwhile. Furthermore, Yin stated that

> *Case studies, like experiments, are generalizable to theoretical propositions and not to populations or universes. In this sense, the case study, like the experiment, does not represent a "sample," and the investigator's goal is to expand and generalize theories (analytic generalization) and not to enumerate frequencies (statistical generalization).*[50]

A third potential drawback of case studies is that they may require long and arduous efforts to describe and report the results owing to the need to present adequate documentation. (Think about the complexity of untangling the differences between French and American societies.) This criticism may stem from confusing the case study with particular methods of data collection, such as participant observation (discussed in chapter 8), which often requires a long period of data collection.[51] But, case studies should not be ruled out as an appropriate research design due to this historic association.

Finally, in spite of the enthusiasm for case studies, considerable debate remains about just how strong causal inferences can be in these designs. Consider table 6–9 again.[52] If our hypothetical study had discovered that France and the United States had the same values on *all* the independent variables, we would conclude that none of the hypotheses in this instance holds. And, as we stressed in chapter 2, that might be an important conclusion, given that falsification of propositions is one of the goals of science. But instead the conclusion seems to be that having a deep-seated social class system is at least a necessary condition for the emergence of socialism. Yet the result is hardly definitive. If, for example, the "real" cause of the dependent variable is not identified and explicitly included in the analysis, this design cannot detect it. Or it is plausible that the nonexplanatory variables (e.g., industrialization, common language) "interact" or have a simultaneous joint effect on the dependent variable. In a design of the sort illustrated in table 6–9, it is impossible to know.[53] Furthermore, this argument assumes causation is deterministic: once *X* appears, *Y always* follows. Yet, many, if not most scholars regard probabilistic causation—if *X* appears, then *Y probably* follows—as a more realistic description of the way the world works. Is it possible that deep socioeconomic cleavages do not always produce socialist movements? The method of difference provides no foolproof answer.[54]

Still, in many circumstances the case study design can be an informative and appropriate research design. The design permits a deeper understanding of causal processes, the explication of general explanatory theory, and the development of hypotheses regarding difficult-to-observe phenomena. Much of our understanding of politics and political processes comes from case studies of individual presidents, senators, representatives, mayors, judges, statutes, campaigns, treaties, policy initiatives, and wars. The case study design should be viewed as complementary to, rather than inconsistent with, other experimental and nonexperimental designs.

Focus Group.   A focus group consists of a small number of individuals (about twenty, say) who meet in a single location and discuss with a leader a topic or research stimulus such as a proposed campaign brochure. A focus group can superficially resemble an experiment, but no effort is usually made to assign participants randomly to treatment and control groups or to systematically introduce an experimental variation. The deliberations may or may not be (surreptitiously) recorded or observed by others on the research team. This approach lends itself nicely to market research but for the reasons just mentioned is seldom used to make causal inferences.

Focus groups have become somewhat controversial in politics because, critics assert, the results often encourage candidates, groups, and parties to take "safe" or noncontroversial positions on issues. Some seemingly daring policy proposals, for example, have been thoroughly researched in focus groups to ease the minds of political consultants that their candidates stood very little risk by adopting them. Yet, these small-group discussions can be used to create hypotheses that can then be tested in larger surveys. Suppose you want to conduct a poll on your campus about physician-assisted suicide. You might begin with a focus-group discussion to see generally what students think about the issue. The verbal reports might then assist you in developing some specific items to place in a questionnaire.

Cross-Sectional Designs: Surveys and Aggregate Analysis

Perhaps the most common nonexperimental research design is cross-sectional analysis. In a **cross-sectional design**, measurements of the independent and dependent variables are taken at approximately the same time,[55] and the researcher does not control or manipulate the independent variable, the assignment of subjects to treatment or control groups, or the conditions under which the independent variable is experienced. If the units of analysis are individuals, the study is often called a *survey* or poll; if the subjects are geographical entities, such as states or nations or other groupings of units, the term *aggregate analysis* is frequently applied. In either situation, the units are simply measured or observed and the data recorded. In surveys, the respondents themselves report their exposure to various factors. In aggregate analysis, the investigator only observes which units have what values on the variables. The measurements are used to construct, with the help of statistical methods, posttreatment quasi-experimental and quasi-control groups that have naturally occurred, and the measurements of the dependent variable are used to assess the differences between these groups. Data analysis, rather than physical manipulation of variables, is the basis for making causal inferences.

Although this approach makes it far more difficult to measure the causal effects that can be attributed to the presence or introduction of independent variables (treatments), it has the virtues of allowing observation of phenomena in more natural, realistic settings; increasing the size and representativeness of the populations studied; and allowing the testing of hypotheses that do not lend themselves easily to experimental treatment. In short, cross-sectional designs improve external validity at the expense of internal validity.

The example presented at the beginning of the chapter illustrates a particularly simple cross-sectional study. Recall that we tried to assess the effects of negative campaigning on the likelihood of voting by interviewing (that is, surveying) a sample of citizens and then dividing the respondents into different categories according to *their* answers to questions of this sort: "Did you happen to see or read any campaign ads? How many? How many seemed to attack the opponent?" We could then sort respondents by their self-reported level of exposure to negativity. Notice that since there is no random assignment, only self-reports, we do not control who is in each group by forcing people to view differing levels of negative advertising. The groups are simply observed. (Figure 6–9 shows a "reconstructed" layout.) If the groups differed by their rate of voting, we would have a relationship but would not demonstrate cause and effect. Suppose, for instance, we find that M_1 (the percentage of those who viewed six or more negative ads who also reported voting) is less than M_2, which in turn is less than M_3.

Because of our research design and our inability to ensure that those with less and those with more exposure were alike in every other way, we could not necessarily conclude that campaign tone determines the propensity to vote. And note that this is true no matter how large our sample is. With a survey design, then, we typically have to employ data analysis techniques to control for potential confounders that may affect both the independent and dependent variables. If we wanted to control for these factors, we would have to include appropriate questions in the survey and then use statistics to hold them constant. Suppose we thought that education independently affected the propensities to watch a lot of television and to not vote. In a survey, we include a question about the level of the respondents' schooling, as indicated in figure 6–10. Here we have formed six, nonrandomized groups and can compare their participation rates, *M*, as before. Presumably if education is creating the (spurious) relationship between voting and viewing habits, the *M*s would all be about the same except for sampling and measurement error. If, however, advertising does affect motivations even after controlling for education, the average measurements in the groups would vary (e.g., under the hypothesis being considered, M_1 and M_2 would be less than, say, M_3 and M_4).

FIGURE 6–9
Logic of Survey Design

		NR$_1$: More than 6 ads	M_1
Questionnaire: "Did you see any negative commercials? How many?"	Assignment based on responses →	NR$_2$: 1 to 6 ads	M_2
		NR$_3$: None	M_3

NR$_i$ = nonrandomized group based on questionnaire responses; that is, quasi-treatment and control groups; M_i = measurement on dependent variable: percentage of group who report voting.

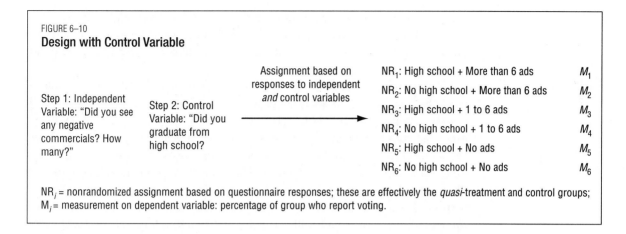

FIGURE 6–10
Design with Control Variable

Step 1: Independent Variable: "Did you see any negative commercials? How many?"

Step 2: Control Variable: "Did you graduate from high school?

Assignment based on responses to independent *and* control variables

NR_1: High school + More than 6 ads M_1
NR_2: No high school + More than 6 ads M_2
NR_3: High school + 1 to 6 ads M_3
NR_4: No high school + 1 to 6 ads M_4
NR_5: High school + No ads M_5
NR_6: No high school + No ads M_6

NR_i = nonrandomized assignment based on questionnaire responses; these are effectively the *quasi*-treatment and control groups; M_i = measurement on dependent variable: percentage of group who report voting.

Incidentally, it might be possible to analyze this same problem with cross-section aggregate data, but we would still confront the same difficulties. For example, we might treat "campaigns for House of Representatives" as the unit of analysis. Then for each campaign in our survey, we would try to determine (a) the proportion of radio, print, and television ads that attack the opposition (presumably we would have a objective standard for judging advertisements negative, positive, or neutral) and (b) the percent of the electorate in each district that actually cast a ballot. We might find that where campaigns employed a lot of negative advertising (more than 50 percent, say), turnout was substantially lower than in those races involving less negativity. Again, there would be an association—the more negative the campaign, the lower the participation. But, and this is the essential point, we would be unable to infer causality. It is possible, after all, that the "negative" House races also or coincidentally took place in regions where turnout is generally low because of historical and economic factors, whereas the "clean" elections occurred where levels of participation are generally higher. Of course, we could control for past turnout, but that would not eliminate the possibility that some other, unmeasured variable is creating a spurious relationship between campaign tone and voting.

In essence, the limitations of the cross-sectional design—that is, lack of control over exposure to the independent variable and inability to form pure experimental and control groups—force us to rely on data analysis techniques to isolate the impact of the independent variables of interest. This process requires researchers to make their comparison groups equivalent by holding relevant extraneous factors constant and then observing the relationship between independent and dependent variables, a procedure described more fully in chapter 13. Yet holding these factors constant is problematic, since it is very difficult to be sure that all relevant variables have been explicitly identified and measured. It is important to stress that if a causal variable is not recognized and brought into the analysis, its effects are nonetheless still operative, even though we may not be aware of them.

Let's wrap up this section by recalling from chapter 4 the inferential problems raised by aggregate data analysis; to wit, conclusions based on aggregates may or may not apply to individuals. Using data from the 1950s on counties in the American south as the unit of analysis, two political Scientists, Donald Matthews and James Prothro, found that the level of voting registration of African Americans was *negatively* correlated with median years of schooling among whites.[56] That is, the higher the level of whites' education in a county, the lower the proportion of blacks who were registered. The data, however, pertain to counties. And, as the authors knew full well, it can be misleading, even fallacious, to extrapolate to the behavior of individuals from information gathered on aggregations. In chapter 4, we called this type of inference an "ecological fallacy." Aggregate data analysis can be extremely helpful for the study of many social and political topics, but it is always necessary to keep in mind the nature of the units of analysis to which conclusions apply. If you have measured, say, counties, your conclusion will, strictly speaking, apply to them and not individuals or other kinds of units.

LONGITUDINAL (TIME SERIES) DESIGNS

Longitudinal or **time series designs** are characterized by the availability of measures of variables at different points in time. As with the other designs, the researcher does not control the introduction of the independent variable(s) and must rely on data collected by others to measure the dependent variable rather than personally conducting the measurements. On the other hand, time series designs have two distinct advantages: (1) change in the level of variables or conditions can be measured and modeled, and (2) it is sometimes easier to decide time order or which comes first, *X* or *Y*.

Additional benefits of longitudinal studies include the fact that they can in principle estimate three kinds of effects: age, period (history), and cohort. Age effects can be considered a direct measure of (chronological) time and be assessed like other variables. As in cross-sectional work, an investigator may be interested in the effect of age on political predispositions or ideology. (It is commonly asserted that as people age, they become more politically conservative.) But in addition, in longitudinal analysis a period (interval of time) may be thought of as an indicator of history during a period, and the consequences on individuals are **period effects.** It is the "history" that occurs during the period, not chronological age, that matters. During the late 1960s and early 1970s, for example, events such as Watergate and the Vietnam War adversely affected many citizens' (young and old alike) trust in government, whether they were young or old. When that era passed, its effects on newer generations dissipated. So those who lived through those stormy times might have much different beliefs and opinions than do younger people.

Another way of interpreting period effects is to consider cohorts. A **cohort** is defined as a group of people who all experience a significant event in roughly the same time. A birth cohort, for instance, consists those born in a given year or period; an "event" cohort is those who shared a common experience, such as their first entry into the labor force at a particular time. It is often hypothesized that individuals in one cohort will, because of their shared background, behave differently than individuals in a different cohort. To take one example, people born in the years immediately after World War II (the baby boomers) may have different political attitudes and affiliations than those who were born in the 1980s. Note that cohort, period, and age effects are inescapably related because "cohort (year of birth) = period (year of event) + age (years since birth)."[57] There are, in short, a number of ways of understanding longitudinal research; the choice depends on the analyst's interests.

TREND ANALYSIS   Former Congressman Lee Hamilton noted, "There's a funny thing going on in our national politics right now: Everyone deplores polarization, but it just keeps getting worse."[58]

Indeed, a quick survey of the political landscape *seems* to indicate a deep and growing divide between conservatives and liberals and between Republicans and Democrats. Its existence is conventional wisdom. Surprisingly, perhaps, some academic research finds that claims of a wide and widening chasm between Americans may be overdrawn.[59] To know if Americans are becoming more polarized—more sharply divided between strong liberals and strong conservatives with relatively few in the middle—we must answer three questions:

1. Exactly who is polarized?

2. What does *polarized* mean?

3. Has the division been growing?

We can answer the first two questions quickly. Political scientists distinguish between polarization among elites and among the general public. There is evidence that among leaders in Washington, D.C., especially, the two parties have become more partisan and the ideological divide between then is as broad as it has ever been. But the same may not be true for average citizens. How do we measure the distance between the ideological groups? Again political scientists turn to questionnaires and survey data. The General Social Survey, a collaborative research project housed at the National Opinion Research Center (NORC) at the University of Chicago, has been conducting national surveys on a yearly basis for more than two decades. Many of the questionnaires across the years contained this question:

> *We hear a lot of talk these days about liberals and conservatives. I'm going to show you a seven-point scale on which the political views that people might hold are arranged from extremely liberal—point 1—to extremely conservative—point 7. Where would you place your-self on this scale?*[60]

For purposes of our study, we categorized respondents into four categories: strong liberal, liberal, moderate (including "slightly" liberal and "slightly" conservative individuals), conservative, and strong conservative.

To address the third question, we turn to **trend analysis**. As the term implies, the analysis of a trend starts with measurements or observations on a dependent variable of interest taken at different times (usually twenty or more) and attempts to determine whether and why the level of the variable is changing. A simple approach for numeric data is to plot some appropriate summary measure of the dependent variable at different times. Figure 6–11 shows the percentage of respondents in each ideology category for twenty-five years from 1974 to 2010. If

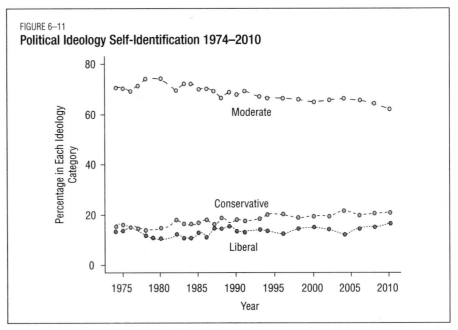

FIGURE 6–11
Political Ideology Self-Identification 1974–2010

Source: James A. Davis, Tom W. Smith, and Peter V. Marsden, *General Social Surveys, 1972–2010* (Chicago: National Opinion Research Center, 2011).

Note: Ideology grouped in three categories.

there is increased polarization, we should be able to spot it in the graph. And we see immediately that all the lines are more or less flat over the period; the percentage of moderates has decreased slightly, while the percentages of liberals and conservatives have risen slightly.

By itself, a graph of one variable over time cannot tell us *why* a variable is trending up or down or even moving randomly. For that analysis, we need slightly more advanced statistical tools and more data. For the latter purpose, an investigator needs to introduce additional variables and measure them over time. This type of analysis takes (roughly speaking) this form:

$$Y_t = f\left(Y_{t-1} + Y_{t-2} \ldots + Xs_t + Xs_{t-1} + Xs_{t-2} \ldots\right),$$

where the Ys and Xs are measures of the dependent (Y) and independent (X) variables at the current (latest) time (t) and at previous times ($t-1$, $t-2$, ... etc.) and f means "is a function of" or "is produced by."[61] When data are measured at many different points, as illustrated in figure 6–11 above, statistical procedures called *time series analysis* are often employed. Note also that, although the previous examples pertain to changing proportions in samples of individuals, trends in aggregate variables (e.g., crime or poverty rates in urban areas) can also be investigated.

ALTERNATIVE RESEARCH STRATEGIES

To study a phenomenon like the effects of the media on voters or the behavior of federal justices, political scientists most commonly employ one of the experimental or nonexperimental designs described above. This propensity stems from their commitment to verify hypotheses empirically and strive for valid causal inferences. But these approaches hardly exhaust the possibilities. We now briefly describe an alternative that flows from the quest for scientific knowledge but that relies on totally different tactics.

Formal Modeling

Anyone who has ever seen or perhaps built a model airplane knows full well that these replicas do not fly passengers or carry cargo or drop bombs. They are simply *representations* of reality. Nevertheless, they can be quite useful, and not just for entertainment. At the very least, they suggest what a "real" airplane looks like, and many can even be used for scientific purposes. Aeronautical engineers, for example, use models to see how certain wing shapes affect a plane's stability or what a sudden downdraft will do to its structural integrity. So, even though model planes may be totally unrealistic in one sense, they can still be useful, even essential, devices for learning about flight. Models, it turns out, are also quite useful in political science.

A **formal model** (frequently termed an "analytic model" or just "model") is a simplified and abstract representation of reality that can be expressed verbally, mathematically, or in some other symbolic system and that purports to show how variables or parts of a system tie together.[62] One might think of a model as a refined or formal or extended metaphor. Samuel Freeman summarized the purpose of models in the natural and behavioral sciences:

> Models . . . are commonly used in the natural and social sciences to acquire knowledge of real world conditions. . . . The point of such idealizations is to filter out irrelevant considerations and concentrate on the interplay of causes and factors most relevant to the determination of the phenomena under consideration.[63]

The main parts of a model are (1) a set of "primitives," or undefined terms or words whose meaning is taken for granted; (2) a collection of assumptions, that is, statements or assertions whose validity is again taken for granted but are explicitly stated; (3) definition of the model's basic units; (4) a body of rules or logic for linking the parts of the model together and making deductions; and (5) various derived propositions that are true by virtue of the rules used to deduce them. They may not be empirically supported, as we will see.

A modeler has to start someplace, so the most elemental parts of the system have to be taken as given. It is also necessary to make some assumptions. As an example, many political scientists assume—they do not prove with data—that people are "rational" in a sense to be discussed below. These assumptions are akin to the axioms used in geometry. What can make a model powerful is the application of rules, such as the rules of algebra or symbolic logic, that allow one to move from base terms and assumptions to validly derived statements. As noted, the conclusions in a model are true if the rules have been correctly applied—period. These statements may or may not hold in the real world. But most modelers believe that they will be approximately empirically valid and that, if the model is a good one, the understanding they provide more than compensates for inaccuracies in the predictions.

For an example of formal modeling, let us return to the question of why people do and do not vote. This time we will approach the question from a theoretical perspective. All models by definition simplify reality, but the one that follows is an especially unsophisticated or bare-bones version presented only for illustrative purposes.[64] Consider a single citizen. We assume that this person has desires or wants, which in modeling are often called "utilities." This individual may desire lower taxes, an end to federal gun control, and less military spending.[65] Denote the sum of the utilities as U. See? The model is already becoming abstract, and we are taking the meaning of *utility* more or less for granted. In any event, we can introduce some additional notation to clarify the amount of utility this person would get from two parties or candidates. Let, for instance, U_A be the value party (or candidate) A brings to the voter on these three issues *if* it comes to power. Similarly let U_B stand for the utility the other party (or candidate) brings if it takes office.

Now the model *assumes* that voters are rational, which means that they try to maximize or get the most value or utility from their actions. This conception or definition of rationality is usually termed "subjective" or "psychological" because what is getting maximized is internal mental states such as expected happiness and contentment, states that are hard to measure objectively. It is as though people mentally calculate the difference between the utilities from A and B and use the result to guide their decisions: vote for A if U_A is greater than U_B; vote for B if U_B is higher; and abstain if U_A equals U_B. (Why? For the answer see below.) No one actually does exactly this, of course, but people may behave *as though* they did.[66] More formally, we might symbolize the comparison of utilities, which we can call a "party differential," as follows:

$$U_{AVB} = U_A - U_B.$$

Note this important point: if U_{AVB} equals zero, the person sees no difference between the parties or candidates (the utilities from each are identical), has no incentive to vote, and thus abstains.[67]

To this point we have introduced a few terms (e.g., *utility*) and one key assumption—namely, voters are rational, meaning that they vote for the alternative that brings them the most pleasure or, in the modeler's language, they maximize utility. From these elements, we use the rules of algebra to derive predictions of how a person will behave. (It is just simple algebra that if U_A equals U_B, their difference is zero. And, by assumption, if an action brings zero utility, it is not taken.) True, the conclusion appears rather trivial—people vote for their most preferred party—but we can expand the model to reach a startling conclusion.

The model implicitly assumes that people have preferences and can easily act on them. But that presumption may be too simplistic because it does not take into account "information and transaction costs." That is, potential voters have to take time to find out where the parties stand on the relevant issues. That task may seem relatively trivial, but it's not. Politics has to compete with a lot of matters of importance to voters, including job and family demands, desire for relaxation and entertainment, and health issues. To become informed about electoral politics requires at least spending a fair amount of time listening or reading about the campaign. There may even be monetary costs, as in the expense of newspapers and magazines. In addition, parties and candidates frequently obscure their stands on issues or try to distort those of their opponents. And to make matters worse, potential voters have to inconvenience themselves to get registered, find the polling place, and take the time to actually vote.[68] A lot of these costs may not seem like much, but research tells us that they probably affect political behavior. So let us factor in a term C for the cost of becoming informed and going to the poll. Admittedly, this is an abstract term, since people do not literally summarize their expenses in a single number. Still, it does represent symbolically what people must *feel* when allocating their time and energy to certain tasks.

Now we can make the prediction that if C is greater than or equal to the absolute value of U_{AVB}, our hypothetical citizen will feel that the cost of voting outweighs any utility derived from one candidate bringing more utility than another. In symbols, if

$$|U_{AVB}| \leq C,$$

then the costs of voting exceed the benefits that one or the other party (or candidate) brings, and we again predict abstention.

There is another possible difficulty that we can model. Everyone must know that in any sizable election the probability that any one vote will be decisive is minuscule. For example, how likely is it that any one person's vote will determine the outcome of a contest for state representative that brings thousands of people to the polls? Elections are just not that close. (How many elections are decided by a margin of 5,001 to 5,000?) So any rational person must reason that it is not going to make a huge difference in the outcome if he or she stays home on election day. That is to say, the chances of reaping the benefits from a favorite party taking power are not affected by anything any particular voter does. And our citizen's participating or not will in all likelihood not affect a favorite party's chances of winning or losing. There are just too many votes being cast for a single one to be decisive.

To see what taking this small probability into account does to the model of turnout, let the likelihood that a vote is decisive be P. This number will be exceedingly small in any realistic election, say 1 in 10,000. And if we discount a person's utility derived from one party over another, the result will also be exceedingly small, almost approaching zero as a matter of fact. The discounting (or multiplication) of utility by P (that is, $P|U_{AVB}|$) is called the "expected" or "subjectively expected" utility of A versus B.

Example: If the expected benefit of A over B is 100 units of utility, and the probability of casting the deciding vote and thus actually bringing about that amount of utility is 1 in 10,000, then the result is 0.01. Now this should be compared with the cost of voting. After all, doesn't everyone compare expected gains with the costs of obtaining them? Any cost of becoming informed and voting over that amount, say 1 unit of utility, will mean the *rational* voter has no incentive to participate. And since we assume all voters are rational and that all make similar calculations, we deduce that *no one* will ever vote!

Once again this result may seem far-fetched. But it is a conclusion of many models of voting, and the fact that many seemingly rational people vote anyway has even earned the title "the paradox of voting."[69] This paradox has been so troubling that it has occupied dozens and dozens of social scientists who have tried to figure out why this logically deduced conclusion flies in the face of the reality that many, many people do, in fact, vote.

Perhaps we can rescue our model by introducing another kind of "utility" above and beyond that obtained by seeing one party or another elected. This additional value might come from the pleasure one receives just by participating in politics and knowing that widespread apathy could undermine democracy.[70] Let us call this new factor E, which means the extra utility or value brought by being active in civic life. It enters the potential voter's "calculation" as an additional or extra utility.

The deductions follow logically from the premises. They are true despite what really happens in the real world. If you are troubled by this situation, you might maintain that the model has a kind of "internal" validity, but its external validity is low because the results do not generalize to any meaningful population. This is a reasonable argument, and it brings us to a discussion of the value of formal models in political science.[71]

Many social scientists think that modeling as a research method has many advantages. Models, they believe, lead to clear and precise thinking. As Morris Fiorina put it, modeling requires that we put "all the cards on the table."[72] For a model to be useful, definitions have to be unambiguous and assumptions made explicit. If these conditions hold and the rules are known and accepted, other researchers can verify the deductions. We may not like the way a term has been defined or an assumption introduced. But if we at least know what the model says, we can suggest alternatives and find and correct errors. Verbal theories or histories, by contrast, often contain hidden or vaguely defined terms and assumptions, and because of these ambiguities, people often talk past one another. Models also tend to be compact. They do away with all but the essential aspects of a problem. True, they may oversimplify, but simplification may be necessary when studying complex political phenomena. Besides, almost any kind of research involves such narrowing of problems to manageable proportions and the reliance on simplifying postulates, a point sometimes forgotten by those critical of this technique.

Finally, political scientists apply formal modeling techniques in a surprisingly wide variety of areas, from international relations (e.g., coalition formation, the outbreak of war, arms races) to the behavior of organizations and groups (e.g., legislative and judicial decision making, roll-call voting and committee assignments in Congress) to individual behavior (e.g., candidate preferences, candidate campaign tactics). Indeed, the procedures now occupy a prominent place in many professional journals and graduate school curricula.

We conclude this section by noting that despite the growing popularity of modeling in the social sciences, it has numerous critics who are especially upset at the use of assumptions to make a model "work." The rationality premise, for instance, causes concern because it is defined in ways that many find odd. Is a chain-smoker who buys cigarettes at the lowest possible cost rational? Formal modelers would say, "Yes, if he or she acts to maximize (subjective or psychological) utility." But probably no doctor would agree.[73]

Simulation

Simulation offers a different way to design and carry out empirical research, whether or not it is quantitative. For our purposes, we define a **simulation** as a representation of a system by a device in order to study its behavior over time. The units of analysis are not discrete individuals like those in a sample survey. Rather, the fundamental interest lies in a process or structure, such as a large organization, a legislative body, or a party system, which has several or many components. To the extent that individuals enter into a simulation, their behavior as a collectivity (e.g., a crowd, a committee, a coalition) is the main interest. The "device" for investigating the phenomenon can be a computer program, a board game, role-playing, or some other method that allows the investigator to see how the system's components interact and change. At least for investigative purposes, the system or process is usually thought of as "closed," or not subject to external forces.

A major consideration in simulation studies is time. They emphasize the dynamic interaction of the internal elements: If one part changes, what happens to the others? Are there feedback loops or paths of reciprocal causation? Does the system evolve to an equilibrium state, or does it spin out of control? Consequently, simulations are normally "run." From a starting point or set of "givens," the pieces are made to interact in order to see two things: how each affects and is affected by the others and what happens to the overall state of the system at different time intervals or "iterations."

Creating simulations requires knowing as much about the subject matter as possible. They are, therefore, not very helpful for exploratory work, but they are useful for discovering "emergent" properties that cannot be found in static models or easily calculated by conventional means. If the investigator has a good idea of a system's constituents and how they interrelate but cannot easily predict what happens when they start functioning together over a period, a series of runs may provide insights not available by computation or deduction. Consequently, simulations work best or are most informative when a researcher has a solid, extensive body of knowledge with which to work.

You may be familiar with simulations, although not by that name. Some games like Monopoly are examples of simulations. Role-playing exercises such

as mock parliaments and model courtrooms are simulations that teach participants legislative or judicial behavior. But simulations are also widely used for
academic and applied purposes to study complex phenomena that cannot be
investigated with laboratory or survey tools. Many simulations appear in the
press, as in models of the economy constructed in an attempt to determine future
levels of employment or inflation. In making these models, economists set certain parameters and then let one or more factors vary. What will happen, they
might ask, if people suddenly decide to retire early? What will happen to productivity? To health care costs? To Social Security trust funds? As another example,
the Congressional Budget Office (CBO), a nonpartisan research arm of Congress,
routinely tries to predict the likely effects of alternative policy options (a tax cut,
perhaps) on the state of government spending or on the economy as a whole.
The natural sciences, as you may know, frequently resort to simulations to investigate complex phenomena such as the effect of accumulating greenhouse gases
(e.g., carbon dioxide) on the global climate.

A demonstration of simulation techniques would take us too far a field since
it is an increasingly fertile subbranch of the social sciences.[74] Simulations have
become an integral part of the social sciences. A great deal of what we think we
know about the world comes partly from simulation studies.

CONCLUSION

In this chapter, we have discussed why choosing a research design is an
important step in the research process. A design enables the researcher to
achieve his or her research objectives and can lead to valid, informative conclusions. We presented two basic types of research designs—experimental
and nonexperimental—along with a couple of alternative approaches. We discussed their advantages and disadvantages. Experimental designs—which
allow the researcher to exercise control over the independent variable, the
units of analysis, and their environment—are often preferred over nonexperimental designs because they enable the researcher to establish sounder
causal explanations. Therefore, experimental designs are generally stronger in
internal validity than nonexperimental ones. However, it may not always be
possible or appropriate to use an experimental design. Thus, nonexperimental
observation may also be used to test hypotheses in a meaningful fashion and
often in a way that increases the external validity of the results. In these
instances, causal assertions rest on weaker grounds and frequently have to be
approximated by statistical means (see chapter 13). Yet, the basic objectives
of research designs, whether experimental or nonexperimental, are the same.

A single research design may not be able to avoid all threats to internal and
external validity. Researchers often use several designs together so that the

weaknesses of one can be overcome by the strengths of another. Also, findings based on research with a weak design are likely to be more readily accepted if they corroborate findings from previous research that used different designs.

Terms Introduced

Case study design. A comprehensive and in-depth study of a single case or several cases. A nonexperimental design in which the investigator has little control over events.

Classical randomized experimental design. An experiment with the random assignment of subjects to experimental and control groups with a pretest and posttest for both groups.

Cohort. A group of people who all experience a significant event in roughly the same time frame.

Control group. A group of subjects that does not receive the experimental treatment or test stimulus.

Correlation. A statement that the values or states of one thing systematically vary with the values or state of another; an association between two variables.

Cross-sectional design. A research design in which measurements of independent and dependent variables are taken at the same time; naturally occurring differences in the independent variable are used to create quasi-experimental and quasi-control groups; extraneous factors are controlled for by statistical means.

Demand characteristics. Aspects of the research situation that cause participants to guess the purpose or rationale of the study and adjust their behavior or opinions accordingly.

Experiment. Research using a research design in which the researcher controls exposure to the test factor or independent variable, the assignment of subjects to groups, and the measurement of responses.

Experimental effect. Effect, usually measured numerically, of the experimental variable on the dependent variable.

Experimental group. A group of subjects that receives the experimental treatment or test stimulus.

Experimental mortality. A differential loss of subjects from experimental and control groups that affects the equivalency of groups; threat to internal validity.

External validity. The ability to generalize from one set of research findings to other situations.

Field experiment. Experimental designs applied in a natural setting.

Formal model. A simplified and abstract representation of reality that can be expressed verbally, mathematically, or in some other symbolic system and that purports to show how variables or parts of a system are interconnected.

Internal validity. The ability to show that manipulation or variation of the independent variable actually causes the dependent variable to change.

Intervention analysis. A nonexperimental time series design in which measurements of a dependent variable are taken both before and after the "introduction" of an independent variable.

Multiple-group design. Experimental design with more than one control and experimental group.

Period effect. An indicator or measure of history effects on a dependent variable during a specified time.

Policy evaluation. Objective analysis of economic, political, cultural, or social effects of public policies.

Posttest design. Research design in which the dependent variable is measured after, but not before, manipulation of the independent variable.

Pretest. Measurement of the dependent variable prior to the administration of the experimental treatment or manipulation of the independent variable.

Quasi-experimental design. A research design that includes treatment and control groups to which individuals are not assigned randomly.

Randomization. The random assignment of subjects to experimental and control groups.

Repeated-measurement design. A plan that calls for making more than one measure or observation on a dependent variable at different times over the course of the study.

Research design. A plan specifying how the researcher intends to fulfill the goals of the study; a logical plan for testing hypotheses.

Selection bias. Bias due to the assignment of subjects to experimental and control groups according to some criterion and not randomly; threat to internal validity.

Simulation. A simple representation of a system in order to study its behavior.

Small-*N* design. A research design in which the researcher examines one or a few cases of a phenomenon in considerable detail.

Statistical regression. Change in the dependent variable due to the temporary nature of extreme values; threat to internal validity.

Test stimulus or test factor. The independent variable introduced and controlled by an investigator in order to assess its effects on a response or dependent variable.

Time series design. A research design (sometimes called a longitudinal design) featuring multiple measurements of the dependent variable before and after experimental treatment.

Trend analysis. Research design that measures a dependent variable at different times and attempts to determine whether the level of the variable is changing and, if it is, why.

Suggested Readings

Campbell, Donald T., and Julian C. Stanley. *Experimental and Quasi-Experimental Designs for Research.* Chicago: Rand McNally, 1966.

Cook, Thomas D., and Donald T. Campbell. *Quasi-Experimentation: Design & Analysis Issues for Field Settings.* New York: Houghton Mifflin, 1979.

Creswell, John W. *Research Design: Qualitative and Quantitative Approaches.* Thousand Oaks, Calif.: Sage, 1994.

Downs, Anthony. *An Economic Theory of Democracy.* New York: Harper and Row, 1957.

Hakim, Catherine. *Research Design: Strategies and Choices in the Design of Social Research.* Contemporary Social Research Series no. 13. London: Allen and Unwin, 1987.

Gerring, John. "What Is a Case Study and What Is It Good For?" *American Political Science Review* 98, no. 2 (2004): 341–54.

Laver, Michael. *Private Desires, Political Action: An Invitation to the Politics of Rational Choice.* Thousand Oaks, Calif.: Sage, 1997.

Menard, Scott. *Longitudinal Research.* A Sage University Paper: Quantitative Applications in the Social Sciences no. 07–076. Newbury Park, Calif.: Sage, 1991.

Sambanis, Nicholas. "Using Case Studies to Expand Economic Models of Civil War." *Perspectives on Politics* 2, no. 2 (2004): 259–79. Available at http://www.apsanet.org/imgtest/sambanis PoP (june 04).pdf.

Sekhon, Jasjeet S. "Quality Meets Quantity: Case Studies, Conditional Probability, and Counterfactuals." *Perspectives on Politics* 2, no. 2 (2004): 281–93. Available at http://sekhon.berkeley.edu/papers/QualityQuantity.pdf.

Spector, Paul E. *Research Designs.* A Sage University Paper: Quantitative Applications in the Social Sciences no. 07–023. Beverly Hills, Calif.: Sage, 1981.

Vandaele, Walter. *Applied Time Series and Box-Jenkins Models.* New York: Academic Press, 1983.

Yin, Robert K. *Case Study Research: Design and Methods.* Rev. ed. Applied Social Research Methods Series, vol. 5. Newbury Park, Calif.: Sage, 1989.

Notes

1. Jim Geraghty, "Arlen Specter's Secret Attack Ad Against Joe Sestak," *National Review Online,* April 20, 2010, http://www.nationalreview.com/campaign-spot/4520/arlen-specters-secret-attack-ad-against-joe-sestak/.

2. See, for example, Stephen Ansolabehere, Shanto Iyengar, Adam Simon, and Nicholas Valentino, "Does Attack Advertising Demobilize the Electorate?" *American Political Science Review* 88, no. 4 (1994): 829–38. Available at http://weber.ucsd.edu/~tkousser/Ansolabehere.pdf.

3. Compare: "Negative campaign advertising has a more deleterious impact on the electoral process than that demonstrated by prior empirical research. Issue attack ads lead citizens to believe—erroneously—that they know the targeted candidate's ideological position. The greater the number of negative ads broadcast about a candidate, the more likely citizens believe they know the targeted candidate's ideological position. Candidates' commercials

create a false certainty among citizens, a belief that they know more than they actually do" (Jeffrey W. Koch, "Campaign Advertisements' Impact on Voter Certainty and Knowledge of House Candidates' Ideological Positions," *Political Research Quarterly* 61, no. 4 [2008]: 619.) versus "Upon close examination, however, we see no evidence that even the most despised of candidate messages—negative, uncivil, trait-based messages—are harmful to the democratic engagement of the polity" (Deborah Jordan Brooks and John G. Geer, "Beyond Negativity: The Effects of Incivility on the Electorate," *American Journal of Political Science* 51, no. 1 [2007]: 12. Available at http://oucommcapstone.wikispaces.com/file/view/Brooks + and + Geer.pdf.).

4. See chapters 13 and 14 for a more thorough discussion of spurious relationships.

5. For a review of experimentation in political science, see Rose McDermott, "Experimental Methods in Political Science," *Annual Review Political Science* 5, no. 1 (2002): 31–61. Available at http://www.sant.ox.ac.uk/people/knicolaidis/mcdermott.pdf.

6. Ansolabehere, Iyengar, Simon, and Valentino, "Does Attack Advertising Demobilize the Electorate?"

7. See Donald T. Campbell and Julian C. Stanley, *Experimental and Quasi-Experimental Designs for Research* (Chicago: Rand McNally, 1966), 5–6; and Paul E. Spector, *Research Designs,* A Sage University Paper: Quantitative Applications in the Social Sciences no. 07–023 (Beverly Hills, Calif.: Sage, 1981), 24–27. Four components of an ideal experiment are identified by Kenneth D. Bailey in *Methods of Social Research* (New York: Free Press, 1978), 191.

8. If you have trouble following this idea, imagine that you have a large can of marbles, most of which are red but a few of which are blue. Now, draw randomly from the can a single marble and put it in a box. Then draw another marble—again randomly—and put this one in a second box. Repeat this process nineteen more times. At the end, you should have two boxes of twenty marbles each. If you have selected them randomly, there should be approximately the same proportion of red and blue marbles in *each* box. If you started with a can holding 90 percent red marbles and 10 percent blue, for example, each of the two boxes should hold about eighteen red marbles and two blue ones. These may not be the exact numbers—one, say, might have three blue marbles and the other just one—but these differences will be due solely to chance and will not be statistically significant.

9. There is a vast literature on the meaning of *causation* in the social sciences.

10. A good reference is Donald T. Campbell and David A. Kenny, *A Primer on Regression Artifacts* (New York: Guilford Press, 1999), esp. chap. 3.

11. Martin T. Orne, "On the Social Psychology of the Psychological Experiment: With Particular Reference to Demand Characteristics and Their Implications," *American Psychologist* 17, no. 11 (1962): 776–83.

12. Alan S. Gerber and Donald P. Green, "Field Experiments and Natural Experiments," in *The Oxford Handbook of Political Methodology,* ed. Janet M. Box-Steffensmeir, Henry E. Brady, and David Collier (New York: Oxford University Press, 2008), 358.

13. For an overview, see Thomas D. Cook and William R. Shadish, "Social Experiments: Some Developments over the Past Fifteen Years," *Annual Review of Psychology* 45, no. 1 (1994): 545–80.

14. David Niven, "A Field Experiment on the Effects of Negative Campaign Mail on Voter Turnout in a Municipal Election," *Political Research Quarterly* 59, no. 2 (2006): 204.

15. Ibid., 206.

16. Ibid., 207.

17. For similar studies, see Ted Brader, "Striking a Responsive Chord: How Political Ads Motivate and Persuade Voters by Appealing to Emotions," *American Journal of Political Science* 49, no. 2 (2005): 388–405, available at http://www.uvm.edu/ ~ dguber/POLS234/articles/

brader.pdf; David Dreyer Lassen, "The Effect of Information on Voter Turnout: Evidence from a Natural Experiment," *American Journal of Political Science* 49, no. 1 (2005): 103–18; and David W. Nickerson, Ryan D. Friedrichs, and David C. King, "Partisan Mobilization Campaigns in the Field: Results from a Statewide Turnout Experiment in Michigan," *Political Research Quarterly* 59, no. 1 (2006): 85–97, available at http://www.nd.edu/~dnickers/papers/PartyMobilization.pdf.

18. Note that policy evaluation involves much more than field experiments.

19. David Kershaw and Jerilyn Fair, *The New Jersey Income-Maintenance Experiment: Vol. 1, Operations, Surveys and Administration* (New York: Academic Press, 1976). Also see Joseph A. Pechman and P. Michael Timpane, eds., *Work Incentives and Income Guarantees: The New Jersey Negative Income Tax Experiment* (Washington, DC: Brookings Institution, 1975), esp. chaps. 2 and 3.

20. Margaret E. Boeckmann, "Policy Impacts of the New Jersey Income Maintenance Experiment," *Policy Sciences* 7, no. 1 (1976): 83.

21. Kenneth J. Neubeck and Jack L. Roach, "Income Maintenance Experiments, Politics, and the Perpetuation of Poverty," *Social Problems* 28, no. 3 (1981): 308–20.

22. Peter H. Rossi and James D. Wright explained: "Interviews with experimental and control households were then undertaken, using traditional sample survey techniques to measure responses to the experimental treatments. Looked upon as surveys, these experiments were long-term panels with repeated measurements of the major dependent . . . variables. . . . Viewed as experiments, the studies were factorial ones in which important . . . treatments were systematically varied"; Rossi and Wright, "Evaluation Research: An Assessment," in *Handbook of Research Design and Social Measurement,* 6th ed., ed. Delbert C. Miller and Neil J. Salkind (Thousand Oaks, Calif.: Sage, 2002), 83.

23. Neubeck and Roach, "Income Maintenance Experiments, Politics, and the Perpetuation of Poverty," 310.

24. If this procedure sounds fanciful, consider that natural experiments, in which the occurrence of "treatments" is observed, not manipulated, underlie much scientific, social scientific, and historical analysis. After all, what does a historian of the American Civil War do if not search for its causes? And, needless to say, these causes cannot be randomized or manipulated to test for causal connections.

25. Jared Diamond, "Intra-Island and Inter-Island Comparisons," in *Natural Experiments of History,* ed. Jared Diamond and James A. Robinson (Cambridge, Mass.: Belknap Press of Harvard University Press, 2010), 120–41.

26. Ibid., 120–21.

27. As Diamond explained, "even if the human societies of Haiti and the Dominican Republic had been culturally, economically, and politically identical (which they have not been), the Haitian part of Hispaniola would still have faced serious environmental problems" (ibid.).

28. Ibid., 125.

29. Ibid., 128.

30. Incidentally, Diamond's approach embodies the principles of John Stuart Mill's (1850) "method of comparison," which we explain later.

31. Jacob S. Hacker and Paul Pierson, "Winner-Take-All Politics: Public Policy, Political Organization, and the Precipitous Rise of Top Incomes in the United States," *Politics & Society* 38, no. 2 (2010): 152–204. Available at http://pas.sagepub.com/content/38/2/152.full.pdf.

32. Ibid., 196.

33. For example, "The shift toward a much more favorable tax regime for the wealthy has occurred largely through policy enactments. The bulk of these have occurred under Republican congressional majorities and Republican presidents (although often with significant Democratic support)" (ibid., 186).

34. The canonical source is G. E. P. Box and G. C. Tiao, "Intervention Analysis with Applications to Economic and Environmental Problems," *Journal of the American Statistical Association* 70, no. 349 (1975): 70–79, ftp://ftp.uic.edu/pub/depts/econ/hhstokes/e537/Box_Tiao_March_75.pdf.

35. Theda Skocpol, *States and Social Revolutions* (New York: Cambridge University Press, 1979), 36.

36. See Richard F. Fenno Jr., *Home Style: House Members in Their Districts* (Boston: Little, Brown, 1978).

37. Robert K. Yin, *Case Study Research: Design and Methods*, rev. ed., Applied Social Research Methods Series, vol. 5 (Newbury Park, Calif.: Sage, 1989), 47.

38. Ibid., 17–19.

39. Ibid., 21.

40. Alexander L. George, "Case Studies and Theory Development: The Method of Structured, Focused Comparison," in *Diplomacy: New Approaches in History, Theory, and Policy*, ed. Paul Gordon Lauren (New York: Free Press, 1979), 46; and Skocpol, *States and Social Revolutions*, chap. 1.

41. Benjamin I. Page and Robert Y. Shapiro, "Effects of Public Opinion on Policy," *American Political Science Review* 77, no. 1 (1983): 186.

42. Yin, *Case Study Research: Design and Methods*, 53.

43. See, among countless other sources, Werner Sombart, *Why Is There No Socialism in the United States?* (White Plains, N.Y.: International Arts and Sciences Press, 1976), first published in German in 1906; and Seymour Martin Lipset, *The First New Nation: The United States in Historical and Comparative Perspective* (New York: Basic Books, 1963).

44. Seymour Martin Lipset and Gary Marks, *It Didn't Happen Here: Why Socialism Failed in the United States* (New York: W. W. Norton, 2000), 16.

45. John Stuart Mill, *A System of Logic, Ratiocinative and Inductive: Being a Connected View of the Principles of Evidence and the Methods of Scientific Investigation* (New York: Harper, 1850), 225, http://www.archive.org/details/systemoflogicrat01milliala.

46. See Merrilee H. Salmon, *Introduction to Logic and Critical Thinking*, 2nd ed. (San Diego, CA: Harcourt Brace Jovanovich, 1989), 109–15.

47. Skocpol, *States and Social Revolutions*, is an excellent example of seminal research that explicitly uses Mill's method.

48. Yin, *Case Study Research: Design and Methods*, 21–22.

49. Ibid., 21.

50. Ibid., 23.

51. Ibid.

52. The literature discussing the pros and cons of small-*N* research, especially its applicability to causal inference, includes, among many others, Gary King, Robert Keohane, and Sidney Verba, *Designing Social Inquiry: Scientific Inference in Qualitative Research* (Princeton, N.J.: Princeton University Press, 1994); James Mahoney, "Strategies of Causal Analysis in Small-*N* Analysis," *Sociological Methods and Research* 28, no. 4 (2000): 387–424; and Stanley Lieberson, "Small *N*'s and Big Conclusions: An Examination of the Reasoning in Comparative Studies Based on a Small Number of Cases," *Social Forces* 70, no. 2 (1991): 307–20, http://www.wjh.harvard.edu/soc/faculty/lieberson/Small_Ns_and_Big_Conclusions.pdf.

53. Lieberson, "Small *N*'s and Big Conclusions," 312–13.

54. For an extended discussion, see King, Keohane, and Verba, *Designing Social Inquiry: Scientific Inference in Qualitative Research*; Douglas Dion, "Evidence and Inference in the Comparative Case Study," *Comparative Politics* 30, no. 2 (1998): 127–45; it presents a more optimistic picture of the possibilities of causal inference in small-*N* research.

55. Although the measurements may be taken over a period of days or even weeks, cross-sectional analysis treats them as though they were obtained simultaneously.

56. Donald R. Matthews and James W. Prothro, "Social and Economic Factors and Negro Voter Registration in the South," *American Political Science Review* 57, no. 1 (1963): 36–38. Available at http://www.rochester.edu/college/psc/signorino/courses/405/data/Matthews_Prothro_1963_APSR_March.pdf.

57. See Scott Menard, *Longitudinal Research,* A Sage University Paper: Quantitative Applications in the Social Sciences no. 07–076 (Newbury Park, Calif.: Sage, 1991), 7.

58. Lee H. Hamilton, "The Changes Necessary to Make American Politics Less Polarized," *Deseret News,* December 6, 2010, http://www.deseretnews.com/article/700088722/The-changes-necessary-to-make-American-politics-less-polarized.html.

59. See, among others, Alan I. Abramowitz, *The Disappearing Center: Engaged Citizens, Polarization, and American Democracy* (New Haven, Conn.: Yale University Press, 2010); Geoffrey C. Layman and Thomas M. Carsey, "Party Polarization and 'Conflict Extension' in the American Electorate," *American Journal of Political Science* 46, no. 4 (2002): 786–802; Morris P. Fiorina and Samuel J. Abrams, "Political Polarization in the American Public," *Annual Review of Political Science* 11 (2008): 563–88, available at http://www.sociology.uiowa.edu/nsfworkshop/JournalArticleResources/Fiorina_Abrams_Political_Polarization_2008.pdf.

60. GSS 1972–2008 Cumulative Dataset, http://www.norc.org/GSS + Website/.

61. In practice, relationships of this sort are thought of as probabilistic, not deterministic, so a random error term would be added.

62. The word *model* used alone can be misleading because social scientists employ it for many different purposes. But in this context we give it a particular meaning, namely, the activities described below.

63. Samuel Freeman, "A New Theory of Justice," *New York Review of Books,* October 14, 2010, 59.

64. A classic work that builds a more thorough model of voter turnout (and many other political phenomena) is Anthony Downs, *An Economic Theory of Democracy* (New York: Harper and Row, 1957); also see William H. Riker and Peter C. Ordeshook, "A Theory of the Calculus of Voting," *American Political Science Review* 62, no. 1 (1968): 25–42, http://www.uky.edu/~rford/Home_files/Riker_1968APSR.pdf.

65. Notice that in this version of rationality, the wishes do not have to be logically consistent. The desire for lower taxes may be inconsistent with less military spending. But political scientists generally take preferences as given. This, in turn, is a sore point with the critics of formal models.

66. Isn't this just a formalization of statements such as "Well, on the whole I just prefer Bush over his opponent"?

67. This deduction comports with the commonly heard complaint from nonvoters: "There ain't a dime's worth of difference between ——— and ———."

68. Not everyone in society can bear these costs equally. College graduates may find them less onerous than high school dropouts, which partly explains why those who are less educated do not vote as regularly as those with more education.

69. John A. Ferejohn and Morris P. Fiorina, "The Paradox of Not Voting: A Decision Theoretic Analysis," *American Political Science Review* 68, no. 2 (1974): 525–36.

70. Downs, in *An Economic Theory of Democracy,* added exactly this sort of ad hoc term to his model. He called it the "long-run participation value."

71. Donald P. Green and Ian Shapiro provided a major critique of formal models in *Pathologies of Rational Choice Theory: A Critique of Applications in Political Science* (New Haven, Conn.: Yale University Press, 1994). Their analysis particularly faults many models for leading to

trivial conclusions and empirically invalid predictions. These points have been rebutted by several social scientists in Jeffrey Friedman, ed., *The Rational Choice Controversy: Economic Models of Politics Reconsidered* (New Haven, Conn.: Yale University Press, 1996).

72. Morris P. Fiorina, "Formal Models in Political Science," *American Journal of Political Science* 19, no. 1 (1975): 137.

73. Green and Shapiro, *Pathologies of Rational Choice Theory,* and Friedman, *The Rational Choice Controversy,* explore this issue in greater detail.

74. See, for example, Nigel Gilbert and Klaus G. Troitzsch, *Simulation for the Social Scientist,* 2nd ed. (Maidenhead, England: Open University Press, 2005). A very good place to explore the possibilities of computer simulation and its application to political and social problems is the NetLogo Project's Web site at http://ccl.northwestern.edu/netlogo/index.shtml.

SAMPLING

IN A STUDY OF WHY PEOPLE do and do not participate in surveys, researchers at the Pew Research Center found that both willing and reluctant participants expressed skepticism about polling validity: "many in each group (65% and 68%, respectively) doubted that a random sample of 1,500 people can 'accurately reflect the views' of the American public."[1] It is easy to find examples of these doubts on the Internet. In response to the question, "Are presidential election polls valid?" one person wrote:

> Regardless of the whole +/–3% hoopla, my wife believes that polls are not accurate. Her arguments are as follows:
> Democrats are more outspoken than Republicans. Exhibit A: We live in one of the top conservative states in America, and the polls indicate a huge McCain advantage here, but we still see more Obama bumper stickers and lawn signs. Exhibit B: According to what I saw in the media, democrats protested more angrily at the RNC than did Republicans at the DNC. . . . Democrats are less likely to hang up when the pollster calls. This kind of goes along with #1 above, but dems will be eager to voice their opinion, whereas reps aren't as boisterous![2]

In response to the question on Answerbag.com, "How valid are polls? Who participates? How do we know these participants tell the truth?" one person responded:

> I saw a poll on the local news station in my area that actually claimed to be a poll of "all registered voters" in the area. My phone never rang!!! And neither did any person I know in my area who is in fact a registered voter. I didn't get one phone call, not one mailer, not one knock on my door. So that's what I think of polls. :)[3]

Our task in this chapter, then, is to provide some answers about the believability of polling. Actually, there are two general questions. First, exactly what are samples, and how are they collected? Second, what kind of information do they supply? Do they really provide precise measures of opinions, or do they just offer rough approximations? That is, how much confidence can we place in statements about a population given observations derived from a very few of its members? We begin answering these questions with a description of sampling techniques and reserve for later in the chapter a discussion of inferences based on samples.

THE BASICS OF SAMPLING

The essence of the empirical methodology is the verification of propositions with observations and data. For example, Gelpi, Feaver, and Reifler studied public opinion and the war in Iraq to investigate a widespread perception: as casualties in a military conflict increase, popular support for it declines.[4] The researchers found some merit to this claim but identified other factors, especially beliefs about the chances of success, that are stronger predictors of public support. Where and how, one might wonder, do the observations for their research come from? In this instance, the source would be, theoretically, every citizen's answer to a series of questions about President George W. Bush, the conduct of the war, the prospects for success, and the war's connection to terrorism.

Of course, putting the question to every citizen would be impractical. So most researchers collect information on a much smaller set of individuals.[5] As we just noted, however, that strategy raises another issue: If an investigation of public opinion rests on 100 or even 1,000 observations, can it really say anything about the millions of Americans who comprise the general public? Can it, in other words, lead to reliable and valid conclusions? To answer this question, we need to know a little about sampling.

The fundamentals are quite simple, at least in theory (see figure 7–1). Suppose we want to assess Americans' level of support for the war in Iraq. At the outset, we need to clarify what we mean by

KEEP TERMS STRAIGHT

Do not be confused by the term *population*, which, as the text indicates, means simply a collection of things. We could define a population as the people living in New Castle, Delaware. But a population could also consist of a set of geographical areas, such as the voting districts in New Castle County. In the first case, the units of analysis are individuals; in the second case, they are aggregates of individuals.

Americans. More formally, we need to define or specify an appropriate population. In the figure, the population is defined to be all adult (aged eighteen and older) citizens not residing in institutional settings (for example, prisons, hospitals) in the United States in 2006. A **population** is any well-defined set of units of analysis or, put another way, all the units of analysis to which a hypothesis applies. It does not necessarily refer to people. A population might be all the adults living in a geographical area, such as a country or state, or working in an organization. But it could equally well be a set of counties, corporations, government agencies, events, magazine articles, or years. What is important is that the

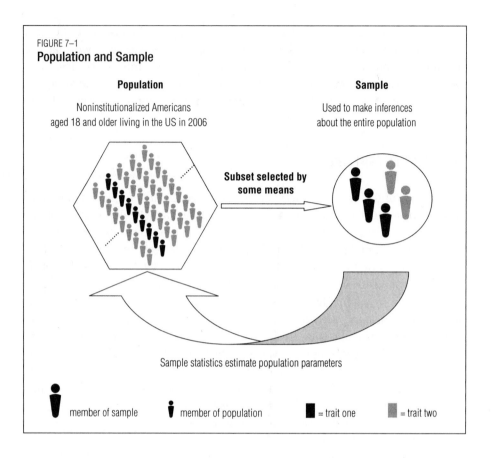

FIGURE 7–1
Population and Sample

Population

Noninstitutionalized Americans
aged 18 and older living in the US in 2006

Sample

Used to make inferences
about the entire population

**Subset selected by
some means**

Sample statistics estimate population parameters

= member of sample   = member of population   ■ = trait one   ▨ = trait two

population be carefully and fully defined and that it be relevant to the research question.[6] The polygon in Figure 7–1 represents the population of adult American citizens. Since there are millions and millions of citizens, the diagram only symbolizes this huge number. In this hypothetical analysis, our claims refer to these people, not to Germans or Mexicans or children or any other group.

Since it is impossible to interview everyone, a more practical approach is to select just a "few" members of the population for further investigation. This is where sampling comes in. A **sample** is any subset of units collected in some manner from a population. (In Figure 7.1, the sample consists of just five out of millions of people.) The sample size and *how* its members are chosen determine the quality (that is, the precision and reliability) of inferences about the whole population. The important thing to clarify is the method of selection and the number of observations to be drawn.

Once a sample has been gathered, its features or characteristics of interest can be examined and measured. These measures, or **sample statistics** as they are known, are used to approximate the corresponding population values, or parameters. That's the idea behind the arrow: we use sample statistics to estimate population characteristics (parameters). It may be intuitively obvious that the sample statistics will not exactly equal the corresponding values, but, as we demonstrate in this chapter, if we follow suitable procedures, they will be reasonably close.

Population or Sample?

A researcher's decision whether to collect data for a population or for a sample is usually made on practical grounds. If time, money, and other costs were not considerations, it would almost always be better to collect data for a population, because we would then be sure that the observed cases accurately reflecte the population characteristics of interest. However, in many if not most instances, it is simply not possible or feasible to study an entire population. Imagine, for instance, the difficulty of attempting to interview every adult in even a small city. Since research is costly and time-consuming, researchers must weigh the advantages and disadvantages of using a population or a sample. The advantages of taking a sample are often savings in time and money. The disadvantage is that information based on a sample is usually less accurate or more subject to error than is information collected from a population.

The point is more subtle than it first appears. In the late 1990s, Congress and President Bill Clinton debated the merits of taking a sample instead of interviewing the entire population when conducting the 2000 Census. Many members of Congress (mainly Republicans) argued that the Constitution requires a complete enumeration of the people. But Clinton and the Census Bureau argued that trying to tally everyone leads to so many errors that many groups are undercounted, in particular, undocumented aliens and inhabitants of inner cities and rural areas. It would be more accurate, they maintained, to draw careful samples of target populations and conduct quality interviews and measurements. (We should note that politics formed the context of this dispute; after all, innumerable government grants as well as seats in the House of Representatives are awarded according to population size.)

Some studies simply do not lend themselves to sampling. For example, case studies, which are often quite useful and lead to scientific understanding, involve the detailed examination of just one or a few units.[7] Usually these are selected by a kind of judgmental process described below.

Consider, as an example, a political scientist who wants to test some hypotheses regarding the content of televised political campaign commercials. The project requires an examination of the content of numerous commercials, which is the unit of analysis. From the standpoint of accuracy, it would be preferable to have data on the total population of televised commercials (in other words, to have available for measurement every campaign commercial that ever aired). But undertaking this type of analysis is simply impossible because no such data bank exists anywhere, nor does anyone even know how many such commercials have been televised across the country since they first appeared. Consequently, the researcher will have to rely on a sample of available commercials to test the hypotheses—a decision that is practical, necessary, and less costly, but perhaps subject to error.[8]

For reasons of necessity and convenience, political science researchers often collect data on a sample of observations. In fact, public opinion and voting behavior researchers almost always rely on samples. This means, however, that they must know how to select good samples. They also must appreciate the implications of relying on samples for testing hypotheses if they want to claim that their findings for the sample accurately reflect what they would find if they were to test the hypothesis on the whole population.

Fundamental Concepts

As noted in the previous section, a sample is simply a subset of a larger population, just as a sample of blood is a subset of all the blood in your body at one moment in time. If the sample is selected properly, the information it yields may be used to make inferences about the whole population. Since sampling is always used in public opinion surveys, it is often thought of in connection with that activity. Sampling arises whenever a researcher takes measurements on a subset of a population, however defined, covered by the hypothesis being investigated. Whatever empirical findings emerge from a sample from a specified population will apply to that and only that population. It would be a mistake, for instance, to sample campaign speeches from the last four presidential elections and then generalize to *all* American presidential rhetoric. By contrast, a sample drawn from a population of campaign speeches given by all presidents could be used to generalize to that population of speeches.

Before proceeding further, we should note that what usually matters most is that the data are obtained according to well-established rules. To understand why, we need to review some terms commonly used in discussions of sampling.[9]

Social scientists are interested mainly in certain characteristics of populations, such as averages, differences between groups, and relationships among variables. If any one of these traits can be quantified as a number, we call it a **population parameter.** Population parameters are typically denoted by capital English or Greek letters. Often θ is used to refer to a population parameter in general. A proportion, such as the proportion of Americans who support the war in Iraq at a particular time, typically is designated P or π (the Greek letter pi).

An **estimator** is a sample statistic based on sample observations that estimates the numerical value of a population characteristic, or parameter. A specific estimator of a population characteristic or attribute calculated from sample data is called a sample statistic. Like population parameters, these are typically denoted by symbols or letters. Frequently, we use a hat (^) over a character to denote a sample statistic; in some situations, a lowercase letter is used, for example, a lowercase p for a sample proportion. Sometimes, though, another symbol is used. The population mean (average) is almost always symbolized by μ (the lowercase Greek mu), but in this case, nearly everyone lets $\bar{Y}$, not $\hat{\mu}$, stand for the sample mean.

An **element** (frequently called a unit of analysis) is a single occurrence, realization, or instance of the objects or entities being studied. Elements in political science research are often individuals, but they also can be states, cities, agencies, countries, campaign advertisements, political speeches, wars, social or professional organizations, crimes, or legislatures, just to name a few.

As noted previously, a population is a collection of elements defined according to a researcher's theoretical interest. Sometimes this is referred to as the *theoretical population*. It may, for example, consist of all campaign speeches given by major candidates for president in the last four presidential elections. Or it may be all international armed conflicts that have occurred in the past 200 years. The key is to be clear and specific. If you refer to presidential campaign speeches as the focus of your research, at some point you should make clear which speeches in what time periods constitute the population.

For reasons that we discuss shortly, a population may be stratified—that is, subdivided or broken up into groups of similar elements—before a sample is drawn. Each **stratum** is a subgroup of a population that shares one or more characteristics. For example, we might divide the population of campaign speeches in the last four presidential elections into four strata, each stratum containing speeches from one of the four elections. In a study of attitudes of university students, the student body may be stratified by academic class, major, and GPA. The chosen strata are usually characteristics or attributes thought to be related to the dependent variables under study.

The particular population from which a sample is *actually* drawn is called a **sampling frame,** and it must be specified clearly. Technically speaking, all elements that are part of the population of interest to the research question should be part of the sampling frame. If they are not, any data collected may not be representative of the population. Often, however, sampling frames are incomplete, as the following example illustrates.

Suppose a researcher evaluates community opinion about snow removal by interviewing every fifth adult entering a local supermarket. The

DON'T BE INTIMIDATED BY SYMBOLS AND FORMULAS

Empirical social scientists frequently use symbols or letters as a shorthand way to describe terms. These devices allow for greater precision in expression. But there is no need to panic when you come across them. Authors are usually very clear in describing exactly what a symbol means.

In this book, we generally use capital English and lowercase Greek letters to designate population parameters (for example, the mean or proportion) and the same symbols with hats over them to denote corresponding sample statistics. One important exception is that in this book, $\bar{Y}$ stands for the sample mean. Also, P refers to the population proportion, and p refers to the sample proportion.

sampling frame would consist of all adults entering the supermarket while the researcher was standing outside. This sampling frame could hardly be construed as including all adult members of the community unless all adult members of the community made a trip to the supermarket when the researcher was there. Furthermore, use of such a sampling frame would probably introduce distortions into the results. Perhaps many of the people who stayed at home rather than going to the supermarket considered the trip too hazardous because of poor snow removal. The closer the sampling frame is to the population of interest or theoretical population, the better.

Sometimes lists of elements exist that constitute the sampling frame. For example, a university may have a list of all students, or the Conference of Mayors may have a list of current mayors of cities with 50,000 residents or more. The existence of a list may be enticing to a researcher, since it removes the need to create one from scratch. But lists may represent an inappropriate sampling frame if they are out-of-date or incorrect or do not really correspond to the population of interest. A common example would be if a researcher used a telephone directory as the sampling frame for interviewing sample households within the service area. Households with unlisted numbers would be missed, some numbers would belong to commercial establishments or no longer be working, and recently assigned numbers would not be included. Consequently, the telephone book could constitute an inaccurate or inappropriate sampling frame for the population in that area. Researchers should carefully check their sampling frames for potential omissions or erroneously included elements. Consumers of research should also carefully examine sampling frames to see that they match the populations researchers claim to be studying.

An example of a poll that relied on an incomplete sampling frame is the infamous *Literary Digest* poll of 1936. Despite being based on a huge sample, it predicted that the winner of the presidential election would be Alf Landon, not Franklin D. Roosevelt. This poll relied on a sample drawn from telephone directories and automobile registration lists compiled by the investigators. At that time, telephone and automobile ownership were not as widespread as they are today. Thus, the sampling frame overrepresented wealthy individuals.[10] The problem was compounded by the fact that in the midst of the Great Depression, an unprecedented number of poor people voted, and they voted overwhelmingly for Roosevelt, the eventual landslide winner.

A newer problem with the use of telephone directories is that so many people have unlisted numbers that reliance on a printed list will quite possibly lead to a biased sample. To deal with this problem, a procedure known as **random digit dialing** (RDD) has been developed. In effect, numbers are dialed randomly.[11] In this way, all telephone owners can potentially be contacted, whether they have listed numbers or not.[12] The existence of millions of cell phones has further complicated the situation. Hence, even a sampling frame consisting of randomly generated telephone numbers may still be an incomplete listing of households. Finally, it is estimated that 90 to 98 percent of all households have telephones.[13] Therefore, if the survey population is *all* households in the United States, a telephone sample will not be entirely representative of that population.

In many instances, a list of the complete population may not exist, or it may not be feasible to create one. It may be possible, however, to make a list of groups. Then the researcher could sample this list of groups and enumerate the elements only in those groups that are selected. In this case, the initial sampling frame would consist of a list of groups, not elements.

For example, suppose you wanted to collect data on the attitudes and behavior of civic and social service volunteers in a large metropolitan area. Rather than initially developing a list of all such volunteers—a laborious and time-consuming task—you could develop a list of all organizations known to use volunteers. Next, a subset of these organizations could be selected, and then a list of volunteers could be obtained for only this subset.

A **sampling unit** is an entity listed in a sampling frame. In simple cases, the sampling unit is the same as an element. In more complicated sampling designs, it may be a collection of elements. In the previous example, organizations are the sampling units.

TYPES OF SAMPLES

Researchers make a basic distinction among types of samples according to how the data are collected. We mentioned earlier that political scientists often select a sample, collect information about elements in the sample, and then use those data to talk about the population from which the sample was drawn. In other words, they make inferences about the whole population from what they know about a smaller group. If a sampling frame is incomplete or inappropriate, **sample bias** will occur. In such cases, the sample will be unrepresentative of the population of interest, and inaccurate conclusions about the population may be drawn. Sample bias may also be caused by a biased selection of elements, even if the sampling frame is a complete and accurate list of the elements in the population.

Suppose that in the survey of opinion on snow removal mentioned earlier, every adult in the community did enter the supermarket while the researcher was there. And suppose that instead of selecting every fifth adult who entered, the researcher avoided individuals who appeared to be in a hurry or in poor humor (perhaps because of snowy roads). In this case, the researcher's sampling frame was fine, but the sample itself would probably be biased and not representative of public opinion in that community. Because of the concern over sample bias, it is important to distinguish between two basic types of samples: probability and nonprobability samples. A **probability sample** is simply a sample for which each element in the total population has a known probability of being included in the sample. This knowledge allows a researcher to calculate how accurately the sample reflects the population from which it is drawn. By contrast, a **nonprobability sample** is one in which each element in the population has an *unknown* probability of being selected. Not knowing the probabilities of inclusion rules out the use of statistical theory to make inferences. Whenever possible, probability samples are preferred to nonprobability samples.

In the next several sections, we consider different types of probability samples: simple random samples, systematic samples, stratified samples (both proportionate and disproportionate), cluster samples, and telephone samples. We then examine nonprobability samples and their uses.

Simple Random Samples

In a **simple random sample,** each element and combination of elements has an *equal* chance of being selected. A list of all the elements in the population must be available, and a method of selecting those elements must be used that ensures that each element has an equal chance of being selected.[14] We review two common ways of selecting a simple random sample so that you can see how elements are given an equal chance of selection.

Note first that despite the seeming simplicity of the idea of "random," drawing a truly random sample can be quite difficult in practice. Try writing down 100 (much less 1,000) random integers. If you are like most people, the chances are that subtle patterns will creep into the list. You may subconsciously, for example, have a slight predilection for sevens, in which case your list will contain too many of them and too few of other numbers. This is not just an academic issue but a practical problem that confronts researchers in all fields.

Here's an instructive case that illustrates the difficulty. As the war in Vietnam wore on and opposition to it grew, the US government tried to make the draft fairer so that members of all segments of society, not just the poor and people of color, would be liable for duty. Obviously, no one could reach into the population and pick men at random. Another method was needed. The Selective Service, the agency in charge of the draft, came up with a random lottery. The basic idea seemed simple enough: the likelihood that a young man would be drafted into the army was to be determined randomly by writing every day of the year on separate slips of paper, placing the slips in separate capsules, and putting all the capsules in a barrel. After turning the drum, days would be drawn randomly. On December 1, 1969, in full view of a national television audience, the dates were drawn one after another and given a number. The first date, September 14, was assigned the number 1, and eligible men born on that day would be the first to be drafted, if they were not otherwise exempted. Another date was drawn, assigned the number 2, and those with that birthday were second in line. The process was repeated for all the days of the year. The Selective Service estimated that anyone with a number of 200 or higher would probably not be called. So, if a person's birthday was drawn early on, there was a good chance that he would have to serve. Others would be more fortunate. Randomness supposedly ensured the system's fairness.

But observers quickly noticed that people with low numbers (and hence likely to be drafted) tended to be born in the latter months of the year. In fact, there was what we call in chapter 13 a substantial negative correlation between day of birth (1–366) and draft number. In the minds of many, the selection process was clearly not random. If you were born in, say, January or February, you had some-what *less* chance of being called up than someone born in October, November, or December—not the same chance! What happened? The capsules, which were placed in the drum sequentially so the latter days of the year were on top, may have been insufficiently mixed. This would increase the likelihood that the last days put in were most likely to be the first taken out.[15]

Problems of this sort plague research. Another way to select elements at random from a list is by assigning a number to each element in the sample frame and then using a random numbers table, which is simply a list of random numbers, to select a sample of numbers. A computer can also create random numbers for this purpose. However it is done, those units having the chosen numbers associated with them are included in the sample.

Suppose, for instance, we have a population of 3,000 elements and wish to draw from it a sample of 150. First we number each member of the population, 1, 2, 3, and so on, up to 3,000. Then we can start at a random place in a random numbers table and look across and down the columns of numbers to identify our selections. Each time a number between 0001 and 3000 appears, the element in the population with that number is selected. If a number appears more than once, that number is ignored after the first time, and we simply go on to another number (i.e., sampling without replacement). For example, if we combine the adjacent cells of the first two columns in Table 7–1 (a table of random integers), we would have the following, random numbers: 4633, 2339, 9816, 2038, and 0869. Because 0869, 2038, and 2339 fall between 0001 and 3,000, they (or more

TABLE 7–1
Fifty Random Numbers

46	33	35	65	86	18	16	15	43	77
23	39	49	87	40	97	45	85	63	23
98	16	97	48	06	86	93	11	07	24
20	38	05	54	41	28	32	55	29	93
08	69	12	40	80	32	45	85	33	35

Note: The fifty pseudo-random integers lie between 0 and 99 and were computer generated.

TABLE 7–2

An Abbreviated List of Supreme Court Nominees, 1787–2011

No.	Nominee	Birth Year
1	Jay, John	1745
2	Rutledge, John	1739
3	Cushing, William	1732
4	Harrison, Robert H.	1745
5	Wilson, James	1742
6	Blair, John, Jr.	1732
7	Iredell, James	1751
8	Johnson, Thomas	1732
9	Paterson, William	1745
10	Rutledge, John	1739
11	Cushing, William	1732
12	**Chase, Samuel**	**1741**
. . .	. . .	. . .
162	Scalia, Antonin	1936
163	Bork, Robert H.	1927
164	Kennedy, Anthony McLeod	1936
165	**Souter, David H.**	**1939**
166	Thomas, Clarence	1948
167	Ginsburg, Ruth Bader	1933
168	Breyer, Stephen G.	1938
169	Roberts, John G., Jr.	1955
170	Miers, Harriet E.	1945
171	Alito, Samuel A., Jr.	1950
172	Sotomayor, Sonia Maria	1954

Source: Lee Epstein, Thomas G. Walker, Nancy Staudt, Scott A. Hendrickson, and Jason M. Roberts, U.S. Supreme Court Justices Database, January 26, 2010, http://epstein.law.north western.edu/research/justicesdata.html.

Note: Duplicate names deleted.

precisely, the elements to which they are assigned) would be included in the sample. Doing the same for the next two columns, we would include elements 0554 and 1240. As long as we do not deliberately look for a certain number, we may start anywhere in the table and use any system to move through it. Of course, for a real project, we would automate the entire process by having a computer select the 150 random numbers that meet our criterion.[16]

In later chapters, we will analyze the voting behavior of Supreme Court justices. The U.S. Supreme Court Justices Database contains information on approximately 170 men and women who have been nominated to serve on the Supreme Court since 1789 (see Table 7–2). (Several individuals were nominated more than once, but for now we ignore this problem. It comes up again with systematic sampling.) We treat this pool of subjects as a population. True, it is a very small population, and if we were being technically accurate, we would adjust our statistical analysis accordingly. (This adjustment involves applying a "finite" correction factor.)

Suppose we want a sample of 10 nominees. A computer pseudo-random number generator spits out these numbers: 46 165 121 60 54 74 132 76 12 159. Hence, we would select the 46th, 165th, 121st, . . . nominee from the list for analysis. (In the table, Samuel Chase and David Souter would be the only ones picked for the study.

Simple random sampling requires a list of the members of the population. Whenever an accurate and complete list of the target population is available and is of manageable size, a simple random sample can usually be drawn. For example, a random sample of members of Congress could be drawn from a list of all 100 senators and 435 representatives. A simple random sample of countries could be chosen from a list of all the countries in the world, or a random sample of American cities with more than 50,000 people could be selected from a list of all such cities in the United States. The problem, as we will see, is that obtaining such a list is not always easy or even possible.

Systematic Samples

Assigning numbers to all elements in a list and then using random numbers to select elements may be a cumbersome procedure. Fortunately, a **systematic sample,** in which elements are selected from a list at predetermined intervals, provides an alternative method that is sometimes easier to apply. It, too, requires a list of the target population. But the elements are chosen from the list systematically rather than randomly. That is, every Kth element on the list is selected, where K is the number that will result in the desired number of elements being selected. This number is called the **sampling interval,** or the "skip" or number of elements between elements that are drawn, and is simply $K = N/n$, where N is the "population" size and n is the desired sample size.

Go back to the Supreme Court nominees. We could treat the database as a list with $N = 172$ entries. If we wanted a sample of size $n = 10$, we would divide the total by 10 to get the sampling fraction or interval: $K = 172/10$, or about 17. So starting at a random point, we could take every 17th name. (If we started at 11, we would include the 11th, 28th, 45th, . . . nominees.)

Systematic sampling is useful when dealing with a long list of population elements. It is often used in product testing. Suppose you have been given the job of ensuring that a firm's tuna fish cans are sealed properly before they are delivered to grocery stores. And assume that your resources permit you to test only a sample of tuna fish cans rather than the entire population of tuna fish cans. It would be much easier to systematically select every 300th tuna fish can as it rolls off the assembly line than to collect all the cans in one place and randomly select some of them for testing.

Despite its advantages, systematic sampling may result in a biased sample in at least two situations.[17] One occurs if elements on the list have been ranked according to a characteristic. In that situation, the position of the random start will affect the average value of the characteristic for the sample. For example, if students were ranked from the lowest to the highest GPA, a systematic sample with students 1, 51, and 101 would have a lower GPA than a sample with students 50, 100, and 150. Each sample would yield a GPA that presented a biased picture of the student population.

The second situation leading to bias occurs if the list contains a pattern that corresponds to the sampling interval. Suppose you were conducting a study of the attitudes of children from large families and you were working with a list of the children by age in each family. If the families included in the list all had six children and your sampling interval was six (or any multiple of six), then systematic sampling would result in a sample of children who were all in the same position among their siblings. If attitudes varied with birth order, then your findings would be biased.

A survey of soldiers conducted during World War II offers a good example of a case in which a pattern in the list used as the sampling frame interfered with the selection of an unbiased systematic sample.[18] The list of soldiers was arranged by squad, with each squad roster arranged by rank. The sampling interval and squad size were both ten. Consequently, the sample consisted of all persons who held the same rank, in this case squad sergeant. Clearly, sergeants might not be representative of all soldiers serving in World War II.

Stratified Samples

A **stratified sample** is a probability sample in which elements sharing one or more characteristics are grouped and elements are selected from each group in proportion to the group's representation in the total population. Stratified samples take advantage of the principle that the more homogeneous the population, the easier it is to select a representative sample from it. Also, if a population is relatively homogeneous, the size of the sample needed to produce a given degree of accuracy will be smaller than for a heterogeneous population. In stratified sampling, sampling units are divided into strata with each unit appearing in only one stratum. Then a simple random sample or systematic sample is taken from each stratum.

A stratified sample can be either proportionate or disproportionate. In proportionate sampling, a researcher uses a stratified sample in which each stratum is represented in proportion to its size in the population—what researchers call a **proportionate sample.** For example, let's assume we have a total population of 500 colored balls: 50 each of red, yellow, orange, and green and 100 each of blue, black, and white. We wish to draw a sample of 100 balls. To ensure a sample with each color represented in proportion to its presence in the population, we first stratify the balls according to color. To determine the number of balls to sample from each stratum, we calculate the **sampling fraction,** which is the size of the desired sample divided by the size of the population. In this example, the sampling fraction is 100/500, or one-fifth of the balls. Therefore, we must sample one-fifth of all the balls in each stratum.

Since there are 50 red balls, we want one-fifth of 50 or 10 red balls. We could select these 10 red balls at random or select every fifth ball with a random start between 1 and 5. If we followed this procedure for each color, we would end up with a sample of 10 each of red, yellow, orange, and green balls and 20 each of blue, black, and white balls. Note that if we selected a simple random sample of 100 balls, there is a finite chance (albeit slight) that all 100 balls would be blue or black or white. Stratified sampling guarantees that this cannot happen, which is why stratified sampling results in a more representative sample. Some deviation from proportional representation will occur, however, depending on the sampling interval, the random start, and the number of sampling units in a stratum.

In selecting characteristics on which to stratify a list, you should choose characteristics that are expected to be related to or affect the dependent variables in your study. If you are attempting to measure the average income of households in a city, for example, you might stratify the list of households by education, sex, or race of household head. Because income may vary by education, sex, or race, you would want to make sure that the sample is representative with respect to these factors. Otherwise the sample estimate of average household income might be biased.

If you were selecting a sample of members of Congress to interview, you might want to divide the list of members into strata consisting of the two major parties, or the length of congressional service, or both. This would ensure that your sample accurately reflected the distribution of party and seniority in Congress. Or if you were selecting a sample of television news stories from NBC, CBS, Fox, CNN, and ABC to analyze, you might want to divide the population of news stories into five strata based on the network of origin to ensure that your sample contained an equal number of stories from each of the networks.

Some lists may be inherently stratified. Telephone directories are stratified to a degree by ethnic groups, because certain last names are associated with particular ethnic groups. Lists of Social Security numbers arranged consecutively are stratified by geographical area, because numbers are assigned based on the applicant's place of residence.

In the examples of stratified sampling we have considered so far, we assured ourselves of a more representative sample in which each stratum was represented in proportion to its size in the population. There may be occasions, however, when we wish to take a **disproportionate sample.** In such cases, we would use a stratified sample in which elements sharing a characteristic are underrepresented or overrepresented in our sample.[19]

For example, suppose we are conducting a survey of 200 students at a college in which there are 500 liberal arts majors, 100 engineering majors, and 200 business majors for a total of 800 students. If we sampled from each major (the strata) in proportion to its size, we would have 125 liberal arts majors, 25 engineering majors, and 50 business majors. If we wished to analyze the student population as a whole, this would be an acceptable sample. But if we wished to investigate some questions by looking at students in each major separately, we would find that 25 engineering students were too small a sample from which to draw inferences about the population of engineering students.

To get around this problem, we could sample disproportionately—for example, we could include 100 liberal arts majors, 50 engineering majors, and 50 business majors in our study. Then we would have enough engineering students to draw inferences about the population of engineering majors. The problem now becomes evaluating the student population as a whole, since our sample is biased due to an undersampling of liberal arts majors and an oversampling of engineering majors. Suppose engineering students have high GPAs. Our sample estimate of the student body's GPA would be biased upward because we have oversampled engineering students. Therefore, when we wish to analyze the total sample, not just students in a particular major, we need some method of adjusting our sample so that each major is represented in proportion to its real representation in the total student population.[20]

Table 7–3 shows the proportion of the population of each major and the mean GPA for each group in a hypothetical sample of college students. To calculate an unbiased estimate of the overall mean GPA for the college, we could use a **weighting factor,** a mathematical factor used to make a disproportionate sample representative. In this example, we would multiply the mean GPA for each major by the proportion of the population of each major (that is, the weighting factor).[21] Thus, the mean GPA would be .625(2.5) + .125(3.3) + .25(2.7) = 2.65.

Disproportionate stratified samples allow a researcher to represent more accurately the elements in each stratum and ensure that the overall sample is an accurate representation of important strata within the target population. This is done by weighting the data from each stratum when the sample is used to estimate characteristics of the target population. Of course, to accomplish disproportionate stratified sampling, the proportion of each stratum in the target population must be known.

Cluster Samples

Thus far, we have considered examples in which a list of elements in the sampling frame exists. There are, however, situations in which a sample is needed but no list of elements exists and to create one would be prohibitively expensive. A **cluster sample** is a probability sample in which the sampling frame initially consists of clusters of elements. Since only some of the elements are to be selected in a sample, it is unnecessary to be able to list all elements at the outset.

In cluster sampling, groups or clusters of elements are identified and listed as sampling units. Next a sample is drawn from this list of sampling units. Then, for the sampled units only, elements are identified and sampled. For example, suppose we wanted to take an opinion poll of 1,000 persons in a city for which there is no complete list of city residents. We might begin by obtaining a map of the city and identifying and listing all blocks. This list of blocks becomes the sampling frame from which a small number of blocks are sampled at random or systematically. (The individual blocks are sometimes called the *primary sampling units.*) Next we would go to the selected blocks and list all the dwelling units in those blocks. Then a sample of dwelling units would be drawn from

---

TABLE 7–3
Stratified Sample of Student Majors

	Liberal Arts	Engineering	Business	Total
Number of students	500	100	200	800
Proportion or weight	.625	.125	.25	1.00
Size of sample	100	50	50	200
Sample mean grade point average	2.5	3.3	2.7	2.65

Note: Hypothetical data.

each block. Finally, the households in the sampled dwellings would be contacted, and someone in each household would be interviewed for the opinion poll. Suppose there are 500 blocks and, from these 500 blocks, 25 are chosen at random. On these 25 blocks, a total of 4,000 dwelling units or households are identified. One-quarter of these households will be contacted because a sample of 1,000 individuals is desired. These 1,000 households could be selected with a random sample or a systematic sample.

Note that even though we did not know the number of households ahead of time, each household has an equal chance of being selected. The probability that any given household will be selected is equal to the probability of one's block being selected times the probability of one's household being selected, or $25/500 \times 1,000/4,000 = 1/80$. Thus, cluster sampling conforms to the requirements of a probability sample.

Our example involved only two samples or levels (the city block and the household). Some cluster samples involve many levels or stages and thus many samples. For example, in a national opinion poll, the researcher might list and sample states, list and sample counties within states, list and sample municipalities within counties, list and sample census tracts within municipalities, list and sample blocks within census tracts, and finally list and sample households—a total of six stages.

An advantage of cluster sampling is that it allows researchers to get around the problem of acquiring a list of elements in the target population. Cluster sampling also reduces fieldwork costs for public opinion surveys, because it produces respondents who are close together. For example, in a national opinion poll, respondents will not come from every state. This reduces travel and administrative costs.

A drawback to cluster sampling is greater imprecision. Errors that arise by virtue of taking samples instead of enumerating an entire population occur at each stage of the cluster sample. For example, a sample of states will not be totally representative of all states, a sample of counties will not be totally representative of all counties, and so on. The random errors at each level must be added to arrive at the total sampling error for a cluster sample.

In cluster sampling, the researcher must decide how many elements to select from each cluster. In the previous example, the researcher could have selected 2 individuals from each of the 500 blocks (requiring no selection of blocks), or 1,000 individuals from 1 of the blocks (making the selection of the particular block terribly important), or some other combination in between (40 individuals from 25 blocks, 25 individuals from 40 blocks, and so on). But how does the researcher decide how many units to sample at each stage?

We know that samples are more accurate when drawn from homogeneous populations. Generally, elements within a group are more similar than are elements from two different groups. Thus, households on the same block are more likely to resemble each other than are households on different blocks. Sample size can be smaller for homogeneous populations than for heterogeneous populations and still be as accurate. (If a population is totally homogeneous, a sample of one element will be accurate.) Therefore, sampling error could be reduced by selecting many blocks but interviewing only a few households from each block. Following this reasoning to the extreme, we could select all 500 blocks and sample 2 households from each block. This approach, however, would be very expensive, since every household in the city would have to be identified and listed, thus defeating the purpose of a cluster sample. The desire to maximize the accuracy of a sample must be balanced with the need to reduce the time and cost of creating a sampling frame. Sometimes stratification can be used in conjunction with cluster sampling to reduce sampling error by creating more homogeneous sampling units. States can be grouped by region, census tracts by average income, and so forth before the selection of sample elements occurs.

Systematic, stratified (both proportionate and disproportionate), and cluster samples are acceptable and often more practical alternatives to the simple random sample. In each case, the probability of a particular element's being selected is known; consequently, the accuracy of the sample can be determined. The type of sample chosen depends on the resources a researcher has available and the availability of an accurate and comprehensive list of the elements in a well-defined target population.

SAMPLING IN THE REAL WORLD

Later in the book, we analyze data from *United States Citizenship, Involvement, Democracy (CID) Survey, 2006,* a nationwide study of political participation. The projected employed a multistage sampling design. A reconstruction of the steps taken to identify and interview respondents shows just how complex (and arduous) sampling can be:[22]

1. *Population:* "Eligible respondents were household members, males or females, age 18 years old and older. . . . The sample was designed to specifically represent the adult population residing in occupied residential housing units, and by definition excluded residents of institutions, group quarters, or those residing on military bases."

2. *Sampling frame:* All residential units.

3. *Stratification levels:* The four standard census regions and metropolitan areas.

4. *Clusters:* "Within each primary stratum, all counties, and by extension every census tract, block group and household, were ordered in a strict hierarchical fashion. . . . Within each metropolitan stratum, MSAs [metropolitan statistical areas] and their constituent counties were arrayed by size (i.e., number of households). Within each MSA, the central-city county or counties were listed first, followed by all non-central-city counties. In the four non-metropolitan strata, states and individual counties within each state were arrayed in serpentine order, North-to-South, and East-to-West. Within county, Census Tracts and Block Groups were arrayed in numerical sequence, which naturally groups together households within cities, towns, and other minor civil divisions (MCDs)."

5. *Selecting households:* "Within each sample PSU [primary sampling unit], two block groups (BG) were selected at random, without replacement. . . . All residential housing units within a sample BG were then identified using the U.S. Postal Service Delivery Sequence File (DSF) and one address selected at random. The next four-teen residential addresses were then identified, along with any intervening commercial, vacant, or seasonal units. The result was a designated walking list that was supplied to each interviewer, along with a map showing the exact segment location, streets, addresses, etc. The street/address listing typically captures about 98% of all occupied housing units."

6. *Interviewer instructions:* "Interviewers were given street/address listings with 15 addresses, and were instructed to work the first ten pieces to a maximum of six callbacks. In order to properly manage the release of sample and strive to work all released sample to its maximum attempts, interviewers were asked to check in once they had attained five interviews or worked the first ten pieces to final dispositions or six active attempts, whichever came first. Throughout the field period the field director made daily decisions regarding whether each inter-viewer should continue working their first ten pieces or be provided more sample to work. Again, the overall goal was to attain a maximum number of attempts with as little sample as possible within a limited field period and an overall goal of approximately 1,000 completed interviews."

It is perhaps clear now why phone and Internet surveys are so popular.

Nonprobability Samples

A nonprobability sample is a sample for which each element in the total popula-tion has an unknown probability of being selected. Probability samples are usu-ally preferable to nonprobability samples because they represent a large population fairly accurately and it is possible to calculate how close an estimated characteristic is to the population value. In some situations, however, probability sampling may be too expensive to justify (in exploratory research, for example), or the target population may be too ill-defined to permit probability sampling (this was the case with the television commercials example discussed earlier). Researchers may feel that they can learn more by studying carefully selected and perhaps unusual cases than by studying representative ones. A brief description follows of some of the types of nonprobability samples.

With a **purposive sample,** a researcher exercises considerable discretion over what observations to study, because the goal is typically to study a diverse and usually limited number of observations rather than to analyze a sample repre-sentative of a larger target population. Richard F. Fenno Jr.'s *Home Style,* which describes the behavior of eighteen incumbent representatives, is an example of research based on a purposive sample.[23] Likewise, a study of journalists that concentrated on prominent journalists in Washington, D.C., or New York City would be a purposive rather than a representative sample of all journalists.

In a **convenience sample,** elements are included because they are convenient or easy for a researcher to select. A public opinion sample in which interviewers haphazardly select whomever they wish is an example of a convenience sample. A sample of campaign commercials that consists of those advertisements that a researcher is able to acquire or a study of the personalities of politicians who have sought psychoanalysis is also a convenience sample, as is any public opinion survey consisting of those who volunteer their opinions. Convenience samples are most appropriate when the research is exploratory or when a target population is impossible to define or locate. But like other nonprobability samples, convenience samples provide estimates of the attributes of target populations that are of unknown accuracy.

A **quota sample** is a sample in which elements are sampled in proportion to their representation in the population. In this respect, quota sampling is similar to proportionate stratified sampling. The difference between quota sampling and stratified sampling is that the elements in the quota sample are not chosen in a probabilistic manner. Instead, they are chosen in a purposive or convenient fashion until the appropriate number of each type of element (quota) has been found. Because of the lack of probability sampling of elements, quota samples are usually biased estimates of the target population. Even more important, it is impossible to calculate the accuracy of a quota sample.

A researcher who decided to conduct a public opinion survey of 550 women and 450 men and who instructed his interviewers to select whomever they pleased until these quotas were reached would be drawing a quota sample. A famous example of an error-ridden quota sample is the 1948 Gallup Poll that predicted that Thomas Dewey would defeat Harry Truman for president.[24]

In a **snowball sample,** respondents are used to identify other persons who might qualify for inclusion in the sample.[25] These people are then interviewed and asked to supply appropriate names for further interviewing. This process is continued until enough persons are interviewed to satisfy the researcher's needs. Snowball sampling is particularly useful in studying a relatively select, rare, or difficult-to-locate population such as draft evaders, political protesters, drug users, or even home gardeners who use sewage sludge on their gardens—a group estimated to constitute only 3 to 4 percent of households.[26]

We have discussed the various types of samples that political science researchers use in their data collection. Samples allow researchers to save time, money, and other costs. However, this benefit is a mixed blessing for by avoiding these costs, researchers must rely on information that is less accurate than if they had collected data on the entire target population. Now we consider the type of information that a sample provides and the implications of using this information to make inferences about a target population.

SAMPLES AND STATISTICAL INFERENCE: A GENTLE INTRODUCTION

We spent a lot of time in earlier parts of this book talking about the use of statistics in research. For example, statistical techniques sometimes let us compensate for the lack of physical control or manipulation of variables in experiments.

Equally important, statistics underlies the process of making inferences about populations from samples. Here we describe some of the basic ideas in nonmathematical terms.

Let's return to a previous example. We want to measure support for President Bush's handling of the war in Iraq. Figure 7–2 illustrates our problem. On one hand, at any given time a presumably *unknown* proportion of Americans back the president's policies, but we have little or no idea what that percentage is. (In an earlier section, we called this percentage a *parameter.*) If we had absolutely no knowledge of American politics, we might think it could be anywhere from 0 to 100 percent. Usually, however, an investigator has a rough idea of the public's attitudes, but even so the parameter could run from, say, 25 to 75 percent. That still leaves a lot of room for doubt, so we need to do better than this ballpark guess.

Suppose we were to draw (at random) a sample of ten adult Americans and count the number who are supportive. (Look at the right side of Figure 7–2.) Here we see that four out of ten, or 40 percent, of the respondents are supportive. This number, the sample statistic or estimator, provides an estimate of the population proportion. Not having any other information, we might take it as our best approximation of public opinion on the matter. But just how good is it? Can we really say anything about the attitudes of millions of Americans based on a sample of just ten people? Before making a judgment, let's examine sampling and inference in a bit more detail.

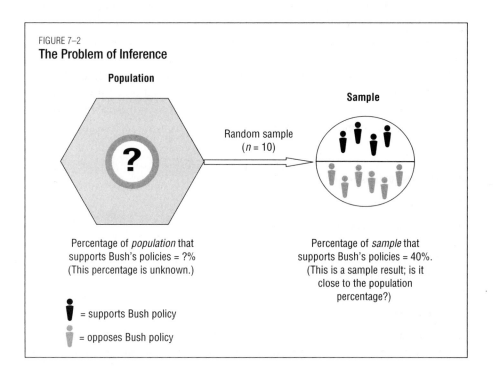

FIGURE 7–2
The Problem of Inference

Samples provide only estimates or approximations of population attributes. Occasionally these "guesses" may be right on the money. Most of the time, however, they will differ from the "true" or population parameter. When we report a sample statistic, we always assume there will be a margin of error, or a difference between the reported and actual values. For example, a finding that 40 percent of a random sample backs the president's goals and policies does not mean that exactly 40 percent of the public is sympathetic. It means merely that *approximately* 40 percent are. In other words, researchers sacrifice some precision whenever they rely on samples instead of enumerating and measuring the entire population. How much precision is lost (that is, how accurate the estimate is) depends on how the sample has been drawn and its size.

Where does the loss of precision or accuracy come from? The answer is chance or luck of the draw. If you flip a coin ten times, you probably won't get exactly five heads, even if the coin is fair or the probability of heads is one-half. Randomness seems to be an innate feature of nature, at least on the scale at which we observe it. Just as with our coin toss, a random sample of ten (or even much larger) is not likely to produce precisely the value of a corresponding population parameter. But, if we follow proper procedures and certain assumptions have been met (for example, the sample is a simple random sample from an infinite population), a sample statistic approximates the numerical value of a population parameter. If a population percentage really is 40, it is unlikely (*but not impossible*) for a sample result to be, say, 5 or 10 or 99 percent or some other "extreme" value. More likely, the sample estimate will be something like 30 or 35 or 45 or 50 percent. The difficulty is figuring out how far off the estimate is likely to be in any individual case. Here is where statistics helps.

The major goal of **statistical inference** is to make supportable conjectures about the unknown characteristics of a population based on sample statistics. The study of statistics partly involves defining much more precisely what *supportable* means. To make this clear, we introduce in a nontechnical way three concepts:

- Expected values
- Standard errors
- Sampling distributions

Although these terms may appear at first sight to have technical meanings, they can be given common-sense interpretations.

Expected Values

Let's look at a relatively simple example. A candidate for the state senate wants to know how many independents live in her district, which has grown rapidly in the past ten years. Although the Bureau of Elections reports that 25 percent of registered voters declined to name a party, she believes that the records are badly out-of-date. She asks you to conduct a poll to estimate the proportion of citizens, aged eighteen and older, who registered as independents rather than as Democrats or Republicans.

Suppose you interview ten *randomly* chosen adults living in the district and discover that two of them registered as independents.[27] Based on this finding, you could report that 20 percent of voters are registered independents. Intuitively, however, you know that this estimate may be off by quite a bit, because you interviewed only ten people. The true proportion may be very different.

Now suppose for the moment that the Bureau of Elections's records are still accurate: one-fourth, or 25 percent, of the population is registered as independents, or, in more formal terms, $P = .25$, where P stands for the value of the population parameter. Of course, no one knows the population value because at the time of your poll it is unobserved, but we will pretend that we do in order to illustrate the ideas of sampling and inference. Your first estimate, .20, then, is a little bit below the true value. This difference is called the **sampling error,** which is the discrepancy between an observed and a true value that arises because only a portion of a population is observed.

What you need is some way to measure the amount of error or uncertainty in the estimate so that you can tell your client what the margin of error is. That is, you want to be able to say, "Yes, my estimate is probably not equal to the real value, but chances are that it is close." What exactly do words like *chances are* and *close* mean?

To answer those questions, imagine taking another, totally independent sample of ten adults from the same district and calculating the proportion of independents. (We will assume that not much time has passed since the first sample, so the probability of being an independent is still 25 percent.) This time the estimate turns out to be .30.

Repeating the procedure once more, you find that the next estimated proportion of independents is .40. This estimate, while quite high, is still possible. And after you take a fourth independent sample, you find that the estimated proportion, .20, is again wide of the mark. So far, two of your estimates have been too large, two too low, and none exactly on target. But notice that the average of the estimates, $(.20 + .30 + .40 + .20)/4 = .275$, is not far from the real value of .25.

What would happen, you might wonder, if you repeated the process indefinitely? That is, what would happen if you took an infinite number of independent samples of $N = 10$ and calculated the proportion of independents in each one?[28] (Throughout this discussion, we use N to denote the size of a sample.) After a while, you would have an extended list of sample proportions or percentages. What would their distribution look like? Figure 7–3 gives an idea. In

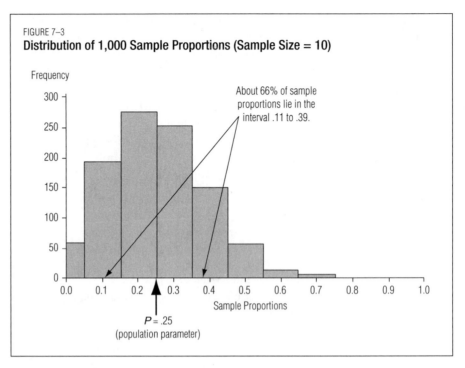

FIGURE 7–3
Distribution of 1,000 Sample Proportions (Sample Size = 10)

Source: Simulated data.

Note: Mean of 1,000 sample proportions is .248.

brief, we programmed a computer to take 1,000 samples (each of size 10) from a hypothetical population in which $P = .25$. This technique permits us to investigate the behavior of a huge number of sample outcomes.

The separate sample proportions are spread around the true value ($P = .25$) in a bell-curve-shaped distribution, that is, a curve with a single peak and more or less symmetric or equal tails. A few of the estimates are quite low, even close to zero, while a few more of them are way above .25. (The frequencies can be determined by looking at the y-axis, the vertical line.) Yet the vast majority is in the range .05 to .45, and the center of the distribution (the average of the 1,000 sample proportions) is near .25, the actual population value. Indeed, the average of the 1,000 proportions in this particular data set is .248, which lies very close to the true value! This is no coincidence, as we will see.

This illustration highlights an important point about samples and the statistics calculated from them. If statistics are calculated for each of many, many independently and randomly chosen samples, their average or mean will equal the corresponding true, or population, quantity, no matter what the sample size. Statisticians refer to this mean as the **expected value** (*E*) of the estimator. This idea can be stated more succinctly. If θ (theta) represents a population parameter or characteristic such as a proportion or mean, then $\hat{\theta}$ stands for a sample estimator of that characteristic. We can then write

$$E(\hat{\theta}) \;=\; \theta,$$

which reads, "The expected (or long-run) value of the estimator equals the corresponding value for the population from which the sample has been drawn."

In the case of a sample proportion based on a simple random sample, we have

$$E(p) \;=\; P,$$

where *p* is the estimated proportion, and the equation reads, "The expected (or long-run, or average) value of sample proportions equals the population proportion, *P.*"

In plain words, although any particular estimate result may not equal the parameter value of the population from which the data come,[29] if the sampling procedure were to be repeated an infinite number of times and a sample estimate calculated each time, then the average, or mean, of these results would equal the true value. This fact gives us confidence in the sampling method, though not in any particular sample statistic. Since Figure 7–3 includes only 1,000 estimates, not an infinite number, it only illustrates what can be demonstrated mathematically for many types of sample statistics.

Measuring the Variability of the Estimates: Standard Errors

Besides telling us the expected value for the population, statistical theory also tells us that sample proportions will fall above and below the true value in a predictable manner, as suggested by Figure 7–3. That is, there is variation or variability in the outcomes. As we just observed, most of the sample proportions fall between .05 and .45 (or 5 and 45 percent). A few will be much larger or smaller, but they will be the exceptions. Consequently, we can use a graph like that shown in Figure 7–3 to determine approximately the likelihood of getting a particular sample result *if* the true value of the population from which the samples have been drawn is .25. For example, what are the chances of getting a sample proportion of .29 if the population proportion is .25? The answer: very likely. Why? Because statistics tells us that most sample results will be close to the true value. But suppose a sample proportion turns out to be .75. If the true number is .25, is this a likely result? Look at the figure. It suggests that a value that far from .25 occurs only rarely. So the answer might be "A sample proportion of .75 is possible but not very probable." (You can use the areas in the rectangles to "guesstimate" the chances.)

The fact that statistics behave in this manner helps us make inferences. To anticipate the material in later chapters, let us continue to hypothesize that the true proportion is .25. Now assume that a sample of ten produces a proportion of .19. Given that such a result is reasonably possible—look at Figure 7–3 once again—we might conclude that this hypothesis cannot be rejected. However, if the sample result turned out to be .9, we would be justified in concluding that the hypothesis does not hold water and should be rejected. Why? Because .9 is an unlikely result given that $P = .25$.

Of course, we could be making a mistake. It is possible that the true proportion is .25 even though our sample estimate is way above that number. If we did reject the hypothesis (that is, $P = .25$), we would be wrong. Yet the chances of making this kind of error are relatively small. That's what people mean when they say they have confidence in an estimate. (Confidence does not equal certainty, just as in legal trials judgments are based on the standard of reasonable doubt, not absolute, infallible knowledge.)

The mathematical term for the variation around the expected value is the standard error of the estimator, or **standard error** for short. Loosely speaking, the standard error provides a numerical indication of the variation in our sample estimates. (Like all statistical indicators, it has its own symbol, $\hat{\sigma}$.) The standard error in this example is .14.[30] As of now, this number has no obvious meaning, but, as shown later, it can be used to make probability statements such as "roughly two-thirds of the sample proportions lie in the interval between .11 and .39." So now you can tell your client, the senator, that based on just the first (and presumably the only) sample you have taken, the true proportion of independents in the district is probably somewhere between 11 and 39 percent with the best bet being 25 percent. When she asks what you mean by *probably*, you can tell her, "I am about 66 percent sure." (You might be able to recognize this point by looking at the frequencies represented by the bars in the graph.)

Not surprisingly, your first estimate may not be very helpful to the campaign, which must decide how to target its limited resources. After all, if the percentage of independents in the district is as low as 11 percent, the senator might follow one strategy, but if it is 39 percent or more, she might do something else. As a result, the senator would like you to narrow the range of uncertainty. What can you do? The answer may be obvious: take a larger sample.

Imagine that you increase the sample size to 50 registered voters ($N = 50$) from the population in which P is still .25 and then note the estimated proportion. This time, you might find that 15 respondents out of 50, or 30 percent, are independents. Because of our omniscience, we know this estimate is a bit too large. But, as before, let us repeat the process. If you drew 1,000 independent random samples, each containing 50 observations, and plotted the distribution of the estimated proportions, you would get a graph similar to the one in Figure 7–4.

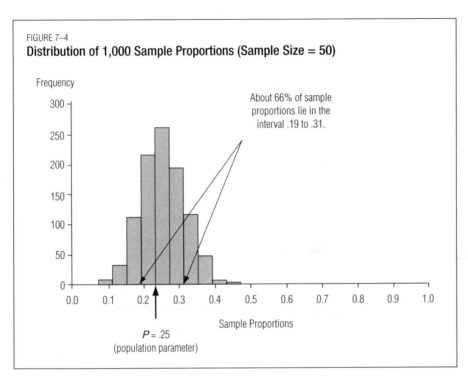

FIGURE 7–4
Distribution of 1,000 Sample Proportions (Sample Size = 50)

Frequency

About 66% of sample
proportions lie in the
interval .19 to .31.

$P = .25$
(population parameter)

Sample Proportions

Source: Simulated data.

Note: Mean of 1,000 sample proportions is .252.

For the hypothetical data shown in Figure 7–4, the mean of the 1,000 sample proportions is .252, a value quite near the true number.[31] The figure illustrates once again what can be shown mathematically, namely, that the distribution of Ps is approximately bell shaped, with the expected or long-run value of sample estimates being equal to the true proportion of the population from which the samples have been collected. Also, notice that the distribution is not as spread out as the one depicted in Figure 7–3. In our statistical language, the standard error is smaller, .06 now versus .14 previously. Hence, about two-thirds of the sample proportions fall in the interval .19 to .31, which is about half the width of the one based on ten cases; very few fall in the tails of the distribution. So increasing the sample size gives us more confidence that .252 is near the true value.

To cement the point, let us repeat the simulation using a much larger sample, $N = 500$. The result appears in Figure 7–5. It, too, shows that the average of the sample proportions is close to the true value and that the variability of the estimates, the sampling error, has been greatly reduced.

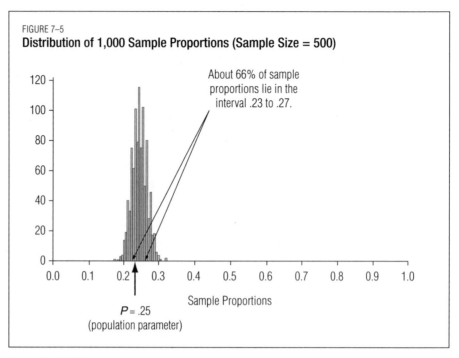

FIGURE 7–5
Distribution of 1,000 Sample Proportions (Sample Size = 500)

Source: Simulated data.

Note: Mean of 1,000 proportions is .250.

This finding illustrates the generalization that the sample size affects the magnitude of sampling variation: the larger the sample, the smaller the standard error. That statement, in turn, implies that as sample sizes increase, the range of sample estimators decreases. (This fact may be consistent with your intuition that large samples should be more accurate than small ones.) But keep in mind that the expected value of sample estimators does not depend on the sample size. Instead, it is the confidence placed in them that does.

Table 7–4 summarizes the results for samples of size 10, 50, and 500. For instance, the row labeled "10" contains the results of taking 1,000 independent samples (each of $N = 10$) from a population in which $P = .25$. The average of the 1,000 sample proportions is .248, the standard error is .14, the interval containing about 66% of the sample proportions is .11 to .39, and the lowest and highest proportions are 0 and .70. Similarly, the next row contains the results of 1,000 samples of $N = 50$. For these sets of simulated data, the average of the sample proportions is always close to the true value no matter how large the sample, again illustrating the argument about expected values. But, and herein lies the crux of the argument, the measures of variability of the proportions decrease

TABLE 7–4

Properties of Samples of Different Sizes

Sample Size	66% Average (Mean)[a]	Standard Error[b]	Confidence Interval	Minimum Proportion	Maximum Proportion	Range of Proportions
10	.248	.14	.11–.39	0	.70	.70
50	.252	.06	.19–.31	.1	.48	.38
500	.250	.02	.23–.27	.19	.32	.13

[a] Each mean is the average of 1,000 sample proportions taken from a population in which the true probability (the parameter of interest in this case) $P = .25$.

[b] This term measures the variation or variability of the sample proportions. It indicates the magnitude of sampling error.

considerably as the sample sizes get larger. The numbers may seem small to you, but notice that the variability of the sample results based on 10 cases (.14) is more than twice as large as the corresponding number for the samples of size 50 (.06).

What does all this mean in plain English? Small sample sizes are not invalid or worthless. The expected values of many of their sample statistics will equal the population parameters. But estimates based on small samples may be imprecise in the sense that any specific estimate may be much too high or low to be useful. Whether or not this is the case depends on the study's purposes.

Sampling Distributions

Let's tie things together by introducing the last concept on our list, sampling distributions. Figures 7–3, 7–4, and 7–5 offer an inkling of what the term *sampling distribution* means. A **sampling distribution** of a sample statistic is a theoretical expression that describes the mean, variation, and shape of the distribution of an infinite number of occurrences of the statistic when calculated on samples of size N drawn independently and randomly from a population. Think of it as a statistical tool for calculating the probability that sample statistics fall within certain distances of the population parameter. The sample information cannot, of course, tell us exactly where within the range of values the population parameter lies. But it allows us to make an educated guess.

A general method for making such an inference is quite simple. Let $\hat{\theta}$ be a sample statistic that estimates some population parameter, θ. (In the previous example, when we knew the population parameter was a proportion, we called these p and P, respectively.) Since θ is unknown, we want to surround an estimate of it with a range or interval of values that includes it with some known probability. (For example, Is the population parameter "probably" between 20 and 30?) This range can be found by adding and subtracting some multiple of the standard error.

For some sample statistics obtained from random samples, we can say that the interval $\hat{\theta} \pm 1.96\sigma_{\theta}$ has a 95 percent probability of containing the population value. (To be clear about the point, the previous statement means that if we drew 100 independent samples from a population having a parameter θ, we believe that about 95 out of the 100 estimated intervals would include this value. The parameter does not "bounce" around; it is a constant. Rather, the intervals vary from sample to sample.) Obviously you need to know how to calculate the standard error and where numbers like 1.96 come from. We explain this in chapter 12. For now only the basic idea is important. By taking the estimator and adding and subtracting some multiple of the standard error, we can obtain a confidence interval for the statistic and interpret this range to mean "there is such and such a probability that the calculated interval includes the population value."

This reasoning underlies poll results reported in the media. You may occasionally see reports of sample-based information that imply that the sample results are precise estimates of the target population. During the 2004 presidential election campaign, for example, you may have seen newspaper headlines declaring "Bush Leads Kerry, 52% to 48%." Such reports can be misleading. No probability sample can produce exact estimates of the voting intentions of the population. Although the poll results may have been 52 percent for Bush, we know that such estimates are subject to sampling error.

HOW LARGE A SAMPLE?

Ideally, sample estimates of the target population are equal to the purposes of the research. As we learned earlier, the key to controlling sampling error is the sample size. Generally, the larger the sample, the smaller the sampling error, as measured by the standard error. Given that sample size figures so prominently in sampling distributions, you might think that by increasing N you could reduce uncertainty to near zero. However, the relationship between sample size and sampling error is exponential rather than linear. For example, to cut sampling error in half, the sample size must be quadrupled. This means that researchers must balance the costs of increasing sample size with the size of the sampling error they are willing to tolerate.

Table 7–5 shows the relationship between sample size and the margin of error for Gallup Poll–type samples.[32] In public opinion research, increasing sample size may be too costly. Survey analysts usually draw samples of 1,500 to 2,000 people (regardless of the size of the target population). This yields a margin of error (about ±3 percent) at a cost that is within reach for at least some survey organizations.

The question of how large a sample should be thus depends not so much on bias or no bias (after all, the

TABLE 7–5

The Relationship between Sample Size and Sampling Error

Sample Size	Confidence Interval (percent)
4,000	±2
1,500	±3
1,000	±4
600	±5
400	±6
200	±8
100	±11

Source: Charles W. Roll Jr. and Albert H. Cantril, *Polls: Their Use and Misuse in Politics* (New York: Basic Books, 1972), 72. Copyright © 1972 Charles W. Roll, Albert H. Cantril. Reprinted by permission of Basic Books, a member of the Perseus Books Group.

Note: This table is based on a 95 percent confidence level and is derived from experience with Gallup Poll samples.

expected value of a statistic based on even a very small sample is unbiased, as we saw above) as on how narrow an interval a researcher needs for a given level of confidence. For exploratory projects in which a rough approximation is adequate, a sample need not be huge. But when researchers attempt to make fine distinctions, they must collect more data.

We can illustrate this point with still another example. Assume that we want to estimate a population mean, and suppose further that we want to be 99 percent certain about our estimate. (Notice that we have established a specific level of confidence—99 percent certainty.) To achieve this level of confidence, how wide off the mark can our estimate be and still be useful? Once we answer this question, we can choose an appropriate sample size. For example, if we want to say with 99 percent certainty that the interval $25,500 to $28,500 contains the true mean, then we would need a sample of a certain size (perhaps 200). But if we want to be 99 percent certain that the mean lies between $26,500 and $26,600—a mere $100 difference—then we will need a much larger sample.[33]

Decisions about sample sizes involve trade-offs. Perhaps our senate candidate wants an estimated proportion to be within 1 or 2 percent of the true value, but does she have sufficient funds to collect a large enough survey? If not, she might have to settle for a wider confidence interval.[34]

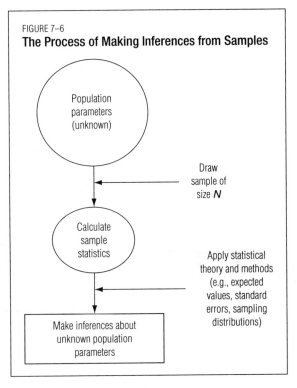

FIGURE 7–6
The Process of Making Inferences from Samples

Population parameters (unknown)

Draw sample of size *N*

Calculate sample statistics

Apply statistical theory and methods (e.g., expected values, standard errors, sampling distributions)

Make inferences about unknown population parameters

CONCLUSION

In this chapter, we discussed what it means to select a sample out of a target population, the various types of samples that political scientists use, and the kinds of information they yield. Figure 7–6 provides an intuitive summary of sampling in the research process.

The following guidelines may help researchers who are deciding whether or not to rely on a sample as well as students who are evaluating research based on sample data:

- If cost is not a major consideration, and the validity of the measures will not suffer, it is generally better to collect data for the complete target population than for just a sample of that population.

- If cost or validity considerations dictate that a sample be drawn, a probability sample is usually preferable to a nonprobability sample. The accuracy of sample estimates can be determined only for probability samples. If the desire to represent a target population accurately is not a major concern or is impossible to achieve, then a nonprobability sample may be used.

- Probability samples yield estimates of the target population. All samples are subject to sampling error. No sample, no matter how well drawn, can provide an exact measurement of an attribute of, or relationship within, the target population.

Fortunately, statistical theory gives us methods for making systematic inferences about unknown parameters and for objectively measuring the probabilities of making inferential errors. This information allows the researcher and the scientific community to judge the tenability of many empirical claims.

Terms Introduced

Cluster sample. A probability sample that is used when no list of elements exists. The sampling frame initially consists of clusters of elements.

Convenience sample. A nonprobability sample in which the selection of elements is determined by the researcher's convenience.

Disproportionate sample. A stratified sample in which elements sharing a characteristic are underrepresented or overrepresented in the sample.

Element. A particular case or entity about which information is collected; the unit of analysis.

Estimator. A statistic based on sample observations that is used to estimate the numerical value of an unknown population parameter.

Expected value. The mean or average value of a sample statistic based on repeated samples from a population.

Nonprobability sample. A sample for which each element in the total population has an unknown probability of being selected.

Population. All the cases or observations covered by a hypothesis; all the units of analysis to which a hypothesis applies.

Population parameter. A characteristic or an attribute in a population (not a sample) that can be quantified.

Probability sample. A sample for which each element in the total population has a known probability of being selected.

Proportionate sample. A probability sample that draws elements from a stratified population at a rate proportional to the size of the samples.

Purposive sample. A nonprobability sample in which a researcher uses discretion in selecting elements for observation.

Quota sample. A nonprobability sample in which elements are sampled in proportion to their representation in the population.

Random digit dialing. A procedure used to improve the representativeness of telephone samples by giving both listed and unlisted numbers a chance of selection.

Sample. A subset of observations or cases drawn from a specified population.

Sample bias. The bias that occurs whenever some elements of a population are systematically excluded from a sample. It is usually due to an incomplete sampling frame or a nonprobability method of selecting elements.

Sample statistic. The estimator of a population characteristic or attribute that is calculated from sample data.

Sampling distribution. A theoretical (nonobserved) distribution of sample statistics calculated on samples of size N that, if known, permits the calculation of confidence intervals and the test of statistical hypotheses.

Sampling error. The difference between a sample estimate and a corresponding population parameter that arises because only a portion of a population is observed.

Sampling fraction. The proportion of the population included in a sample.

Sampling frame. The population from which a sample is drawn. Ideally it is the same as the total population of interest to a study.

Sampling interval. The number of elements in a sampling frame divided by the desired sample size.

Sampling unit. The entity listed in a sampling frame. It may be the same as an element, or it may be a group or cluster of elements.

Simple random sample. A probability sample in which each element has an equal chance of being selected.

Snowball sample. A sample in which respondents are asked to identify additional members of a population.

Standard error. The standard deviation or measure of variability or dispersion of a sampling distribution.

Statistical inference. The mathematical theory and techniques for making conjectures about the unknown characteristics (parameters) of populations based on samples.

Stratified sample. A probability sample in which elements sharing one or more characteristics are grouped and elements are selected from each group in proportion to the group's representation in the total population.

Stratum. A subgroup of a population that shares one or more characteristics.

Systematic sample. A probability sample in which elements are selected from a list at predetermined intervals.

Weighting factor. A mathematical factor used to make a disproportionate sample representative.

Suggested Readings

Govindarajulu, Zakkula. *Elements of Sampling Theory and Methods.* Upper Saddle River, N.J.: Prentice Hall, 1999.

Kish, Leslie. *Survey Sampling.* New York: John Wiley & Sons, 1995. (Originally published 1965.) This is the classic treatment of this subject.

Levy, Paul S., and Stanley Lemeshow. *Sampling of Populations: Methods and Applications.* 3rd ed. New York: Wiley, 1999.

Lohr, Sharon L. *Sampling: Design and Analysis.* Pacific Grove, Calif.: Duxbury Press, 1999.

Rea, Louis M., and Richard A. Parker. *Designing and Conducting Survey Research: A Comprehensive Guide.* 2nd ed. San Francisco: Jossey-Bass, 1997.

Rosnow, Ralph L., and Robert Rosenthal. *Beginning Behavioral Research: A Conceptual Primer.* 3rd ed. Upper Saddle River, N.J.: Prentice Hall, 1998.

Notes

1. Pew Research Center for the People and the Press, "Possible Consequences of Non-Response for Pre-Election Surveys: Race and Reluctant Respondents," May 16, 1998, http://people-press.org/1998/05/16/possible-consequences-of-non-response-for-pre-election-surveys/.

2. "Are Presidential Election Polls Valid?" *Yahoo! Answers,* last modified 2008, http://answers.yahoo.com/question/index?qid = 20081007203232AAt2nug/.

3. "How Valid are Polls? Who Participates? How Do We Know These Participants Tell the Truth?" *Answerbag.com,* last modified October 29, 2008, http://www.answerbag.com/q_view/1012158/.

4. Christopher Gelpi, Peter D. Feaver, and Jason Reifler, "Success Matters: Casualty Sensitivity and the War in Iraq," *International Security* 30, no. 3 (2005/2006): 7–46.

5. It would not only be impractical but perhaps inaccurate as well. Social scientists generally believe that for *some* purposes, trying to contact and study every person in a population may lead to more errors than if a smaller sample were investigated.

6. A related concern is the size of the population. In fact, no population of real "things" has an infinite number of members, but we nevertheless treat populations as if they were infinite for most purposes.

7. For a good discussion, see Gary King, Robert O. Keohane, and Sidney Verba, *Designing Social Inquiry: Scientific Inference in Qualitative Research* (Princeton, N.J.: Princeton University Press, 1994).

8. Richard A. Joslyn, *Mass Media and Elections* (Reading, Mass.: Addison-Wesley, 1984).

9. This discussion of terms used in sampling is drawn primarily from Earl R. Babbie, *Survey Research Methods* (Belmont, Calif.: Wadsworth, 1973), 79–81.

10. Ibid., 74–75.

11. Random digit dialing has become increasingly sophisticated. For more details on how it works and for a list of references, see Johnny Blair, Shanyang Zhao, Barbara Bickart, Ralph Kuhn, and Yung Chiao Kang, "Sample Design for Household Telephone Surveys: A Bibliography 1949–1996," Survey Research Center University of Maryland at College Park, http://www.musc.edu/bmt738/German/sampbib.html.

12. For various methods of random digit dialing, see E. Laird Landon Jr. and Sharon K. Banks, "Relative Efficiency and Bias of Plus-One Telephone Sampling," *Journal of Marketing*

Research 14, no. 3 (1977): 294–99; K. Michael Cummings, "Random Digit Dialing: A Sampling Technique for Telephone Surveys," *Public Opinion Quarterly* 43, no. 2 (1979): 233–44; Robert M. Groves and Robert Louis Kahn, *Surveys by Telephone: A National Comparison with Personal Interviews* (New York: Academic Press, 1979); and Joseph Waksberg, "Sampling Methods for Random Digit Dialing," *Journal of the American Statistical Association* 73, no. 361 (1978): 40–46.

13. James H. Frey, *Survey Research by Telephone* (Beverly Hills, Calif.: Sage, 1983), 22.

14. When used to describe a type of sample, *random* does not mean haphazard or casual; rather, it means that every element has a known probability of being selected. Strictly speaking, to ensure an equal chance of selection, *replacement* is required, that is, putting each selected element back on the list before the next element is selected. In *simple* random sampling, however, elements are selected without replacement. This means that on each successive draw, the probability of an element's being selected increases because fewer and fewer elements remain. But for each draw, the probability of being selected is equal among the remaining elements. If the sample size is less than one-fifth the size of the population, the slight deviation from strict random sampling caused by sampling without replacement is acceptable. See Hubert M. Blalock Jr., *Social Statistics,* 2nd ed. (New York: McGraw-Hill, 1972), 513–14.

15. This episode has been studied extensively. See, for example, Stephen E. Fienberg, "Randomization and Social Affairs: The 1970 Draft Lottery," *Science* 171, no. 3968 (1971): 255–61; and Stephen E. Fienberg, "Randomization for the Selective Service Draft Lotteries," in *Statistics by Example: Finding Models,* ed. Frederick Mosteller, Joint Committee on the Curriculum in Statistics and Probability, National Council of Teachers of Mathematics (Reading, Mass.: Addison-Wesley, 1973), 1–13.

16. These numbers are sometimes called "pseudo-random" because computers use an algorithm to generate a string of digits, and if you knew that algorithm and its starting place, you could re-create the list exactly. But once produced, the numbers pass all sorts of mathematical tests of randomness. For a more advanced discussion, see Micah Altman, Jeff Gill, and Michael P. McDonald, *Numerical Issues in Statistical Computing for the Social Scientist* (Hoboken, N.J.: Wiley-Interscience, 2003), especially chapters 2 and 3.

17. Blalock, *Social Statistics,* 515.

18. Babbie, *Survey Research Methods,* 93.

19. There are two reasons to use disproportionate sampling in addition to obtaining enough cases for statistical analysis of subgroups: the high cost of sampling some strata and differences in the heterogeneity of some strata that result in differences in sampling error. A researcher might want to minimize sampling when it is costly or increase sampling from heterogeneous strata while decreasing it from homogeneous strata. See Blalock, *Social Statistics,* 518–19.

20. Ibid., 521–22.

21. We could have obtained the same results by multiplying the GPA of each student by the weighting factor associated with the student's major and then calculating the mean GPA for the whole sample.

22. Marc M. Howard, James L. Gibson, and Dietlind Stolle, *United States Citizenship, Involvement, Democracy (CID) Survey, 2006* (Ann Arbor, Mich.: Inter-university Consortium for Political and Social Research, 2007).

23. Richard F. Fenno Jr., *Home Style: House Members in Their Districts* (Boston: Little, Brown, 1978).

24. Babbie, *Survey Research Methods,* 75.

25. Snowball sampling is generally considered to be a nonprobability sampling technique, although strategies have been developed to achieve a probability sample with this method.

See Kenneth D. Bailey, *Methods of Social Research* (New York: Free Press, 1978), 83. The "reputational approach" discussed in Chapter 2 could be considered an example of this type of sample.

26. Jane W. Bergsten and Stephanie A. Pierson, "Telephone Screening for Rare Characteristics Using Multiplicity Counting Rules," in *1982 Proceedings of the Section on Survey Research Methods* (Alexandria, Va.: American Statistical Association, 1982), 145–50. Available at http://www.amstat.org/sections/srms/proceedings/.

27. The following remarks assume that we have a simple random sample, meaning (just as a reminder) that each member of the sample has been selected randomly and independently of all the others. We assume the same throughout the discussion in this section.

28. This procedure, called sampling with replacement, is premised on the assumption that, at least theoretically, people will sooner or later be interviewed twice or more. We ignore this nuance, because it does not affect the validity of the conclusions in this case.

29. Indeed, in all likelihood it will not exactly equal the population value.

30. It is easy enough to calculate from the formula:

$$\sigma_p = \sqrt{P(1-P)/N}.$$

In the present case, the standard error is as follows:

$$\sigma_p = \sqrt{P(1-P)/N} = \sqrt{(.25)(.75)/10} = .14.$$

31. Note, too, that it is close to the value obtained from the 1,000 samples, where $N = 10$. So the average of the Ps based on samples of 10 is not much different from the average based on samples of 50.

32. The decision about appropriate sample size depends on many factors, including the type of sample, attributes being measured, heterogeneity of the population, and complexity of the data analysis plan. A more complete discussion of these factors may be found in Royce Singleton Jr., Bruce C. Straits, Margaret M. Straits, and Ronald J. McAllister, *Approaches to Social Research* (New York: Oxford University Press, 1988), 158–63; and Edwin Mansfield, *Basic Statistics: With Applications* (New York: Norton, 1986), 287–94.

33. Sample size is not the only factor that affects statistical inferences. For a somewhat advanced discussion, see Dennis D. Boos and Jacqueline M. Hughes-Oliver, "How Large Does n Have to Be for Z and t Intervals?" *American Statistician* 54, no. 2 (2000): 121–28.

34. Sampling error also depends on the type of sample drawn. For a given sample size, a simple random sample provides a more accurate estimate of the target (that is, a smaller margin of error) than does a cluster sample. Sampling error is also smaller for an attribute that is shared by almost all elements in the sample than for one that is distributed across only half of the sample elements. Finally, sampling error is reduced if the sample represents a significant proportion of the target population—that is, if the sampling fraction is greater than one-fourth of the target population. Because this is unusual, however, the effect of the sampling fraction on sampling error is generally minuscule.

MAKING EMPIRICAL OBSERVATIONS

Direct and Indirect Observation

TYPES OF DATA AND COLLECTION TECHNIQUES

POLITICAL SCIENTISTS TEND TO USE three broad types of empirical observations, or data collection methods, depending on the phenomena they are interested in studying. Interview data, discussed in chapter 10, are derived from individuals. This type of data collection may involve interviewing a representative cross-section of the national adult population or a select group of political actors, such as committee chairs in Congress. It may involve face-to-face interviews or interviews conducted over the phone or through the mail or Internet. It may involve highly structured interviews in which a questionnaire is followed closely or less structured, open-ended discussions. Regardless of the particular type of interview setting, however, the essentials of the data collection method are the same: the data come from responses to the verbal or written cues of the researcher, and the respondent knows these responses are being recorded.

In addition to interview data, political scientists use documents (newspapers, photographs, video clips, hearing testimony, press releases, letters, and diaries) as well as statistical data that exist in various archival records. We refer to these sources of data collectively as the written record. This type of data collection, known as document analysis (the subject of chapter 9), relies heavily on the record-keeping activities of government agencies, private institutions, interest groups, media organizations, and even private citizens. Also included in what we refer to as the written record are data collected first as interview data but then aggregated and reported in summary form for groups of individuals. For example, unemployment statistics are derived from the Census Bureau's Current Population Survey, a household survey conducted each month. What sets document analysis apart from other data collection methods is that the researcher is usually not the original collector of the data and the original reason for the collection of the data may not have been to further a scientific research project. The record keepers may be unaware of how the data they collect will ultimately be used, and the phenomena they record are not generally personal beliefs and attitudes of individuals, which are more typically collected through interviews, although diaries and letters could provide such information.

Finally, data may be collected through physical observation, discussed further in this chapter. The researcher collects data on political behavior by observing either the behavior itself (**direct observation**) or some physical trace of the behavior (indirect observation). Unlike interviewing, this method of data collection does not rely on people's verbal responses to verbal stimuli presented by the researcher but rather on firsthand examination of activities, behavior, events, or the like. Furthermore, those whose behavior is being directly or indirectly observed may be unaware that they are being observed.

Choosing among Data Collection Methods

A political scientist's choice of data collection method depends on many factors. One important consideration is the validity of the measurements that a particular method will permit. For example, a researcher who wants to measure the crime rate of different cities may feel that the crime rates reported by local police departments to the FBI are not sufficiently accurate to support a research project. The researcher may be concerned that some departments overreport and some underreport various criminal acts or that some victims of crimes may fail to report the crimes to the police, hence rendering that method of collecting data and measuring the crime rate unacceptable. Therefore, the researcher may decide that a more accurate indication of the crime rate can be attained by interviewing a sample of citizens in different cities and asking them how much crime they have experienced themselves.

Also reflecting a concern over the validity of measurements, Susan J. Carroll and Debra J. Liebowitz noted that scholars of women and politics have criticized the use of survey research to study the political participation of women.[1] One problem is that existing conceptions of what is considered "political," and hence what is asked about in survey questions, may not fully capture the range of women's political activity. Carroll and Liebowitz suggested that researchers look at the issue inductively, that is, study women's activities and determine in what ways their activities are political. For this approach, observation, in-depth interviews, and focus groups, rather than structured questionnaires, are more appropriate data collection methods.

A political scientist is also influenced by the **reactivity** of a data collection method—the effect of the data collection itself on the phenomena being measured. When people know their behavior is being observed and know or can guess the purpose of the observation, they may alter their behavior. As a result, the observed behavior may be an unnatural reaction to the process of being observed. People may be reluctant, for example, to admit to an interviewer that they are anti-Semitic or have failed to vote in an election. Thus, many researchers prefer unobtrusive or nonreactive measures of political behavior, because they believe that the resulting data are more natural or real.

The population covered by a data collection method is another important consideration for a researcher. The population of interest determines whose behavior the researcher observes. One type of data may be available for only a few people, whereas another type may permit more numerous, interesting, and worthwhile comparisons. A researcher studying the behavior of political consultants, for example, may decide that relying on the published memoirs of a handful of consultants will not adequately cover the population of consultants (not to mention the validity problems of the data) and that it would be better to seek out a broad cross-section of consultants and interview them. Or a researcher interested in political corruption may decide that interviewing a broad cross-section of politicians charged with various corrupt practices is not feasible and that data (of a different kind) could be obtained for a more diverse set of corrupt acts from accounts published in the mass media.

Additionally, cost and availability are crucial elements in the choice of a data collection technique. Some types of data collection are simply more expensive than others, and some types of observations are made more readily than others. Large-scale interviewing, for example, is very expensive and time-consuming, and the types of questions that can be asked and behaviors that can be observed are limited. Although the costs of data generated through interviews or the written record may be high, the cost of firsthand observation through the expenditure of time (if the researcher does it) or money (if the researcher pays others to do it) will generally be even higher. Data from archival records are usually much less expensive, since the record-keeping entity has borne most of the cost of collecting and publishing the data. With the increased use of computers, many organizations are systematically collecting data of interest to researchers. A disadvantage, however, may be that the data must be made available by the record-keeping organization, which can refuse a researcher's request or take a long time to fill it.

Observation is generally an example of **primary data**—that is, data recorded and used by the researcher making the observations—whereas data from interviews or the written record can be primary data or **secondary data**—data used by a researcher who did not personally collect the data. Most data collected through direct observation are recorded in the form of personal notes, recordings, and transcripts. These data are less likely to be publicly available because notes, in particular, are highly individualized and intended to help the person taking the notes remember observations. Hence, they would be relatively dissatisfactory to others even if they were made publicly available.

The high cost of direct and indirect observation means that most students will not have the resources to make their own observations for use in a research paper, except in the most limited fashion. Students will often find suitable data generated through interviews or the written record for free in publicly available data archives (see chapters 9 and 10), but students wishing to use data generated through direct or indirect observation must usually rely on their own ability to make the observations. For example, you might be able to use observations made during your internship with a political campaign in an analysis of election strategy, but you are not likely to have the time to make firsthand observations across multiple campaigns. In most cases, it will be more cost-effective to rely on other, more readily available sources of data for research projects.

In addition to these factors, researchers must consider the ethical implications of their proposed research. In most cases, the research topics you are likely to propose will not raise serious ethical concerns, nor will your choice of method of data collection hinge on the risk it may pose to human subjects. Nevertheless, you should be aware of the ethical issues and risks to others that can result from social science research, and you should be aware of the review process that researchers are required to follow when proposing research involving human subjects.

In accordance with federal regulations, universities and other research organizations require faculty and students to submit research proposals involving human subjects for review by an **institutional review board** (often called a human subject review board). There may be some variation in practice concerning unfunded research, but the proper course of action is to contact your institution's research office for information regarding the review policy on human subjects. There are three levels of review: some research may be exempt, some may require only expedited review, and some research will be subject to full board review. Even if your research project seems to fit one of the categories of research exempt from review, you must request and be granted an exemption.[2]

Three ethical principles—respect for persons, beneficence, and justice—form the foundation for assessing the ethical dimensions of research involving human subjects. These principles were identified in the *Belmont Report,* a report of the National Commission for the Protection of Human Subjects of Biomedical and Behavioral Research.[3] The principle concerning respect for persons asserts that individuals should be treated as autonomous agents and that persons with diminished capacity are entitled to protection. *Beneficence* refers to protecting people from harm as well as making efforts to secure their well-being. The principle of justice requires researchers to consider the distribution of the benefits and burdens of research.

The principle of respect for persons requires that subjects be given the opportunity to choose what shall or shall not happen to them. **Informed consent** means that subjects are to be given information about the research, including the research procedure, its purposes, risks, and anticipated benefits; alternative procedures (where therapy is involved); how subjects are selected; and the person responsible for the research. In addition, the subject is to be given a statement offering him or her the opportunity to ask questions and to withdraw from the research at any time. This information and statement should be conveyed in a manner that is comprehensible to the subject, and the consent of the subject must be voluntary.

An assessment of risks and benefits relates directly to the beneficence principle by helping to determine whether risks to subjects are justified and by providing information useful to subjects for their informed consent. The justice principle is often associated with the selection of subjects insofar as some populations may be more likely to be targeted for study; one example is prison populations, particularly in the past.

In this chapter and in chapters 9 and 10, the relative advantages and disadvantages of each of the major data collection methods are examined with respect to the factors of validity, reactivity, population coverage, cost, and availability. We also point out the ethical issues raised by some applications of these data collection methods.

OBSERVATION

Although observation is more generally a research tool of anthropologists, psychologists, and sociologists, observation has been used by political scientists to study political campaigning, community politics, leadership and executive decision making, program implementation, judicial proceedings, the US Congress, and state legislatures. In fact, any student who has had an internship, kept a daily log or a diary, and written a paper based on his or her experiences has used this method of data collection.

Every day we "collect data" using observational techniques. We observe some attribute or characteristic of people and infer some behavioral trait from that observation. For example, we watch the car in front of us swerve between traffic lanes and conclude that the driver has been drinking. We observe the mannerisms, voice pitch, and facial expressions of a student making a presentation in one of our classes and decide that the person is exceptionally nervous. Or we decide that most of the citizens attending a public hearing are opposed to a proposed project by listening to their comments to each other before the start of the hearing. The observational techniques used by political scientists are only extensions of this method of data collection. They resemble everyday observations but are usually more self-conscious and systematic.

Observations may be classified in at least four ways: (1) direct or indirect, (2) participant or nonparticipant, (3) overt or covert, and (4) structured or unstructured. The most basic distinction is whether an observation is direct or indirect.[4] For example, a direct method of observing college students' favorite studying spots in classrooms and office buildings would involve walking around the buildings and noticing where students are. An indirect method of observing the same behavior would be to arrive on campus early in the morning before the custodial staff and measure the number of food wrappers, soda cans, and other pieces of debris at various locations.

In **participant observation,** the investigator is "both an actor and a specta-tor," that is, a regular participant in the activities or group being observed. [5] For example, someone who studies political campaigns by becoming actively involved in them is a participant observer. Researchers who attended meetings and rallies of the Greater Boston Tea Party to observe and interview tea party activists considered themselves to be participant observers.[6] A researcher does not, however, have to become a full-fledged member of the group to be a par-ticipant observer. Some mutually acceptable role or identity must be worked out. For example, Ruth Horowitz did not become a gang member when she studied Chicano youth in a Chicago neighborhood.[7] She hung around with gang mem-bers, but as a nonmember. She did not participate in fights and was able to decline when asked to conceal weapons for gang members. A nonparticipant observer does not participate in group activities or become a member of the group or community. For example, an investigator interested in hearings held by public departments of transportation or city council meetings could observe those proceedings without becoming a participant.

A third way to characterize observation is by noting whether it is overt or covert. In **overt observation,** those being observed are aware of the investiga-tor's presence and intentions. In **covert observation,** the investigator's presence is hidden or undisclosed, and his or her intentions are disguised. For example, observation was used in a study to measure what percentage of people washed their hands after using the restroom. Research involving covert observation of public behavior of private individuals is not likely to raise ethical issues as long as individuals are not or cannot be identified and disclosure of individuals' behavior would not place them at risk. Note that elected or appointed public officials are not shielded by these limitations. Ethical standards and their appli-cation or enforcement have changed, and it is likely that many earlier examples of participant observation research, especially those involving covert observa-tion, would not receive approval from human subject review boards today. For example, social scientists Mary Henle and Marian B. Hubble once hid under beds in students' rooms to study student conversations.[8]

In **structured observation,** the investigator looks for and systematically records the incidence of specific behaviors. In **unstructured observation,** all behavior is considered relevant, at least at first, and recorded. Only later, upon reflection, will the investigator distinguish between important and trivial behavior.

DIRECT OBSERVATION

The vast majority of observation studies conducted by political scientists involve direct observation, in which the researcher observes actual behavior, with the observation more likely to occur in a natural setting than in a labora-tory. As a student, you are not likely to conduct your own observation research in a laboratory. Again, observation may be structured or unstructured. The term **field study** is typically used to refer to open-ended and wide-ranging, rather than structured, observation in a natural setting. This type of study or data collection method is also referred to as **ethnography**, which Wedeen defined as "immersion in the place and lives of people under study."[9]

Observation in a laboratory setting gives a researcher the advantage of having control over the environment of the observed. Thus, the researcher may be able to use a more rigorous experimental design than is possible in a natural, uncontrolled setting. Also, observation may be easier and more convenient to record and preserve, since one-way windows, videotape machines, and other observational aids are more readily available in a laboratory.

A disadvantage of laboratory observation is that subjects usually know they are being observed and therefore may alter their behavior, raising questions about the validity of the data collected. The use of aids that allow the observer to be physically removed from the setting and laboratories that are designed to be as inviting and as natural as possible may lead subjects to behave more naturally and less self-consciously.

An example of an attempt to create a natural-looking laboratory setting may be found in Stanley Milgram and R. Lance Shotland's book *Television and Antisocial Behavior*.[10] These researchers were interested in the effect of television programming on adult behavior, specifically in the ability of television drama to stimulate antisocial acts such as theft. They devised four versions of a program called *Medical Center*, each with a different plot, and showed different versions to four different audiences. Some of the versions showed a character stealing money, and those versions differed in whether the person was punished for the theft or not. The participants in the study were then asked to go to a particular office at a particular time to pick up a free transistor radio, their payment for participating in the research study. When they arrived in the office (the laboratory), they encountered a sign that said the radios were all gone. The researchers were interested in how people would react and specifically in whether they would imitate any of the behaviors in the versions of *Medical Center* that they had seen (such as the theft of money from see-through plastic collection dishes). Their behavior was observed covertly via a one-way mirror. Once the subjects left the office, they were directed to another location where they were, in fact, given the promised radio. (This experiment, reported in 1973, raises some serious ethical issues about deceiving research subjects and causing them harm.)

Direct observation in natural settings has its own advantages. One advantage of observing people in a natural setting is that people generally behave as they would ordinarily. Furthermore, the investigator is able to observe people for longer periods than would be possible in a laboratory. In fact, one of the striking features of field studies is the considerable amount of time an investigator may spend in the field. It is not uncommon for investigators to live in the community they are observing for a year or more. William F. Whyte's classic study of life in an Italian slum, *Street Corner Society,* was based on three years of observation (1937–1940), and Marc Ross's study of political participation in Nairobi, Kenya, took more than a year of field observation.[11] To study the behavior of US representatives in their districts, Richard Fenno traveled intermittently for almost 7 years, making 36 separate visits and spending 110 working days in 18 congressional districts.[12] Ruth Horowitz spent three years researching youth in an inner-city Chicano community in Chicago.[13] Raphael Schlembach observed activists participating in the Camp for Climate Action in the United Kingdom over a period of four years.[14]

Sometimes researchers have no choice but to observe political phenomena as they occur in their natural setting. Written records of events may not exist, or the records may not cover the behavior of interest to the researcher. Relying on personal accounts of participants may be unsatisfactory because of participants' distorted views of events, incomplete memories, or failure to observe what is of interest to the researcher. Joan E. McLean suggested that researchers interested in studying the decision-making styles of women running for public office need to spend time with campaigns in order to gather information as decisions are being made, rather than rely on postelection questionnaires or debriefing sessions.[15]

Open-ended, flexible observation is appropriate if the research purpose is one of description and exploration. For example, Fenno's research purpose was to study "representatives' perceptions of their constituencies while they are actually in their constituencies."[16] As Fenno explained, his visits with representatives in their districts

> were totally open-ended and exploratory. I tried to observe and
> inquire into anything and everything these members did. I worried
> about whatever they worried about. Rather than assume that I
> already knew what was interesting, I remained prepared to find inter-
> esting questions emerging in the course of the experience. The same
> with data. The research method was largely one of soaking and pok-
> ing or just hanging around.[17]

In these kinds of field studies, researchers do not start out with particular hypotheses that they want to test. They often do not know enough about what they plan to observe to establish lists and specific categories of behaviors to look for and record systematically. The purpose of the research is to discover what these might be.

Some political scientists have used observation as a preliminary research method.[18] For example, James A. Robinson's work in Congress provided firsthand information for his studies of the House Rules Committee and of the role of Congress in making foreign policy.[19] Ralph K. Huitt's service on Lyndon B. Johnson's Senate majority leader staff gave Huitt inside access to information for his study of Democratic Party leadership in the Senate.[20] And David W. Minar served as a school board member and used his experience to develop questionnaires for his comparative study of several school districts in the Chicago area.[21] As mentioned earlier, Carroll and Liebowitz suggested observing women's activities in order to identify behaviors with political effect that have not previously been included in measures of political activity; subsequent surveys could then include questions that ask about such behaviors.[22]

You may look upon an internship, volunteer work, or participation in a community or political organization as an opportunity to conduct your own research using direct observation. More than likely, your research will be a case study in which you are able to compare the real world with theories and general expectations suggested in course readings and lectures. If you are fortunate, your case may turn out to be a critical or deviant case study.

Most field studies involve participant observation. An investigator cannot be like the proverbial fly on the wall, observing a group of people for long periods of time. Usually he or she must assume a role or identity within the group that is being studied and participate in the activities of the group. As noted earlier, many political scientists who have studied Congress have worked as staff members on committees and in congressional offices. In addition to interviewing influential Latinos in Boston, Carol Hardy-Fanta joined the community group Familias Latinas de Boston while conducting her research on Latina women and politics. As she pointed out, this strategy complemented her research interviews:

> *Joining the community group Familias Latinas de Boston allowed me to gain an in-depth understanding of one community group over an extended period. Participating in formal, organized political activities such as manning the phone bank at the campaign office of a Latino candidate and attending political banquets, public forums, and conferences and workshops provided another means of observing how gender and culture interacted to stimulate—or suppress—political participation. I also joined protest marches and rallies and tracked down voter registration information in Spanish for a group at Mujeres Unidas en Acción. In addition, I learned much from informal interactions: at groups on domestic violence, during lunch at Latino community centers, and during spontaneous conversations with Latinos from many countries and diverse backgrounds. As I talked to people in community settings and observed how they interacted politically, the political roles of Latina women and the gender differences in how politics is defined emerged. Thus, multiple observations were available to check what I was hearing in the interviews about how to stimulate Latino political participation, and how Latina women and Latino men act politically.[23]*

Acceptance by the group is necessary for the investigator to benefit from the naturalness of the research setting. Negotiating an appropriate role for oneself within a group may be a challenging and evolving process. As Chicago gang researcher Ruth Horowitz pointed out, a researcher may not wish, or be able, to assume a role as a "member" of the observed group. Personal attributes (gender, age, ethnicity) of the researcher or ethical considerations (gang violence) may prevent this.[24] The role the researcher is able to establish also depends on the setting and the members of the group.

> *I was able to negotiate multiple identities and relationships that were atypical of those generally found in the research setting, but that nonetheless allowed me to become sufficiently close to the setting members to do the research. By becoming aware of the nature, content, and consequences of these identities, I was able to use the appropriate identity to successfully collect different kinds of data and at the same time avoid some difficult situations that full participation as a member might have engendered.[25]*

Investigators using participant observation often depend on members of the group they are observing to serve as **informants,** persons who are willing to be interviewed about the activities and behavior of themselves and of the group to which they belong. An informant also helps the researcher interpret group behavior. A close relationship between the researcher and the informant may help the researcher gain access to other group members, not only because an informant may familiarize the researcher with community members and norms but also because the informant, through close association with the researcher, will be able to pass on information about the researcher to the community.[26] Some participant observation studies have one key informant; others have several. For example, Whyte relied on the leader of a street corner gang whom he called "Doc" as his key informant, while Fenno's eighteen representatives all could be considered informants.[27] In fact, interviewing members of the group being observed is an integral part of participation observation in most cases.

Although a valuable asset to researchers, informants may present problems. A researcher should not rely too much on one or a few informants, since they may give a biased view of a community. And if the informant is associated with one faction in a multifaction community or is a marginal member of the community (and thus more willing to associate with the researcher), the researcher's affiliation with the informant may inhibit rather than enhance access to the community.[28]

Participant observation offers the advantages of a natural setting, the opportunity to observe people for lengthy periods so that interaction and changes in behavior may be studied, and a degree of accuracy or completeness that documents or recall data, such as that obtained in surveys, cannot provide. Observing a city council or school board meeting or a public hearing on the licensing of a locally undesirable land use will allow you to know and understand what happened at the event far better than reading official minutes or transcripts. However, this method has some noteworthy limitations as well.

The main problem with direct, participant observation as a method of empirical research for political scientists is that many significant instances of political behavior are not accessible for observation. The privacy of the voter in the voting booth is legally protected, US Supreme Court conferences are not open to anyone but the justices themselves, political consultants and bureaucrats do not usually wish to have political scientists privy to their discussions and decisions, and most White House conversations and deliberations are carefully guarded. Occasionally, physical traces of these private behaviors become public—such as the Watergate tapes of Richard Nixon's conversations with his aides—and disclosures are made about some aspects of government decision making, such as congressional committee hearings and Supreme Court oral arguments. Typically, however, access is the major barrier to directly observing consequential political behavior.

Another disadvantage of participant observation is lack of control over the environment. A researcher may be unable to isolate individual factors and observe their effect on behavior. Participant observation is also limited by the small number of cases that are usually involved. For example, Fenno observed only eighteen members or would-be members of Congress—too few for any sort of statistical analysis. He chose "analytical depth" over "analytical range"; in-depth observation of eighteen cases was the limit that Fenno thought he could manage intellectually, professionally, financially, and physically.[29] Whyte observed one street corner gang in depth, although he did observe others less closely.[30] Because of the small numbers of cases, the representativeness of the results of participant observation has been questioned. But, as we stressed in our discussion of research designs (chapter 6), the number of cases deemed appropriate for a research topic depends on the purpose of the research. Understanding how people function in a particular community may be the knowledge that is desired, not whether the particular community is representative of some larger number of communities.

Participant observation is often used as one of several data collection methods in a single study. For example, Williamson, Skocpol, and Coggin used fieldwork observations and personal interviews along with an e-mail questionnaire of Massachusetts tea party activists to supplement data from national surveys of the demographic and attitudinal characteristics of tea party activists and information on activism and ideology from local and regional tea party Web sites, among other sources.[31] J. C. Sharman used surveys and interviews as well as participant observation in his study of the adoption of anti-money-laundering policies in developing countries.[32]

Unstructured participant observation also has been criticized as invalid and biased. A researcher may selectively perceive behaviors, noting some while ignoring others. The interpretation of behaviors may reflect the personality and culture of the observer rather than the meaning attributed to them by the observed themselves. Moreover, the presence of the observer may alter the behavior of the observed, no matter how skillfully the observer attempts to become accepted as a nonthreatening part of the community.

Fieldworkers attempt to minimize these possible threats to data validity by immersing themselves in the culture they are observing and by taking copious notes on everything going on around them, no matter how seemingly trivial. Events without apparent meaning at the time of observation may become important and revealing upon later reflection. Of course, copious note taking leads to what is known as a "high dross rate"; much of what is recorded is not relevant to the research problem or question as it is finally formulated. It may be painful for the investigator to discard so much of the material that was carefully recorded, but it is standard practice with this method.

Another way to obtain more valid data is to allow the observed to read and comment on what the investigator has written and point out events and behavior that may have been misinterpreted. This check on observations may be of limited or no value if the person being observed cannot read or if the written material is aimed at persons well versed in the researcher's discipline and therefore is over the head of the observed.

Researchers' observations may be compromised if the researchers begin to overidentify with their subjects or informants. "Going native," as this phenomenon is known, may lead researchers to paint a more complimentary picture of the observed than is warranted. Researchers combat this problem by returning to their own culture to analyze their data and by asking colleagues or others to comment on their findings.

A demanding, yet essential, aspect of field study is note taking. Notes can be divided into three types: mental notes, jotted notes, and field notes. Mental note taking involves orienting one's consciousness to the task of remembering things one has observed, such as "who and how many were there, the physical character of the place, who said what to whom, who moved about in what way, and a general characterization of an order of events."[33] Because mental notes may fade rapidly, researchers use jotted notes to preserve them. Jotted notes consist of short phrases and keywords that will activate a researcher's memory later when the full field notes are written down. Researchers may be able to use tape recorders if they have the permission of those being observed.

Taped conversations do not constitute "full" field notes, which should include a running description of conversations and events. For this aspect of field notes, John Lofland advised that researchers should be factual and concrete, avoid making inferences, and use participants' descriptive and interpretative terms. Full field notes should include material previously forgotten and subsequently recalled. Lofland suggested that researchers distinguish between verbal material that is exact recall, paraphrased or close recall, and reasonable recall.[34]

Field notes should also include a researcher's analytic ideas and inferences, personal impressions and feelings, and notes for further information.[35] Because events and emotional states in a researcher's life may affect observation, they should be recorded. Notes for further information provide guidance for future observation—to fill in gaps in observations, call attention to things that may happen, or test out emerging analytic themes.

Full field notes should be legible and should be reviewed periodically, since the passage of time may present past observations in a new light to the researcher or reveal a pattern worthy of attention in a series of disjointed events. Creating and reviewing field notes is an important part of the observational method. Consequently a fieldworker should expect to spend as much time on field notes as he or she spends on observation in the field. Fortunately, computerized text analysis programs exist to help analyze field notes and interviews.

INDIRECT OBSERVATION

Indirect observation, the observation of physical traces of behavior, is essentially detective work.[36] Inferences based on physical traces can be drawn about people and their behavior. An unobtrusive research method, indirect observation is nonreactive: subjects do not change their behavior because they do not know they are being studied.

Physical Trace Measures

Researchers use two methods of measurement when undertaking indirect observation. An **erosion measure** is created by selective wear on some material. For example, campus planners at one university observed paths worn in grassy areas and then rerouted paved walkways to correspond to the most heavily trafficked routes. Other examples of natural erosion measures include wear on library books; wear and tear on selected articles within volumes; and depletion of items in stores, such as by sales of newspapers.

The second measurement of indirect observation is the **accretion measure,** which measures a phenomenon as manifested through the deposition and accumulation of materials. Archaeologists and geologists commonly use accretion measures in their research by measuring, mapping, and analyzing accretion of materials. Other professions find them useful as well. Eugene Webb and his colleagues reported a study in which mechanics in an automotive service department recorded radio dial settings to estimate radio station popularity.[37] This information was then used to select radio stations to carry the dealer's advertising. The popularity of television programs could be measured by recording the drop in water level in community water-storage systems while commercials are aired, since viewers tend to use the toilet only during commercials when watching very popular shows. Or the reverse could be explored to test the popular wisdom that commercials shown during the Superbowl are more popular than the game itself. Similarly, declines in telephone usage could indicate television program popularity. The presence of fingerprints and nose prints on glass display cases may indicate interest as well as reveal information about the size and age of those attracted to the display. The effectiveness of various antilitter policies and conservation programs could also be measured using physical trace evidence, and the amount and content of graffiti may represent an interesting measurement of the beliefs, attitudes, and mood of a population.

One of the best-known examples of the use of accretion measures is W. L. Rathje's study of people's garbage.[38] He studied people's behavior based on what they discarded in their trash cans. One project involved investigating whether poor people wasted more food than those better off; they did not.

Indirect observation typically raises fewer ethical issues than direct observation because the measures of individual behavior are taken after the individuals have left the scene, thus ensuring anonymity in most cases. However, Rathje's studies of garbage raised ethical concerns because some discarded items (such as letters and bills) identified the source of the garbage. Although a court ruled in Rathje's favor by declaring that when people discard their garbage, they have no further legal interest in it, one might consider sorting through a person's garbage to be an invasion of privacy. In a study in which data on households were collected, consent forms were obtained, codes were used to link household information to garbage data, and then the codes were destroyed. Rathje's assistants in another garbage study were instructed not to examine any written material closely.

It is also possible that garbage may contain evidence of criminal wrongdoing. Twice during Rathje's research, body parts were discovered, although not in the bags collected as part of the study. Rathje took the position that evidence of victimless crimes should be ignored but evidence of serious crimes should be reported. Of course, the publicity surrounding Rathje's garbage study may have deterred disposal of such evidence. This raises the problem of reactivity: To what extent might people change their garbage-disposing habits if they know there is a small chance that what they throw away will be examined?

This example also illustrates the possibility that indirect observation of physical traces of behavior may border on direct observation of subjects if the observation of physical traces quickly follows their creation. In some situations, extra measures may have to be taken to preserve the anonymity of subjects.

Another good example of the use of accretion measures is Kurt Lang and Gladys Engel Lang's study of the MacArthur Day parade in Chicago in 1951.[39] Gen. Douglas MacArthur and President Harry S. Truman were locked in an important political struggle at the time, and the Langs wanted to find out how much interest there was in the parade. They used data on mass-transit passenger fares, hotel reservations, retail store and street vendor sales, parking lot usage, and the volume of ticker tape on the streets to measure the size of the crowd attracted by MacArthur's appearance.

Validity Problems with Indirect Observation

Although physical trace measures generally are not subject to reactivity to the degree that participant observation and survey research are, threats to the validity of these measures do exist. Also, erosion and accretion measures may be biased. For example, certain traces are more likely to survive because the materials are more durable. Thus, physical traces may provide a selective, rather than complete, picture of the past. Differential wear patterns may be due not to variation in use but to differences in material. Researchers studying garbage must be careful not to infer that garbage reflects all that is used or consumed. Someone who owns a garbage disposal, for example, generally discards less garbage than someone who doesn't.

Researchers should exercise caution in linking changes in physical traces to particular causes. Other factors may account for variation in the measures. Webb and his colleagues suggested that several physical trace measures be used simultaneously or that alternative data collection methods be used to supplement physical trace measures.[40] For example, physical trace measures of the use of recreational facilities, such as which trash cans in a park fill up the fastest, could be supplemented with questionnaires completed by park visitors on facility usage.

Caution should also be used in making inferences about the behavior that caused the physical traces. For example, wear around a particular museum exhibit could indicate either the number of people viewing the exhibit or the amount of time people spent near the exhibit shuffling their feet. Direct observation could determine the answer, but in cases where the physical trace measures occurred in the past, this solution is not possible.

Examples of the use of indirect observation in political science research are not numerous. Nevertheless, this method has been used profitably, and you may be able to think of cases where it would be appropriate. For example, you could assess the popularity of candidates by determining the number of yard signs appearing in a community. Or you could estimate the number of visitors and level of office activity of elected representatives by noting carpet wear in office entryways. Although this would not be as precise as counting visitors, it would allow you to avoid posting observers or questioning office staff.

Indirect observation, when used ingeniously, can be a low-cost research method free from many of the ethical issues that surround direct observation. Let us now turn to a consideration of some of the ethical issues that develop in the course of fieldwork and in simple, nonexperimental laboratory observations.

ETHICAL ISSUES IN OBSERVATION

Ethical dilemmas arise primarily when there is a potential for harm to the observed. The potential for serious harm to subjects in most observational studies is quite low. Observation generally does not entail investigation of highly sensitive, personal, or illegal behavior, because people are reluctant to be observed in those circumstances and would not give their informed consent. Nor do fieldwork and simple laboratory observation typically involve experimental manipulations of subjects and exposure to risky experimental treatments. Nonetheless, harm or risks to the observed may result from observation. They include (1) negative repercussions from associating with the researcher because of the researcher's sponsors, nationality, or outsider status; (2) invasion of privacy; (3) stress during the research interaction; and (4) disclosure of behavior or information to the researcher resulting in harm to the observed during or after the study. Each of these possibilities is considered here in turn.

In some fieldwork situations, contact with outsiders may be viewed as undesirable behavior by an informant's peers. Cooperation with a researcher may violate community norms. For example, a researcher who studies a group known to shun contact with outsiders exposes informants to the risk of being censured by their group.

Social scientists from the United States have encountered difficulty in conducting research in countries that have hostile relations with the United States.[41] Informants and researchers may be accused of being spies, and informants may be exposed to harm for appearing to sympathize with "the enemy." Harm may result even if hostile relations develop after the research has been conducted. Military, Central Intelligence Agency, or other government sponsorship of research may particularly endanger the observed.

A second source of harm to the observed results from the invasion of privacy that observation may entail. Even though a researcher may have permission to observe, the role of observer may not always be remembered by the observed. In fact, as a researcher gains rapport, there is a greater chance that informants may view the researcher as a friend and reveal to him or her something that could prove to be damaging. A researcher does not always warn, "Remember, you're being observed!" Furthermore, if a researcher is being treated as a friend, such a warning may damage rapport. Researchers must consider how they will use the information gathered from subjects. They must judge whether use in a publication will constitute a betrayal of confidence.[42] Even when a subject being interviewed does not consider the research to be an invasion of privacy, the subject may feel stress if the topic of conversation is emotionally painful.

Much of the harm to subjects in fieldwork occurs as a result of publication. They may be upset at the way they are portrayed, subjected to unwanted publicity, or depicted in a way that embarrasses the larger group to which they belong. Carelessness in publication may result in the violation of promises of confidentiality and anonymity. And value-laden terminology may offend those being described.[43]

CONCLUSION

Observation is an important research method for political scientists. Observational studies may be direct or indirect. Indirect observation is less common but has the advantage of being a nonreactive research method. Direct observation of people by social scientists has produced numerous studies that have enhanced knowledge and understanding of human beings and their behavior. Fieldwork—direct observation by a participant observer in a natural setting—is the best-known variety of direct observation, although direct observation may take place in a laboratory setting. Observation tends to produce data that are qualitative rather than quantitative. Because the researcher is the measuring device, this method is subject to particular questions about researcher bias and data validity. Since there is an evolving relationship between the observer and the observed, participant observation is a demanding and often unpredictable research endeavor. Part of the demanding nature of fieldwork stems from the difficult ethical dilemmas it raises.

As a student you may find yourself in the position of an observer, but it is more likely that you will be a consumer and evaluator of observational research. In this position you should base your evaluation on many considerations: Does it appear that the researcher influenced the behavior of the observed or was biased in his or her observation? How many informants were used, a few or only one? Does it appear likely that the observed could have withheld significant behavior of interest to the researcher? Are generalizations from the study limited because observation was made in a laboratory setting or because of the small number of cases observed? Were any ethical issues raised by the research? Could they have been avoided? What would you have done in a similar situation? Asking these questions will help you evaluate the validity and ethics of observational research.

 Terms Introduced

Accretion measures. Measures of phenomena through indirect observation of the accumulation of materials.

Covert observation. Observation in which the observer's presence or purpose is kept secret from those being observed.

Direct observation. Actual observation of behavior.

Erosion measures. Measures of phenomena through indirect observation of selective wear of some material.

Ethnography. A type of field study in which the researcher is deeply immersed in the place and lives of the people being studied.

Field study. Open-ended and wide-ranging (rather than structured) observation in a natural setting.

Indirect observation. Observation of physical traces of behavior.

Informants. Persons who are willing to be interviewed about the activities and behavior of themselves and of the group to which they belong. An informant also helps the researcher engaged in participant observation to interpret group behavior.

Informed consent. Procedures that inform potential research subjects about the proposed research in which they are being asked to participate; the principle that researchers must obtain the freely given consent of human subjects before they participate in a research project.

Institutional review board. Panel to which researchers must submit descriptions of proposed research involving human subjects for the purpose of ethics review.

Overt observation. Observation in which those being observed are informed of the observer's presence and purpose.

Participant observation. Observation in which the observer becomes a regular participant in the activities of those being observed.

Primary data. Data recorded and used by the researcher who is making the observations.

Reactivity. Effect of data collection or measurement on the phenomenon being measured.

Secondary data. Data used by a researcher that were not personally collected by that researcher.

Structured observation. Systematic observation and recording of the incidence of specific behaviors.

Unstructured observation. Observation in which all behavior and activities are recorded.

Suggested Readings

Fenno, Richard F., Jr. *Home Style: House Members in Their Districts.* Boston: Little, Brown, 1978. See esp. the introduction and appendix, "Notes on Method: Participant Observation."

Jaggar, Alison M. *Just Methods: An Interdisciplinary Reader.* Boulder, Colo.: Paradigm, 2008.

Piccolo, Francesco Lo, and Huw Thomas, eds. *Ethics and Planning Research.* Burlington, Vt.: Ashgate, 2009.

Reason, Peter, and Hilary Bradbury, eds. *The SAGE Handbook of Action Research: Participative Inquiry and Practice.* 2nd ed. Thousand Oaks, Calif.: Sage, 2008.

Sieber, Joan. E. *Planning Ethically Responsible Research: A Guide for Students and Internal Review Boards.* Applied Social Research Methods Series vol. 31. Newbury Park, Calif.: Sage, 1992.

———, ed. *The Ethics of Social Research: Fieldwork, Regulation, and Publication.* New York: Springer-Verlag, 1982.

Smyth, Marie, and Emma Williamson, eds. *Researchers and their 'Subjects': Ethics, Power, Knowledge and Consent.* Bristol, UK: Policy Press, 2004.

Wedeen, Lisa. "Reflections on Ethnographic Work in Political Science." *Annual Review of Political Science* 13, no. 1 (2010): 255–72.

Williamson, Vanessa, Theda Skocpol, and John Coggin. "The Tea Party and the Remaking of Republican Conservatism." *Perspectives on Politics* 9, no. 1 (2011): 25–43.

Notes

1. Susan J. Carroll and Debra J. Liebowitz, "Introduction: New Challenges, New Questions, New Directions," in *Women and American Politics: New Questions, New Directions,* ed. Susan J. Carroll (Oxford, UK: Oxford University Press, 2003), 1–29.

2. Exemption categories are as follows: "1. Research conducted in established or commonly accepted educational settings, involving normal educational practices, such as (a) research on regular and special education instructional strategies or (b) research on the effectiveness of or the comparison among instructional techniques, curricula, or classroom management methods. 2. Research involving the use of educational tests (cognitive, diagnostic, aptitude, achievement), survey procedures, interview procedures, or observation of public behavior, unless (a) information obtained is recorded in such a manner that human subjects can be identified, directly or through identifiers linked to the subjects, AND (b) any disclosure of the human subjects' responses outside the research could reasonably place the subjects at risk of criminal or civil liability or be damaging to the subjects' financial standing, employability, or reputation. 3. Research involving the use of education tests, survey procedures, interview procedures, or observation of public behavior that is not exempt under category 2, if (a) the human subjects are elected or appointed public officials or candidates for public office or (b) federal statute(s) requires without exception that the confidentiality of the personally identifiable information will be maintained throughout the research and thereafter. 4. Research involving the collection or study of existing data, documents, records, pathological specimens, or diagnostic specimens, if these sources are publicly available or if the information is recorded by the investigator in such a manner that subjects cannot be identified directly or through identifiers linked to the subjects. 5. Research and demonstration projects that are conducted by or subject to the approval of department or agency heads and that are designed to study, evaluate, or otherwise examine (a) public benefit or service programs, (b) procedures for obtaining benefits or services under those programs, (c) possible changes in or alternatives to those programs or procedures, or (d) possible changes in methods or levels of payment for benefits or services under those programs. 6. Taste and food quality evaluation and consumer acceptance studies, (a) if wholesome foods without additives are consumed or (b) if a food is consumed that contains a food ingredient at or below the level and for a use found to be safe, or agricultural chemical or environmental contaminant at or below the level found to be safe, by the Food and Drug Administration or approved by the Environmental Protection Agency or the Food Safety and Inspection Service of the U.S. Department of Agriculture." From United States Office of the Federal Register, *Code of Federal Regulations: Title 45, Public Welfare; Part 46, Protection of Human Subjects* (Washington, D.C.: US Government Printing Office, 1977), Part 46.101(b). These exemptions do not apply to research involving prisoners, fetuses, pregnant women, or human in vitro fertilization. Exemption 2 does not apply to children except for research involving observations of public behavior when the investigator does not participate in the activities being observed.

3. National Commission for the Protection of Human Subjects of Biomedical and Behavioral Research, *The Belmont Report: Ethical Principles and Guidelines for the Protection of Human*

Subjects of Research (Washington, D.C.: US Government Printing Office, 1979), http://ohsr
.od.nih.gov/guidelines/belmont.html.

4. Eugene J. Webb, Donald T. Campbell, and Richard D. Schwarz, *Nonreactive Measures in the Social Sciences,* 2nd ed. (Boston: Houghton Mifflin, 1981).

5. Lisa Wedeen, "Reflections on Ethnographic Work in Political Science," *Annual Review of Political Science* 13, no. 1 (2010): 255–72.

6. Vanessa Williamson, Theda Skocpol, and John Coggin, "The Tea Party and the Remaking of Republican Conservatism," *Perspective on Politics* 9, no. 1 (2011): 25–43.

7. Ruth Horowitz, "Remaining an Outsider: Membership as a Threat to Research Rapport," *Journal of Contemporary Ethnography* 14, no. 4 (1986): 409–30.

8. Mary Henle and Marian B. Hubble, "'Egocentricity' in Adult Conversation," *Journal of Social Psychology* 9, no. 2 (1938): 227–34.

9. Wedeen, "Reflections on Ethnographic Work in Political Science."

10. Stanley Milgram and R. Lance Shotland, *Television and Antisocial Behavior: Field Experiments* (New York: Academic Press, 1973).

11. William F. Whyte, *Street Corner Society: The Social Structure of an Italian Slum,* 3rd ed. (Chicago: University of Chicago Press, 1981); and Marc H. Ross, *Grass Roots in an African City: Political Behavior in Nairobi* (Cambridge, Mass.: MIT Press, 1975).

12. Richard F. Fenno Jr., *Home Style: House Members in Their Districts* (Boston: Little, Brown, 1978).

13. Ruth Horowitz, *Honor and the American Dream: Culture and Identity in a Chicano Community* (New Brunswick, N.J.: Rutgers University Press, 1983).

14. Raphael Schlembach, "How do Radical Climate Movements Negotiate Their Environmental and Their Social Agendas? A Study of Debates within the Camp for Climate Action (UK)," *Critical Social Policy* 31, no. 2 (2011): 194–215.

15. Joan E. McLean, "Campaign Strategy," in *Women and American Politics: New Questions, New Directions,* ed. Susan J. Carroll (Oxford, UK: Oxford University Press, 2003), 53–71.

16. Fenno, *Home Style: House Members in Their Districts,* xiii.

17. Ibid., xiv.

18. Jennie-Keith Ross and Marc Howard Ross, "Participant Observation in Political Research," *Political Methodology* 1 (1974): 65–66.

19. James A. Robinson, *The House Rules Committee* (Indianapolis, Ind.: Bobbs-Merrill, 1963); and James A. Robinson, *Congress and Foreign Policy-Making: A Study in Legislative Influence and Initiative* (Homewood, Ill.: Dorsey Press, 1962). Also, extensive firsthand observations of Congress are reported in many of the articles in Raymond E. Wolfinger, ed., *Readings on Congress* (Englewood Cliffs, N.J.: Prentice Hall, 1971).

20. Ralph K. Huitt, "Democratic Party Leadership in the Senate," *American Political Science Review* 55, no. 2 (1961): 333–44.

21. David W. Minar, "The Community Basis of Conflict in School System Politics," in *The New Urbanization,* ed. Scott Greer et al. (New York: St. Martin's Press, 1968), 246–63.

22. Carroll and Liebowitz, "Introduction: New Challenges, New Questions, New Directions."

23. Carol Hardy-Fanta, *Latina Politics, Latino Politics: Gender, Culture, and Political Participation in Boston* (Philadelphia: Temple University Press, 1993), xiv.

24. Horowitz, "Remaining an Outsider: Membership as a Threat to Research Rapport," 412.

25. Ibid., 413.

26. Ross and Ross, "Participant Observation in Political Research," 70.

27. Whyte, *Street Corner Society;* Fenno, *Home Style: House Members in Their Districts.*

28. Ross and Ross, "Participant Observation in Political Research."

29. Fenno, *Home Style: House Members in Their Districts,* 255.

30. Whyte, *Street Corner Society.*

31. Williamson, Skocpol, and Coggin, "The Tea Party and the Remaking of Republican Conservatism."

32. J. C. Sharman, "Power and Discourse in Policy Diffusion: Anti-Money Laundering in Developing States," *International Studies Quarterly* 52, no. 3 (2008): 635–56.

33. John Lofland, *Analyzing Social Settings: A Guide to Qualitative Observation and Analysis* (Belmont, Calif.: Wadsworth, 1971), 102–03.

34. Ibid., 105.

35. Ibid., 106–7.

36. Webb, Campbell, and Schwartz, *Nonreactive Measures in the Social Sciences,* 4.

37. Ibid., 10–11.

38. See discussion of Rathje's work in ibid., 15–17.

39. Kurt Lang and Gladys Engel Lang, *Politics and Television* (Chicago: Quadrangle Books, 1968).

40. See Webb, Campbell, and Schwartz, *Nonreactive Measures in the Social Sciences,* 27–32.

41. See Myron Glazer, *The Research Adventure: Promise and Problems of Field Work* (New York: Random House, 1972), 25–48, 97–124.

42. See Fenno, *Home Style: House Members in Their Districts,* 272.

43. For a discussion and examples of value-laden terminology in published reports of participant observers, see ibid.

DOCUMENT ANALYSIS:

Using the Written Record

IN THIS CHAPTER WE DESCRIBE DOCUMENT ANALYSIS—how empirical observations can be made using the **written record,** which is composed of documents, reports, statistics, manuscripts, and other written, oral, or visual materials.

Political scientists turn to the written record when the political phenomena that interest them cannot be measured through personal interviews, with questionnaires, or by direct observation. For example, interviewing and observation are of limited utility to researchers interested in large-scale collective behavior (such as civil unrest and the budget allocations of national governments) or in phenomena that are distant in time (Supreme Court decisions during the Civil War) or space (defense spending by different countries).

The political phenomena that have been observed through written records are many and varied—for example, judicial decisions concerning the free exercise of religion, voter turnout rates in gubernatorial elections, the change over time in Soviet military expenditures, and the incidence of political corruption in the People's Republic of China.[1] Of the examples of political science research described in chapter 1 and referred to throughout this book, Lane Kenworthy and Jonas Pontusson's and Jacob S. Harker and Paul Peterson's studies of income inequality; Thomas Holbrook and Brianne Heidbreder's study of voter turnout rates; Wesley T. Milner, Steven C. Poe, and David LeBlang's investigation of governments' violation of human rights; Richard L. Hall and Kristina C. Miler's study of congressional oversight activity; Jeffrey A. Segal and Albert D. Cover's investigation of the ideology of Supreme Court justices; and several of the studies of the impact of negative campaign advertisements all depended on written records for the measurement of important political concepts.[2] Not all portions of the written record are equally useful to political scientists. Hence, we discuss the major components of the written record of interest to political scientists and how researchers use those components to measure significant political phenomena.

Generally speaking, use of the written record raises fewer ethical issues than either observation or interviewing. Research involving the collection or study of existing data, documents, or records often does not pose risks to individuals, because the unit of analysis for the data is not the individual. Also, issues of risk are not likely to arise where records are for individuals, as long as individuals cannot be identified directly or through identifiers linked to them (organizations often go to great lengths to delete possible personal identifying information) or where the records are publicly available, as in the case of the papers of public figures such as presidents and members of Congress. However, allowing researchers access to their private papers may pose some risk to private individuals. Thus, access to private papers may be subject to conditions designed to protect the individuals involved.

TYPES OF WRITTEN RECORDS

Some written records are ongoing and cover an extensive period; others are more episodic. Some are produced by public organizations at taxpayers' expense; others are produced by business concerns or by private citizens. Some are carefully preserved and indexed; other records are written and forgotten. In this section, we discuss two types of written records: the episodic record and the running record.

The Episodic Record

Records that are not part of an ongoing, systematic record-keeping program but are produced and preserved in a more casual, personal, and accidental manner are called **episodic records.** Good examples are personal diaries, memoirs, manuscripts, correspondence, and autobiographies; biographical sketches and other biographical materials; the temporary records of organizations; and media of temporary existence, such as brochures, posters, and pamphlets. The episodic record is of particular importance to political historians, since much of their subject matter can be studied only through these data.

The papers and memoirs of past presidents and members of Congress could also be classified as part of the episodic record, even though considerable resources and organizational effort are invested in their preservation, insofar as the content and methods of organization of these documents vary and the papers are not available all in the same location.

To use written records, researchers must first gain access to the materials. Gaining access to the episodic record is sometimes particularly difficult.[3] Locating suitable materials can easily be the most time-consuming aspect of the whole data collection exercise.

Researchers generally use episodic records to illustrate phenomena rather than as a basis for the generation of a large sample and numerical measures for statistical analysis. Consequently, quotations and other excerpts from research materials are often used as evidence for a thesis or hypothesis. That is to say, their analyses are qualitative rather than quantitative. Over the years, social scientists have conducted some exceptionally interesting and imaginative studies of political phenomena based on the episodic record. We describe two particular studies that used the episodic record to illuminate important political phenomena.

Economics and the U.S. Constitution.   In 1913 the historian Charles Beard published a book about the US Constitution in which he made imaginative use of the episodic record.[4] Beard's thesis was that economic interests prompted the framing of the Constitution. He reasoned that if he could show that the framers and pro-Constitution groups were familiar with the economic benefits that would ensue upon ratification of the Constitution, then he would be able to argue that economic considerations were central to the Constitution debate. If, in addition, he could show that the framers themselves benefited economically from the system of government established by the Constitution, the case would be that much stronger. Beard tested this thesis, which has stimulated a good deal of controversy, with a variety of data from the episodic record.

The first body of evidence presented by Beard measured the property holdings of those present at the 1787 Constitutional Convention. These measures, which Beard admitted are distressingly incomplete, are derived largely from six types of sources: biographical materials, such as James Herring's multivolume *National Portrait Gallery* and the *National Encyclopedia of Biography;* census materials, in particular the 1790 census of heads of families, which showed the number of slaves owned by some of the framers; US Treasury records, including ledger books containing lists of securities; records of individual state loan offices; records concerning the histories of certain businesses, such as the *History of the Bank of North America* and the *History of the Insurance Company of North America;* and collections of personal papers stored in the Library of Congress.

From these written records Beard was able to discover the occupations, land holdings, number of slaves, securities, and mercantile interests of the framers. This allowed him to establish a plausible case that the framers were not economically disinterested when they met in Philadelphia to "revise" the Articles of Confederation.

Beard coupled his inventory of the framers' personal wealth with a second body of evidence concerning their political views. His objective was to demonstrate that the framers realized and discussed the economic implications of the Constitution and the new system of government. By using the existing minutes of the debate at the convention; the personal correspondence and writings of some of the framers; and the *Federalist Papers* by James Madison, Alexander Hamilton, and John Jay—which were written to persuade people to vote for the Constitution—Beard was able to demonstrate that the framers were concerned about, and cognizant of, the economic implications of the Constitution they wrote.

A third body of evidence allowed Beard to analyze the distribution of the vote for and against the Constitution. Where the data permitted, Beard measured the geographical distribution of the popular vote in favor of ratification and compared this with information about the economic interests of different geographical areas in each of the states. He also attempted to measure the personal wealth of those present at the state ratification conventions and then related those measures to the vote on the Constitution. These data were gleaned from the financial records of the individual states, records of the US Treasury Department, and historical accounts of the ratification process in the states.

Through this painstaking and time-consuming reading of the historical record, Beard constructed a persuasive (although not necessarily proven) case for his conclusion that "the movement for the Constitution of the United States was originated and carried through principally by four groups of personal interests which had been adversely affected under the Articles of Confederation: money, public securities, manufactures, and trade and shipping."[5]

PRESIDENTIAL PERSONALITY. A second example of the use of the episodic record may be found in James David Barber's *The Presidential Character*.[6] Because of the importance of the presidency in the American political system and the extent to which that institution is shaped by its sole occupant, Barber was interested in understanding the personalities of the individuals who had occupied the office during the twentieth century. Although he undoubtedly would have preferred to observe directly the behavior of the fourteen presidents who held office between 1908 and 1984 (when he conducted his study), he was forced instead to rely on the available written materials about them.

For Barber, discerning a president's personality meant understanding his style, worldview, and character. Style is "the President's habitual way of performing his three political roles: rhetoric, personal relations, and homework." A president's worldview is measured by his "primary, politically relevant beliefs, particularly his conceptions of social causality, human nature, and the central moral conflicts of the time." And character "is the way the President orients himself toward life." Barber believed that a president's style, character, and worldview "fit together in a dynamic package understandable in psychological terms" and that this personality "is an important shaper of his Presidential behavior on nontrivial matters." But how is one to measure the style, character, and worldview of presidents who are dead or who will not permit a political psychologist access to their thoughts and deeds? This is an especially troublesome question when one believes, as Barber did, that "the best way to predict a President's character, world view, and style is to see how they were put together in the first place . . . in his early life, culminating in his first independent political success."[7]

Barber's solution to this problem was to use available materials on the twentieth-century presidents he studied, including biographies, memoirs, diaries, speeches, and, for Richard Nixon, tape recordings of presidential conversations. Barber did not use all the available biographical materials. For example, he "steered clear of obvious puff jobs put out in campaigns and of the quickie exposés composed to destroy reputations."[8] He quoted frequently from the biographical materials as he built his case that a particular president was one of four basic personality types. Had these materials been unavailable or of questionable accuracy (a possibility that Barber glosses over in a single paragraph), measuring presidential personalities would have been a good deal more difficult, if not impossible.

Barber's analysis of the presidential personality was exclusively qualitative; the book contains not one table or graph. He used the biographical material to categorize each president as one of four personality types and to show that the presidents with similar personalities exhibited similar behavioral patterns when in office. In brief, Barber used two dimensions—activity-passivity (how much energy does the man invest in his presidency?) and positive-negative affect (how does he feel about what he does?)—to define the four types of presidential personality (table 9–1).

Barber's research is a provocative and imaginative example of the use of the episodic record—in this case, biographical material—as evidence for a series of generalizations about presidential personality. Although Barber did not empirically test his hypotheses in the ways that we have been discussing in this book, he did accumulate a body of evidence in support of his assertions and presented his evidence in such a way that the reader can evaluate how persuasive it is.[9]

TABLE 9–1
Presidential Personality Types

Positive-Negative Affect	Activity-Passivity	
	Active	Passive
Positive	Franklin D. Roosevelt Harry S. Truman John F. Kennedy Gerald Ford Jimmy Carter	William Howard Taft Warren Harding Ronald Reagan
Negative	Woodrow Wilson Herbert Hoover Lyndon Johnson Richard Nixon	Calvin Coolidge Dwight Eisenhower

Source: Based on data from James David Barber, *The Presidential Character,* 3rd ed. (Englewood Cliffs, N.J.: Prentice Hall, 1985). Courtesy of James David Barber, James B. Duke Professor of Science, Emeritus, Duke University, Durham, N.C.

The Running Record

Unlike the episodic record, the **running record** is more likely to be produced by organizations than by private citizens, it is carefully stored and easily accessed, and it is available for long periods of time. The portion of the running record that is concerned with political phenomena is extensive and growing. The data collection and reporting efforts of the US government alone are impressive, and if you add to that the written records collected and preserved by state and local governments, interest groups, publishing houses, research institutes, and commercial concerns, the quantity of politically relevant written records increases quickly. Reports of the US government, for example, now cover everything from electoral votes to electrical rates, taxes to taxi cabs, and, in summary form, fill a thousand pages in the *Statistical Abstract of the United States,* published annually by the US Bureau of the Census. What makes the running record especially attractive as a resource is that many data sets are now housed online. The *Statistical Abstract,* for example, can be found at www.census.gov/compendia/statab/.

There are far too many sources of the running record to list them here, but a quick look at some popular sources will help you understand the array that is available. If you are interested in elections and campaigns, you can visit the Federal Election Commission at www.fec.gov and find financial records filed by candidates, interest groups, and political parties, or you can visit privately operated Web sites, like www.opensecrets.org, that offer processed reports in an easy-to-read and use format. Or you might visit the Web sites administered by the secretaries of state to find state-level election returns or summaries of election law changes over time or the America Votes series to find election results for national and some state and local elections. Alternatively, if you are interested in the lawmaking process, Congress makes the text and legislative histories of bills, committee reports, hearings, congressional votes, and the *Congressional Record* available in print or online at www.thomas.gov with a useful search engine to find needed documents. Or you can search for similar material through nongovernmental sources like the Inter-university Consortium for Political and Social Research archive or in print in the *CQ Almanac* or in CQ Press's *Politics in America.* Finally, you can find a wealth of information related to foreign affairs in *World Resources,* published by the World Resources Institute in collaboration with the United Nations Environment Programme and the United Nations Development Programme or in the Central Intelligence Agency's *World Fact Book* at www.cia.gov/library/publications/the-world-factbook/index.html. As you can imagine, the references listed here represent only a small fraction of the available records. Each reference has its own advantages and disadvantages, and you should take care to understand exactly what is and what is not included in each reference before using it.

THE POLICY AGENDAS PROJECT.   The Policy Agendas Project (www.policyagendas
.org) offers many sources of data linked by public policy topics, and it is a significant resource for those doing research in public policy. It seeks to provide users
with an easy one-source way to track long-term policy changes at the national
level of government across many different arenas. According to the Web site,

> The Policy Agendas Project is an ambitious attempt to provide truly
> comparable measures of policy changes in the United States since the
> Second World War. Systematic policy comparisons across time have
> often eluded students of public policy because of the absence of a
> valid and reliable set of categories of policy activity. The Policy Agen-
> das Project is a reliable tool for tracking policy changes in the United
> States, analogous to the National Income Accounts used by econo-
> mists to track the state of the economy. Users can be assured that our
> reported measures of policy change have the same fundamental
> meaning across time, something that cannot be guaranteed without
> the meticulous coding and reliability standards we impose.
>
> Modern information technology allows users of this website to trace,
> graph, and download policy changes in many different arenas at the
> click of a mouse. By providing direct information on the sources of
> our measures of policy changes, this website also allows users to
> access the original material, which provides the historical context of
> policy choice.
>
> The unique contribution of the Policy Agendas Project is that many of
> our datasets allow users to immediately download and access full
> text source policy documents from linked websites. A long-term objec-
> tive of the Project is to provide a systematic gateway to a virtual digi-
> tal policy library through a 'guided search' function.[10]

At the heart of this project is a comprehensive list of public policy topics
(table 9–2). Each topic is divided into dozens of subtopics to better organize the
broad policy areas. Finally, each topic and subtopic is assigned a unique identification number that is used in each of the data sets available on the Web site.

The Web site is updated continually with new and more recent data. As of
this writing, it includes data sets in six distinct areas, as shown in table 9–3.
Each of these data sets is a useful source of data in its own right, but the policy
codes linking these data make this Web site especially important. There are both
quantitative and textual data here.

In addition to the main Policy Agendas site, there are several partner sites.
The Congressional Bills Project (www.congressionalbills.org), created by E. Scott
Adler and John Wilkerson at the University of Washington, includes data on
every congressional bill from 1947 to 2008. This Web site uses the same policy
codes used on the Policy Agendas Project so that data from both sites may be

easily combined. The Comparative Agendas Project (www.comparativeagendas.org) extends the Policy Agendas Project to the European Union and eleven countries in addition to the United States. Finally there is a Pennsylvania Policy Database Project (www.temple.edu/papolicy/).

The Running Record and Episodic Record Compared

There are three primary advantages to using the running record rather than the episodic record. The first is cost, in both time and money. Since the costs of collecting, tabulating, storing, and reporting the data in the running record are generally borne by the record keepers themselves, political scientists are usually able to use these data inexpensively. Researchers can often use the data stored in the running record by photocopying a few pages of a reference book, purchasing a government report or data file, or downloading data into a spreadsheet. In fact, the continued expansion of the data collection and record-keeping activities of the national government has been a financial boon to social scientists of all types.

A second, related advantage is the accessibility of the running record. Instead of searching packing crates, deteriorated ledgers, and musty storerooms, as users of the episodic record often must do, users of the running record more often handle reference books, government publications, and computer printouts. Many political science research projects have been completed with only the data stored in the reference books and government documents of a decent research library.

A third advantage of the running record is that, by definition, it covers a more extensive period than does the episodic record. This permits the type of longitudinal analysis and before-and-after research designs discussed in chapter 6. Although the episodic record helps explain the origins of and reasons for a particular event, episode, or period, the running record allows the measurement of political phenomena over time.

The running record presents problems, however. One is that a researcher is at the mercy of the data collection practices and procedures of the record-keeping

TABLE 9–2
Policy Agendas Project Policy Topics

1. Macroeconomics
2. Civil Rights, Minority Issues, and Civil Liberties
3. Health
4. Agriculture
5. Labor, Employment, and Immigration
6. Education
7. Environment
8. Energy
10. Transportation
12. Law, Crime, and Family Issues
13. Social Welfare
14. Community Development and Housing Issues
15. Banking, Finance, and Domestic Commerce
16. Defense
18. Space, Science, Technology and Communications
19. Foreign Trade
10. International Affairs and Foreign Aid
20. Government Operations
21. Public Lands and Water Management

Major Topic Codes Greater than 21 (Additional NYT [*New York Times*] Codes)

24. State and Local Government Administration
26. Weather and Natural Disasters
27. Fires
28. Arts and Entertainment
29. Sports and Recreation
30. Death Notices
31. Churches and Religion
99. Other, Miscellaneous, and Human Interest

Source: Policy Agendas Project, "Topic Codebook," retrieved August 18, 2011, from http://www.policyagendas.org/page/topic-codebook/.

TABLE 9–3
Policy Agendas Project Datasets

Congress

- **Congressional Hearings**

    This dataset contains information summarizing each U.S. Congressional hearing from 1946 to 2008 (87,896 hearings). Using the Congressional Information Service (CIS) Abstracts, we code each hearing by our system of policy content codes. Other variables, including committee and subcommittee, are also available. Other variables, including committee and subcommittee, are also available. Identification variables link our records to the original CIS source material. Note: Research making use of the congressional hearings dataset should bear in mind that the hearings for the last year available on our website are incomplete. This is due to the CIS archival system.

- **Congressional Quarterly Almanac**

    This dataset contains information from all articles in the main chapters of the CQ Almanac from 1948 to 2007 (14,028 records). Each CQ Almanac article typically covers one legislative initiative; when an article contains information about several different public laws or bills, it is divided so that each record in our dataset contains information about one legislative initiative. Each record is coded according to our policy content scheme. Several other variables concerning each legislative initiative (e.g., bill numbers, Public Law number if applicable, committees involved, primary sponsors, etc.) are also included. Identification variables link our records to the original CQ source material as well as to our Public Laws dataset. A note of caution, article length has varied over the span of this dataset.

- **Public Laws**

    This dataset contains information about each public law passed from 1948 to 2007 (19,215 records). Each record is coded by our policy content scheme and other variables. Identification variables allow linkage to the CQ Almanac dataset. The dataset directly links users to the full text (starting with the 104th Congress) and bill summary (starting with the 93rd Congress) information found on THOMAS and other public domain websites.

- **Most Important Laws**

    This dataset identifies 576 of the most important laws from 1948 through 1998, based on the number of lines of CQ Almanac coverage they receive (with adjustments made between 1948 and 1961 for below-average levels of CQ coverage).

- **Roll Call Votes**

    The Congressional Roll Call Voting dataset codes every congressional roll call vote from 1946 to 2004 using the Policy Agendas Project content coding system. In addition, this dataset standardizes information from multiple sources into an easily utilized format.

- **Committee Codebook**

    Committee codes are found in the hearings, laws, and CQ Almanac datasets. These codes assign a unique number to each congressional committee associated with a particular record in each of the datasets.

Presidency

- **Executive Orders**

    This dataset contains information about each executive order issued from 1945 to 2003 (3,800 records). Each record is coded by our system of policy content scheme and other variables, including the president's party, whether the order was issued during a time of divided government, and whether the order was issued at the beginning or end of a presidential term.

■ State of the Union Speeches

This dataset contains information on each quasi-statement in the Presidential State of the Union Speeches from 1946 to 2005 (18,854 records). Each quasi-statement is coded according to our system of policy content categories and other variables. Users can directly link to full text versions of the speech for further analysis.

Supreme Court

■ Supreme Court Cases

The Supreme Court dataset contains information on each case on the Court's docket from from 1944 to 2006 (8,776 records), and is the only publicly available dataset to examine the Court's agenda from a policy perspective. Cases are coded according to our policy content scheme codes and include additional variables such as the Court's ruling in cases in which one was issued. The accompanying codebook addresses Court-specific coding issues and serves as a reference guide for those unfamiliar with the Court's terminology and procedures.

Public Opinion

■ Gallup's Most Important Problem

This dataset contains the responses to Gallup's Most Important Problem question aggregated at the annual level from 1946 to 2007 (1,240 records) and coded by major topic.

News Media

■ New York Times Index

This dataset is a systematic random sample of the New York Times Index from 1946 to 2005 (46,458 records). The sample includes the first entry on every odd-numbered page of the Index. Each entry is coded by Policy Agendas major topics and includes other variables such as the length, date and location of the story and whether it addressed government actions.

■ New York Times Index Weights

This dataset provides information on the number of pages in the New York Times Index and an estimate of the number of articles per page for each of the years included in our Index dataset. These weights address the occasional newspaper format changes that systematically alter the number of articles on each page and the variation in the size of the New York Times and its Index over time.

Budget Authority

■ Budget

This dataset provides annual data, adjusted for inflation, of U.S. Budget Authority from FY 1947 through FY 2008. Using Office of Management and Budget Functions and Subfunctions, we have revised the data to be consistent over time.

■ Budget-Policy Crosswalk

This file compares the Policy Agendas Project topic codes with the OMB codes used in the Budget dataset to assess how well they correspond. A "1" represents nearly complete correspondence, while a "5" represents significant divergence.

■ Budget Resources

These pages highlight the main issues concerning the study of budgetary outcomes across countries and time. A brief glossary of budgetary terminology and data sources from international, national, and research institutions are provided.

Source: Policy Agendas Project, "Datasets & Codebooks," retrieved August 18, 2011, from http://www.policyagendas .org/page/datasets-codebooks#codebook.

organizations themselves. Researchers are rarely in a position to influence record-keeping practices; they must rely instead on what organizations such as the US Census Bureau, Federal Election Commission, and Policy Agendas Project decide to do. A trade-off often exists between ease of access and researcher influence over the measurements that are made. Some organizations—some state and local governments, for example—do not maintain records as consistently as researchers may like. One colleague found tracing the fate of proposed constitutional amendments to the Delaware State Constitution to be a difficult task. Delaware is the only state in which voters do not ratify constitutional amendments. Instead, the state legislature must pass an amendment in two consecutive legislative sessions between which a legislative election has occurred. Thus, constitutional amendments are treated like bills, and tracking them depends on the archival practices of the state legislature. Even when clear records are kept, such as election returns for mayoral contests, researchers may face a substantial task in collecting the data from individual cities, because the only returns from the largest cities are reported in various statistical compilations.

Another, related disadvantage of the running record is that some organizations are not willing to share their raw data with researchers. The processed data that they do release may reflect calculations, categorizations, and aggregations that are inaccurate or uninformative. Access to public information is not *always* easy. More problems may be encountered when trying to obtain public information that shares some of the characteristics of the episodic record, for example, such as information on the effect of specific public programs and agency activities. Emily Van Dunk, a senior researcher at the Public Policy Forum, a nonpartisan, nonprofit research organization that conducts research on issues of importance to Wisconsin residents, noted that obtaining data from state and local government agencies can be difficult at times and offered tips for researchers.[11]

Finally, it is sometimes difficult for researchers to find out exactly what an organization's record-keeping practices are. Unless the organization publishes a description of its procedures, a researcher may not know what decisions have guided the record-keeping process. This can be a special problem when these practices change, altering in an unknown way the measurements reported.

Although the running record has its disadvantages, political scientists often must rely on it if they wish to do any empirical research on a particular topic. To illustrate some of the problems with using written records, we conclude this section with a description of PollingReport.com, one of many Web sites dedicated to providing users with national- and state-level public opinion data.

Presidential Job Approval

PollingReport.com is a popular source of public opinion polling data, PollingReport.com provides national poll results, free of charge, from well-known polling organizations such as Gallup, Pew, and Quinnipiac and news organizations such as CNN, CBS, and the *Los Angeles Times*. The Web site also offers state-level poll results to paid subscribers. In this section, we focus on the data available for free.

PollingReport.com organizes its poll results into the following categories: the State of the Union, Elections, In the News, National Security, and Issues. As shown in figure 9–1, each of these categories offers a number of subtopics of interest. The State of the Union category, for example, includes subtopics covering each branch of the federal government—President Obama, Congress, and the Supreme Court—as well as the "Direction of the country," "National priorities," and "Consumer confidence." Likewise, the Issues category is divided into several subtopics. A great deal of useful public opinion data may be found among these many subtopics.

FIGURE 9–1
Subtopics Used by PollingReport.com

Source: PollingReport.com, http://www.pollingreport.com/.

FIGURE 9–2
Presidential Support Data at PollingReport.com

Source: PollingReport.com, "President Obama: Job Ratings," http://www.polling report.com/obama.htm.

Let's assume that you are interested in studying public support for the president. The one place to start would be by finding data on President Obama's job approval ratings, which are perhaps the most direct indicator of support for the president. By clicking on the President Obama subtopic under State of the Union, you will find several different kinds of presidential support data (figure 9–2). Polling Report.com provides data on the "Obama Administration," "Job ratings," and "Favorability ratings." You will want to explore each of these options, looking for differences in polling questions and responses. We will explore President Obama's job ratings poll results in this example. You can click on "Major polls" to find poll results from various polling organizations that answer a question similar to ABC News/ *Washington Post* poll's job approval rating question: "Do you approve or disapprove of the way Barack Obama is handling his job as president?" or "Daily tracking," which will give you the results of the Gallup poll question asked virtually daily since January 2009. A portion of these results is shown in figure 9–3. From this page, you can access polling results for questions asking about President Obama's handling of specific issues. These data could be used to investigate how opinions about the handling of specific issues affect assessments of overall job performance.

PollingReport.com has many advantages for students using the written record. First, and perhaps most important, PollingReport.com offers free, high-quality data at an easy-to-use Web site. The results found at Polling Report.com are from the same professional polling organizations that news organizations around the country rely on. Second, students have access to multiple surveys administered during different periods using very similar question wording. But as valuable as PollingReport.com is, it shares some disadvantages with other examples of the running record. Perhaps most glaring are the lack of consistency and regularity in the poll results provided on the Web page. Even though the president's job approval rating question is one of the most frequently asked questions in national political surveys, others questions are not asked with similar frequency or duration. This is not an indictment of PollingReport.com but

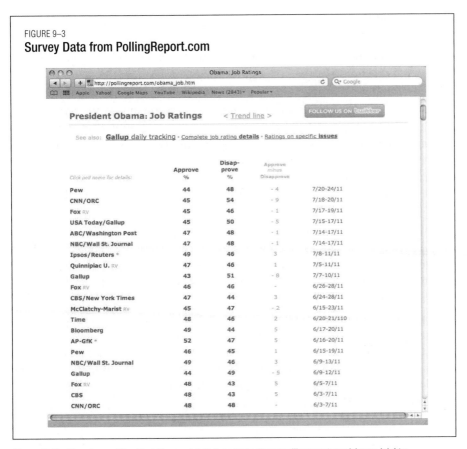

FIGURE 9–3
Survey Data from PollingReport.com

Source: PollingReport.com, "President Obama: Job Ratings," http://www.pollingreport.com/obama_job.htm.

a symptom of the fact that PollingReport.com can report only the data made available by other polling organizations. Although those other organizations provide a great deal of data, sometimes a large number of surveys are administered at the same time whereas no data are available for other time periods. And, although a great many organizations are listed on the Web site, it does not include all polling organizations.

Finally, PollingReport.com provides poll results from the Bush and Clinton administrations, but results from previous administrations are not available. If you wish to compare President Obama's approval ratings with those of other previous presidents, you will have to search for those results elsewhere. These are only some of the potential problems that might be encountered with Polling Report.com or other examples of the running record. Problems like these generally will not prevent you from using such sources, but they can be a nuisance depending on the purpose of your research project.

CONTENT ANALYSIS

Those who rely on the written record, such as Charles Beard and James David Barber, often extract excerpts, quotations, or examples from documents to support an observation or relationship. Alternatively, a researcher might measure the number of times the president references the economy in the State of the Union address. This use of the written record via systematic coding and classification of its contents is an example of **content analysis.** We can think of document analysis, much like other forms of analysis, as taking both a qualitative and a quantitative form. In the earlier examples, we can label Beard and Barber's use of the written record as qualitative because they used the words of others or interpreted written documents without the use of a numeric coding scheme to provide evidence for their arguments. Alternatively, we can label the use of State of the Union addresses as quantitative because quantitative content analysis enables us to "take a verbal, nonquantitative document and transform it into quantitative data." A researcher "first constructs a set of mutually exclusive and exhaustive categories that can be used to analyze documents, and then records the frequency with which each of these categories is observed in the documents studied."[12] This is exactly what Segal and Cover had to do with newspaper editorials to produce a quantitative measure of the political ideologies of Supreme Court justices.[13] In this section, we focus primarily on quantitative content analysis for use in statistical analyses, but remember that a qualitative approach to documents can be just as useful, if not more so, depending on the purpose of a research project.

Content Analysis Procedures

The first step in content analysis is to decide what materials to include in the analysis. This selection, of course, is guided by the topic, theory, existing research, etc. If a researcher is interested in the political values of candidates for public office, position papers and campaign speeches might be suitable. Or if a researcher is interested in what liberals are currently thinking about the role of government in society, liberal opinion magazines or blogs might be used. Krippendorff referred to these materials as the "sampling units" and defined these as "units that are distinguished for selective inclusion in an analysis."[14] The list of materials germane to the researcher's subject thus makes up a "sampling frame." Once the appropriate sampling frame has been selected, then any of the possible types of samples described in chapter 7—random, systematic, stratified, cluster, and nonprobability—could be used. Of course, it may be the case that the sampling frame corresponds to the population and that all units of the population will be studied. For example, you might have all State of the Union addresses and wish to analyze all of them.

The second task in any content analysis is to define the "recording or coding units," that is, "the units that are distinguished for separate description, transcription, recoding, or coding."[15] For example, from a given document, news item, video clip, or other material, the researcher may want to code (1) each word or sentence fragment, (2) each character or actor, (3) each sentence, (4) each paragraph, or (5) each item in its entirety. The choice of the recording or coding unit depends on the categories of content that are going to be measured. In choosing the recording unit, the researcher usually considers the correspondence between the unit and the content categories (stories may be more appropriate than words to determining whether crime is a topic of concern, whereas individual words or sentences rather than larger units may be more appropriate to measuring the traits of political candidates). Generally, if the recording unit is too small, it will be unlikely to possess any of the content categories. If the recording unit is too large, however, it will be difficult to measure the single category of a content variable that it possesses (in other words, the case will possess multiple values of a given content variable). For example, a paragraph or a story may contain both positive and negative evaluations of a candidate. The selection of the appropriate recording unit is often a matter of trial and error, adjustment, and compromise in the pursuit of measures that capture the content of the material being coded.

The third task, therefore, is to choose categories of content that are going to be measured. These categories are the variables you want to focus on in your study. This process is in many respects the most important part of any content analysis, because the researcher must measure the content in such a way that it relates to the research topic and must define this content so that the measures of it are both valid and reliable. So, for example, researchers studying the prevalence of crime in the news might take a sample of the front pages of newspapers or half-hour nightly news programs and measure the amount of content that either deals with crime or does not.

Suppose we were coding the presence of Hispanics in televised entertainment programming. For each program we could count (1) whether there was at least one Hispanic present, (2) how many Hispanics there were, (3) how much time Hispanics were on the screen, and (4) how favorable the portrayal of Hispanics was or how important the portrayal of Hispanics was for the overall story. In these examples, the sampling unit and the recording unit would be the same. However, if you wanted to measure the personality traits of Hispanic prime-time television characters—such as strength, warmth, integrity, humility, and wisdom—and the sex, age, and occupation of those characters, the program would be the sampling unit, and the individual character would be the recording unit.

As another example, if you wanted to measure the orientation of governors toward the role of government, you might use State of the State addresses. Within each address, you could code each sentence as being either positive about government or government employees, neutral, or negative. In this case, the recording unit would be the sentence, not the whole address.

Finally, a researcher has to devise a system of enumeration for the content being coded. The presence or absence of a given content category can be measured, or the measurement may be of the "frequency with which the category appears," the "amount of space allotted to the category," or the "strength or intensity with which the category is represented."[16]

The validity of a content analysis can usually be enhanced with a precise explanation of the procedures followed and content categories used. Usually the best way to demonstrate the reliability of content analysis measures is to show intercoder reliability. **Intercoder reliability** simply means that two or more analysts, using the same procedures and definitions, agree on the content categories applied to the material analyzed. The more the agreement, the more the researcher can feel confident that the meaning of the content is not heavily dependent on the particular person doing the analysis. If different coders disagree frequently, then the content categories have not been defined with enough clarity and precision.

Content analysis is a commonly used technique in some areas of inquiry such political communications. Content analysis may be used to analyze the content of a large number of lengthy, semistructured interviews after they are transcribed. Today many social scientists are conducting content analyses with the help of computer programs known as computer-aided text analysis (CATA). Software can read and store text and search for various patterns of words or even look for ideas implied by the text. Many of the programs have become quite sophisticated. Besides doing the actual content analysis, they write reports and calculate summary statistics. Because there are now so many of these programs, their operation is outside the scope of this book.[17]

News Coverage of Campaigns

A frequent subject of content analysis is press coverage of election campaigns. Given the importance of how candidates are presented and how the electoral process is treated in the news, political scientists have been interested for some time in accurately and systematically describing and explaining campaign news coverage. Most of these studies have investigated whether candidates receive favorable or unfavorable coverage; whether news coverage relays useful information to the American electorate; whether the press accurately presents the complex and lengthy presidential nomination process; and whether journalists are, in general, objective, accurate, fair, and informative.

One example of a content analysis of this type is a study of campaign coverage in 1998 and 2002 by Andrew W. Barrett and Lowell W. Barrington, who wanted to investigate whether there were discernable differences in the favorableness of visual images of political candidates and if these differences were consistent with the "political atmosphere" of the news organizations.[18] We discuss the procedures they followed as such a study is within the capabilities of advanced undergraduate students. We also provide an example of what a code sheet might look like for coding a photograph in table 9–4.

From the outset, Barrett and Barrington decided to select the newspapers for their study. They noted that most research on visual news images had been focused on television. Furthermore, newspapers contain fewer visual images, and photographs are likely to be used repeatedly during a campaign. Readers of the newspapers are also likely to see view photographs for longer than they see the fleeting images presented on television news. Thus, the impact of an image is likely to be greater for newspaper coverage. Finally, Barrett and Barrington argued it is easier to determine the political atmosphere for newspapers than it is for many television stations.

They chose to collect photographs of candidates in seven different statewide and local races in 1998 and 2002 from seven Midwestern newspapers based on availability of the papers and for practical reasons. They argued that there was no reason to believe that the practice of photographic favorableness would be different in the Midwest than the rest of the United States. They collected 435 photographs (all of the candidate photographs contained in the newspapers during the election cycles) for their study.

Each photograph was coded as being unfavorable or favorable by three coders. Basic characteristics of favorable and unfavorable photographs were discussed with the coders, but they were not given a checklist of attributes. Instead, they were just asked for their quick impression of the photograph and to code it on a scale, ranging from –2 (*highly unfavorable*) to 2 (*highly favorable*). Barrett and Barrington argued that while this may appear to be a relatively subjective approach to measurement, it is natural and similar to average readers' reaction to pictures. Furthermore, the coders' impressions were quite consistent, as indicated by a high intercoder reliability statistic. Each photograph was also coded into four size categories, and the favorableness scale was multiplied by the size to create an overall favorableness rating ranging from –8 to 8.

Document analysis was also used to measure the independent variable in this study. Political atmosphere of the paper was measured in two ways: first and most simply was which candidate the newspaper endorsed at the end of the general election period. While this is a very clear measurement, it took place after most of the photographs had appeared, interfering with causal claims. Therefore, Barrett and Barrington also assessed the political atmosphere of papers over time by seeking to identify a consistent pattern of endorsement in major statewide and national races in the election year in question and the previous two even-year elections. If this analysis failed to show that a paper consistently endorsed

TABLE 9–4

Possible Coding Sheet for Content Analysis of Campaign Photographs

Photographs Newspaper _____ Year _____
Name of candidate: _____

| Candidate's party: | 1 Democrat | | | | 2 Republican |

Favorableness of photograph:

	−2	−1	0	1	2
	Highly				Highly
	Unfavorable				Favorable

Size of photograph (actual size ranges need to be specified)

Very small head shot	1____
Small	2____
Medium	3____
Large	4____

Political atmosphere of newspaper:

Opposite to candidate	−1
Mixed	0
Same as candidate	1

Democratic or Republican candidates, a sample of editorials was drawn, and those dealing with major, ideologically divisive issues were evaluated as being strongly Republican, leaning Republican, neutral, leaning Democratic, or strongly Democratic. In the end, only one newspaper was coded as "mixed," being in neither the Republican nor Democratic camp.

Some of their results are shown in table 9–5. Overall, six of the seven newspapers examined had statistically significant levels of bias in their selection of photographs corresponding to at least on the two measures of political atmosphere.

A Simple Computer Content Analysis

You can use your Internet browser to find and analyze speeches or other printed records if you keep careful records of your work. As an example, suppose you wanted to compare the relative emphasis placed on education and jobs by governors in their State of the State addresses, comparing speeches in 2002 to those in 2011. Fortunately, Stateline.org has compiled addresses for all fifty states going back to 2000 (www.stateline.org/live/resources/Speech + Archives/). This time frame will suit our purposes just fine, but if we wanted to include addresses over a longer time, we would have to look elsewhere for earlier addresses. When you locate a particular address, you could use the browser's "Find in page" feature to look for the words *education, school, jobs,* and *economy.* The "Find in page" feature will highlight the word in the document and give you the number of times the word is found (see figure 9–4). You can record these counts and other information about the speeches in a data matrix. We could add more variables to the data matrix, for example, the party of the governor, if we thought that this variable might influence what issues or themes governors emphasized. A portion of such a data matrix is included in figure 9–5.

TABLE 9–5

Favorableness of Candidate Photographs (Weighted by Photograph Size) in the Eleven Races Examined

Race	Newspaper	"Political Atmosphere"	Party of Candidate	# of Pict.	Mean Favorableness (SE)	Difference[a]	Same as Endorsed	Same as Political Atmosphere
1998 IL Senate	*Chicago Tribune*	Rep	Dem	21	1.86 (0.45)			
			Rep	14	2.40 (0.43)	+0.54	Yes	Yes
1998 OH Senate	*Cincinnati Enquirer*	Rep	Dem	5	−0.27 (0.27)			
			Rep	9	1.15 (0.54)	+1.42*	Yes	Yes
1998 OH Senate	*Columbus Dispatch*	Rep	Dem	10	0.17 (0.33)			
			Rep	12	0.25 (0.39)	+0.08	Yes	Yes
1998 WI Senate	*Milwaukee Journal Sentinel*	Dem	Dem	23	1.20 (0.29)	+1.33**	Yes	Yes
			Rep	16	−0.13 (0.35)			
1998 WI Senate	*Wisconsin State Journal* (Madison)	Mixed	Dem	14	0.76 (0.23)	+1.28**	Yes	(NA)
			Rep	9	−0.52 (0.39)			
2002 MO Senate	*St. Louis Post-Dispatch*	Dem	Dem	23	0.71 (0.34)			
			Rep	22	0.95 (0.43)	+0.24	No	No
2002 IL Governor	*Chicago Tribune*	Rep	Dem	17	1.06 (0.65)			
			Rep	19	1.30 (0.43)	+0.24	Yes	Yes
2002 WI Governor	*Capital Times* (Madison)	Dem	Dem	25	2.27 (0.47)	+1.37*	Yes	Yes
			Rep	20	0.90 (0.33)			
2002 WI Governor	*Milwaukee Journal Sentinel*	Dem	Dem	26	1.86 (0.48)	+0.07	Yes	Yes
			Rep	22	1.79 (0.79)			
2002 WI Governor	*Wisconsin State Journal* (Madison)	Mixed	Dem	52	1.15 (0.19)	+0.00	No	(NA)
			Rep	52	1.15 (0.19)			
2002 Milw. Cty. Exec.	*Milwaukee Journal Sentinel*	Dem	Dem	12	2.61 (0.49)	+1.69*	Yes	Yes
			Rep	12	0.92 (0.66)			

Note: **Statistically significant at *p* < .01 level, one-tailed; * significant at *p* < .05, one-tailed.

[a] Significance levels for the difference of means tests based on independent-samples *t*-tests, with assumption of unequal variances.

Source: Andrew W. Barrett and Lowell W. Barrington, "Bias in Newspaper Photograph Selection," *Political Research Quarterly* 58, no. 4 (2005): 609-618. Copyright © SAGE Publications. Reprinted by Permission of SAGE Publications.

FIGURE 9–4
Example of Search for "education" in 2002 Hawaii State of State Message

Following is the partial text of Gov. Ben Cayetano's annual State of the State address, delivered on January 22, 2002:

Mr. President, Mr. Speaker, Members of the Legislature, Lt. Governor Hirono, Mayors Harris, Apana, and Kim, Admiral Blair, Governor and Mrs. Waihee, members of the Consular Corps, distinguished guests and my fellow citizens. Aloha. . . .

Keep in mind that education makes up 52% of our State General Fund Budget and this time, I cannot spare the Department of Education from carrying its fair share of budget cuts. Our state programs servicing the sick, poor and disadvantaged suffered greatly during the first four years of my administration. And, except for adjustments to the costs for Felix, simply cannot be cut anymore.

Our second task is to continue our efforts to strengthen our economic infrastructure. September 11th demonstrated what we all know: Hawaii's economy is over-dependent on tourism. Diversifying our economy will strengthen it and make it less vulnerable to the ups and downs in tourism. Over the past seven years—we have focused on healthcare, biotechnology and high technology.

Since 1995, we've taken some big steps toward diversification. To encourage the development of high technology, we approved one of the most progressive high tech laws in the nation. We've provided additional funding for the University's College of Engineering and aggressively solicited high tech business. In spite of the dot-com crisis, we've made some progress. In technology, according to the Center for Digital Government and the Progress & Freedom Foundation, Hawaii now ranks 13th in Technology Management, 15th in Electronic Commerce and Business Regulation, and 23rd for Taxation Revenue Systems in 2001. Considering Hawaii was ranked near the bottom only a few years ago these are signs our high technology industry is growing.

It has long been part of my vision to make Hawaii the premier Healthcare Center of the Pacific. Your approval of the UH's new $300 million bio-medical research center in Kakaako was a major step [toward] this goal. The new school will not only train doctors, it will also have a strong research component, which will create hundreds of jobs[—]good, high skilled jobs for our people. About five years ago, I expressed my belief that a biotech industry was a natural for Hawaii. Some thought I was dreaming. I was, and the new bio-medical research center will help that dream come true. In fact, Kamehameha Schools and the Ward Estates, two major landowners in Kakaako[,] are prepared to develop a biotech park for biotech companies which will be attracted by the new Center. I won't be governor when the Center is built and the biotech park is established, but I expect you to invite me to the dedication ceremonies. Healthcare, Biotechnology and High Tech have been my priorities. I am certain there are other opportunities which we are not aware [of] today. Our job is to find or create them.

But new economic opportunities will mean little if our young people do not have the education and background to compete for them. And that is why I am pushing for more improvements to our public education system. Education is the great equalizer. It certainly has been for me. And that['s] why over the past seven years, in spite of our state's fiscal problems, we have given education our top priority. That's why we spared the DOE from budget cuts and cut other departments more to make up the difference. That's why we built more new schools and facilities than any other administration. That's why we increased the pay for teachers, boosting the pay for starting teachers from $25,000 in 1997 to $34,300 in 2003[,] a nearly $10,000 increase in just six years.

Today, our starting teachers earn more than their counterparts in Arizona, Colorado, Oregon, Washington, Nevada, and New Mexico. Our new contract with our teachers provides more than just a pay raise, it is a step toward a culture which focuses on accountability and professional development, rather than just seniority. For example, under the new contract, a teacher who acquires certification by the National Board for Professional Teacher Standards will receive a $5,000 salary differential. Acquiring national certification is no easy process. It requires hard work, study over a two-year period. But it is a tool that gives teachers an incentive to improve their

FIGURE 9–4   Continued

professional skills and increase their compensation as well. So far, only seven Hawaii public school teachers have achieved it[—]each one of them is an excellent teacher. The two teachers who earned their national certification this year are here today. And, I'd like to introduce them to you. First, Teresa Tugadi—a special education teacher at Pohakea Elementary School—and Lisa Yanase who teaches at Waialua Elementary School. The good news is that there are about 50 more public school teachers who will enroll in the program. The bad news—is that you will have to find the extra money to pay for them. I suggest you pay them[—]it will be well worth it.

The statewide teacher strike we experienced was not just about money[—]it was about doing what had to be done to improve the quality of public education. We need teachers who have the training and skills to provide a quality education to our children. And, we need ways to find out who the good teachers are, reward them, and help the teachers who need improvement to get better. We should not settle for mediocrity. After all, a public education system that teaches its students how to read, but not how to distinguish what is worth reading[,] is not a very good school system at all. To paraphrase social commentator, Fran Lebowitz, if we are truly serious about preparing our children for the future, don't teach them to subtract, teach how to deduct. Good teachers know the difference between subtraction and deduction. Our contract is designed to produce good teachers. . . .

Source: Adapted from Ben Cayetano, "Hawaii State of the State Address 2002," January 22, 2002, http://www.stateline.org/live/details/speech?contentId= 16122.

FIGURE 9–5

Example Data Matrix Showing Results of Content Analysis of State of the State Addresses

CASE	STATE	YEAR	EDUCATION	SCHOOL	JOBS	ECONOMY
1	ALABAMA	2002	11	35	17	1
2	ALABAMA	2011	12	5	6	5
3	COLORADO	2002	14	25	4	6
4	COLORADO	2011	11	2	10	0
5	HAWAII	2002	15	21	8	17
6	HAWAII	2011	9	4	3	3
7	KANSAS	2002	9	9	2	2
8	KANSAS	2011	8	7	6	8
9	MASSACHUSETTS	2002	14	6	8	4
10	MASSACHUSETTS	2011	5	7	9	4

ADVANTAGES AND DISADVANTAGES OF THE WRITTEN RECORD

Using documents and records, or what we have called the written record, has several advantages for researchers. First, it allows us access to subjects that may be difficult or impossible to research through direct, personal contact because they pertain either to the past or to phenomena that are geographically distant. For example, late-eighteenth-century records permitted Beard to advance and test a novel interpretation of the framing of the US Constitution. This study would not have been possible had no records been available from this period.

A second advantage of data gleaned from archival sources is that the raw data are usually nonreactive. As we mentioned in previous chapters, human subjects often consciously or unconsciously establish expectations or other relationships with investigators, which can influence their behavior in ways that might confound the results of a study. But those writing and preserving the records are frequently unaware of any future research goal or hypothesis or, for that matter, that the fruits of their labors will be used for research purposes at all. State loan officers during the late 1700s had no idea that some two hundred years later, a historian would use their records to discover why some people were in favor of revising the Articles of Confederation. This nonreactivity has the virtue of encouraging more accurate and less self-serving measures of political phenomena.

Record keeping is not always completely nonreactive, however. Record keepers are less likely to create and preserve records that are embarrassing to them, their friends, or their bosses; that reveal illegal or immoral actions; or that disclose stupidity, greed, or other unappealing attributes. Richard Nixon, for example, undoubtedly wished that he had destroyed or never made the infamous Watergate tapes, which revealed the extent of his administration's knowledge of the 1972 break-in at Democratic National Committee headquarters. Today many record-keeping agencies employ paper shredders to ensure that a portion of the written record does *not* endure. Researchers must be aware of the possibility that the written record has been selectively preserved to serve the record keepers' own interests.

A third advantage of using the written record is that sometimes the record has existed long enough to permit analyses of political phenomena over time. The before-and-after research designs discussed in chapter 6 may then be used. For example, suppose you are interested in how changes in the 55-mile-per-hour speed limit (gradually adopted by the states and then later dropped by many states on large stretches of their highway systems) affected the rate of traffic accidents. Assuming that the written record contains data on the incidence of traffic accidents over time in each state, you could compare the accident rate before and after changes in the speed limit in those states that changed their speed limit. These changes in the accident rate could then be compared with the changes occurring in states in which no change in the speed limit took place. The rate changes could then be "corrected" for other factors that might affect the rate of traffic accidents. In this way an interrupted time series research design could be used, a research design that has some important advantages over cross-sectional designs. Because of the importance of time, and of changes in phenomena over time, for the acquisition of causal knowledge, a data source that supports longitudinal analyses is a valuable one. The written record more readily permits longitudinal analyses than do either interview data or direct observation.

A fourth advantage to researchers of using the written record is that it often enables us to increase sample size above what would be possible through either interviews or direct observation. For example, it would be terribly expensive and time-consuming to observe the level of spending by all candidates for the House of Representatives in any given year. Interviewing candidates would require a lot of travel, long-distance phone calls, or the design of a questionnaire to secure the necessary information. Direct observation would require gaining access to many campaigns. How much easier and less expensive it is to contact the Federal Election Commission in Washington, D.C., and request the printout of campaign spending for all House candidates. Without this written record, resources might permit only the inclusion of a handful of campaigns in a study; with the written record, all 435 campaigns can easily be included.

This raises the fifth main advantage of using the written record: cost. Since the cost of creating, organizing, and preserving the written record is borne by the record keepers, researchers are able to conduct research projects on a much smaller budget than would be the case if they had to bear the cost themselves. In fact, one of the major beneficiaries of the record-keeping activities of the federal government and of news organizations is the research community. It would cost a prohibitive amount for a researcher to measure the amount of crime in all cities larger than 25,000 or to collect the voting returns in all 435 congressional districts. Both pieces of information are available at little or no cost, however, because of the record-keeping activities of the FBI and the Elections Research Center, respectively. Similarly, using the written record often saves a researcher considerable time. It is usually much quicker to consult printed government documents, reference materials, computerized data, and research institute reports than it is to accumulate data ourselves. The written record is a veritable treasure trove for researchers.

Collecting data in this manner, however, is not without some disadvantages. One problem mentioned earlier is selective survival. For a variety of reasons, record keepers may not preserve all pertinent materials but rather selectively save those that are the least embarrassing, controversial, or problematic. It would be surprising, for example, if political candidates, campaign consultants, and public officials saved correspondence and memoranda that cast disfavor on themselves. Obviously, whenever a person is selectively preserving portions of the written record, the accuracy of what remains is suspect. This is less of a problem when the connection between the record keeper's self-interest and the subject being examined by the researcher is minimal.

A second, related disadvantage of the written record is its incompleteness. Large gaps exist in many archives due to fires, losses of other types, personnel shortages that hinder record-keeping activities, and the failure of the record maker or record keeper to regard a record as worthy of preservation. We all throw out personal records every day; political entities do the same. It is difficult to know what kinds of records should be preserved, and it is often impossible for record keepers to bear the costs of maintaining and storing voluminous amounts of material.

Another reason records may be incomplete is simply because no person or organization has assumed the responsibility for collecting or preserving them. For example, before 1930, national crime statistics were not collected by the FBI, and before the creation of the Federal Election Commission in 1971, records on campaign expenditures by candidates for the US Congress were spotty and inaccurate.

A third disadvantage of the written record is that its content may be biased. Not only may the record be incomplete or selectively preserved, but it also may be inaccurate or falsified, either inadvertently or on purpose. Memoranda or copies of letters that were never sent may be filed, events may be conveniently forgotten or misrepresented, the authorship of documents may be disguised, and the dates of written records may be altered; furthermore, the content of government reports may tell more about political interests than empirical facts. For example, Soviet and East European governments apparently released exaggerated reports of their economic performance for many years, and scholars (and investigators) attempting to reconstruct the actions in the Watergate episode have been hampered by alterations of the record by those worried about the legality of their role in it. Often, historical interpretations rest upon who said or did what, and when. To the extent that falsifications of the written record lead to erroneous conclusions, the problem of record-keeping accuracy can bias the results of a research project. The main safeguard against bias is the one used by responsible journalists: confirming important pieces of information through several dissimilar sources.

A fourth disadvantage is that some written records are unavailable to researchers. Documents may be classified by the federal government, they may be sealed (that is, not made public) until a legal action has ceased or the political actors involved have passed away, or they may be stored in such a way that they are difficult to use. Other written records—such as the memoranda of multinational corporations, campaign consultants, and Supreme Court justices—are seldom made public because there is no legal obligation to do so and the authors benefit from keeping them private.

Finally, the written record may lack a standard format because it is kept by different people. For example, the Chicago budget office may have budget categories for public expenditures different from those used in the San Francisco budget office. Or budget categories used in the Chicago budget office before 1960 may be different from the ones used after 1960. Or the French may include items in their published military defense expenditures that differ from those included by the Chileans in their published reports. Consequently, a researcher often must expend considerable effort to ensure that the formats in which the records of different entities can be made comparable.

Despite these limitations, political scientists have generally found that the advantages of using the written record outweigh the disadvantages. The written record often supplements the data we collect through interviews and direct observation, and in many cases it is the only source of data on historical and cross-cultural political phenomena.

CONCLUSION

The written record includes personal records, archival collections, organizational statistics, and the products of the news media. Researchers interested in historical research, or in a particular event or time in the life of a polity, generally use the episodic record. Gaining access to the appropriate material is often the most resource-consuming aspect of this method of data collection, and the hypothesis testing that results is usually more qualitative and less rigorous (some would say more flexible) than with the running record. Increasingly, gaining access is less of a problem as more and more documents are scanned and available online.

The running record of organizations has become a rich source of political data as a result of the record-keeping activities of governments at all levels and of interest groups and research institutes concerned with public affairs. The running record is generally more quantitative than the episodic record and may be used to conduct longitudinal research. Measurements using the running record can often be obtained inexpensively, although the researcher frequently relinquishes considerable control over the data collection enterprise in exchange for this economy.

One of the ways in which a voluminous, nonnumerical written record may be turned into numerical measures and then used to test hypotheses is through a procedure called content analysis. Content analysis is most frequently used by political scientists interested in studying media content, but it has been used to advantage in studies of political speeches, statutes, and judicial decisions.

Through the written record, researchers may observe political phenomena that are geographically, physically, and temporally distant from them. Without such records, our ability to record and measure historical phenomena, cross-cultural phenomena, and political behavior that do not occur in public would be seriously hampered.

Terms Introduced

Content analysis. A systematic procedure by which records are transformed into quantitative data.

Episodic record. Record that is not part of a regular, ongoing record-keeping enterprise but instead is produced and preserved in a more casual, personal, or accidental manner.

Intercoder reliability. Demonstration that multiple analysts, following the same content analysis procedure, agree and obtain the same measurements.

Running record. A written record that is enduring and easily accessed and covers an extensive period of time.

Written record. Documents, reports, statistics, manuscripts, and other recorded materials available and useful for empirical research.

Suggested Readings

Grbich, Carol. *Qualitative Data Analysis: An Introduction.* Thousand Oaks, Calif.: Sage, 2007.

Krippendorff, Klaus. *Content Analysis: An Introduction to Its Methodology.* 2nd ed. Thousand Oaks, Calif.: Sage, 2004.

Miller, Delbert C., and Neil J. Salkind. *Handbook of Research Design and Social Measurement.* 6th ed. Newbury Park, Calif.: Sage, 2002.

Riffe, Daniel, Stephen Lacy, and Frederick G. Fico. *Analyzing Media Messages: Using Quantitative Content Analysis in Research.* 2nd ed. Mahwah, N.J.: Lawrence Erlbaum Associates, 2005.

Roberts, Carl W., ed. *Text Analysis for the Social Sciences: Methods for Drawing Statistical Inferences from Text and Transcripts.* Mahwah, N.J.: Lawrence Erlbaum Associates, 1997.

Van Dunk, Emily. "Getting Data through the Back Door: Techniques for Gathering Data from State Agencies." *State Politics and Policy Quarterly* 1, no. 2 (2001): 210–18.

Webb, Eugene J., Donald T. Campbell, Richard J. Schwartz, and Lee Sechrest. *Unobtrusive Measures.* Rev. ed. Thousand Oaks, Calif.: Sage, 2000.

Notes

1. Frank Way and Barbara J. Burt, "Religious Marginality and the Free Exercise Clause," *American Political Science Review* 77, no. 3 (1983): 652–65; Samuel C. Patterson and Gregory A. Caldeira, "Getting Out the Vote: Participation in Gubernatorial Elections," *American Political Science Review* 77, no. 3 (1983): 675–89; William Zimmerman and Glenn Palmer, "Words and Deeds in Soviet Foreign Policy: The Case of Soviet Military Expenditures," *American Political Science Review* 77, no. 2 (1983): 358–67; and Alan P. L. Liu, "The Politics of Corruption in the People's Republic of China," *American Political Science Review* 77, no. 3 (1983): 602–23.

2. Lane Kenworthy and Jonas Pontusson, "Rising Inequality and the Politics of Redistribution in Affluent Countries," *Perspectives on Politics* 3, no. 3 (2005): 449–71, available at http://www.u.arizona.edu/~lkenwor/pop2005.pdf; Jacob S. Hacker and Paul Pierson, "Winner-Take-All Politics: Public Policy, Political Organization, and the Precipitous Rise of Top Incomes in the United States," *Politics & Society* 38, no. 2 (2010): 152–204; Thomas Holbrook and Brianne Heidbreder, "Does Measurement Matter? The Case of VAP and VEP in Models of Voter Turnout in the United States," *State Politics & Policy Quarterly* 10, no. 2 (2010): 159–81; Wesley T. Milner, Stephen C. Poe, and David Leblang, "Security Rights, Subsistence Rights, and Liberties: A Theoretical Survey of the Empirical Landscape," *Human Rights Quarterly* 21, no.2 (1999) 403–43; Richard C. Hall and Kristina Miler, "What Happens After the Alarm? Interest Group Subsidies to Legislative Overseers," *Journal of*

Politics 70, no. 4 (2008): 990–1005; Jeffrey A. Segal and Albert D. Cover, "Ideological Values and the Votes of U.S. Supreme Court Justices," *American Political Science Review* 83, no. 2 (1989): 557–65, available at http://www.uic.edu/classes/pols/pols200mm/Segal89.pdf; Stephen D. Ansolabehere, Shanto Iyengar, and Adam Simon, "Replicating Experiments Using Aggregate and Survey Data: The Case of Negative Advertising and Turnout," *American Political Science Review* 93, no. 4 (1999): 901–10; Stephen D. Ansolabehere, Shanto Iyengar, Adam Simon, and Nicholas Valentino, "Does Attack Advertising Demobilize the Electorate?" *American Political Science Review* 88, no. 4 (1994): 829–38, available at http://weber.ucsd.edu/~tkousser/Ansolabehere.pdf; Martin P. Wattenberg and Craig Leonard Brians, "Negative Campaign Advertising: Demobilizer or Mobilizer?" *American Political Science Review* 93, no. 4 (1999): 891, available at http://weber.ucsd.edu/~tkousser/Wattenberg.pdf; and Richard R. Lau and Ivy Brown Rovner, "Negative Campaigning," *Annual Review of Political Science* 12 (2009): 285–306.

3. Charles A. Beard reported that he was able to use some records in the US Treasury Department in Washington, D.C., "only after a vacuum cleaner had been brought in to excavate the ruins." See Beard, *An Economic Interpretation of the Constitution of the United States* (New York: Macmillan, 1913), 22.

4. Ibid.

5. Ibid., 324.

6. James David Barber, *The Presidential Character: Predicting Performance in the White House,* 3rd. ed. (Englewood Cliffs, N.J.: Prentice Hall, 1985).

7. Ibid., 4–5.

8. James David Barber, *The Presidential Character: Predicting Performance in the White House* (Englewood Cliffs, N.J.: Prentice-Hall, 1972), ix.

9. A critique of Barber's analysis may be found in Garry Wills, *The Kennedy Imprisonment: A Meditation on Power* (Boston: Little, Brown, 1982).

10. University of Texas at Austin Policy Agendas Project, "About Policy Agendas Project," retrieved August 18, 2011, from http://www.policyagendas.org/aboutus/.

11. Emily Van Dunk, "Getting Data through the Back Door: Techniques for Gathering Data from State Agencies," *State Politics and Policy Quarterly* 1, no. 2 (2001), 210–18.

12. Kenneth D. Bailey, *Methods of Social Research,* 2nd ed. (New York: Free Press, 1982), 312–13.

13. Segal and Cover, "Ideological Values and the Votes of U.S. Supreme Court Justices."

14. Klaus Krippendorff, *Content Analysis: An Introduction to Its Methodology,* 2nd ed. (Thousand Oaks, Calif.: Sage, 2004), 98.

15. Ibid., 99.

16. Bailey, *Methods of Social Research,* 319.

17. For a discussion of computer-assisted text analysis, see Krippendorff, "Computer Aids," chap. 12 in *Content Analysis: An Introduction to Its Methodology;* Daniel Riffe, Stephen Lacy, and Frederick G. Fico, "Computers," chap. 9 in *Analyzing Media Messages: Using Quantitative Content Analysis in Research.* 2nd ed. (Mahwah, N.J.: Lawrence Erlbaum Associates, 2005), 208–24; and Roel Popping, "Computer Programs for the Analysis of Texts and Transcripts," in *Text Analysis for the Social Sciences: Methods for Drawing Statistical Inferences from Text and Transcripts,* ed. Carl W. Roberts (Mahwah, N.J.: Lawrence Erlbaum Associates, 1997), 209–24.

18. Andrew W. Barrett and Lowell W. Barrington, "Bias in Newspaper Photograph Selection," *Political Research Quarterly* 58, no. 4 (2005): 609–18.

SURVEY RESEARCH AND INTERVIEWING

POSSIBLY THE MOST HOTLY CONTESTED ISSUES in the first decade of twenty-first-century American politics was the passage of Patient Protection and Affordable Care Act (PPACA), frequently labeled by its critics as "Obamacare" after President Barack Obama. Among many, many objections (and possibly because of them) opponents claim the law, which aims at providing universal health insurance for Americans, is bitterly opposed by a vast majority of citizens. Typical of comments directed at the legislation is this *Washington Examiner* editorial: "Six months ago, President Obama, Senate Majority Leader Harry Reid and House Speaker Nancy Pelosi *rammed Obamacare down the throats of an unwilling American public* [emphasis added]."[1] Indeed, the public's disapproval was seen as one reason why Republicans won control of the House of Representatives and nearly gained a majority in the 2010 congressional elections.

Yet, one can reasonably ask, How do we know that the people had to have the law "crammed" down their throats. The obvious answer is that "polls say so." That response, of course, simply raises new issues. Which polls? Who sponsored them? What do they really show? And, by the way, how reliable is polling for measuring public opinion?

Most readers are no doubt familiar with this form of argumentation because even a cursory glance at the news demonstrates how pervasive polling has become in American politics. Polls are part and parcel of the efforts of many groups not just to study public opinion but also to use it for political ends. So it behooves anyone who wants to understand debates about public policies and issues to become familiar with this activity.

More generally, polling or, as we call it, survey research, is an indispensable tool in social and political research. Suppose we want to know whether or not Americans are "isolationists" or "internationalists" when it comes to foreign affairs. We might try to answer the question by making indirect or unobtrusive observations, such as reading letters to the editor in a dozen or so newspapers and coding them as pro or con involvement. Or we might observe protest demonstrations for or against various international activities to see what kinds of people seem to be participating. But these indirect methods probably would not tell us what we wanted to know. It would seem far preferable (and maybe even easier) to ask citizens up front how they felt about world affairs and the proper US role in them. This was Miroslav Nincic's strategy, for he relied heavily on poll data in his article "Domestic Costs, the U.S. Public, and the Isolationist Calculus."[2] And it is used by countless other political scientists who feel that the best way to measure people's preferences, beliefs, opinions, and knowledge about current events is to ask them.

In this chapter, we explain two related methods of collecting data from people: (1) survey research, which involves collecting information via a questionnaire or **survey instrument** (a carefully structured or scripted set of questions that may be administered face-to-face, by telephone, by mail, by Internet, or by other means) and (2) **interviewing**, which involves direct and personal communication with individuals in a less formal and less structured situation—more in the nature of a constrained conversation. Although we describe both techniques in a moment, for now let us just say that these approaches range from talking to one or a handful of people to gathering data from 1,000 or more people across an entire nation. In either approach, the researcher is trying to get at what people think and do by asking them for self-reports.

Because both methods rely on interpersonal communication, they might seem to entail no special considerations: just think of some questions and ask them. This is not the case, however. To see why, refer to the research described in chapter 1 regarding voter turnout. As you may recall, the issue boils down to who votes and who doesn't. Political scientists have developed all sorts of hypotheses and theories to answer the question, but testing them rests on a seemingly simple and straightforward but in reality quite difficult task: determining who actually voted in any given election. You might think it would be easy to ask people, "Did you vote in the last election?" And that is precisely what most survey researchers do. The problem is that often two-thirds to three-fourths of the respondents claim to have voted. But we know from vote counts reported by election officials that these survey estimates must be too high, for voter turnout rarely exceeds 50 percent and is often much less. So the questionnaire method usually overestimates participation. Overcounting of voters calls into question conclusions based on the replies to these questions.[3]

As a result, the design and implementation of surveys and interviews have to be scrutinized. We begin with a thorough discussion of the problem of obtaining accurate information about attitudes and beliefs by asking people questions rather than by directly observing their behavior. This background puts us in a position to examine survey and interview methods carefully and thoroughly.

FUNDAMENTALS: ENSURING VALIDITY AND RELIABILITY

Since survey and interview methods produce only indirect measures of attitudes and behavior, measurement problems, as discussed in chapter 5, come to the fore. In particular, what is recorded on a piece of paper or an audiotape is usually not an exact, error-free measure of a object. This is particularly true when the objects are attitudes, beliefs, or self-described behavior. An observed "score" (for example, a response to a question) is composed of a true or real (but unobserved) measure plus various types of error. The errors may be random or systematic. Random errors arise by chance or happenstance and (it is hoped) cancel one another out. A systematic error, by contrast, results when a measuring device consistently over- or underestimates a true value, as when a scale always reads two pounds less than a person's real weight. The goal of any research design, of course, is to minimize these errors. Stated differently, our investigative procedures have to ensure validity and reliability. A valid measure produces an accurate or true picture of an object, whereas a reliable one gives consistent results (measurements) across time and users. In the case of survey research, attaining both goals can be a daunting but surmountable problem. This is an important point for making sense of claims based on polls.

Let's think about a naive view of survey research. A pollster asks a man if he supports or opposes civil unions, a legal status that gives gay and lesbian couples rights equal to or similar to those enjoyed by traditionally married people. When asking such a question, most people expect that most of the time the responses will be a precise representation of what the respondent intends or thinks and that all parties understand the question. In the case of a supposedly objective scientific method such as survey research, the replies appear to be straightforward statements that accurately express a person's real feelings. It is usually assumed, in other words, that the response is unproblematic; that *approve* means "approve" and there is nothing more to the story than that.

To see what can go wrong, consider figure 10–1. It shows that a fully formed attitude does not simply sit in someone's mind isolated from all other mental states. Instead, a verbalized or a written opinion that is stimulated by a question is a distillation of a number of beliefs, hopes, desires, and motivations. Furthermore, one person who hears the phrase *civil union* may not be familiar with the term, whereas another, perhaps more informed about current events, may realize the question deals with marriage for homosexual couples. They may express opposing views, but the opinions can be based on unrelated beliefs about the subject. Or, if both people reply with, say, "approve," they may do so for different reasons. Even though two people may give the same response, the answers may not be comparable when this opinion is associated with other attitudes or behaviors. And consider that even if two people share a common understanding of the term, they may differ greatly in other respects: the intensity of their feelings about the matter, their willingness to cooperate with the research, or their desire to "please" the interviewer by giving a socially acceptable response. We must also factor in the interviewer's characteristics (for example, demeanor, race, gender) and the context of the research (for example,

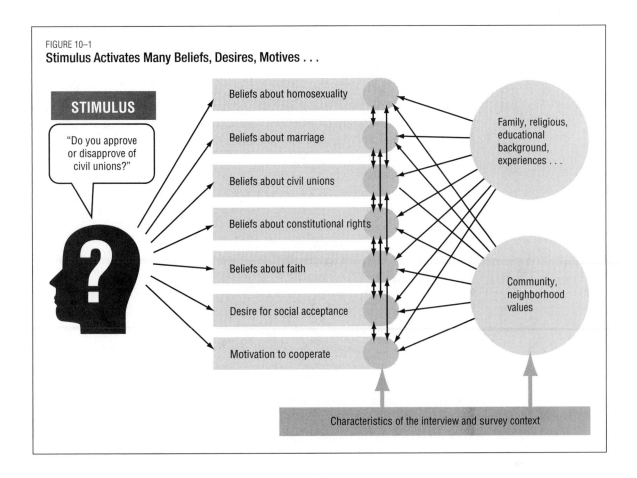

FIGURE 10–1
Stimulus Activates Many Beliefs, Desires, Motives . . .

nature of the sponsoring organization, time constraints on participants). The net result is that an interview, even one carried out over the phone or using a mail survey, involves a complex set of potential interactions that can confuse the interpretation of responses.

To deal with problems of this nature, even in the simplest situations, we need to ensure that several assumptions have been met, including the following (for simplicity, let *R* stand for the respondent and *I* for the interviewer):

- The requested information must be available to *R* (that is, not forgotten or misunderstood).
- *R* must know what is to *I* a relevant and appropriate response.
- *R* must be motivated to provide *I* with the information.
- *R* must know how to provide the information.
- *I* must accurately record *R*'s responses.

- The responses must reflect R's meanings, not I's.

- Other users of the data must understand the questions and answers the same way R and I do.

We are not trying to overanalyze the situation. The point is that if questionnaires and interviews are to produce any useful information, they must take into account the mental context of the respondent and the interview situation. For that reason, we spend the greater portion of this chapter discussing crucial topics such as question wording, questionnaire layout, administrative protocols, efforts to balance demands for completeness versus costs, ways of motivating cooperation, and interviewer characteristics and deportment. These factors contribute to the validity and reliability of the measurements or observations obtained through questionnaires and interviews.

SURVEY RESEARCH

The term *survey research* has two broad meanings. In the context of research design, it indicates an alternative data collection method to experiments, simulations, and formal modeling. Instead of manipulating an independent variable, for instance, to see the effect on behavior, the survey design asks people if they have been exposed to some factor and, if so, by how much, and then it relates the responses to other questions about their behavior. In this chapter, we use the term a bit more specifically to mean research based on direct or indirect interview methods. Simply stated, a group of individuals respond to or fill out more or less standardized questionnaires. (The questionnaires may take different forms to investigate different hypotheses, but they do not involve freewheeling or spontaneous conversations.) Also known as opinion polling, administering questionnaires is one of the most familiar political science research methods.

As the use of surveys has grown, so too has the amount of research on the method itself. This research tries to improve the validity and reliability of the method while keeping costs manageable. We now know more about many aspects of survey research than was known when it was first used, much to the benefit of researchers and consumers of survey research.

We begin with a review of the types of surveys and some of their important characteristics. Then we take up response quality and question wording, the heart and soul of this type of research.

Types of Surveys

A survey solicits information by posing a standard set of questions and stimuli to a sample of individuals drawn from an appropriate target population (see chapter 7). The forms of the instrument and means of administration vary widely depending on a host of factors ranging from cost to comprehensiveness. Table 10–1 lists the main types of surveys along with a few of their properties or characteristics. As you can see from the table, surveys range from personal or face-to-face interviews to contacting subjects by mail or telephone to more or less hit-or-miss methods such as posting questions on a Web site or leaving them in a public area. As Floyd J. Fowler pointed out, researchers may be able to combine mail, telephone, and personal interviews in a research project to take advantage of the particular strengths of each type.[4] Often, however, researchers must make compromises in choosing a survey instrument. As Don A. Dillman noted, "The use of any [of these types] requires accepting less of certain qualities to achieve others, the desirability of which cannot be isolated from a consideration of the survey topic and the population to be studied."[5]

Perhaps the most familiar surveys are those conducted personally or face-to-face. The interviewer typically follows a structured questionnaire that is administered to all members of the sample, although sometimes different forms are used with slightly different question wording and order. Not only are the same questions asked of everyone, but the manner in which they are posed is also standardized to the maximum extent possible. The results are then coded or transcribed for further analysis. Moreover, for a variety of reasons, the principal investigator does not usually conduct the interviews but uses paid or volunteer assistants. Hence, this kind of research can be quite expensive.[6]

Academic and commercials polls are increasingly being conducted in whole or part by mail, phone, or computer. A mail survey, which may be preceded by an introductory letter, has to be self-contained with clear questions and instructions

TABLE 10–1
Types and Characteristics of Surveys

Type of Survey	Overall Cost[a]	Potential Completion Rate[b]	Characteristics Sample-Population Congruence	Questionnaire Length[c]	Data-Processing Costs
Personal/face-to-face	High	High to medium	Potentially high	Long-medium	High
Telephone	Medium	Medium	Medium	Medium-short	High to low
Mail	Low	Low	Medium	Medium-short	Medium
E-mail	Low	Depends but low	Low	Medium-short	High to low
Internet	Low	Depends but low	Low	Medium-short	High to low
Group administration	Very low	High once group is convened	Depends on group selection process	Variable	High to low
Drop-off/pick-up	Very low	Low	Low	Short	Low

[a] Costs of design, administration, and processing

[b] Assumes a general target population (see text): high = greater than 75 percent; medium = 30 to 75 percent; low = less than 30 percent.

[c] *Length* can refer to the number of questions or the time to complete (see text).

for completing and returning it. Motivating participants, anticipating misunderstandings, and obtaining unambiguous results demands a lot of careful planning and pretesting. It also requires a list of addresses drawn from the population of interest. Although somewhat less expensive, phone interviews raise a number of tricky problems of their own (discussed below). Nevertheless, the basic idea is the same: pose a series of questions or stimuli and record the responses.

The explosive growth in e-mail and Internet use has led many researchers to adapt these technologies to survey research. Some researchers send questionnaires via e-mail. Just as with mail surveys, the objective is to identify and contact potential participants and send them a questionnaire to be filled out and returned. In this case, the task is carried out electronically. The use of e-mail has some significant advantages (for example, distribution and processing costs are reduced), but it is hard to apply to general populations. Not everyone uses e-mail, or it may be difficult or impossible to establish a list of addresses that conforms with a desired target population (for example, people living in poverty). A related approach is the Web or Internet survey. Here participants are somehow directed or enticed to visit a site where they answer questions by filling out computer-generated forms. This form of research engenders a lot of suspicion—sampling is again a major issue—but some large organizations (Zogby Interactive and Harris Poll Online, to name two) encourage people to register in order to participate in their ongoing polls. The results, the sponsors claim, are both accurate and influential.[7]

Finally, it is possible, even necessary sometimes, to prepare a survey that is administered to a group (for example, a political science class or visitors to a senior center) or made available at a public location (library, museum, dormitory lounge). The finished forms are then collected or returned to the same or another convenient spot. The results are generally suspect in some people's minds and probably not publishable because they may not be representative, but the method offers considerable savings in effort and cost. For this reason they are commonly used at schools and colleges.

As might be expected, each of these types has advantages and disadvantages. The entries in Table 10–1 are merely suggestive and comparative and have to be interpreted flexibly. A phone survey, for example, generally has to be shorter (in time necessary to complete it) than a personal interview because respondents to the former may be reluctant to tie up a phone line or may be distracted by those around them. Given an interesting topic, plenty of forewarning, and trained interviewers, however, it is possible to hold people's attention for longer periods.

Characteristics of Surveys

COST.   Any type of survey research takes time and incurs at least some expenses for materials. Among the factors determining survey costs are the amount of professional time required for questionnaire design, the length of the questionnaire, the geographical dispersion of the sample, callback procedures, respondent selection rules, and availability of trained staff.[8] Personal interviews are the most expensive to conduct because interviewers must, after being trained, locate and contact subjects, a frequently time-consuming process. For example, some well-established surveys ask interviewers to visit a household and, if the designated subject is not available, make one or more callbacks. National in-person surveys also incur greater administrative costs. Regional supervisory personnel must be hired and survey instruments sent back and forth between the researcher and the interviewers. Mail surveys are less expensive but require postage and materials. Electronic surveys (for example, e-mail or Internet) do not necessitate interviewer time but must still be set up by individuals with technical skills. Although mail surveys are thought to be less expensive than telephone polls, Fowler argued that the cost of properly executed mail surveys is likely to be similar to that of phone surveys.[9] Thus, when deciding among personal interviews, telephone interviews, and mail surveys, researchers must consider cost and administrative issues.

Compared with personal interviewing, telephone surveys have several administrative advantages.[10] Despite the cost of long-distance calls, centralization of survey administration means that training of telephone interviewers may be easier, and flexible working hours are often attractive to the employees. But the real advantages to telephone surveys begin after interviewing starts. It is possible to exercise greater supervision over interviewers and give them prompt feedback. Also, callers can easily inform researchers of any problems they encounter with the survey. Coders can begin coding data immediately. If they discover any errors, they can inform interviewers before a large problem emerges. With proper facilities, interviewers may be able to code respondents' answers directly on computer terminals. In some cases, the whole interview schedule may be computerized, with questions and responses displayed on a screen in front of the interviewer. These are known as computer-assisted telephone interviews (CATIs). Computer and telephone technologies gives telephone surveys a significant time advantage over personal interviews and mail surveys. Telephone interviews may be completed and data analyzed almost immediately.[11] On the downside, people tend to be home mostly in the evenings and weekends, but calls made during these hours often meet resistance. This problem used to be aggravated by an explosion in the use of telemarketing; now, however, with the advent of "do-not-call" lists, the situation may not as dire as it once was.

Telephone surveys are particularly good for situations in which statistically rare subgroups must be reached or estimated. For example, a telephone survey was used to estimate the disabled population in an area (the only problem being that the number of hearing-impaired people was underestimated).[12] A large sample was required to obtain enough disabled persons for the survey. Where large samples are required, telephone surveys are one-half to one-third the cost of personal interviews.[13] Telephone interviews cut down on the cost of screening the population. In some cases, telephone surveys may be used to locate appropriate households, and then the survey itself may be completed by personal interview. Telephone surveys are also best if the research must be conducted in a short period of time; personal surveys are not as fast, and mail surveys are quite slow.

Almost needless to say, group surveys (those that are distributed to members of groups who might be expected to fill them out at a group meeting or online) and drop-off surveys (questionnaires that are left in public places like libraries, malls, or offices with collection boxes on-site) are least expensive. After all, they require minimal administrative and personnel costs to gather the data. On the other hand, the questionnaires still have to be carefully constructed and tested. This is particularly true if the investigator is not in a position to provide guidance or answer questions during survey administration.

COMPLETION RATES.   One of the maddening characteristics of many commercial polls is that they often do not indicate how many people refused to take part in the survey. As a typical example, a CBS poll contained the following information: "This poll was conducted by telephone on August 2–3, 2011 among 960 adults nationwide."[14] This number, however, most likely refers to the number of complete or nearly complete questionnaires and not to the refusals to participate in the survey in the first place. This information can be important to have.

A completion rate or **response rate** refers to the proportion of persons initially contacted who actually participate. In a mail survey, for instance, the denominator is the total number of questionnaires sent out, not the number returned. Three distinguished researchers, Robert M. Groves, Robert B. Cialdini, and Mick P. Couper, succinctly summarized the significance of this quantity for the social sciences:

> Among the alternative means of gathering information about society, survey research methods offer unique inferential power to known populations. . . . This power, however, is the cumulative result of many individual decisions of sample persons to participate in the survey. When full participation fails to obtain, the inferential value of the method is threatened.[15]

We need to explore this point in slightly greater detail. If the response rate is low, either because individuals cannot be reached or because they refuse to participate, the researchers' ability to make statistical inferences for the population being studied may be limited. Also, those who do participate may differ systematically from those who do not, creating other biases. Increasing the size of the survey sample to compensate for low response rates may only increase costs without alleviating the problem.

Most of what we know about response rates comes from studies of personal interview, mail, and telephone surveys. It is difficult, perhaps impossible in some cases, to measure participation levels in electronic and drop-off studies. At one time, response rates were clearly superior for personal interview surveys of the general population than for other types of surveys. Response rates of 80 to 85 percent were often required for federally funded surveys.[16] Higher response rates were not uncommon. By the 1970s, however, response rates for personal interview surveys declined. In 1979 it was reported that in "the central cities of large metropolitan areas the final proportion of respondents that are located *and* consent to an interview is declining to a rate sometimes close to 50 percent."[17]

In general, the decrease in response rates for personal interview surveys has been attributed to both an increased difficulty in contacting respondents and an increased reluctance among the population to participate in surveys. There are more households now in which all adults work outside the home, which makes it difficult for interviewers to get responses. Moreover, pollsters continually worry about public resistance to their craft.[18]

In large cities, nonresponse can be attributed to several additional factors: respondents are less likely to be home or are more likely to be people who do not have a full command of English, or both; interviewers are less likely to enter certain neighborhoods after dark; and security arrangements in multiple-unit apartment buildings make it difficult for interviewers to reach potential respondents. Moreover, many individuals such as undocumented immigrants or people receiving welfare benefits are often skittish about talking to "official-looking" strangers. Because of poor working conditions, it is hard to find skilled and experienced interviewers to work in large cities. In smaller cities and towns also, people have shown an increased tendency to refuse to participate in surveys.[19]

Higher refusal rates may be due to greater distrust of strangers and fear of crime as well as to the increased number of polls. For example, in one study of respondents' attitudes toward surveys, about one-third did not believe that survey participation benefited the respondent or influenced government.[20] An equal number thought that too many surveys were conducted and that too many personal questions were asked. Some survey researchers feared that the National Privacy Act, which requires researchers to inform respondents that their participation is voluntary, would lead to more refusals. However, one study found that privacy concerns and past survey experience were more frequent reasons for refusal than was being informed of the voluntary nature of participation.[21]

Some of these findings about why people do not participate in personal interview surveys raise the possibility that survey research of all types may become increasingly difficult to conduct. The increased nonresponse has reduced the advantage of the personal interview over mail and telephone surveys. In fact, Dillman, using his "total design method" for mail and telephone surveys, has achieved response rates rivaling those for personal interviews.[22] He concluded that the chance someone will agree to be surveyed is best for the personal interview but that telephone interviews are now a close second, followed by mail surveys. Other research comparing response rates of telephone and personal interview surveys has also found little difference.[23]

It is often thought that personal interviews can obtain higher response rates because the interviewer can ask neighbors the best time to contact a respondent who is not at home, thus making return visits more efficient and effective. But repeated efforts by interviewers to contact respondents in person are expensive. Much less expensive are repeated telephone calls.

Two norms of telephone usage have contributed to success in contacting respondents by phone and completing telephone interviews.[24] First, most people feel compelled to answer the phone if they are home when it rings. A telephone call represents the potential for a positive social exchange. With the increase in telephone solicitation and surveys, this norm may be revised, however. Caller ID and answering machines can be used to screen and redirect unwanted calls. Thus, telephone surveys may increasingly become prearranged and conducted after contact has been established by some other method.

A second norm of telephone usage is that the initiator should terminate the call. This norm gives the interviewer the opportunity to introduce himself or herself. And in a telephone interview the introductory statement is crucial (see the following discussion on motivation). Because the respondent lacks any visual cues about the caller, the initial response is one of uncertainty and distrust. Unless the caller can quickly alleviate the respondent's discomfort, the respondent may refuse to finish the interview. For this reason, telephone interviews are more likely to be terminated before completion than are personal interviews. It is harder to ask an interviewer to leave than it is simply to hang up the phone.

One advantage of mail surveys is that designated respondents who have changed their address may still be reached, since the US Postal Service forwards mail for about a year. It is not as easy in phone surveys to track down persons who have moved. In personal and telephone interviews, it is also harder to change the minds of those who initially refuse to be interviewed, since personal contact is involved and respondents may view repeated requests as harassment. Recontacts made by mail are less intrusive than are those by other means.[25]

Because of the importance attached to high response rates, much research on how to achieve them has been conducted. For example, an introductory letter sent prior to a telephone interview has been found to reduce refusal rates.[26] In fact, such letters may result in response rates that do not differ significantly from those for personal surveys.[27] Researchers have also investigated the best times to find people at home. One study found that for telephone interviews, evening hours are best (6:00 to 6:59, especially), with little variation by day (weekends excluded).[28] Another study concluded that the best times for finding someone at home were late afternoon and early evening during weekdays, although Saturday until four in the afternoon was the best time overall.[29]

Because mail surveys usually have the poorest response rates, many researchers have investigated ways to increase responses to them.[30] Incentives (money, pens, and other token gifts) have been found to be effective, and prepaid incentives are better than promised incentives. Follow-up, prior contact, type of postage, sponsorship, and title of the person who signs the accompanying letter are also important factors in improving response rates. Telephone calls made prior to mailing a survey may increase response rates by alerting respondents to the survey's arrival. Telephone calls also are a quick method of reminding respondents to complete and return questionnaires. Good follow-up procedures allow a researcher to distinguish between respondents who have replied and those who have not without violating the anonymity of respondents' answers.[31] Generally, mail surveys work best when the population is highly literate and interested in the research problem.[32]

In sum, response rates are an important consideration in survey research. When evaluating research findings based on survey research, you should check the response rate and what measures, if any, were taken to increase it. Should you ever conduct a survey of your own, a wealth of information is available to help you to achieve adequate response rates.

SAMPLE-POPULATION CONGRUENCE.   **Sample-population congruence,** which refers to how well the sample subjects represent the population, is always a major concern. Here we are speaking of how well the individuals in a sample represent the population from which they are presumably drawn. Bias can enter either through the initial selection of respondents or through incomplete responses of those who agree to take part in the study. In either case a mismatch exists between the sample and the population of interest. These problems arise to varying degrees in every type of survey.

Some of the cheapest and easiest surveys, such as drop-off or group questionnaires, encounter difficulties in matching sampling frames with the target population, as figure 10–3 suggests. Suppose, for example, you wanted to survey undergraduates at your college about abortion. One option would be to draw a sample of names and addresses from the student directory. Assuming all currently enrolled students are correctly listed there, the sampling frame (the directory) should closely match the target population, the undergraduate student body. A random sample drawn from the list would presumably be representative. If instead you left a pile of questionnaires in the library, you would have much less control over who responds. Now your "sample" might include graduate students, staff, and outside visitors. It would then be difficult to draw inferences about the student body. One solution would be to add a "filter" question

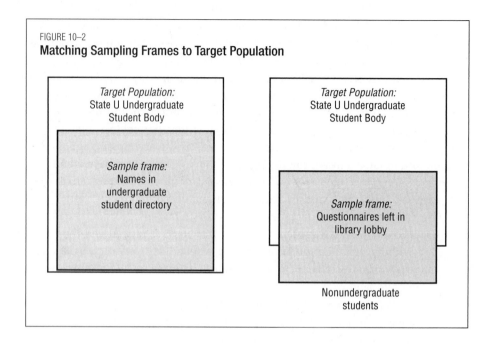

FIGURE 10–2
Matching Sampling Frames to Target Population

Target Population:
State U Undergraduate
Student Body

Sample frame:
Names in
undergraduate
student directory

Target Population:
State U Undergraduate
Student Body

Sample frame:
Questionnaires left in
library lobby

Nonundergraduate
students

(e.g., "Are you a freshman, sophomore, . . . ?") to sort out nonstudents, but the potential for problems can easily be imagined.[33]

Recall from chapter 7 that when all members of a population are listed, theoretically there is an equal opportunity for all members to be included in the sample. Only rarely, however, are all members included. Personal interviews based on cluster samples in which all the households of the last sampled cluster or area are enumerated and then selected at random, which gives each household an equal chance of being selected, are likely to be more representative than are mail or telephone surveys based on published lists, which are often incomplete.

Telephone surveys attempt to improve the representativeness of samples with a procedure called random digit dialing (the use of randomly generated telephone numbers instead of telephone directories; see chapter 7) and by correcting for households with more than one number. Thus, people who have unlisted numbers or new numbers may be included in the sample. Otherwise, a telephone survey may be biased by the exclusion of these households. Estimates of the number of households in the United States that do not have phones vary from 2 to 10 percent, whereas only about 5 percent of dwelling units are missed with personal interview sampling procedures.[34]

A relatively recent technical innovation has put a wrinkle into telephone interviewing: the rise of cell-phone-only users. During the competitive 2004 presidential election, polling companies and media outlets worried that unless this growing group could be included in their sampling frames, predictions about the outcome could be in error. That is, if interest lies in surveying the general public, and a small but noticeable fraction of people are excluded from the sample frame, bias might creep into the study. Apparently there was some basis for concern. According to a Pew Research Center report, in 2006 about 7 to 9 percent of Americans relied on cell phones instead of landlines or combinations of cell and landline phones. More ominously, this subpopulation differs from the general public in several significant ways. Cell-phone-only individuals tend to be younger, earn less, and hold somewhat more "liberal" views on social issues (for example, abortion, gay marriage) compared with the populace as a whole.[35] The study also pointed out that cell-phone-only users are easier to contact than landline users, but doing so is more difficult and expensive, and that response rates are lower and refusal rates are higher among cell-phone-only users. Nevertheless, by making statistical adjustments, the Pew Center found that substantive conclusions about attitudes on political issues were not greatly distorted. Still, this is an area in need of additional research.

Sometimes researchers make substitutions if respondents cannot or will not participate. Substituting another member of a household may bias results if the survey specifically asks about the respondent rather than the respondent's household, which is why many professional and academic research designs insist that a presampled individual, not a replacement, be interviewed. Substituting another household from the same block for personal surveys might be better than substituting another telephone number, because city blocks tend to be homogeneous, whereas there is no way to estimate the similarity of households reached by telephone. Substitution of respondents in mail surveys may pose a special problem, since the researcher cannot control whether the intended respondent or another member of the household completed the questionnaire. The extent of bias introduced by substitution of respondents depends on the nature of the survey.

As mentioned earlier, one of the major reasons for worry about sample-population congruence is the possibility that those who are not included will differ from those who are.[36] Some evidence of this likelihood appears in the literature. African Americans, for example, have been found to be more likely to refuse telephone interviews.[37] Refusals also are more common among older, middle-class persons; urban residents; and westerners.[38]

The amount of bias introduced by nonresponses due to refusal or unavailability varies, depending on the purpose of the study and the explanatory factors stressed by the research. For example, if urbanization was a key explanatory variable and refusals were concentrated in urban areas, the study could misrepresent respondents from urban areas because the urban respondents who agreed to participate could differ systematically from those who refused. The personal interview provides the best direct opportunity to judge the characteristics of those who refuse and to estimate whether their refusals will bias the analysis.[39]

The bottom line is that you should always ascertain how well sample proportions match the population of interest on key demographic variables (e.g., age, gender, ethnicity). Nearly every survey analyst takes this first step, even if the results are not always reported.

QUESTIONNAIRE LENGTH.   Subject fatigue is always a problem in survey research. Thus, if a survey poses an inordinate number of questions or takes up too much of the respondents' time, the respondents may lose interest or start answering without much thought or care. Or they may get distracted, impatient, or even hostile. And keeping people interested in the research is exactly what is needed.

A survey needs to include enough questions to gather the data necessary for the research topic, but a good rule of thumb is to keep the survey as short as possible. Given that general advice, how many questions are too many? It is almost impossible to give a precise answer. This is why hypotheses have to be stated carefully. A fishing expedition will in all likelihood end up producing little useful information. Getting the length right is another reason why repeated pretesting is crucial. By trying out the questionnaire on the same types of subjects who will be included in the final study, it is possible to head off respondent weariness.

Unless the pool of participants is especially well motivated (see below), three or four dozen items may be the limit. Especially when there is only a limited possibility to interact with subjects (e.g., with mail, Internet and e-mail, or drop-off surveys), the number of questions should be kept to a minimum (within the confines of the project's goals, of course). Alternatively, the questionnaire should take less than, say, 40 minutes (and, for phone surveys, much less time). This seems to be about the time needed for surveys conducted by government and academic institutions. A respondent's attention may be held longer in some situations than in others; hence, some questionnaires can be longer. Personal interviews generally permit researchers to ask more questions than do phone or mail surveys, and certainly more than can be asked on dropped-off forms, especially if experienced and personable interviewers do the interviewing. But again, researchers need to experiment before going into the field.

IS THE SAMPLE GOOD ENOUGH?

Survey analysts commonly compare their sample results with known population quantities. They do so by asking a few questions about demographic characteristics such as gender, age, and residency (e.g., urban versus rural). If these quantities are known for the target population, the sample results can be compared with the known quantities and any discrepancies noted.

Suppose, for example, that you wanted to survey undergraduates at a college but had limited resources and had to rely on a relatively low-cost class or drop-off procedure (see text). You might ask students in several large introductory courses to participate in your study. Imagine that your questionnaire asks about gender, class (e.g., freshman, sophomore), residency (in-state or out-of-state), and living arrangements (e.g., dorm, off-campus apartment). The registrar or office of institutional research probably makes these data available online or in print. Finding them should not be a major problem. Compare the sample percentages with those for the entire school. If the sample percentages are low or high in a category, you can factor that into your analysis. This method works for any group or population for which adequate measures of common traits are available.

DATA-PROCESSING ISSUES. Finally, although technology is making data collection, preparation, and analysis easier, data processing remains an important subject. After the surveys have been collected, the answers still have to be tabulated. And that requirement can be costly. Consider a written questionnaire administered to 500 people that contains 50 agree-disagree items plus 10 other questions for a total of 60. The responses will simply be marks on pieces of paper. These data need to be coded (translated) in such a way that a computer can process them. (Usually an "agree" answer would be coded as, say, a 1 and a "disagree" as a 5.) If all of the responses can be given numeric codes, there will be 60 × 500 or 30,000 bits of data to record. If, however, any of the questions are open-ended, with respondents replying in their own words, this information has to be transcribed and coded. The task used to be done laboriously by hand. If proper forms have been used, scanners can be put to work. Otherwise, the numbers or codes still have to be entered manually. In the days of IBM cards and keypunches, these chores were the bane of the survey researcher. Since the late 1990s, software has become available for this purpose, although it can be expensive and requires training to use.[40] And, as might be expected, skeptics wonder if machines can ever really decode verbatim transcripts.

Data-processing costs are a major reason for the adoption of Internet and even telephone surveys (CATIs). In the latter case, an operator uses a monitor and software to guide the interviewer through the questionnaire and record the data. One company puts it this way:

> The most important aspect of a CATI system is that it uses computers to conduct the interviews. Because a computer controls the questionnaire, skip patterns are executed exactly as intended, responses are within range, and there are no missing data. And, because answers are entered directly into the computer, data entry is eliminated—data analysis can start immediately.[41]

The software also dials the numbers, records no-answers, and handles many other administrative details.

Response Quality

As we said at the outset, it is easy to take respondents' answers at face value. But doing so can be a mistake. A mere checkmark next to "approve" may or may not indicate a person's true feelings. Also, political scientists and other specialists often forget that not everyone shares their enthusiasm for or knowledge of current events. What is exciting to one person may bore another. If you are a political science major, terms and names like *party identification, World Trade Organization, Senate filibuster, Muammar Muhammad al-Gaddafi* and *Senator Harry Reid* may have a clear meaning. But the public as a whole may not be nearly as familiar with them. Or they may be aware of issues such as *global warming* and *greenhouse gases* but not comprehend *volatile organic compounds* or CO_2 *emissions*. Nor will they always understand a question the way you do. You may know that *Roe v. Wade* invalidated state laws outlawing abortion, but a person in the street may only be aware that a controversial Supreme Court decision "legalized" abortion. Asking about *Roe v. Wade* might produce too many "don't know" or "no opinion" responses. Equally important, people may be reluctant to express their opinions to strangers, even if they can do so anonymously, or they may view social research as trivial or a waste of time. Finally, everyone seems to be busy; what is in your mind a short interview may be a major interference in someone else's busy life. All of these factors may affect the quality of the data obtained through a survey or an interview.

These observations lead to some important guidelines. You can apply them in your own research and, more important, should be on the lookout for how others handle (or do not handle) them.

- Motivate respondents. Good survey researchers try hard not just to induce people to take part in their studies but also to do so as enthusiastically as possible. They want more than perfunctory responses; they hope participants will be careful and thoughtful.

- Always pretest a questionnaire with the types of respondents to be included in the study, not just your friends or colleagues. Find out ahead of time what works and what doesn't.

- Be neat, organized, professional, and courteous.

- If you are using interviewers, train them especially in the skill and art of putting subjects at ease and probing and clarifying. The more experience they have, the better. Make sure they don't betray any political, ethnic, gender, age, class, or other biases that would affect the truthfulness of responses.

- Have reasonable expectations. It is not possible to conduct "the perfect study." As desirable as a personal or mail survey may be, it may not feasible. So think about adopting an alternative and making it as rigorous as your resources allow. Regardless of the choice, keep in mind that some types of surveys have advantages over others in regard to response quality.

These guidelines pertain to **response quality,** which refers to the extent to which responses provide accurate and complete information. It is the key to making valid inferences. Response quality depends on several factors, including the respondents' motivations, their ability to understand and follow directions, their relationship with the interviewer and sponsoring organization, and, most important, the quality of the questions being asked. Indeed, this last point is so important that we discuss it in a separate section.

ENGAGING RESPONDENTS.   To engage respondents, it is important to get off on a good footing by introducing yourself, your organization, your purpose, your appreciation of their time and trouble, your nonpartisanship, your awareness of the importance of anonymity, and your willingness to share your findings. Here, for example, is how the *Washington Post* began one of its telephone surveys:

> *Hello, I'm (NAME), calling for the* Washington Post *public opinion poll. We're not selling anything, just doing an opinion poll on interesting subjects for the news.*[42]

This introduction is short and businesslike but friendly. The interviewers have no doubt rehearsed the message countless times so that they can repeat it with confidence and professionalism.

In general, interviewers are expected to motivate the respondents. Generally it has been thought that warm, friendly interviewers who develop a good rapport with respondents motivate them to give quality answers and to complete the survey. Yet some research has questioned the importance of rapport.[43] Friendly, neutral, "rapport-style" interviews in which interviewers give only positive feedback no matter what the response may not be good enough, especially if the questions involve difficult reporting tasks. Both types of feedback—positive ("yes, that's the kind of information we want") and negative ("that's only two things")—may improve response quality. Interviewers also may need to instruct respondents about how to provide complete and accurate information. This more businesslike, task-oriented style has been found to lead to better reporting than rapport-style interviewing.[44]

Interviewer style appears to make less difference in telephone interviews, perhaps because of the lack of visual cues the respondent can use to judge the interviewer's sincerity.[45] Even something as simple as intonation, however, may affect data quality. Interviewers whose voices go up rather than down at the end of a question appear to motivate a respondent's interest in reporting.[46]

Despite the advantages of using interviewers to improve response quality, the interviewer-respondent interaction may also bias a respondent's answers. The interviewer may give a respondent the impression that certain answers are expected or are correct. For example, interviewers who anticipate difficulties in persuading respondents to respond or to report sensitive behavior have been found to obtain lower response and reporting rates.[47] The age, gender, or race of the interviewer may affect the respondent's willingness to give honest answers. For example, on questions about race, respondents interviewed by a member of another race have been found to be more deferential to the interviewer (that is, try harder not to cause offense) than those interviewed by a member of their own race.[48] Education also has an impact on race-of-interviewer effects: less-educated blacks are more deferential than better-educated blacks, and better-educated whites are more deferential than less-educated whites.[49]

Interviewer bias, which occurs when the interviewer influences the respondent's answers, may have a larger effect on telephone surveys than in-person surveys.[50] Because of its efficiency and because telephone interviewers, even for national surveys, do not need to be geographically dispersed, telephone interviewing requires fewer interviewers than does personal interviewing to complete the same number of interviews. Centralization of telephone interviewing operations, however, allows closer supervision and monitoring of interviewers, making it easier to identify and control interviewer problems. For both personal and telephone interviewers, training and practice is an essential part of the research process.

PROBING.   As just noted, politics is not on the top of everyone's mind. Consequently, it is often necessary to tease out responses. An interviewer can probe for additional information or clarification. He or she can gently encourage the respondent to think a bit or add more information rather than just provide an off-the-cuff answer. For example, suppose you want to know how people feel about presidential candidates. You could, as many polls do, list a number of qualities or characteristics that respondents can apply to the choices. But this technique assumes that you know what people are thinking. By contrast, if you simply ask a subject, "What do you think about Candidate X?" the first reply is often something like "Hmm . . . not much" or "She's a jerk." This may or may not be a true feeling, and in all likelihood it is not complete. Often, however, people pause a moment before responding. A trained interviewer waits a short while for the person to gather his or her thoughts. If the answer is not totally clear, the interviewer can ask for clarification. This is how the American National Election Studies, a series of major academic surveys, handle the problem. The lead-in begins, "Now I'd like to ask you about the good and bad points of the major candidates for President. . . . Is there anything in particular about [name of candidate] that might make you want to vote for him?" The questionnaire then reads:

"IF R [the respondent] SAYS THERE IS SOMETHING THAT WOULD MAKE R VOTE [for the candidate]:
QUESTION:

(What is that?)
INTERVIEWER INSTRUCTION:

{PROBE: ANYTHING ELSE? UNTIL R SAYS NO}[51]

Survey Type and Response Quality

The ability to obtain quality responses differs according to the type of survey used. Although with mail and drop-off surveys, an interviewer cannot probe for additional information or clarification, these surveys may have an advantage in obtaining truthful answers to threatening or embarrassing questions because anonymity can be assured and answers given in private. A mail survey also gives the respondent enough time to finish when it is convenient; this enables the respondent to check records to provide accurate information, something that is harder to arrange in telephone and personal interviews.

Disadvantages of the mail survey include problems with open-ended questions. (As we see in the next section, an open-ended question asks for the respondent's own words, as in "Is there anything in particular that you like about the Republican Party?" The respondent can say whatever he or she thinks.) Some respondents may lack writing skills or find answering at length a burden. No interviewer is present to probe for more information, clarify complex or confusing questions, motivate the respondent to answer tedious or boring questions, or control who else may contribute to or influence answers.

Personal and telephone interviews share many advantages and disadvantages with respect to obtaining quality responses, although some important differences exist. Several of the advantages of personal and telephone interviews over mail surveys stem from the presence of an interviewer. As noted earlier, an interviewer may obtain better-quality data by explaining questions, probing for more information to open-ended questions, and making observations about the respondent and his or her environment. For example, in a personal interview, the quality of furnishings and housing may be an indicator of income, and in a telephone interview, the amount of background noise might affect the respondent's concentration. In a personal interview, the interviewer may note that another household member is influencing a respondent's answers and take steps to curtail this influence. Influence by others is generally not a problem with telephone interviews, since only the respondent hears the questions. One response-quality problem that does occur with telephone interviews is that the respondent may not be giving the interviewer his or her undivided attention. This may be difficult for the interviewer to detect and correct.

Numerous studies have compared the response quality of personal and telephone interviews. One expected difference is in answers to open-ended questions. Telephone interviewers lack visual cues for probing. Thus, telephone interviews tend to be quick paced; pausing to see if the respondent adds more to an answer is more awkward on the telephone than in person. Research findings, however, have been mixed. One study found that shorter answers were given to open-ended questions in telephone interviews, especially among respondents who typically give complete and detailed responses; another study found no difference between personal and telephone interviews in the number of responses to open-ended questions.[52] Asking an open-ended question early in a telephone survey helps to relax the respondent, reduce the pace of the interview, and ensure that the respondent is thinking about his or her answers.[53]

Response quality may be lower for telephone interviews than for face-to-face interviews because of the difficulty of asking complex questions or questions with many response categories over the phone. Research has found more acquiescence, evasiveness, and extremeness in telephone survey responses than in personal survey responses. In addition, phone respondents give more contradictory answers to checklist items and are less likely to admit to problems.[54] This finding contradicts the expectation that telephone interviews result in more accurate answers to sensitive questions because of reduced personal contact.

Researchers using personal and telephone interviews have developed techniques to obtain more accurate data on sensitive topics.[55] Problems often can be avoided simply by careful wording choice. For example, for questions about socially desirable behavior, a casual approach reduces the threat by lessening the perceived importance of the topic. The question, "For whom did you vote in the last election?" could inadvertently stigmatize nonvoting. Here, once more, is how the American National Election Studies put the question:

> *In talking to people about elections, we often find that a lot of people were not able to vote because they weren't registered, they were sick, or they just didn't have time. How about you—did you vote in the elections this November?*[56]

In other words, giving respondents reasons for not doing something perceived as socially desirable reduces threat and may cut down on overreports of the behavior.

A different approach to the problem of obtaining accurate answers to sensitive questions is the **randomized response technique** (RRT).[57] Examples might be "Have you ever had an abortion?" or "Have you used marijuana in the past month?" or "Do you believe gays should have the same legal rights as other people?" The RRT technique allows respondents to answer these kinds of sensitive questions truthfully without the interviewer's knowing the question being answered. For example, the interviewer gives the respondent a card with two questions, one sensitive and one not sensitive. A device such as a coin or a box with two colors of beads is used to randomly determine which question the respondent will answer. If a coin is used, the respondent will be instructed to answer one question if the result is a heads and the other if tails shows up. The respondent flips the coin and, without showing the interviewer the outcome of the toss, answers the appropriate question. One can then use probability theory to estimate the distribution of sensitive responses. The accuracy of RRT depends on the assumption that a respondent will answer both the sensitive and nonsensitive questions truthfully. Success in obtaining accurate information depends on the respondent's ability to understand the method and follow instructions and on his or her belief that the random-choice device is not rigged.[58] The technique seems to work better when the nonsensitive question deals with a socially positive activity, further reducing the stigma attached to a yes response.[59]

Research has found RRT to be superior to other methods of asking threatening questions, such as having the respondent answer a direct question and return it in a sealed envelope.[60] For example, use of RRT produced higher estimates of abortion than previous measures.[61] RRT can be used for telephone as well as personal interviews. Random-choice devices can be supplied by the respondent—thus eliminating suspicion that the device is fixed—or they can be mailed by the researcher to the respondent.[62] However, since the method can be expensive and cumbersome, it is not widely used in public opinion research.

Question Wording

The central problem of survey and interview research is that the procedures involve a structured interaction between a social scientist and a subject. This is true even if the method used involves indirect contact, such as a mail or an Internet survey. Since the whole point of survey research is to accurately measure people's attitudes, beliefs, and behavior by asking them questions, we need to spend time discussing good and bad questions. Good questions prompt accurate answers; bad questions provide inappropriate stimuli and result in unreliable or inaccurate responses. When writing questions, researchers should use objective and clear wording. Failure to do so may result in incomplete questionnaires and meaningless data for the researcher. The basic rule is this: *the target subjects must be able to understand and in principle have access to the requested information.* Try to put yourself in the respondent's place. Would an ordinary citizen, for example, be able to reply meaningfully to the question, "What's your opinion of the recently passed amendments to the Import/Export Bank Authorization?"

OBJECTIVITY AND CLARITY.   Certain types of questions make it difficult for respondents to provide reliable, accurate responses. These include double-barreled, ambiguous, and leading questions. A **double-barreled question** is really two questions in one, such as "Do you agree with the statement that the situation in Iraq is deteriorating and that the United States should increase the number of troops in Iraq?" How does a person who believes that the situation in Iraq is deteriorating but who does not wish an increase in troops answer this question? Or someone who doesn't feel the situation is worse but nevertheless believes that more troops would be advisable? And how does the researcher interpret an answer to such a question? It is not clear whether the respondent meant for his or her answer to apply to both components or whether one component was given precedence over the other.

INTERLUDE: THE HEALTH CARE DEBATE AND WHY QUESTION WORDING MATTERS

Before proceeding with an examination of the dos and don'ts of question wording, we present a substantive example of the importance of question wording.

The chapter began by mentioning how groups use polls to advance their causes. The reason is obvious: public support is a potent resource in any democratic conflict. An organization that asserts the people support its objectives may have an advantage over its opponents. After all, what slogan beats "The American people want it!"? And it is usually a snap to find a poll that, if looked at in the right way, can be interpreted as a proving there is a mandate for nearly any cause. The health care debate that roiled American politics during President Obama's first term is a case in point.

We pointed out in the beginning of the chapter that the Patient Protection and Affordable Care Act (aka "Obamacare") has been opposed on many grounds. Among the strongest objections is the assertion that the "people don't want it." Republicans have been especially vocal in making this point. Here, for example, is Congressman Steve King, Republican of Iowa:

> On March 23, 2010, President Obama defied the wishes of the American people and signed ObamaCare into law. At the time, supporters of the unconstitutional law claimed that Americans would warm up to ObamaCare as they began to realize what was in it. This claim was unlikely then, and recent polling indicates that it is completely without merit now. . . . The lesson derived from these results? Americans increasingly favor repeal, and their position on this matter is hardening.[63]

Given its deep hostility to the Act and gains it made in the 2010 midterm elections, the GOP not surprisingly set its sights on a total repeal of the new law or, barring that, complete "defunding" of key programs to prevent its implementation. Democrats naturally stand on the opposite side. Although they don't explicitly argue that public opinion backs them, they predict voters will "come around" when they start benefiting from PPACA's many provisions.

Since both sides resort to polling to bolster their arguments, we might think this would be an easy dispute to settle. Alas, things are not quite so simple. Consider the results taken from several organizations in the first months of 2011. (*Note:* These questions come from polls conducted by various organizations. All entail national samples of about 1,000 individuals and were conducted during roughly the same period, in early 2011.)

- Do Americans approve of the PPACA? Not really, according to many polls taken in early 2011, one year after the reform's passage.

Survey	Good thing/Favor %	Bad thing/oppose %	Unsure %
Gallup Poll*	46	44	10
CNN/ORC§	37	59	5
Kaiser Family Foundation†	42	46	13
CBS News Poll‡	33	51	16
Average	39.5%	50%	11%

*Gallup Poll, March 18–19, 2011. *N* = 1,038 adults nationwide.

§CNN/Opinion Research Corporation Poll, March 11–13, 2011. *N* = 1,023 adults nationwide.

†Kaiser Family Foundation Health Tracking Poll, March 8–13, 2011. *N* = 1,202 adults nationwide.

‡CBS News Poll, February 11–14, 2011. *N* = 1,031 adults nationwide. "Strongly approve" and "somewhat approve" responses are combined as are disapprovals.

- Do they therefore want it repealed? Senator Jim DeMint (R-SC) thinks so:

  Republicans are standing with the American people who are demanding we repeal this government takeover of health care.[64]

- But from aggregate numbers it is not clear. Overall, in fact, it appears the country is closely divided. Maybe then we need to dig under the surface. As the data imply, but certainly do not demonstrate, there doesn't seem to be a stampede for repeal.

Survey	Repeal %	Let Stand %	Unsure %
CBS News/New York Times Poll[*]	40%	48%	12%
NBC News/Wall Street Journal[§]	45	46	9
CNN/Opinion Research Corporation Poll.[†]	50	42	8
Average	45%	44.7	9.7%

[*]CBS News/*New York Times* Poll, January 15–19, 2011. N = 1,036 adults nationwide.

[§]NBC News/*Wall Street Journal* Poll conducted by the polling organizations of Peter Hart (D) and Bill McInturff (R), January 13–17, 2011. N = 1,000 adults nationwide. Those "strongly" and "not so strongly" combined; the same for those "opposed."

[†]CNN/Opinion Research Corporation Poll, January 14–16, 2011. N = 1,014 adults nationwide.

- Of course, any public official will probably respond to those he or she hears most frequently and loudly. Being a Republican from a conservative state, Senator DeMint might naturally infer a groundswell of opposition to the law. So when trying to fathom the public's mind, it helps to break down further who is saying what.

Party Identification	Repeal %	Let It Stand %	Unsure %
Republican	73	16	11
Independent	38	45	17
Democrat	16	77	6
Total sample	**40**	**48**	**12**

"Do you think Congress should try to repeal the health care law that was passed last year, or should they let it stand?"

Source: CBS News/*New York Times* Poll, January 15–19, 2011. N = 1,036 adults nationwide.

- The figures suggest that in the aggregate, the people are divided; attitudes are strongly correlated with partisanship. In order to know where the public stands, one has to take account of the various groups. Independents split slightly in favor of letting the reforms alone, and they—along with the Democrats, who are overwhelmingly in favor—counterbalance Republicans, who are more or less united in opposition. The ambiguity of public opinion on the matters deepens when examining attitudes and beliefs in more detail. Rather than simply counting "for" and "against" respondents, we should look for clues to *how* respondents interpret key terms. It's tempting, for example, to assume the response "Oppose" means "against the health care bill passed in 2010." But consider these results.

(Box Continued)

(Box Continued)

| | **Pro Health Care Reform Responses** | | | |
	Favor %	Oppose—Not Liberal Enough %	Oppose—Too Liberal %	Unsure %
CNN/Opinion Research Corporation Poll	37	13	43	7

"As you may know, a bill that makes major changes to the country's health care system became law last year. Based on what you have read or heard about that legislation, do you generally favor or generally oppose it?" If oppose: "Do you oppose that legislation because you think its approach toward health care is too liberal, or because you think it is not liberal enough?"

Source: CNN/Opinion Research Corporation Poll, March 11–13, 2011. *N* = 1,023

- Respondents were first asked whether or not they oppose the reform package, and then those who were opposed were asked if the bill was too liberal or not liberal enough. Most (43%) objected because it was too "liberal," an understandable reaction given the legislation's liberal origins and support. But note also that 13 percent understood *oppose* differently; for them the act was objectionable because it did not go far enough in the direction favored by Democrats and progressives who advocate for even greater involvement in health care than the bill provides. So again, the answer to the question, "What do the voters want?" is not entirely obvious. (Needless to say, this conclusion rests on the assumption that those surveyed understood *liberal* in the same way. That may be doubtful.)

- Survey analysts often want to gauge the level of knowledge that undergirds opinions. In early 2011, House and Senate Republicans made strenuous, widely publicized attempts to repeal PPACA, but as of August of that year they had not succeeded. Many voters however, seemed confused. A Kaiser Foundation poll posed this question: "As far as you know, which comes closest to describing the current status of the health reform law that was passed last year? It is still the law of the land. OR, It has been repealed and is no longer law." The responses:[65]

  o Still the law: 52%

  o Has been repealed: 22%

  o Unsure: 26%

  Barely more than half the sample knew the law was still in force. Nearly one in five thought it had been repealed, and over a quarter were not certain. What to make of this? One implication is that some opinions may not be set in stone; if people "knew" more, their thoughts about the policy might change.

- This and the previous finding point to a potential Achilles' heel in survey research: the dependence on language. Pollsters must constantly strive to establish shared frames of reference so interviewer and subject comprehend and apply words the same way. Equally important is trying to grasp the set of beliefs (thoughts about what is "real") and evaluations of beliefs (that is, attitudes toward what is believed—"Is this a good or bad state of affairs?") that underlie spoken opinions, which are frequently uttered on the spur of the moment. Below are attitudes toward various provisions of the new law. Once these are taken into account, one has a far more nuanced understanding of popular reactions to the legislation.

	Favor %	Oppose %	Neither/Unsure/Refused %
Employer mandate*	59	32	10
Limits on coverage§	59	34	7
Prior conditions†	50	34	17
Mandate to obtain insurance‡	31	59	10

* "Do you favor, oppose, or neither favor nor oppose a law requiring most medium-size and large companies to offer health insurance to their employees or pay money to the government as a penalty if they don't?"

"Do you favor, oppose, or neither favor nor oppose a law saying that an insurance company cannot stop selling health insurance to one of their customers if that person gets a serious illness?"

† "Do you favor, oppose, or neither favor nor oppose a law requiring insurance companies to sell health insurance to a person who is currently sick or has had a serious illness in the past, which would probably cause most Americans to pay more for health insurance?"

‡ "Do you favor, oppose, or neither favor nor oppose a law that would require every American to have health insurance, or pay money to the government as a penalty if they do not, unless the person is very poor?"

Source: AP-GfK Poll conducted by GfK Roper Public Affairs & Corporate Communications, January 5–10, 2011. *N* = 1,001 adults nationwide.

- Except for the personal mandate, some provisions of the reform seem acceptable to perhaps a majority or plurality of Americans. The exception, the requirement that everyone purchase some form of health insurance, is wildly unpopular, perhaps because it touches on issues of individual freedom and responsibility. Whatever the case, it seems to be a stretch to argue that voters oppose the reforms in their entirety.

- It is also important to inquire into the policy implications of public opinion. One proposal for getting rid of Obamacare is to "defund" it by choking off appropriations necessary for the law's implementation. But many citizens, even Republicans, seem to be wary of this approach.

Party Identification	Approve %	Disapprove %	Unsure %
Republican	57	34	10
Independent	38	49	13
Democrat	12	82	6
Average	35	55	10

Question: "Some members of Congress have said they may stop funding for the new health care law. Regardless of how you feel about the new health care legislation, would you approve or disapprove if Congress stopped funding for the new health care law?"

Source: CBS News Poll, February 11–14, 2011. *N* = 1,031 adults nationwide.

- Finally, since all of these data illustrate role language plays in decoding poll reports, we conclude with an issue that comes up later: "leading" questions or questions phrased in such a manner as to intentionally or encourage a response in one direction or another. A Fox News survey asked its participants this question:

   Some Americans choose not to buy health insurance even though they can afford it. The president's plan requires all Americans who can afford it to have some form of health insurance or else pay a penalty. Failure to pay the penalty would result in an even larger fine, a jail sentence of up to one year, or both. Do you think the government should be able to require all Americans who can afford it to have health insurance or pay a penalty, or not?[66]

- The results were as follows:

   o "Yes," government should be able to require participation: 28%

   o "No," should not: 69%

   o "Unsure": 4%

The upshot, then, is that how one frames an issue partly determines the public's expressed or verbalized stances on it. Advocacy groups of course have to take into account this phenomenon, but as social scientists we have to be aware of it as well. The following sections describe in more detail some considerations when writing or evaluating questionnaires.

Despite a conscious effort by researchers to define and clarify concepts, words with multiple meanings or interpretations may creep into questions. An **ambiguous question** is one that contains a concept that is not defined clearly. An example would be the question, "What is your income?" Is the question asking for family income or just the personal income of the respondent? Is the question asking for earned income (salary or wages), or should interest and stock dividends be included? Similarly, the question "Do you prefer Brand A or Brand B?" is ambiguous. Is the respondent telling us which brand is purchased or which brand would be purchased if there were no price difference between the brands?

Ambiguity also may result from using the word *he.* Are respondents to assume that *he* is being used generically to refer both to men and women or to men only? If a respondent interprets the question as applying only to men and would respond differently for women, it would be a mistake for the researcher to conclude that the response applies to all people.[67]

Researchers must avoid asking leading questions. A **leading question,** sometimes called a reactive question, encourages respondents to choose a particular response because the question indicates that the researcher expects it. The question "Don't you think that global warming is a serious environmental problem?" implies that to think otherwise would be unusual. Word choice may also lead respondents. Research has shown that people are more willing to help "the needy" than those "on welfare." Asking people if they favor "socialized medicine" rather than "national health insurance" is bound to decrease affirmative responses. Moreover, linking personalities or institutions to issues can affect responses. For example, whether or not a person liked the governor would affect responses to the following question: "Would you say that Governor Burnett's program for promoting economic development has been very effective, fairly effective, not too effective, or not effective at all?"[68] There are numerous other ways to lead the respondent, such as by characterizing one response as the preference of others, thereby creating an atmosphere that is anything but neutral.[69]

Polls conducted by political organizations and politicians often include leading questions. For example, a 1980 poll for the Republican National Committee asked, "Recently the Soviet armed forces openly invaded the independent country of Afghanistan. Do you think the U.S. should supply military equipment to the rebel freedom fighters?"[70] Before accepting any interpretation of survey responses, we should check the full text of a question to make sure that it is neither leading nor biased.

Indeed, some campaigns, parties, and political organizations have begun converting survey research into a form of telemarketing through a technique called **push polls.** Interviewers, supposedly representing a research organization, feed respondents (often) false and damaging information about a candidate or cause under the guise of asking a question. The caller may ask, for example, "Do you agree or disagree with Candidate X's willingness to tolerate terrorism in our country?" The goal, of course, is not to conduct research but to use innuendo to spread rumors and lies.

Questions should be stated in such a way that they can produce a variety of responses. If you simply ask, "Do you favor cleaning up the environment—yes or no?" almost all the responses will surely be yes. At the same time, the alternatives themselves should encourage thoughtful replies. For instance, if the responses to the question "How would you rate President Obama's performance so far?" are (1) great, (2) somewhere between great and terrible, and (3) terrible, you probably are not going to find very much variation, since the list practically demands that respondents pick choice (2). Also, an alternative should be available for each possible situation. For example, response options for the question "For whom did you vote in the 2008 presidential election?" should list John McCain and Barack Obama, as well as other candidates (for example, Ralph Nader) and certainly should include generic "other" and "did not vote" options. (The section on "question type" discusses this topic in more depth.)

Other kinds of bias can creep into questionnaires. As Margrit Eichler demonstrated, gender bias may occur if, for example, a respondent is asked to agree or disagree with the following statement: "It is generally better to have a man at the head of a department composed of both men and women employees." This wording does not allow the respondent to indicate that a woman is preferable as the department head. It would be better to rephrase the statement as "What do you think is generally better: to have a woman or a man at the head of a department that is composed of both men and women employees?" and to give respondents the opportunity to indicate that a man is better, a woman is better, or there is no difference.[71]

Use of technical words, slang, and unusual vocabulary should be avoided, since respondents may misinterpret their meaning. Questions including words with several meanings will result in ambiguous answers. For example, the answer to the question, "How much bread do you have?" depends on whether the respondent thinks of bread as coming in loaves or dollar bills. The use of appropriate wording is especially important in cross-cultural research. For researchers to compare answers across cultures, questions should be equivalent in meaning. For example, the question, "Are you interested in politics?" may be interpreted as "Do you vote in elections?" or "Do you belong to a political party?" The interpretation would depend on the country or culture of the respondent.

Questions should be personal and relevant to the respondent. For example, in a questionnaire on abortion, the question "Have you ever had an abortion?" could be changed to "Have you [your wife, girlfriend] ever had an abortion?" This will permit the researcher to include the responses of men as well as women.

Attention to these basic guidelines for question wording increases the probability that respondents will interpret a question consistently and as intended, yielding reliable and valid responses. Luckily every researcher does not have to formulate questions anew. We discuss archival sources of survey questions later in this chapter.

Question Type

The form or type of question as well as its specific wording is important. There are two basic types of questions: closed-ended and open-ended. A **closed-ended question** provides respondents with a list of responses from which to choose. "Do you agree or disagree with the statement that the government ought to do more to help farmers?" and "Do you think that penalties for drunk driving are too severe, too lenient, or just about right?" are examples of closed-ended questions.

A variation of the closed-ended question is a question with multiple choices for the respondent to accept or reject. A question with multiple choices is really a series of closed-ended questions. Consider the following example: "Numerous strategies have been proposed concerning the federal budget deficit. Please indicate whether you find the following alternatives acceptable or unacceptable: (a) raise income taxes, (b) adopt a national sales tax, (c) reduce military spending, (d) reduce spending on domestic programs."

In an **open-ended question,** the respondent is not provided with any answers from which to choose. The respondent or interviewer writes down the answer. An example of an open-ended question is "Is there anything in particular about BARACK OBAMA that might make you want to vote for him?[72]

CLOSED-ENDED QUESTIONS: ADVANTAGES AND DISADVANTAGES.   The main advantage of a closed-ended question is that it is easy to answer and takes little time. Also, the answers can be precoded (that is, assigned a number) and the code then easily transferred from the questionnaire to a computer. Another advantage is that answers are easy to compare, since all responses fall into a fixed number of predetermined categories. These advantages aid in the quick statistical analysis of data. With open-ended questions, by contrast, the researcher must read each answer, decide which answers are equivalent, decide how many categories or different types of answers to code, and assign codes before the data can be computerized.

Another advantage of closed-ended questions over open-ended ones is that respondents are usually willing to respond on personal or sensitive topics (for example, income, age, frequency of sexual activity, or political views) by choosing a category rather than stating the actual answer. This is especially true if the answer categories include ranges. Finally, closed-ended questions may help clarify the question for the respondent, thus avoiding misinterpretations of the question and unusable answers for the researcher.

Critics of closed-ended questions charge that they force a respondent to choose an answer category that may not accurately represent his or her position. Therefore, the response has less meaning and is less useful to the researcher.

Also, closed-ended questions often are phrased so that a respondent must choose between two alternatives or state which one is preferred. This may result in an oversimplified and distorted picture of public opinion. A closed-ended question allowing respondents to pick more than one response (for example, with instructions to choose all responses that apply) may be more appropriate in some situations. The information produced by such a question indicates which choices are acceptable to a majority of respondents. In fashioning a policy that is acceptable to most people, policy makers may find this knowledge much more useful than simply knowing which alternative a respondent prefers.

Just as the wording of a question may influence responses, so too may the wording of response choices. Changes in the wording of question responses can result in different response distributions. Two questions from the 1960s concerning troop withdrawal from Vietnam illustrate this problem.[73] A June 1969 Gallup Poll question asked,

> *President Nixon has ordered the withdrawal of 25,000 United States troops from Vietnam in the next three months. How do you feel about this—do you think troops should be withdrawn at a faster rate or a slower rate?*

The answer "same as now" was not presented but was accepted if given. The response distribution was as follows: faster, 42 percent; same as now, 29 percent; slower, 16 percent; no opinion, 13 percent.

Compare the responses with those to a September–October 1969 Harris Poll in which respondents were asked,

> *In general, do you feel the pace at which the president is withdrawing troops is too fast, too slow, or about right?*

Responses to this question were as follows: too slow, 28 percent; about right, 49 percent; too fast, 6 percent; no opinion, 18 percent.

Thus support for presidential plans varied from 29 to 49 percent. The response depended on whether respondents were directly given the choice of agreeing with presidential policy or had to mention such a response spontaneously.

Response categories may also contain leading or biased language and may not provide respondents with equal opportunities to agree or disagree. Response distributions may be affected by whether the researcher asks a **single-sided question,** in which the respondent is asked to agree or disagree with a single substantive statement, or a **two-sided question,** which offers the respondent two substantive choices. An example of a one-sided question is

> *Do you agree or disagree with the idea that the government should see to it that every person has a job and a good standard of living?*

An example of a two-sided question is

> *Do you think that the government should see to it that every person has a job and a good standard of living, or should it let each person get ahead on his or her own?*

With a single-sided question, a larger percentage of respondents tend to agree with the statement given. Forty-four percent of the respondents to the single-sided question given above agreed that the government should guarantee employment, whereas only 30.3 percent of the respondents to the two-sided question chose this position.[74] Presenting two substantive choices has been found to reduce the proportion of respondents who give no opinion.[75]

Closed-ended questions may provide inappropriate choices, thus leading many respondents to not answer or to choose the "other" category. Unless space is provided to explain "other" (which then makes the question resemble an open-ended one), it is anybody's guess what "other" means. Another problem is that errors may enter into the data if the wrong response code is marked. With no written answer, inadvertent errors cannot be checked. A problem also arises with questions having a great many possible answers. It is time-consuming to have an interviewer read a long list of fixed responses that the respondent may forget. A solution to this problem is to use a response card. Responses are typed on a card that is handed to the respondent to read and choose from.

OPEN-ENDED QUESTIONS: ADVANTAGES AND DISADVANTAGES. Unstructured, free-response questions allow respondents to state what they know and think. They are not forced to choose between fixed responses that do not apply. Open-ended questions allow respondents to tell the researcher how they define a complex issue or concept. As one survey researcher in favor of open-ended questions pointed out,

> *Presumably, although this is often forgotten, the main purpose of an interview, the most important goal of the entire survey profession, is to let the respondent have his say, to let him tell the researcher what he means, not vice versa. If we do not let the respondent have his say, why bother to interview him at all?*[76]

Sometimes researchers are unable to specify in advance the likely responses to a question. In this situation, an open-ended question is appropriate. Open-ended questions are also appropriate if the researcher is trying to test the knowledge of respondents. For example, respondents are better able to *recognize* names of candidates in a closed-ended question (that is, pick the candidates from a list of names) than they are able to *recall* names in response to an open-ended question about candidates. Using only one question or the other would yield an incomplete picture of citizens' awareness of candidates.

Paradoxically, a disadvantage of the open-ended question is that respondents may respond too much or too little. Some may reply at great length about an issue—a time-consuming and costly problem for the researcher. On the other hand, if open-ended questions are included on mail surveys, some respondents with poor writing skills may not answer, which may bias responses. Thus, the use of open-ended questions depends on the type of survey. Another problem is that interviewers may err in recording a respondent's answer. Recording answers verbatim is tedious. Furthermore, unstructured answers may be difficult to code, interpretations of answers may vary (affecting the reliability of data), and processing answers may become time-consuming and costly. For these reasons, open-ended questions are often avoided—although unnecessarily, in Patricia Labaw's opinion:

> I believe that coding costs have now been transferred into data-processing costs. To substitute for open questions, researchers lengthen their questionnaires with endless lists of multiple choice and agree/disagree statements, which are then handled by sophisticated data-processing analytical techniques to try to massage some pattern or meaning out of the huge mass of pre-coded and punched data. I have found that a well-written open-ended question can eliminate the need for several closed questions, and that subsequent data analysis becomes clear and easy compared to the obfuscation provided by data massaging.[77]

Question Order

The order in which questions are presented to respondents may also influence the reliability and validity of answers. Researchers call this the **question-order effect.** In ordering questions, the researcher should consider the effect on the respondent of the previous question, the likelihood of the respondent's completing the questionnaire, and the need to select groups of respondents for certain questions. In many ways, answering a survey is a learning situation, and previous questions can be expected to influence subsequent answers. This presents problems as well as opportunities for the researcher.

The first several questions in a survey are usually designed to break the ice. They are general questions that are easy to answer. Complex, specific questions may cause respondents to terminate an interview or not complete a questionnaire because they think it will be too hard. Questions on personal or sensitive topics usually are left to the end. Otherwise, some respondents may suspect that the purpose of the survey is to check up on them rather than to find out public attitudes and activities in general. In some cases, however, it may be important to collect demographic information first. In a study of attitudes toward abortion, one researcher used demographic information to infer the responses of those who terminated the interview. She found that older, low-income women were most likely to terminate the interview on the abortion section. Since their group matched those who completed the interviews and who were strongly opposed to abortion, she concluded that termination expressed opposition to abortion.[78]

One problem to avoid is known as a **response set,** or straight-line responding. A response set may occur when a series of questions have the same answer choices. Respondents who find themselves agreeing with the first several statements may skim over subsequent statements and check "agree" on all. This is likely to happen if statements are on related topics. To avoid the response-set phenomenon, statements should be worded so that respondents may agree with the first, disagree with the second, and so on. This way the respondents are forced to read each statement carefully before responding.

Additional question-order effects include saliency, redundancy, consistency, and fatigue.[79] Saliency is the effect that specific mention of an issue in a survey may have in causing a respondent to mention the issue in connection with a later question: the earlier question brings the issue forward in the respondent's mind. For example, a researcher should not be surprised if respondents mention crime as a problem in response to a general question on problems affecting their community if the survey had earlier asked them about crime in the community. Redundancy is the reverse of saliency. Some respondents, unwilling to repeat themselves, may not say crime is a problem in response to the general query if earlier they had indicated that crime was a problem. Respondents may also strive to appear consistent. An answer to a question may be constrained by an answer given earlier. Finally, fatigue may cause respondents to give perfunctory answers to questions late in the survey. In lengthy questionnaires, response-set problems often arise due to fatigue.[80]

The learning that takes place during an interview may be an important aspect of the research being conducted. The researcher may intentionally use this process to find out more about the respondent's attitudes and potential behavior. Labaw referred to this as "leading" the respondent and noted it is used "to duplicate the effects of information, communication and education on the respondent in real life."[81] The extent of a respondent's approval or opposition to an issue may be clarified as the interviewer introduces new information about the issue.

In some cases, such education *must* be done to elicit needed information on public opinion. For example, one study set out to evaluate public opinion on ethical issues in biomedical research.[82] Because the public is generally uninformed about these issues, some way had to be devised to enable respondents to make meaningful judgments. The researchers developed a procedure of presenting "research vignettes." Each vignette described or illustrated a dilemma actually encountered in biomedical research. A series of questions asking respondents to make ethical judgments followed each vignette. Such a procedure was felt to provide an appropriate decision-making framework for meaningful, spontaneous answers and a standard stimulus for respondents. A majority of persons, even those with less than a high school education, were able to express meaningful and consistent opinions.

If there is no specific reason for placing questions in a particular order, researchers may vary questions randomly to control question-order bias. Computerized word processing of questionnaires makes this an easier task.[83]

Question order also becomes an important consideration when the researcher uses a **branching question,** which sorts respondents into subgroups and directs these subgroups to different parts of the questionnaire, or a **filter question,** which screens respondents from inappropriate questions. For example, a marketing survey on new car purchases may use a branching question to sort people into several groups: those who bought a car in the past year, those who are contemplating buying a car in the next year, and those who are not anticipating buying a car in the foreseeable future. For each group, a different set of questions about automobile purchasing may be appropriate. A filter question is typically used to prevent the uninformed from answering questions. For example, respondents in the 1980 National Election Study were given a list of presidential candidates and asked to mark those names they had never heard of or didn't know much about. Respondents were then asked questions only about those names that they hadn't marked.

Branching and filter questions increase the chances for interviewer and respondent error.[84] Questions to be answered by all respondents may be missed. However, careful attention to questionnaire layout, clear instructions to the interviewer and the respondent, and well-ordered questions will minimize the possibility of confusion and lost or inappropriate information.

Questionnaire Design

The term **questionnaire design** refers to the physical layout and packaging of the questionnaire. An important goal of questionnaire design is to make the questionnaire attractive and easy for the interviewer and the respondent to follow. Good design increases the likelihood that the questionnaire will be completed properly. Design may also make the transfer of data from the questionnaire to the computer easier.

Design considerations are most important for mail questionnaires. First, the researcher must make a favorable impression based almost entirely on the questionnaire materials mailed to the respondent. Second, because no interviewer is present to explain the questionnaire to the respondent, a mail questionnaire must be self-explanatory. Poor design increases the likelihood of response error and nonresponse. Whereas telephone and personal interviewers can and should familiarize themselves with questionnaires before administering them to a respondent, the recipient of a mail questionnaire cannot be expected to spend much time trying to figure out a poorly designed form.

USING ARCHIVED SURVEYS

Now that you have a better idea of what surveys are and how they are properly designed and administered, it is important to understand the costs and benefits of designing and administering your own survey to collect data versus using survey questions written by or data collected by someone else. Because of the high costs involved in designing and administering a survey and the concerns about validity and reliability of the data, most students who want to design their own survey would be remiss if they did not at least consult existing surveys. In this section, we explain how you can search for survey questions and data in archives and what you can expect to find.

Advantages of Using Archived Surveys

Although some students can rely on funding from their universities for research (usually a couple hundred dollars to defray costs), most students will not have access to such funds. Without funding, most students wishing to collect survey data to analyze in a research paper will turn to the least expensive options available. The most popular source of survey data for students is a sample of undergraduate students. These efforts generally involve less expensive collection measures like in-class group surveys or surveys conducted via e-mail or the Internet. Given the limitations on available resources, these are acceptable choices, and students designing and administering their own surveys will undoubtedly learn a great deal about the pitfalls of survey research when choosing this option. Firsthand experience can be invaluable to fully understanding survey design and administration, and the experience cannot be replicated simply by reading a textbook on the subject.

One of the biggest drawbacks of students designing and administering their own surveys is that the questions, the survey form, and the administration will likely be of quite low quality without considerable input from an instructor or an advisor. Although this is not a problem if a survey is intended to be a learning exercise, students hoping to collect high-quality data from their own survey might be disappointed with the results. To be able to make valid conclusions based on the data, students should consider instead using survey questions written by professionals. Such questions are widely available for free to students through publicly available archives. In chapter 9, we discussed the availability of preprocessed or preanalyzed data in regard to document analysis. The data to which we referred are useful to students because someone else has already worked with the raw data, or answers to survey questions, and produced results in the form of tables, figures, or statistical output. In this chapter, we focus instead on the survey questions and the raw survey data, or the unvarnished answers to survey questions. These data can be more difficult to work with, but they will lend greater flexibility to students in analyzing data and making conclusions.

There are many advantages to drawing upon professional surveys for use in your own. First and foremost, imagine that you are ready to embark on a research project for which you will need survey data. You would be safe in assuming that using data someone else collected would save a great deal of time, effort, and resources. The key, of course, is finding data that will allow you to test your hypotheses and answer your research questions. Fortunately, myriad data archives are publicly available, with surveys and sample data collected from many different populations and about many topics. Second, using a professionally designed survey should lead to better data, collected from answers to well-written questions. Having taken a data analysis course, and read this chapter, students should have a good idea of what to look for in a survey design to determine the quality of the questions and, subsequently, the data. Third, using a professional survey can help convince readers that the results reported in a research report are valid because the questions used to collect the data have been used by others, potentially in published, peer-reviewed work.

INTERVIEWING

Interviewing is simply the act of asking individuals a series of questions and recording their responses. The interaction may be face-to-face or over the phone.[85] In some cases, the interviewer asks a predetermined set of questions; in others, the discussion may be more spontaneous or freewheeling; and in still others, both structured and unstructured formats are used. The key is that an interview, like a survey, depends on the participants sharing a common language and understanding of terms. And whereas a formal questionnaire, once constructed, limits opportunities for empathetic understanding, an in-depth interview gives the interviewer a chance to probe, to clarify, to search for deeper meanings, to explore unanticipated responses, and to assess intangibles such as mood and opinion intensity.

Perhaps one of the finest examples of the advantages of extended interviews is Robert E. Lane's study of fifteen "urban male voters."[86] Although the sample seems small, Lane provided evidence that it is representative of working- and middle-class men living in an Atlantic seaboard town he calls "Eastport." More important for his purposes, his method—a series of extended and taped individual interviews lasting a total of ten to fifteen hours per subject—allowed him to delve into the political consciousness of his subjects in a way no cut-and-dried survey could.

Among many other topics, Lane explored these men's attitudes toward "equality" and a hypothetical movement toward an equalitarian society. Of course, he could have written survey-type questions that would have asked respondents if they agreed or disagreed with this or that statement. Instead, he let his subjects speak for themselves. And what he found turned out to be very interesting and unexpected.

> The upper working class, and the lower middle class, support specific measures embraced in the formula "welfare state," which have equalitarian consequences. But, so I shall argue, many members of the working class do not want equality. They are afraid of it. In some ways they already seek to escape from it.[87]

Why did he come to this startling conclusion? Because during his long interviews he uncovered several latent patterns in the men's thinking, patterns that would have been difficult to anticipate and virtually impossible to garner from a standardized questionnaire. For example, when asked about the desirability of greater equality of opportunity and income, one man, Sullivan, a railroad firefighter, said,

> I think it's hard. . . . Supposing I came into a lot of money, and I moved into a nice neighborhood—class—maybe I wouldn't know how to act then. I think it's very hard, because people know that you just—word gets around that you . . . never had it before you got it now. Well, maybe they wouldn't like you . . . maybe you don't know how to act.[88]

Lane termed this response a concern with "social adjustment" and found that others shared the sentiment. He discovered another source of unease: those in the lower classes would not necessarily deserve a "promotion" up the social ladder. Thus, Ruggiero, a maintenance worker, believed "There's laziness, you'll always have lazy people," while another man said,

> But then you get a lot of people who don't want to work; you got welfare. People will go on living on that welfare—they're happier than hell. Why should they work if the city will support them.[89]

The research uncovered similar fears that Lane's subjects experienced when envisioning an equalitarian society. They believed such a society would be unfair to "meritorious elites," would entail the loss of "goals" (if everyone is equal, why work?), and would cause society to "collapse."

Our quick review of Lane's research should not be interpreted as an argument that his is the definitive study. One could, in fact, interpret some of the men's statements quite differently. But the men of Eastport, like all citizens, had mixed, frequently contradictory thoughts, and only after hours of conversation and considerable analysis of the transcripts could Lane begin to classify and make sense of them.

The Ins and Outs of Interviewing

Interviewing, as we use the term, differs substantially from the highly structured, standardized format of survey research.[90] There are many reasons for this difference.

First, a researcher may lack sufficient understanding of events to be able to design an effective, structured survey instrument or schedule of questions. The only way for researchers to learn about certain events is to interview participants or eyewitnesses directly. Second, a researcher is usually especially interested in an interviewee's own interpretation of events or issues and does not want to lose the valuable information that an elite "insider" may possess by unduly constraining responses. As one researcher put it, "A less structured format is relatively exploratory and stresses subject rather than researcher definitions of a problem."[91]

Finally, some people, especially elites or those in positions of high standing or power, may resent being asked to respond to a standardized set of questions. In her study of Nobel laureates, for example, Harriet Zuckerman found that her subjects soon detected standardized questions. Because these were people used to being treated as individuals with minds of their own, they resented "being encased in the straitjacket of standardized questions."[92] Therefore, those who interview elites often vary the order in which topics are broached and the exact form of questions asked from interview to interview.

In this method, eliciting valid information may require variability in approaches.[93] Interviewing is not as simple as lining up a few interviews and chatting for a while. The researcher using the in-depth interview technique must consider numerous logistical and methodological questions. Advance preparation is extremely important. The researcher should study all available documentation of events and pertinent biographical material before interviewing a member of an elite group. Advance preparation serves many purposes. First, it saves the interviewee's time by eliminating questions that can be answered elsewhere. The researcher may, however, ask the interviewee to verify the accuracy of the information obtained from other sources. Second, it gives the researcher a basis for deciding what questions to ask and in what order. Third, advance preparation helps the researcher to interpret and understand the significance of what is being said, to recognize a remark that sheds new light on a topic, and to catch inconsistencies between the interviewee's version and other versions of events. Fourth, the researcher's serious interest in the topic impresses the interviewee. At no time, however, should the researcher dominate the conversation to show off his or her knowledge. Finally, good preparation buoys the confidence of the novice researcher who is interviewing important people.

The ground rules that will apply to what is said in an interview should be made clear at the start.[94] When the interview is requested, and at the beginning of the interview itself, the researcher should ask whether confidentiality is desired. If he or she promises confidentiality, the researcher should be careful not to reveal a person's identity in written descriptions. A touchy problem in confidentiality may arise if questions are based on previous interviews. It may be possible for an interviewee to guess the identity of the person whose comments must have prompted a particular question.

A researcher may desire and promise confidentiality in the hope that the interviewee will be more candid.[95] Interviewees may request confidentiality if they fear they may reveal something damaging to themselves or to others. Some persons may want to approve anything written based on what they have said. In any event, it often is beneficial to the researcher to give interviewees a chance to review what has been written about them and the opportunity to clarify and expand on their comments. Sometimes a researcher and an interviewee may disagree over the content or interpretation of the interview. If the researcher has agreed to let an interviewee have final say on the use of an interview, the agreement should be honored. Otherwise, the decision is the researcher's—to be made in light of the needs of the investigation.

Sometimes, gaining access to influential people is difficult. They may want further information about the purpose of the research or need to be convinced of the professionalism of the researcher. Furthermore, many have "gatekeepers" who limit access to their bosses. It is advisable to obtain references from people who are known to potential interviewees. For example, suppose you want to talk to a few state senators. Try getting your own representative to make a few phone calls or write an introductory letter. Sometimes a person who has already been interviewed will assist a researcher in gaining access to other elites. Having a letter of recommendation or introduction from someone who knows the subject can be extremely helpful in this regard.

Two researchers encountered particular access problems in their study of the 1981 outbreaks of civil disorder in several British cities when they attempted to interview community activists.[96] These activists, whom the researchers termed the "counter-elite" or the "threatened elite," were reluctant to cooperate, even hostile. They feared that the findings might be abused, that the research was for the benefit of the establishment and part of a system of oppression, and that cooperation would jeopardize their standing in their community. Unlike conventional elites, they did not assume that social science research was useful.

Whom to interview first is largely a theoretical decision. Interviewing persons of lesser importance in an event or of lower rank in an organization first allows a researcher to become familiar with special terminology used by an elite group and more knowledgeable about a topic before interviewing key elites. It also may bolster a researcher's experience and confidence. Lower-level personnel may be more candid and revealing about events because they are

ASK THE RIGHT QUESTIONS

The importance of thoroughly researching a topic before conducting elite interviews cannot be stressed enough. In addition to the guidelines discussed in the text, ask yourself this question: Can the information be provided only (or at least most easily) by the person being interviewed? If you can obtain the answers to your questions from newspapers or books, for example, then it is pointless to take up someone's time going over what is (or should be) already known. If, however, the subject believes that only she or he can help you, then you are more likely to gain her or his cooperation. Looking and acting professional is absolutely essential. So, for example, do not arrive at the interview wearing a ball cap or without paper and pen.

able to observe major participants and have less personal involvement. Talking to superiors first, however, may indicate to subordinates that being interviewed is permissible. Moreover, interviewing key elites first may provide a researcher with important information early on and make subsequent interviewing more efficient. Other factors, such as age of respondents, availability, and convenience, may also affect interview order.

A tape recorder or handwritten notes may be used to record an interview. There are numerous factors to consider in choosing between the two methods. Tape recording allows the researcher to think about what the interviewee is saying, to check notes, and to formulate follow-up questions. If the recording is clear, it removes the possibility of error about what is said. Disadvantages include the fact that everything is recorded. The material must then be transcribed (an expense) and read before useful data are at hand. Much of what is transcribed will not be useful—a problem of elite interviewing in general. A tape recorder may make some interviewees uncomfortable, and they may not be candid even if promised confidentiality; there can be no denying what is recorded. Sometimes the researcher will be unfamiliar with recording equipment and will appear awkward.

Many researchers rely on handwritten notes taken during an interview. It is important to write up interviews in more complete form soon after the interview, while it is still fresh in the researcher's mind. Typically this takes much longer than the interview itself, so enough time should be allotted. Only a few interviews should be scheduled in one day; after two or three, the researcher may not be able to recollect individual conversations distinctly. How researchers go about conducting interviews will vary by topic, by researcher, and by respondent.

Although interviews are usually not rigidly structured, researchers still may choose to exercise control and direction in an interview. Many researchers conduct a semistructured or flexible interview—what is called a **focused interview**—when questioning elites. They prepare an interview guide, including topics, questions, and the order in which they should be raised. Sometimes alternative forms of questions may be prepared. Generally the more exploratory the purpose of the research, the less topic control exercised by the researcher. Researchers who desire information about specific topics should communicate this need to the person being interviewed and exercise enough control over the interview to keep it on track.

Interviewing is difficult work. A researcher must listen, observe nonverbal behavior, think, and take notes all at the same time. Maintaining appropriate interpersonal relations is also required. A good rapport between the researcher and subject, although it may be difficult to establish, facilitates the flow of information. How aggressive should a researcher be in asking questions? This issue is often debated. Although aggressive questioning may yield more information and allow the researcher to ferret out misinformation, it also may alienate or irritate the interviewee. Zuckerman used the tactic of rephrasing the interviewee's comments in extreme form to elicit further details, but in some cases the Nobel laureates expressed irritation that she had not understood what they had already said.[97]

Establishing the meaningfulness and validity of the interview data is important. The data may be biased by the questions and actions of the interviewer. Interviewees may give evasive or untruthful answers. As noted earlier, advance preparation may help an interviewer recognize remarks that differ from established fact. Examining the remarks' plausibility, checking for internal consistency, and corroborating them with other interviewees also may determine the validity of an interviewee's statements. John P. Dean and William Foote Whyte argued that a researcher should understand an interviewee's mental set and how it might affect his or her perception and interpretation of events.[98] Raymond L. Gordon stressed the value of being able to empathize with interviewees to understand the meaning of what they are saying.[99] Lewis Dexter warned that interviews should be conducted only if "interviewers have enough relevant background to be sure that they can make sense out of interview conversations or . . . there is reasonable hope of being able to . . . learn what is meaningful and significant to ask."[100]

Despite the difficulties, interviewing is an excellent form of data collection, particularly in exploratory studies or when thoughts and behavior can be described or expressed only by those who are deeply involved in political processes. Interviewing often provides a more comprehensive and complicated understanding of phenomena than other forms of research designs, and it provides researchers with a rich variety of perspectives.

CONCLUSION

In this chapter, we discussed two ways of collecting information directly from individuals—through survey research and interviewing. Whether data are collected over the phone, through the mail, or in person, the researcher attempts to elicit information that is consistent, complete, accurate, and instructive. This goal is advanced by being attentive to questionnaire design and taking steps to engage and motivate respondents. The choice of an in-person, telephone, or mail survey can also affect the quality of the data collected. Interviews of elite populations require attention to a special set of issues and generally use a less structured type of interview.

Although you may never conduct an elite interview or a public opinion survey of your own, the information in this chapter should help you evaluate the research of others. Polls, surveys, and interview data have become so prevalent in American life that an awareness of the decisions made and problems encountered by survey researchers is needed to independently judge conclusions drawn from such data.

Terms Introduced

Ambiguous question. A question containing a concept that is not defined clearly.

Branching question. A question that sorts respondents into subgroups and directs these subgroups to different parts of the questionnaire.

Closed-ended question. A question with response alternatives provided.

Double-barreled question. A question that is really two questions in one.

Filter question. A question used to screen respondents so that subsequent questions will be asked only of certain respondents for whom the questions are appropriate.

Focused interview. A semistructured or flexible interview schedule used when interviewing elites.

Interviewer bias. The interviewer's influence on the respondent's answers; an example of reactivity.

Interviewing. Interviewing respondents in a nonstandardized, individualized manner.

Leading question. A question that encourages the respondent to choose a particular response.

Open-ended question. A question with no response alternatives provided for the respondent.

Push poll. A poll intended not to collect information but to feed respondents (often) false and damaging information about a candidate or cause.

Questionnaire design. The physical layout and packaging of a questionnaire.

Question-order effect. The effect on responses of question placement within a questionnaire.

Randomized response technique. A method of obtaining accurate answers to sensitive questions that protects the respondent's privacy.

Response quality. The extent to which responses provide accurate and complete information.

Response rate. The proportion of respondents selected for participation in a survey who actually participate.

Response set. The pattern of responding to a series of questions in a similar fashion without careful reading of each question.

Sample-population congruence. The degree to which sample subjects represent the population from which they are drawn.

Single-sided question. A question in which the respondent is asked to agree or disagree with a single substantive statement.

Survey instrument. The schedule of questions to be asked of the respondent.

Two-sided question. A question in which two substantive alternatives are provided for the respondent.

Suggested Readings

Aldridge, Alan, and Kenneth Levine. *Surveying the Social World.* Buckingham, UK: Open University Press, 2001.

Bradburn, Norman, Seymour Sudman, and Brian Wansink, "Asking Questions." Rev. ed. San Francisco: Jossey-Bass, 2004.

Braverman, Marc T., and Jana Kay Slater. *Advances in Survey Research.* San Francisco: Jossey-Bass, 1998.

Converse, J. M., and Stanley Presser. *Survey Questions: Handcrafting the Standardized Questionnaire.* Beverly Hills, Calif.: Sage, 1986.

Dillman, Don A. *Mail and Electronic Surveys.* New York: Wiley, 1999.

Frey, James H., and Sabine M. Oishi. *How to Conduct Interviews by Telephone and in Person.* Thousand Oaks, Calif.: Sage, 1995.

Nesbary, Dale. *Survey Research and the World Wide Web.* Needham Heights, Mass.: Allyn & Bacon, 1999.

Newman, Isadore, and Keith A. McNeil. *Conducting Survey Research in the Social Sciences.* Lanham, Md.: University Press of America, 1998.

Patten, Mildred L. *Questionnaire Research: A Practical Guide.* 2nd ed. Los Angeles: Pyrczak, 2001.

Rea, Louis M., and Richard A. Parker. *Designing and Conducting Survey Research.* San Francisco: Jossey-Bass, 1997.

Sapsford, Roger. *Survey Research.* Thousand Oaks, Calif.: Sage, 1999.

Tanur, Judith M., ed. *Questions about Questions.* New York: Russell Sage Foundation, 1992.

Weisberg, Herbert F. *The Total Survey Approach.* Chicago: University of Chicago Press, 2005.

Notes

1. "*Examiner* Editorial: Obamacare Is Even Worse Than Critics Thought," *Washington Examiner,* September 22, 2010, http://washingtonexaminer.com/opinion/examiner-editorial-obamacare-even-worse-critics-thought/.

2. Miroslav Nincic, "Domestic Costs, the U.S. Public, and the Isolationist Calculus," *International Studies Quarterly* 41, no. 4 (1997): 593–610.

3. See Robert F. Belli, Michael W. Traugott, Margaret Young, and Katherine A. McGonagle, "Reducing Vote Overreporting in Surveys: Social Desirability, Memory Failure, and Source Monitoring," *Public Opinion Quarterly* 63, no. 1 (1999): 90–108; and Janet M. Box-Steffensmeier, Gary C. Jacobson, and J. Tobin Grant, "Question Wording and the House Vote Choice: Some Experimental Evidence," *Public Opinion Quarterly* 64, no. 1 (2000): 257–70.

4. Floyd J. Fowler, *Survey Research Methods,* rev. ed. (Newbury Park, Calif.: Sage, 1988), 61.

5. Don A. Dillman, *Mail and Telephone Surveys: The Total Design Method* (New York: Wiley, 1978), 40.

6. Indeed, a large (1,000 or more respondents) national survey using probability sampling of the sort explained in chapter 7 might cost more than $100,000.

7. The Harris organization said, for example, "By participating, you'll not only have your say in matters that affect you, you'll also be able to see the results from the surveys you complete. You can then compare your opinions and experiences to many others'—people who are like, and unlike, you. Occasionally, you may participate in surveys whose results will be published in national or international media"; Harris Interactive Inc., "Harris Poll Online," retrieved March 27, 2007, from http://www.harrispollonline.com/. Zogby stressed its accuracy: "The strength of the results of the 2004 Presidential election has validated the new method. Zogby Interactive accurately predicted the winner in 85 percent of the states that it polled, while by state, the poll was within 4 points on average"; Zogby International, "Welcome to the Zogby Interactive," retrieved March 27, 2007, from http://interactive.zogby .com/.

8. Fowler, *Survey Research Methods*, 68.

9. Ibid.

10. Robert M. Groves and Robert L. Kahn, *Surveys by Telephone: A National Comparison with Personal Interviews* (New York: Academic Press, 1979); and James H. Frey, *Survey Research by Telephone* (Beverly Hills, Calif.: Sage, 1983).

11. Frey, *Survey Research by Telephone*, 24–25.

12. Howard E. Freeman, K. Jill Kiecolt, William L. Nicholls II, and J. Merrill Shanks, "Telephone Sampling Bias in Surveying Disability," *Public Opinion Quarterly* 46, no. 3 (1982): 392–407.

13. Ibid.

14. "Poll: Disapproval of Congress Hits All-Time High," *CBS News Political Hotsheet* (blog), August 4, 2011, http://www.cbsnews.com/8301-503544_162-20088388-503544.html.

15. Robert M. Groves, Robert B. Cialdini, and Mick P. Couper, "Understanding the Decision to Participate," *Public Opinion Quarterly* 56, no. 4 (1992): 474.

16. Earl R. Babbie, *Survey Research Methods* (Belmont, Calif.: Wadsworth, 1973), 171.

17. Groves and Kahn, *Surveys by Telephone*, 3.

18. See, for example, Burns W. Roper, "Evaluating Polls with Poll Data," *Public Opinion Quarterly* 50, no. 1 (1986): 10–16.

19. Charlotte G. Steeh, "Trends in Nonresponse Rates, 1952–1979," *Public Opinion Quarterly* 45, no. 1 (1981): 40–57.

20. Laure M. Sharp and Joanne Frankel, "Respondent Burden: A Test of Some Common Assumptions," *Public Opinion Quarterly* 47, no. 1 (1983): 36–53. Note that another survey found that people had generally favorable beliefs about polls (Roper, "Evaluating Polls with Poll Data"), but even the author of this study worried that the public might grow weary and distrustful of polling.

21. Theresa J. DeMaio, "Refusals: Who, Where, and Why," *Public Opinion Quarterly* 44, no. 2 (1980): 223–33.

22. Dillman, *Mail and Telephone Surveys*.

23. See Theresa F. Rogers, "Interviews by Telephone and in Person: Quality of Responses and Field Performance," *Public Opinion Quarterly* 40, no. 1 (1976): 51–65; and Groves and Kahn, *Surveys by Telephone*. Response rates are affected by different methods of calculating rates for the three types of surveys. For example, nonreachable and ineligible persons may be dropped from the total survey population for telephone and personal interviews before response rates are calculated. Response rates to mail surveys are depressed because all nonresponses are assumed to be refusals, not ineligibles or nonreachables. Telephone response rates may be depressed if nonworking but ringing numbers are treated as nonreachable but eligible respondents. Telephone companies vary in their willingness to identify working numbers. If noneligibility is likely to be a problem in a mail survey, ineligibles should be

asked to return the questionnaire anyway so that they can be identified and distinguished from refusals.

24. Frey, *Survey Research by Telephone,* 15–16.

25. Herschel Shosteck and William R. Fairweather, "Physician Response Rates to Mail and Personal Interview Surveys," *Public Opinion Quarterly* 43, no. 2 (1979): 206–17.

26. Don A. Dillman, Jean Gorton Gallegos, and James H. Frey, "Reducing Refusal Rates for Telephone Interviews," *Public Opinion Quarterly* 40, no. 1 (1976): 66–78.

27. Fowler, *Survey Research Methods,* 67.

28. Gideon Vigderhous, "Scheduling Telephone Interviews: A Study of Seasonal Patterns," *Public Opinion Quarterly* 45, no. 2 (1981): 250–59.

29. Michael F. Weeks, Bruce L. Jones, R. E. Folsom, and Charles H. Benrud, "Optimal Times to Contact Sample Households," *Public Opinion Quarterly* 44, no. 1 (1980): 101–14.

30. See J. Scott Armstrong, "Monetary Incentive in Mail Surveys," *Public Opinion Quarterly* 39 (1975): 111–16; Arnold S. Linsky, "Stimulating Responses to Mailed Questionnaires: A Review," *Public Opinion Quarterly* 39, no. 1 (1975): 82–101; James R. Chromy and Daniel G. Horvitz, "The Use of Monetary Incentives in National Assessment Household Surveys," *Journal of the American Statistical Association* 73 (1978): 473–78; Thomas A. Heberlein and Robert Baumgartner, "Factors Affecting Response Rates to Mailed Questionnaires: A Quantitative Analysis of the Published Literature," *American Sociological Review* 43, no. 4 (1978): 447–62; R. Kenneth Godwin, "The Consequences of Large Monetary Incentives in Mail Surveys of Elites," *Public Opinion Quarterly* 43, no. 3 (1979): 378–87; Kent L. Tedin and C. Richard Hofstetter, "The Effect of Cost and Importance Factors on the Return Rate for Single and Multiple Mailings," *Public Opinion Quarterly* 46, no. 1 (1982): 122–28; Anton J. Nederhof, "The Effects of Material Incentives in Mail Surveys: Two Studies," *Public Opinion Quarterly* 47, no. 1 (1983): 103–11; Charles D. Schewe and Norman G. Cournoyer, "Prepaid vs. Promised Monetary Incentives to Questionnaire Response: Further Evidence," *Public Opinion Quarterly* 40, no. 1 (1976): 105–07; James R. Henley Jr., "Response Rate to Mail Questionnaire with a Return Deadline," *Public Opinion Quarterly* 40 (1976): 374–75; Thomas A. Heberlein and Robert Baumgartner, "Is a Questionnaire Necessary in a Second Mailing?" *Public Opinion Quarterly* 45, no. 1 (1981): 102–08; and Wesley H. Jones, "Generalizing Mail Survey Inducement Methods: Population Interactions with Anonymity and Sponsorship," *Public Opinion Quarterly* 43, no. 1 (1979): 102–11.

31. For detailed instructions on improving the response rate to mail surveys, see Dillman, *Mail and Telephone Surveys.*

32. Fowler, *Survey Research Methods,* 63.

33. And, of course, you still would not have a probability sample. See chapter 7.

34. Groves and Kahn, *Surveys by Telephone,* 214; and Frey, *Survey Research by Telephone,* 22.

35. Pew Research Center for People & the Press, "The Cell Phone Challenge to Survey Research," May 15, 2006, http://people-press.org/2006/05/15/the-cell-phone-challenge-to-survey-research/.

36. For research estimating the amount of bias introduced by nonresponse due to unavailability or refusal, see F. L. Filion, "Estimating Bias Due to Nonresponse in Mail Surveys," *Public Opinion Quarterly* 39, no. 4 (1975–96): 482–92; Michael J. O'Neil, "Estimating the Nonresponse Bias Due to Refusals in Telephone Surveys," *Public Opinion Quarterly* 43, no. 2 (1979): 218–32; and Arthur L. Stinchcombe, Calvin Jones, and Paul Sheatsley, "Nonresponse Bias for Attitude Questions," *Public Opinion Quarterly* 45, no. 3 (1981): 359–75.

37. Carol S. Aneshensel, Ralph R. Frerichs, Virginia A. Clark, and Patricia A. Yokopenic, "Measuring Depression in the Community: A Comparison of Telephone and Personal Interviews," *Public Opinion Quarterly* 46, no. 1 (1982): 110–21.

38. DeMaio, "Refusals: Who, Where, and Why," 223–33; and Steeh, "Trends in Nonresponse Rates," 40–57.

39. Dillman, *Mail and Telephone Surveys.*

40. See, for example, Matthew B. Miles and A. Michael Huberman, *Qualitative Data Analysis: An Expanded Sourcebook,* 2nd ed. (Thousand Oaks, Calif.: Sage, 1995); and Renata Tesch, *Qualitative Research: Analysis Types and Software Tools* (Bristol, Penn.: The Falmer Press, 1990).

41. SawTooth Technologies, "WinCati for Computer-Assisted Telephone Interviewing," retrieved March 11, 2007, from http://www.sawtooth.com/.

42. *Washington Post* Virginia Governor Poll #2, October [computer file], ICPSR04522-v1 (Horsham, Penn.: Taylor Nelson Sofres Intersearch [producer], 2005; Ann Arbor, Mich.: Interuniversity Consortium for Political and Social Research [distributor], March 9, 2007), retrieved March 31, 2007, from http://www.icpsr.umich.edu/.

43. See Willis J. Goudy and Harry R. Potter, "Interview Rapport: Demise of a Concept," *Public Opinion Quarterly* 39, no. 4 (1975): 529–43; and Charles F. Cannell, Peter V. Miller, and Lois Oksenberg, "Research on Interviewing Techniques," in *Sociological Methodology 1981,* ed. Samuel Leinhardt (San Francisco: Jossey-Bass, 1981), 389–437.

44. Rogers, "Interviews by Telephone and in Person."

45. Ibid.; and Peter V. Miller and Charles F. Cannell, "A Study of Experimental Techniques for Telephone Interviewing," *Public Opinion Quarterly* 46, no. 2 (1982): 250–69.

46. Arpad Barath and Charles F. Cannell, "Effect of Interviewer's Voice Intonation," *Public Opinion Quarterly* 40, no. 3 (1976): 370–73.

47. Eleanor Singer, Martin R. Frankel, and Marc B. Glassman, "The Effect of Interviewer Characteristics and Expectations on Response," *Public Opinion Quarterly* 47, no. 1 (1983): 68–83; and Eleanor Singer and Luane Kohnke-Aguirre, "Interviewer Expectation Effects: A Replication and Extension," *Public Opinion Quarterly* 43, no. 2 (1979): 245–60.

48. Patrick R. Cotter, Jeffrey Cohen, and Philip B. Coulter, "Race-of-Interviewer Effects in Telephone Interviews," *Public Opinion Quarterly* 46, no. 2 (1982): 278–84; and Bruce A. Campbell, "Race of Interviewer Effects among Southern Adolescents," *Public Opinion Quarterly* 45, no. 2 (1981): 231–44.

49. Shirley Hatchett and Howard Schuman, "White Respondents and Race-of-Interviewer Effects," *Public Opinion Quarterly* 39, no. 4 (1975–76): 523–28; and Michael F. Weeks and R. Paul Moore, "Ethnicity of Interviewer Effects on Ethnic Respondents," *Public Opinion Quarterly* 45, no. 2 (1981): 245–49.

50. See Singer, Frankel, and Glassman, "The Effect of Interviewer Characteristics and Expectations on Response"; Groves and Kahn, *Surveys by Telephone;* Dillman, *Mail and Telephone Surveys;* and John Freeman and Edgar W. Butler, "Some Sources of Interviewer Variance in Surveys," *Public Opinion Quarterly* 40, no. 1 (1976): 79–91.

51. Adapted from American National Election Study (ANES) 2004, "HTML Codebook Produced July 14, 2006," accessed March 10, 2007, from http://sda.berkeley.edu/.

52. See Groves and Kahn, *Surveys by Telephone;* and Lawrence A. Jordan, Alfred C. Marcus, and Leo G. Reeder, "Response Styles in Telephone and Household Interviewing," *Public Opinion Quarterly* 44, no. 2 (1980): 210–22.

53. Dillman, *Mail and Telephone Surveys.*

54. Jordan, Marcus, and Reeder, "Response Styles"; Groves and Kahn, *Surveys by Telephone.* See also Rogers, "Interviews by Telephone and in Person."

55. For example, see Seymour Sudman and Norman M. Bradburn, *Asking Questions: A Practical Guide to Questionnaire Design* (San Francisco: Jossey-Bass, 1982), 55–86; Jerald G. Bachman

and Patrick M. O'Malley, "When Four Months Equal a Year: Inconsistencies in Student Reports of Drug Use," *Public Opinion Quarterly* 45, no. 4 (1981): 536–48.

56. American National Election Study (ANES) 2004, "HTML Codebook Produced July 14, 2006," accessed March 10, 2007, from http://sda.berkeley.edu/.

57. RRT was first proposed by Stanley L. Warner in "Randomized Response," *Journal of the American Statistical Association* 60, no. 309 (1965): 63–69. Available at http://www.cs.utsa.edu/~wzhang/dbpapers/ppdm/JASA65-warner-randomResponse.pdf.

58. Frederick Wiseman, Mark Moriarty, and Marianne Schafer, "Estimating Public Opinion with the Randomized Response Model," *Public Opinion Quarterly* 39, no. 4 (1975–76): 507–13.

59. S. M. Zdep and Isabelle N. Rhodes, "Making the Randomized Response Technique Work," *Public Opinion Quarterly* 40, no. 4 (1976): 531–37.

60. Ibid.

61. Iris M. Shimizu and Gordon Scott Bonham, "Randomized Response Technique in a National Survey," *Journal of the American Statistical Association* 73, no. 361 (1978): 35–39.

62. Robert G. Orwin and Robert F. Boruch, "RRT Meets RDD: Statistical Strategies for Assuring Response Privacy in Telephone Surveys," *Public Opinion Quarterly* 46, no. 4 (1982): 560–71.

63. Steve King, "Public Wants ObamaCare Repealed, And I Can Do It," *Florida Political Press* (blog), March 26, 2011, http://www.floridapoliticalpress.com/2011/03/26/public-wants-obamacare-repealed-and-i-can-do-it/.

64. Quoted in Daniel Sayani, "Senate Republicans Seek to Repeal ObamaCare," *New American*, February 2, 2011, http://thenewamerican.com/usnews/health-care/6150-senate-republicans-seek-to-repeal-obamacare/.

65. Kaiser Family Foundation, February 3–6, 2011, reported in *Polling Report: Health Policy*, accessed March 30, 2011, from http://www.pollingreport.com/health.htm.

66. FOX News/Opinion Dynamics Poll, December 14–15, 2010, *Polling Report: Health Policy*, accessed March 20, 2011, from http://www.pollingreport.com/health.htm. $N = 900$ registered voters nationwide.

67. Margrit Eichler, *Nonsexist Research Methods: A Practical Guide* (Winchester, Mass.: Allen and Unwin, 1988), 51–52.

68. Charles H. Backstrom and Gerald Hursh-Cesar, *Survey Research*, 2nd ed. (New York: Wiley, 1981), 142, 146.

69. Ibid., 141.

70. Republican National Committee, *1980 Official Republican Poll on U.S. Defense and Foreign Policy*.

71. Eichler, *Nonsexist Research Methods*, 43–44.

72. American National Election Study (ANES) 2008, "HTML Codebook Produced April 12, 2011," http://sda.berkeley.edu/D3/NES08new/Doc/hcbk.htm.

73. John P. Dean and William Foote Whyte, "How Do You Know If the Informant Is Telling the Truth?" in *Elite and Specialized Interviewing*, ed. Lewis Anthony Dexter (Evanston, Ill.: Northwestern University Press, 1970), 127.

74. Raymond L. Gordon, *Interviewing: Strategy, Techniques, and Tactics* (Homewood, Ill.: Dorsey, 1969), 18.

75. Dexter, *Elite and Specialized Interviewing*, 17.

76. Patricia J. Labaw, *Advanced Questionnaire Design* (Cambridge, Mass.: Abt Books, 1980), 132.

77. Ibid., 132–33.

78. Ibid., 117.

79. Norman M. Bradburn and William M. Mason, "The Effect of Question Order on Responses," *Journal of Marketing Research* 1, no. 4 (1964): 57–61.

80. A. Regula Herzog and Jerald G. Bachman, "Effects of Questionnaire Length on Response Quality," *Public Opinion Quarterly* 45, no. 4 (1981): 549–59. Available at http://www.uta. edu/faculty/richarme/MARK%205338/Articles/Herzog.pdf.

81. Labaw, *Advanced Questionnaire Design,* 122.

82. Glen D. Mellinger, Carol L. Huffine, and Mitchell B. Balter, "Assessing Comprehension in a Survey of Public Reactions to Complex Issues," *Public Opinion Quarterly* 46, no. 1 (1982): 97–109.

83. William D. Perrault Jr., "Controlling Order-Effect Bias," *Public Opinion Quarterly* 39, no. 4 (1975): 544–51.

84. Donald J. Messmer and Daniel T. Seymour, "The Effects of Branching on Item Nonresponse," *Public Opinion Quarterly* 46, no. 2 (1982): 270–77.

85. Occasionally the investigator may obtain the information from some form of written communication.

86. Robert E. Lane, "The Fear of Equality," *American Political Science Review* 53, no. 1 (1959): 35–51. The complete results of Lane's work are found in his *Political Ideology: Why the Common Man Believes What He Does* (New York: Free Press, 1963).

87. Lane, "The Fear of Equality," 35.

88. Ibid., 46.

89. Ibid., 44–45.

90. There are exceptions to this general rule, however. See John Kessel, *The Domestic Presidency* (Belmont, Calif.: Duxbury, 1975). Kessel administered a highly structured survey instrument to Richard Nixon's Domestic Council staff.

91. Joseph A. Pika, "Interviewing Presidential Aides: A Political Scientist's Perspective," in *Studying the Presidency,* ed. George C. Edwards III and Stephen J. Wayne (Knoxville: University of Tennessee Press, 1982), 282.

92. Harriet Zuckerman, "Interviewing an Ultra-Elite," *Public Opinion Quarterly* 36, no. 2 (1972): 167.

93. Gordon, *Interviewing: Strategy, Techniques, and Tactics,* 49–50.

94. Dom Bonafede, "Interviewing Presidential Aides: A Journalist's Perspective," in *Studying the Presidency,* ed. George C. Edwards III and Stephen J. Wayne (Knoxville: University of Tennessee Press, 1982), 269.

95. Richard F. Fenno Jr., *Home Style: House Members in Their Districts* (Boston: Little, Brown, 1978), 280.

96. Margaret Wagstaffe and George Moyser, "The Threatened Elite: Studying Leaders in an Urban Community," in *Research Methods for Elite Studies,* ed. George Moyser and Margaret Wagstaffe (London: Allen and Unwin, 1987), 186–88.

97. Zuckerman, "Interviewing an Ultra-Elite," 174.

98. Dean and Whyte, "How Do You Know If the Informant Is Telling the Truth?" 127.

99. Gordon, *Interviewing: Strategy, Techniques, and Tactics,* 18.

100. Dexter, *Elite and Specialized Interviewing,* 17.

MAKING SENSE OF DATA:

First Steps

IN THEORY WE ARE NEARING THE TOP OF THE LEARNING CURVE. Probably the hardest part of the research process is picking a "good" topic. But once it is selected and major concepts and hypotheses have been defined and operationalized, gathering the necessary information becomes a relatively straightforward, if time-consuming, task. The logical next move is to interpret the findings and draw conclusions about the tenability of the propositions. This step is usually a matter of applying substantive knowledge and judgment. Frequently, however, verifying empirical claims requires a more analytical or systematic approach. Here is where statistics can play a role.

Many students wonder why they spend a semester or more studying statistical methods. After all, aren't topics such as current events, politics in general, law, foreign affairs, voting, and legislatures more interesting? Why bother with something as formal as data collection and analysis? To repeat our sermon in chapter 1, we offer two compelling reasons. First, for better or worse, you need to understand a few basic statistical concepts and methods in order to understand what your—or other people's—numbers mean. Second, good citizenship requires an awareness of statistical concepts. To one degree or another, many issues and policies involve statistical arguments. A story in a widely read Saint Louis Web site, for instance, states flatly that "the trend toward greater income inequality has been apparent since the early 1980s—the decade when Gordon Gekko, a fictional character in Oliver Stone's *Wall Street,* first extolled the virtues of greed."[1] Yet, conclusions of this sort have been vigorously challenged, especially by conservative economists and journalists. So, who's right? Statistics may provide a partial answer.[2]

This chapter takes readers the first steps down the road to understanding applied statistics. Data analysis encompasses three activities: *data exploration, making inferences about hypotheses,* and using the information to *describe and explain* (the term of trade these days is *model*) political phenomena. This chapter covers the first subject; the others are discussed subsequently.

We proceed slowly because the concepts, though not excessively mathematical, do require thought and effort to comprehend. But it will be worth the effort because the knowledge will make you not just a better political science student but also a better citizen.

THE DATA MATRIX

Most of the statistical reports you come across in both the mass media and scholarly publications show only the final results of what has been a long process of gathering, organizing, and analyzing a large body of data. But knowing what goes on behind the scenes is as important as understanding the empirical conclusions. Conceptually, at least, the first step is the arrangement of the observed measurements into a **data matrix**, which is simply an array of rows and columns that stores observed values of variables. Separate rows hold the data for each case or unit of analysis. If you read across one row, you see the specific values that pertain to that case. Each column contains the values on a single variable for all the cases. The column headings list the variable names. (A data frame looks like a worksheet in a "spreadsheet" program, such as Excel.) To find out where a particular case stands with regard to a particular variable, just look for the row for that case and read across to the appropriate column.

Table 11–1 provides an example, one that pertains to the issue raised in chapters 1 and 2, inequality and power. This matrix contains data for twenty-one developed countries. The Gini index, named after Italian statistician Corrado Gini, measures (in this instance) income inequality. A country with a score of 0 on the index has complete equality in income; everyone has the same income. Higher numbers indicate greater inequality, with a value of 100 indicating total inequality; that is one person has all the income. Union density is the percentage of employees who are members of trade unions. We use it as a measure of the inverse of business power. "Political culture," a rather contrived variable, attempts to capture differences between continental European and British-American political traditions and institutions.

Data Description and Exploration

As presented in table 11–1, the data are not very helpful, partly because they overwhelm the eye and partly because it is hard to see even what an average value is, much less the degree of variability or range of values. (For a much larger data matrix—one with, say, 5,000 rows and 50 variables—the difficulties of interpretation are even worse.) Nor does a matrix reveal many patterns in the data or tell us much about what causes low or high scores. Still, its creation is an essential initial step in data analysis. Moreover, it represents pictorially how text and numbers are stored in a computer. We can instruct a computer program, for example, to sum all the numerical values in column 2 (Gini) and divide by 21 to obtain the overall average Gini score.

TABLE 11–1

Inequality and Socioeconomic Measures for Twenty-One Developed Democracies

Country	Gini Index	Union Density (2003)	Social Expenditures (% GDP) (2004)	Percentage of Seats in Legislature Held by "Left-Wing" Parties (2004)	Aged Population (in thousands)	Political Culture
Australia	35.2	23.1	18.777	44.8	2,882	Anglo-American
Austria	29.1	35.7	28.184	56.0	1,283	European
Belgium	33.0	55.6	26.627	60.3	1,790	European
Canada	32.6	28.2	16.569	56.7	4,141	Anglo-American
Denmark	24.7	72.5	27.873	67.9	809	European
Finland	26.9	74.8	25.972	42.4	822	European
France	32.7	8.2	29.452	34.6	9,994	European
Germany	28.3	23.2	27.836	58.5	15,897	European
Greece	34.3	24.5	19.861	49.7	1,989	European
Ireland	34.3	36.3	16.187	56.2	450	Anglo-American
Italy	36.0	34.0	26.151	8.9	10,935	European
Japan	24.9	20.3	18.811	48.7	24,876	—
Luxembourg	30.8	42.3	24.190	51.1	64	European
The Netherlands	30.9	22.4	21.747	54.2	2,270	European
New Zealand	36.2	22.6	18.049	55.4	485	Anglo-American
Norway	25.8	53.0	24.777	28.2	676	European
Spain	34.7	16.2	21.152	47.6	7,186	European
Sweden	25.0	78.0	30.384	66.3	1,548	European
Switzerland	33.7	17.8	27.776	50.2	1,200	European
UK	36.0	29.2	21.880	59.0	9,570	Anglo-American
USA	40.8	12.6	16.436	46.5	36,301	Anglo-American

Sources: Klaus Armingeon, Romana Careja, Sarah Engler, Panajotis Potolidis, Marlène,Gerber, and Philipp Leimgruber, "Comparative Political Data Set III 1990–2008; Jelle Visser, "Union Membership Statistics in 24 Countries," Monthly Labor Review 129, no. 1 (2006), http://www.bls.gov/opub/mlr/2006/01/art3abs.htm); Duane Swank, "Electoral, Legislative, and Government Strength of Political Parties by Ideological Group in Capitalist Democracies, 1950–2006: A Database," http://www.marquette.edu/polisci/faculty_swank.shtml.

To go from raw data to meaningful conclusions, you begin by summarizing and exploring the information in the matrix. Several kinds of tables, statistics, and graphs can be used for this purpose. Different statistical procedures assume different levels of measurement. Recall from chapter 5 that we distinguished four broad types of measurement scales:

1. *Nominal:* Variable values are unordered names or labels. (Examples: ethnicity, gender, country of origin)

2. *Ordinal:* Variable values are labels having an implicit but unspecified or measured order. Numbers may be assigned to categories to show ordering or ranking, but strictly speaking, arithmetic operations (e.g., addition) are inappropriate. (Example: scale of ideology)

3. *Interval:* Numbers are assigned to objects such that interval differences are constant across the scale, but there is no true or meaningful zero point. (Examples: temperature,[3] intelligence scores)

4. *Ratio:* In addition to having the properties of interval variables, these scales have a meaningful zero value. (Examples: income, percentage of the population with a high school education)

A statistical technique that is appropriate for interval scales, for example, may not be useful or may be misleading when applied to ordinal scales.[4] In the discussion that follows, we clarify which techniques apply to which kinds of variables.

In the following sections we show how to summarize a large batch of numbers with

■ tables (e.g., frequency distributions, cross-tabulations);

■ a single number or range of numbers (e.g., mean, maximum and minimum values); and

■ graphs (e.g., bar charts).

Frequency Distributions, Proportions, and Percentages

An **empirical frequency distribution** is a table that shows the number of observations having each value of a variable. More generally, a distribution "lists" a variable's possible values and how frequently they occur. The number of observations, also called the frequency or count, in the kth category of a variable is often represented by f_k. By the way, the adjective *empirical* emphasizes the fact that we are tallying observed data; later, we talk about "theoretical" distributions, which are mathematical models.

A frequency distribution is usually accompanied by a number called a **relative frequency,** which simply transforms the raw frequency into a proportion or percentage. A *proportion*—the ratio of a part to a whole—is calculated by dividing the number of observations (f_k) having property k, or individuals who gave a particular response, by the total number of observations (N). A *percentage,* or "parts per 100," is found by multiplying a proportion by 100 or, equivalently, moving the decimal two places to the right. Percentages are especially popular because the quantities communicate information that is often more meaningful and easier to grasp than plain frequencies.

Table 11–2 shows the distribution of 995 responses to a question regarding the level of influence wealthy people wield in politics: "Do you agree strongly, agree, are uncertain, disagree, or disagree strongly with . . . ? The rich and powerful people in this country have too much influence on politics." The survey, "United States Citizenship, Involvement, Democracy," was conducted by Georgetown

TABLE 11–2
Empirical Frequency Distribution: Beliefs about Power in the United States

Too Much Influence	Frequency	Proportion	Relative Frequency (percentage)	Cumulative Frequency (percentage)
Strongly agree	333	.34	33.5	33.5
Agree	533	.54	53.6	87.1
Uncertain	38	.04	3.8	90.9
Disagree	75	.08	7.5	98.4
Disagree strongly	16	.02	1.6	100.0
Totals	995	1.01	100	

Question: "Do you agree strongly, agree, are uncertain, disagree, or disagree strongly with . . . ? The rich and powerful people in this country have too much influence on politics."

Source: Marc M. Howard, James L. Gibson, and Dietlind Stolle, *United States Citizenship, Involvement, Democracy (CID) Survey, 2006* (Washington, D.C.: Georgetown University, Center for Democracy and Civil Society (CDACS), 2007. Distributed by Ann Arbor, Mich.: Inter-university Consortium for Political and Social Research ICPSR Study No.: 4607.

University's Center for Democracy and Civil Society (CDACS) and the European Social Survey (ESS). Besides counts and proportions, this frequency distribution also includes **cumulative proportions** (or percentages), which tell the reader what portion of the total is at or below a given point.

We can learn a lot from a table like table 11–2, which, incidentally, is available in almost every statistical computer program. A quick glance reveals that Americans (or at least those in this sample) generally believe the rich have too much influence. How do we reach this conclusion? Let's take the table apart piece by piece.

The first column lists the response categories, and the second simply records how many respondents, out of 995, gave each response (e.g., 333 "agree strongly"). But is this a large or small number? More useful indicators are proportions and relative frequencies. Here we see that about a third (.33) fall in the first category and about half in the second (.54). Percentages put these proportions in a clearer perspective because we see that 33 and 54 percent are in the two "agree" categories. Most informative perhaps is the last column, "Cumulative frequency (percentage)." It shows that the overwhelming majority of survey participants might agree with Hacker and Pierson's assessment that there is an unequal distribution of power in American politics.[5] In fact, a major advantage of empirical frequency distributions is that they show both the "middle" value or values and how spread out around the middle the data are.

PROBABILITIES. Let's look at the frequency distribution once more to glean further information and interpretations. Start with the number of people who "strongly agree." Table 11–2 shows that 333 people gave that response. Knowing that 333 people in a sample pick the first response tells us very little. So we calculated the proportion $p = 333/995 = .33$. We can also interpret this number as a probability. (We will continue to use the same symbol, p.) So you might prefer to read "$p = .33$" as saying, "The probability of a randomly selected adult American giving a 'strongly agree' response to the question is about .33" or "there are about 33 chances in 100 that a person will select that label."

MISSING DATA, PERCENTAGES, AND PROPORTIONS. Let's conclude this section by nailing down a very important point. When calculating and describing proportions or percentages, it is essential to have a firm grasp on the base, or denominator, of all these numbers. Since the proportion of observations in kth category is

$$p_k = \frac{f_k}{N}$$

we see that its value will be affected by the total number of cases. If N includes invalid or missing data, it might make the proportion seem smaller than we would expect. Conversely, in many analyses, we might want to know the proportion out of *all* observations (valid or not) that are in the kth category. Hence, the inclusion or exclusion of missing values in the calculation of percentages or proportions will affect our understanding of their substantive meaning. Here's an example.

As we observed in the chapter on survey research, not everyone is willing to identify with a party or to publicly take a side on a controversial issue. Look at table 11–3, based on data from the 2004 National Election Study (NES), one of a biennial academic

HOW IT'S DONE

Proportions and Percentages

Consider a nominal or ordinal variable, Y, with K values or categories and N observations. Let f_k be the frequency or number of observations in the kth category or class. (k goes from 1 to K.)

$\sum\limits_{k=1}^{k}$ means to add frequencies or proportions starting at

1 and stopping at k.

The proportion or relative frequency of cases in the kth category is $\frac{f_k}{N} = p_k$.

The cumulative proportion in the kth category is

$$\sum_{k=1}^{k} p_k = p_1 + p_2 + \ldots p_k.$$

The percentage of cases in the kth category is $\frac{f_k (100)}{N}$.

survey series of public opinion and voting. One question was, "A working mother can establish just as warm and secure a relationship with her children as a mother who does not work. (Do you agree, neither agree nor disagree, or disagree with this statement)?" It shows that 152 people out of a total of 1,212 (12.6 percent) did not offer a substantive response to the question or their responses were for one reason or another not recorded. We thus have two totals. The first is the sample size (often designated by capital N), that is, the total of all the cases in the study, regardless of whether or not information is available for each and every person. Second, there is a subtotal of "valid" or recorded responses for each item. Look at the fourth row, where you will find substantive, or valid, responses. (The total is 311 + 138 + 610 = 1,059.) The percentages of the valid responses are not the same as the total percentages. (Pay attention to the last column, which contains cumulative percentages. About 42 percent of the sample either "agree" or "neither agree nor disagree" with the statement.)

TABLE 11–3
The Effect of Missing Data on Percentages

Response	Frequency	Percentage of All Respondents	Percentage Valid Responses	Cumulative Percentage
Agree	311	25.7	29.4	29.4
Neither agree nor disagree	138	11.4	13.0	42.4
Disagree	610	50.3	57.6	100
Valid Responses	1,059	—	100	
Missing	152	12.5		

Question: A working mother can establish just as warm and secure a relationship with her children as a mother who does not work.

Source: National Election Study (Ann Arbor, MI: University of Michigan, Center for Political Studies, 2004).

When describing your results, and especially when calculating percentages or proportions, it is essential to keep the two totals separate and to use the one most appropriate to your study's purposes. In this case, 29.4 percent *of those (1,059) respondents with substantive or valid responses* agreed that a working woman can establish "just as warm and secure a relationship" with the family as a stay-at-home mom. In the complete data set, the value was 25.7 percent, a difference of about 3 or 4 percentage points. Here the numbers differ only slightly, but such will not always be the case. (By the way, are you surprised that more than half of the subjects in this survey disagreed with the statement about working mothers?)

The differences in percentages between those with a valid response and the complete data set may be considerable. Why might this be important? Imagine that someone tells you that a survey proves that 80 percent of Americans favor stem cell research. You might assume that since only 20 percent are opposed, there must be overwhelming sentiment for this scientific activity. But suppose 1,000 people took part in the poll, and only 200 gave "approve" or "disapprove" responses. All the others were recorded as "don't know what stem cell research is," "no opinion," or "refused." In this case the "80 percent" in favor could be misleading. Table 11–4 shows the hypothetical distribution responses.

TABLE 11–4
The Effect of Missing Data

	Raw Frequency	Percentage of Total N	Percentage of "Valid" N
Approve	160	16	80
Disapprove	40	4	20
Subtotal	200	—	100
Missing	800	80	
Total	1,000	100	

We see that only 20 percent of the *total* sample took a substantive position. For the overwhelming number of respondents, there is no interpretable or meaningful response, so you might hesitate to make sweeping generalizations about the public, given these data. The lesson: Always be aware of the base of a percentage calculation.[6] If you choose to present only the valid responses, you should also tell your audience which categories have been excluded and the number of cases in each.

DESCRIPTIVE STATISTICS

Frequency distributions, like those displayed in tables 11–2, 11–3, and 11–4, help us make sense of a large body of numbers and consequently are a good first step in describing and exploring the data. They have, however, a couple of shortcomings. First, and perhaps most obvious, it would be nice to have one, two, or at most a few numerical indicators that would in some sense describe the crucial aspects of the information at hand rather than keeping track of many relative frequencies, proportions, or percentages. Another problem with the frequency distributions is that they aren't much help in describing quantitative (interval and ratio) variables, for which there is often just one observation for each observed value of the variable. If you refer to table 11–1, for instance, you can see that the twenty-one nations have different Gini scale scores. For these reasons, analysts turn to descriptive statistics.

A **descriptive statistic** is a number that, because of its definition and formula, describes certain characteristics or properties of a batch of numbers. These descriptive indicators have two important applications:

1. As the name suggests, they provide a concise summary of variables. If interpreted carefully and in conjunction with knowledge of the subject matter, they can help answer questions such as "What is the typical (average) level of inequality in democracies" or "How partisan are Americans?"

2. The word *statistic* in the term reminds us that these measures underlie statistical inference, the process of estimating unknown or unmeasured population characteristics from a sample. For example, if a sample shows that 10 percent more women than men identify themselves as strong Democrats, can we say the difference holds for the adult population of Americans as a whole? What is *the best* guess of the size of the gender gap? On what grounds does the answer rest? Assuming certain assumptions have been met and the data come from a probability sample, nearly all of the statistics we present in this and later chapters have the properties of not only describing data but also of being mathematically justifiable estimators of population parameters.

What kinds of statistics are used? In this section, we describe statistics for measuring central tendency, variation, and the occurrence or rates of events or properties. In later chapters, we introduce statistics that describe the association or connection between two variables. We further organize the statistics by level of measurement.

Measures of Central Tendency

Formally speaking, a measure of **central tendency** locates the middle or center of a distribution, but in a more intuitive sense it describes a typical case. A measure of central tendency applied to table 11–1 can tell you the average or typical Gini coefficient or unionization level of the twenty-one countries shown.

THE MEAN. The most familiar measure of central tendency is the **mean**, called the average in everyday conversation. A simple device for summarizing a batch of numbers, it is calculated by adding the values of a variable and dividing the total by the number of values. For example, if we want the mean of the variable "union density" for the 21 developing nations in table 11–1, we just add the values and divide by 21:

$$\bar{Y} = \frac{\begin{array}{c}(23.1 + 35.7 + 55.6 + 28.2 + 72.5 + 74.8 + 8.2 + 23.2 + 24.5 + 36.3 + 34.0 + \\ 20.3 + 42.3 + 22.4 + 22.6 + 53.0 + 16.2 + 78.0 + 17.8 + 29.2 + 12.6)\end{array}}{21} = 34.79$$

The mean, denoted $\bar{Y}$ (read as "Y bar"), is thus 34.79 percent; we can say that on average, about 35 percent of employees in these countries are unionized.

The mean is appropriate for interval and ratio (that is, truly quantitative) variables, but it is sometimes applied to ordinal scales in which the categories have been assigned numbers, as in the previous example. After all, everyone uses the mean to get grade point averages (GPAs), which are usually based on assigning a value of 4.0 for an A and so forth. Another substantive example is the mean political ideology as measured in the 2004 NES data mentioned above. The questionnaire asks respondents to place themselves on a 7-point liberalism-conservatism scale, for which the responses are coded 1 for "extremely liberal," 2 for "liberal," 3 for "slightly liberal," 4 for "moderate," 5 for "slightly conservative," 6 for "conservative," and 7 for "extremely conservative."

HOW IT'S DONE

The Mean

The mean is calculated as follows:

$$\bar{Y} = \frac{\displaystyle\sum_{i=1}^{N} Y_i}{N},$$

where i refers to the ith member of the sample and the

symbol $\dfrac{\displaystyle\sum_{i=1}^{N} Y_i}{N}$ means summing Y values starting with

$i = 1$, $i = 2$, i . . . and continuing until all N values of Y have been added.

(These integers have no inherent meaning; they are just a way of coding the data.) The mean of the 1,059 cases with valid (that is, nonmissing) values is 4.28. Since the center of the scale, 4, represents a middle-of-the-road position, a mean scale score of 4.28 suggests that the sample is very slightly conservative.

As we will say countless times, numbers do not speak for themselves. A mean ideology score of 4.28 does lean a tad in the conservative direction, but is there a practical consequence? Just how conservative is public opinion? These are questions statistics cannot answer. Only a political scientist or journalist can. The result, by the way, agrees with many academic studies showing that Americans are not particularly ideological in their politics.

TABLE 11–5
Hypothetical Incomes in Two Communities

Community A	Community B
$10,000	$10,000
10,000	10,000
12,000	12,000
18,000	18,000
20,000	20,000
22,000	22,000
25,000	25,000
28,000	28,000
30,000	30,000
200,000	30,000
$\bar{Y} = \$37,500$	$\bar{Y} = \$20,500$

Of course, summarizing even quantitative data with a single figure has a potential disadvantage because the message contained in one number provides incomplete information. How many times have you heard a claim like "My GPA doesn't reflect what I got out of college?" Or suppose a classmate has a GPA of 3.0 (on a 4.0 grade scale). It is impossible to learn from that indicator alone whether she excelled in some courses and struggled in others or whether she consistently received Bs.

Furthermore, although the mean is widely known and used, it can mislead the unwary. Here's a simple illustration. Suppose you have been told that Community A has a lower crime rate than Community B. You hypothesize that the gap stems partly from differences in economic well-being. To test this supposition, you take a random sample of 10 households per community, obtain the family income of each household, and compute the means for both neighborhoods. The results appear in table 11–5. The mean income of Community A is $37,500; the mean for Community B is $20,500. Since Community A has a higher average (look at the bottom row of the table), you might believe the hypothesis holds water.

On closer inspection, however, note that the incomes are identical in each community except for the last one. These two families have substantially different earnings. Concentrating on just the mean income of the communities and ignoring any large values would give you the erroneous impression that people in Community A are financially much better off than people in Community B. In reality only one family in A is much better off than others in B. Could this one family explain the difference? Possibly, but before deciding, look at how the mean is calculated. For both communities, the first nine numbers add to 10,000 + 10,000 + 12,000 + . . . + 30,000 = 175,000. For Community A the last income, $200,000, brings this total to $375,000, which when divided by 10 (the number of cases), gives a mean of $37,500. But for Community B the last addition is $30,000, for a total of $205,000. When the total is divided by 10, we get a mean of $20,500. This example illustrates how one (or a few) extreme or very large (or small) values can affect or skew the numerical magnitude of the mean (and other statistics). For this reason, other measures of central tendency, known as **resistant measures,** which are not sensitive to one or a few extremes values, are frequently used.

THE TRIMMED MEAN.   Because the mean is susceptible or sensitive to a few very large or small values—in statistical argot, it is "not resistant to outliers"—analysts sometimes modify its calculation by dropping or excluding some percentage of the largest and smallest values. The result is called the **trimmed mean.** This tactic automatically removes the influence of the discrepant values. Return to the previous example, in which we want to compare the incomes of Communities A and B. If we drop the first and last observations from each community, we have 8 cases each, and the means are both $20,625.

$$\overline{Y}_{\text{trimmed}} = \left(\frac{\begin{array}{c} 10{,}000 + 12{,}000 + 18{,}000 + 20{,}000 + \\ 22{,}000 + 25{,}000 + 28{,}000 + 30{,}000 \end{array}}{8} \right) = 20{,}625.$$

THE MEAN AS A PREDICTOR

The mean is used mainly to describe the central tendency of a distribution. Throughout the remaining chapters, however, we put it to a slightly different use. Sometimes it becomes a benchmark for making predictions. Suppose, to take a hypothetical situation, you had a large group of people about whom you knew nothing—not their race, gender, family background, . . . nothing. Then, you are asked to select a person at random and guess her annual income. Since you have no information, you might feel lost, but you could go to a reference source such as the Bureau of Economic Analysis in the Commerce Department. There you might find that in 2010, the mean per capita personal income in the United States was $40,584.[7] In the absence of any other information, a first approximation to the person's yearly income would be about $41,000. A bit more formally, this prediction is based on a "model":

Model 1: Predicted income $=$ mean income or $\hat{Y} = \overline{Y}$.

The little hat over the Y means "predicted," and the equation can be read as "the predicted value of Y equals the mean of Y."

Of course, this method of prediction is going to lead to lots of errors. But suppose you have an additional piece of information, say years of education completed. Since there is a strong connection between education and earnings, we would expect to make fewer prediction errors knowing how educated a person is. Using the added data, we have a new model:

Model 2: Predicted income $=$ mean income $+$ "effect of education," or $\hat{Y} = \overline{Y} + $ education effect.

If your subject has a doctorate degree, you might predict that she would earn twice the national average; if she only finished grade school, her income might be lower than average. Whatever the case, much statistical analysis can be viewed as a comparison of the explanatory power two models. Alternatively and equivalently, we can estimate the education effect to determine how much it raises or lowers the mean.

Seen this way, the communities have the same standard of living.

Most software programs will produce trimmed means along with the standard arithmetic mean. The usual default is to exclude the highest and lowest 5 percent of values, but some programs let the user choose the percentage. (In our example, we effectively dropped 20 percent, but only because we had such an artificially low number of cases.)

To further demonstrate the effects of trimming, let's look at the variable "Aged population (in thousands)" that appears in table 11–1. A variable of this sort is often part of the "dependency" indicators that measure a nation's demand for social services. We make two points and an aside. First, the calculation of the trimmed mean is straightforward: we order the populations from smallest to largest, drop 10 percent (or about 2 observations) from each end, and calculate the mean of the remaining 17 cases.

$$\bar{Y}_{\text{trimmed}} = \left(\frac{\begin{array}{l} 485 + 676 + 809 + 822 + 1,200 + 1,283 + \\ 1,548 + 1,790 + 1,989 + 2,270 + 2,582 + 4,141 + \\ 7,186 + 9,570 + 9,894 + 10,935 + 15,897 \end{array}}{17} \right) = 4,304.53$$

Second, note that this value is considerably smaller than the original (unadjusted) mean (6,436.57). What happened? Notice that one country in particular (the United States) has an elderly population about 570 times larger the country at the bottom of the scale (Luxembourg) and about 75 times that of two other countries. So in the full data set, one very large value drags the mean way above what might regard as the "typical" population size. Of course, in this case that result makes sense. And this point leads to our aside: raw numbers such as population counts are often uninterpretable or misleading. Instead, the normal practice is to use a scaled or normed indicator such as the "percentage of the total population that is 65 or older." For the same reason we analyze union density, not the absolute number of unionized workers.

How valid is this procedure? It might seem like a case of lying with statistics. Yet statisticians regard it as standard practice because they feel the technique adjusts for the effects of a few extreme values. (As we explain later, variation of the data is also reduced.)

Inasmuch as trimming adjusts the arithmetic mean by dropping a small percentage of cases, it is, like the arithmetic mean, appropriate for interval or ratio scales but typically would not be applied to ordinal scales.

THE MEDIAN. A measure of central tendency that is fully applicable to ordinal as well as interval and ratio data is the median. The **median** is a (not necessarily

TABLE 11–6
Calculation of the Median

Rank	Over 65 Population
1	64
2	450
3	485
4	676
5	809
6	822
7	1,200
8	1,283
9	1,548
10	1,790
11 Middle value	1,989
12	2,270
13	2,882
14	4,141
15	7,186
16	9,570
17	9,994
18	10,935
19	15,897
20	24,876
21	36,301

Median = 1,989.

Source: Table 11–1.

unique) value that divides a distribution in half. That is, half the observations lie above the median and half below it. Stated differently, to find the median, we need to locate the middle of the distribution.

You can find the middle of an *odd* number of observations by arranging them from lowest to highest and counting the same number of observations from the top and bottom to find the middle. If, for example, the data consist of 21 cases, you will count up 11 observations and the middle observation will be the 12th. To continue with a previous example, look at table 11–6. It lists the ordered over-65 population values.

If you have lots of observations, an easy way to find the middle one is to apply the following formula:

$$mid_{obs} = \frac{(N + 1)}{2}$$

For the previous example, this formula yields $(21 + 1)/2 = 11$, as it should.

If, however, the number of observations is *even*, a modification is required because the middle observation number will contain a 0.5, for example, $(22 + 1)/2 = 11.5$.) What to do? Simply use the observations above and below mid_{obs} and average their values. Suppose we had another country in table 11–1 whose "senior" population (again in thousands) was 6,700. Then the middle values would be the 11th and 12th, and the median would be the arithmetic mean of the two countries corresponding to those cases: $(1,989 + 2,270)/2 = 2,129.50$.

The median, like the trimmed mean, is a resistant measure (see the previous section) in that extreme values (outliers) do not overwhelm its computation. Figure 11–1 shows the calculation of the median for the two hypothetical communities discussed earlier. Recall that the means of the two differed quite a bit: $\bar{Y}_A = \$37,000$ versus $\bar{Y}_B = \$20,500$ But the medians are identical: $\$21,000$. This reflects the fact that the incomes and, hence, the standards of living in the two areas are essentially the same. Consequently, if A's crime rate is lower than B's, the cause may be something other than wealth.

THE MODE. A common measure of central tendency, especially for nominal and categorical ordinal data, is the **mode**, or modal category. It is

HOW IT'S DONE

The Median

This procedure is practical if the number of cases, *N*, is not large (say, fewer than 30 to 40):

1. Sort the values of the observations from lowest to highest.

2. If the number of cases is an odd number, locate the middle one and record its value. This is the median.

3. If the number of cases is an even number, locate the two middle values. Average these two numbers. The result is the median.

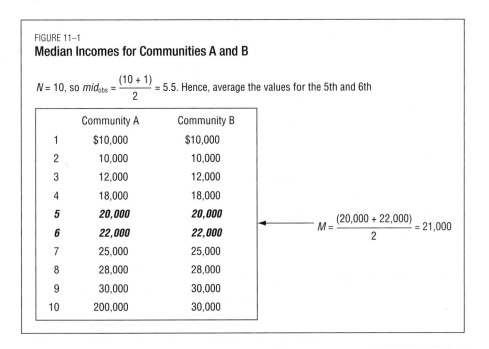

FIGURE 11–1

Median Incomes for Communities A and B

$N = 10$, so $mid_{obs} = \dfrac{(10 + 1)}{2} = 5.5$. Hence, average the values for the 5th and 6th

	Community A	Community B
1	$10,000	$10,000
2	10,000	10,000
3	12,000	12,000
4	18,000	18,000
5	**20,000**	**20,000**
6	**22,000**	**22,000**
7	25,000	25,000
8	28,000	28,000
9	30,000	30,000
10	200,000	30,000

$$M = \frac{(20,000 + 22,000)}{2} = 21,000$$

simply the category with the greatest frequency of observations. As an example, start with table 11–2, which shows the distribution of responses to the partisanship indicator. The modal (most frequent) category was "Agree," with 533 responses. It is worth paying attention to the substantive meaning of a statistic like this one. After all, it tells us that the modal "belief" about the influence on government is that "the rich and powerful" have too much of it.

The mode has less utility in describing interval and ratio data per se, but it is helpful in describing the *shape* of distributions of all kinds of variables. When one category or range of values has many more cases all than the others, we describe the distribution as being *unimodal,* which is to say it has a single peak. But there can be more than two dominant peaks or spikes in the distribution, in which case we speak of *multimodal* distributions. The term *rectangular* is typically used to describe a distribution that has roughly the same number or proportion of observations in each category. Graphs are often more useful than tables for investigating the "shape" of a distribution, as we will see later.

Measures of Variability or Dispersion

We come now to a key concept in statistics: variation, or the differences among the units on a variable. Naturally we want to know what a typical case in our study looks like. But equally important, we need to take stock of the variability among the cases and understand why this variation arises.

GENERAL REMARKS.   Go back to table 11–1. Consider the "Aged population" variable, the data in the sixth column. The figures (in thousands) range from 64 to 36,301 with many values in between. We might conclude that on this variable at least, the nations are quite different or varied or heterogeneous. Now examine "political culture," a categorical variable. Even a glance reveals that there are only two classes and that most countries in this table have what we call a "European" political culture. Thus, there is not much variation in this variable; rather, the nations are more homogeneous.

PROPERTIES OF MEASURES OF VARIATION.   Ideally, a single summary number would clearly express the exact amount of variation in a variable. That way we could precisely or objectively compare variability among groups of objects or apportion it among known and unknown causes. In fact, many single indices of variation exist, but many lack a simple, commonsense interpretation. Let's use the symbol V for some as yet undefined statistical measure of variation. In the limiting case, if all the units in a batch of data have the same value, V is zero. All measures have at least this property. And this trait seems reasonable only because it is impossible for there to be less than zero variation; hence, V will always be equal to or greater than zero. But does V have an upper limit? Nearly all of the measures considered herein do not have an upper bound, which means that they can take on any positive value subject to constraints of the measurement scales. Unfortunately, the interpretation of the numerical value of a measure of variation is not always obvious. Suppose you are told that V equals 2.0. What exactly does this mean? The number will be a mere abstraction unless you understand V's definition and the theoretical or practical context of the variable it describes. Even then the meaning may not be intuitively satisfying, so it is often helpful to interpret measures of variability with the help of other statistics and graphs.

The properties of measures of variation or **dispersion** described in this book can be summed up in three statements:

1. If there is *no* variability (all the scores have the same value), the measure will equal 0.

2. The measure will always be a positive number (there can't be less than no variation).

3. The greater the variability in the data, the larger the numerical value of the measure.

THE RANGE.   For interval- and ratio-level scales, the **range** is a particularly simple measure of gross variation: it is just the largest (maximum) value of a variable minus the smallest (minimum) value:

$$\text{Range} = \text{maximum} - \text{minimum}.$$

Look carefully at the union densities (union members as percentage of the work-force) in table 11–1. The largest value is 78 percent (Sweden), and the smallest is 8.2 percent (France). The range in union density is therefore 78 − 8.2 or 69.8 percent. In plain language, an enormous disparity exists in labor organization in this sample. Now consider spending on "social" programs (e.g., unemployment compensation, pension, and so on) as a percentage of gross domestic product. (See the fourth column of Table 11-1.) Following the spirit of Hacker and Pierson's argument, we might interpret this variable as a measure of the consequences of the distribution of power, since these benefits accrue largely to individuals rather than to corporations or private institutions. In any event, it varies between a low of 16.2 percent (Ireland) and a high of 30.4 percent (Sweden) for a range of 14.2 percent.

An aside: Sweden has both the largest union densities *and* expenditure percentage, while the United States has the lowest spending percentage and second lowest union density. Do you suppose the data support a hypothesis: "The greater labor's strength in a society, the greater its social expenditures?" You can check this assertion with the techniques described in subsequent chapters. At this point, we merely emphasize that data exploration are an essential first step in moving from numbers to hypotheses then to conclusions.

Finally, suppose we had another variable, "level of economic development," coded 1 for developed, 2 for underdeveloped. Surely all the nations listed in table 11–1 would score 1, and there would be no variation. Maximum and minimum values would be 1, and the range (if we treated the codes as actual integers) would be 0. This demonstrates the property that when all units have the same value, a measure of variation (such as the range) will be 0.

INTERQUARTILE RANGE.   Finding the range, of course, requires sorting or ordering the data from largest to smallest or at least finding the maximum and minimum values. Computers make this chore easy, even with a large data set. Another measure of variation, the interquartile range, is easily computed from data ordered in this way.

Imagine that, after ordering your data, you divide them into four equal-sized batches. The first bunch would contain 25 percent of the cases, the next would have 25 percent, the next 25 percent, and the last the remaining 25 percent. The division points defining these groups are called quartiles, abbreviated Q. Now, find the range as before but use the third and first quartiles as the maximum and minimum. Their difference is the **interquartile range** (IQR):

$$IQR = Q3 - Q1,$$

where Q3 stands for the third quartile (sometimes it's called the 75th percentile because 75 percent of the cases lie below it) and Q1 is the first (or 25th percentile). Since the interquartile range, a single number, indicates the difference or distance between the third and second quartiles, the middle 50 percent of observations lie between these values.

Another way to think about the computation of the IQR is to obtain the median, which divides the data in half. Then, find the medians of *each* half; these medians will be the first and third quartiles.

Let's look at the calculation for the Gini coefficients in table 11–1. Remember, a value close to 0 indicates complete equality, and larger numbers mean greater inequality, with (in this case) 100 signifying maximum inequality. Figure 11–2 shows how the IQR is calculated for the 21 nations in table 11–1. We first find the location of the median: $(N + 1)/2 = (21 + 1)/2 = 11$). Then we find the first quartile by taking the median of the first 11 observations, which is the score for the $(11 + 1)/2 = $ 6th case, Germany). Its value is Q1 = 28.3. Similarly, the third quartile is found by calculating the median of the largest 11 values: Q3 = 34.7. The IQR is thus 34.7—28.3 = 6.4. We can explain these numbers as saying that three-quarters of the developed countries have Gini scores between about 28 and

FIGURE 11–2
The Quartiles and Interquartile Range

Rank	Country	Gini		
1	Denmark	24.7		
2	Japan	24.9		
3	Sweden	25.0		
4	Norway	25.8		
5	Finland	26.9		
6	*Germany*	*28.3* ←	Q1 = 28.3	
7	Austria	29.1		
8	Luxembourg	30.8		
9	Netherlands	30.9		
10	Canada	32.6		
11	*France*	*32.7* ←	M = 32.7	IQR = 37.7 − 28.3 = 6.4
12	Belgium	33.0		
13	Switzerland	33.7		
14	Greece	34.3		
15	Ireland	34.3		
16	*Spain*	*34.7* ←	Q3 = 34.7	
17	Australia	35.2		
18	Italy	36.0		
19	UK	36.0		
20	New Zealand	36.2		
21	USA	40.8		

35 points. (By contrast, the median for 127 countries across the world is 39.5 and the IQR is 13.5, about twice the IQR for the nations in table 11–1. So, we conclude—no surprise—that the world at large is more varied in terms of income inequality than the industrial democracies.)

Quartiles, the range, and the interquartile range (as well as the median) have the property that we have been calling resistance: extreme or outlying values do not distort the picture of the majority of cases. This is a major advantage, especially in small samples. The next set of measures of variability reveal how data diverge from a measure of central tendency.

Deviations from Central Tendency

These statistics evaluate deviations from means. A deviation from the mean is simply a data point's distance from the mean.[8] Let's take a hypothetical case. Suppose the mean of a variable is 50. If a particular observation has a value of, say, 49, it deviates from the mean by 1 unit. Another case that has a score of 20 departs from the mean by 30 units. Now, suppose we find out how far each observation's score is from the mean and total these deviations. We would then have the beginnings of a measure of variation. Artificial data demonstrate the point (table 11–7). We have three samples each containing just three observed values.

The first data set clearly has no variation. The numbers in the second set are almost the same, while those in the third exhibit considerable diversity. The measures of variation to be discussed combine the deviations (the third set of columns) into a single indicator that summarizes the data.

THE VARIANCE. The **variance** is the average or *mean* of squared deviations, or the average of all the squared differences between each score and the mean. Denoted σ^2, the variance can be found by subtracting the mean from each score, squaring the result (a squared deviation), and adding up all the squared deviations and dividing by N. When the data are for a sample, the variance is the sum of the squared deviations divided by $N - 1$. So, to calculate the variance for the Gini numbers in table 11–1, simply find the mean (31.71) and squared deviation

---

TABLE 11–7
Deviations from the Mean

Observed Values			Mean	Deviations from the Mean			Interpretation
50	50	50	50	0	0	0	No deviation implies no variation.
49	50	51	50	−1	0	1	Small deviations imply little variation.
20	50	80	50	−30	0	30	Large deviations imply considerable variation.

Note: Hypothetical data.

TABLE 11–8
Calculating the Variance and Standard Deviation of Gini Scores

	Country	Gini	Deviation = Gini − Mean	Deviation Squared
1	Australia	35.2	3.5	12.3
2	Austria	29.1	−2.6	6.8
3	Belgium	33	1.3	1.7
4	Canada	32.6	0.9	0.8
5	Denmark	24.7	−7	49.0
6	Finland	26.9	−4.8	23.0
7	France	32.7	1	1.0
8	Germany	28.3	−3.4	11.6
9	Greece	34.3	2.6	6.8
10	Ireland	34.3	2.6	6.8
11	Italy	36	4.3	18.5
12	Japan	24.9	−6.8	46.2
13	Luxembourg	30.8	−0.9	0.8
14	The Netherlands	30.9	−0.8	0.6
15	New Zealand	36.2	4.5	20.3
16	Norway	25.8	−5.9	34.8
17	Spain	34.7	3	9.0
18	Sweden	25	−6.7	44.9
19	Switzerland	33.7	2	4.0
20	UK	36	4.3	18.5
21	USA	40.8	9.1	82.8
Totals			0.0	400.2

Variance: $\sigma^2 = \dfrac{400.2}{21-1} = 20.01$.

Standard deviation: $\sqrt{\sigma^2} = \sqrt{\dfrac{400.2}{21-1}} = 4.47$.

Source: Table 11–1.

Note: Some totals subject to rounding errors.

from the mean, then add to get the total, 400.2. Divide this sum by $N-1$, or 20, to get the variance: 20.01. Table 11–8 illustrates the steps. When calculating the variance for a sample, $N-1$ appears in the denominator for technical reasons. (Here we treat the data in table 11–1 as a sample.) Since N and $N-1$ are close when N is large, you can think of the variance and sample variance as a kind of average of squared deviations.[9]

The variance and sample variance follow the rules of a measure of variation: the greater the dispersion of data about the mean, the higher the value of the variance. If all the values are the same, variance equals zero. And it is always nonnegative. The variance is a fundamental concept in mathematical and applied statistics, as we shall see shortly.

THE STANDARD DEVIATION FOR A POPULATION AND A SAMPLE.   The most commonly computed and calculated measure of variation is the **standard deviation**, which we denote by σ for a population and by $\hat{\sigma}$ for a sample. The standard deviation is simply the square root of the variance or, for a sample, $\hat{\sigma} = \sqrt{\hat{\sigma}^2}$.

The standard deviation (and the variance), like the mean, is sensitive to extreme values. As a quick example to illustrate this property, in table 11–9, we slightly alter the three hypothetical data sets given in table 11–7.

The first group of numbers (50, 50, 50) has no variation—the numbers' deviations from the mean are 0—and, in keeping with our conception of a measure of variation, the standard deviation, σ, is 0. The next set (49, 50, 51) has almost no variability, and its standard deviation works out to 1. Inasmuch as we haven't identified a measurement scale, this number does not have much theoretical or practical meaning. But it is quite small (less than 1 unit) and indicates very little dispersion among the values. The last group (49, 50, 80) has one outlying value, at least compared to the other two, and the standard deviation is more than 21 units. Is there that much variation? According to σ, the answer is yes. But the last value (80) contributes virtually everything to the total and hence inflates the magnitude of the statistic.

We also want to demonstrate the effect of outliers—a few values far above or below the mean on the magnitude of variance and standard deviation. Instead of drawing on the previous example, let's turn to the "population over 65" variables that we

HOW IT'S DONE

The Variance for a Sample

The variance is calculated as follows:

$$\hat{\sigma}^2 = \frac{\sum\limits_{i=1}^{N} (Y_i - \bar{Y})^2}{N-1},$$

where Y_i stands for the ith value, $\bar{Y}$ is the mean of the variable, and N is the sample size.

To simplify calculations, you can use

$$\hat{\sigma}^2 = \frac{\sum\limits_{i=1}^{N} Y_i^2 - \dfrac{\left(\sum\limits_{i=1}^{N} Y_i\right)^2}{N}}{N-1}.$$

TABLE 11–9
Calculation of the Standard Deviation

Data Set 1	Squared Deviations	Data Set 2	Squared Deviations	Data Set 3	Squared Deviations
50	$(50 - 50)^2 = 0$	49	$(49 - 50)^2 = 1$	49	$(49 - 50)^2 = (-1)2 = 1$
50	$(50 - 50)^2 = 0$	50	$(50 - 50)^2 = 0$	50	$(50 - 50)^2 = 0$
50	$(50 - 50)^2 = 0$	51	$(51 - 50)^2 = 1$	80	$(80 - 50)^2 = (30)2 = 900$
$\bar{Y} = 50$	Sum = 0	$\bar{Y} = 50$	Sum = 2	$\bar{Y} = 50$	Sum = 901
	$\hat{\sigma} = \sqrt{\dfrac{0}{3-1}} = 0$		$\hat{\sigma} = \sqrt{\dfrac{2}{3-1}} = 1$		$\hat{\sigma} = \sqrt{\dfrac{901}{3-1}} = 21.22$

looked at previously. You may recall that at least two countries (the United States and Japan) have aged populations that are way beyond the average. Let's calculate these statistics for the full complement of countries and for a reduced set created by dropping the two largest values. For the full data (N = 21), the sum of squared deviations is the humungous number 1,727,430,137, which, when divided by 21 − 1 = 20, produces the sample variance, $\hat{\sigma}^2$ = 86,371,506.9. Taking the square root yields $\hat{\sigma}$ = 9,293.63, the sample standard deviation. (Fortunately, technology comes to our aid in finding the variance and standard deviation since laptops, pocket calculators, and even smartphones usually have applications that do the dirty work. But it never hurts to perform the calculations by hand if there are not too many cases.) The corresponding values for the abbreviated data (that is, with the United States and Japan deleted) are $\hat{\sigma}^2$ = 20,707,234.5, which is about three times smaller than the original variance, and $\hat{\sigma}$ = 4,550.52, which is about half the size of standard deviation for all 21 countries.

We cannot emphasize enough the importance of carefully exploring data with summary statistics and looking out for cases that may unduly sway the interpretation of the results. The lesson in all of this is that you should not rely on a single number to summarize or describe your data. Rather, use as much information as is reasonable and take your time interpreting each variable. Computers spit out results, but they never interpret them.

In any event, what does sample standard deviation of 9,293.63 tell us about the variable? At this point it is difficult to provide a quick, intuitive interpretation. Understanding the standard deviation becomes easier as we flesh out some additional concepts and you gain experience.

HOW IT'S DONE

The Standard Deviation for a Sample

The standard deviation is calculated as follows:

$$\hat{\sigma} = \sqrt{\frac{\sum_{i=1}^{N}(Y_i - \bar{Y})^2}{N-1}},$$

where Y_i stands for the ith value, $\bar{Y}$ is the mean of the variable, and N is the population size.

If you have a calculator that accumulates sums, you can apply this calculating formula:

$$\hat{\sigma} = \sqrt{\frac{\sum_{i=1}^{N}Y_i^2 - \dfrac{\left(\sum_{i=1}^{N}Y_i\right)^2}{N}}{N-1}}.$$

MORE ON THE INTERPRETATION OF THE STANDARD DEVIATION. The significance of the standard deviation in statistics is illustrated by considering a common situation. Suppose a large set of data have a distribution approximately like the one shown in figure 11–3. What we see there is a "bell-shaped" distribution (often called a **normal distribution**) with the following features:

- The bulk of observations lies in the center, where there is a single peak.

- More specifically, in a normal distribution, half (50 percent) of the observations lie *above* the mean and half lie *below* it.

■ The mean, median, and mode have the same numerical values.

■ Fewer and fewer observations fall in the tails of the distribution.

■ The spread of the distribution is symmetric: one side is the mirror image of the other.

If data have such a distribution, the frequency or proportion of cases lying between any two values of the variable can be described by "distances" between the mean and standard deviations. Following what Alan Agresti called the "empirical rule," the spread of observations can be described this way:[10]

■ Approximately 68 percent of the data lie between $\bar{Y} - \sigma$ and $\bar{Y} + \sigma$. Read this as "68 percent of the observations are between plus and minus one standard deviation of the mean." For example, if the mean of a variable is 100 and its standard deviation is 10, then about 68 percent of the cases will have scores somewhere between 90 and 110.

■ Approximately 95 percent of the cases will fall between $\bar{Y} - 2\sigma$ and $\bar{Y} + 2\sigma$. In the first example, 95 percent or so would be between 80 and 120.

■ Almost all of the data will be between $\bar{Y} - 3\sigma$ and $\bar{Y} + 3\sigma$.

This feature of the standard deviation and the normal distribution has an important practical application. For all suitably transformed normal distributions, the areas between the mean and the various distances above and below it, measured in standard deviation units, are precisely known and have even been tabulated (see appendix A). Figure 11–3 illustrates this information for one and two standard deviation units above and below the mean.

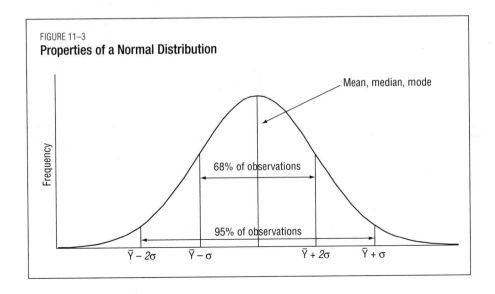

FIGURE 11–3
Properties of a Normal Distribution

Frequency

Mean, median, mode

68% of observations

95% of observations

$\bar{Y} - 2\sigma$ $\bar{Y} - \sigma$ $\bar{Y} + 2\sigma$ $\bar{Y} + \sigma$

TABLE 11–10
Summary of Descriptive Statistics

Statistic	Symbol (if any)	Description (what it shows)	Resistant to Outliers	Most Appropriate For
Measures of Central Tendency				
Mean	$\bar{Y}$	Arithmetic average: Identifies center of distribution	No	Interval, ratio scales
Trimmed mean	$\bar{Y}_{trimmed}$	Arithmetic mean with a certain percentage of cases dropped from each end of the distribution	Yes	Interval, ratio scales
Median	M	Identifies middle value: 50% of observations lie above, 50% below	Yes	Interval, ratio, ordinal, scales; ranks
Mode	Mode	Identifies the category (or categories) with highest frequencies	No	Categorical (nominal, ordinal) scales
Measures of Variation				
Range	Range	Maximum − minimum	NA	Interval, ratio scales
Interquartile range	IQR	Middle 50% of observations	Yes	Interval, ratio scales; ranks
Variance	σ^2	Average of squared deviations	No	Interval, ratio scales
Standard deviation	σ	Square root of average of squared deviations	No	Interval, ratio scales

How do we know these percentages? Because mathematical theory proves that normal distributions have this property. Of course, if data are not perfectly normally distributed, the percentages will only be approximations. Yet many naturally occurring variables do have nearly normal distributions, or they can be transformed into an almost normal distribution (for instance, by converting each number to a logarithm).

We conclude this section with table 11–10, which summarizes the descriptive statistics discussed in this chapter.

GRAPHS FOR PRESENTATION AND EXPLORATION

In statistics the maxim "A picture is worth a thousand words" has a special place. We have already discussed the difficulty of using a large data matrix and the need to condense information to a few descriptive numbers. But even those numbers can be uninformative, if not misleading. A major development since the 1980s has been an emphasis on graphic displays to explore and analyze data.[11] These visual tools may lead you to see aspects of the data that are not revealed by tables or a single statistic, and they assist with developing and testing models.

In particular, for any data matrix, a well-constructed graph can answer several questions at one time:

- *Central tendency:* Where does the center of the distribution lie?
- *Dispersion or variation:* How spread out or bunched up are the observations?
- *The shape of the distribution:* Does it have a single peak (one concentration of observations within a relatively narrow range of values) or more than one?
- *Tails:* Approximately what proportion of observations is in the ends of the distribution or in its tails?
- *Symmetry or asymmetry (also called skewness):* Do observations tend to pile up at one end of the measurement scale, with relatively few observations at the other end? Or does each end have roughly the same number of observations?
- *Outliers:* Are there values that, compared with most, seem very large or very small?
- *Comparison:* How does one distribution compare to another in terms of shape, spread, and central tendency?
- *Relationships:* Do values of one variable seem related to those of another?

Figure 11–4 illustrates some ways a variable (Y) can be distributed. Panel A displays a symmetric, unimodal (one-peak) distribution, which we previously called bell-shaped or normal. Panel B depicts a rectangular distribution; in this case, each value or range of values has the same number of cases. Panel C shows a distribution that, although unimodal, is **negatively skewed** or skewed to the left. In other words, there are a few observations on the left or low end of the scale, and most observations are in the middle or high end of the scale. Finally, panel D represents the opposite situation: there are comparatively few observations on the right or high end of the scale. The curve is skewed to the right or **positively skewed.** These are ideal types. No empirical distribution will look exactly like any one of them. Yet if you compare these shapes with the graphs of your own data, you can quickly approximate the kind of distribution you have.

Why is it important to look at the shape of a distribution? For one thing, many statistical procedures assume that variables have an approximately normal distribution. And, if they do not, they can sometimes be mathematically changed or transformed into a bell-shaped configuration.

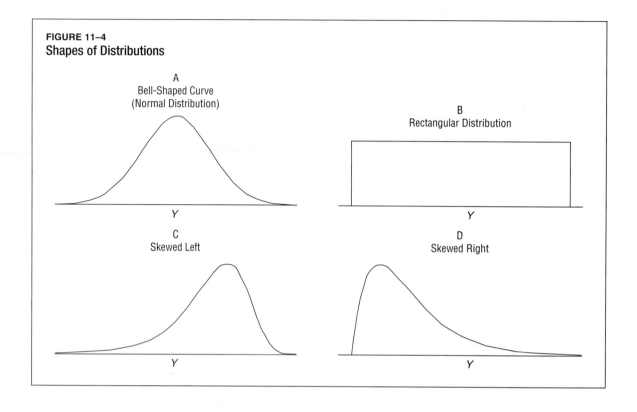

FIGURE 11–4
Shapes of Distributions

A
Bell-Shaped Curve
(Normal Distribution)

B
Rectangular Distribution

Y

Y

C
Skewed Left

D
Skewed Right

Y

Y

We can somewhat arbitrarily divide graphs into two general varieties, aimed at two audiences:

1. *Presentation graphs:* Some graphs are intended to be end products. Everyone has seen bar graphs and pie diagrams. The mass media use them to summarize information or even to prove a point, and they commonly appear in books on policy and politics. They are appropriate for summarizing data to be published or otherwise publicly disseminated.

2. *Exploratory graphs:* Graphic analysis works in the background to assist in the exploration of data. As a matter of fact, one of the most vigorous research activities in applied statistics is the search for newer and better ways to visualize quantitative and qualitative information. Beginning with techniques developed in the 1970s by John Tukey and others, research on the visualization of data has become a growth industry.[12] Sometimes these exploratory graphs appear in published research literature, but they are mainly for the benefit of the analyst and are intended to tease out aspects of data that numerical methods do not supply. These diagrams amount to

all-in-one devices that simultaneously display various aspects of data, such as central tendency, variation, and shape.

Designing and Drawing Graphs

As we said, a literal picture may be worth a thousand words, but only if it shows what the photographer intends. Computers have greatly simplified the task of constructing graphs with a few keystrokes. Yet this computational power will create problems if overused. Remember, a graph is supposed to provide the viewer with a visual description of the data. Computers may churn out wonderful-looking charts. But many of them add so many extra features, such as three-dimensional bars, exploded slices, cute little icons, or colorful fills, that the data easily get lost in the ink. Edward Tufte called these doodads "chartjunk."[13] It is usually best to keep lines and areas as simple as possible so that readers can easily see the point being conveyed. More important, the essence of successful graphing is to ensure that the viewer can accurately perceive the data and any relations among variables.[14] The image should not distort the data. The graphical elements (e.g., size of plotting symbols, colors, axes, etc.) should reflect the actual relationships and trends in the data. Graph designers introduced the term *lie factor* to quantify this notion:[15]

$$\text{Lie factor} = \frac{\text{Size of effect displayed in graph}}{\text{Size of effect in data}}.$$

Many statisticians and social scientists regard a graph as a story about the data. Like any story, it should be well told and not drone on and on.

Here are some tips. They are very general. Their purpose is merely to alert you to the fact that unless helped by humans, computers are not especially good at telling stories.

- Small amounts of data (few cases) usually don't need to be summarized by graph. A table (e.g., frequency distribution) is often a better way to present small amounts numerical information.

- A table that spans several pages, however, may overwhelm a reader unless it's meant to be part of a databook. But graphs can provide a succinct summary, especially if one wants to emphasize trends or patterns and looking at individual data points is not essential to the story.

- Pick an appropriate type of graph. We see shortly that categorical (nominal and ordinal) variables require or are best suit to one variety, quantitative variables to another. A mixture of variable types (one nominal and one continuous, for example) may require special attention.

■ Think carefully about the axes and how they relate to the scale of the data. There are two considerations: the range of data values and how they are measured on the graph and the physical dimensions of the plot. Suppose, as we do shortly, you want plot carbon dioxide (CO_2) emissions against year. If the time axis is 5 1/2 inches wide, the increase over the years may look relatively flat; but if the axis is only 2 inches, the rates may seem to soar. Consider the data's maximum and minimums before setting the axes' limit(s). Both axes should be proportional to the data's limits. The viewer should have little problem understanding the range. Scale the axes to show trends in a reasonable way (e.g., figure 11–5.) Is there a meaningful zero point? Including it may or may not be appropriate.

■ Clearly label axes and graphical elements (e.g., bars, lines, symbols). Note the measurement units in labels, titles, and legends (e.g., "Population [in thousands]," "Spending [as percent of GDP]").

■ Use sufficient tick or "hash" marks so the reader can quickly estimate quantities.

■ Don't "clip" (not include) extreme values that are part of the data unless absolutely necessary and clearly noted. It is sometimes necessary to cut an axis, but make sure everyone knows what you are doing and why.

■ If possible, identify interesting or extreme values, but if the graph contains a lot of points (more than, say, 30 or 40), labeling all of them may leave an unreadable mess on the page. Use text (sparingly) to point out interesting features of the data. Suppose a plot of GDP per capita versus total expenditures on health (as a fraction of GDP) reveals a clear pattern (the greater the wealth, the greater the spending) but one country lies out of the mainstream. It would be worth identifying this country on the graph.

■ Independent variables usually (but do not always) appear on the x- or horizontal axis. A common exception is when comparing categories of a nominal or ordinal factors in terms of a quantitative variable. Then, analysts frequently list the classes along the y- or vertical axis and extend bars or boxes or whatever into the graph (from left to right) to show magnitudes along the horizontal scale.

■ Again, the size of the graphical elements has to be proportional to the data they represent. Only use the size of a graphical element, such as a bar or circle, to show differences in data; keep these elements the same size otherwise. Suppose you are using bars to show the percentages of a sample that are liberal and conservative. If the liberal bar is twice as wide as the one for conservatives (1 inch versus 1/2 inch), the relative proportions may be distorted in the viewer's eye, even if the actual numbers appear in the graph. Politicians along with statisticians know that the visual often dominates the verbal.

- If you are using bars or pie slices to represent data, it helps to arrange them in a logical order. If the variable is ordinal, then list the categories from lowest to highest. Similarly, group common categories together. Typically in charts that show the relative proportions of individuals who self-identify with one or the other US political party, strong to weak Democrats are placed next to each other, as are Republicans, with independents placed in the middle. Imagine what the picture would look like if the categories were randomly scattered.

- Don't crowd the graph with too much data or information. For example, a pie chart (see figure 11–6[b]) with more than ten or twelve slices may be hard to read; important interesting differences can get lost in the ink.

- Avoid 3-D effects like the plague unless they help tell your story. Of course, a three-dimensional graph may be necessary for a multiple-variable display, but normally not to dramatize or beautify. Avoid unneeded decorations.

- Include a title.

- Indicate the source and date of the data if possible.

- Points are usually better than icons.

- Colors are useful to show different categories, etc., but as in this book, the graph has to stand on its own in black and white. As Web page designers are well aware, your viewer may not have the same viewing device you used to create the image. And don't use more colors than data values.

- A rule of thumb: When it comes to graphing, the less ink on the page, the better.

As an example of some of these issues, consider the debate about global warming. Most climatologists argue that dramatic increases in carbon dioxide (CO_2)—a "greenhouse gas"—emissions have risen so steeply as a result of human activities that the earth's average temperature is rising to the point where human well-being is threatened. Let's lay aside the pros and cons of the argument and instead look at how one can use a graph to inform and misinform citizens. Figure 11–5 shows the trend in CO_2 emissions, in parts per million (ppm), over the past half century or so. Consider two ordinary citizens. One who looks at only figure 11–5(a) might say, "Why shucks, the levels haven't changed hardly t'all. What's the worry?" The second, however, sees only the second and thinks, "Oh my God! The levels are skyrocketing." Why the different reactions? Exactly the same data have been plotted, but the y-axes are different. In (a), the limits are 0 and 500. Yet the maximum and minimum of the series are 313 and 393, respectively a spread of 80 ppm. This difference gets swallowed in the y-axis, making the trend look almost level. The second is closer to the mark, but still the y-limits are now the minimum and maximum values.[16] The graph seems to surge

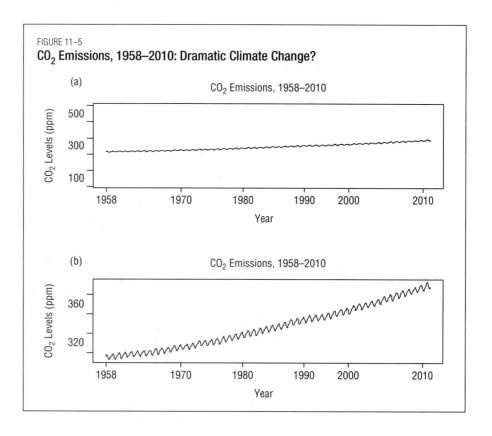

FIGURE 11–5

CO$_2$ Emissions, 1958–2010: Dramatic Climate Change?

(a)   CO$_2$ Emissions, 1958–2010

(b)   CO$_2$ Emissions, 1958–2010

from the bottom and crash into the top of the frame. Neither graph is flat out lying. It's just that the length of the x-axis (compared to the y-scale) and the different limits of the y-scale create differing visual impressions, especially among casual viewers. Although this sort of squished presentation commonly appears in journals, it might be preferable to use a larger plotting region. In other respects, though, the graphs are relatively concise, informative, and clean.

Also, be sure to title charts and graphs and provide clear labels for variables and both axes where appropriate. Do not use abbreviations that mean nothing to a general reader. Also, use annotations (text and symbols) judiciously to highlight features of the data you believe the viewer should study. In other words, make your graphs as self-contained as possible.

Presentation Graphs: Bar Charts and Pie Charts

Numerical information can be presented in many ways, the most common of which are bar charts and pie diagrams. A **bar chart** is a series of bars in which the height of each bar represents the proportion or percentage of observations that are in the category. A **pie chart** is a circular representation of a set of observed values in which the entire circle (or pie) stands for all the observed values and each slice of the pie is the proportion or percentage of the observed values in each category.

Figure 11–6 presents a bar chart and a pie diagram of the party identification data found by the United States Citizen 2006 Study mentioned earlier in connection with partisanship (see table 11–2). This time we plot party identification coded as "Strong Democrat," "Democrat," "Lean Democrat," Independent," "Lean Republican," "Republican," and "Strong Republican." Both chart types tell the same story: Democrat is the modal category, and there are slightly more self-identified Democrats than Republicans, relatively few "leaners" (in this sample), a roughly rectangular distribution (most categories, except the leaning Republicans, differ by not much more than 8 percent). In a presentation, you would include one chart *or* the other.

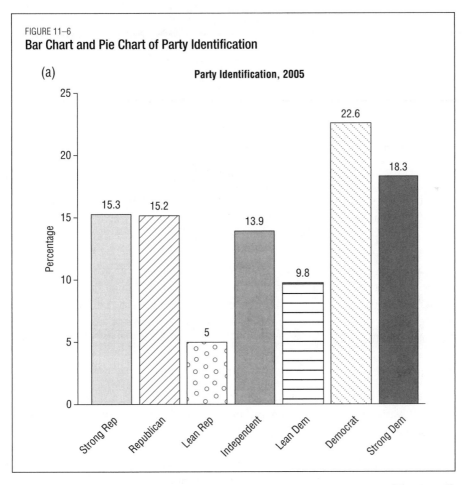

FIGURE 11–6
Bar Chart and Pie Chart of Party Identification

(a)   **Party Identification, 2005**

(Continued)

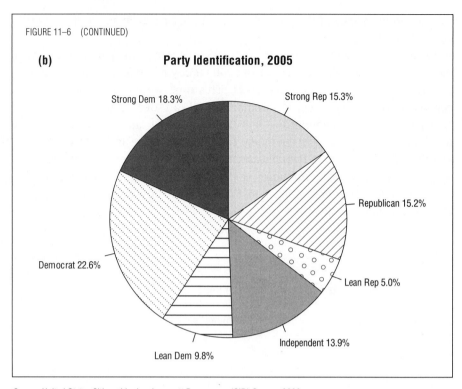

FIGURE 11–6   (CONTINUED)

(b)   **Party Identification, 2005**

Source: United States Citizenship, Involvement, Democracy (CID) Survey, 2006.

Both types of graphs are most useful when the number of categories or values of a variable is relatively small and the number of cases is large. They most commonly display percentages or proportions. Be careful about constructing a bar chart or a pie diagram when you have, say, a dozen or more categories. By the same token, these graphs will not reveal much if you have fewer than ten or fifteen cases. And you have to make sure the graphic elements (bars and slices) are proportional to the data. Unless there is a substantive reason to do otherwise, keep miscellaneous and missing value categories out of the picture.

Exploratory Graphs

The graphs in this section display empirical frequency distribution for different types of variables. They can be presented formal reports but are often used behind the scenes to explore the properties of a batch of numbers in one picture.

DOT CHART.   A dot chart displays *all* of the observed values in a batch of numbers as dots along a horizontal or vertical line that represents the variable. Since it shows the entire data set, the number of observations should be relatively small, for example, fewer than fifty. The great advantage of this plot is that it presents the main features of a distribution. To construct a simple dot chart, draw a horizontal line that stands for the variable. Below the line, print a reasonable number of values of the variable. Finally, using the data scores to position the dots, draw one dot above the line for each observation.

Figure 11–7 shows a simple dot chart of union density rates in the developed countries introduced in table 11–1. It shows at a glance which countries have low and high densities. The United States and France (perhaps surprisingly) have the lowest levels, while only two (Sweden and Finland) are 75 percent or above. The mean and median appear to be between 30 and 50 percent. (Actually the median is 28.2 percent, and the mean is 34.8 percent.) We see clearly that the two "outlying" Scandinavian countries (Sweden and Finland) pull the median down from the mean. This result, in turn, tells us that the distribution is skewed slightly toward the lower end of the scale.

INSPECT GRAPHS FIRST

Participants in debates frequently use graphs to bolster their arguments. In most instances, it's a good idea to scan a graph before reading the author's claims about what it says. The application of data analysis to real-world problems is at least as much a matter of good judgment as it is an exact science. A researcher, who will have a lot invested in demonstrating a point, may see great significance in a result, whereas your independent opinion might be "big deal." You can maintain this independence by first drawing your own conclusions from the visual evidence and then checking them against the writer's assessments. If you don't study the information for yourself, you become a captive, not a critic, of the research.

In view of widespread and widely publicized labor protest in France, we might wonder if we have made a recording error for France (8 percent). Consequently, it is necessary to check the recorded value against the original data. As it happens, the percentage is approximately correct, but according to a European Community publication, "in membership terms the French trade union movement is one of the weakest in Europe with only 8% of employees in unions. . . . But despite low membership and apparent division French trade unions have strong support in elections for employee representatives and are able to mobilise French workers to great effect."[17] The case shows that a graph such as a dot chart can reveal situations that might warrant further investigation, not only to check the data's accuracy but also to explain the apparent anomaly. And it would also be worth pondering why, among all these industrial nations, the United States has such a comparatively anemic labor movement.

The dot chart is actually quite versatile, and depending on available software, it can display combinations of categorical factors against a quantitative dependent variable. (In this simple example, the independent variable is "country," and the category labels are just the country names.) It is common practice, for example, to sort the values of the dependent variable from lowest to highest and display the ordered data. Or one can use symbols and colors to highlight important features.

HISTOGRAMS.   A **histogram** is a type of bar graph in which the height and area of the bars are proportional to the frequencies in each category of a nominal or

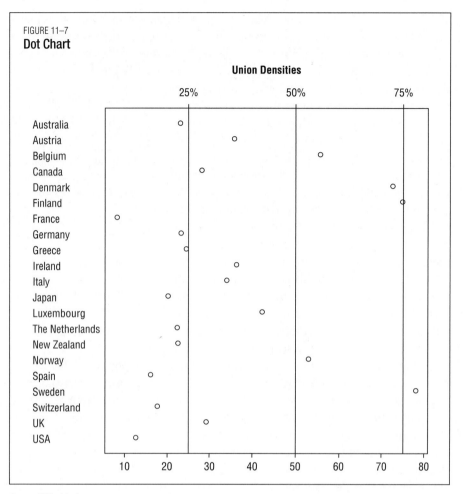

FIGURE 11–7
Dot Chart

Source: Table 11–1.

ordinal variable or of a continuous variable in intervals. If the variable is continuous, such as age or income, construct a histogram by dividing the variable into intervals, or bins, counting the number of cases in each one, and then drawing the bars to reveal the proportion of total cases falling in each bin. If the variable is nominal or ordinal with a relatively few discrete categories, just draw bar sizes so as to reflect the proportion of cases in each class.

A histogram, like other descriptive graphic devices, reduces a data matrix in such a way that you can easily see important features of the variable. For example, you can quickly see modes if there are any, the shape of the distribution (that is, whether or not it is skewed), and even extreme values. It helps to annotate your exploratory graphs with summary statistics so that you have everything required for analysis in one place.

Figure 11–8 shows a histogram of women's ages from the 2004 National Election Study. (Several midpoints of the intervals are shown on the x-axis.) It is important to examine this variable because (1) we want to make sure the sample distribution approximates the population and (2) if discrepancies exist, we can identify and adjust for them. Although a couple of spikes can be observed in this distribution, the overall appearance is very roughly normal or bell shaped. The graph succinctly sums up the more than 600 female respondents in the sample. Notice among other things that the middle of the distribution, as measured by both the mean and the median, is just about 47. The lower end of the scale is truncated because females less than 18 years of age were ineligible for participation in the study. The "location" statistics (Q1, median, and Q3) are instructive: 50 percent of the women are somewhere between 33 and 60 years old, and fully 25 percent are older than 60 years.

If you have to construct a histogram by hand (unlikely in this computer-dominated era), draw a horizontal line and divide it into equal-sized intervals or bins for the variable. The y-axis shows the frequency or proportion of observations in each interval. Simply count the number of units in each group and draw a bar proportionate to its share of the total. Suppose you have a total of 200 cases, of which 20 fall in the first interval. The bar above this interval should show that 20 observations, or 20/200 = 10 percent of the observations, are in it.

Most statistical programs, even elementary ones, easily draw histograms. This capability comes in handy because an investigator may want to try creating

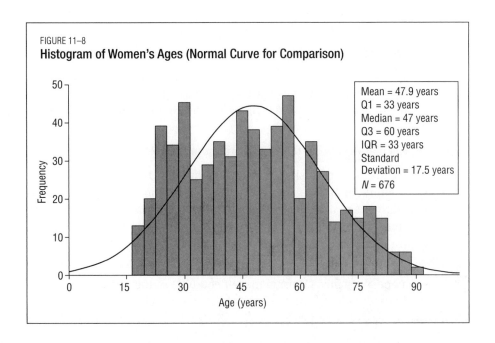

FIGURE 11–8
Histogram of Women's Ages (Normal Curve for Comparison)

Mean = 47.9 years
Q1 = 33 years
Median = 47 years
Q3 = 60 years
IQR = 33 years
Standard Deviation = 17.5 years
N = 676

histograms on a given data set using many different numbers of intervals. Histograms are helpful, as we have indicated, because they summarize both the spread of the values and their average magnitude. They are, however, quite sensitive to the delineations or definitions of the cut points or bins. By *sensitive*, we mean that the shape of the distribution can be affected by the number and the width of the intervals. Some programs do not give the user much control over the intervals, so be cautious when using them.

BOXPLOT.   Perhaps the most useful graphic device for summarizing and exploring interval and ratio level data is the boxplot. It does not display individual points but does explicitly and simultaneously let you see several descriptive statistics: Q1, the median, Q3, and what are called the "lower" and "upper" whiskers, which for now can be thought of as fences beyond which any data points far from the "ordinary" lie. (We discuss these a bit more later.) What is more, it can be annotated in various ways to reveal even more information. Boxplots are sometimes called box-and-whisker plots because they appear to have a whisker at each end of a box.

Constructing a boxplot (even with paper and pencil) is relatively simple:

1. Find the maximum and minimum, the first and third quartiles, the interquartile range (IQR), and the median.

2. Draw a horizontal line to indicate the scale of the variable. Mark off intervals of the variable. Be sure to fully label the scale.

3. Above the line, say about half an inch or so, draw a small vertical line to indicate the median. It should correspond to the appropriate value on the scale.

4. Next, draw short vertical lines of the same size above the scale to indicate Q1 and Q3.

5. Sketch a rectangle with the two quartiles (Q1 and Q3) at the ends. The median will be in the box somewhere. The height of the rectangle does not matter.

6. Next, calculate 1.5 times the interquartile range, IQR.

7. Calculate the "lower whisker." The lower whisker is the *maximum* of either (1) the minimum of the variable *or* (2) 1.5 times the IQR. In symbols, the lower whisker equals the maximum of (minimum[variable], 1.5 × IQR.) (It looks complicated, but in reality you get used to doing this pretty quickly, and most statistical software does the work automatically.) Call this quantity "LW" for short.

8. Draw a line a distance LW from the left end (Q1) of the box.

9. Do the same for the "upper whisker." This time, however, you take the *minimum* of either (1) the maximum of the variable *or* (2) 1.5 times the IQR. More succinctly, the upper whisker is the lesser of the maximum value of the variable or 1.5 × IQR. Call the result "UW."

10. Draw a line from the third quartile (Q3) to the point UW.

11. Place points or symbols to indicate the actual location of extreme values. These should be labeled with the observation name or number.

12. Give the graph a title and properly label the *x*-axis.

This may seem complicated, so let's look at an example, this time using a different variable: "percent of legislative seats held by leftist (e.g., Democrats in America) parties." (See table 11–1; the data are from 2004.) In later chapters, we will invoke this variable as a possible causal factor affecting social-welfare expenditures and equality, as Hacker and Pierson's study suggests. The boxplot

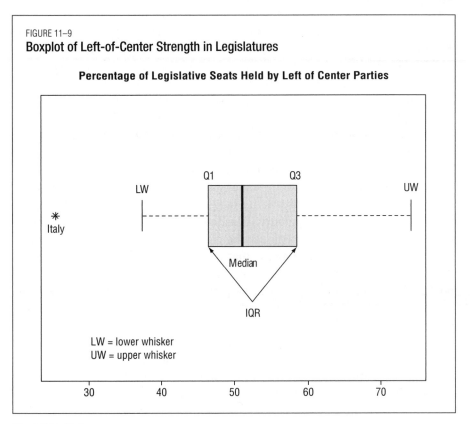

FIGURE 11–9
Boxplot of Left-of-Center Strength in Legislatures

Percentage of Legislative Seats Held by Left of Center Parties

LW = lower whisker
UW = upper whisker

Source: Table 11–1.

in figure 11–9 gives us a bird's-eye view of the distribution. The bottom scale is measured in percentages. The solid line in the middle of the box represents the median, which we can see is slightly more than 50 percent. (The actual number is 52.1 percent.) The lines at the end of the box, marked Q1 and Q3, are the first and third quartiles. (The precise boundaries of the box are 46.5 and 58.5.) They show that in about 75 percent of these nations, left-wing parties hold between roughly 47 and 59 percent of the seats in the legislatures in 2004. The lower and upper whiskers show the location of extreme values. The boxplot has been annotated to show its main features. In most circumstances, you wouldn't bother with these explanatory notes. That is, the notations on the graph ("median," "Q1," "Q3," and so forth) are not usually included because viewers supposedly understand this kind of graph. We include them merely for instructional purposes. We now have a graphical summary of the "left party strength" variable.

TIME SERIES PLOT.   Political scientists frequently work with variables that have been measured or collected at different points in time. In a time series plot, the x-axis marks off time periods or dates, whereas the y-axis represents the variable. These sorts of plots frequently appear in newspapers and magazines and could well be described as a type of presentation graph. However, they are also helpful in exploring trends in data in preparation for explaining or modeling them.

The time series plot in figure 11–10 shows the decline in President George W. Bush's approval ratings from the beginning of his first term in January 2001 to January 2007. The graph contains the results of ninety-six polls, and, to simplify the presentation, we assumed that they were taken during equally spaced intervals.

One of the characteristics of time series data is that they appear to "seesaw" around a trend: there is frequently some or a lot of random variation in addition to the trend itself. You can observe this in figure 11–10, which contains innumerable peaks and valleys. The pattern in this figure seems clear, but with other data the variation may obscure or confuse the picture. Hence, some software optionally applies a "smoothing" process that in a sense averages out the ups and downs. (The math underlying this procedure goes way beyond the scope of this book.) The smoothed data can then be plotted as a line that better reveals the trend, if one exists. In the figure, the downward sloping line amid the swarm of points represents the smoothed data. It demonstrates that, despite a few reversals, the president's approval ratings plunged steadily during his terms of office. (This situation, incidentally, is not unusual in presidential politics, a fact that you could check by obtaining and plotting approval ratings for other presidents.)

Table 11–11 summarizes the kinds of graphs we have discussed and offers a few tips on their proper use.

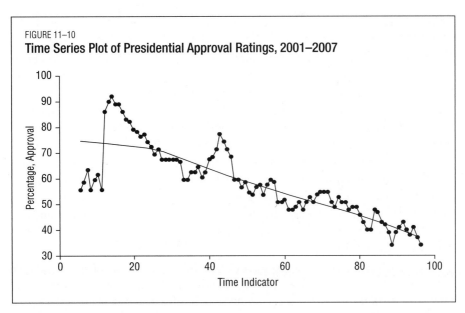

FIGURE 11–10
Time Series Plot of Presidential Approval Ratings, 2001–2007

Source: "Washington Post-ABC News Poll," Washington Post, January 20, 2007; http://www.washingtonpost.com/wp-srv/politics/poll_012007.htm. Accessed October 12, 2007. Reprinted by permission.

Note: Percentage approving or strongly approving President Bush, February 8, 2001–January 2007.

TABLE 11–11
Typical Presentation and Exploratory Graphs

Type of Graph	What Is Displayed	Most Appropriate Level of Measurement	Number of Cases	Comments
Bar chart or pie diagram	Relative frequencies (percentages, proportions)	Categorical (nominal, ordinal)	3–10 categories	Common presentation graphic
Dot chart	Frequencies, distribution shape, outliers	Quantitative (interval, ratio)	$N < 50$ cases	Displays actual data values
Histogram	Distribution shape	Quantitative	$N > 50$ cases	Essential exploratory graph for interval or ratio variables with a large number of cases
Boxplot	Distribution shape, summary statistics, outliers	Quantitative	$N > 50$ cases	Can display several distributions; actual data points, an essential exploratory tool
Time series plot	Trends	Quantitative (percentages, rates)	$10 < N < 100$	Common in presentation and exploratory graphics

Note: Entries are guidelines, not hard-and-fast rules.

WHAT'S NEXT

So far we have described and explored our data sets with various numbers, tables, and graphs. If we have carried out our research competently, we have the beginnings of a quantitative analysis that will eventually lead (we expect) to some answers to our substantive questions (what explains cross-national variation in inequality or welfare spending or why some people become more active in politics than others). If, as in the case of the comparative data of table 11–1, we have a complete set of cases (countries), we can proceed to a more thorough analysis of the hypotheses. On the other hand, think about the survey or poll data we touched on (e.g., the National Election Study). This material comes from a *sample* and thus raises a question: Are the results a reflection or indicator of reality, or do they merely represent chance and would differ considerably if we drew another sample?

Consider this problem. The United States Citizenship, Involvement, Democracy study contains a variable measuring political activity, "the total number of political acts that a respondent has undertaken in the previous 12 months." The mean number is 2.03. An average of two activities per person might suggest that Americans are kind of apathetic. But how reliable is this estimate? After all, it comes from a sample. Maybe in the population as a whole, people are more involved than the sample showed. Or perhaps they are even less involved. Political scientists frame this problem as follows.

Recast the substantive question into a very precise statement of what is supposed to be the state of the real world and what kind of evidence it would take to disconfirm or falsify this supposition. This crucial step is called stating a *statistical* hypothesis. A statistical hypothesis differs from the kinds we've discussed before. These are statements that the world is in a specific state, such as "The real average or mean number of political activities is 2.0." Since the hypothesis has been stated so clearly, we should be able to find a way to disconfirm it.

Because we cannot interview or record the political activities of everyone in all fifty states, we need a sample. The sample, in turn, yields a sample estimate, which we compare to the hypothesized value.

While making the comparison, first ask, "How different are the two numbers really?" Then, ask how likely it is that the observed difference arose purely by chance and another sample might give a totally different estimate. Or is it the case that the discrepancy between observed and hypothesized value is too large to be explained by chance?

Use statistical theory and methods to make a probabilistic statement about the likelihood that the hypothesis is false. This step is called "testing" a statistical hypothesis. Note the adjective *statistical*. Whatever the result of a statistical test, a political or social theory may or may not be cast into doubt.

Therefore, one has to use the statistical results plus substantive expertise, common sense, and knowledge of basic statistical principles to interpret the results more generally.

Fortunately, obtaining this level of familiarity is not especially difficult. The next chapter adopts a gentle pace to explain these steps.

Terms Introduced

Bar chart. A graphic display of the data in a frequency or percentage distribution.

Central tendency. The most frequent, middle, or central value in a frequency distribution.

Cumulative proportion. The total proportion of observations at or below a value in a frequency distribution.

Data matrix. An array of rows and columns that stores the values of a set of variables for all the cases in a data set.

Descriptive statistic. A number that, because of its definition and formula, describes certain characteristics or properties of a batch of numbers.

Dispersion. The distribution of data values around the most frequent, middle, or central value.

Empirical frequency distribution (*f*). The number of observations per value or category of a variable.

Histogram. A type of bar graph in which the height and area of the bars are proportional to the frequencies in each category of a nominal variable or intervals of a continuous variable.

Interquartile range. The middle 50 percent of observations.

Mean. The sum of the values of a variable divided by the number of values.

Median. The category or value above and below which one-half of the observations lie.

Mode. The category with the greatest frequency of observations.

Negatively skewed. A distribution of values in which fewer observations lie to the left of the middle value and those observations are fairly distant from the mean.

Normal distribution. A distribution defined by a mathematical formula and the graph of which has a symmetrical, bell shape; in which the mean, the mode, and the median coincide; and in which a fixed proportion of observations lies between the mean and any distance from the mean measured in terms of the standard deviation.

Pie chart. A circular graphic display of a frequency distribution.

Positively skewed. A distribution of values in which fewer observations lie to the right of the middle value and those observations are fairly distant from the mean.

Range. The distance between the highest and lowest values or the range of categories into which observations fall.

Relative frequency. Percentage or proportion of total number of observations in a frequency distribution that have a particular value.

Resistant measure. A measure of central tendency that is not sensitive to one or a few extreme values in a distribution.

Standard deviation. A measure of dispersion of data points about the mean for interval- and ratio-level data.

Trimmed mean. The mean calculated by excluding a specified proportion of cases from each end of the distribution.

Variance. A measure of dispersion of data points about the mean for interval- and ratio-level data.

Suggested Readings

Abelson, Robert P. *Statistics as Principled Argument.* Hillsdale, N.Y.: Lawrence Erlbaum, 1995.

Agresti, Alan. *An Introduction to Categorical Data Analysis.* New York: Wiley, 1996.

Agresti, Alan, and Barbara Finlay. *Statistical Methods for Social Sciences.* Upper Saddle River, N.J.: Prentice Hall, 1997.

Cleveland, William S. *Visualizing Data.* Summit, N.J.: Hobart Press, 1993.

Jacoby, William. *Statistical Graphics for Univariate and Bivariate Data.* Thousand Oaks, Calif.: Sage, 1997.

Lewis-Beck, Michael. *Data Analysis: An Introduction.* Thousand Oaks, Calif.: Sage, 1995.

Tufte, Edward R. *Beautiful Evidence.* Cheshire, Conn.: Graphics, 2006.

———. *The Visual Display of Quantitative Information.* 2nd ed. Cheshire, Conn.: Graphics, 2001.

Velleman, Paul, and David Hoaglin. *Applications, Basics, and Computing of Exploratory Data Analysis.* Pacific Grove, Calif.: Duxbury Press, 1983.

Notes

1. The Editorial Board, "Record Income Inequality Threatens Democracy," *STLToday.com*, September 30, 2010, http://www.stltoday.com/news/opinion/columns/the-platform/article_94a224e8-cce0–11df-a34d-0017a4a78c22.html.

2. We write "partial" because much of the debate turns on how income and inequality are defined and measured.

3. One metric, the Kelvin scale of temperature, does have an absolute zero, the point at which atoms do not move and heat and energy are absent. The zero points on the other temperature scales are arbitrary.

4. Occasionally, however, it is useful to treat the numbers assigned to the categories of an ordinal or ranking scale as if they were really quantitative.

5. Jacob S. Hacker and Paul Pierson, "Winner-Take-All Politics: Public Policy, Political Organization, and the Precipitous Rise of Top Incomes in the United States," *Politics & Society* 38, no. 2 (2010): 152–204.

6. Unfortunately, it is often impossible to make the distinction in published work, especially in the mass media, because the authors simply do not provide the necessary information. This is why we encourage researchers to report total frequencies along with percentages.

7. US Department of Commerce, Bureau of Economic Analysis, "Per Capita Personal Income by State, 1990 to 2010," released September 2010, http://bber.unm.edu/econ/us-pci.htm.

8. Incidentally, instead of using the means, we could explore deviations from the median. But we will not pursue that topic here.

9. The theoretical or population definition of the variance uses N, the population size, in the denominator instead of $(N - 1)$.

10. Alan Agresti and Barbara Finlay, *Statistical Methods for the Social Sciences* (Upper Saddle River, N.J.: Prentice Hall, 1997), 60.

11. The literature on this topic is vast. For guidelines for presenting accurate and effective visual presentations, Edward Tufte is indispensable. His *The Visual Display of Quantitative Information* (Cheshire, Conn.: Graphics, 1983) is a classic. For an introduction to graphic data exploration, see William Jacoby, *Statistical Graphics for Univariate and Bivariate Data* (Thousand Oaks, Calif.: Sage, 1997).

12. John Tukey, *Exploratory Data Analysis* (New York: Addison-Wesley, 1977).

13. Tufte, The Visual Display of Quantitative Information, 107–21.

14. Kevin J. Keen, *Graphics for Statistics and Data Analysis with R* (Boca Raton, Fla.: CRC Press, 2010), 11. Chapter 1 of this book succinctly describes the "principles of statistical graphics."

15. Cited in Keen, *Graphics for Statistics and Data Analysis with R,* 18.

16. Needless to say, the graphs are only suggestive. The next step is to attempt to "model" the data. This task lies beyond the scope of the book. But we should note that trends are not easy to analyze because they can be the result of real changes caused by some set of factors or of random fluctuations or both. You might be amazed at how a process can drift randomly and yet appear to be a true increase or decrease.

17. Worker-Participation.eu, "Trade Union," http://www.worker-participation.eu/National-Industrial-Relations/Countries/France/Trade-Union/.

STATISTICAL INFERENCE

SOMEONE BENT ON A QUANTITATIVE ANALYSIS of a political phenomenon often has a sample, not a complete population, of observations. Based on just this comparative handful of cases out of potential thousands or millions, the investigator has to decide which results or effects occurred by happenstance and which are real manifestations of reality. More specifically, the first part of *Political Science Research Methods* showed you how to transform substantive questions into testable hypotheses. If these propositions are quantitative and are investigated with a sample, it is necessary to take another step: create and test a statistical hypothesis.

Statistical hypotheses have two important characteristics that we need to clarify right off the bat:

1. They are succinct and precise assertions about population parameters, such as a mean equals a certain value, a pair of proportions do not differ, or a numerical indicator of a relationship between two variables is zero.

2. They are stated in such a manner that data plus statistical theory allow us to reject them with a known degree of confidence that we are not making a mistake.

As we move on, we will clarify and expand on these points. Since we are going to be talking about samples it might be worth briefly reviewing chapter 7, especially the section "Samples and Statistical Inference." The nub of the problem is this: A social scientist believes that some characteristics of an unmeasured population are worth investigating, particularly if they might help resolve substantive controversies. The trouble is that a scholar or a policy analyst cannot study and measure every member or unit in the population. Instead it is necessary to take a sample and make inferences on the basis of sample measurements.

As obvious and mundane as that statement appears, it points to an extremely important fact about both scholarship and practical politics: a great deal of what is known or thought to be known about the world is based on sampling and the inferences drawn from the samples. Therefore, even if you have no intention of becoming an empirical social scientist, as a citizen and consumer of political arguments you should understand the concepts and logic behind statistical inference.

Before continuing, let's recall some statistical vocabulary. These concepts have been discussed in various places earlier in the book, but it will help to review them.

- A *population* refers to any well-defined set of objects such as people, countries, states, organizations, and so on. The term doesn't simply mean the population of the United States or some other geographical area.

- A *sample* is a subset of the objects drawn in some known manner. If the selection is made so that each case is chosen independently of all the others and each has an equal chance of being drawn, then the subset is considered to be a simple random sample, also called a random sample or even just a sample. We use those three labels interchangeably from here on out because when we make statistical inferences, we always assume the data derive from a simple random sample. (Violations of this assumption don't always spell disaster in empirical research. As long as the probabilities of being included in the sample are known, you can adapt most procedures and formulas accordingly. But that discussion goes far beyond the scope of this book.)

- Populations are frequently described by numerical features we call *parameters*. A population parameter may be the proportion of people in the United States who identify as political independents, for instance. A parameter, in short, is a number that describes a specific feature of a population.

- A *sample statistic* or *estimator*, as we call it, is a numerical summary of a sample that corresponds to a population parameter of interest and is used to estimate the population value. An example is the mean income in a sample that can be used to estimate the average income of the population from which the sample derives.

Statistical presentations rely heavily on symbols, and ours is no exception, although we attempt to keep them to a minimum. With that in mind, N stands for the number of cases or observations in the sample. Also, in line with what we have been doing, we let capital letters stand for variables. We may even embellish them to symbolize aspects of these variables as, for example, $\bar{Y}$ (read "Y bar") is the mean or average of the variable Y.

Make sure you understand the difference between sample statistics and population parameters. We usually, but not always, label the latter with Greek letters. Thus, for example, the Greek letter mu (μ) designates the population mean. In many books, Greek letters with a caret or hat ($\wedge$) over them denote sample estimators, but no consensus exists on the best typographical style. Hence, we use a mixture of symbols. The context and the text itself will, we believe, make clear what statistic is under discussion.

In a nutshell, the goal of statistical inference is to make a statement about a parameter, which is unknown, based on a sample statistic, which is available.[1]

TWO KINDS OF INFERENCE

Now we dig a little deeper. Statistical inference means many things to many people, but for us it involves two core activities:

1. *Hypothesis testing:* Many empirical claims can be translated into specific statements—hypotheses—about a population, which can be confirmed or disconfirmed with the aid of probability theory. To take a simple example, the assertion that there is *no* gender gap in American politics can be restated as "Hypothesis: Men's mean liberalism scores equal women's mean liberalism scores."

2. *Point and interval estimation:* The goal here is to estimate unknown population parameters from samples and to surround those estimates with confidence intervals. Confidence intervals suggest the estimate's reliability or precision.

We discuss each activity in turn.

Hypothesis Testing

The problem with depending on samples is that we cannot be sure whether any particular result arises because of a real underlying phenomenon in the population or because of sampling error. As a consequence, we are forced to make inferences. A common inferential tool is hypothesis testing. These tests involve translating propositions into statistical language and using probability to test them. A statistical hypothesis asserts that a population parameter μ equals a particular value such as 10 or 20. This assertion is evaluated in light of a sample statistic. That's really about all there is to it.

Although hypotheses are simple to state, testing them entails a few concepts that can confuse beginners. So we start with an intuitive explanation. Imagine playing a game of chance with someone you don't know very well. Suppose you and your opponent agree to toss a coin. If heads comes up, he wins a dollar; if tails comes up, you win the dollar. Naturally, you assume that the coin is fair, which effectively means the probability or chances of obtaining a head on a single flip is one-half. In addition, the outcome of any one toss is independent of the ones before and after it, and the probability of heads stays constant. The game consists of the opponent tossing the coin ten times. Your main concern is where you stand at the end of the game. If the coin and opponent are fair, you would expect to break even, maybe winning or losing a couple of dollars, but not much more.

The game starts, and to your consternation your opponent gets nine out of ten heads. You are down eight dollars. (Why eight dollars?)[2] But you're no sucker, and you walk away before paying, saying, "You're a cheat!" Your decision leaves your adversary fuming, and he yells back, "The game was fair. You're a chiseler." As far-fetched as the idea sounds, this experience can be construed as a parable of a statistical hypothesis test.

Let's reconstruct the game and its conclusion in statistical terms. In the abstract, a hypothesis test involves several steps, some of which are supposed to be made before any data are collected. The following list is a reconstruction or idealization of the test procedure, and it will make more sense when viewed in context of the cases to follow.

1. Starting with a specific verbal claim or proposition, recast it as a hypothesis about a population parameter: "My opponent is a gentleman. He plays fair, and so the chances of getting a heads are the same as the chances of tails, namely, one-half."

2. More precisely, state a **null hypothesis.** This is a statement that a population parameter equals a specific value. (*Note:* A null hypothesis never sets a range of values.) Letting P stand for probability, you can often state a null hypothesis in this way: H_0: $P = .5$, which reads, "The null hypothesis is that the probability of 'producing' heads is one-half." After all, the very essence of a fair coin is that the probability of heads is one-half. In many research reports, the null hypothesis (H_0) is that something (for example, a mean or a proportion) equals zero.[3] Hence, the word *null*—because zero represents no effect, such as no difference. But keep in mind that a null hypothesis can be an assertion that a population parameter equals any *single* number such as 0.5 or 100.

3. Specify an **alternative hypothesis,** such as "The parameter does *not* equal the number in the null hypothesis [or is greater or less than it is]." In the present case, the alternative hypothesis is that the coin is *not* fair, which when translated into statistical lingo is H_A: $P \neq .5$. This particular alternative simply asserts that the probability of heads is not one-half but something greater or lesser. Such an open-ended hypothesis is called two-sided, which means that a sample result's deviating too far in either direction from the null hypothesis will be cause for rejection. If only outcomes greater (or less) than the null hypothesis matter, a one-sided hypothesis can be formulated: H_A: $P > .5$ or H_A: $P < .5$. So, depending on your alternative hypothesis, if the opponent throws "too many" heads *or* tails, you may challenge the fairness of the game.

4. Identify the sample estimator that corresponds to the parameter in question. In the example at hand, the population parameter—the probability of

heads—must be estimated from the "data," namely, a series of 10 flips of a coin. A logical sample statistic is p, the sample proportion of heads in 10 tries.

5. Determine how this sample statistic is distributed in repeated random samples. That is, specify the sampling distribution of the estimator. Before the game begins (before data are gathered), we want to know the likelihood of various outcomes in 10 tosses of a fair coin. In other words, we want the chances of getting 10 heads in 10 flips ($p = 1.0$), 9 heads ($p = .9$), 8 heads ($p = .8$), and so on down to 0 heads ($p = 0$). A sampling distribution provides this kind of information. Briefly stated, it is a function that shows the probabilities of obtaining possible values for a statistic *if* a null hypothesis is true. We use it to assess the possibility that a particular sample result could have occurred by chance.

6. Make a decision rule based on some criterion of probability or likelihood. It is necessary to determine probable and improbable values of the statistic if the null hypothesis is true. In the social sciences, a result that occurs with a probability of .05 or less (that is, 1 chance in 20) is considered unusual and consequently is grounds for rejecting a null hypothesis. Other thresholds (for example, .01, .001) are common, and you are free to adopt a different decision rule.

7. In light of the decision rule, define a critical region according to the following logic: Assume the null hypothesis is true. Draw a sample from a population and calculate the sample statistic. Under the null hypothesis, only a certain set of outcomes of a random process or sample should arise regularly. If you toss a fair coin 10 times, you expect heads to come up *about* half the time. If you see 10 heads (or 10 tails) in 10 tosses, you will suspect something is amiss. The critical region consists of those outcomes deemed so unlikely to occur *if* the null hypothesis is true that, should one of them actually appear, you have cause to reject the null hypothesis. The demarcation points between probable and improbable results are called critical values. They define areas of "rejection" and "nonrejection." If a result falls at or beyond a critical value, the null hypothesis is rejected in favor of the alternative; otherwise, H_0 is not rejected. In this game, you might think, "If my opponent tosses 9 or more heads *or* 9 or more tails, I'm going to reject the hypothesis that the coin is fair. Those outcomes are just too unlikely to happen if the coin is unbiased." According to this rule, the critical values are 1 and 9 because should one of them (or one even more "extreme," that is, 0 or 10) occur, you will reject the hypothesis of fairness (figure 12–1). The other possible outcomes—2 heads, 3 heads, . . ., 8 heads—are not in the critical region and hence provide no reason for rejection.

8. In theory, these choices are made in advance of any data collection (for example, before the game begins). The probability claims that back your

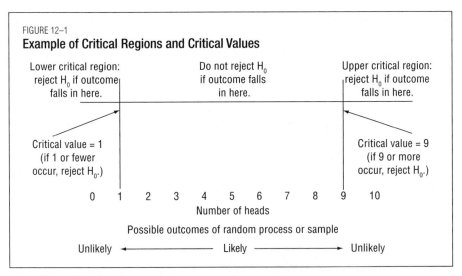

FIGURE 12–1

Example of Critical Regions and Critical Values

Lower critical region: reject H_0 if outcome falls in here.

Do not reject H_0 if outcome falls in here.

Upper critical region: reject H_0 if outcome falls in here.

Critical value = 1 (if 1 or fewer occur, reject H_0.)

Critical value = 9 (if 9 or more occur, reject H_0.)

0 1 2 3 4 5 6 7 8 9 10
Number of heads

Possible outcomes of random process or sample

Unlikely ◄———————— Likely ————————► Unlikely

Note: In this example, there are two critical regions and thus two critical values.

conclusions will be invalid if you first obtain the data, look at them, and *then* make your decision rules.

9. Collect a random sample and calculate the sample estimator. (Start the game.)

10. Calculate the observed test statistic. A test statistic converts the sample result into a number that can be compared with the critical values specified by your decision rule and critical values. Most of the time a computer will do the number crunching for you. What is important is that you understand what the test does and doesn't say.

11. Examine the observed test statistic to see if it falls in the critical region. If it does, reject the null hypothesis. If not, do not reject the hypothesis. In the coin-flipping example, if the final tally is, let's say, 8 heads, you may be suspicious, but you don't reject H_0. However, suppose the outcome is 9 heads, 1 tail. This outcome does lie in the critical region and would lead to a rejection of the null hypotheses.

12. Make a practical or theoretical interpretation of the findings and take appropriate action. At most, the result of a hypothesis test is a bit of information. You have to couple the statistical result with other evidence to know whether you have uncovered something of practical or theoretical value. Recall from chapter 2 that inference is not the same as deductive proof. So the results of a statistical test, no matter how carefully carried out, prove very little by themselves.

Let's now explore aspects of these steps in more detail, beginning with the notion of what inference entails.

TYPES OF ERRORS IN INFERENCE. To paraphrase dictionary definitions, inference refers to reasoning from available information or facts to reach a conclusion. The end product, however, is not guaranteed to be true. It might in fact turn out to be incorrect. This possibility certainly arises in the case of statistical inference, in which values of unknown population characteristics such as means or probabilities are estimated and hypotheses about those characteristics are tested.

This discussion implies that errors can arise in statistical inferences. Take hypothesis testing, the essence of which is making a decision about a null hypothesis. We can make two kinds of mistakes, as illustrated in table 12–1.

The first type of mistake is to reject a true null hypothesis. Going back to the coin-tossing dispute, suppose that (1) the coin really is fair (that is, H_0: $P = .5$ is true), (2) ahead of time you have decided to reject H_0 if 0, 1, 9, or 10 heads occurs (this is your critical region), (3) your opponent obtains 9 heads in 10 flips, and (4) you reject the hypothesis and accuse the person of being unfair. Given that the coin is fair ($P = .5$), you have made a mistake. Statisticians call this mistake a **type I error**: the incorrect or mistaken rejection of a true null hypothesis.

As you might have surmised, the probability of committing a type I error is the "size" of the critical region. It is designated by small Greek letter alpha (α). Thus, α = the probability of a type I error given the decision rule, critical value, and sample size.

Before we explain further, let's look again at table 12–1 to examine another possibility, namely, failing to reject a null hypothesis that is false. Suppose you are a trusting soul and, prior to the game, establish a small critical region: to wit, you will reject H_0 only if the opponent tosses 10 out of 10 heads (that is, you limit the size of your critical region to the single outcome 10). You play the game, and the outcome is 9 heads, which this time does not equal or exceed your critical value. The null hypothesis is *not* rejected. But what if the person really is a cheat? What if, in other words, P does *not* equal .5 but instead equals, say, .9. This time, H_0 should have been discarded. In this case, where the result does not fall in the critical region and you do not reject H_0, you have made a mistake of a different sort: a **type II error,** that is, failing to reject a false null hypothesis.

The probability of committing a type II error (normally designated with the lowercase Greek letter beta, β) depends on how far the true value of the population

---

TABLE 12–1

Types of Inferential Errors

	In the "Real" World, the Null Hypothesis Is . . .	
Decision is to	True	False
Accept H_0	Correct decision	Type II error
Reject H_0	Type I error	Correct decision

parameter is from the hypothesized one. Assuming a fixed α level (the probability of making a type I error) and a fixed sample size, N, suppose the null hypothesis is H_0: P = .5. If the true P is .6, it may be hard to reject the null hypothesis even though it should be rejected, and β will be relatively large. But if P = .9, it will be easier to reject H_0, and β will be relatively small. We cannot go into more detail because the necessary background information would take us too far afield, except to note that for a fixed α, the probability of a type II error (β) decreases as the sample size increases.[4] In a life-or-death showdown, you might be better off having the opponent toss the coin many more times than 10.

Now that we have identified two possible inferential errors, we need to consider how to measure and control the probability of their occurrence.

SAMPLING DISTRIBUTIONS.   On several occasions in this chapter and previous ones, we have mentioned sampling distributions. Yet it is worth explaining the concept once more because it is so important to statistical inference.

Here again is the general idea. Given an indefinitely large number of independent samples each of size N, a sampling distribution is a mathematical function that indicates the probability of different values of the estimator occurring.[5] As another way of understanding the concept, think of a sampling distribution as a picture of the variability of sample results. Grasping this idea takes a bit of imagination because a sampling distribution is a theoretical concept rather than something observed in the course of research.

Imagine that you take an endless number of independent samples of size N from a fixed population that has a mean of μ and a standard deviation σ. Each time, you calculate the sample mean, $\bar{Y}$, and the standard deviation, $\hat{\sigma}$. In the end, you will have literally thousands of $\bar{Y}$s. If you drew a graph of their distribution, much like the histogram shown in figure 11–8, the result would be what is called a sampling distribution. How do we know? Statistical theory demonstrates that the distribution of sample means is normal with these two characteristics: the mean of the sampling distribution is μ (the population mean), and its standard deviation is $\hat{\sigma}/\sqrt{N}$. The standard deviation of a sampling distribution is called the standard error of the mean (on computer-generated reports, it is usually denoted by "s.e." or "se. mean" or some such abbreviation). If the population standard deviation is unknown, as it almost always is, the standard error has to be estimated by using the sample standard deviation, and calculating it as $\hat{\sigma}/\sqrt{N}$.

The expression for the standard error implies that as N gets larger and larger, the standard error decreases in numerical value. The lesson

HOW IT'S DONE

Calculating the Standard Error of the Mean

The standard error is calculated as follows:

$$\hat{\sigma}_{\bar{Y}} = \frac{\hat{\sigma}}{\sqrt{N}},$$

where $\hat{\sigma}$ is the sample standard deviation and N is the sample size.

here is that as N increases, you would expect the sample estimate to get closer and closer to the true value (μ). It might not be exactly on target, but with large samples, the average of the estimates should congregate around this value. The standard error is a measure of the imprecision in the estimators, and we use it again and again.

All of this discussion is theoretical, but you can grasp the gist of it by considering a simple example. Let's return to the coin-tossing contest. There are 10 flips of a supposedly fair coin per game. At the end, the proportion (p) of heads is counted. Suppose you were to compete a billion times more, each time recording the proportion of heads that come up in the 10 tosses. How often would you see 10 out of 10 heads, 9 out of 10 heads, 8 out of 10 heads, and so forth?

Statistics proves that a distribution, called the binomial, answers those questions. The binomial is an equation that takes as input the hypothesized probability of heads (the general term is the *hypothesized probability of a success*) and the number of tosses (more generally, the *number of trials*) and gives the relative frequency or probability of each possible outcome. We do not give the formula here,[6] but table 12–2 shows an example of the binomial distribution as it pertains to 10 tosses of a supposedly fair coin. Interpret the table as follows: In 10 flips of a coin for which the probability of heads is $P = .5$, the chances of getting exactly no heads or $p = 0$ is .001, or 1 in 1,000.[7] Similarly, the likelihood of 1 head in 10 trials is about .01 or 1 in a 100. At the other end of the scale, the probability of getting all heads is also quite remote, .001.

By the way, since this sampling distribution assumes that $P = .5$, you might expect to get on average 5 heads half of the time. The table, though, shows that the probability of obtaining *exactly* 5 heads in 10 flips is roughly .25. As counterintuitive as the probability seems, it is a fact.

The lesson is that a sampling distribution such as the binomial shows you the probabilities of various possible sample outcomes. Therefore, when you observe a particular result, you can decide whether it is unusual and, thus, whether to reject a hypothesis.

The binomial is merely one of many sampling distributions. Different sample estimators require different distributions for inference. In this book, we talk mainly about four others: the normal distribution, the t distribution, the chi-square distribution, and the F distribution. This list may seem intimidating, but all four work pretty much the same way as the binomial.

CRITICAL REGIONS AND CRITICAL VALUES. Refer to table 12–2, which shows a binomial distribution, as you read this section. Remember that a critical region is a set of possible values of a sample result, the actual occurrence of any one of which will cause the null hypothesis to be rejected. When setting a critical

TABLE 12–2

Binomial Sampling Distribution ($N = 10$)

Outcome	Probability of Outcome
0	.001
1	.010
2	.044
3	.117
4	.205
5	.246
6	.205
7	.117
8	.044
9	.010
10	.001

region and the corresponding critical points that define it, we have a couple of choices. For one, we determined the size of the regions by selecting the probability of making a type I error, α. Assume the choice is to reject if either zero or 10 heads appear in the sample of 10 coin tosses. Go back to the table and add up the probabilities of getting either zero or 10 heads in 10 attempts. You should see that it is .001 + .001 = .002. This is the size of the critical region. More generally, the size of a critical region is the total probability of a sample result's landing in it under the null hypothesis. So in the present situation, under the decision rule, the size of the critical region is α = .002.

This probability is quite small, so you might consider it a conservative test. We use the term *conservative* because only two rare events will lead to rejection of the null hypothesis. You might gain a clearer understanding of this point by thinking about changing the decision rule, that is, by changing the size of the critical region. If you were untrusting, you might tolerate almost no deviation from what you thought was a fair game. Hence, the rejection area could be 0, 1, 2, 8, 9, or 10 heads. If any of those numbers comes up, you question the opponent's honesty. Now, what is the size of the critical region or, put differently, what is the probability of making a type I error (falsely accusing the opponent of cheating)? Again, add the probabilities of the outcomes in your rejection region: .001 + .010 + .044 + .044 + .010 + .001 = .110. This means you have about 11 chances out of 100 of incorrectly rejecting the null hypothesis. Is it too big a risk?

Unhappily, there is no right or wrong answer because statistical analysis cannot be divorced from practical or substantive considerations. Instead, it is always necessary to ask, "What are the costs of a mistaken decision?" If rejection of your opponent's integrity leads to gunplay, perhaps you want to be conservative by choosing critical values that minimize a type I error. On the other hand, if there is little or no downside to a false accusation of unfairness—maybe you don't know the person well and can leave the relationship without pain—you might be less rigorous or demanding and choose the .11 level.

Whatever the verdict, it is made with a certain probability of a type I error and this probability is called the level of significance.

LEVELS OF SIGNIFICANCE. All of this background comes to a head in the notion of **statistical significance**, perhaps one of the most used (and abused) terms in empirical analysis. To claim that a result of a hypothesis test is statistically significant is to assert that a (null) hypothesis has been rejected with a specified probability of making a type I error. The three commonest levels of significance in political science are .05, .01, and .001, but you should not be chained to these standards.

Before explaining, let's decode the following statement: "The result is significant at the .05 level." Translated into common usage, the statement means that a researcher has set up a null hypothesis, drawn a sample, calculated a sample statistic or estimator, and found that its particular value would occur by chance at most only 5 percent of the time. Because the outcome is deemed unlikely in the circumstances, the null hypothesis is rejected. This might be a mistake, but the probability of making a mistake is only .05. That's the long and short of "level of significance." Once you get used to the vocabulary, the idea becomes less daunting.

The popular and scholarly literatures contain a variety of ways to phrase this idea. For example, let's assume that you have established a less-than-stringent critical region and will reject the null hypothesis of a fair coin if your adversary gets 8, 9, or 10 heads in 10 chances. In this new circumstance, the critical value is 8 because if the result of the contest is 8 *or more* heads, the null hypothesis is rejected. Furthermore, the size of the critical region is .044 + .010 + .001 = .055 (see table 12–2). One way of expressing this decision rule is to say the "test is being conducted at the .055 level." Furthermore, if you do reject the null hypothesis, it is common to express the finding as "significant at the .055 level." Sometimes, the alpha symbol is used in the declaration, as in "the hypothesis is rejected at α = .055." These statements all mean the same thing: you consider your sample result *so* unlikely given the truth of the null hypothesis (and other assumptions including independent random trials, accurate counting, and so forth) that you are willing to reject the null hypothesis and entertain the alternative, H_A.

Conversely, with the same decision rule, if the opponent gets 7 heads, then the result does not equal or exceed the critical value (8) or lie in the critical region. Now you might write, "not significant at the .055 level" or "failed to reject at α = .055."

More generally, the media often report that something is "statistically significant" or is "not statistically significant" and let the matter drop there. What lies behind such statements is that someone has conducted a statistical test and rejected (or did not reject) the null hypothesis. The sample size and α level almost never get reported, so the claim of (in)significance by itself does not reveal much information. Before we go into more detail about whether or not statistical significance should be considered a big deal, we need to wrap up some loose ends of hypothesis testing.

READING TABLES OF STATISTICAL RESULTS

The text mentions a number of forms for presenting the results of a hypothesis test. In most scholarly presentations, the format is far more succinct. Authors give a table of sample results (e.g., p = .8) and place a typographical symbol (e.g., an asterisk "*") next to them. Then, at the bottom of the table (or somewhere else), a brief explanation will appear, such as "* prob < .05," which means a null hypothesis is rejected at the .05 level. If a null hypothesis is not rejected, you sometimes see "NS" for "not significant" or no accompany mark next to the estimate.

ONE- OR TWO-SIDED TESTS. You may or may not have noticed that in the previous section, we pulled a fast one. In the very first coin-tossing scenario, a decision rule was to reject if the observed number of heads turned out to be 0 or 10. In effect, we were using both ends of the sampling distribution, which meant that a low or high number of heads would count against the null hypothesis. But for the last example, we changed the rejection criterion to consider only 8, 9, or 10 heads as evidence against the hypothesis. This time, just one (the upper) end of the binomial distribution (the high values) constituted the critical region. The former case is called a two-sided test of significance, whereas the latter is called (sensibly enough) a one-sided test.

The difference, of course, is that both small and large values of the sample result count in a two-sided test, whereas in a one-sided test either the low or high results (but not both!) make up the critical region. More precisely, a two-sided test requires two critical values and two critical regions, one for small values and one for large ones. With a one-tailed test, only one critical value and region are relevant.

So which kind of test do you use? The substantive goals of the research ultimately determine the response. One thing is certain: *try to make a test of significance as informative as possible.* If previous research or common sense suggests that a population parameter will be larger than the one in the null hypothesis, use a one-sided test. For example, assume you watch your opponent in action against other players and his coin generally comes up heads. As an alternative to H_0: P = .5, you might establish the alternative hypothesis H_A: P > .5 and thus use the upper tail of the distribution for the critical region, say, 8 or more heads. This is a one-tailed test. That way, if the final result is 7 or fewer (even 0 or 1) heads, you won't reject the null hypothesis. But if you cannot predict in which direction the population parameter might be—that is, if you have no reason to expect large or small P values—you have to use a two-sided test.

COMPARING OBSERVED TEST STATISTICS TO CRITICAL VALUES.   We made the coin-toss example simple in order to explain different aspects of hypothesis testing. One simplification was the sampling distribution, which was based on the probability of success (heads) equaling .5 and 10 trials (tosses). Although we did not supply the formula for the binomial distribution, we produced a table that listed every possible sample outcome and the probability of its occurrence under the null hypothesis. We could thus directly link a realized result (say, 9 heads) to a probability and decide whether or not that result was probable. Imagine that we bumped up the number of trials (tosses) to 1,000. Now, a similar table of the binomial would have to have 1,000 rows, one for each possible result (for example, 0 heads out of 1,000 tries, 1 head, . . . , 999 heads, 1,000 heads). Besides being impracticable, this strategy is unnecessary.

In the applications covered in this book, we use sampling distributions that have tabular summaries. To find critical values, all we have to do is decide on a level of significance and look up the critical values that define the critical region. Suppose, for instance, we want a two-tailed test of some hypothesis at the .01 level. This means we want the total area of the critical region to be .01. To find critical values that create an area that size, we use a tabulation of an appropriate sampling distribution.

In the previous example, the observed test statistic was p, the observed proportion of heads, and we compared it directly to critical values to reach a decision about whether or not to reject the null hypothesis. In most instances, however, it is not possible to compare a sample value directly to a critical value obtained from some distribution. Instead, we need to convert the estimator into an *observed test statistic,* which is a function of the sample data. Many test statistics take the following general form:

$$\text{Observed test statistic} = \frac{(\text{Sample estimate} - \text{Hypothesized populatation parameter})}{\text{Estimated standard error of sample statistic}}.$$

To remind you, a standard error is the standard deviation of a sampling distribution. When needed, we always provide the required formula, and statistical software always computes standard errors along with other hypothesis test information.

The decision to reject or not reject the null hypothesis depends on the comparison between the observed test statistic and the critical value.

- Two-tailed test: reject H_0 if the absolute value of the test statistic is greater than or equal to the critical value.

- One-tailed test: Check to make sure sample estimate is consistent with H_A. (e.g. is in the correct tail). If so, reject H_0 if the absolute value of the test statistic is greater than or equal to the critical value.

Figure 12–2 summarizes the steps in hypothesis testing. It is time now to put these ideas to work on a "real" problem.

Significance Tests of a Mean

Suppose someone tells you the "average American has left the middle of the road and now tends to be somewhat conservative." You, however, are not so sure. You think that the average American is not conservative. This situation could be tested using responses to a 7-point ideology scale with 1 representing "extremely liberal," 4 "moderate" or "neither liberal nor conservative," and 7 "extremely conservative." A 5 on this scale represents a slightly conservative position. So, the above claim can be interpreted as saying that the mean ideology score of voting-age individuals is 5. The null hypothesis is, thus, H_0: $\mu = 5$, where μ is the population mean ideology score. Given the way the problem has been set up, the alternative hypothesis is H_A: $\mu < 5$.

So, the statistic for this test is the sample mean of liberalism-conservatism scores. For this example, let's set $\alpha = .05$ for the level of significance. The next

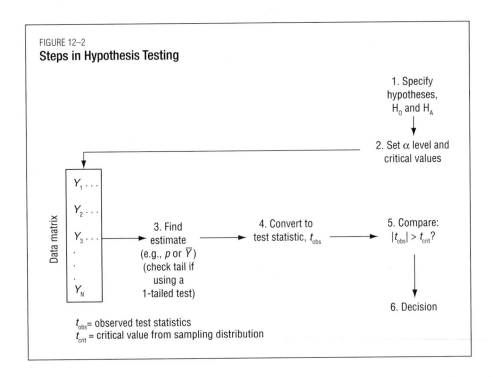

FIGURE 12–2
Steps in Hypothesis Testing

1. Specify
hypotheses,
H_0 and H_A

2. Set α level and
critical values

Data matrix

$Y_1 \cdots$

$Y_2 \cdots$

$Y_3 \cdots$

Y_N

3. Find
estimate
(e.g., p or $\overline{Y}$)
(check tail if
using a
1-tailed test)

4. Convert to
test statistic, t_{obs}

5. Compare:
$|t_{obs}| > t_{crit}$?

6. Decision

t_{obs} = observed test statistics
t_{crit} = critical value from sampling distribution

step is to specify an appropriate sampling distribution and gather the data for the test. When testing a hypothesis about a mean, you will use the sample size to determine the appropriate sampling distribution.

SMALL-SAMPLE TEST OF A MEAN.   If the sample is small—less than or equal to about 25—statistical theory asserts that the appropriate sampling distribution for a test about a mean is the t distribution. A graph of this distribution is a symmetrical (bell-shaped) curve with a single peak. It resembles the normal distribution described in conjunction with the standard deviation but is a bit "fatter" in that it has more area in its tails. The shape of the t distribution depends on the sample size (N) and is thus a "family" of distributions. But as N gets larger, the t distribution approaches the shape of the normal distribution; at $N = 30$ or 40, they are essentially indistinguishable.

To use the t distribution for a small-sample hypothesis test of a mean, follow these steps:

1. Determine the size of the sample to be collected. This number, N, should be less than or equal to 30. Otherwise, use the normal distribution, as explained in the next section.

2. Find the degrees of freedom (*df*) by calculating $N - 1$. The degrees of freedom is for now an abstract concept that we do not explain. But in this situation it is always the sample size minus 1.[8]

3. Choose the level of significance and directionality of the test, a one- or two-tailed test at the α level.

Given these choices, find the critical value(s). Looking at a tabulation of a *t* distribution (see appendix B for an example), go down the rows of the table until you locate the degrees of freedom. Move across the row until you find the column that corresponds to the area of the size of the designated level of significance. The number at the intersection of the degrees of freedom row and area under the curve column is the critical value. Call this number t_{crit}.

At this point, you would now collect the sample data, find the sample mean, and compute the observed test statistic. In keeping with the general formula given above, the observed *t* is found by subtracting the hypothesized mean from the observed mean and dividing by the estimated standard error.

The observed value, labeled t_{obs}, is then compared to the critical value, and a statistical decision is made according to the following rule:

HOW IT'S DONE

Calculating the Observed *t*

The observed *t* is calculated as follows:

$$t_{obs} = \frac{(\bar{Y} - \mu)}{\hat{\sigma}/\sqrt{N}},$$

where $\bar{Y}$ is the sample mean, μ is the hypothesized population mean, $\hat{\sigma}$ is the sample standard deviation, and N is the sample size.

If $|t_{obs}| \geq t_{crit}$, reject H_0; otherwise, do not reject.

In plain English, if the absolute value of the observed test statistic is greater than or equal to the critical value, reject the null hypothesis; if the observed *t* is smaller than the critical value, do not reject it.

Let's test the statistical hypothesis that the mean liberalism-conservatism score for the population is 5. Suppose we use a small sample of 25 observations from

---

TABLE 12–3

Example Setup of a *t*-Test for the Mean

Null hypothesis	H_0: $\mu = 5$
Alternative hypothesis	H_A: $\mu < 5$
Sampling distribution[a]	*t* distribution
Level of significance	$\alpha = .05$
Direction	one-tailed
Critical value (*df* = 25 − 1 = 24)	$t_{crit\,(.05)} = 1.711$

[a] *t* distribution required for small-sample ($N \leq 30$) test of the mean.

the 2004 National Election Study (NES). Table 12–3 outlines the test guidelines. It shows that we are using a one-sided test at the .05 level of significance. As a reminder, this means that if we observe a sample result greater than the critical value, 1.711, we reject the null hypothesis that the population mean liberalism-conservatism score is 5.

Figure 12–3 shows how the critical value was found from the *t* distribution shown in appendix B. (For the sake of brevity, many table entries have been deleted.)

The level of significance, .05, is found by looking in the second column. The degrees of freedom for this problem is calculated as 25 − 1 = 24, so we use the 24th row. The intersection of this row and the third column leads to the critical value, 1.711. Therefore, if the observed test statistic equals or is greater than 1.711, we reject the null hypothesis in favor of the alternative. Otherwise, we do not reject.

To set the test in motion we need to find the sample estimate, in this case, the sample mean. Assume we drew a sample of 25 cases from the 2004 NES data and found the sample mean liberalism-conservatism score to be 4.44, with a standard deviation of 1.23. This observed mean is slightly below the hypothesized average. Thus, our sample estimate is consistent with the alternative hypothesis. To make an obvious point, if the sample mean had been .5 or higher, we would proceed no further as we are conducting a one-tailed test and such an outcome would not allow us to reject the null hypothesis. In this case, we can proceed

FIGURE 12–3
Finding the *t* Value

Level of significance = total size of critical region for one-sided test.
(Probability of type I error (α level)

Degrees of Freedom *(df)*	Alpha Level for One-Tailed Test						
	(.05)	.025	.01	.005	.0025	.001	.005
	Alpha Level for Two-Tailed Test						
	.10	.05	.02	.01	.005	.002	.001
. . .	. . .	. . .	. . .	. . .	. . .	. . .	. . .
21	1.721	2.080	2.518	2.831	3.135	3.527	3.819
22	1.717	2.074	2.508	2.819	3.119	3.505	3.792
23	1.714	2.069	2.500	2.807	3.104	3.485	3.767
(24)	(1.711)	1.064	2.492	2.797	3.091	3.467	3.745
25	1.708	2.060	2.485	2.787	3.078	3.450	3.725
. . .	. . .	. . .	. . .	. . .	. . .	. . .	. . .

df = 25 − 1 = 24   Critical value for α = .05 with 24 *df*.

Source: Excerpt from "Critical Values from *t* Distribution," appendix table B, p. 620.

and the big question is, Does this result give us any grounds for rejecting the hypothesis that the population mean is 5? To find out, we must convert the sample mean to an observed t, which we can compare with the critical value:

$$t_{obs} = \frac{(\bar{Y} - \mu)}{\frac{\hat{\sigma}}{\sqrt{N}}} = \frac{(4.44 - 5)}{\frac{1.23}{\sqrt{25}}} = \frac{-.56}{.246} = -2.28.$$

The denominator is the standard error. It is what we use to scale the difference between the sample mean and the hypothesized mean to fit a tabulated sampling distribution such as the t. Notice that the test statistic can be negative, but we are only interested in its absolute value (that is, disregarding the negative sign). And since $|t_{obs}| = 2.28$ is greater than 1.711 (the critical value), we reject the null hypothesis. The implication is that Americans are not as conservative as hypothesized, and at this point the best estimate of the true mean is 4.44, a very slightly conservative value.

To cement your understanding of this section, use the sample information provided and the decision rule to test the hypothesis that H_0: $\mu = 4$. We have supplied all the necessary information. Then, for further practice, pick a different decision criterion, say, $\alpha = .01$ for the level of significance.[9]

Computer programs now perform most statistical analyses. Although the advantages in saved time and effort are obvious, it is essential to understand what the computer output is telling us. That's why we invest so much time in going over the ideas behind hypothesis testing. But whether as a student or in another capacity, you are likely to be a consumer of software-generated reports. Figure 12–4 illustrates the results of a small-sample t-test cranked out by a popular software package. Once the abbreviations have been explained, the meaning of the numbers should present no problem. The only extra information is the "P" in the last column; it stands for "p-value." Instead of indicating that the result is significant at, say, the .05 level, this program, like most others of its kind, gives the probability of getting a t statistic *at least as large as the one actually observed if the null hypothesis is true*. In the present case, in which the sample mean is 4.44, the evidence is that a population value of 5 is not very likely. More precisely, the probability of a sample mean this far or farther from the hypothesized value is only about .016 or 16 chances in 100.

Finally, given the ubiquity of computers, you might as well take advantage of their services and follow this rule: whenever the p-value is available, report it and not an arbitrary level of significance. Why follow this advice? Compare these two assertions:

1. The result is significant at the .05 level.

2. The p-value is .016.

FIGURE 12–4

Results from a Small-Sample Test of a Mean (Example *t*-Test Results from a Software Package)

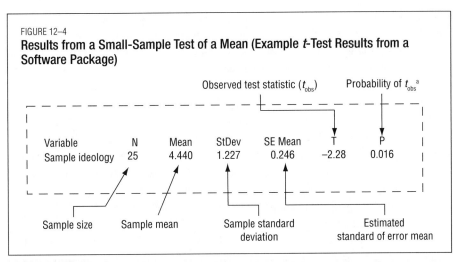

Source: See Table 11-1.

[a] The probability of observing a *t* statistic this large or larger under the null hypothesis that $\mu = 5$.

The first statement tells us only that the probability of the result (or one more extreme) is less than .05. But is it .04? Or .02? The second statement indicates that under the null hypothesis the probability of the result (or one more extreme) is .016; this statement is more specific.

LARGE-SAMPLE TEST OF A MEAN.   In the previous example, we drew a sample of a sample, which gave us a small sample size. This time, let's rely on a larger sample. The *t* distribution, we noted, is a collection of distributions, the shape and areas of which depend on the sample size. But as *N* grows larger, the distributions get closer and closer to the normal distribution. More specifically, an important theorem in statistics states that, given a random sample of 30 or more cases, the distribution of the mean of a variable (*Y*) is approximately a normal distribution with a mean equal to μ (the mean of the population from which the sample was drawn) and a standard deviation of $\hat{\sigma}_{\bar{Y}} = \hat{\sigma}/\sqrt{N}$. As noted previously, $\hat{\sigma}_{\bar{Y}}$ (read "sigma hat sub *Y* bar") represents the standard error of the mean. It measures how much variation (or imprecision) there is in the sample estimator of the mean. For us, the theorem boils down to the fact that we can test large-sample means with a standard normal distribution.

The standard normal distribution is specified by an equation, the graph of which is a unimodal, symmetrical (bell-shaped) curve. This particular distribution has a mean of zero and a standard deviation of 1. (Figure 11–3 displays a graph of the standard normal distribution.) Recall from the previous discussion of the standard deviation and the empirical rule that the areas between the mean and any point along the horizontal axis have been tabulated. (Appendix A contains such a table.) So if you travel up from the mean a certain distance, you can easily find how much of the area under the curve lies beyond that point. Thinking of these areas as probabilities, you can thus establish critical regions and critical values. The values along the horizontal scale, called *z* **scores**, are multiples of the standard deviation. For example, $z = 1.96$ means 1.96 standard deviations above the mean.

Although this is our first application of the standard normal distribution to assess a hypothesis such as $H_0: \mu = 5$, the general logic and methods explained previously apply here. We need only use a different table and compute a slightly different test statistic to be compared with critical values. More concretely, we need to establish null and alternative hypotheses, choose a decision rule, find appropriate critical regions, draw the sample, calculate the observed test statistic, and make a decision.

Figure 12–5 shows you how to use the tabulated distribution to find critical values. Suppose, as we have, that we have a large sample ($N > 30$) and want to test $H_0: \mu = 5$ at the .01 level with a two-tailed test. We need two critical regions,

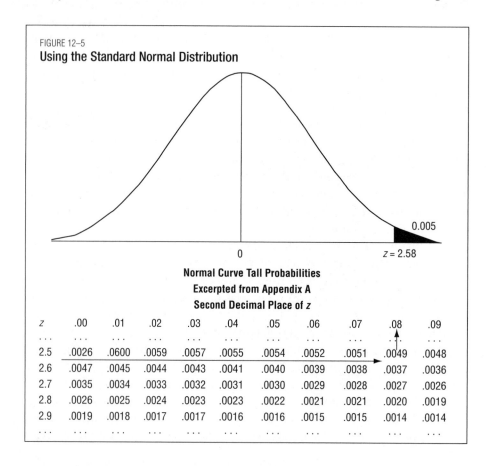

FIGURE 12–5
Using the Standard Normal Distribution

Normal Curve Tail Probabilities
Excerpted from Appendix A
Second Decimal Place of z

z	.00	.01	.02	.03	.04	.05	.06	.07	.08	.09
...	...	...	...	...	...	...	...	...	.	...
2.5	.0026	.0600	.0059	.0057	.0055	.0054	.0052	.0051	.0049	.0048
2.6	.0047	.0045	.0044	.0043	.0041	.0040	.0039	.0038	.0037	.0036
2.7	.0035	.0034	.0033	.0032	.0031	.0030	.0029	.0028	.0027	.0026
2.8	.0026	.0025	.0024	.0023	.0023	.0022	.0021	.0021	.0020	.0019
2.9	.0019	.0018	.0017	.0017	.0016	.0016	.0015	.0015	.0014	.0014
...	...	...	...	...	...	...	...	...	...	...

but their total area must equal .01 to give the desired level of significance. This requirement means that the size of each tail region must be .01/2 = .005. The numbers appearing in the body of the table show the area or proportion of the distribution lying above the z scores defined by the row and column headings. For example, scan down the column under "z" until you come to the row marked "2.5." This corresponds to a z value of 2.5. Now move across the row until you come to the entry ".0049." Then move up the column to the top row under "Second Decimal Place of z." There you should see ".08." The combination of the row label (2.5) and column label (.08) gives 2.58 (just add 2.5 and .08). The area at and above this z score is .0049 or about .005. That's the size of the region we want, so the critical value for the test is 2.58. In probability language, 2.58 creates a critical region for which (assuming H_0 is true) the probability of a sample result's landing in it is .005.

The table gives values only for the upper half of the distribution, but the normal is symmetric, so –2.58 (note the minus sign) defines an area at the lower end equal to about .005. Consequently, if we get an observed test statistic that is greater than or equal to either –2.58 or + 2.58, we will reject the null hypothesis at the .01 level. Once again, .01 can be thought of as the probability of making a type I error (or incorrectly rejecting a true null hypothesis).

To help secure the procedure in your mind, let's find the critical values for (1) a two-tailed test at the .05 level and (2) a one-tailed test at the .002 level.

1. Since we want a two-tailed test, we have to divide .05 in half and look for the z value in the table that marks off the .05/2 = .025 proportion of the distribution. Look in appendix A for ".0250," the size of the critical region. When you have found it, look at the row and column labels (you may want to use a straight edge). The row should be "1.9" and the column ".06" so that the critical value is 1.9 + .06 = 1.96. This value is compared to the observed z to arrive at a decision.

2. We need be concerned with only one end of the distribution. Therefore, search the bottom of the table for ".002." Again, when it has been located, the conjunction of row and column labels should be "2.88." You would compare this number to the observed z to make the decision.

A concrete example may clarify the procedure. Once more let's assess the possibility that Americans are as a whole slightly conservative in their political views; that is, that μ = 5. But to vary the presentation, we conduct the test at the .01 level and use a two-sided test, so the alternative hypothesis is H_A: μ ≠ 5. To carry out the test with the 2004 NES data, we have to find the sample mean ideology score ($\bar{Y}$) and the sample standard deviation ($\hat{\sigma}$). With these numbers in hand, we can calculate the observed test statistic, which in this case is called the

TABLE 12–4
Large-Sample Test of a Mean

Null hypothesis	H_0: $\mu = 5$
Alternative hypothesis	H_A: $\mu \neq 5$
Sampling distribution	Standard normal
Level of significance	$\alpha = .01$
Size of each critical region	.005
Critical value	$z_{crit} = 2.58$
Sample size	920
Sample mean ($\bar{Y}$)	4.27
Estimated population standard deviation ($\hat{\sigma}$)	1.47
Estimated standard error ($\hat{\sigma}_{\bar{Y}}$)	.048
Observed test statistic	$z_{obs} = -15.21$

observed z. Its formula has the same outward appearance as that of the observed t. We just subtract the sample mean from the hypothesized mean and divide by the estimated standard error, which you may recall is $\hat{\sigma}_{\bar{Y}} = \hat{\sigma}/\sqrt{N}$.

Table 12–4 summarizes the test criteria, sample values, and decision for testing the hypothesis that the average population liberalism-conservatism score is 5.

The observed z is calculated as follows:

$$z_{obs} = \frac{(\bar{Y} - \mu)}{\frac{\hat{\sigma}}{\sqrt{N}}} = \frac{(4.27 - 5)}{\frac{1.47}{\sqrt{920}}} = \frac{-.73}{.048} = -15.21.$$

The absolute value of this result greatly exceeds the chosen critical value (2.58), so the null hypothesis would be rejected. As a matter of fact, the observed z exceeds *any* value in the tabulated standard normal. Consequently, we would conclude that the probability of making a type I error is vanishingly small. Figure 12–6 shows how most software represents the probability (as 0.000). This does not mean that there is *no* possibility the null hypothesis is true; it only suggests a very small likelihood that cannot be presented conveniently.

What are we to make of this highly significant result? It could be presented with great fanfare. We might declare that, based on our statistical evidence, Americans can in no way be construed as being even slightly conservative. After all, the findings, which are based on a reputable scholarly survey, are significant at considerably below the .001 level. The next section, however, argues that such a claim may be unwarranted. Besides, the sample mean is 4.27, a value ever so

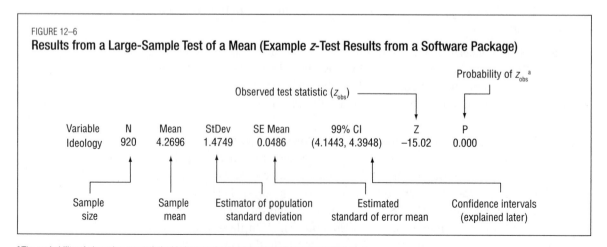

FIGURE 12–6
Results from a Large-Sample Test of a Mean (Example *z*-Test Results from a Software Package)

[a] The probability of observing a *z* statistic this large or larger under the null hypothesis that $\mu = 5$.

slightly in the conservative direction. And how much does a somewhat arbitrary ideology scale reveal about attitudes, and how much substantive or practical importance can we place on scale score differences of 0.5 or even 1.0? The soundest conclusion seems to be that the public is in the middle of the political road or just a bit to the right.

Testing Hypotheses about Proportions

Throughout this book, and indeed throughout political science, we everywhere come across proportions and their first cousins, percentages. So one might ask if one could form a statistical hypothesis about them. It is possible and actually straightforward to do so. Our logic and procedure are exactly the same for a proportion, which can be thought of as a kind of mean. Suppose, for example, we want to estimate the proportion of citizens who donate money to political organizations and causes. After asking our question of a randomly drawn sample, we could record the responses as 0 for "No" and 1 for "Yes." After the surveys have been tallied, we could find the average, which would just be the total of the scores divided by the sample size:

$$\frac{(0+0+0+0+\ldots+1+1+1+1\ldots)}{N} = \frac{Total\ Number\ of\ 1s}{N} = \hat{p}$$

which as we see is just the proportion of respondents coded 1 or the proportion saying yes. We treat $\hat{p}$ as a sample estimator of the population proportion, P. The test that P equals a particular value follows the same procedure used for the mean:

1. State null and alternative hypotheses.

2. Determine the sampling distribution of $\hat{p}$.

3. Decide on a decision rule (α level, test direction, critical value).

4. Obtain the data and calculate the estimator and its sample standard error.

5. Compare this result to the chosen critical value.

6. Decide whether or not to reject the null hypothesis.

Sample distributions of proportions depend on the sample size used in their construction: for small samples (≤ 30), the t distribution is appropriate, while for larger samples, the z or standard normal takes over. Assuming the truth of the null hypothesis, the sampling distribution will have a mean P and a standard error (deviation) $\hat{\sigma}_{\hat{p}}$:

$$\hat{\sigma}_{\hat{p}} = \sqrt{\frac{\hat{p}(1-\hat{p})}{N-1}},$$

where $\hat{p}$ is the sample proportion, $1 - \hat{p} = \hat{q}$ (sometimes referred to as q hat) is the proportion *not* in the category of interest, and N is the sample size. We use this to find the observed test statistic in the usual way:

$$\text{Observed test statistic} = \frac{\text{Sample proportion} - \text{Hypothesized proportion}}{\text{Standard error of proportion}} = \frac{\hat{p} - P}{\hat{\sigma}_{\hat{p}}} = t_{\text{obs}} \text{ or } z_{\text{obs}}.$$

We use data from the United States Citizenship, Involvement, Democracy study to gauge the level of political contributions. The questionnaire asked its participants, "During the last 12 months, have you done any of the following? Donated money to a political organization or group." As suggested earlier, those saying "no" were coded 0; those saying "yes" received scores of 1. The estimated proportion turns out to be 202/995 = 0.203. (There were 995 valid responses out of which 202 had made political donations.) Given this particular sample, $\hat{p} = .2$ is our best estimate of the true level of public giving. Now, suppose we believed on the basis of small pilot surveys and other information that the real proportion is .3. Do we have reason to believe that our sample result differs (meaningfully) from the hypothesized value, $P = .3$?

Since the true value could be larger or smaller than .3, the alternative hypothesis is that P is either less or greater than .3, which leads to a two-tailed test. This "test of a proportion" has the usual layout, with the main difference being the statistic of interest is now a proportion. We calculate the standard error as

$$\hat{\sigma}_{\hat{p}} = \sqrt{\frac{(.20)(1-.2)}{995-1}} = \sqrt{\frac{.16}{994}} = .0128.$$

So the test statistic is

$$z_{\text{obs}} = \frac{(\hat{p} - P)}{\hat{\sigma}_{\hat{p}}} = \frac{(.2030 - .3)}{.0128} \approx -7.578.$$

(We have used more precision for the calculations than are reported in the text.) Table 12–5 summarizes the steps.

A small-sample test of a proportion follows the same procedure but uses the t distribution in place of the standard normal.

STATISTICAL SIGNIFICANCE AND THEORETICAL IMPORTANCE. We declared at the outset of the discussion on inference that people depend on the knowledge generated from samples. An integral part of that knowledge is the concept of statistical significance. Policy makers, politicians, journalists, academics, and laypeople frequently try to prove a point by claiming something to the effect that "studies indicate a statistically significant difference between A and B" or that "there is no statistically significant association between X and Y." Hypothesis testing has become a common feature of both social and scientific discourse.

As empirical political scientists, we are happy that people resort to data and statistics to justify their positions. (Chapter 2 discussed the value of scientific epistemology.) Nevertheless, great confusion exists about what "significance" really entails. We have given you a lot of background about what goes into hypothesis testing and the assertions that something is or is not significant. Keep in mind, though, that these tests rest on specific assumptions and procedures, and making meaningful generalizations from samples depends on how thoroughly these assumptions and procedures are satisfied.

Sometimes when a person says that "findings are statistically significant," the implication is that a possibly earth-shattering discovery has been produced. But several factors affect the decision to reject or not reject a null hypothesis (figure 12–7). The first thing that bears on a result is the objective or real situation in the world. There may indeed be differences between men and women and between developed and developing nations. A generic expression for this idea is that effects exist, and social scientists, like scientists in general, want to discover and measure these effects. But the hard truth is that a significance test does not prove that a meaningful effect has been uncovered. Too many other factors can cloud the interpretation of a hypothesis test.

A major factor is the sample size. All other things being equal, the larger the sample, the easier it is to find significance, that is, to reject a null hypothesis. Why? The sample size does its work through the standard error, the measure of a sample estimator's precision or, loosely speaking, its closeness to the population value it estimates. If N is relatively small, sample estimates of a parameter will jump all over the place. But when N is relatively large, sample estimates tend to be close to one another. This variation shows up in the magnitude of the standard error, which in turn goes into the formulas for observed test statistics.

TABLE 12–5
Large-Sample Test of a Proportion

Null hypothesis	H_0: $P = .3$
Alternative hypothesis	H_A: $P \neq .3$
Sample size	995
Sample statistic	Sample proportion
Sampling distribution	Standard normal (z)
Level of significance	$\alpha = .01$
Size of each critical region	.005
Critical value	$z_{crit} = 2.57$
Sample proportion of "yes"	0.203
Estimated population standard deviation ($\hat{\sigma}$)	.40
Estimated standard error ($\hat{\sigma}_Y$)	.0128
Observed test statistic	$z_{obs} = -7.578$

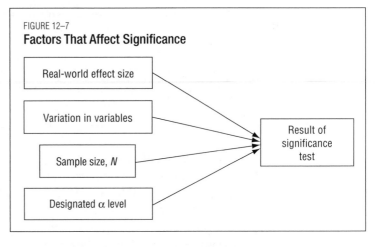

FIGURE 12–7
Factors That Affect Significance

To demonstrate the point, suppose a null hypothesis is H_0: μ = 100. Further, assume the sample mean is $\bar{Y} = 105$ and $\hat{\sigma} = 50$. (We will use the z statistic for illustrative purposes.) Let the sample size increase from 25 to 100 to 400 to 900. The observed z values are as follows:

$$z_{obs1} = \frac{(\bar{Y} - \mu)}{\dfrac{\hat{\sigma}}{\sqrt{N}}} = \frac{(105 - 100)}{\dfrac{50}{\sqrt{25}}} = \frac{5}{\dfrac{50}{5}} = \frac{5}{10} = .5.$$

$$z_{obs2} = \frac{(105 - 100)}{\dfrac{50}{\sqrt{100}}} = \frac{5}{\dfrac{50}{10}} = \frac{5}{5} = 1.0.$$

$$z_{obs3} = \frac{(105 - 100)}{\dfrac{50}{\sqrt{400}}} = \frac{5}{\dfrac{50}{20}} = \frac{5}{2.5} = 2.0.$$

$$z_{obs4} = \frac{(105 - 100)}{\dfrac{50}{\sqrt{900}}} = \frac{5}{\dfrac{50}{30}} = \frac{5}{1.6667} = 3.0.$$

The lesson is that a relatively small departure of a sample mean from the hypothesized mean becomes more and more statistically significant as the sample size increases, when everything else remains the same. This kind of argument backs up an old saying popular among statistics teachers: "You can *always* prove something if you take a large enough sample." A less cynical view is that "statistical significance is not the same thing as substantive significance."

Even more disturbing perhaps is the fact that you can influence whether something is found to be statistically significant by changing the decision rule or level of significance, or by making other decisions.[10] Consequently, when you are confronted with statistical arguments, the key questions should always be "Does the reported effect have theoretical or practical or substantive import, and what research choices went into finding it?"

CONFIDENCE INTERVALS AND CONFIDENCE LEVELS: REPORTING ESTIMATES OF POPULATION PARAMETERS

Recall from chapter 7 that, according to sampling theory, if we take many samples to obtain estimates of a population parameter, our estimates will be normally distributed and cluster around the true value of the population parameter. Sampling distributions tell us the probability that our estimates fall within certain distances of the population parameter. This probability is known as the **confidence level.** The **confidence interval** refers to the range of likely values associated with a given probability or confidence level. Thus, for every confidence level, a particular confidence interval exists.

The general form of the confidence interval is as follows:

Estimated parameter value ± standard error × critical value.

Let's return to the question of ideology in America. Look back at figure 12–6. You will see the sample mean, $\bar{Y} = 4.2696$; the standard deviation $\hat{\sigma} = 1.4749$; and the standard error of the mean, $\hat{\sigma}_{\bar{Y}} = 1.4749/\sqrt{920} = .0486$. Let's start out with a 99 percent confidence level. Since we have a large sample, we use the table of z scores to find the critical value. We need to find the critical value associated with 1 percent ($\alpha = .01$) of the distribution in the tails. The table reports the percentage of estimates likely to fall in one tail. So we need to divide .01 by 2, which is .005. Then we look in appendix A for this value. Looking at figure 12–5, we find .049, which corresponds with a z score of 2.58. This is our critical value. Substituting 2.58 into the above equation, we find that our confidence interval is $4.2696 \pm .0486 \times 2.58$, or between 4.144 and 4.395. Thus we can say that we are 99 percent confident that the actual mean in the population is between the values of 4.144 and 4.395. Figure 12–6 shows the confidence interval for the 99 percent confidence level. If, for instance, you want the 95 percent interval, then α is .05. The z score defining the upper $\alpha/2 = .05/2 = .025$ tail area of the standard normal distribution is 1.96.

As another example, refer to our test of a proportion. Based on a sample of about 1,000, we estimated that about 20 percent of Americans ($\hat{p} = 0.203$) gave money to a political organization in the year before the study. We also investigated the hypothesis that the true or population proportion of donors is .3. Based on that test result, we rejected the null hypothesis (at the .01 level) that P is in fact 0.3. But we never bothered to say what the true value might be. Confidence intervals provide a range of possibilities.

As with the mean, the form of the intervals' calculation is as follows: the estimated proportion plus and minus the critical value times the standard error ($\hat{\sigma}_{\hat{p}}$) In the present case, $\hat{p} = 0.203$, the standard error is $\hat{\sigma}_{\hat{p}} = .013$, and the critical value obtained from the appendix is 2.57. Applying these quantities gives the lower and upper bounds of the 99 percent confidence level:

$$Lower = 0.203 - .013(2.57) \approx .170.$$
$$Upper = 0.203 + .013(2.57) \approx .236.$$

Hence, the interval extends from about .17 (17 percent) to .24 (24 percent). Notice, by the way, that the interval does not contain the hypothesized value, $P = .3$. As we will see, the confidence intervals give us two pieces of information for the price of one: the estimated proportion is about .2, *and* we can reject the notion that it is as high as .3.

The same procedure is followed using the t distribution for small samples. Suppose the mean number of physicians per 100,000 people for a sample of 17 developed nations is 321 with a standard deviation of 72.4. To report the range of values that might include the unknown population mean of the number of physicians with a 95 percent confidence level, we would find the critical value for $\alpha = .05$ for a two-tailed test with 16 degrees of freedom. The critical value is 2.120. To calculate the interval, we must first calculate the standard error for the sample, which is $72.4/\sqrt{17}$ or 17.56. Thus, the 95 percent confidence interval is $321 \pm 17.56 \times 2.120$, or between 283.77 and 385.23. You interpret these two numbers as saying, "We are 95 percent sure that the average number of physicians per 100,000 people of the developed world lies somewhere between roughly 283.77 and 358.23 physicians. We are not 100 percent positive, but the evidence is overwhelmingly in that direction." (As before, let us stress the fine point that our confidence actually lies in the method of obtaining the confidence limits—we believe that 95 times out of 100 the technique will return a pair that covers the true value. We are not 95 percent certain about a particular interval.)

HOW IT'S DONE

The Construction of Confidence Intervals

Calculate the confidence interval for population parameter θ based on sample of size N and level of significance α:

1. Obtain an estimate of θ.

2. Find the standard error of θ, or $\hat{\sigma}_{\hat{\theta}}$.

3. Determine the critical value based on α, the desired level of significance.

4. Multiple the standard error by the critical value.

5. Add and subtract this product from the sample estimate.

Here's a very important and useful tip. You can learn a lot from a confidence interval that you can't get from just one statistic: the sample mean. Confidence intervals, in a sense, suggest a span of plausible values for a parameter. By the same token, they indicate values that are implausible. For example, the interval in the previous example strongly suggests that the mean number of physicians per 100,000 persons of all the developed nations is not, say, 400; it's even less likely to be 600. Why? These values fall outside the interval. Or, to anticipate the next section, suppose someone claims that the mean for these nations is a meager 200. This argument can be considered to be a statistical hypothesis and can be tested. Since the hypothesized value falls beneath the lower confidence interval, you have reason to doubt it.

Now flip around the argument. Suppose another research team estimates the average number of physicians to be 295. Although this value lies considerably below our estimate of 321, is it really inconsistent? Remember, we are pretending that the data come from random samples, so both estimates inevitably have some imprecision. Our confidence interval, however, goes from about 283 to slightly more than 358. Hence, it includes the alternative estimate. On just these grounds, we can't argue that the other estimate is wrong, and neither can they say that ours is wrong.

There is a rule of thumb in statistics as in life: the more certain you need to be, the more information you have to have. In the case of confidence intervals, the higher the assurance you have to have, the wider your interval will be for a given sample size. Table 12–6 illustrates this point. In it we calculate 80 percent, 90 percent, 95 percent, and 99 percent confidence intervals for the mean GNP of the developing nations. The first column gives the different degrees of confidence requested. The last column shows the widths of the resulting intervals; you might loosely interpret these numbers as the "margins of error" in the estimate. Notice that as you go down the table, this error margin increases. Stated differently, if you can be content with a ballpark guess, say 80 percent intervals, then the difference between the upper and lower limits is 4,730.90 – 2,847.10 = 1,883.80, or about $1,884. But if you want to be as close as possible, or 99 percent certain, the interval becomes twice as wide, a whopping $4,076. This example is based on just nineteen cases. To tell the story one more time, the estimator of the population mean is not wrong or invalid—but it is imprecise.

If you want narrower interval widths while still being, say, 95 percent confident, then you have to increase the sample size. Table 12–7 tells you what you get for larger and larger samples. As N increases, the interval widths shrink. If you could somehow take a very large sample of developing nations—you cannot, of course, but just imagine—you could increase the estimator's precision from almost $3,000 to less than $500. The downside is the expense of collecting the extra data.

These statements, incidentally, may remind you of something mentioned earlier: the larger the sample size, the smaller the standard error. This notion comes into play here because confidence intervals are partly a function of the standard error. If the standard error decreases, so does the width of the corresponding confidence interval.

The bottom line is that statistical inference demands a balance between exactitude and sample sizes. If you want or need to be more exact, you need a bigger sample. But whether or not you need to be more or less exact is *not* a matter of statistics; it is essentially a substantive or practical question. Our feeling is that in an exploratory study in which the investigator is entering new territory, precision

TABLE 12–6
Confidence Intervals Calculated for Four Different Confidence Levels

Sample mean = 3,789
$N = 19$

Percent confidence	Confidence Interval		
	Upper limit	Lower limit	Interval width
80	4,730.9	2,847.1	1,883.8
90	5,017.0	2,561.0	2,456.0
95	5,276.9	2,301.1	2,975.9
99	5,827.2	1,750.8	4,076.4

TABLE 12–7

Confidence Intervals for Various Sample Sizes at 95 Percent Level of Confidence

Sample mean = 3,789

Sample size (N)	Upper limit	Lower limit	Interval width
19	5,276.9	2,301.1	2,975.8
50	4,644.7	2,933.3	1,711.3
100	4,393.1	3,184.0	1,210.1
1,000	4,023.8	3,554.2	469.69

may not be as important as making sure the sample is drawn correctly and the measurements are made and recorded carefully and accurately. Only when a lot is riding on the accuracy of estimates will huge sample sizes be essential.

Using Confidence Intervals to Test for Significance

We have stressed that a confidence interval gives you a range of likely values of the population parameter besides the one actually observed. This range turns out to be handy because you can tell at a glance whether or not a hypothesized value falls in that interval.

Let's return to the question of ideology in America. Look back at figure 12–6, which reports the results of a test of the hypothesis that H_0: μ = 5. You should see the sample mean, $\bar{Y} = 4.2696$; the standard deviation $\hat{\sigma}$ = 1.4749; and the standard error of the mean, $\hat{\sigma}_{\bar{Y}}$ = $1.4749/\sqrt{920}$ = .0486. The 99 percent confidence intervals are also reported; they range from about 4.14 to 4.39. This interval does not contain the hypothesized value, so you have reason to reject H_0.

In many instances, confidence intervals provide at least as much information as a statistical hypothesis test. We say "at least as much" because a hypothesis test just indicates whether or not a null hypothesis has been rejected. A confidence interval also supplies a set of possible values for the parameter.

CONCLUSION

In this chapter, we started down the road to understanding statistical inference, including hypothesis testing and estimation. We leave you with some guidelines for improving your research and evaluating that of others.

No single summary statistic does or can say everything important about even a small amount of data. Consequently, you should rely on several summary measures and graphs, not just one.

Look at each variable individually. How much variation is there? What form does its distribution have? Are there any "problem" observations? Does it seem to have an association with other variables? What kinds?

If this sounds like a lot of work, think carefully *before* collecting any data. Just because a variable is in a collection doesn't mean you have to include it in your study. Ask what will be just enough to support or refute a hypothesis.

Most readers probably will not be in a position to analyze much more than six to ten variables. True, computers make number crunching easy. But it is very hard to take in and discuss in substantive terms a mass of tables, graphs, and statistics. You are probably better off studying a small data set thoroughly than analyzing a big one perfunctorily.

Try to understand the principles of statistical inference and think continually about the topic or phenomenon being studied and the practical or real-world meaning of the results. Do not get hung up on technical jargon.

A well-thought-out and carefully investigated hypothesis that the data do not support can be just as informative and important as a statistically significant result. It is not necessary to report only "positive" findings; in fact, it's misleading. Chapter 2 discussed the roles that replication and falsification play in science. If you are studying a claim that lots of people believe and discover that your data do not support it, you will have made a positive contribution to knowledge.

Terms Introduced

Alternative hypothesis. A statement about the value or values of a population parameter. A hypothesis proposed as an alternative to the null hypothesis.

Confidence interval. The range of values into which a population parameter is likely to fall for a given level of confidence.

Confidence level. The degree of belief or probability that an estimated range of values includes or covers the population parameter.

Null hypothesis. A statement that a population parameter equals a single or specific value. Often a statement that the difference between two populations is zero.

Statistical significance. The probability of making a type I error.

Type I error. Error made by rejecting a null hypothesis when it is true.

Type II error. Error made by failing to reject a null hypothesis when it is not true.

z **score.** The number of standard deviations by which a score deviates from the mean score.

Suggested Readings

Abelson, Robert P. *Statistics as Principled Argument.* Hillsdale, N.Y.: Lawrence Erlbaum, 1995.

Agresti, Alan. *An Introduction to Categorical Data Analysis.* New York: Wiley, 1996.

Agresti, Alan, and Barbara Finlay. *Statistical Methods for Social Sciences.* Upper Saddle River, N.J.: Prentice Hall, 1997.

Agresti, Alan, and Christine Franklin. *Statistics: The Art and Science of Learning from Data.* Upper Saddle River, N.J.: Prentice Hall, 2007.

Lewis-Beck, Michael. *Data Analysis: An Introduction.* Thousand Oaks, Calif.: Sage, 1995.

Velleman, Paul, and David Hoaglin. *Applications, Basics, and Computing of Exploratory Data Analysis.* Pacific Grove, Calif.: Duxbury Press, 1983.

Notes

1. We are using the singular *parameter* and *statistic* to save time, but in practice our analysis often involves sets of parameters and statistics, as when we carry out a test to see if two or more population means differ and, if so, how and by how much.

2. From your nine losses, you are down $9, but your one win gets you back $1 for a net loss of $8.

3. Frequently a null hypothesis is known ahead of time to be false. Suppose, for example, that you tested the hypothesis that the mean income of political liberals in America is zero (H_0: $\mu = 0$). This proposition is nonsensical, and testing it would provide no information because any sample result would reject it. Yet surprisingly many studies in effect conduct such tests.

4. The probability of detecting and thus rejecting a false null hypothesis is called the power of the test and equals $1 - \beta$, where β is the probability of a type II error. Power is an extremely important issue in statistics. Many commonly used inferential tests may have relatively low power. Excellent introductions to the topic are Jacob Cohen, *Statistical Power Analysis for the Behavioral Sciences*, 2nd ed. (Hillsdale, N.J.: Erlbaum, 1988); and Jacob Cohen, "A Power Primer," *Psychological Bulletin* 112, no. 1 (1992): 155–59, available at http://www.math.unm.edu/~schrader/biostat/bi02/Spr06/cohen.pdf.

5. Building statistical inference on the idea of repeated samples initially makes students uneasy since it is indeed a difficult concept. Even more interesting is that it bothers many researchers in the field. For a readable introduction to this debate, see Bruce Western, "Bayesian Analysis for Sociologists," *Sociological Methods and Research* 28, no. 1 (1999): 7–11.

6. The probability of getting exactly Y successes in N trials, $\Pr(Y)$, given that the probability of a success is P, is

$$\Pr(Y) = \frac{N!}{Y!(N-Y)!} P^Y (1-P)^{N-Y},$$

where "!" denotes "factorial." The term means obtain the product of all integers less than or equal to a given integer. Example: $3! = 3 \times 2 \times 1 = 6$.

7. Actually it's a little less, .000977, to be a bit more precise, but we have rounded the results.

8. We need degrees of freedom because the t distribution is really a family of distributions, each based on a degree of freedom. When N gets larger and larger, the t distribution becomes approximately normal, and we can use it when $N \geq 30$.

9. We get $t_{obs} = 1.789$, which with 24 degrees of freedom is barely greater than the critical value of 1.711. Hence, we would reject this null hypothesis and perhaps conclude that the public on average sits just barely to the right of center. If you test the hypothesis at the .01 level, you need a different critical value. With 24 degrees of freedom, we see that the critical value at the $\alpha = .01$ level is 2.492. According to this standard, we would *not* reject the null hypothesis. The bottom line here seems to be that the typical American is more or less in the middle of the road when it comes to politics.

10. A point that the figure illustrates but that we do not go into here is that the amount of variation in the data also affects all kinds of statistical results, not just hypothesis tests. It seems logical to regard variation as a property of the world and to acknowledge that all you can do is measure it. Yet, in reality, research design—that is, the choices social scientists consciously or unconsciously make—affects observed variation. An excellent and accessible discussion of this sort of problem is Charles Manski, *Identification Problems in the Social Sciences* (Cambridge, Mass.: Harvard University Press, 1995).

INVESTIGATING RELATIONSHIPS BETWEEN TWO VARIABLES

THE METHODS EXPLAINED IN CHAPTER 11 gave us a way to describe and summarize a batch of numbers—we called it a data matrix, or a rectangular array, in which rows hold data for cases and columns hold values of variables—in order to see important properties of variables one at a time. Tables, descriptive statistics, and graphs, for example, show us what a "typical case" looks like (central tendency), how much variability there is in the observations (dispersion), and what the overall pattern of data looks like (shape of the distribution). Collecting this information is an essential first step, but most of the issues and controversies we have come across in this book involve the associations or connections among two or more variables. In chapter 1, to take one instance, we were interested not just in levels of civic involvement (e.g., voter turnout) per se but rather in what explains the variation in participation. Why are some people active, others passive? Chapter 1 also raised the issue of economic inequality. Chapter 11 introduced a variable, the Gini index, that assigns countries scores on an equality-inequality scale that runs from 0 (total inequality) to 100 (maximum equality). Now we need to tools to explain differences in Gini scores. Such methods provide a way to test hypotheses such as "The stronger working-class political power is, the less inequality there is."

This chapter, then, takes up the investigation of relationships between two variables. Generally speaking, a statistical relationship between two variables exists if the values of the observations for one variable are associated with or connected to the values of the observations for the other. For example, if as people get older they become more politically active, then the values of the dependent variable (voting or not voting) are associated with the values of the independent variable (age). Therefore, the observed values for the two variables are related. Knowing that two variables are related lets us make predictions, because if we know the value of one variable, we can predict (subject to error) the value in the other. But many other questions arise. How "strong" is the relationship? What is its direction or shape? Is it a causal one? Does it change or disappear if other variables are brought into the picture? If the relationship has been detected in a sample, can we conclude that it holds for the population?

As we stressed in chapter 6, the existence of a relationship between independent and dependent variables does not necessarily imply causality. It may or may not be the case that the independent variable "causes" the dependent variable. For example, Stephen D. Ansolabehere, Shanto Iyengar, Adam Simon, and Nicholas Valentino's study of the effects of negative campaign advertising raised the possibility that "attack" ads actually caused a decline in turnout.[1] The problem, we saw there, is that even if a relationship exists between exposure and participation, it might be spurious. The observation of a relationship is really only a launch pad for the search for causal knowledge, a search that is generally long and difficult. Observing the existence, direction, strength, and statistical significance of a

Examine Variables One by One

Before undertaking a bivariate or multivariate analysis, examine each variable one by one. First note the types: Are they categorical (ordinal or nominal), quantitative (interval and ratio scales), or a mixture?

For categorical variables look for the following:

- Order among categories
- The modal (most frequent) category
- The distribution of cases into each category and overall shape of the distribution of cases across the categories (skewed, uni- or bimodal, etc.)
- Nearly empty categories that might be combined
- Categories not of substantive interest that can be dropped (e.g., missing value codes)

For quantitative variables look for the following:

- Missing values
- Summary statistics such as mean, median, range, variance (standard deviation)
- Range of variables; any limits such as 0 to 1 or 0 to 100; whether negative values are possible and what they mean
- Shape of the distribution
- Substantive interpretation of scales: What does a one-unit increase or decrease in the variable mean in practical or theoretical terms?
- Any outliers or extreme values

For all variables think about the following:

- Which variables are (plausibly) dependent?
- Which variables are independent or explanatory?
- Which variables might be causal?

Use this information to pick an appropriate statistical method and interpret the results.

relationship is a fairly objective process in which one can use well-established analytical techniques and sensible conventions to evaluate the evidence. We leave reaching conclusions about causal relationships to the next chapter.

We start with general remarks about two-variable relationships and then describe several methods for measuring and interpreting them and, when samples are involved, assessing their statistical significance. We employ both numerical and graphical techniques for this purpose.

THE BASICS OF IDENTIFYING AND MEASURING RELATIONSHIPS

Determining how the values of one variable are related to the values of another is one of the foundations of empirical social science inquiry. This determination touches on several matters that we consider in the following sections:

- The level of measurement of the variables: Different kinds of measurement necessitate different techniques.

- The "form" of the relationship: One can ask if changes in X move in lockstep with increases (or decreases) of Y or whether there is a more complicated connection.

- The strength of the relationship: It is possible that some levels of X will *always* be associated with certain values of Y; more commonly, though, there is only a tendency for the values to covary, and the weaker the tendency, the less the "strength" of the relationship.

- Numerical summaries of relationships: Social scientists strive to boil down all the different aspects of a relationship to a single number that reveals the type and strength of the association. These numerical summaries, however, depend on how relationships are defined.

- Conditional relationships: The variables X and Y may seem to be related in some fashion, but in there is always the possibility that appearances are deceiving. Chapter 6 discussed "spurious" relationships, which means that once a third factor is brought into the analysis, the perceived relationship between two variables may disappear. (A trivial example is the correlation between stork populations and birth rates that vanishes after population density is considered.) A major activity in statistical analysis is studying how the inclusion of additional variables affects the form and strength of relationships.

Level of Measurement

Just as the level of measurement of a variable was important in the selection of appropriate descriptive statistics, so too is it important in selecting the appropriate

TABLE 13–1
Levels of Measurement and Statistical Procedures: A Summary

Type of Dependent Variable	Type of Independent Variable(s)	Procedure
Quantitative	Dichotomous[*]	Difference of means boxplots
Quantitative	Categorical (nominal or ordinal)	One-way analysis of variance
	More than two	(ANOVA) Boxplots
Categorical (nominal or ordinal)	Categorical (nominal and/or ordinal)	Cross-classification tables analysis: measures of association Log-linear models Association models
Quantitative	Quantitative and/or categorical	Linear regression Scatterplots
Dichotomous[*]	Quantitative and/or Categorical (nominal and/or ordinal)	Logistic regression Effect plots

[*]A dichotomous variable has two categories.

method for investigating relationships between variables. Procedures for measuring relationships are summarized in table 13–1.[2]

Types of Relationships

A relationship between two variables, Y and X, can take one of several forms (use figure 13–1 as a reference.)

■ General association: The values of one variable, Y say, tend to be associated with specific values of the other variable, X. This definition places no restrictions on how the values relate; the only requirement is that knowing the value of one variable helps to know or predict the value of the other. For example, if religion and party identification are associated, then certain members of certain sects should tend to identify with certain political parties. Discovering that a person is Catholic should say something about his or her partisanship. If there is no connection at all between the values of Y and X, we assert that they are *independent* of one another. (Statistical independence gets discussed in a later section of this chapter.)

■ Monotonic correlation:

  o Positive: When high values of one variable are associated with high values of the other and, conversely, low values are associated with low values. On a graph, X-Y values drift upward from left to right (see figure 13–1a.)

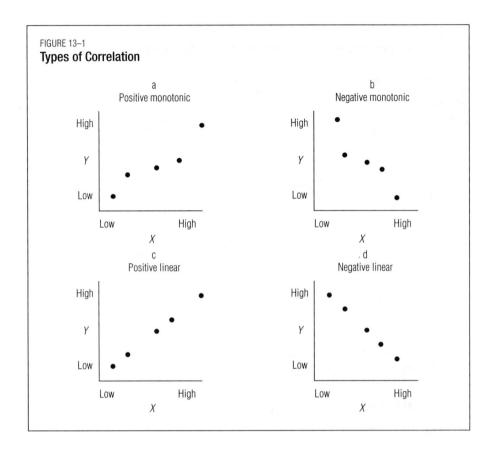

FIGURE 13–1

Types of Correlation

A line drawn through the graph will be curved but *never goes down once it is on its way up.*

- ○ Negative: High values of *Y* are associated with low values of *X*, and—equally—low values of *Y* are associated with high values of *X*. A graph of *Y-X* pairs drifts downward from left to right and never turns back up.

- ■ Linear correlation: A particular type of monotonic relationship in which plotted *Y-X* points fall on (or at least, close to) a straight line. Perhaps you recall from algebra that the equation for a straight line that slopes upward from left to right is $Y = a + bX$, where *a* and *b* are constants. (Figure 13–1c shows an example of a positive linear correlation.) If the plotted values of *Y* and *X* fall on a straight line that slopes downward from left to right, the relation is called a negative correlation. The graph of the equation $Y = c + dX$, where *d* is negative, represents a negative correlation (see figure 13–1d).

Variables may have other forms, as when values of X and Y increase together until some threshold is met and then decline. Since these curvilinear patterns of association are hard to analyze, we set them aside in this book. In any case, the important point is that the first step in data analysis is the examination of plots to determine the approximate form or type of relationship.

Strength of Relationship

Virtually no relationship has a cut-and-dried or "perfect" form. There are, in other words, degrees of association, so it makes sense to talk about their strength. The graph in figure 13–2 provides an intuitive idea of what is meant by "strength." Observe that in the first example (a), the values of X and Y are tied tightly together; you could even imagine a straight line passing through or very near most of the points.

In the second illustration, by contrast, the X-Y points seem spread out, and no simple line or curve would connect them. Yes, there *is* a tendency for the values to be associated—as X increases, so does Y—but the connection is rather weak. There are, as a matter of fact, a couple of exceptions.

We always encourage you to examine graphs of relationships among variables. But as essential as the visual devices are, they almost always need to be supplemented by numerical indices that in a "word" describe the form and strength of relationships. The general term for these statistics is measures of association.

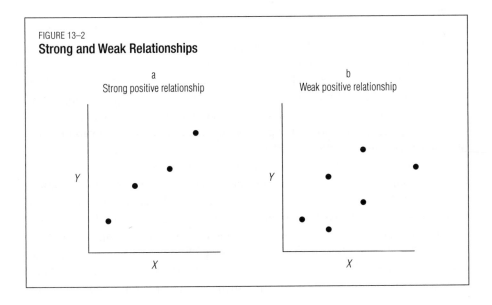

FIGURE 13–2
Strong and Weak Relationships

Numerical and Graphical Procedures

As in the case of a single variable, we can employ three general types of tools to summarize and describe two-variable (or bivariate) relationships:

- Tables (e.g., two-way and multiway cross-classifications or cross-tabulations)
- Graphs (e.g., scatterplots, boxplots)
- Single numbers (e.g., measures of association, correlation coefficients)

The first two were touched on in chapter 11, so we'll come back to them later. For the moment, let's concentrate measures of association and correlation, perhaps the two concepts one most needs to understand in order to evaluate scholarly literature and political discourse.

A **measure of association** describes in a single number or index the kind and strength of relationship between the values of two variables. The remainder of this chapter contains a half dozen or so such indicators, and most social science programs crank them out automatically. Furthermore, to an extent that is probably misguided, these numbers are used to support theoretical or policy claims, much as the results of statistical tests do (see chapter 12). It is imperative, then, to develop a feel for what the numbers do (and do not!) say about possibly complex relationships. In other words, it might be desirable to distill the relationship between economic development and the emergence of democracy down to a single number. Yet in reality there are no such numbers. Instead, an analyst has to know the definitions of measures of association and how they apply in different situations.

Nevertheless, a computer program might report that a coefficient of association between X and Y is .35. What does that mean? More important, what does that number tell you about a research problem?

At the most general level, if there is an association between, say, X and Y, then if one knows a person's particular value on X, it is possible to predict his or her value on Y. Knowing a person's gender, for example, allows a researcher to predict the individual's position on capital punishment, assuming the variables are associated. Of course, if the variables are not related according to the definition, then the coefficient will suggest that no prediction is possible. The coefficients we describe in this chapter (1) assume a particular level of measurement—nominal, ordinal, interval, or ratio—and (2) rest on a specific conception of association. Stated differently, each coefficient measures a specific type of association, and to interpret (translate) its numerical value into everyday language, you have to grasp the kind of association it is measuring. Two variables can be strongly associated according to one coefficient and weakly (or not all) by another. Therefore, whenever we describe a measure such as the correlation coefficient, we need to explain what kind of relationship it is intended to measure.

With these thoughts in mind, we present two broad approaches: measures based on proportional reduction in error and measures based on explained variation. Not every coefficient fits into one or the other of these categories, but many do, and the categories provide a convenient way to interpret the numerical magnitudes of the coefficients.

Here are some important properties of commonly used coefficients.

- Null value: Usually, but not always, zero indicates no association, but there are important exceptions to this rule of thumb.

- Maximum value: Some coefficients do not have a maximum value; they can be in theory very small or very large. Many, however, are bounded: normally their upper and lower limits are 1.0 and –1.0. When a coefficient attains a bound, variables are said to be perfectly associated according to the coefficient's definition.

- Strength of relationship: Subject to lower and upper boundaries, a coefficient's absolute numerical value increases with the strength of the association. So, for example, a coefficient of .6 would indicate a stronger relationship than one of .3. (But the relationship would not necessarily be twice as strong. It all depends on how the statistic is defined.)

- Level of measurement: As indicated above, nominal, ordinal, and quantitative (ratio and interval) variables each require their own type of coefficient. You can, of course, pretend that ordinal scales are numeric and calculate a statistic intended for quantitative data—plenty of people do—but since lots of research has gone into measures of association for different levels of measurement and satisfactory alternatives exist, you should be able to find one or two that will fit your data.

- Symmetry: The numerical magnitudes of some indices depends on which variable, Y or X, is considered independent. These are asymmetric measures. The value of a coefficient calculated with Y as dependent may very well differ from the same indicator using X as the dependent variable. A symmetric measure keeps the same value no matter which variable is treated as dependent or independent.

- Standardized or unstandardized: The measurement scale on which variables are measured affects the numerical value of some measures, whereas others are not so affected.

- Comparison: Coefficients calculated on different variables or different data sets can be compared numerically, but the comparisons are not necessarily of substantive or practical importance.

We now take up specific indicators or methods for assessing or investigating or measuring two-variable relationships.

TABLE SUMMARIES OF CATEGORICAL VARIABLE ASSOCIATIONS

A **cross-tabulation** shows the joint or bivariate relationship between two catego-rized (nominal and/or ordinal) variables. To start the explanation, let's return to a previous topic, political participation. Studies cited in the first chapter have found that several variables—socioeconomic status, political interest, and parti-sanship among them—affect the decision to vote or stay at home. Perhaps, these kinds of variables also explain variation in other forms of participation.

An obvious hypothesis is "The greater one's party loyalty, the greater one's willingness to spend time and money on politics." We can use the partisanship scale developed in chapter 11 to demonstrate how a cross-tabulation can assist in hypothesis testing. Recall that this indicator attempts to tap into the degree or intensity of partisan feelings, not their political direction. Hence, "independents" are coded 1; "leaning Democrats or Republicans" get 2; those who simply iden-tify with either party, but not strongly, receive scores of 3; and, finally, the strong partisans of either party (those who said they "strongly" identified with their party) are 4. This is an ordinal scale that extends from 1, "least partisan," to 4, "most partisan," with (we hope) more or less equally spaced psychological lev-els in between. For the moment, we are not going to take advantage of the quasi-numerical scale and instead treat it as a simple categorical variable.

The data in table 13–2 provide a simple test of the hypothesis that partisan-ship is related to political activity—in this case, donating money to a political organization or cause. "Reading" the table is straightforward. The sample con-sists of 134 nonpartisans, those who state no preference for either party. Simi-larly, there are 141 "weak" partisans who lean toward one or the other party but do not identify with either; 359 moderates (Democrats or Republicans); and 322 highly partisan individuals, those who use the adjective "strong" to describe

TABLE 13–2
Level of Partisanship: Donating Money

Donated money	Nonpartisan (independent)	Weak	Moderate	Strong
No, did not donate	91.8%	71.6%	87.5%	68.0%
	(123)	(101)	(314)	(219)
Yes, donated	8.2%	28.4%	12.5%	32.0%
	(11)	(40)	(45)	(103)
Totals	100%	100%	100%	100%
	(134)	(141)	(359)	(322)

Question: "During the last 12 months, have you done any of the following? Donated money to a political organization or group."

Source: United States Citizenship, Involvement, Democracy Survey, 2006.

Note: Cell entries are percentages and (frequencies).

their party affiliations. (See the row labeled "Totals.") Next consider how the independents are distributed on the dependent variable, donated or not. We see that 123 or about 92 percent ($123/134 \approx .92$) of them report not having contributed in the last year. By the same token, fewer than 9 percent did donate. (Look at the next row down marked "Yes, donated.") Going across the "Yes" row, it is apparent that as partisanship increases, so too does the proportion of respondents who contribute. In fact we find a 24 percentage point difference between strong and nonpartisan: 8 percent versus 32 percent. The behavior of those in the middle partisan categories fits the pattern, except that for some reason the "weak" group gives more than the "moderates" do. (These sorts of anomalies arise all the time in survey research and invite us to think carefully about our measurements and data analysis. Did we make a coding mistake, for instance?) Overall, then, we could conclude that the research hypothesis is tenable.[3] We might even say there is a positive monotonic correlation (with the exception just noted).

The previous example was especially simple because we skipped some nuances such as what to do with missing values. Cross-tabulations are a foundation of data analysis, and grasping what they reveal (and do not reveal) about relationships will stand you in good stead as a student of political science and politics. When you get used to them, displays like these are easy to understand.

HOW IT'S DONE

Building a Cross-Tabulation

Suppose you have a dependent or response variable (Y) with two categories, A and B, and another (X) with three levels, L, M, and H. To construct a cross-tabulation, find each observation's scores on Y and X and the cell in a table that corresponds to these values. Mark the observation's position with a tally mark ("/"). Do the same for all N cases and write the totals in each cell. Add across the rows and then down the columns to obtain the row and column *marginal* totals. Convert to proportions or percentages as needed. Make sure each combination of Y-X scores appears in one and only one cell. Of course, hardly anyone follows this "by-hand" procedure except the smallest polls. The work is done with electronic processing equipment. But this is essentially the logic computers follow. And knowing the underlying process may further clarify the table's meaning.

Categories of variable Y	Categories of variable X			Totals of row tallies
	L	M	H	
A	⧸⧸⧸⧸ //	⧸⧸⧸⧸ ⧸⧸⧸⧸ //	⧸⧸⧸⧸	24
	7	12	5	
B	//	⧸⧸⧸⧸/	⧸⧸⧸⧸ ///	16
	2	6	8	
Totals of column tallies	9	18	13	40

Here is a slightly more complicated example. In the wake of the 2010 midterm elections, there was a lot of talk about growing polarization in American politics. It might be worthwhile to investigate the behavior and attitudes of highly partisan voters vis-á-vis their less engaged neighbors. The Citizenship, Involvement, Democracy (CID) survey used in table 13–3 asked, "Which statement best describes your preference: Politics should be about finding a compromise between people with different views OR Politics should be about sticking to your convictions, and fighting to implement them." Given the purported increase in divisiveness in politics, one wonders how partisans and nonpartisans answered this question.[4] Table 13–3 provides a tentative answer. (The underlying hypothesis might be "The greater the feelings of party loyalty, the less the willingness to compromise one's principles.")

Analyze the table as before by thinking about what the percentages refer to. In the row titled "Finding compromise," we see that about 30 to 40

CATEGORIES WITH "TOO FEW" CASES

A widely accepted rule of thumb asserts that percentages based on twenty or fewer observations are not reliable indicators and should not be reported or should be reported with "warning signs." Suppose, for example, a survey contained only fifteen respondents in a category of the independent variable, such as Asian Americans. If you try to find the percentage of this group that identify as, say, strong Republicans, the resulting estimate will be based on such a small number (15) that many readers and analysts may not have confidence in it. Two possible solutions come to mind. First, use a symbol (for example, †) to indicate "too few cases." Alternatively, the category could be combined with another one to increase the total frequency. The text gives some examples.

TABLE 13–3

Level of Partisanship: Finding Compromise versus Sticking to Your Convictions

Position on compromise	Nonpartisan (independent)	Weak	Moderate	Strong
Finding compromise	40.91% (54)	40.43% (57)	32.50% (117)	31.15% (100)
Lean toward finding compromise	26.52 (35)	35.46 (50)	34.72 (125)	33.64 (108)
Can't say	5.30 (7)	4.96 (7)	5.28 (19)	5.92 (19)
Lean toward sticking to convictions	9.85 (13)	9.22 (13)	11.94 (43)	15.58 (50)
Sticking to convictions	17.42 (23)	9.93 (14)	15.56 (56)	13.71 (44)
Totals	100% (132)	100% (141)	100% (360)	100% (321)

Question: "Politics should be about finding a compromise between people with different views OR Politics should be about sticking to your convictions, and fighting to implement them."

Source: United States Citizenship, Involvement, Democracy Survey, 2006.

Note: Cell entries are percentages and (frequencies).

percent of *all* partisan groups choose to compromise rather than dig in. Now go to the next row, to the category "lean" toward compromising. Again the percentages are not too different. Indeed, combining the first two rows reveals that the overwhelming majority of all partisanship levels supports trying to compromise. The strongest partisans (those in the last column) seem to think as everyone else does.

This table, incidentally, is an example of a "negative" finding. Such *nil* relationships often go unreported because they seem not have discovered anything important. Before burying such findings, however, an analyst should think carefully about two things:

1. Was the hypothesis stated accurately? Do the operational indicators—the questions on the survey—adequately capture the meaning of the concepts? Were the data correctly coded and analyzed? In other words, might some deficiency in the research design or analysis have led to the false rejection of the proposition?

2. As important, if the hypothesis really is viable and correctly tested, is the commonplace belief about growing hostility in American politics exaggerated? Perhaps the "pundit" class—those who are interested and active in politics—divide more sharply on party lines than the public does. If so, polarization may be an "elite," not mass, phenomenon.

Whatever the case, don't give up on a hypothesis because data do not support it. Sure, it may have been a rotten idea to begin with. On the other hand, there may be substantively and methodologically interesting and important reasons for the nonassociation.

When the categories of the independent variable are arrayed across the *top* of the table—that is, they are the column labels—it is essential that the percentages add to 100 down the columns. These are called *column percentages*. You might think of the respondents in each column as a subsample. Look at table 13-4, which compares male and female party affiliation. Suppose we want to know how the males differ among themselves on partisanship. It is necessary to use the column totals as the bases (denominators) for the percentage calculations. Thus, for the 581 men, the percentage identifying as "strong Democrats" (11.9%) *plus* the percentage identifying as "weak Democrats" (15.0%) *plus* the percentage

TABLE 13–4

Cross-tabulation of Gender by Party Identification

Party Identification	Gender	
Response Category	Male	Female
Strong Democrat	11.9% (69)	20.9% (128)
Weak Democrat	15.0% (87)	16.2% (99)
Independent-leaning Democrat	18.6% (108)	16.5% (101)
Independent	10.2% (59)	9.3% (57)
Independent-leaning Republican	14.5% (84)	9.1% (56)
Weak Republican	13.9% (81)	11.1% (68)
Strong Republican	16.0% (93)	17.0% (104)
Total N = 1,194	100.1% (581)	100.1% (613)

Source: 2004 National Election Study.

Note: Totals subject to rounding error.

TABLE 13–5

Row Percentages Are Not the Same as Column Percentages

Party Identification Response Category	Gender		
	Male	Female	Total
Strong Democrat	35.0%	65.0%	100%
	(69)	(128)	(197)
Weak Democrat	46.8%	53.2%	100%
	(87)	(99)	(186)
Independent-leaning Democrat	51.7%	48.3%	100%
	(108)	(101)	(209)
Independent	50.9%	49.1%	100%
	(59)	(57)	(116)
Independent-leaning Republican	60.0%	40.0%	100%
	(84)	(56)	(140)
Weak Republican	54.4%	45.6%	100%
	(81)	(68)	(149)
Strong Republican	47.2%	52.8%	100%
	(93)	(104)	(197)

Source: 2004 National Election Study.

Note: Numbers in parentheses are frequencies.

identify as "leaning Democrat" (18.6%) . . . and so forth down through all the response categories equals 100 percent. The same is true for women: the total of column percentages sums to 100 percent. It is this arrangement of percentages that allows us to compare the relative frequencies of responses between men and women.

Suppose you asked a computer to give you percentages by row totals or obtain *row percentages.* Table 13–5 suggests what might result and the possible difficulties of interpretation. If you were not careful, you might conclude that there was a huge gender difference on "strong Democrat," 35 percent versus 65 percent. But this is not what the numbers mean. There are 197 strong Democrats in the sample (look in the last column), of which 35 percent are men and 65 percent women. It would be reasonable to say that strong Democrats tend to be composed overwhelmingly of women whereas independents are about half male and half female. Still, if in your mind one variable (e.g., party identification) depends on another variable (e.g., gender) and you want to measure the effect of the latter on the former, make sure the percentages are based on the independent variable category totals.

MEASURING STRENGTH OF RELATIONSHIPS IN TABLES

Do the data in table 13–4 support the hypothesis of a "gender gap"? As we just indicated, a careful examination of the column percentages suggests that the hypothesis has only minimal support. Why? Because a scrutiny of the partisanship distributions by gender does not show much difference. Yet it would be desirable to have a more succinct summary, one that would reveal the strength of the relationship between gender and party identification.

The strength of an association refers to how different the observed values of the dependent variable are in the categories of the independent variable. In the case of cross-classified variables, the strongest relationship possible between two variables is one in which the value of the dependent variable for every case in one category of the independent variable differs from that of every case in another category of the independent variable. We might call such a connection a *perfect relationship,* because the dependent variable is perfectly associated with the independent variable; that is, there are no exceptions to the pattern. If the results can be applied to future observations, a perfect relationship between the independent and dependent variables enables a researcher to predict accurately a case's value on the dependent variable given a known value of *X.*

A weak relationship would be one in which the differences in the observed values of the dependent variable for different categories of the independent variable are slight. In fact, the weakest observed relationship is one in which the distribution is identical for all categories of the independent variable—in other words, one in which no relationship appears to exist.

To get a better handle on strong versus weak relationships as measured by a cross-tabulation, consider the hypothetical data in tables 13–6 and 13–7. Assume we want to know if a connection exists between people's region of residency and attitudes about continuing the war in Iraq. (The hypothesis might be that southerners and westerners are more favorable than citizens in other parts of the country.) The frequencies and percentages in table 13–6 show no relationship between the independent and dependent variables. The relative frequencies (that is, percentages) are identical across all categories of the independent variable. Another way of thinking about nil relationships is to consider that knowledge of someone's value on the independent variable does not help predict his or her score on the dependent variable. In table 13–6, 48 percent of the easterners pick

TABLE 13–6

Example of a Nil Relationship between Region and Opinions about Keeping Troops in Iraq

	Region			
Opinion	East	Midwest	South	West
Favor keeping troops in Iraq	48% (101)	48% (103)	48% (145)	48% (97)
Favor bringing troops home	52% (109)	52% (111)	52% (158)	52% (106)
Total *N* = 930	100% (210)	100% (214)	100% (303)	100% (203)

Note: Hypothetical responses to the question, "Do you favor keeping a large number of US troops in Iraq until there is a stable government there OR do you favor bringing most of our troops home in the next year?"

TABLE 13–7

Example of a Perfect Relationship between Region and Opinions about Keeping Troops in Iraq

Opinion	Region			
	East	Midwest	South	West
Favor keeping troops in Iraq	0%	0%	100%	100%
	(0)	(0)	(303)	(203)
Favor bringing troops home	100%	100%	0%	0%
	(210)	(214)	(0)	(0)
Total	100%	100%	100%	100%
N = 930	(210)	(214)	(303)	(203)

Note: Hypothetical responses to the question, "Do you favor keeping a large number of US troops in Iraq until there is a stable government there OR do you favor bringing most of our troops home in the next year?"

"keeping," but so do 48 percent of the westerners, and for that matter, so do 48 percent of the inhabitants of the other regions. The conclusions are that (1) slightly more than half of the respondents in the survey want American troops brought home and (2) that there is *no* difference among the regions on this point. Consequently, the hypothesis that region affects opinions would not be supported by this evidence.

Now look at table 13–7, in which there is a strong—one might say nearly perfect—relationship between region and opinion. Notice, for instance, that 100 percent of the easterners and Midwesterners favor bringing the troops home, whereas 100 percent of the southerners and westerners have the opposite view. Or, stating the situation differently, knowing a person's region of residence lets us predict his or her response.

Most observed contingency tables, like table 13–5, fall between these extremes. That is, there may be a slight (but not nil) relationship, a strong (but not perfect) relationship, or a "moderate" relationship between two variables. Deciding which is the case requires the analyst to examine carefully the relative frequencies and determine if there is a substantively important pattern. When asked, "Is there a relationship between *X* and *Y*?" the answer will usually not be an unequivocal yes or no. Instead, the reply rests on judgment. If you think yes is right, then make the case by describing differences among percentages between categories of the independent variable. If, however, your answer is no, then explain why you think any observed differences are more or less trivial. A little later in the chapter, we present some additional methods and tools that help measure the strength of relationships.

Direction of a Relationship

In addition to assessing the strength of a relationship, one can also examine its "direction." The **direction of a relationship** shows which values of the independent variable are associated with which values of the dependent variable. This is an especially important consideration when the variables are ordinal or have ordered categories such as "high," "medium," and "low" or "strongly agree" to "strongly disagree" or the categories can reasonably be interpreted as having an underlying categorical spectrum, such as "least" to "most" liberal.

Table 13–8 displays the relationship between a scale of political liberalism (call it X) and a measure of opinions about gun control (Y). Both variables have an inherent order. The ideology variable can be thought of as running from lowest to highest liberalism, while responses to the question about firearms might be considered as going from least to most restrictive control.[5]

Take a moment to study the numbers in the table; we guarantee it will pay off in the long run. Start with the "most" liberal category. About two-thirds of respondents in this category (65.4%) are also "most" supportive of restricting gun purchases. That is, there is a tendency for "high" values of ideology to be associated with a "high value" of gun control. Now look in the last column, the "most conservative." You should see that a clear majority of these respondents (63.8%) are in the "least" enthusiastic category of Y, the dependent variable. Here, we have a case of "low" values tending to be linked to "low" values. The middle group (independent thinkers maybe) are more or less split between being for and against making it more difficult for people to buy firearms.

TABLE 13–8
Attitudes toward Gun Control by Liberalism

| | Liberalism Scale (X) | | | |
Make It Easier or Harder to Buy a Gun (Y)	Least conservative	Medium (middle of the road)	Most conservative	Total
Least favorable to guns (make it much harder to buy)	65.4% (72)	43.5% (226)	28.2% (50)	43.2% (348)
Medium (make it harder)	14.5% (16)	17.0% (88)	7.9% (14)	14.6% (118)
Most favorable to guns (make it easier to buy plus "same as now")	20.0% (22)	39.5% (205)	63.8% (113)	42.2% (340)
Total	100% (110)	100% (519)	100% (177)	100% (806)

Source: 2004 National Election Study.

Sometimes it helps to draw a sketch of the results. Consider the top row. The percentages decline as the one moves from "least" (66.5%) to "most" (28.2%) conservative. If you plot these numbers on a simple X-Y graph with equally spaced intervals for the X variable, you can see that the line decreases almost linearly, which can be interpreted simply as "The more conservative a person, the less favorable he or she feels toward stricter gun laws." (The percentage of each category saying "stricter" declines precipitously as one moves from liberals to independents to conservatives.) The upward-sloping line (positive slope) can be interpreted similarly. It shows the percentages in the third row, "make laws easier or keep the same," are plotted on the line that slants upward from left to right, which can be read as "The more conservative (the less liberal) an individual, the less favorable to controls" (see figure 13–3.) In both instances, we see at least monotonic correlation. (If you were to plot the middle row percentages, what would the line look like on the graph?)

This figure is merely a heuristic device for understanding the data's practical meaning. A more formal method, suitable for presentations and papers, is the "stacked bar chart." Generally speaking, it is better to leave bivariate frequency distributions in tabular form so long as they contain the necessary numbers of cases and information about coding decisions. Interestingly, there are actually quite a few sophisticated graphical tools for summarizing cross-tabulations, even those with more than two variables.

We should add that the association between these two variables, although not perfect by the standards set forth earlier, is quite strong. Why this conclusion? As a preview of things to come, try this thought experiment. Suppose you were asked to predict how Americans would respond to a question about making gun control tougher. In the absence of any other information, you might take the "marginal" distribution of responses to the question in table 13–8 as a first approximation. (The marginal totals are in the rightmost column of the table.) Thus, you could reply, "Well most citizens are either for stricter controls (43.2%) or for leaving things as they are (42.2%) with a smattering of people (14.6%) in between." But suppose that you *also* knew people's political leanings. This knowledge would help you improve your predictions, because the least conservative (most liberal) individuals are apt to want stronger controls while conversely the most conservative (least liberal) respondents by and large favor leaving matters as they stand. So knowing a person's ideology enhances your predictive power. This idea—the proportional reduction in error—underlies several measures of association we will discuss shortly.

Assessing both the strength and type (direction) of a relationship in cross-classification tables requires looking at relative frequencies (percentages) cell by

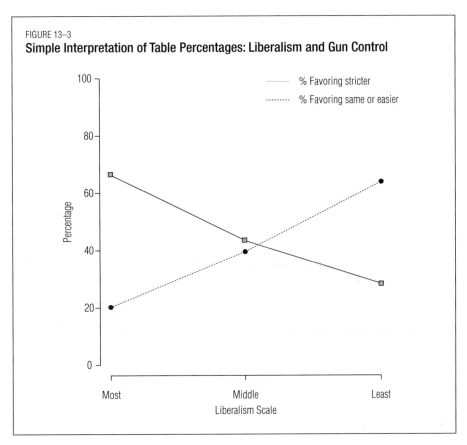

FIGURE 13–3
Simple Interpretation of Table Percentages: Liberalism and Gun Control

———— % Favoring stricter

·········· % Favoring same or easier

Source: Table 13–8.

cell. That is not at all a bad practice. But statisticians have developed sophisticated methods for distilling the frequencies down to single numbers or "modeling" them in such a way that hard-to-see features become apparent. We next introduce a few of the ideas.

Coefficients for Ordinal Variables

So far we have examined the relationship between two categorical variables by inspecting percentages in the categories of the independent variable. To fathom their messages, we have used rough sketches and visual inspection of the tables themselves. However, if the analysis involves many tables or tables that have many cells, another way of summarizing the information is needed. Here we introduce four correlation coefficients for ordinal variables.

TABLE 13–9

TABLE 13–9

Table with Concordant, Discordant, and Tied Pairs

Variable Y	Variable X		
	High	Medium	Low
High	Alex	Dawn	Gus
Medium		Ernesto	Hera
Low	Carl	Fay	Ike
			Jasmine

These statistics, much like the descriptive statistics given in chapter 11, represent the data in a table with a single summary number that measures the strength and direction of an association. (You might want to review the introductory section that lists the properties of these indicators.) Among the most common statistics are **Kendall's tau-*b*, Kendall's tau-*c*, Somers' *D*** (two versions), and **Goodman and Kruskal's gamma**—named after the individuals who developed them. Most computer programs calculate these and other coefficients as well. They are similar, but not identical, in how they summarize the contents of a two-way frequency table.

We will not go into the details of their calculation, partly because software makes them so readily available, but instead concentrate on their numerical meaning. Nevertheless, a bit of background won't hurt. Each coefficient compares *pairs* of cases by determining whether those pairs are "concordant," "discordant," or "tied." These can be slippery concepts, so look at table 13–9. It contains nine individuals (cases).

- A *concordant pair* is a pair in which one individual is *higher* on *both* variables than the other case. Alex and Ernesto are concordant because Alex is higher on *Y* and *X*. Alex is also concordant with Fay, Hera, Ike, and Jasmine. There are other concordant pairs such as Dawn-Hera and Ernesto-Ike.

- A *discordant pair* is one in which one case is *lower* on one of the variables but *higher* on the other. Gus, for example, has a higher score on *Y* but a lower score on *X* compared to either Ernesto, Fay, or Carl. Therefore, these pairs "violate" the expectation that as one variable increases, so does the other.

- A *tied pair* is a pair in which both observations have the same value on one or both variables. There are lots of tied pairs in this table: Alex and Dawn are tied on *Y* (they both are in the "high" category), Alex and Carl are tied on *X* (but not *Y*), and Ike and Jasmine are tied on both *X* and *Y*. (There are several others in the table.).

All of the ordinal coefficients of association (tau-*b*, tau-*c*, Somers' *D*, and gamma) use the probability or number of pairs of different kinds to summarize the relationship in a table. In a population, they measure the probability of a randomly drawn pair of observations being concordant minus the probability of being discordant with respect to *Y* and *X*:

$$\text{Measure} = p_{\text{concordance}} - p_{\text{discordance}},$$

where p means probability. They differ only in whether the probabilities are conditional on the presence or absence of ties. Gamma, for example, is defined as

$$\gamma = p_{C|\text{no ties}} - p_{D|\text{no ties}}.$$

In plain language, it is the probability that a randomly drawn pair will be concordant on Y and X, given that it is not tied, minus the corresponding probability of discordance. An "excess" of concordant pairs over discordant pairs suggests a positive relationship; if discordant pairs are more likely, then the correlation will be negative.

In samples, the basic comparison made is between the number of concordant and discordant pairs. If both types of pairs are equally numerous, the statistic will be zero, indicating no relationship. If concordant pairs are more numerous, the coefficient will be positive; if discordant pairs are outnumber concordant pairs, the statistic will be negative. The degree to which concordant or discordant pairs predominate, or one kind of pair is more frequent than the other, affects the magnitude of the statistic. Hence, if only the main diagonal were filled with observations, all the pairs would be concordant, and the statistic would be +1—a perfect, **positive relationship** (see table 13–10a). If only the minor (opposite) diagonal were filled with observations, all the pairs would be discordant, and the statistic would be –1—a perfect, **negative relationship** (see table 13–10b).

Gamma can attain its maximum (1 or –1) even if not all of the observations are on the main diagonal because it ignores all tied pairs. The others measures (tau-*b*,

TABLE 13–10
Perfect Positive and Negative Relationships

	a. Every Pair Concordant (Perfect Positive Relationship)		
	Variable *X*		
Variable *Y*	High	Medium	Low
High	Arthur		
Medium		Candy	
Low			Ed
	b. Every Pair Discordant (Perfect Negative Relationship)		
	Variable *X*		
Variable *Y*	High	Medium	Low
High			Faith
Medium		Guy	
Low	Hilary		

TABLE 13–11
Perfect Monotonic Relationship

Variable Y	Variable X			
	Very High	Medium High	Medium Low	Very Low
Very High	Abe			
Medium High		Bertha		
Medium Low			Claudio	
Very Low				Darby
Gamma $(\hat{\gamma})$ = 1.0.				

HOW IT'S DONE

Computing Ordinal Measures of Association

Let C = number of concordant pairs,

D = the number of discordant pairs,

T_X = the number of pairs tied only on X,

T_Y = the number of pairs tied only on Y,

T_{XY} = the number of pairs tied on both X and Y, and

m = the minimum of I or J, where I and J are the numbers of categories of Y and X, respectively.

Gamma: $\hat{\gamma} = \dfrac{(C - D)}{(C + D)}$

Tau-b: $\hat{\tau}_b = \dfrac{(C - D)}{\sqrt{(C + D + T_Y)}\sqrt{(C + D + T_X)}}$

Tau-c: $\hat{\tau}_c = \dfrac{(C - D)}{N^2\left[\dfrac{(m - 1)}{2m}\right]}$

Somers' D: $D_{YX} = \dfrac{(C - D)}{C + D + T_Y}$

Somers' D: $D_{XY} = \dfrac{(C - D)}{C + D + T_X}$

for example) "discount the strength of the relationship by the number of ties in the table."[6] Hence, in table 13–11, gamma would be 1.0, whereas the other coefficients would be slightly less.

In a "real" contingency table, there will be many pairs of all sorts, and counting them can be a nuisance. So we leave their computation to the computer. The formulas for these measures have the same form: one quantity divided by another. The numerator is always the number of concordant minus discordant pairs $(C - D)$. The denominators differ, however, in how they handle ties. Gamma ignores tied pairs altogether, whereas the others incorporate them in different ways.[7] To help you understand them, we list a few of their properties.

- Theoretically, all vary between –1 and 1, with 1 indicating a perfect positive (monotonic) correlation and –1 a perfect negative (monotonic) correlation.

- In practice, you will most likely never see one of these coefficients attain these bounds. Indeed, even for strongly related variables, the numerical values will usually be far from 1 or –1. If any of them reaches, say, .4 or .5 in absolute value, there is an association worth investigating.

- Since zero means no correlation, values in the range of −.1 to .1 suggest a weak relationship.

- All will have the same sign.

- The absolute value of gamma ($\hat{\gamma}$) will always be greater than or equal to that of any of the others. The relationships among tau-*b*, tau-*c*, and Somers' *D* are harder to generalize because they are affected differently by the cross-classification's structure (i.e., number of rows and columns).

- Somers' *D* is an "asymmetric" measure because its value depends on which variable is considered dependent. Therefore, there are really two possible versions: one, D_{YX}, has *Y* as the dependent variable, while the other, D_{XY}, treats *X* as dependent.

- By themselves, the measures are not sufficient to assess how and how strongly one variable is related to another. You should ask the software to calculate all the coefficients *and* spend time visually inspecting the relative frequencies in the table.[8]

The last point is worth emphasizing. None of the coefficients is appropriate if the relationship "curves," in the sense that as *X* increases so does *Y* up to a certain point when an increase in *X* is accompanied by a decrease in *Y*. Consider table 13–12, which contains four observations. There is a "perfect" association: you tell me a person's value on *X*, and I will predict exactly her score on *Y*. Yet the number of concordant pairs (3) equals the number of discordant ones (3), so their difference is zero. This difference ($C - D$) appears in the numerator of all the coefficients, so they would all be nil, implying no relationship. But there is an association; it's just not a correlation.

THE IMPORTANCE OF SCRUTINY. A well-known psychologist and statistician, Robert Abelson, titled a book *Statistics as Principled Argument*. His point was that statistics (either the numbers or the methods) do not speak for themselves. It is

TABLE 13–12
Perfect but Not Monotonic Relationship

	Variable *X*			
Variable *Y*	Very High	Medium High	Medium Low	Very Low
Very High				Doris
Medium High	Adele			
Medium Low		Barbara		
Very Low			Connie	

TABLE 13–13

Cross-classification of Y by X with Majority of Cases in One Row

Y	X		
	1	2	Total
A	550	608	1,158
B	20	7	27
C	12	4	16
Total	582	619	1,201

TABLE 13–14

Comparison of Concordant, Discordant, and Tied Pairs

Type of Pair	Number	Proportion
Concordant	6,130	.01
Discordant	19,540	.02
Tied (on Y, on X, and Y and X)	694,930	.96
Total	720,600	.99

Somers' $D_{YX} = -.04$; Tau-$b = -.10$; gamma $= -.52$.

Source: Table 13–13.

Note: Proportions do not add to 1.00 due to rounding error.

always necessary to make a case for point of view. Here is an example.

Gamma is one of the most widely reported ordinal coefficients. Its numerical value is always greater than or equal to the tau and Somers' measures, which raises the possibility that an investigator wanting to find large relationship might think gamma gives "the most association for the money." One difficulty, however, is that its computation only uses concordant and discordant pairs and ignores all tied pairs. Yet in some tables, the tied pairs greatly outnumber the concordant and discordant ones. Look at the simple tabulation cross-classification of Y by X in table 13–13.

By looking carefully at the row totals, you will see that that the vast majority of observations are in the first row. Stated differently, the marginal total is heavily skewed or concentrated in one category. As a consequence, there are not many concordant or discordant pairs compared to ties (see table 13–14).

If someone reported just gamma (–.52), the conclusion might be that a strong Y-X relationship exists. But we see that about 96 percent of the data have been "thrown out" and that the other coefficients show virtually no relationship.

There are a couple important lessons here. First, always pay attention to the shape of each variable's distribution, a point made emphatically in chapter 11. Social science data sets almost always contain skewed marginal totals on at least a few variables. (The data in this example come from a table analyzed later in the chapter.) Second, try not to rely on just one method, such as ordinal coefficients, to make a substantive claim. In other words, don't rely solely on a coefficient, no matter how convenient and interpretable it is.

TWO EXAMPLES.   Hypothetical data help establish the basic ideas of these ordinal measures of association, but when push comes to shove they do not give much practice understanding actual survey results. Therefore we provide two more tables that explore questions touched on earlier. The first is a cross-tabulation of vote in the 2008 presidential election by self-placement on a seven-point liberalism conservatism scale. The voting variable has only two categories (Barack Obama, Democrat, and John McCain, Republican), but any dichotomous variable (a variable with two categories) can be considered ordinal. You can construe the other variable as measuring the "degree" of conservatism. Since there are $7 \times 2 = 14$ relative frequencies to scrutinize, measures of (monotonic) correlation

TABLE 13–15
2008 Presidential Vote by Party

	Political Ideology						
	1 Least conservative	2	3	4 Middle	5	6	7 Most conservative
Obama	98.80% (56)	94.83% (167)	80.58% (118)	61.44% (203)	30.70% (60)	10.89% (34)	10.17% (5)
McCain	1.20 (1)	5.17 (9)	19.42 (28)	38.56 (127)	69.30 (134)	89.11 (275)	89.83 (46)
Totals	100% (57)	100% (176)	100% (146)	100% (330)	100% (194)	100% (309)	100% (51)

Question: "Where would you place yourself on this (liberalism-conservatism) scale, or haven't you thought much about this?"

Chi square = 517.99; 6 df; gamma = 0.818; tau-b = .564; Somers' D_{YX} = .719, $\hat{\lambda}$ = .575.

Source: The American National Election Studies (ANES; www.electionstudies.org). The ANES 2008 Time Series Study, Stanford University and the University of Michigan [producers].

may help us decide how closely ideology predicts candidate preference. This table is interpreted exactly like all the others: compare categories of ideology by the percentage in each who voted for, say, Obama.[9]

You should be able to detect a clear-cut pattern: as conservatism increases across the table, the propensity to vote for McCain also increases. Examine the percentages. (Notice, by the way, that the "Least" and "Most" conservative categories have relatively few cases in them. We might have combined those cases with the adjacent categories to improve the precision or reliability of the cell proportion estimates.)

All the measures are "large" by the standards of categorical data analysis. Gamma is 0.82, which indicates a strong positive correlation. Why positive? Consider the two variables as having an order: ideology runs from low to high conservatism. It is also legitimate to think of vote as having a numerical dimension, with Obama arbitrarily used as a low value and McCain as high. Consequently, moving along the columns from left to right, we see "low" values of conservatism associated with "low" values of vote (Obama) and high conservatism scores associated with "high" on voting (McCain). It may seem strange, but a dichotomous or two-category variable can often be interpreted this way. As we mentioned earlier, these numbers seldom get close to their maximums ($|1.0|$), and values over .4 to .5 indicate a strong correlation. So taken together, these suggest that ideology is highly correlated with voting. Overall, the conclusion is that position on the liberalism-conservatism spectrum predicts voting. Note, however, that since the data show only covariance and not time order or the operation of other variables, we cannot say this is a causal connection.

To wrap up this section, let us look at the second example, which returns to the idea of a gender gap: Are women more liberal than men and, if so, on what issues? Here the response variable is attitudes toward allowing gays to serve in the military. (These data too come from the 2008 ANES study used earlier.) Table 13–16 shows how gender relates to preferences about gays serving in the military. Conventional wisdom might say the women will be somewhat more open to the idea than men will.

The pattern here might be a bit harder to detect. Step back for a second and look at the column totals, as usual. In raw frequencies, there are more women in the sample than men, a common result in public opinion research. Still, there are enough of each gender to make meaningful comparisons. Note first of all that the vast majority of these respondents (55% + 23% = 78%) favor strongly or favor allowing gays to enlist in the military (the last column contains these totals). So right away we sense that there will not be huge sex differences on this issue. But when we look in the body of the table, we see that two-thirds of the women strongly favor lifting the ban on gay military service, and they are joined by 19 percent more who said simply "favor" (rows 4 and 5 of the table). That's 83 percent in favor! By contrast, the corresponding sum among men is 73 percent, a 10 percentage point difference. Note also that fewer than half of the men strongly favor lifting the ban whereas more than a quarter simply favor lifting

TABLE 13–16
Gays in the Military: A Gender Gap?

Gays serve in military?	Male (0)	Female (1)	Totals
(1) Strongly opposed	18.0% (183)	10.8 % (132)	14.1% (315)
(2) Opposed	9.3% (94)	5.8% (71)	7.4% (166)
(3) Favor	28.5% (289)	18.8% (231)	23.2% (520)
(4) Strongly favor	44.2% (449)	64.6% (794)	55.4% (1,244)
Totals	100% (1,015)	100% (1,229)	100% (2,245)

Summary statistics: gamma = .33, tau-b = .19, tau-c = .21, Somers' D = .21, $\hat{\lambda}$ = 0, χ^2 = 94.29 with 3 df.

the ban. So there is a difference in the distribution of men and women in the two categories on the favor side. If you look at the bottom of the table, a similar conclusion emerges. The ordinal coefficients help a bit. They show first a modest to weak correlation—as we saw from the percentages—and second that the relationship is positive.

In this instance, you can think of the variables as having an underlying order. Attitudes toward gays in the military runs from low to high support. Gender can be treated as if it were a numeric variable by letting men be 0 and women 1.[10] So as you move across and down the table, going in effect from low values on X and Y to high values, a slight positive correlation appears. (We place index numbers in parentheses in the table to illustrate the idea, but of course the measures of correlation introduced here do not in any way depend on numerical scale scores.) Beyond saying that there is a limited correlation which the percentages also reveal, these ordinal statistics do not have a common-sense or easily grasped interpretation. The situation improves slightly with the next coefficient.

A Coefficient for Nominal Data

When one or both of the variables in a cross-tabulation are nominal, ordinal coefficients are not appropriate because the identification of concordant and discordant pairs requires that the variables possess an underlying ordering (one value being higher than another). For these tables, different measures of association are employed. Some of the most useful rest on a *proportional-reduction-in-error* interpretation of association. The basic idea is this: you are asked to *predict* a randomly selected person's category or response level on a variable following two rules. Rule 1 requires you to make the guess in the absence of any other prior information (e.g., predict the individual's position on gun control). The other rule lets you know the person's score on a second variable, which you now take into account in making the prediction (e.g., you now know the individual's gender). Since you are guessing in both situations, you can expect to make some errors, but *if* the two variables are associated, then the using the second rule should lead to fewer errors than following the first.

How many fewer errors depends on how closely the variables are related. If there is no association at all, the expected number of errors should be roughly the same, and the reduction will be minimal. If, on the other hand, the variables are perfectly connected, in the sense that there is a one-to-one connection between the categories of the two variables, you would expect no errors by following rule 2. A "PRE measure" gives the **proportionate reduction in errors**:

$$PRE = \frac{(E_1 - E_2)}{E_1},$$

where E_1 is the number of errors made using rule 1 and E_2 is the number made under rule 2.

Suppose for a particular group of subjects the number of rule 1 errors (E_1) predicting variable scores on Y is 500. Now, think about these possibilities.

1. X has no association with Y. Then even using the individuals' X scores, the expected number of errors will still be 500, and the proportional reduction in errors will be $(500 - 500)/500 = 0$. This is the lower limit of a proportion, and it indicates *no* association.

2. Suppose the categories of X are uniquely associated with those of Y so that if you know X, you can predict Y exactly. The expected number of errors under rule 2 (E_2) will be zero. Consequently, $PRE = (500 - 0)/500 = 1.0$, the upper boundary for the measure. This means *perfect* association (according to this definition). In the third and last situation

3. Assume that Y and X have a moderate relationship. The expected number of errors following rule 2 might be, say, 200. Now we have

$$PRE = \frac{(500 - 200)}{500} = \frac{300}{500} = .6.$$

There is then a 60 percent reduction in prediction errors from knowing the value of X, a result that suggests a modest but not complete association.

LAMBDA.   Many coefficients of association (e.g., gamma) can be defined in such a way as to lead to a *PRE* interpretation. We describe only one, however: **Goodman and Kruskal's lambda**. Lambda is a proportional-reduction-in-error coefficient. As we did earlier, imagine predicting a person's score on a variable in the absence of any other information ("rule 1"). What exactly would be the best strategy? If you did not know anything, you might ask what proportion of the population had characteristic A, what proportion characteristic B, and so forth for all of the categories of the dependent variable of interest. Let's say B was the most common (modal) category. Then, without other information, guessing that each individual was a B would produce fewer prediction errors than if you picked any other category. Why? Well, suppose there were 10 As, 60 Bs, and 30 Cs in a population of 100. Select a person at random and guess his or her category. If you picked, say, A, you would on average be wrong $60 + 30 = 90$ times out of 100 guesses (90% incorrect). If, on the other hand, you chose C, you would be mistaken $10 + 60 = 70$ times (70% errors). Finally, if you guessed the modal (most frequent) category, B, your errors would be on average $10 + 30 = 40$. By choosing B (the mode), you do indeed make some incorrect predictions but many fewer than if you picked any other category. In sum, rule 1 states that, lacking any other data, your best long-run strategy for predicting an individual's class is to choose the modal one, the one with the most observations.

Now suppose you knew each case's score or value on a second variable, X. Say you realized a person fell in (or had property) M of the second variable. Rule 2 directs you to look only at the members of M and find the modal category. Assume that category C is most common among those who are M's. Given that the observation is an M, guessing C would (over the long haul) lead to the fewest mistakes. So rule 2 simply involves using rule 1 *within* each level of X.

The key to understanding lambda, a proportional-reduction-in-error type measure of association, lies in this fact: *if Y and X are associated, then the probability of making an error of prediction using rule 1 will be greater than the probability of making an error with rule 2.* How much greater? The measure of association, lambda (λ), gives the proportional reduction in error:

$$\lambda = \frac{\left(p_{\text{error 1}} - p_{\text{error 2}}\right)}{p_{\text{error 1}}},$$

where $p_{\text{error 1}}$ is the probability of making a prediction error with the first rule and similarly $p_{\text{error 2}}$ is the likelihood of an error knowing X. If the values of X are systematically connected to those of Y, the errors under the second rule will be less probable than those made under rule 1. In this case, lambda will be greater than zero. In fact, if *no* prediction errors result from rule 2, the probability p_{error2} will be zero, and

$$\lambda = \frac{\left(p_{\text{error 1}} - 0\right)}{p_{\text{error 1}}} = \frac{p_{\text{error 1}}}{p_{\text{error 1}}} = 1.0.$$

But of course if X and Y are unrelated, then knowing the value of X will tell you nothing about Y, and in the long run the probability of errors under both rules will be the same. So $p_{\text{error 1}} = p_{\text{error 2}}$ and

$$\lambda = \frac{\left(p_{\text{error 1}} - p_{\text{error 2}}\right)}{p_{\text{error 1}}} = \frac{(0)}{p_{\text{error 1}}} = 0.$$

The upshot is that lambda lies between 0 (no association) and 1.0 ("perfect" association as defined by the prediction rules.) A value of .5 would indicate a 50 percent reduction in errors, which in most situations would be quite a drop and hence suggest a strong relationship. A value of, say, .10—a 10 percent reduction—might signal a weak to nonexistent association. Note that correlation is not an issue here. If there is an X-Y link of whatever kind, lambda should pick it up. Yet, also remember that lambda does *not* take into account the ordering of the categories.

Again, we emphasize the importance of looking at the whole forest (the overall relationship) and not obsessing over a single tree (a measure of association). These kinds of statistics usually depend to a greater or lesser extent on the marginal distributions of the variables. Take care when a preponderance of observations are piled up in one or two categories.[11] For example, the lambda in table 13–15 is .575, which means knowing a person's ideology allows us to predict vote preference reasonably well; we cut prediction errors by more than 50 percent. This result, of course, agrees with our previous conclusion that voting is closely tied to ideology. (If you want to check another of lambda's characteristics, try scrambling the order of the columns in table 13–15. You should get the same result, .575.)

Testing a Cross-tabulation for Statistical Significance

Before taking up methods for describing relationships between other types of variables, we need to pause to think about on this problem. Apart from the hypothetical data, all of the examples presented so far use sample surveys. As samples go, most are quite large with slightly more than 1,000 cases. Nevertheless, since

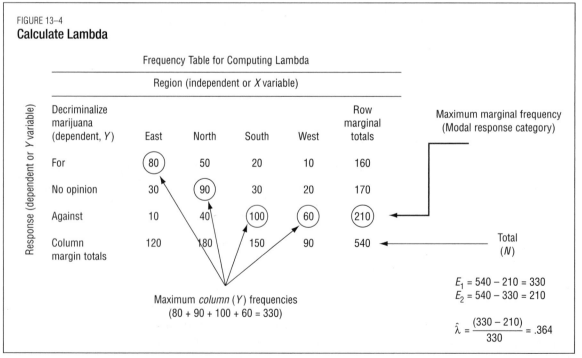

FIGURE 13–4
Calculate Lambda

Source: Hypothetical data.

the totals represent only a tiny fraction of the population, one can always ask, "Do observed relationships reflect true patterns, or did they arise from chance or what is called sampling error?" Chapter 12 introduced concepts for answering that sort of question. Here we apply them to cross-classifications.

STATISTICAL INDEPENDENCE.   At this point it is useful to introduce a technical term that plays a large role in data analysis and that provides another way to view the strength of a relationship. Suppose we have two nominal or categorical variables, X and Y. For the sake of convenience, we can label the categories of the first a, b, c, . . . and those of the second r, s, t, . . . Let $P(X = a)$ stand for the probability that a randomly selected case has property or value a on variable X, and let $P(Y = r)$ stand for the probability that a randomly selected case has property or value r on Y. These two probabilities are called marginal probabilities and refer simply to the chance that an observation has a particular value (a, for instance) irrespective of its value on another. And, finally, $P(X = a, Y = r)$ stands for the joint probability that a randomly selected observation has both property a *and* property r simultaneously. The two variables are **statistically independent** if and only if the

HOW IT'S DONE

Calculating Lambda

To calculate lambda, follow these steps. (For an example using hypothetical data, see figure 13–4.)

1. Look at the cross-tabulation with both sets of marginal frequency (not percent) totals displayed.

2. Decide which variable is dependent.

3. Find the maximum marginal total for the dependent variable.

4. Subtract this total from table total, N, to get errors by method 1: $N -$ (maximum frequency) $= E_1$, the number of predictions errors not knowing the independent variable.

5. In the body of the table, find the maximum frequency within *each* category of the independent variable.

6. Sum the maximums and subtract total from N. Call the result E_2, the number of prediction errors after using knowledge of the independent variable.

7. Calculate lambda:

$$\hat{\lambda} = \frac{(E_1 - E_2)}{E_1}.$$

Note, the numerical value of lambda depends on the choice of independent and dependent variables. Reversing them will usually change $\hat{\lambda}$.

chances of observing a combination of categories is equal to the marginal probability of one category times the marginal probability of the other:

$$P(X = a, Y = r) = [P(X = a)][P(Y = r)] \text{ for all } a \text{ and } r.$$

If, for instance, men are as likely to vote as women, then the two variables—gender and voter turnout—are statistically independent, because, for example, the probability of observing a male nonvoter in a sample is equal to the probability of observing a male times the probability of picking a nonvoter.

In table 13–17, we see that 100 out of 300 respondents are men and that 210 out of the 300 respondents said they voted. Hence, the marginal probabilities are $P(X = m) = 100/300 = .33$ and $P(Y = v) = 210/300 = .7$. The product of these marginal probabilities is $(.33)(.7) = .23$. Also, note that because 70 voters are

TABLE 13–17
Voter Turnout by Gender

Turnout (Y)	Gender (X)		
	Male (m)	Female (f)	Total
Voted (v)	70	140	210
Did not vote (nv)	30	60	90
Total	100	200	300

Note: Hypothetical data. Cell entries are frequencies.

TABLE 13–18
Voter Turnout by Social Class

Turnout (Y)	Social Class (X)		
	Upper (u)	Lower (1)	Total
Voted (v)	100	50	150
Did not vote (nv)	50	100	150
Total	150	150	300

Note: Hypothetical data. Cell entries are frequencies.

male, the joint probability of being male *and* voting is $70/300 = .23$, the same as the product of the marginal probabilities. Since the same relation holds for all other combinations in this data set, we infer that the two variables in table 13–17 are statistically independent.

Now suppose we had the data shown in table 13–18. There the sample consists of 300 respondents, half of whom voted and half of whom did not. The marginal probabilities of voting and not voting are both $150/300 = .5$. It is also clear that the marginal probabilities of being upper- and lower-class equal .5. *If* the two variables were statistically independent, the probability that an upper-class respondent voted would be $(.5)(.5) = .25$. Similarly, the predicted probability (from these marginal totals) that a lower-class individual did not vote would be $(.5)(.5) = .25$. But we can see from *observed* cell frequencies that actual proportions of upper- and lower-class voters are .33 and .17, respectively. Since the observed joint probabilities do not equal the product of the marginal probabilities, the variables are not statistically independent. Upper-class respondents are more likely to vote than are lower-class individuals.

In this context, a test for statistical significance is really a test that two variables in a population are statistically independent. The hypothesis is that in the population, the variables are statistically independent, and we use the observed joint frequencies in a table to decide whether or not this proposition is tenable. Generally speaking, the stronger a relationship is, the more likely it is to be statistically significant, because it is unlikely to arise if the variables are really independent. However, even weak relationships may turn out to be statistically significant in some situations. In the case of cross-tabulations, the determination of statistical significance requires the calculation of a statistic called a chi-square, a procedure we discuss next.

CHI-SQUARE TEST FOR INDEPENDENCE. Table 13–19 pertains to civil liberties. It shows by levels of education attainment the degree of agreement with this statement: "Society shouldn't have to put up with those who have political ideas that are extremely different from the majority." The underlying hypothesis is that tolerance of dissent increases with education. By examining the cell proportions and the measures of association, you can surmise that a modest relationship

TABLE 13–19
Opinion on Civil Liberties: Tolerance of Dissent

Do not put up with extreme differences	Educational Attainment				
	Less than high school	High school graduate	Some post–high school education	College graduate or post graduate	Totals
Agree	45.58%	41.12%	23.17%	20.45%	31.7% (312)
Uncertain	7.65%	9.24%	6.80%	7.30%	7.8% (77)
Disagree	46.77%	49.63%	70.03%	72.25%	60.5% (596)
Totals	100% (154)	100% (312)	100% (270)	100% (249)	100% (985)

Chi square = 56.15 with 6 *df*.

Gamma = .32, tau-*b* = .20, tau-*c* = .19, Somers' D_{yx} = .24, lambda = 0, φ = 0.24.

Question: "Now I would like to ask about public affairs. Please indicate whether you agree. Society shouldn't have to put up with those who have political ideas that are extremely different from the majority." ("Agree strongly" and "agree" responses have been combined as have the disagree categories.)

Source: Citizen, Involvement, Democracy Survey, 2006.

exists between the two variables. (You might reinforce your understanding of the coefficients by interpreting them to yourself.) But is the relationship statistically significant? In the population is there really a relationship between tolerance and education?

Whether or not a relationship is statistically significant usually cannot be determined just by inspecting a cross-tabulation alone; instead, a statistic called **chi square** (χ^2) must be calculated. This statistic essentially compares an observed result—the table produced by sample data—with a "hypothetical" table that would occur if, in the population, the variables were statistically independent. Stated differently, the chi square measures the discrepancy between frequencies actually observed and those we would expect to see if there was no population association between the variables. When each observed cell frequency in a table equals the frequency expected under the **null hypothesis** of independence, chi square will equal zero. Chi square increases as the departures of observed and expected frequencies grow. There is no upper limit to how big the difference can become, but if it passes a certain point—a critical value—there will be reason to reject the hypothesis that the variables are independent.

How is chi square calculated? The observed frequencies are shown in the cross-tabulation in table 13–19.) Expected frequencies in each cell of the table are found by multiplying the row and column marginal totals and dividing by the sample size. As an example, consider the first cell in table 13–19. That cell is in the first row, first column of the table, so multiply the row total, 312, by the column total, 154, and then divide by 985, the total sample size in this table. The result is $(312 \times 154)/985 = 48.78$. This is the *expected* frequency in the first cell of the table; it is what we would expect to get in a sample of 985 (with 312 "agrees" and 154 less than high school graduates) *if there is statistical independence in the population.* This is substantially less than the number we actually have, 70, so there is a difference. What about the other cells?

Let's do another example. If there were no association, how many college graduates would we expect to find in the "Disagree" category? Again, find the corresponding marginal totals (here 596 and 249), multiply them, and divide by 985 to get 150.66, the expected number under the null hypothesis. Notice, we keep repeating the phrase "under the . . ." We want to stress that this procedure can be interpreted as measuring the adequacy of a simple model (the model of no association) to these observed data. If the adequacy or fit is good, we say the model partially explains the data, which in turn is a manifestation of the real world. If the assumption of independence is not supported, we wouldn't anticipate that the expected frequencies would equal the observed ones except by chance.

Table 13–20 contains all of the expected frequencies for table 13–19. The overall measure of fit—the observed test statistic—is found by, in effect, comparing observed and expected frequencies. If the sum of differences is relatively small, do not reject the hypothesis of no association. But, if in the aggregate the discrepancy between observed and expected numbers is large, then the model upon which the expected frequencies are calculated is not a summary of the data, and the decision will be to reject the null hypothesis. So what is a large departure from the expected? The statistic is found by subtracting each expected frequency from its observed counterpart, squaring the difference (no minus sign

TABLE 13–20
Observed and Expected Values under Hypothesis of Independence

Do not put up with extreme differences	Level of Education				
	Less than high school	High school graduate	Some post–high school education	College graduate or postgraduate	Totals
Agree	**70**	**128**	**63**	**51**	**312**
	48.78	*98.8*	*85.5*	*78.9*	
Uncertain	**12**	**29**	**18**	**18**	**77**
	12.0	*24.4*	*21.1*	*19.5*	
Disagree	**72**	**155**	**189**	**180**	**596**
	93.2	*188.8*	*163.4*	*150.7*	
Totals	**154**	**312**	**270**	**249**	**985**

Note: Numbers in boldface font are observed frequencies; those in *italics* are expected frequencies under the hypothesis of statistical independence.

will be left), dividing the quotient by the expected frequency, and then adding the results over all the cells of the table. Hence, for table 13–20 we have

$$\chi^2_{obs} = \frac{(70-49)^2}{70} + \frac{(128-99)^2}{128} + \frac{(63-85)^2}{63} \ldots + \frac{(180-150)^2}{180} = 56.15.^*$$

This is the observed chi square, which we compare to a critical value to help decide whether or not to reject the null hypothesis.

Recall that a statistical hypothesis test entails several steps: specify the null and alternative hypothesis, specify a sample statistic and an appropriate sampling distribution, set the level of significance, find critical values, calculate the observed test statistic, and make a decision. A chi-square test of the statistical independence of Y and X has the same general form.

1. Null hypothesis: X and Y are statistically independent.

2. Alternative hypothesis: X and Y are not independent. The nature of the relationship is left unspecified.

3. Sampling distribution: Choose chi square. This distribution is a family each of which depends on *degrees of freedom* (*df*). The **degrees of freedom** equals the number of rows (I) minus 1 times the number of columns (J) minus 1 or $(I-1)(J-1)$.

4. Level of significance: Choose the probability (α) of incorrectly rejecting a true null hypothesis.

5. Critical value: The chi-square test is always one-tailed. Choose the critical value of chi square from a tabulation to make the critical region (the region of rejection) equal to α.

6. The observed chi square is the sum of the squared differences between observed and expected frequencies, divided by the expected frequency.

7. Reject the null hypothesis if the observed chi square equals or exceeds the critical chi square; that is, reject if $\chi^2_{obs} \geq \chi^2_{critical}$. Otherwise, do not reject.

For the tolerance and education example, the null hypothesis is simply that the two variables are independent. The alternative is that they are not. (Yes, this is an uninformative alternative in that it does not specify *how* education and political tolerance might be related. This lack of specificity is a major criticism of the common chi-square test. But this is nevertheless a first step in categorical data analysis.) For this test, we will use $\alpha = .01$ level of significance. To find a critical value, it is necessary to first find the degrees of freedom, which in this case is $(4-1)(3-1)$, or 6.

---

*results subject to rounding errors.

TABLE 13–21

Relationship between X and Y Based on Sample of 300

| Variable Y | Variable X | | | |
	A	B	C	TOTAL
A	30	30	30	90
B	30	30	36	96
C	40	40	34	114
Total	100	100	100	300

$\chi^2 = 1.38$, 4 *df;* $\phi = .07$.

Note: Hypothetical data.

Then we look in a chi-square table to find the value that marks the upper 1 percent (the .01 level) of the distribution (see appendix C). Read down the first column (*df*) until you find the degrees of freedom (6 in this case) and then go across to the column for the desired level of significance. With 6 degrees of freedom, the critical value for the .01 level is 16.81. This means that if our observed chi square is greater than or equal to 16.81, we reject the hypothesis of statistical independence. Otherwise, we do not reject it.

The observed chi square for table 13–20 is 56.15 with 6 degrees of freedom. (*Always report the degrees of freedom.*) Clearly, this greatly exceeds the critical value (16.81), so we would reject the independence hypothesis at the .01 level. Indeed, if you look at the chi-square distribution table, you will see that (for 6 degrees of freedom) 56.15 is much larger than the highest listed critical value, 22.46, which defines the .001 level. So really this relationship is "significant" at the .001 level. We place quote marks around "significant" to reemphasize that all we have done is reject a null hypothesis. We have not necessarily produced a momentous finding. This statement leads to our next point.

The sample size, *N,* and the distribution of cases across the table always have to be taken into account. Large values of chi square occur when the observed and expected tables are quite different and when the sample size upon which the tables are based is large. A weak relationship in a large sample may attain statistical significance, whereas a strong relationship found in a small sample may not. Keep this point in mind. If *N* (the total sample size) is large, the magnitude of the chi-square statistic will usually be large as well, and we will reject the null hypothesis even if the association is quite weak. This point can be seen by looking at tables 13–21 and 13–22. In table 13–21, the chi square of 1.38 suggest that there is virtually no relationship between the categories *X* and *Y.* In table 13–22, which involves a larger sample size but no other difference, the chi-square statistic (13.8) is now statistically significant (at the .05 level). However, the strength of the relationship between *X* and *Y* is still the same as before, namely, quite small.

The lesson to be drawn here is that when dealing with large samples (say, *N* > 1,500), small, inconsequential relationships can be statistically significant.[12] As a result, we must take care to distinguish between statistical and substantive importance. The fact that

TABLE 13–22

Relationship between X and Y Based on Sample of 3,000

| Variable Y | Variable X | | | |
	A	B	C	TOTAL
A	300	300	300	900
B	300	300	360	960
C	400	400	340	1,140
Total	1,000	1,000	1,000	3,000

$\chi^2 = 13.8$, 4 *df;* $\phi = .07$.

Note: Hypothetical data.

chi square rapidly inflates with increases in the sample size has led statisticians to propose measures that try to take *N* into account. A simple one, **phi** (ϕ), adjusts the observed chi-square statistic by dividing it by *N* and taking the square root of the quotient. (Because of the division by *N*, the statistic is sometimes referred to as the "mean square contingency coefficient.") Yet, like chi square, phi does not have a readily interpretable meaning, so it is mostly used for comparison. (In ideal situations, phi varies between 0 and 1, but in many bivariate distributions, it can exceed 1.) We see in tables 13–21 and 13–22 that phi does not change even though the chi-square statistic

HOW IT'S DONE

The phi Coefficient

Although most software calculates phi as a matter of course, it can be calculated quickly by hand if the observed chi square is available:

$$\varphi = \sqrt{\frac{\chi^2_{\text{obs}}}{N}},$$

where *N* is the sample size.

does. So even though we do not use it much in this book, it comes in handy on occasion. If you look back to table 13–19, you will see that phi = .24, indicating once more the weak to moderate relationship between education and political tolerance.

Generally speaking, the chi-square test is only reliable for relatively large *N*s. Stating exactly how large is difficult because the answer depends on the table's number of rows and columns (or, more formally, its degrees of freedom). Many times, as in a table with many cells (see table 13–20), a sample will be large but the table will contain at least some cells with small frequencies. Very few respondents in the CID study seemed "uncertain," so frequencies in that row are small compared to the others. A rule of thumb directs analysts to be cautious if any cell contains expected frequencies of 5 or fewer, and many cross-classification programs flag these "sparse cells." If you run across this situation, the interpretation of the chi-square value remains the same but should be perhaps advanced with less certainty. Moreover, if the total sample size is less than 20 to 25, alternative procedures are preferable for testing for significance.[13]

Remember: the chi-square statistic in and by itself is not a very good indicator of the strength of an association; rather, it tests the statistical significance of any association that does appear. Assessing relationships is thus a two-step process: (1) measure the strength of the association with percentages, proportions, and coefficients and (2) test to see if the observed results could might have arisen by chance. The first step is the crucial one: make sure the relationship is "worth talking about" and *then* test its significance.

DIFFERENCE-OF-MEANS TESTS

Linear Models

Cross-tabulation is the appropriate analysis technique when both variables are nominal- or ordinal-level measures. When the independent variable is nominal or ordinal and the dependent variable is interval or ratio, however, a contingency table would have far too many columns or rows for a straightforward and meaningful analysis. Moreover a tabular analysis would not take advantage of the information packed in numerical scales. Therefore, other techniques are required. In this situation, we want to compare the means of a quantitative dependent variable (Y) between two or more categories of a categorical (nominal or ordinal) independent variable (X). Intuitively, this approach seems reasonable since a mean is one way to summarize a variable. If the means of various groups or subpopulations differ, then there is possibly a relationship worth exploring.

First consider the graph in figure 13–5. It offers an inkling of what is to come. Our problem is to determine the correlates of political participation. The figure, a multiple boxplot, shows the distribution of "total number of activities that a respondent has engaged in during the previous year" within levels of partisanship.[14] Recall from chapter 11 that boxplots show several pieces of information (e.g., the median, quartiles); now we see this information by each category of the independent variable. (The leftmost box in figure 13–5, for instance, reveals that among the least partisan members of the survey, the median activity level is nearly zero, even though several in this group seem to be quite a bit more active.) On the whole, the four categories of partisanship have roughly the same distributions, but at this point there is no clear pattern. The medians of strong and weak partisans look to be about the same and higher than the "nonpartisan" and "moderate" individuals. We require a more precise procedure than "look to be," but at least we have an idea of what to expect from a more sophisticated analysis.[15]

Statisticians tackle this difficulty by translating the question into a linear model. A linear model is a first crack at explaining how independent variables affect (or cause changes in) a dependent variable. More specifically, it is an equation that relates values of a dependent variable through an additive combination of independent variables plus an error term. In symbols, it is

$$Y_i = \beta_0 + \beta_1 X_{1i} + \ldots + \beta_K X_{Ki} + \varepsilon_i.$$

The model posits that for any individual or case, i, Y_i (a quantitative variable)[16] equals or is a function of a set of one or more independent variables (represented by Xs), which may be quantitative or categorical, and a *random* error. In essence, the model states that a person's value on Y can be predicted from knowledge of the independent variables. The Greek letters stand for unknown population values; the betas in particular give a numerical indicator of how the Xs affect the dependent variable. An important objective is to estimate these unknowns from a sample.

Once a model or, more precisely, its parameters have been estimated, we can use it to make predictions: put in a set of X values, and the outcome is a predicted score for Y. The differences between the observed and predicted Ys are called **residuals:** the residual for the ith score is $\hat{Y}_i - Y_i = $ residual, where $\hat{Y}_i$ is the predicted value for the ith observation and Y_i is the observed score.

So what does this idea have to do with comparing means? At the outset, perhaps not much. But shortly we repackage many types of analyses in the form of linear models. This formation provides a uniform method to analyze all sorts of data. After explaining how to statistically compare two means, we start using the linear model more explicitly in a technique known as **analysis of variance** (ANOVA, or sometimes AOV for short).

Difference of Means and Effect Sizes

The difference between one mean and another is an **effect size**, one of the most basic measures of relationships in applied statistics. The name comes from experimental sciences, in which a goal is to measure the effect of a treatment on the dependent variable. A logical measure of an effect is the difference:

Effect = Mean of treatment group – Mean of control group.

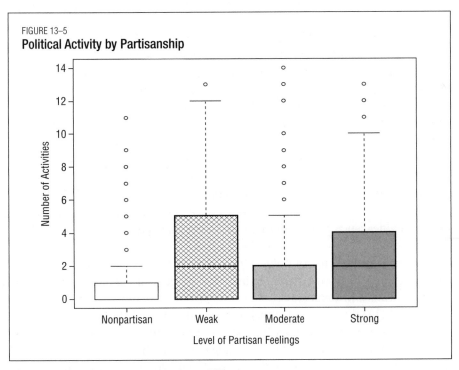

FIGURE 13–5
Political Activity by Partisanship

Source: Citizenship, Involvement, Democracy Survey, 2006.

For those who appreciate more formality, a population effect can be written succinctly as

$$\Delta = \mu_{\text{experimental}} - \mu_{\text{control}},$$

where Δ (capital Greek letter delta) is the effect size and the μ's are the means of the "population" treatment and experimental groups.[17] A logical estimator of Δ is the difference in sample means:

$$\hat{\Delta} = \bar{Y}_{\text{experimental}} - \bar{Y}_{\text{control}}.$$

Capital delta with a "hat" is the symbol for the sample estimator of an effect size, and the $\bar{Y}$s are the sample means for the experimental and control group.

If the research rests on a randomized experiment (see chapter 6), the estimated effect can be used for making causal inferences. In observational studies, on the other hand, such as surveys or aggregate data analysis, making causal claims is a tricky business.

For a change of pace, let's turn to a different substantive question, one that was posed in chapter 1. If justices on the Supreme Court are supposed to follow the law and not their political beliefs, why the hullabaloo over the nomination and confirmation? Shouldn't the best "legal" minds be chosen regardless of ideology or political affiliation? Of course, everyone knows that Supreme Court decisions are determined by more than just objective interpretation of law and precedent. They surely reflect the political views of the justices as well. After all, presidents nominate justices who share their general philosophy. One way to demonstrate the point is to compare judges' rulings by the party of the nominating president.

Look at figure 13–6, which we will refer to on several occasions. (We have tilted the box plot on its side to aid in making comparisons.) It displays the voting record of Supreme Court justices nominated and confirmed since 1950. (There are twenty-three in all.) Decisions have been limited to those involving union activities, such as worker safety and labor management cases. The dependent variable is defined and measured as "the percentage of 'liberal' votes cast by the justice in the area of unions."[18] The point is to identify any meaningful (practical and statistical) differences in behavior between the justices nominated by Republicans and Democrats.

The plot shows a clear difference in the distributions. Besides the medians, which are represented by solid lines in the boxes, we have added the means (67% and 48%). As one might expect, judges selected by Democratic presidents are more liberal on labor issues by approximately 20 percentage points. If you look carefully, you can see that half of or more of the "Democrats" score above

65 percent, whereas the same proportion of "Republicans" lie below 45 percent. No Democratic appointee falls below 50 percent liberal on union-related cases. Once more, we see the interconnection between politics and the economy: organized labor does "better" under Democratic than Republican administrations. And we see later that the stronger the unions are in a country, the less inequality there is. The boxplot shows more. Note, for instance, that there is more variation among Republican-nominated justices than their Democratic counterparts. Finally, this figure hides an important piece of information that is essential in our further analysis, the number of justices in each group.

A boxplot such as figure 13–6 gives us information useful for conducting tests of significance. The estimation of an effect such as the consequences of party affiliation on judicial decision making requires two *independent* samples of size N_1 and N_2. (If the samples are not independent, alternative statistical procedures have to be used.) The size of the samples also matters because small Ns are handled slightly differently than large ones. As you can see, there are only six Democratic justices and seventeen Republicans.[19] In addition, we have to pay attention to the variation (as measured by the standard deviations) of the two populations from which the samples come. If we can assume that population 1's

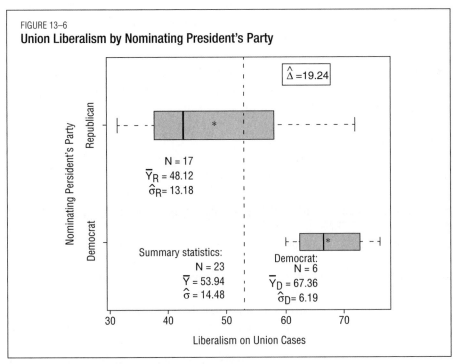

FIGURE 13–6
Union Liberalism by Nominating President's Party

$\hat{\Delta} = 19.24$

N = 17
$\bar{Y}_R = 48.12$
$\hat{\sigma}_R = 13.18$

Democrat:
N = 6
$\bar{Y}_D = 67.36$
$\hat{\sigma}_D = 6.19$

Summary statistics:
N = 23
$\bar{Y} = 53.94$
$\hat{\sigma} = 14.48$

Liberalism on Union Cases

Nominating Persident's Party

Republican

Democrat

Source: Lee Epstein et al., US Supreme Court Justices Database.

standard deviation equals population 2's, the test for significance goes in one direction; if we believe the standard deviations are not the same, we follow a different path. (We will pursue this point in a moment.) The boxplot provides a picture of the variation as well as central tendency, so we can use it for an initial assessment of the variation in the categories of X. Here, we note that the decisions relating to unions of justices nominated by Republican presidents appear to be much less liberal than those of their Democratically nominated colleagues.

Before taking up hypothesis testing, let us pretend that the data come from independent random samples of Supreme Court justices. Furthermore, just as an exercise, let's think of the nominating presidents' parties as "factors" or treatments. We want to assess the "effect" of partisan politics on legal rulings. (This scenario is not required for the analysis, but it may help clarify the interpretation of test results.) The sample mean union liberalism scale scores are 67.36 percent for the Democrats and 48.12 percent for Republicans; the difference is

$$\hat{\Delta} = \bar{Y}_{\text{Democrat}} - \bar{Y}_{\text{Republican}} = 67.36 - 48.12 = 19.24.$$

Hence, the "consequence" of presidential party is a nearly 20 percent increase in liberalism on union cases. The "direction" of the difference, positive, has a nice substantive interpretation: people who are nominated by Democratic presidents tend to vote about 20 percent "more liberal" on union-related cases than do those picked by Republicans. But is this difference statistically significant? Could it have arisen by chance, especially since the samples are small?[20] Note that once this question is answered, we still have to decide if the observed difference is substantively or politically important. A 20 percent difference might be considered large even though it is based on small samples. Given just these data, we easily see why politicians and interest groups fight tooth and nail over judicial appointments.

The statistic $\hat{\Delta}$ is a point estimator of the *population* difference of means. Whenever data come from random samples, one can reasonably ask if the observed effect represents a true difference or is the result of sampling error. This question leads to statistical hypothesis testing. The procedures for testing for the significance of a difference of means depend on (among other considerations) sample sizes. We begin with so-called large-sample tests first.

LARGE SAMPLE DIFFERENCE OF MEANS TEST. We are going to compare two sample means, $\bar{Y}_1$ and $\bar{Y}_2$, based on samples of size N_1 and N_2, respectively. In this section, we assume that both Ns are greater than or equal to 20 There are two equivalent ways to describe the statistic of interest, a *difference of means* and an *effect*. We use the terms interchangeably. The final preliminary point is that the samples have been drawn from populations having means μ_1 and μ_2 and variances σ_1^2 and σ_2^2. For the large-sample tests and confidence intervals, we make no assumptions about these population variances. When it comes time to talk about small samples, we will assume the two variances equal each other.

The judicial data set is small, so we need a larger one to illustrate the large sample test. Thus, we shift back to the gender gap hypothesis about male-female differences on current social and political issues. One commonly heard argument is that women are on average a bit more suspicious and hostile toward the military. The 2004 National Election Study survey contains a question that touches on exactly that possibility; it asked respondents to place themselves on a "thermometer" of feelings toward the military, with 0 degrees being coldest or most negative and 100 degrees being most favorable or positive. Presumably, 50 degrees is the neutral position, neither hot or cold.[21] In the context of American politics, the existence of a gender gap would imply that women have *on average* a slightly less favorable opinion of the military than men do.

Computers perform significance tests practically with the push of a button, but to reinforce your understanding of the logic and assumptions underlying them, we outline the test procedure. The null hypothesis is that thermometer scores are *equal*, or symbolically (letting μ's represent population means),

$$H_0: \mu_{male} = \mu_{female} \; or \; H_0: \mu_{male} - \mu_{female} = 0 \; or \; H_0: \Delta_{\mu_{male-female}} = 0.$$

Here we have stated the null hypothesis in three equivalent ways. Delta (Δ) refers to the "effect" of gender. The alternative hypothesis is that women have on average lower thermometer scores, and it too can be written several ways:

$$H_A: \mu_{female} < \mu_{male} \; or \; H_A: \mu_{female} - \mu_{male} < 0 \; or \; H_0: \Delta_{female-male} < 0.$$

In essence, we are testing whether the population difference of means is zero or negative. Since only values much less than zero are of interest, this is a one-sided test. Let us test at the .01 level of significance, which means that if we should reject the null hypothesis, we may be making a type I error (falsely rejecting H_0), but the chances of doing so are 1 in 100 (.01).

A sample difference of means based on large samples has a normal distribution, so to find an appropriate critical value for testing the null hypothesis, we use the tabulated standard normal distribution or z distribution in appendix A. The critical value has to be chosen in such a way as to make the probability of a type 1 error equal to .01. Recall that the table gives z scores that cut off the upper α proportion of the distribution. The critical value that cuts off .1% (.01) of the area under the normal curve is 2.325. (We interpolated between 2.32 and 2.33.) Any observed test statistic greater than or equal to this value will lead to the rejection of H_0; if it is less, the null hypothesis still stands.

For this test, the effect, $\hat{\Delta}$, is converted to a observed test statistic, z, by the general formula:

$$z_{obs} = \frac{\text{Estimated difference}}{\text{Estimated standard error}}.$$

The standard error in the denominator is the variation of the sampling distribution. The z_{obs} is compared to the critical z to reach a decision: If $|z_{obs}| \geq z_{critical}$, reject H; otherwise, do not reject.

The estimated effect size, $\bar{Y}_{male} - \bar{Y}_{female} = 79.56 - 80.07 = -.52$, is not much to write home about, but is it statistically significant? The test results appear in table 13–23.

The observed test statistic ($z_{obs} = -.393$) is considerably less than the critical value. In view of these data and the way we framed the problem, there is no reason to reject the null hypothesis. More important, the conclusion is that on this issue measured in this way, there appears to be no gender gap. This finding is not, of course, the end of the story. Some of the response variables studied in the section on cross-tabulations *did* reveal a modest male-female divergence on a couple of issues. But it does suggest that gender politics in America may be more complex than conventional wisdom might indicate. (Also, bear in mind the timing of the survey, October to December 2004. The war in Iraq was just a year old, and the shock of 9/11 had not dissipated.)

SMALL-SAMPLE TESTS OF THE DIFFERENCE OF MEANS.   The preceding test assumed relatively large sample sizes. What about smaller ones? We can return to the Supreme Court data in which the subsample sizes are $N_D = 6$ and $N_R = 17$, both less than 30, our arbitrary cutoff for deciding what is small. Given the sample sizes and unequal variances, we have to adjust the test procedures. As in the case of single samples (see chapter 11), when dealing with small Ns, we apply the t distribution instead of the standard normal (z) distribution. Under certain

TABLE 13–23

Large-Sample Difference of Means Test (Gender by Attitudes toward the Military)

Gender	Sample Size	Mean	Standard Deviation	Standard Error of Mean
Male	518	79.56	20.59	.905
Female	531	80.07	21.99	.954

$D = -.52$.

$z_{obs} = -.393$, *p*-value = .614.

Confidence interval for difference of mean: –3.913, 2.878.

Source: 2004 National Election Study.

assumptions, the difference of means approximately follows a t distribution with degrees of freedom, df, that are a function of the sample sizes.

All of these considerations lead to two methods for testing whether one μ differs from another:

■ Method I (Student's t-test): Assume variances are equal ($\sigma_1^2 = \sigma_2^2$)

  ○ $df = N_1 + N_2 - 2$.

■ Method II (Welch t-test): Assume unequal variances ($\sigma_1^2 \neq \sigma_2^2$).

  ○ df is more complicated (see below).

Both cases assume independent random sampling;[22] the dependent variable may or may not be normally distributed.[23]

A quick measure of differences in variation is the "variance ratio":

$$\frac{\hat{\sigma}_1^2}{\hat{\sigma}_2^2}.$$

If the ratio is about 1, the variances are roughly equal; if they differ, the ratio will be less than zero or greater than 1.[24] For the current data, the variance of Republican nominated justices is about four times that of their Democratic counterparts (173.60 versus 38.34). We'll ignore the discrepancy for the moment by assuming equal variances and then later apply method II to determine whether or our conclusion changes when we are more rigorous.

The null hypothesis is that mean union liberalism scores are *equal:*

$$H_0: \mu_{\text{Democrat}} = \mu_{\text{Republican}} \; or \; H_0: \mu_{\text{Democrat}} - \mu_{\text{Republican}} < 0 \; or \; H_0: \Delta_{\mu_{\text{Democrat}}-\mu_{\text{Republican}}} = 0.$$

The alternative is that decision making does not differ (except randomly) by party:

$$H_A: \mu_{\text{Democrat}} \neq \mu_{\text{Republican}}$$

The choice of the alternative hypothesis dictates a two-tailed test (that is, large departures from the hypothesized difference in *either* direction will be grounds for rejecting H_0).

Using the formulas in the box, the calculations for the Supreme Court data are

$$\hat{\sigma}_p = \sqrt{\frac{(6-1)(6.19)^2 + (17-1)(13.18)^2}{6+17-2}} = \sqrt{\frac{2969.33}{21}} = 11.89.$$

Therefore, the standard error turns out to be

$$\hat{\sigma}_{\bar{Y}_1 - \bar{Y}_2} = 11.89\sqrt{\frac{1}{6} + \frac{1}{17}} = 5.69.$$

Calculate Small-Sample Difference of Means Tests

Required sample statistics are as follows:

- N_1 and N_2, the sample sizes
- σ_1^2 and σ_2^2 the sample variances
- $\bar{Y}_1$ and $\bar{Y}_2$, the sample means

Assume $N_1 + N_2 \leq 30$. (Pay attention to subscripts.)

Method I: Variances Equal $(\hat{\sigma}_1 = \hat{\sigma}_2)$

- Step 1: Pooled estimator of common variance:

$$\hat{\sigma}_P = \sqrt{\frac{(N_1 - 1)\hat{\sigma}_1^2 + (N_2 - 1)\hat{\sigma}_2^2}{(N_1 + N_2 - 2)}}.$$

- Step 2: Estimated standard error of difference

$$\hat{\sigma}_{\bar{Y}_1 - \bar{Y}_2} = \hat{\sigma}_P \sqrt{\frac{1}{N_1} + \frac{1}{N_2}}.$$

- Step 3: Observed t

$$t_{obs} = \frac{(\bar{Y}_1 - \bar{Y}_2)}{\hat{\sigma}_{\bar{Y}_1 - \bar{Y}_2}}.$$

- Step 4: Degrees of freedom

$$df = N_1 + N_2 - 2$$

Method II: Variances Unequal $(\sigma_1 \neq \sigma_2)(N_1 \text{ and } N_2 \text{ not necessarily equal})$

- Step 1: Estimated standard error of difference

$$\hat{\sigma}_{\bar{Y}_1 - \bar{Y}_2} = \sqrt{\frac{\hat{\sigma}_1^2}{N_1} + \frac{\hat{\sigma}_2^2}{N_2}}.$$

- Step 2: Observed t

$$t_{obs} = \frac{(\bar{Y}_1 - \bar{Y}_2)}{\hat{\sigma}_{\bar{Y}_1 - \bar{Y}_2}}.$$

- Step 3: Degrees of freedom

$$df = \frac{\left(\frac{\hat{\sigma}_1^2}{N_1} + \frac{\hat{\sigma}_2^2}{N_2}\right)^2}{\left(\left(\frac{\hat{\sigma}_1^2}{N_1}\right)^2 \Big/ (N_1 - 1)\right) + \left(\left(\frac{\hat{\sigma}_2^2}{N_2}\right)^2 \Big/ (N_2 - 1)\right)}.$$

and the observed t is

$$t_{obs} = \frac{19.24}{5.69} = 3.38.$$

The correct degrees of freedom for Method I is $df = N_1 + N_2 - 2$, or in this case $6 + 17 - 2 = 21$. For $\alpha = .01$, the critical t is 2.51. Since $t_{obs} > t_{crit}$, we reject H_0.

So the decision is to reject the null hypothesis that nominated Supreme Court justices nominated by Democratic have the same average union-cases scores as those supported by Republicans.

How much have we learned from this exercise? We observed a difference in judicial behavior, 19.23 percent, which we judge to be statistically significance. This analysis supplies a statistical basis for the conclusion that the Supreme Court is a politicized institution just like the Congress and president.

METHOD II: UNEQUAL SUBPOPULATION VARIANCES (WELCH T-TEST).   If the subpopulations variances are not equal, the t-test performs rather "poorly," in that levels of significance may be erroneous. (Having equal sample sizes, N_1 and N_2, helps, but we use a modification of Method I to make the test when variances are dissimilar.) The procedure generally follows the other means tests, but we have to adjust the degrees of freedom and the standard error. To find the degrees of freedom for the situation we're in—the subpopulation variances differ—the calculations are not as straightforward as before. Fortunately, most software computes the df, although not all programs produce exactly the same result. The formula is

$$df = \frac{\left(\dfrac{\hat{\sigma}_1^2}{N_1} + \dfrac{\hat{\sigma}_2^2}{N_2}\right)^2}{\left(\dfrac{\hat{\sigma}_1^2}{N_1}\right)^2 \bigg/ (N_1 - 1) + \left(\dfrac{\hat{\sigma}_2^2}{N_2}\right)^2 \bigg/ (N_2 - 1)}.$$

where the terms have been defined earlier. In our case, this becomes

$$df = \frac{\left(\dfrac{\hat{\sigma}_1^2}{N_1} + \dfrac{\hat{\sigma}_2^2}{N_2}\right)^2}{\left(\dfrac{\hat{\sigma}_1^2}{N_1}\right)^2 \bigg/ (N_1 - 1) + \left(\dfrac{\hat{\sigma}_2^2}{N_2}\right)^2 \bigg/ (N_2 - 1)} = \frac{\left(\dfrac{6.19^2}{6} + \dfrac{13.18^2}{17}\right)^2}{\dfrac{\left(6.19^2 / 6\right)^2}{5} + \dfrac{\left(13.18^2 / 17\right)^2}{16}} = \frac{275.64}{14.69} = 18.77.$$

Yes, it's a strange degrees of freedom but perfectly proper. In the absence of a computer, we can treat this as approximately 18 and use appendix B to find the corresponding critical value, which is 2.55 (for a one-tailed test at the .01 level). Any observed t value greater than or equal to this number will lead to the rejection of the null hypothesis in favor of the alternative.

The observed test statistic closely resembles the one calculated for large samples. The general form is the hypothesized effect, Δ, subtracted from the observed effect, $\hat{\Delta}$, or the difference in the corresponding subpopulation means, divided by the estimated standard error of $\hat{\Delta}$. The standard error is just the weighted average of the subpopulation variances:

$$\hat{\sigma}_{\bar{Y}_1 - \bar{Y}_2} = \sqrt{\frac{\hat{\sigma}_1^2}{N_1} + \frac{\hat{\sigma}_2^2}{N_2}}.$$

The test statistic is for these data is

$$t_{obs} = \frac{(\bar{Y}_1 - \bar{Y}_2) - (\mu_1 - \mu_2)}{\sqrt{\frac{\hat{\sigma}_1^2}{N_1} + \frac{\hat{\sigma}_2^2}{N_2}}} = \frac{\hat{\Delta}}{\hat{\sigma}_{\bar{Y}_1 - \bar{Y}_2}}.$$

Here is the calculation of the observed difference, its estimated standard error, and the observed t all in one fell swoop (you can get the values from the figure):

$$t_{obs} = \frac{(67.36 - 48.13) - (0)}{\sqrt{\frac{6.19^2}{6} + \frac{13.18^2}{18}}} = \frac{19.23}{3.93} = 4.89.$$

The formula for the standard error looks complicated, but it simply tells us to square the standard deviations in each subpopulation, divide by the respective Ns, add the two quotients, and take the square root. Incidentally, the simplification of the numerator is possible because $\mu_{Democrat} - \mu_{Republican}$ is hypothesized to be zero and $\hat{\Delta} = \hat{\Delta} = \bar{Y}_{Democrat} - \bar{Y}_{Republican}$. Table 13–24 presents the test results.

The observed t (4.89) easily exceeds the critical value (2.55)—in fact, it is greater than all t's with 18 df—so we reject the null hypothesis at the .05 level and indeed at the .001 level. As a reminder, the phrase "p-value $= .000$" at the

---

TABLE 13–24

Small-Sample Difference of Means Test

Nominating Party	Sample Sizes	Mean	Standard Deviation
Democrat	6	67.36	6.19
Republican	17	48.13	12.78

$\hat{\Delta} = 19.23$.

Method I: $\hat{\sigma}_{\bar{Y}_1 - \bar{Y}_2} = 5.93$; $t_{obs} = 3.38$; $df = 21$; $t_{crit} = 2.51$; p-value $= .000$.

99% confidence intervals: 3.80–34.67.

Method II: $\hat{\sigma}_{\bar{Y}_1 - \bar{Y}_2} = 3.38$; $t_{obs} = 4.89$; $df = 18.77$; $t_{crit} = 2.55$; p-value $= .000$.

bottom of table 13-24 is the attained probability of the observed t. This means that *if* the null hypothesis of no difference of means is true, we have found a very, very unusual result, one with a probability is less than .001 or 1 in 1,000. The observed t is close to the value achieved according to Method I (4.89 versus 3.38), so the political conclusion is the same as the one derived from Method I.

CONFIDENCE INTERVALS.   Chapter 12 underscored the value of confidence intervals. Remember, confidence intervals are lower and upper boundaries that probably enclose the population value of an estimator. Go back to table 13-23, which reports the 99 percent confidence intervals for the estimated gender effect. The intervals extend from–3.913 to 2.878. Thus, 99 times out of 100, the intervals will include the population difference of means. In other words, we are 99 percent certain that the difference in men and women's mean thermometer scores lies between–3.913 and 2.878. Since the intervals extend from about –4 to 3, we have reason to believe that zero is a possible value of the population difference of means. What is more, because these limits are based on the same α level used in the test of significance, we have in effect tested the null hypothesis a second way: by observing that the 99 percent confidence intervals included the (null) hypothesized value of zero, we do not reject H_0. The substantive interpretation is thus that there is no difference between men and women on this issue.

CALCULATING CONFIDENCE INTERVALS.   Although you will undoubtedly use packaged statistical software to find confidence intervals, the computation is not difficult. The general form is

Estimated difference of means ± critical value × estimated standard error.

In words, find the critical value appropriate for the alpha level, multiply it by the standard error, and then add and subtract the product to the difference to get the upper and lower bounds. The critical value is the z or t used in a hypothesis test (at the desired α level), and the standard error is the standard error of the difference of means. The precise numbers will depend on sample sizes and on whether or not equal population variances are assumed. For those who want a more precise formulation, confidence intervals for a difference of means or effect are

$$\hat{\Delta} \pm \delta_\alpha \left(\hat{\sigma}_{\bar{Y}_1 - \bar{Y}_2} \right),$$

where $\hat{\Delta}$ is the estimated effect, the δ_α is a critical value for $(1 - \alpha)$ percent confidence intervals, and $\hat{\sigma}_{\bar{Y}_1 - \bar{Y}_2}$ is the estimated standard error of the difference.
There are two situations.

LARGE-SAMPLE INTERVALS.   If the N's are greater than 20, the confidence intervals are

$$\hat{\Delta} + z_{\alpha/2}\hat{\sigma}_{\bar{Y}_1-\bar{Y}_2} \; and \; \hat{\Delta} - z_{\alpha/2}\hat{\sigma}_{\bar{Y}_1-\bar{Y}_2}.$$

Example: Assume $N_1 = N_2 = 100$ and sample standard deviations $\hat{\sigma}_1 = 5$ and $\hat{\sigma}_2 = 4$. If $\bar{Y}_1 = 50$ and $\bar{Y}_2 = 40$, the estimated difference of means is $\hat{\Delta} = 50 - 40 = 10$. The formula for estimated standard error of $\hat{\Delta}$ is

$$\hat{\sigma}_{\bar{Y}_1-\bar{Y}_2} = \sqrt{\frac{\hat{\sigma}_1^2}{N_1} + \frac{\hat{\sigma}_2^2}{N_2}}.$$

For 95 percent confidence intervals, the appropriate critical z is 1.96. (Why?[25]) Hence, the upper limit is

$$10 + 1.96\sqrt{\frac{5^2}{100} + \frac{4^2}{100}} = 10 + 1.96\sqrt{.25 + .16}$$
$$= 10 + 1.96\sqrt{(.41)}$$
$$= 10 + 1.96\,(.64)$$
$$= 10 + 1.255$$
$$= 11.255,$$

and the lower limit is

$$10 - 1.96\sqrt{\frac{5^2}{100} + \frac{4^2}{100}} = 10 - 1.96\sqrt{.25 + .16}$$
$$= 10 - 1.96(.64)$$
$$= 10 - 1.255$$
$$= 8.745.$$

The procedure we used to construct the confidence intervals has a 95 percent chance of including the population difference of means. Loosely speaking, we are 95 percent certain that the interval 8.745 to 11.255 contains the true value of $\mu_1 - \mu_2$.

SMALL-SAMPLE INTERVALS.   Intervals for smaller samples (the Ns are less than 20 or so) have the same general form, except that a critical t with approximately $N_1 + N_2 - 2$ (or as calculated previously with the formula) degrees of freedom

HOW IT'S DONE

Large-Sample Confidence Intervals for a Difference of Means

If N_1 and $N_2 \geq 20$, the $(1 - \alpha)$ percent confidence intervals for $\hat{\Delta} = \bar{Y}_1 - \bar{Y}_2$ are

$$\hat{\Delta} \pm z_{\text{critical}}\hat{\sigma}_{\bar{Y}_1-\bar{Y}_2},$$

where

$$\hat{\sigma}_{\bar{Y}_1-\bar{Y}_2} = \sqrt{\frac{\hat{\sigma}_1^2}{N_1} + \frac{\hat{\sigma}_2^2}{N_2}}.$$

replaces the critical z value. And we use the appropriate standard error depending on the assumption about equal variances.

$$\hat{\Delta} + t_{\alpha/2, N_1 + N_2 - 2} \hat{\sigma}_{\bar{Y}_1 - \bar{Y}_2} \ and \ \hat{\Delta} - t_{\alpha/2, N_1 + N_2 - 2} \hat{\sigma}_{\bar{Y}_1 - \bar{Y}_2}.$$

Example: As before, let $\bar{Y}_1 = 50$ and $\bar{Y}_2 = 40$ (hence, $\hat{\Delta} = 10$) and $\hat{\sigma}_1 = 5$ and $\hat{\sigma}_2 = 4$. This time, however, set $N_1 = N_2 = 10$. Assume first equal population variances. The pooled estimated of the population standard deviation is

$$\hat{\sigma}_{pooled} = \sqrt{\frac{(10-1)5^2 + (10-1)4^2}{10 + 10 - 2}} = \sqrt{\frac{(9)(25) + (9)(16)}{18}} = \sqrt{\frac{369}{18}} = 4.53,$$

from which we find the estimated standard error to be

$$\hat{\sigma}_{\bar{Y}_1 - \bar{Y}_2} = 4.53 \sqrt{\frac{1}{10} + \frac{1}{10}} = 2.02.$$

We want 95 percent confidence intervals, so the necessary critical t is 2.101 (look in appendix B, the row for 18 df and $t_{.025}$). The upper-limit interval turns out to be

$$10 + (2.10)(2.02) = 10 + 4.25 = 14.25,$$

whereas the lower limit is

$$10 - (2.10)(2.02) = 10 - 4.25 = 5.75.$$

As an aside, here are the intervals using the second method. First, the standard error:

$$\hat{\sigma}_{\bar{Y}_1 - \bar{Y}_2} = \sqrt{\frac{\hat{\sigma}_1^2}{N_1} + \frac{\hat{\sigma}_2^2}{N_2}}$$

$$= \sqrt{\frac{5^2}{10} + \frac{4^2}{10}}$$

$$= \sqrt{2.5 + 1.6}$$

$$= 2.02.$$

The degrees of freedom works out to be 16.81. The appropriate critical t for the .01 level of significance, which corresponds to 99 percent confidence intervals, is 2.898. The intervals for the estimated difference ($\hat{\Delta} = 10$) are

$$10 - (2.898)(2.02) = 4.13 \ and \ 10 + (2.898)(2.02) = 15.87.$$

Small-Sample Confidence Intervals for a Difference of Means

Let N_1 and N_2 be the sizes of samples 1 and 2 respectively. Assume if N_1 and $N_2 < 20$.

$(1 - \alpha)$ percent confidence intervals for $\hat{\Delta} = \bar{Y}_1 = \bar{Y}_2$ are

$$\hat{\Delta} \pm t_{\alpha/2, N_1 + N_2 - 2} \hat{\sigma}_{\bar{Y}_1 - \bar{Y}_2}.$$

Method I: σ_1 and σ_2 are equal.

t_{crit} is the t value with $N_1 + N_2 - 2$ degrees of freedom for the chosen α level of significance and $\hat{\sigma}_{\bar{Y}1-\bar{Y}2}$, the estimated standard error of the sample difference of means:

$$\hat{\sigma}_{\bar{Y}_1 - \bar{Y}_2} = \hat{\sigma}_{pooled} \sqrt{\frac{1}{N_1} + \frac{1}{N_2}},$$

and $\hat{\sigma}_{pooled}$ is the pooled estimator of the common population standard deviation:

$$\hat{\sigma}_{pooled} = \sqrt{\frac{(N_1 - 1)\hat{\sigma}_1^2 + (N_2 - 1)\hat{\sigma}_2^2}{N_1 + N_2 - 2}}.$$

Method II: σ_1 and σ_2 are not equal.

t_{crit} is the t value with degrees of freedom calculated as

$$df = \frac{\left(\dfrac{\hat{\sigma}_1^2}{N_1} + \dfrac{\hat{\sigma}_2^2}{N_2}\right)^2}{\left(\left(\dfrac{\hat{\sigma}_1^2}{N_1}\right)^2 \middle/ (N_1 - 1)\right) + \left(\left(\dfrac{\hat{\sigma}_2^2}{N_2}\right)^2 \middle/ (N_2 - 1)\right)}.$$

The appropriate standard error is

$$\hat{\sigma}_{\bar{Y}_1 - \bar{Y}_2} = \sqrt{\frac{\hat{\sigma}_1^2}{N_1} + \frac{\hat{\sigma}_2^2}{N_2}}.$$

These intervals are considerably wider than the previous ones because of the much smaller samples. (Remember from chapter 12 we stressed that, other things being equal, the larger the samples, the smaller the confidence intervals.)

To wrap up, refer first to table 13–23 and note the confidence intervals for the difference of the means between men's and women's scale scores on feelings toward the military. They stretch from –3.913 to 2.878. That is, the difference in means might be negative, meaning women have less favorable attitudes than men, but it could also be positive, meaning that women would feel more favorable toward the military than men. Yet, another possible value is zero. A zero difference, of course, disconfirms the gender gap hypothesis. This conclusion matches the one we made on the basis of just the difference-in-means test itself. This equivalence results from the close connection between hypothesis testing and interval estimation.

Difference of Proportions

Closely related to an analysis of differences of means is the comparison of proportions. Testing for a difference of proportions follows exactly the same steps as the previous tests except for relatively minor adjustments in formulas. When the goal is to measure the difference between two sample proportions, p_1 and p_2, and the data come from two independent samples, place confidence intervals around the estimated difference and test the hypothesis that the population difference of proportions, $P_1 - P_2$, equals a specific value, usually zero. This test has all of the elements of difference-of-means tests, which should not be surprising because we can interpret proportions as a kind of mean. Thus, to check the significance of a difference of proportions, we need the hypotheses (e.g., H_0: $\Delta p = P_1 - P_2 = 0$ and H_A: $\Delta p = P_1 - P_2 \neq 0$), decision rules (e.g., α-level = .01, two-sided test, and corresponding critical value), the estimated difference (i.e., $\hat{\Delta}_{p_1 - p_2}$), degrees of freedom (if samples are small), and the standard error. For a difference of proportions test, the standard error is

$$\hat{\sigma}_{p_1 - p_2} = \sqrt{p^*\left(1 - p^*\right)\left[\frac{1}{N_1} + \frac{1}{N_2}\right]},$$

where p^* is the overall sample proportion in the comparison and the Ns are the respective subsample sizes. For confidence intervals, use

$$\hat{\sigma}_{p_1 - p_2} = \sqrt{\frac{(p_1)(1 - p_1)}{N_1} + \frac{(p_2)(1 - p_2)}{N_2}}.$$

The test statistic has the same general form as the one for the difference of means. For large samples,

$$z_{obs} = \frac{(p_1 - p_2) - (P_1 - P_2)}{\hat{\sigma}_{p_1 - p_2}}.$$

To motivate the discussion, let us stick with the gender gap problem. The 2004 NES survey asked respondents to rate various groups on "feeling thermometers." This time we take attitudes toward "feminists" as the dependent variable, but instead of comparing means, we will investigate the differences in the proportions of men and women who rate feminists "negatively." Thermometer ratings of less than 50 are considered "unfavorable" ratings while scores of 50 and higher are considered "favorable." (This is admittedly an arbitrary dividing line, and we use it merely to illustrate the method. As a rule of thumb, one should apply the statistical technique that preserves the level of measurement.)

Table 13–25 summarizes the data and analysis results. For large samples, a difference of proportion has a normal distribution with mean $P_1 - P_2$ and standard error $\sigma_{p_1 - p_2}$. As a consequence, we compute an observed z to compare with the critical value. For the sake of argument, we choose a two-tailed test at the .05 level. The null hypothesis is therefore $H_0: P_1 = P_2$ or $H_0: P_1 - P_2 = 0$, and the alternative is simply $H_A: P_1 \neq P_2$. The sample sizes ($N_{Male} = 496$, $N_{Female} = 518$) are quite large, so the z distribution is appropriate, and the critical value for the test is 1.96.

The estimated proportions are the cell frequencies divided by the totals (e.g., $p_{Male} = 139/496 = .280$).

Usually (as in the present case) the null hypothesis is simply $H_0: P_1 - P_2 = 0$, and the last term in the numerator drops out. Notice that because the observed test statistic (3.12) is considerably larger than 1.96, the hypothesis that the population proportions are the same is rejected at the $\alpha = .05$ level. In addition, we report that the attained probability of this z is less than .0014, further confirming the decision. In two words, the difference in sample proportions is "statistically

TABLE 13–25

Difference of Proportions Test (Gender by Attitudes toward "Feminists")

| | Gender | | |
Estimated proportion	Male	Female	Total
Proportion negative	.280	.197	.238
	(139)	(102)	(241)
Proportion positive	.720	.803	.762
	(357)	(416)	(773)
Total	1.0	1.0	1.0
	(496)	(518)	(1,014)

Estimated difference, $P_1 - P_2$: .280 − .197 = .083.
$z_{obs} = 3.12$; $z_{crit} = 1.96$.
Since $z_{obs} > 1.96$, reject H_0 at .05 level; p-value < .0014.
Confidence interval: .031, .136.

Source: 2004 National Election Study.

significant." There does appear to be a gap in attitudes toward feminists between men and women.

Before overinterpreting the result, however, note the 95 percent confidence intervals (CI) in table 13–25. They extend from about .03 to .14. In other words, the male-female split could be as small as .03, a difference that might have little if any practical importance. Moreover, the upper limit, .14, may not be large for practical purposes.

We conclude with a methodological and a substantive lesson. We have evidence of a small gender gap in these and previously reported data. Yet it does not seem earth shattering and is not evidence of a major divide in American politics. When it comes to attitudes and partisanship, the gender gap probably pales into insignificance compared with other divisions in society such as racial, regional, class, or ethnic cleavages. The point about statistics is this: examine data from several perspectives. Besides considering the significance of a result measure, think about its magnitude. Once again we see the value of confidence intervals. In this case, they tell us that there might be a modest gap in feelings, but a trivial one is a possibility as well.

In this procedure, the dependent variable is quantitative, and an important measure of the variation is the sum of squared deviations from the mean. To make this concept understandable, consider a variable whose mean is 10. Again, *effect size* means pretty much what the name says: it is a numerical indicator of the impact of an independent variable on a dependent variable. We do not want to get too far ahead, but empirical propositions and theories often stand or fall on effect sizes, not on whether they are "statistically significant."

Analysis of Variance (ANOVA)

ANOVA extends the previous method to the comparison of more than two means. As before, the dependent variable (Y) is quantitative. The independent or explanatory variable (X), sometimes referred to as a treatment or factor, consists of several categories. This procedure treats the observations in the separate categories as independent samples from populations. If the data constitute random samples (and certain other conditions are met), you apply ANOVA to test a null hypothesis such as H_0: $\mu_1 = \mu_2 = \mu_3 \ldots$ and so on, where the μs are the population means of the groups formed by X.

Suppose, for example, that you have a variable (X) with three categories—A, B, and C—and a sample of observations within each of those categories. For each observation, there is a measurement on a quantitative dependent variable (Y). Thus, within every category or group, you can find the mean of Y. ANOVA digs into such data to discover (1) if there are any differences among the means, (2) which specific means differ and by how much, and (3) assuming the observations are sampled from a population, whether the observed differences have arisen by chance or reflect real variation among the categories or groups in X.

More formally, ANOVA rests on a linear model of this form where X has K categories:

$$Y_i = \beta_0 + \beta_1 X_1 + \ldots + \beta_{KX_K} + \varepsilon_i,$$

The Xs are known as indicator or dummy variables, and they jointly and unique describe each observation's particular category membership. β_0 is the overall or grand population mean of Y. (That is, $\beta = \mu$.) The other betas can be interpreted as showing how membership in a specific category can (on average) pull or push one's score on Y away from the grand mean. They are thus the "effects" of X on Y. Instead of having one effect to estimate, we now have several.

EXPLAINED AND UNEXPLAINED VARIATION. The inclusion of the word *variance* in "analysis of variance" may throw you. If the procedure deals with means, why not call it the "analysis of means"? As we said in chapter 2 and elsewhere, the goal of empirical research is to explain differences. In statistics, the variation from all sources is frequently called the total variation. In a sample or observed batch of data, the total variation of a variable is measured by the total sum of squares, which is the summation of the squared deviation of each observation from its mean. Symbolically,

$$TSS = \sum_{i=1}^{N} (Y_i - \bar{Y})^2.$$

Identified and measured variables explain some of this overall variation; the explained part is called, naturally, the explained variation. What's left over is the

TABLE 13–26

Measurements on *Y* within Three Categories of *X*

	Categorical Variable (*X*)		
	A	B	C
	10	20	30
	12	22	32
	14	24	34
	16	26	36
	18	28	38
Number of cases (N_i)	5	5	5
Mean ($\bar{Y}_j$)	14	24	34
Standard deviation ($\hat{\sigma}_j$)	3.16	3.16	3.16

Overall "grand" mean = 24.

unexplained variation. Figure 13–7 may help clarify this point. It shows the data in table 13–26 as a dot chart of individual values. Notice first the considerable variation among the points. By looking at the graph carefully, you may see two kinds of variation. For example, the members of group or category A differ from members of categories B and C. But these observations also vary among themselves. In all three groups, four out of five observations lie above or below their category means. (The mean in A, for instance, is 14, and two scores are above and below it.)

In ANOVA parlance, two types of variation add up to the overall variation, or **total variance**. If we denote the overall variance as *total*, the within-category variance as *within* (or *unexplained*) and the between-group variance as *between* (or *explained*), then the fundamental ANOVA relationship is

Total variance = Within variance + Between variance.

The terms *between* or *explained* refer to the fact that some of the observed differences seems to be due to "membership in" or "having a property of" one category of *X*. That is, on average, the As differ from the Bs. Knowing that a case has characteristic A tells us roughly what its value on *Y* will be. The prediction will not be perfect, however, because of the internal variation among the As. Yet if we could numerically measure these different sources of variability, we could determine what percentage of the total was explained:

Percent explained = (Between/Total) × 100.

If the portion of total variance explained by the independent variable is relatively large, there is reason to believe that at least two of the population means are not equal. You can figure out which are different only by examining graphs and calculating effect sizes.

Now look at figure 13–8. It shows two things: the means of A, B, and C are all the same, and the observations differ among themselves but not because they belong

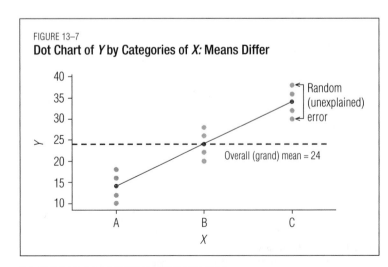

FIGURE 13–7

Dot Chart of *Y* by Categories of *X*: Means Differ

Note: Variation in Y is due to differences in X and "error."

to one or another group. Each level of X has the same mean. So the total variation in scores has nothing to do with levels of the factor. There is no difference among means and hence no explained or between variation. The analysis of the relationship is thus total variation = within variation + zero, and the percent explained variation is zero:

$$\text{Percent explained} = \text{Explained/Total} = 0/\text{total} = 0.$$

The mathematics of ANOVA simply involves quantifying the types of variation and using these numbers to make inferences. The standard measure of variation is the sum of squares, which is a total of squared deviations about a mean. Let's not get bogged down in computations and instead simply express the idea of explained variation with these terms: TSS stands for the total variability in the data (read this as "the total sum of squares"); BSS represents the between means variability ("between sum of squares"); and WSS ("within sum of squares") is the within groups or categories variation. With these definitions we have

$$TSS = BSS + WSS, \text{ and}$$

$$\text{Percent explained} = (BSS/TSS) \times 100.$$

The percent of variation explained is a commonly used (and abused!) measure of the strength of a relationship. In the context of ANOVA, the percent variation explained is sometimes called **eta-squared** (h^2). One of the properties of eta-squared may be obvious: it varies between zero, which means the independent variable (statistically speaking) explains nothing about Y, to 1, which means it accounts for all of the variation. You frequently read something to the effect that "X explains 60 percent of the variation in Y and hence is an important explanatory factor." Whether or not the data justify a statement of this sort depends on a host of considerations, which we take up later.

DO MEANS DIFFER? SIGNIFICANCE TEST FOR ANALYSIS OF VARIANCE. A test of the hypothesis that K subpopulation means are equal (H_0: $\mu_1 = \mu_2 = \mu_3 = \ldots = \mu_K$) rests on several assumptions, especially that the observations in one group are independent of those in the other groups. In addition, we assume large N_Ks and equal population variances (that is, $\sigma^2_1 = \sigma^2_2 = \sigma^2_3 = \ldots \sigma^2_K$). Test results are most often organized and summarized in an ANOVA table like table 13–27.

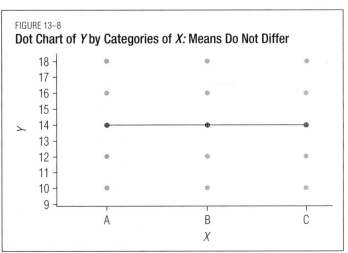

FIGURE 13–8
Dot Chart of Y by Categories of X: Means Do Not Differ

Note: X does not "explain" any variation in Y.

TABLE 13–27

Typical ANOVA Table Format

Source of Variation	Sum of Squares	Degrees of Freedom	Mean Square	Observed F
Between (name of variable)	BSS	$df_{between} = K - 1$	$BMS = BSS/df_{between}$	$F_{obs} = \dfrac{BSS/(K-1)}{WSS/(N-K)} = \dfrac{BMS}{WMS}$
Within (unexplained or error)	WSS	$df_{within} = N - K$	$WMS = WSS/df_{within}$	
Total	TSS	$df_{total} = N - 1$		

Note: Assume X has K categories.

The terms inside the table may seem intimidating at first, but the numbers are straightforward. The sums of squares are calculated from formulas described elsewhere. Each sum of squares has an associated degrees of freedom, df. They are easy to calculate: the between df is the number of categories (K) of the independent variable minus 1, or $K - 1$; and the within df is N, the total sample size, minus the number of categories, or $N - K$. Together they sum to the degrees of freedom for the total sum of squares, or $(K - 1) + (N - K) = N - 1$.

Whenever a sum of squares is divided by its degrees of freedom, the quotient is called a mean square. The between mean square is divided by the within mean square to obtain an observed test statistic called the F statistic. Symbolically,

$$F_{obs, df_{Numerator}, df_{Denominator}} = \frac{\dfrac{SS \text{ between}}{df \text{ for between}}}{\dfrac{SS \text{ error}}{df \text{ for error}}} = \frac{\text{Mean square between}}{\text{Mean square error}}.$$

Like the other statistics we have discussed (for example, chi square, t, and z), the observed F has a distribution called (sensibly enough) the F distribution. As in the case of the t distribution, the F distribution is a family, each member of which depends on *two* degrees of freedom, one for the between component and one for the within component. A decision about the null hypothesis of equal population means is made by comparing F_{obs} to F_{crit}.

The general idea should be familiar by now. Suppose we use the hypothetical data in table 13–26 to test the hypothesis that $\mu_A = \mu_B = \mu_C$ against the alternative that at least two of them differ. (Technically, we should have larger samples, but this is just an illustration.) For this test, we choose the .001 level of significance. Table 13–28 shows the results as they are typically spewed out of a computer.

The observed F is 50, considerably larger than the critical F (with 2 and 12 df at the .001 level) of 12.97. (The critical value is found in appendix D.) First decide on a level of significance, then on the degrees of freedom for the within sum of squares (12) and for the between sum of squares (2). The needed value

TABLE 13–28
ANOVA Results

Source of Variation	Degrees of Freedom (df)	Sum of Squares	Mean Squares	Observed F
Between X	2	1,000	500.0	50.0
Within	12	120	10.0	
Total	14	1,120		
p-level ≈ .000				

Source: Table 13–26.

will be in the third F table. Since F_{obs} exceeds F_{crit}, the null hypothesis is rejected at the .001 level. Indeed, if the null hypothesis were in fact true, the p-value (.000) tells us we have obtained a very improbable result.

What does all this mean? So far, we only know that two or more population means are probably unequal. Without looking at confidence intervals, we do not know which differ or by how much. The precise source of the explained variation is not obvious. Once again, at the risk of beating a dead horse, we emphasize that a significance test provides helpful information but does not relieve you of the duty to scrutinize your data from several angles.

For a "real" example, we return to the question of what motivates political participation. The Citizenship, Involvement, Democracy Survey that we've been using contains an interesting item, "Citizenship Norms," which measures "the public's adherence to different potential citizenship norms." To operationalize the concept, the investigators combined responses to a series of questions—"To be a good citizen, how important is it for a person to be . . . [list items]. 0 is extremely unimportant and 10 is extremely important"[26]—into "factor" scales. Although the scale scores (e.g.,–1.0) have no intrinsic meaning, they nevertheless allow us to compare respondents on their degree of commitment to *active* citizenship (e.g., voting, being involved in politics and voluntary groups, forming and expressing opinions) as opposed to "obedience" norms (e.g., "always obeying the law," serving in the military, paying taxes). The higher the score, the more a person believes citizenship entails active participation, not mere acquiescence to rules. The summary statistics for this variable are $N = 944$, mean $= -0.036$, median $= .057$, standard deviation $= 1.02$, and IQR $= 1.387$. From these data and the histogram (figure 13–9), we see that the sample values seem to be roughly normally distributed with a mean of nearly zero.[27] Note that the means nearly equal the medians and the variation of Y is more or less the same across categories.[28]

But what explains the variation in these scores? Are they associated with other factors that might make these data more intelligible? In particular, how will the average scale scores vary among different groups? Right off the bat we might hypothesize that highly partisan citizens (i.e., people who closely identify with one of the two major American political parties) will tend to believe that good

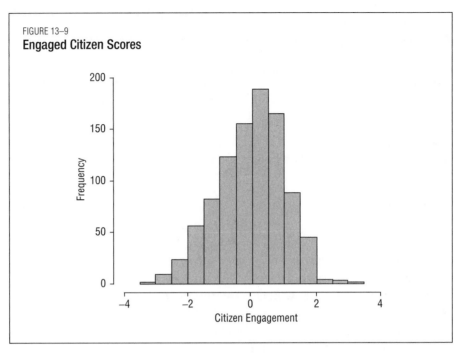

FIGURE 13–9
Engaged Citizen Scores

Source: Citizenship, Involvement, Democracy Survey, 2006.

citizenship involves more than passively following the rules and the obligations of a democracy include articulating and acting on one's opinions. Nonpartisans, by contrast, will stress nonactivist norms.[29] In short, we can propose that mean engagement scores will increase across categories of partisanship. The null and alternative hypotheses are these:

- H_0: $\mu_{Nonpartisan} = \mu_{Weak} = \mu_{Moderate} = \mu_{Strong}$.
- H_A: $\mu_{Nonpartisan} < \mu_{Weak} < \mu_{Moderate} < \mu_{Strong}$.

Figure 13–10 offers a bird's-eye view of the data. From the picture it is apparent that the means vary only roughly in the predicted manner and most means differ only marginally. We immediately have reason to doubt that this proposition is going to hold water.

Still, let's proceed with a formal *F*-test. Even though these are survey data and we can use regression analysis to accomplish the same task (see the following discussion and chapter 14), these data lend themselves to analysis of variance if we think metaphorically: consider the levels of partisanship as "treatments" or factors that are "assigned" to individuals whose responses are then recorded. Our job is to compare mean squares: the "explained" (by partisanship) and the "unexplained." Table 13–29 shows the results.

Calculating Sums of Squares[1]

Let N = total sample size and X be the independent variable with K categories: k = 1, 2,. . . K.

First, get totals, T_k, for *each* group or subpopulation:

$$T_k = \sum_{k=1}^{N_k} Y_{ik}, k = 1, 2, \ldots K.$$

Calculate three quantities:

- Square each subtotal (T_k), divide by N_k, the total number of cases in the kth subpopulation.

$$A = \sum_{k=1}^{K} \frac{T_k^2}{N_k}$$

- Sum all observations, square the result, the divide total by N:

$$B = \frac{\left(\sum_{i=1}^{N} Y_i \right)^2}{N}.$$

- Square each observation and obtain the total:

$$C = \sum_{i=1}^{N} Y_i^2.$$

Finally, the sum of squares are:

- Total sum of squares:

  TSS = C − B.

- Between sum of squares:

  BSS = A − B.

- Within sum of squares:

  WSS = C − A.

Note: If you have a statistical calculator the sum of squares used here and elsewhere can be found by applying the calculating formulas provided below. Most calculators will automatically accumulate both the sum of a set of numbers $\sum_{i=1}^{N} Y_i$ and the sum of their squares $\sum_{i=1}^{n} Y_i^2$.

1. Based on notes prepared by Richard Williams, University of Notre Dame. Available Online: Stats I - http://www.nd.edu/~ rwilliam/stats1/

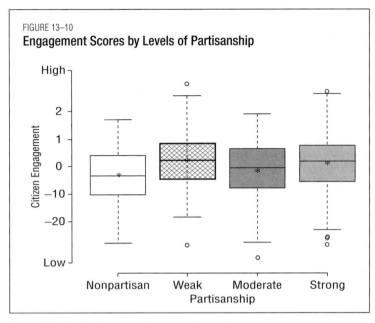

FIGURE 13–10
Engagement Scores by Levels of Partisanship

Source: Citizenship, Involvement, and Democracy Survey, 2006.

We now confront an interesting situation. The boxplot of the category suggests little real difference in average values across levels of partisanship. Yet, the *F* statistic (9.98) is highly significant, which tells us that after rejecting the null hypothesis, we should search for which means differ from which in meaningful ways. So which ones differ? After all, there six comparisons: "strong" versus "nonpartisan," "strong versus "weak," . . ." moderate versus "weak." Are all subpopulations different or only a subset of them? Do any differences have a substantive meaning? A picture might clarify matters.

Carefully, examine figure 13–11. The stars (*) represent the six estimated differences. The bars around them are 99 percent confidence intervals.[30] These intervals contain a range of values that probably includes the true differences. Look, for instance, at the strong-nonpartisan interval shown by third bar from the bottom. It does not include zero as a likely value. So we might conclude that strong partisans in the population have on average higher engagement scores than nonpartisans. (We know the value is "greater" because the difference is positive.) Similarly the next bar indicates that moderates and nonpartisans do not differ significantly because the line includes zero, suggesting that the difference could well be zero. As you go through the graph, you can see that at least two and possibly three pairs of means differ. But apart from these there does not seem to be a clear pattern in the

TABLE 13–29
ANOVA Table and *F*-Test

Source of Variation	Degrees of Freedom (*df*)	Sum of Squares	Mean Squares	Observed *F*
Between (due to partisanship)	3	30.22	10.07	9.98*
Within	940	948.22	1.02	
Total	943	978.44		

*p-level ≈ .000

Source: Citizen, Involvement, Democracy Survey, 2006.

data. Our expectation at the outset was that as partisanship increased, so too would citizen engagement scores. Yet, as figures 13–10 and 13–11 reveal, there is no obvious trend in the data.

We should also compare the magnitudes of the differences. Doing so is difficult, however, because the scale scores are abstract numbers that show respondents' positions on a scale constructed from ten individual items. Thus, the difference between strong partisans and independents is 0.44. It's statistically significant, but is it meaningful? In the absence of an understandable scale, we have to

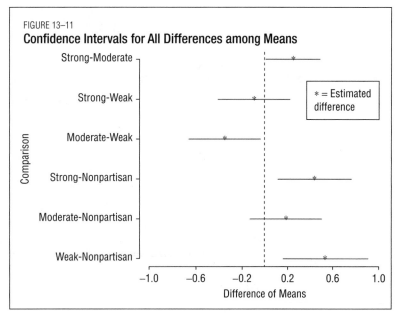

FIGURE 13–11
Confidence Intervals for All Differences among Means

Source: Citizenship, Involvement, Democracy Survey, 2006

rely on patterns and trends as shown by graphs for the most informative interpretation.

In any case, the results demonstrate the limitations of a hypothesis test and the necessity of using a variety of graphs as well as statistics to construct interpretative pictures.

A FINAL NOTE ON ANOVA.   This section has not spent much time on calculations in favor of explaining what the results of ANOVA mean. But there is another reason. Most political scientists analyze "ANOVA-like" data represented as a "linear model." In an earlier chapter, we defined a *model* as a simplified representation of an object or process. We now narrow our scope to *statistical* models, which again simplify reality but describe it with mathematical concepts. Analysis of variance, for example, is often introduced as a procedure for estimating and testing a model of this sort:

$$Y_i = \mu + \beta X_i + \varepsilon_i,$$

where Y is a quantitative dependent variable, μ is the overall or grand mean, X_k represents the value of the kth category of the explanatory factor, the betas are parameters (numbers) that show the decrease in the overall mean produced by moving from one category to another, and ε is a random error. There is nothing really mysterious about this equation. If the overall mean is 20 and $\hat{\beta} = 5$, then moving from one category of X (e.g., becoming "very liberal" instead of just plain liberal), increases the mean from 55 to 55. Procedures shown later lead to a test for the significance of $\hat{\beta}$.

REGRESSION ANALYSIS

The procedure, **regression analysis**, is really a toolbox of methods for describing how, how strongly, and under what conditions an independent and dependent variable are associated. The regression framework is without doubt the meat and potatoes of empirical social and political research because of its versatility. Regression techniques can be used to analyze all sorts of variables having all kinds of relationships. But its value goes even further. In chapter 6 we discussed the difficulty of making causal inferences on the basis of nonexperimental observations. Many scholars believe regression analysis and related approaches act as reasonable surrogates for controlled experiments and can, if applied carefully, lead to causal inferences. As with many other techniques, the first step is to get the overall picture.

Basic Assumptions

A linear regression model for two variables has this form:

$$Y_i = \beta_0 + \beta_1 X_1 + \ldots + \varepsilon_i.$$

The betas are regression parameters (constant and slope), and ε_i is the error terms. Before undertaking estimation and significance tests for the regression

---

A REMINDER ABOUT CONFIDENCE INTERVALS AND TESTS OF STATISTICAL SIGNIFICANCE

In this text, we describe both hypothesis tests and confidence intervals. The former are common in scholarly and popular reports of statistical findings, but the latter, we believe, give you all the information a hypothesis test does and then some.

Suppose you hypothesize that in a population, $A - B = 0$. You conduct a t- or z-test on a sample and reject this hypothesis at the .05 level. This means you are pretty sure A does not equal B. You are not positive, of course, but if you carried out the analysis correctly, there is only a 1 in 20 (.05) chance of rejecting a hypothesis that should not be rejected.

What about finding 95 percent confidence limits for the $A - B$ difference? Notice that $1 - .95 = .05$. The connection between .95 and .05 is not coincidental. A confidence interval puts a positive spin on your inference: you are 95 percent sure that the true difference lies somewhere in the interval. By contrast, a significance test at the .05 level is in a sense a negative statement: you think there's only a 5 percent chance (.05 probability) that you are wrong. But as far as probability theory is concerned, one procedure is as good as another.

So why do we prefer confidence intervals? Because besides allowing you to discard (or not) a hypothesis, confidence intervals explicitly show you possible values of the effect; better still, they are presented in the measurements of the variables in the problem at hand. If you reject the hypothesis that A equals B, you only know that A probably does not equal B. But if the confidence intervals for the difference run from, say, 1 to 2, you may conclude that there is not a meaningful theoretical or practical difference. On the other hand, if the interval extends from 1 to 50, that might suggest something worthy of further investigation.

parameters, we need touch on a topic that we have so far finessed: Under what conditions is it reasonable to develop, estimate, and test linear models? That is, since we only have samples or actual realizations of data, we can only know so much about the population from which they came and the causal mechanisms at work. Much of the rest we have to assume. The assumptions, some of which can be verified to one degree or another, include the following:

- Correct specification: The model includes all the necessary independent variables and excludes the unnecessary ones. By *necessary*, we mean the variables that systematically affect Y. Unnecessary information in the form of irrelevant variables just increases errors of prediction.

- Linearity: The expected value of the dependent variable is a *linear* function of the independent variable. Thus, if X_1 is an explanatory factor, its impact on Y comes in the form of $\beta_0 + \beta_1 X$, not, say, exponentially as in β_1^X. (It is possible, however, to create new variables and use them additively. Hence, we could define $Z = \beta^X$. But of course now a unit change in Z will be harder to interpret.)

- X measured without error: A critical assumption is that the independent variable is measured without systematic error. To take a quick example, suppose we have observed X values but in reality our measurement instrument is faulty, so the observed Xs are a function of "true" values and an error: $X = x + $ error, where x is the actual value. In this situation, regression estimates may be biased, which gives us a reason to think carefully about the independent variables.

- Independent observations: Data are collected in such a fashion that the inclusion of one case has no bearing on the selection of any other (as opposed to, say, sampling ten individuals and then including their best friends).

- Random errors: The error component, which represents the effects of omitted causes of Y, measurement errors *in Y*, and "natural" variation among subjects, must be truly random in the sense that the errors cancel. In statistical language, $E(\varepsilon_i = 0)$, which is read as "the expected (long-range) value of the errors is zero."

- Constant error variance: The variation in errors is the same for each level or value of X. (Want a fancier term? Constant variance is called *homoscedasticity* or *homogeneity* of variance.)

- Normally distributed errors: You can think of the errors added onto the linear model as unseen, unmeasured variables. Nevertheless, they still have a distribution, which (for testing hypotheses) we assume is normal with a mean of zero and variance σ^2.

This list serves an important purpose: to remind us that a modeling technique like linear regression carries a lot of hidden baggage. Just because an analyst ignores them does not mean the effects of violating assumptions go away. A computer can crank out reams of respectable-looking reports without the results being accurate or meaningful. Consequently, there is a vast and continuously growing statistical literature on how bad the violations are and what to do about them. Unfortunately, the topic is too large and complex to explore here. Thus, we generally proceed as if the assumptions were true.[31]

Scatterplots

The real work of empirical political science involves answering "why" questions: Why do some countries develop democratic forms of government? Why do nations go to war? Why are some people Republicans, others Democrats, and still others independent or apolitical? To answer these questions, researchers translate verbal theories, hypotheses, even hunches into models. A model shows how and under what conditions two (or more) variables are related. The beginning point of this process is identifying associations or correlations between pairs of variables, and graphs provide the best first step.

One common graph is the scatterplot. Intended for quantitative data, a **scatterplot** contains a horizontal axis representing one variable and a vertical axis (drawn at a right angle) for the other variable. The usual practice is to place the values of the independent variable along the x-axis and values of the dependent variable along the y-axis. The scales of the axes are in units of the particular variables, such as percents or thousands of dollars. The X and Y values for each observation are plotted using this coordinate system. The measurements for each case are placed at the point on the graph corresponding to the case's values on the variables.

As an example, figure 13–12 shows five Y and X values and how they are plotted on a scatterplot. Each case is located or marked at the intersection of the line extending from the x- and y-axes. The first pair of observations, 5 and 10, appears at the point Y = 5 and X = 10.

Scatterplots are handy because they show at a glance the form and strength of relationships. In this example, increases in X tend to be associated with increases in Y. Indeed, we have drawn a straight line on the graph in such a fashion

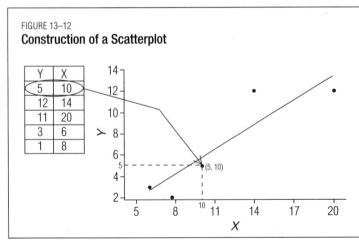

FIGURE 13–12
Construction of a Scatterplot

Y	X
5	10
12	14
11	20
3	6
1	8

Source: Hypothetical data.

that most observations fall on it or very near to it. In the language introduced at the chapter's outset, this pattern of points indicates a strong "positive linear correlation."

For a more realistic illustration, let's return to the discussion of the causes and consequences of inequality. Look at figure 13–13. It shows how union density (percentage of labor force who are members of unions) is related to a measure of income inequality (Gini scores) in twenty-one developed countries. The data, which come from table 11–1, show each nation's values on union density (X) and Gini scale (Y). We have also added a so-called least-squares line to underscore the decreasing, approximately linear pattern of the relationship. Finally, we tagged two countries, Japan and the United States, to illustrate how the graph is constructed. (If you refer to table 11–1, you will see that the union-Gini values for Japan are 20.3 and 24.9, respectively; those for the United States are 12.6 and 40.8.) We see a familiar pattern in the scatter of the points: correlation. It has these features:

A TIP AND A WARNING

If you have large batch of quantitative data (say, more than 500 cases), you can obtain clearer, more interpretable results if you ask your software to first select a *sample* of the data (25 to 75 cases) and plot those numbers. If the sample is truly representative, the plot will reveal the important features of the relationship. Creating a scatterplot from an entire data set may produce a picture filled with so many dots that nothing intelligible can be detected. Furthermore, scatterplots are suitable only for quantitative variables; they are not intended for categorical (nominal and ordinal) data. If you tried, for instance, to get your software to plot party identification by gender, the result would be two parallel lines that would tell you nothing.

- The association is roughly linear; the points lie near a straight line.

- The correlation is negative; the line slants downward, telling us that an increase in unionization is associated with a decrease in inequality. Bluntly stated, the more unions, the less the inequality.

- The correlation is moderately strong: the points don't form a perfect linear pattern, but the configuration is clear enough.

- The two identified cases (Japan and United States) provide further examples of how to interpret the plot. If the straight line is used to predict or estimate a country's Gini coefficient on the basis of union density, we see that Japan has a lower than expected score, while the US score is higher. Similar labor profiles but quite different outcomes. (But in one sense, the errors almost cancel, a point we discuss in greater detail later.) Most of the observations lie nearer the line, which suggests that whatever technique produced the line might provide a method to quantify the correlation more precisely.

Modeling Linear Relationships

The examination of scatterplots is a good first step in describing statistically or modeling a two-variable relationship. Figure 13–13 shows the relationship

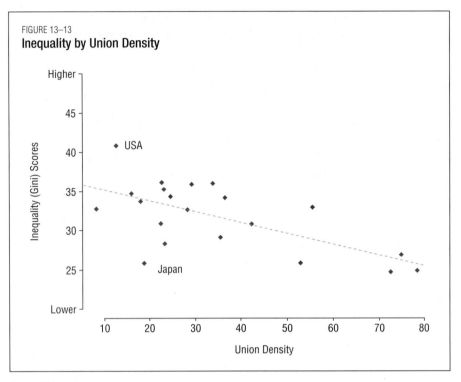

FIGURE 13–13
Inequality by Union Density

Source: Table 11–1.

between union density and a measure of income inequality, the Gini variable, in twenty-one developing nations. It reveals a pattern: *large* values of density are associated with *small* values of inequality, and vice versa. The relationship is by no means perfect, but there does seem to be a negative correlation.

As mentioned earlier, we added a line to underscore the correlation. The slope of this line is a negative number, which means that as we go up the scale on the *x*-axis, we move down the *y*-axis. These ideas can be further clarified by recalling high school algebra. The equation for the graph of a straight line has the general form

$$Y = a + bX.$$

In the equation, *X* and *Y* are variables. The first letter is called the constant and equals the value of *Y* when *X* equals zero (just substitute 0 for *X*). Also, the constant equals the mean of the dependent variable or $a = \bar{Y}$, a fact that turns out to be useful.

The equation for the linear model has a geometric interpretation as well. If the graph of the equation is plotted, *a* is the point where the line crosses the *y*-axis.

The letter *b* stands for the slope of the line, which indicates how much *Y* changes for each one-unit increase in *X*. For a positive *b* (i.e., *b* > 0), if we move up the *X* scale one unit, *b* indicates how much *Y* changes. (If we applied this type of equation to the data shown in figure 13–13, *b* would be negative and would indicate how much *Y*, Gini scores, decline for every unit increase in *X*, union concentration.) If there is no (linear) relationship between the two variables, the slope of the line is zero, and its graph is horizontal and parallel to the *x*-axis.

Note that the line's slope depends partly on the measurement scale of *X*. So, if one were inadvertently to use *Y* as the *in*dependent variable, a slope could be calculated, but its magnitude would in general *not* be the same as if *X* were treated as independent. Recall from the beginning of the chapter that in the language of statistics, the slope is an *asymmetric* parameter.

The Regression Model

Regression analysis can be thought of as applying these ideas to two-variable relationships, where both variables are numeric or quantitative. (Actually, regression analysis is general enough to include categorical variables, but only in special ways. We discuss this possibility in chapter 14.) The goal here is to find an equation, the graph of which "best fits" the data.[32]

What exactly does "fit" mean in this context? In regression, an equation is found in such a way that its graph is a line that minimizes the squared vertical distances between the data points and the line drawn. In figure 13–14, for example, d_1 and d_2 represent the distances of observed data points from an estimated regression line. This mathematical procedure is called least squares and is often called "ordinary least squares," or OLS for short.

There are lots of ways of expressing a linear regression model. As noted several times before, we utilize lowercase Greek letters to denote unknown quantities and Greek letters with hats (^) over them to denote estimators of these numbers. In the two-variable case, the regression model commonly appears as

$$Y_i = \beta_0 + \beta_{YX} X + \varepsilon_i.$$

Pay attention to the subscripts on the second beta. They signify that we are regressing "*Y* on *X*," not the other way around. That is, the dependent variable is *Y* and is listed first in the subscript. The independent variable, *X*, comes second. Always remember this key point: regression analysis is asymmetric in that the choice of dependent variable matters because, as noted in the previous section, the numerical value of the slope (regression coefficient) depends on which

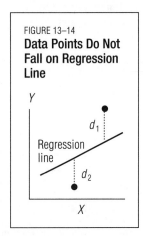

FIGURE 13–14

Data Points Do Not Fall on Regression Line

variable is considered dependent. Throughout we have treated Y as the dependent variable. Were we to switch their roles, we would be regressing X *on* Y. And usually $\beta_{YX} \neq \beta_{XY}$.

Since an important assumption underlying regression is that the errors in the model "cancel out," we sometimes state the model in terms of the expected value of Y:

$$E(Y_i) = \beta_0 + \beta_{YX}X.$$

The notation simply means the average value of Y is a function only of the linear effect of X. If there were no errors, *every* observed Y would equal $\beta_0 + \beta_1 X$, but since prediction errors are inevitable, we can only predict an average value for the dependent variable given a specific X value.

However stated, the two constants are called regression parameters. The first, β_0, is the constant and is interpreted exactly as indicated before: it is the value of Y when X equals zero. (Remember that in the simple case, it also equals the mean of Y.) The second, β_1, is the **regression coefficient** and tells how much Y changes per unit change in X. The regression coefficient is always measured in units of the dependent variable.

The error (ε) indicates that observed data do not follow a neat pattern that can be summarized with a straight line. It suggests instead that an observation's score on Y can be broken into two parts: one that is "due to" the independent variable and is represented by the linear part of the equation, $\beta_0 + \beta_1 X$, and another that is "due to" error or chance, ε. In other words, if we know an observation's score on X and also know the equation that describes the relationship, we can substitute the number into the equation to obtain a *predicted* value of Y. This predicted value will differ from the observed value by the error:

Observed value = Predicted value + Error.

If there are few errors—that is, if all the data lie near the regression line—then the predicted and observed values will be very close. In that case, we would say the equation adequately explains, or fits, the data. In contrast, if the observed data differ from the predicted values, then there will be considerable error, and the fit will not be as good.

Figure 13–15 ties these ideas together. Suppose we consider a particular case. Its scores on X and Y (X_i and Y_i) are represented by a dot (•).

HOW IT'S DONE

Calculation of Estimated Regression Coefficients

The regression coefficient is calculated as follows:

$$\hat{\beta}_{YX} = \frac{N \sum_{i=1}^{N} X_i Y_i - \left(\sum_{i=1}^{N} X_i \right)\left(\sum_{i=1}^{N} Y_i \right)}{N \sum_{i=1}^{N} X_i^2 - \left(\sum_{i=1}^{N} X_i \right)},$$

where N is the number of cases and X_i and Y_i are the X-Y values of the ith case. The regression constant is calculated as follows: $\hat{\beta}_0 = \bar{Y} - \hat{\beta}_{YX} \bar{X}$, where $\bar{Y}$ and $\bar{X}$ are the means of Y and X, respectively, and $\hat{\beta}_{YX}$ is the regression coefficient as calculated.

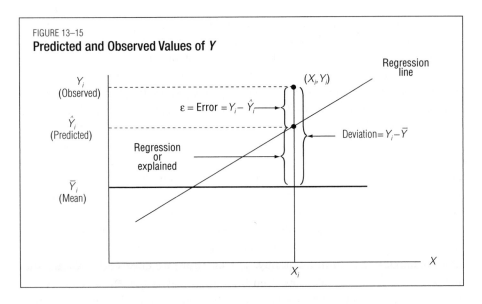

FIGURE 13–15
Predicted and Observed Values of Y

Its score on X is denoted as X_i. If we draw a line straight up from X_i to the regression line and then draw another line to the y-axis, we find the point that represents the predicted value of Y, denoted $\hat{Y}_i$. The difference between the predicted value, $\hat{Y}_i$, and the observed value, Y_i, is called the error or **residual.** Recall that the residual represents the difference between the predicted score based on the regression equation—which is the mathematical equation describing the relationship between the variables—and the observed score, Y_i. (As we see in a moment, it stands for that part of a Y score that is unexplained.) Regression-computing formulas pick values of α and β that minimize the sum of all these squared errors.

Although the minimizing procedure may sound complicated, computer software and many handheld calculators make finding regression equations relatively easy. The tricky part is understanding the results. We do not show the calculations here, but the estimated equation for the regression of Gini scores on union density is

$$\hat{Y}_i = 36.44 - .14\text{union}.$$

What exactly do the numbers 36.44 and –.14 mean?

Interpretation of Parameters

The slope of the line and the y-intercept describe the nature and strength of the connection between the two variables. Again, the y-intercept is the value of the dependent variable when X (the independent variable) = 0, or, stated differently, it is the place where the regression line crosses the y-axis when X = 0.

In the current example the *y*-intercept of 36.44 means that when a country's unionization is zero, its predicted Gini score is about 34.44. This value is, of course, a prediction for a case with no one in organized labor union unions. In many instances, the actual value is not of much substantive interest because a zero value on the independent variable does not make much theoretical sense.

The slope or regression coefficient is a different matter, however. It measures the amount the dependent variable changes when the independent variable, *X*, changes one unit. In this case, the slope of –.14 tells us that for every 1 percent increase in union strength, there is a predicted or estimated *decrease* of .14 units of "inequality." (We label the variables "union strength" and "inequality" to keep reminding us that they refer to politically interesting and important concepts. But the actual measurements—the operational definitions of strength and inequality—were described earlier.) The two variables appear to be linked in the hypothesized way. Remember, the initial substantive problem was to explain cross-national variation in inequality. The literature we cited earlier claims that the large disparities we seen between the richest, say, 1 percent and the rest of the population do not occur by chance but result from political struggle. Our idea is that the better equipped the lower classes are to press their demands, the greater share of the national wealth they can obtain for themselves. When looked at from the narrow point of view of our research design and dataset, this notion seems to hold water.

The value of the regression coefficient (–.14) may seem small and abstract. Here's a simple method to help you better understand its meaning. Try performing some thought experiments in which you systematically substitute "informative" values of *X* into the equation to observe how they affect the dependent variable. Let's take some arbitrary but practically meaningful union density scores and insert them one by one into the estimated equation, $\hat{Y}_i = 36.44 - .14\text{union}$, to see their effects via predicted values. Table13–30 shows the outcome. The entries are obtained by substitution as illustrated here:

$$\hat{Y}_i = 36.44 - .14(0) = 36.44$$
$$\hat{Y}_i = 36.44 - .14(1) = 36.30$$
$$\hat{Y}_i = 36.44 - .14(10) = 35.04$$

. . .

The predicted Gini score of a country without any organized labor (0 percent) is 36.44. Suppose its union rate increased 1 percentage point. Line 3 in the table tells us that its score would drop to 36.30, a decline of .14 units. This amount is exactly the estimated regression coefficient reported above, confirming intuitively that it measures the impact of a one unit change in *X*. Now, is the effect, .14, a big deal or not? It bears repeating that the regression parameter is measured in units of the independent variable, here percent unionization. In practical terms, a 1 percent change in union participation would not much affect a country's labor-relations profile. But what if it increased 10 percent (or 10 units)? The predicted Y is 35.04. When rounded, the decrease is 1.4, which is except for rounding error, 10 times the slope, as it should be.[33] Or, if half a nation's eligible workers belong to unions, the predicted score would be 29.44, about a 7-point decline; if all were unionized it would drop all the way to 22.44. (We are implicitly applying a causal interpretation merely to explain how the regression coefficient can be interpreted.)

True, it is hard to grasp fully numbers like these when the measurement instrument is this abstract. That's why we later resort to a rescaling of a variable like the Gini coefficient. First, however, consider another short example.

TABLE 13–30
Predicted Gini Scores

Interpretation	Selected X Value (Union density)	Predicted Y (Gini)
No unions	0	36.44
1 percent unionized	1	36.30
10 percent unionized	10.00	35.04
Minimum observed	8.20	35.29
25th quantile	22.40	33.30
Median	28.20	32.49
Mean	34.79	31.57
75th quantile	42.30	30.52
Observed maximum	78.00	25.52
100 percent unionization	100	22.44

Briefly return to the debate about the existence of a political gender gap. Those who believe that, for whatever reason, women tend to be more liberal than men need to show that the sexes' political attitudes differ to some extent. The 2008 American National Election Study, part of the series of voting studies we've been using, contains variables for gender and political ideology. The latter is a 7-point scale that extends from 1 (*most liberal–least conservative*) to 7 (*least liberal–most conservative*). For the moment, we can treat the scale scores as if they were numbers and use them in a regression analysis as the dependent variable.

But we now have an independent variable, gender. It has been mentioned several times that a dichotomous variable—that is a variable with two categories—can be given a numerical interpretation by assigning numeric codes to the two categories. It is especially helpful to use codes 0 and 1. This coding scheme is called "dummy." Thus, men are coded 0, women 1. A "one-unit" change in this variable simply means moving from one category to the next. (Again, we are speaking metaphorically because such changes are usually physically impossible or meaningless.) In short, we want to predict ideology based on one's gender. After crunching the numbers, the estimated equation is $\hat{Y}_i = 4.24 - .18$ (*gender*)

The regression constant in the case of dummy coding has a particularly clear interpretation: it is the mean of Y for the members of the category coded 0. Try putting 0 in the above equation. What do you get? The answer ($\hat{Y}_i = 4.24 - .18(0) = 4.24$) is the average liberalism-conservatism score among just women. The "effect" of being a male is to reduce the mean ideology score by .18 units: $\hat{Y}_i = 4.24 - .18(1) = 4.06$ (This number, as you might have guessed, is the mean ideology score for men.) Whether or not this result is worth shouting about remains to be seen. The answer depends on how well the data fit the model.

Remember: the regression parameter is asymmetric. In symbols, $\beta_{YX} \neq \beta_{XY}$, except in certain situations. Had we used Gini rates as the dependent variable (thereby considering union density as independent) we would get a different equation:

$$\hat{Y}_{(union)} = 126.52 - 2.89X_{(Gini)}.$$

This equation is completely different from the previous one. (Of course, the same interpretation applies—"A change of 1 in Gini score is accompanied by (causes) a decrease of about 2.89 percent in unionization."—and in this context leads to the same theoretical conclusion, namely that inequality and union strength are negatively related. But in other situations, mixing the order of variables may lead to nonsensical results, especially if there is a hint of causality in the analysis. Suppose, for example, you were studying the interaction between age and annual income. If you treated age as the dependent variable and regressed it on income, the resulting regression coefficient could be interpreted "as a one dollar increase in income leads to a specified amount of aging"—clearly a silly conclusion. The moral is to ponder the choice of dependent and independent variables.

Measuring the Fit of a Regression Line: R^2

Let us pause for a moment to glance at figure 13–15 again. Earlier in the chapter, we introduced a term called the total sum of squares (*TSS*). It was the sum of squared deviation from the mean. Now, by examining figure 13–15 you can see that an observation's *total* deviation from the mean, denoted $Y_i - \bar{Y}$, can be divided into two additive parts. The first is the difference between the mean and the predicted value of *Y*. Let's label that portion as the "regression," or "explained," part (*RegSS*). It is explained in the sense that a piece of the deviation from the overall mean is accounted for or attributable to *X*, the independent variable. The second component of the total deviation is called "residual sum of squares" (*ResSS*) and measures prediction errors. This term is frequently labeled the "unexplained sum of squares" because it represents the differences between our predictions—that is, $\hat{Y}$—and what is actually observed. If all the predictions were perfect, there would be no errors, and the residual sum of squares errors would be zero. The residual sum of squares provides the numerator of the "conditional" standard deviation of *Y*, a statistic used later on to test hypotheses and construct confidence intervals.

These three quantities are identical to the ones presented earlier in connection with the analysis of variance, except two of them have slightly different names—they are now called the "regression" and "error" residual sum of squares. (Their computing formulas also differ slightly.) Yet the same fundamental relationship still holds:

$$TSS = RegSS + ResSS.$$

The total sum of squares (*TSS*) represents all the variation in the data, explained or not, whereas the regression sum of squares (*RegSS*) corresponds to that part of this total that is "explained" (in a statistical sense) by the independent variable via the regression equation. So, as in ANOVA, we can calculate the "proportion of total variation explained by *X*" as

$$R^2 = RegSS/TSS$$

This measure (R^2) is known as **R-squared** and is one of the most commonly reported statistics in the social sciences.[34] For example, if R^2 is multiplied by 100, the result is often interpreted as the percentage of (total) variation in *Y* that *X* "explains." R^2's popularity derives partly from its simplicity and partly from the belief that it indicates how well a regression model fits data.[35]

Table 13–31 shows the sums of squares from the regression of telephone availability on infant mortality. The explained variation is .56, which, statistically speaking, means that *X* explains somewhat more than half of the variation in *Y*.

An R^2 of .56 means that about 40 percent of the variation in Gini scores is statistically "explained" by union density. This result once again suggests a modest correlation between the two variables. The evidence is consistent with the hypothesis that to the extent that workers are politically empowered, inequality is reduced, but lots more information is needed to support a causal connection.

An important property of *R*-squared is that it is symmetrical, meaning that it has the same value no matter which variable is treated as dependent. This is a key difference from the regression coefficient, which does change depending on the choice of dependent variable. Also, *R*-squared must be at least zero; it cannot be negative because it is the quotient of two squared terms.

Figure 13–16 offers some additional insights into the properties and interpretation of *R*-squared. In the first set of graphs (a), we see that if all the data points lie on a straight line, there will be no residual or unexplained deviations, and consequently *X* explains 100 percent of the variation in *Y*. This is true for both perfect positive ($\hat{\beta} > 0$) or negative ($\hat{\beta} < 0$) relationships. Hence, R^2 equals 1. However, if the points have a general tendency to lie on a positively or negatively sloping line, R^2 will be less than 1 but will indicate that some portion of the variation in *Y* can be attributed to *X*. (See section b of figure 13–16.) Finally, if no linear relationship exists between *X* and *Y*, R^2 will be zero. A value of zero means only that there is no relationship describable by a straight line. It does *not* mean statistical independence. The variables may have no association at all, or they may be strongly curvilinearly related or connected in some other fashion (see figure 13–16, section c). In both situations, R^2 will be zero or close to zero, but the

TABLE 13–31

Regression Sums of Square and *R*-Squared and *r*

Source	Value
Regression (*RegSS*)	27,032
Residual (*ResSS*)	21,270
Total (*TSS*)	48,302
$R^2 = 27,032/48,302 = .56 \ (56\%); \ r = -.75.$	

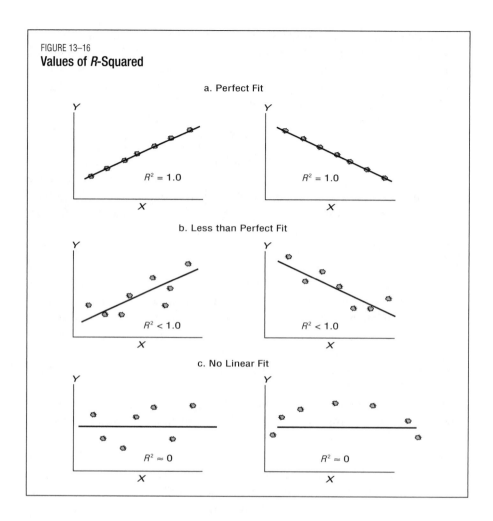

FIGURE 13–16
Values of *R*-Squared

a. Perfect Fit

$R^2 = 1.0$

$R^2 = 1.0$

b. Less than Perfect Fit

$R^2 < 1.0$

$R^2 < 1.0$

c. No Linear Fit

$R^2 \approx 0$

$R^2 \approx 0$

meaning will differ. A good way to spot the difference is to examine a plot of *Y* versus *X*. A scatterplot can help you determine the pattern your data come closest to.

In regression analysis, the term *explained* has a different meaning than it does in day-to-day conversation. In statistics, it means that the variation in one variable can be mathematically divided into two quantities. One, the so-called explained part, is the squared sum of differences between predicted values and the overall mean. These are strictly statistical terms. Thus, we might find a large *R*-squared between two variables (for example, literacy and economic development), which in statistical terms implies that a lot of variation has been explained. But this finding does not necessarily indicate that we really understand why and how countries with higher literacy rates achieve more economic development. In fact, as we explained in chapter 6, a relationship can be spurious, meaning that a false connection is caused by other factors. Always be cautious when confronted with seemingly large values of R-squared.

Here is a different slant on R-squared. If you think of the regression equation as a method for making predictions, then R-squared can be understood as a proportional-reduction-in-error (*PRE*) measure for assessing the strength of a relationship. Faced with a quantitative variable, Y, and lacking any other information, your best guess of a case's value on that variable would be the mean, $\bar{Y}$. When X is known, however, a better guess is achieved from the predicted value produced by the regression of Y on X. It can be shown that the reduction in errors is exactly R-squared. Consequently, in the previous example, we could state the error rate in predicting the dependent variable from knowledge of union structure is reduced about 40 percent.

The Correlation Coefficient

A close kin of R-squared is the **correlation coefficient,** a measure of the strength and direction of the linear correlation between two quantitative variables. The definition and computation of the correlation coefficient, denoted r, depend on standardizing the covariation between Y and X by dividing by their standard deviations. To find the covariation between two variables, you multiply the "deviations from the mean"—as shown in chapter 12, a deviation is a value minus the mean—and add them together. This total is then divided by the variables' standard deviations.

We listed many general properties of measures of association at the beginning of this chapter, and you may wish to refresh your memory because the correlation coefficient exhibits many of those properties. Known under a variety of labels—the product-moment correlation, Pearson's r, or, most plainly, r—this coefficient reveals the direction of a regression line (positive

HOW IT'S DONE

Calculating Sums of Squares and R^2

Let Y_i and X_i be the values for the ith case on Y and X, respectively;

let $\hat{\beta}$ be the regression coefficient from regressing Y on X; let N be the number of cases in the sample; let $\hat{Y}_i$ be the predicted value for ith observation; and let s_X^2 be the sample variance of X (the *independent*) variable found by dividing the total variation in X $\left(\sum_{i=1}^{N}\left(X_i - \bar{X}\right)^2\right)$ by N, not $N - 1$.

Total Sum of Squares:

$$TSS = \sum_{i=1}^{N}(Y_i - \bar{Y})^2 = \sum_{i=1}^{N} Y_i - \frac{\left[\sum_{i} Y_i\right]^2}{N}.$$

$$RegSS = \sum_{i=1}^{N}(\hat{Y}_i - \bar{Y})^2 = \hat{\beta}_{YX}\sum_{i=1}^{N} Y_i X_i = N\hat{\beta}_{YX}^2 s_X^2.$$

$$ResSS = TSS - RegSS$$

$$R^2 = \frac{RegSS}{TSS}.$$

HOW IT'S DONE

The Correlation Coefficient

The (Pearson) correlation coefficient is calculated as follows:

$$r = \frac{\sum_{i=1}^{n}(Y_i - \bar{Y})(X_i - \bar{X})}{(N-1)\hat{\sigma}_Y \hat{\sigma}_X},$$

where Y_i and X_i are the values on Y and X of the ith observation; $\bar{Y}$ and $\bar{X}$ are the means of Y and X, respectively; $\hat{\sigma}_Y$ and $\hat{\sigma}_X$ are the sample standard deviations of Y and X, respectively; N is the sample size; and the summation is over all pairs of data points.

or negative) and how closely observations lie near it. Its properties include the following:

- It is most appropriate if the relationship is approximately linear.

- Its value lies between –1 and 1. The coefficient reaches the lower limit when Y and X are perfectly negatively correlated, which is to say all the data lie on a straight line sloping downward from left to right. Its maximum value (1) is achieved when the variables are perfectly positively correlated.

- It will equal zero if there is no linear correlation or, to be more exact, when the slope is zero.

- The closer r is to either of its maximum values, the stronger the correlation. The nearer to zero, the weaker the correlation. (Consequently, r = .8 or –.8 implies a stronger relationship than r = .2 or –.2.)

- It has the same sign as the regression coefficient. (For example, if $\hat{\beta}$ is negative, r will be, too.)

- Unlike the regression parameter, it is symmetric in that its numerical value does not depend on which variable is considered dependent or independent.

- The correlation coefficient is scale independent in that its magnitude does not depend on either variable's measurement scale. It does not matter if, say, X is measured in dollars or thousands of dollars; the value r stays the same. This is not true of the regression coefficient.

Because of the last property, the correlation coefficient can be regarded as a kind of regression coefficient that does not depend on the units of Y or X. As a matter of fact, r has this association with the slope:

$$r = \left(\frac{\hat{\sigma}_X}{\hat{\sigma}_Y} \right) \hat{\beta},$$

where the $\hat{\sigma}$s are the sample standard deviations of X and Y. (As an aside, notice that r is partly a function of the size of the standard deviations. Given two samples with identical $\hat{\beta}$'s between Y and X, the one with the larger standard deviation, $\hat{\sigma}_X$, will *appear* to have the larger r and hence the larger linear correlation. But the magnitude of the relationship may be simply a function of the variability of X, not any intrinsic strength of the relationship.) We discuss the pros and cons of this feature of r in the next section.

Looking at the analysis of inequality, we see that the correlation between unionization and values of the Gini coefficients is -.63. This indicates a strong negative (linear) correlation.

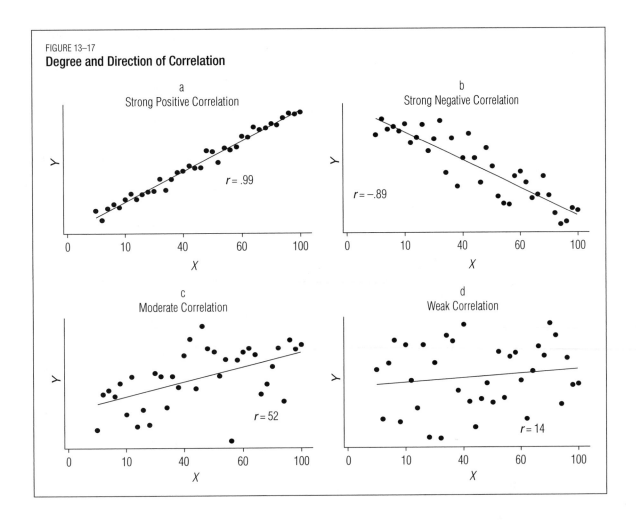

FIGURE 13–17
Degree and Direction of Correlation

a
Strong Positive Correlation

$r = .99$

b
Strong Negative Correlation

$r = -.89$

c
Moderate Correlation

$r = 52$

d
Weak Correlation

$r = 14$

To grasp the meaning of the numerical values of the correlation, try studying the patterns in figure 13–17. In graphs (a) and (b), most of the data lie near a straight line, and r is close to either its maximum value of 1 or its minimum value of –1. By contrast, graphs (c) and (d) show what you are likely to encounter in data analysis, moderate to weak relationships. Observe that the sign of r reflects the direction of the correlation. In each of these graphs, the data "behave very well" (this is a term statisticians commonly use): either there is a correlation or there isn't. Look, however, at figure 13–18. It illustrates a highly curvilinear relationship. A strong connection exists between Y and X—knowing the value of one would help you accurately predict values of the other—but the correlation coefficient ($r = -.15$) might suggest a weak relationship, until you

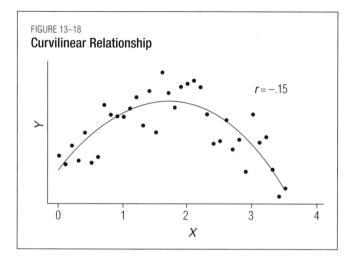

FIGURE 13–18
Curvilinear Relationship

$r = -.15$

remember that it measures the fit to a line. Once again, we stress the importance of examining scatterplots along with numbers. You are not likely to encounter such a strongly curved relationship in typical social science data, but it is important to remember that at this level of study, regression performs "best" when associations are linear or can be transformed to linearity.

Standardized Regression Coefficients

The regression coefficient indicates how much Y changes—in values of the dependent variable—for a one-unit change in X. If you were relating years of education (X) to annual wages (Y), the regression parameter would be expressed in, say, dollars. As an example, an estimated coefficient of 1.25 should be thought of and interpreted as "There is a 1.25-unit increase in Y for every 1 unit increase in the independent variable." (Earlier we found that the regression coefficient of Gini scores on union density equaled –0.14, or a 1 percent growth in union membership is associated with a decline (note the minus sign) of .14 units on the Gini scale. In many, if not most cases, this measure of association is exactly what is needed.

Yet social scientists sometimes prefer a "scale-free" statistic. For example, if independent variables had a common scale, their effect or impact could be compared unequivocally. (This statement rests on a major caveat discussed below.) Let's say a research team wants to explain variation in inequality. The problem with the regression coefficient is that a "one-unit change in X" means different things depending on the measurement scale. If X is income measured in dollars (a unit is $1), the coefficient may have a very small numerical value; if it is measured in thousands of dollars (a unit is $1,000), the coefficient will be larger.

To solve this problem, researchers often rescale all variables so that a one-unit change has common meaning. The results are called **standardized variables**. To obtain them, you subtract the mean (of the variable) from each value and divide by the standard deviation. Consider a variable, X. Its sample mean is $\bar{X}$ and its standard deviation is $\hat{\sigma}_X$. Denoting the corresponding standardized value of X with lowercase x, the standardization is

$$x_i = \frac{(X_i - \bar{X})}{\hat{\sigma}_x}.$$

Keep a close eye on the symbols: lowercase letters denote standardized variables, whereas uppercase letters represent the raw data. After standardization, the unit of measurement becomes "standard deviations." Thus, a one-unit change in x is a one standard deviation change. To clarify, think of union density as X; a one-unit change is a 1 percent change. Then, standardize the variable to get x, standardized union density. A one-unit increase now means one standard deviation change.

The minimum union density in table 13–32 is 8.2 percent. When standardized, this becomes –1.29. Note the minus sign. The interpretation is that the minimum value lies 1.29 standard deviations *below* the mean. Similarly, the maximum is 2.09 standard deviations above the mean.

Standardized variables have several interesting and (for statisticians) important features. First, the mean and standard deviation of the recalibrated variables are always zero and 1.0, respectively. (Standardization is based on the fact that deviations from a mean add to zero.) Table 13–33 illustrates the technique for standardizing a variable and its properties.

More important, the advantage of standardization lies in the seeming simplicity of regression results. For example, when both X and Y are standardized and y is regressed on x, the resulting equation simplifies to

$$\hat{y}_i = \hat{\beta}^* x_i$$

where $\hat{\beta}^*$ is the regression coefficient for the standardized data.

TABLE 13–32

Raw and Standardized Union Density Scores

Example Values	Union Density	Standardized Union Density
Minimum	8.2%	–1.29
Mean	34.79%	0
Standard deviation	20.63%	1.0
Maximum	78%	2.09

TABLE 13–33

Example of Raw Scores Converted to Standardized Values

Observation I	Raw Score (X_i)	Raw Deviation $(X_i - \bar{X})$	Squared Deviation $(X_i - \bar{X})^2$	Standardized Score (x_i)	Squared Deviations $(X_i - \bar{X})^2 = x_i^2$
1	10	10 – 15 = –5	25	–1.34	1.79
2	12	12 – 15 = –3	9	–0.80	.64
3	14	14 – 15 = –1	1	–.27	.07
4	16	16 – 15 = 1	1	.27	.07
5	18	18 – 15 = 3	9	0.80	.64
6	20	20 – 15 = 5	25	1.34	1.79
Sums	90	0	70	0	5

Raw scores:

Mean of X: $\bar{X} = 90/6 = 15$.

Standard deviation of X: $\hat{\sigma}_X = \sqrt{70/5} = 3.74$.

Standardized scores:

Mean of x: $\bar{x} = 0/6 = 0$.

Standard deviation of x: $\hat{\sigma} = \sqrt{\dfrac{5}{5}} = 1.0$.

Notice that there is no constant (α): whenever Y and X have been standardized, the regression constant drops out. Also pay attention to $\hat{\beta}^*$. Called the **standardized regression coefficient,** this number is interpreted as in the usual way, except that now a one-unit change in x is a *one-standard-deviation change.* In other words, the independent variable's effect is measured in standard deviations of y, not the scale of the original dependent variable. A standardized coefficient has the same sign as its unstandardized cousin. The only difference is in numerical values and interpretations.

Incidentally, in two-variable regression, the standardized slope equals the correlation coefficient. Thus, it is not surprising that after standardizing the union and Gini variables, we find that $\hat{\beta}^*$ is $-.63$, the same value reported in the section on correlation.

The standardized regression coefficient tells us that a one-standard-deviation increase in union density corresponds to a .63-standard-deviation *decrease* in economic inequality. At the end of the day, though, the coefficients $\hat{\beta}$ and $\hat{\beta}^*$ differ numerically, but the overall picture they convey stays the same: the two variables are negatively correlated.

So, aside from simplifying the equation, why bother with standardized variables? Some social scientists believe that standardized regression coefficients enable you to rank the "relative importance" of independent variables on a dependent variable.[36] Imagine that you are trying to explain political participation. Your study includes (1) education in years of schooling, (2) annual family income in dollars, and (3) degree of partisanship measured on a 5-point scale (1 for "least partisan" to 5 for "highly partisan"). The literature tells you to expect a positive relationship between all three variables and the indicator of participation. But some authors say socioeconomic factors are more important explanations of political behavior than are political leanings; others disagree completely. So you perform an analysis and find the regression coefficients for education, income, and partisanship to be, respectively, .0001, .5, and 1. Numerically, $\hat{\beta}_{partisanship}$ is larger than either of the other two; hence, psychology seems more important than economic class. The problem is that since the variables have different measurement scales, the coefficients cannot be compared directly. If, however, you standardize all of the variables, the standardized coefficients might turn out to be .8, .5, and .2, in which case the socioeconomic variables seem to have the strongest relationship.

Although calculating standardized variables may be a good idea, their use in the preceding example works only if the independent variables are independent of one another, a situation that rarely arises in observational studies. In addition, even if you wish to take advantage of the standardized version, you should calculate the nonstandardized coefficient as well.

Inference for Regression Parameters: Tests and Confidence Intervals

This section builds on the ideas presented in chapter 12 and in previous sections regarding hypothesis testing. You may wish to review those topics briefly before proceeding.

Like any other statistical procedure, regression can be applied to sample or population data. In the present context, we assume that in a specified population a relationship exists between X and Y and that one way of describing it is with the regression coefficient β. This unknown quantity must be estimated with β, the sample regression coefficient. Briefly, we want to test the statistical hypothesis, H_0: $\beta_1 = 0$ (or some specified value) against H_A: $\beta_1 \neq 0$ (or perhaps, $\beta_1 < 0$ or $\beta_1 > 0$). The test for its significance can go in two directions, both of which end up in essentially the same place. We describe the first here and save the other for the next chapter.

Under the assumptions stated at the beginning of the regression section (independent sampling, normally distributed errors, and so forth), we can test the null hypothesis that the constant and regression coefficient equal a particular value, typically zero. The estimated regression coefficient has a t distribution with $N - 2$ df. (When N becomes large—roughly 30 or more cases—the t blends into the standard normal distribution, for which a z statistic is appropriate.) The null hypothesis is usually simply H_0: $\beta_1 = 0$. This possibility is tested against a two-sided ($\beta \neq 0$) or one-sided ($\beta < 0$ or $\beta > 0$) alternative. The test statistic has the typical form—the estimated coefficient divided by the estimated standard error:

$$t_{\text{obs}} \frac{\hat{\beta}}{\hat{\sigma}_{\hat{\beta}}},$$

where $\hat{\sigma}_{\hat{\beta}}$ is the estimated standard error of the regression coefficient. Remember that if an estimator is calculated from many, many independent samples, these sample statistics will have a distribution, called the sampling distribution, with its own mean and standard deviation. When $\hat{\beta}$ is the statistic, its sampling distribution is the t distribution (the standard normal for a large N), which has mean β and standard error or deviation $\hat{\sigma}_{\hat{\beta}}$. Confidence intervals can be constructed in the usual way:

$$\beta \pm t_{(1-\alpha)/2.\ N-2}\ \hat{\sigma}_{\hat{\beta}},$$

where $t_{(1-\alpha)/2.\ N-2}$ is the value in appendix B that cuts off the upper $\alpha/2$ proportion of the distribution.

For example, earlier we estimated the regression of Gini scores on union density. The estimate turnout to be $-.14$ with a standard error of $\hat{\sigma}_{\hat{\beta}1} = .04$. It appears to be a small number, but is it statistically significantly different from zero? The sample size, $N = 21$, is less than 30, so we use a t distribution with $N - 2 = 21 - 2 = 19$ degrees of freedom to find the critical t at the .01 level, two-tailed test. It is 2.861. The observed t is

$$t_{obs} = \frac{\hat{\beta}_1}{\hat{\sigma}_1} = \frac{-.14}{.04} = -3.5.$$

This is a bit larger than the critical value, so we reject the null hypothesis at the .01 level and conclude that the population β_1 is probably is not zero. Our best estimate is that it is about $-.14$. A test of the regression constant, β_0 is conducted in exactly the same manner: obtain the observed t statistic by dividing the estimated constant by its standard error. Recall that the regression constant for the inequality data is 36.43 with a standard error of 1.56, so the observed t is $36.43/1.56 = 23.35$, which also greatly exceeds the critical value. Normally, regression results are displayed as in table 13–34. Symbols such as asterisks (*) are frequently used to denote the achieved significance, as shown in the table. (Sometimes they appear next to the names of the coefficients and sometimes next to the coefficients themselves, as in this table.)

Confidence intervals also appear in the table (in parentheses). They are found by

$$\hat{\beta}_j \pm t_{\alpha/2=.01/2=.005,19}\hat{\sigma}_{\sigma_j}$$
$$= -.14 \pm 2.861(.04)$$
$$= -.25, -.03.$$

Estimates of the constant usually do not have much practical meaning, but these days reporting them for quantities of interest (e.g. the regression coefficient that measures the impact of unionization on inequality) is required. Note that neither set of intervals includes zero, a fact consistent with the hypothesis test. As we explained in the last chapter, confidence intervals provide both a test of a statistical hypothesis and a range of plausible values for the coefficients.

TABLE 13–34
Regression of Gini on Union Density

Coefficient	Estimate (confidence intervals)	Standard Error	Observed t	Probability
Constant ($\hat{\beta}_0$)	36.44*** (31.98, 40.90)	1.56	23.35	.000
Coefficient ($\hat{\beta}_1$) Gini on union density	−.14** (−0.25,−0.03)	.04	−3.5	.002

Critical t for .01 level (two-tailed) with 19 *df:* 2.861.

** = significant at .01; *** = significant at .001.

Case Studies in Two-Variable Regression

We bring the chapter to a close by analyzing three additional examples. This analysis presents no really new ideas, but it does underscore our central theme: statistics requires more than the mechanical application of software to a pile of numbers. Instead, it requires clear thinking about what the data mean for the substantive problem. Doing so in turn requires a systematic approach:

■ Examine each variable's summary statistics.

■ Use graphs wherever possible and helpful.

■ Always keep the units of analysis and measurement scales in mind.

CASE 1: LITERACY AND ECONOMIC DEVELOPMENT, A NONLINEAR RELATIONSHIP.   The variables are GDP per capita (X) (measured in dollars)—an operational indicator of development—and literacy rates (Y) (percentage of adult population that is literate) in ninety-seven countries ranging from Angola to Zambia for the year 2004.[37] Table 13–35 shows the summary statistics.

Note these points:

■ The difference between the median and mean GDP is quite large, with the mean being about two and a half times bigger. Also, three-quarters of the countries have GDPs below about $3,312 (see Q3) whereas the maximum is $34,340, a huge disparity. All of this adds up to the fact that the distribution is heavily skewed to the right.

■ The opposite is true of literacy: it is skewed to the left. The minimum is just 19 percent, but in the bulk of the counties, at least two-thirds of the citizens can read. If fact, in one-quarter of the cases, literacy is virtually universal (i.e., third quartile = 96%). In addition, compare the median and median: this time the mean is somewhat smaller, suggesting that a few low values are pulling the average down. The "typical" literacy rate is not 79 percent as the mean suggests but closer to 87 percent (see the median in the table.) The conclusion? A relatively few nations have high levels of *il*literacy; most don't.

■ GDP is measured in dollars. Therefore, a one-unit change in this variable doesn't amount to much. To get a meaningful idea of the impact of GDP on education, we will be better off asking what a $500 or even $1,000 increase does.

TABLE 13–35
Summary Statistics for GDP and Literacy in Ninety-Seven Countries

Variable	Minimum	Q1	Median	Mean	Q3	Maximum	Standard Deviation
GDP (in dollars)	$87.5	$67.41	$1,323	$3,181	$3,312	$34,340	$5,435.54
Literacy (percentage)	19.0%	67.4%	86.7%	78.6%	96.3%	99.8%	21.0%

Now look at figure 13–19. The graph itself shows what at first sight looks like a very peculiar scatterplot. Some of the points have been identified to illustrate once again the basic idea of such a graph. It shows each unit's values on the two variables, literacy and per capita GDP. The skewness of the data can be seen in the accompany boxplots. Remember, a boxplot gives a snapshot (but an informative one) of the data's main features. We see, for instance, that the median GDP is about $1,320. (The bar in the middle of the box stands for the median; read over to the scale to get its approximate value.)

The graph tells two stories. Or rather there are two substantive conclusions, one for the poorer nations and another for the richer ones. Have a look the plot of the points on the left of the dotted line, which marks off the first quartile.

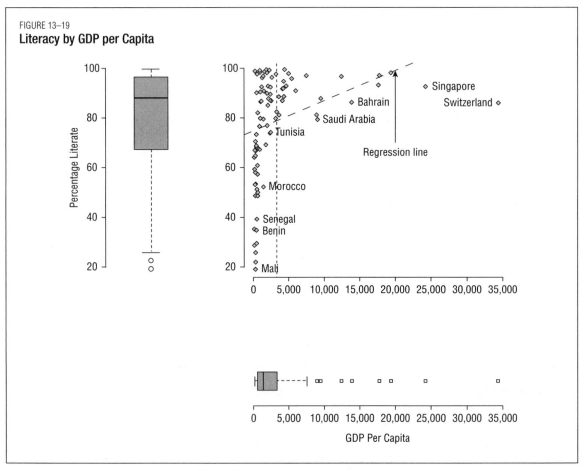

FIGURE 13–19
Literacy by GDP per Capita

They seem stacked one atop the other. Let's try to tease some meaning out of the stack. In these countries, it appears that even relatively small increases in per capita GDP bring noticeably higher levels of literacy *or* possibly nations can boost reading skills while remaining quite poor. But after a certain point, no amount of income can raise literacy because the maximum is 100 percent. For example, even though Cyprus has a GDP per capita approximately one-third of Switzerland's, its literacy rate is about 10 points higher. This finding suggests that education may be affected by more than just material resources; surely culture, tradition, history, and social organization play a role. But the effect depends on the level of GDP. Such a situation is called "interaction," as we see in the following chapter.

What can we make of this relationship? Table 13–36 presents the results of the regression of literacy on income. The table is organized in a fashion common in scholarly publications. Below the estimated coefficients (in parentheses) are their standard errors. You can figure out the observed test statistic merely by dividing the standard error into the coefficient (e.g., $74.71/2.36 = t_{obs} = 31.66$). Since there are 97 observations in the study, which is considerably more than 30, we can use the standard normal (z) distribution to find the probability that if the null hypothesis is true (H_0: $\beta_0 = 0$), we would get a z value of 31.66 or greater. It's practically zero. Hence, the highly significant test result. One conclusion is that overall there is not a linear but a curved or nonlinear correlation between the variables. Income's effects, in other words, are not constant across the full range of GDP. As development progresses, it has less and less effect on literacy. That's the substantive inference. A regression of literacy on GDP produces an estimated model: $\hat{Y}_i = 74.71 + .001GDP$.

The regression coefficient $\hat{\beta}_{Literacy \sim GDP} = .001$ looks tiny, but remember the measurement issue: GDP is measured in dollars (not in hundreds or thousands of dollars), so a one dollar increase or decrease is associated with less than 1 percent change in literacy levels. However, if we changed income by, for instance, $1,000, the effect on literacy would be $1,000 \times .001 = 1$ percent. At this point this still doesn't seem like such a big deal, but wait.

We also see that although both coefficients are highly significant (we do not accept the hypothesis that they are zero), the fit of the data to the model is weak, as measured by R^2 anyway. This lack of fit stems from the curved relationship.

Remember that a basic assumption of regression analysis is that the relationship be linear. If it is not, a common response is to transform the data in such a way to "straighten" them out by transforming the raw scores into a variable that will have a straight-line relationship with dependent variable. Lots of rescalings

TABLE 13–36

Regression Results: Literacy on Income

Variable	Raw Data	Logged Data
Constant	74.71***	9.56
	(2.36)	(9.11)
GDP per capita	0.001**	9.66***
	(0.00038)	(1.25)

$R^2_{raw} = .10$ $R^2_{logged} = .39$

** = significant at .01; *** = significant at .001.

are possible, and many tools exist for finding the optimal ones. Here we confine ourselves to taking the logarithm of GDP.[38] By the way, it should be mentioned that the logarithmic transformation of income data is quite common (almost mandatory) in economics and policy sciences.

You can see the result of the transformation in figure 13–20. Notice first that literacy has been left untouched. But by using the *log* of GDP per capita, we have made its distribution much less skewed. (Compare the new boxplot with the previous one. The median and mean are now, respectively, 7.19 and 7.15 on the log scale.) More important, the relationship appears more linear. Notice, however, that at the lower end of the log scale, several countries lie a considerable distance from the estimated regression line. These points don't fit as neatly as we might expect and perhaps warrant further investigation. The estimated coefficients, standard errors, and significance levels appear in the rightmost column of table 13–36. In this case, the coefficient for logged GDP is significant at the .001 level, but the constant no longer is. This once again forces us to ask if there is a substantive meaning for this term.

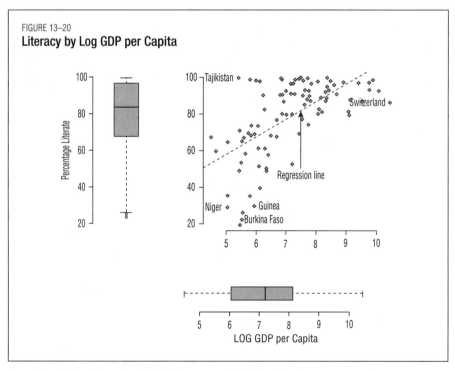

FIGURE 13–20
Literacy by Log GDP per Capita

Source: Cross-National Research on USAID's Democracy and Governance Programs.

More generally, how does one know which variables should be altered and by what method? There are systematic procedures for finding the best (most efficient) transformations. We cannot go into those techniques here. Instead, we suggest you engage in trial and error. Any measure of variable involving income will be a candidate for a logarithmic transformation. You can also try taking the square root of a variable or, going in the other direction, raise the variable to a power such as 1.5 or 2 (that is, for instance, $Y^{1.5}$ or Y^2).[39]

There are many other ways to tackle data like these. An appealing method is to treat the nations as a pool of developed and less developed economies. We could, for example, sort the countries in to two groups based on whether they are below or at or above the third income quartile. That is, those with GDPs greater than or equal to \$3,312 can be classified "Higher" and the others "Lower." By splitting the data this way, we can run two regressions, one for each group. The results, shown in table 13–37, confirm what the previous analysis pointed to as the interaction between wealth and literacy.

As should be apparent, each regression coefficient for the literacy data applied only to *lower* GDP countries ($N = 72$) is significant at the .001 level. Divide the estimates by their standard errors (in braces {}) to find the observed z statistics and use the z-table in appendix A to find the probability that if the betas were zero, you would obtain a z-observed this large or larger. The confidence intervals tell you in an instant that neither set of limits contains zero and so the null hypotheses should probably be rejected. Figure 13–21 summarizes the previous analysis. We have, for example, printed the regression lines for both groups of countries. The one on the right is parallel to the x-axis because $\beta_{\text{Literacy} \sim \text{GDP}}$ is zero to three decimal places; a change in GDP does nothing for literacy in these countries.

TABLE 13–37
Regression Estimates for Two Groups

Parameter	Lower GDP ($N = 72$) Estimate (99% confidence intervals) [standard error]	Higher GDP ($N = 25$) Estimate (99% confidence intervals) [standard error]
Constant, β_0	58.54*** (49.25–67.84) {3.51}	91.66*** (85.88–97.43) {2.05}
Regression, $\beta_{\text{Literacy} \sim \text{GDP}}$	0.015*** (0.008–0.023) {0.003}	.0000 (−0.0005–0.0004) {0.0002}

*** = significant at $\alpha = .001$ level.

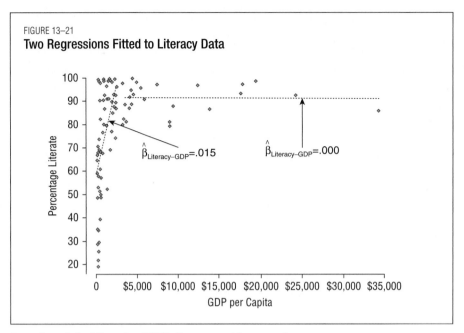

FIGURE 13–21
Two Regressions Fitted to Literacy Data

$\hat{\beta}_{\text{Literacy–GDP}}=.015$ $\hat{\beta}_{\text{Literacy–GDP}}=.000$

Source: Cross-National Research on USAID's Democracy and Governance Programs.

CASE 2: SURGICAL PROCEDURES AND PHYSICIAN AVAILABILITY—THE EFFECTS OF OUTLIERS. We now look at still another example of the importance of combing graphs, statistics, and general knowledge for obtaining substantively meaningful results. In order to do so, we look at an issue that plagues modern democracies, soaring health care costs. Just as the sample mean and standard deviation are sensitive to outlying or "deviant" values, so too are the regression parameter ($\hat{\beta}$) and correlation coefficient (r). The point is best demonstrated with an example.

The media sometimes reports that health care costs continue to rise partly because Americans may be "overtreated." The argument runs as follows. To the extent that medical facilities and physicians are available, they will be utilized. Consequently, areas densely populated with, say, MRI devices will experience higher rates (per capita) of use than in places where they are scarce. Figure 13–22 takes a slightly different view of the problem. It shows the relationship between the number of surgical procedures carried out in the fifty states plus the District of Columbia by the number of surgical specialists. (Both variables have been converted to per capita indices.) The plot in figure 13–22a seems to back up the notion that more surgeons are accompanied by more surgeries. Naturally, it is possible that specialists migrate to places with a lot of sick people. On the

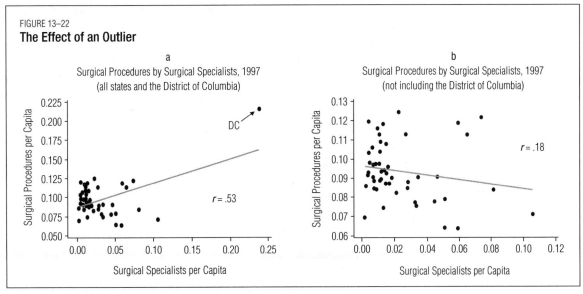

FIGURE 13–22
The Effect of an Outlier

a
Surgical Procedures by Surgical Specialists, 1997
(all states and the District of Columbia)

b
Surgical Procedures by Surgical Specialists, 1997
(not including the District of Columbia)

Source: Health Care State Rankings, 1999 (Morgan Quitno Press).

other hand, it seems more probable that availability drives usage. The correlation coefficient (.53) supports a claim of a relatively strong positive correlation between operations and surgeons.

Yet even a cursory glance at the distribution might raise suspicions, for one point lies far from all the others. It is the value for the District of Columbia, which has a high density of surgical specialists and operations. (The city is known for its many and famous health centers.) You may recall from chapter 11 that a "distant" point is called an outlier. Sitting far from all the other states, D.C. is a prime example of an outlier. Correlation and regression are functions of the sums squared deviations from means, and if one or two observations differ greatly from the others, their deviations will contribute a disproportion amount to the totals. In technical terms, an outlier can exert great "leverage" on the numerical values of coefficients. That this is the case here can be seen in figure 13–22b. It displays the procedures by specialists for all the data *except* D.C. With that outlier removed—a valid, even necessary step in data analysis—the linear correlation disappears; the correlation coefficient $r = -.18$, has changed direction and moved into the "weak" range.

Statisticians know full well that standard regression models are not "robust" against problems such as leverage points and recommend paying attention to and adjusting for them. Luckily, most regression software offers the option of flagging these kinds of data.

CASE 3: JUDICIAL DECISION MAKING—INVESTIGATING LACK OF FIT AND RESIDUALS.
We close the chapter by returning to judicial decision making. Remember the question of whether there is an association (possibly causal) between the nominating president's ideology and the ideological tenor of Supreme Court decisions. The analysis presented previously suggested why judicial nominations are the subject of bitter political disputes. Will we arrive at the same conclusion if we explore slightly different variables? Here we use the "Economic Liberalism Score of the Nominating President" as the independent variable and a "variable represents the percentage of 'liberal' votes cast by [justices] in the area of economics" as the dependent or response variable.[40] Both variables run from 0 to 100 percent, with larger numbers indicating greater liberalism. As before, we analyzed justices seated after 1950 and exclude two, John Roberts and Samuel Alito, both of whom had incomplete information on their voting records. The total N is 21.[41]

As usual, start with a scatterplot (figure 13–23). This is an ordinary plot that reveals a linear positive correlation between the two variables: the more "liberal" the nominating president, the more "liberal" the decisions. The slanted dotted line is the graph of the estimated regression. Note also that most points, 14 out of 21 or about 71 percent, fall on the conservative side of the presidency scale. This of course demonstrates once again that more conservative and presumably Republican presidents have had a crack at filling vacancies. (Don't forget, though, that the analysis does not include the Obama administration.) But if you study the vertical axis, you see that at least two (Warren and Brennan) of these more conservative appointees have (surprisingly?) liberal voting records and one (Whittaker) is apparently far more conservative than the president who chose him. We have identified these individuals.

A statistical analysis lends support to the hypothesis of a positive linear connection: the simple correlation is $r = .51$, and the estimated regression coefficient is

$$\hat{Y}_i = 37.69^{***} + .34^{*}\text{Presideology},$$
$$(6.32) \qquad (.13)$$

where the stars signify that both coefficients are statistically significant, one at the .001 level (the constant), the other at the .05 level (the regression coefficient.)

The three labeled justices, however, might encourage us to take a closer look. First, we would recheck the data matrix to make certain the data have been correctly entered. More important, we might inquire into the circumstances of their nominations or into their backgrounds. Is there anything that might explain their anomalous positions? All three, for example, were nominated by the moderately conservative Dwight Eisenhower, a man without a strict ideological axe to grind. Thus, it is perhaps not too surprising that these justices' decisions span a wide spectrum. (Earl Warren had been a former Republican governor of California, and his subsequent rulings took some observers by surprise.) One might then

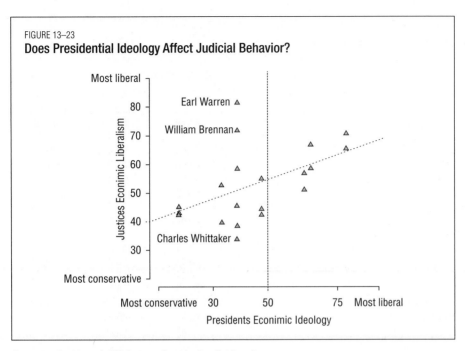

FIGURE 13–23
Does Presidential Ideology Affect Judicial Behavior?

Source: Lee Epstein et al., "US Supreme Court Justices Database."

wonder about the effects of these three people on the model's overall fit. (The R^2 is .26.) Would it help to treat these cases differently? Table 13–38 helps clarify the situation.

The table contains the raw data plus two important additional components: the predicted values of the dependent variable $(\hat{Y}_i)$, found by applying the regression equation to the economic and presidential ideology scores, and the residuals, which measure the difference between observed and predicted Ys: $r_i = (Y_i - \hat{Y}_i)$ As explained under the discussion of how regression models are estimated, the residuals measure the line's "lack of fit." The table highlights the three largest residuals, which—no shocker here—belong to Warren, Brennan, and Whittaker.

What do you suppose would happen if these three observations were removed from the analysis? It should come as no surprise that all our measures of goodness of fit would improve (i.e., increase), as seen in table 13–39, especially the last column. Observe that even though their numerical values have changed hardly at all, all the terms in the estimated regression equation for the incomplete data are now highly significant. Usually when N is decreased, achieving significance becomes harder. Here, however, we have improved the fit by eliminating the three justices with the largest residuals.

TABLE 13–38
Supreme Court Justices

Justice	President Ideology X_i	Economic Ideology Y_i	$\hat{Y}_i$	$r_i = (Y_i - \hat{Y}_i)$
Warren, Earl*	**38.8**	**81.59**	**50.37**	**31.22**
Harlan, John*	38.8	38.40	50.37	−11.97
Brennan, William*	**38.8**	**71.66**	**50.37**	**21.29**
Whittaker, Charles*	**38.8**	**33.78**	**50.37**	**−16.59**
Stewart, Potter*	38.8	45.52	50.37	−4.85
White, Byron*	65.4	58.39	59.29	−0.90
Goldberg, Arthur	65.4	66.67	59.29	7.38
Fortas, Abe	78.2	70.67	63.58	7.09
Marshall, Thurgood	78.2	65.21	63.58	1.63
Burger, Warren	47.7	42.58	53.35	−10.77
Blackmun, Harry	47.7	55.02	53.35	1.67
Powell, Lewis	47.7	44.44	53.35	−8.91
Stevens, John	38.8	58.45	50.37	8.08
O'Connor, Sandra Day	17.6	43.17	43.26	−0.09
Rehnquist, William	17.6	45.05	43.26	1.79
Scalia, Antonin	17.6	42.31	43.26	−0.95
Kennedy, Anthony	17.6	44.66	43.26	1.40
Souter, David	33.1	52.55	48.46	4.09
Thomas, Clarence	33.1	39.71	48.46	−8.75
Ginsburg, Ruth Bader	63.1	56.78	58.52	−1.74
Breyer, Stephen	63.1	50.97	58.52	−7.55
* Nominated by Dwight Eisenhower.				

Source: Lee Epstein et al., "US Supreme Court Justices Database."

TABLE 13–39
The Effects of Case Deletion

Data	Regression Equation	Measures of Fit
Full (N = 21)	$\hat{Y}_i = 37.69^{***} + .34^*$ Preseconomic.	$R^2 = .26$ $r = .51$
Incomplete (N = 18)	$\hat{Y}_i = 34.45^{***} + .37^*$ Preseconomic.	$R^2 = .59$ $R = .77$

* = significant at .05 level; *** = significant at .001 level.

Or have we? One might wonder about the propriety of selectively removing data that do not "agree" with one's hypothesis. Ordinarily there is little to recommend the practice. One of our goals here was to encourage a careful examination of the data in substantive terms to see why an estimated model may not fit what one thought was a good idea. Perhaps something about the Eisenhower presidency runs counter to the practice of basing judicial appointments on rigorous ideological tests. Our second objective is more pedagogical: we want to introduce the concept of residual analysis. Most statisticians use residuals to check assumptions and look for transformations that make these assumptions more tenable. But this is a vast and technical subject that we leave for the next chapter and further reading.[42]

CONCLUSION

This chapter has shown how to measure the existence, direction, strength, and statistical significance of relationships between two variables. We have emphasized the difference between association and causation. The particular techniques used—cross-tabulation, difference-of-means test, analysis of variance, regression analysis, and correlation—all lead to inferential evidence but in no sense "prove" anything. This warning is especially apt for the examples presented above. Stripped as they are of theoretical, contextual, and statistical rigor necessary to warrant being used as evidence, these examples have been presented as merely learning devices. What is especially important is to keep both technique and substance in proper perspective. One way of doing so is always to ask yourself, "What does this finding mean in the real world?" That we have tried to do by constantly going back and forth to the data and its real-world implications. We can, however, strength our case by adding additional variables.

Terms Introduced

Analysis of variance. A technique for measuring the relationship between one nominal- or ordinal-level variable and one interval- or ratio-level variable.

Chi square. A statistic used to test whether a relationship is statistically significant in a cross-classification table.

Correlation coefficient. In regression analysis, a measure of the strength and direction of the linear correlation between two quantitative variables; also called product-moment correlation, Pearson's r, or r.

Cross-tabulation. Also called a cross-classification or contingency table, this array displays the joint frequencies and relative frequencies of two categorical (nominal or ordinal) variables.

Degrees of freedom. A measure used in conjunction with chi square and other measures to determine if a relationship is statistically significant.

Difference-of-means test. A technique for measuring the relationship between one nominal- or ordinal-level variable and one interval- or ratio-level variable.

Direction of a relationship. An indication of which values of the dependent variable are associated with which values of the independent variable.

Effect size. How and how much a change in one variable affects another variable, often measured as the difference between one mean and another, often between a treatment group and control group.

Eta-squared. A measure of association used with the analysis of variance that indicates what proportion of the variance in the dependent variable is explained by variance in the independent variable.

Goodman and Kruskal's gamma. A measure of association between ordinal-level variables.

Goodman and Kruskal's lambda. A measure of association between one nominal- or ordinal-level variable and one nominal-level variable.

Kendall's tau-*b* and tau-*c*. Measures of association between ordinal-level variables.

Measures of association. Statistics that summarize the relationship between two variables.

Negative relationship. A relationship in which high values of one variable are associated with low values of another variable.

Null hypothesis. The hypothesis that there is no relationship between two variables in the target population.

Phi. An association measure that adjusts an observed chi-square statistic by the sample size.

Positive relationship. A relationship in which high values of one variable are associated with high values of another variable.

Proportionate reduction in error (*PRE*) measure. A measure of association that indicates how much the knowledge of the value of the independent variable of a case improves prediction of the dependent variable compared to the prediction of the dependent variable based on no knowledge of the case's value on the independent variable. Examples are Goodman and Kruskal's lambda, Goodman and Kruskal's gamma, eta-squared, and R-squared.

Regression analysis. A technique for measuring the relationship between two interval- or ratio-level variables.

Regression coefficient. A measure that tells how much the dependent variable changes per unit change in the independent variable.

Residuals. Differences between observed values of a dependent variable and those predicted by a specified model (e.g., linear regression).

R-squared. The proportion of the total variation in a dependent variable explained by an independent variable.

Scatterplot. A graph that plots joint values of an independent variable along one axis (usually the x-axis) and a dependent variable along the other axis (usually the y-axis).

Somers' *D*. A measure of association between ordinal-level variables.

Standardized regression coefficient. A coefficient that measures the effects of an independent variable on a dependent variable in standard deviation units.

Standardized variable. A rescaled variable obtained by subtracting the mean from each value of the variable and dividing the result by the standard deviation.

Statistical independence. Property of two variables where the probability that an observation is in a particular category of one variable and a particular category of the other variable equals the simple or marginal probability of being in those categories.

Total variance. A numerical measure of the variation in a variable, determined by summing the squared deviation of each observation from the mean.

Suggested Readings

Achen, Christopher. *Interpreting and Using Regression.* Sage University Paper Series on Quantitative Applications in the Social Sciences, series no. 29. Beverly Hills, Calif.: Sage, 1982.

Agresti, Alan. *An Introduction to Categorical Data Analysis.* New York: Wiley, 1996.

Agresti, Alan, and Barbara Finlay. *Statistical Methods for the Social Sciences.* 3rd ed. Upper Saddle River, N.J.: Prentice Hall, 1997.

Faraway, Julian J. *Linear Models with R.* New York: Chapman & Hall/CRC, 2005.

Fox, John. *Applied Regression Analysis and Generalized Linear Models.* 2nd ed. Los Angeles: Sage, 2008.

Lewis-Beck, Michael S., ed. *Basic Statistics.* Vol. 1. Newbury Park, Calif.: Sage, 1993.

Velleman, Paul, and David Hoaglin. *The ABC's of EDA: Applications, Basics, and Computing of Exploratory Data Analysis.* Duxbury, Mass., Duxbury Press, 1981.

Notes

1. Stephen D. Ansolabehere, Shanto Iyengar, Adam Simon, and Nicholas Valentino, "Does Attack Advertising Demobilize the Electorate?" *American Political Science Review* 88, no. 4 (1994): 829–38. Available at http://weber.ucsd.edu/~tkousser/Ansolabehere.pdf.

2. In reality, there are many techniques for analyzing relationships at a given level of measurement. The ones presented in this chapter are the most common and least complicated.

3. Keep in mind the difference between a research and statistical hypothesis. The latter is usually stated as saying there is no relationship between variables. Were it subject to a statistical test, it would be rejected.

4. Chapter 11 discusses the construction of this variable. Briefly, based on responses to a question asking respondents if they identified with a party, responses coded "strong" Democrats and Republicans were classified as most partisan, independents least partisan. Those with weak to moderate party attachments fell in the middle two categories.

5. These labels represent an interpretation we have imposed on the question responses. It would be perfectly legitimate, for instance, to redefine the ideology scale as the "degree of conservatism." What matters is that you keep straight in your mind how the variables are treated and make your explanations consistent with that definition.

6. You might think of ties as a "penalty" for the imprecise measurement classification involves. But however they are interpreted, tied pairs count against all the measures except gamma

in the sense that the more ties, the smaller the numerical value of the coefficient. See H. T. Reynolds, *The Analysis of Cross-Classifications* (New York: The Free Press, 1977): 69–79.

7. For further information about the calculation of each of these statistics, see Alan Agresti and Barbara Finlay, *Statistical Methods for the Social Sciences,* 3rd ed. (Upper Saddle River, N.J.: Prentice Hall, 1997), 272–82.

8. Partly because these coefficients do not generally describe the complexities of relationships between categorical variables, they have fallen out of favor with many social scientists. Sociologists and statisticians have developed methods for modeling the multiplicity of interactions often found among categories in a table. We touch on a few techniques later in the chapter but leave the bulk of them to more advanced texts. A good introduction is Alan Agresti, *Analysis of Ordinal Categorical Data* (New York: Wiley, 1984).

9. By the way, these and the other survey data have been "weighted" in order to ensure that the final samples approximate the US population. Chapter 7 explains the rationale for weighted samples. The only wrinkle is that sometimes we report fractional frequencies. Just round these to the nearest whole number.

10. We could have used any two numbers, such as 1 and 2 or 10 and 21. These numbers don't enter into any calculations, but they have marvelous properties in quantitative analysis.

11. Many of these statistics attempt in one way or another to take into account the number of categories and the distribution of cases among them. Going into more detail would take us too far astray.

12. Note, however, that small effects can in some circumstances have theoretical or substantive importance.

13. See Agresti and Finlay, *Statistical Methods for the Social Sciences,* 264–65 for more information and ideas about how to proceed.

14. Marc Morjé Howard, James L. Gibson, and Dietlind Stolle, "The U.S. Citizenship, Involvement, Democracy Survey," Center for Democracy and Civil Society (CDACS), Georgetown University, 2005.

15. Since the dependent variable is a "count" of activities, certain statistical issues come up, and a full analysis of the data might require techniques that go beyond this text.

16. It can also be a dichotomous or two-category variable.

17. The quotes around "population" are necessary because, technically speaking, there are *no* population experimental and treatment group means. These are hypothetical or theoretical quantities. They could exist only if a researcher could somehow conduct an experiment on an entire population and at the same time treat it as a control. This is a subtle point but one that has far reaching consequences for how the results of experimental and observational studies are interpreted. An excellent and accessible introduction to this topic is Christopher Winship and Stephen L. Morgan, "The Estimation of Causal Effects from Observational Data," *Annual Review of Sociology* 25 (1999): 659–706. Available at http://www.wjh .harvard.edu/soc/faculty/winship/winship_causal_observational_99.pdf.

18. Lee Epstein, Thomas G. Walker, Nancy Staudt, Scott A. Hendrickson, and Jason M. Roberts, *Codebook: US Supreme Court Justices Database,* January 26, 2010. Available at http:// epstein.usc.edu/research/justicesdata.pdf.

19. Here is an interesting point to consider. The data go back to 1950, yet just six out of twenty-four justices were nominated by Democratic presidents. It would be fair to say that Republicans have had a chance to influence the nomination process, but the ideological results (e.g., repealing the *Roe v. Wade* decision) have not panned out according to their expectations. It would interesting to think about the reasons why.

20. Needless to say, we do not have samples; the data consist of the entire population. Testing for significance is more of a numerical exercise than an absolute requirement to make

generalizations about Supreme Court politics. Nevertheless, for expository purposes we proceed as if we had a simple random sample of justices.

21. The actual question is, "I'll read the name of a person [or institution] and I'd like you to rate that person using something we call the feeling thermometer. Ratings between 50 degrees and 100 degrees mean that you feel favorable and warm toward the person. Ratings between 0 degrees and 50 degrees mean that you don't feel favorable toward the person and that you don't care too much for that person. You would rate the person at the 50 degree mark if you don't feel particularly warm or cold toward the person. . . . Still using the thermometer, how would you rate the following . . ." (American National Election Study [ANES], *2004 HTML Codebook,* July 14, 2006; The American National Election Studies (http://www.electionstudies.org/; The 2004 National Election Study [dataset]. Ann Arbor: University of Michigan, Center for Political Studies [producer and distributor]).

22. There is a vast literature on the analysis of "paired" or matched samples in which members of one group are selected to match some characteristics of members of the other one. See Agresti and Finlay, *Statistical Methods for the Social Sciences,* 226–32.

23. Nonnormality seems to be most troublesome when one or both subpopulation distributions are skewed.

24. There are tests for equality of variances but none performs especially well in all circumstances. See Agresti, and Finlay, *Statistical Methods for the Social Sciences,* 220–24. For a more technical discussion, see Richard J. Larsen and Morris L. Marx, *An Introduction to Mathematical Statistics and Its Applications* (Englewood Cliffs, N.J., Prentice-Hall, 1981), 329–33.

25. Because that value cuts off the upper $.05/2 = .025$ portion of the standard normal distribution. Check appendix A.

26. Howard, Gibson, and Stolle, "United States Citizenship, Involvement, Democracy (CID) Survey," 159.

27. As a refresher of chapter 11, you could test the hypothesis that the population mean of engagement is zero. What test would you use?

28. In technical terms this is homoscedasticity (equal variances).

29. For a classic discussion of the definition and analysis of *subject* and *citizen* norms, see Gabriel A. Almond and Sidney Verba's *The Civic Culture: Political Attitudes and Democracy in Five Nations* (Princeton, N.J.: Princeton University Press, 1963).

30. An important technical issue arises in the calculation of these intervals. As we said when discussing difference of means tests, it is usually not advisable to compute a series of *t*- or *z*-tests to see which means differ. The reason is that probability statements—"the difference between group *X* and group *Y* is significant at the .01 level"—will be incorrect unless all tests are truly independent of one another. With more than two comparisons on the same data, this requirement is not met. Hence, statisticians use "simultaneous inference" to construct tests and confidence intervals. The particular application used here is called "Tukey's 'Honest Significant Difference'" method after John Tukey, a preeminent statistician at Bell Labs. See Brian. S. Yandell, *Practical Data Analysis for Designed Experiments* (New York: Chapman and Hall/CRC, 2007).

31. A thorough treatment of the assumptions underlying regression analysis is John Fox's *Applied Regression Analysis and Generalized Linear Models,* 2nd ed. (Thousand Oaks, Calif.: Sage, 2008), chap. 6.

32. Consider, for example, a model that contains two types of variables—one group measuring demographic factors and another measuring attitudes and beliefs. The investigator might want to know if the demographic variables can be dropped without significant loss of information.

33. *X* was increased $1 \times 10 = 10$.

34. *R*-squared is also called the "multiple correlation coefficient," "multiple *R*," and the "coefficient of determination." These terms usually come into play when analyzing the effect of several independent variables.

35. Computer programs usually report the calculated or obtained probability of the observed chi-square, so we do not even have to look up a critical value in a table.

36. That is, $P + (1 - P) = 1$.

37. Data of these sort are widely available. For various (and irrelevant) reasons, we used Steven Finkel, Andrew Green, Aníbal Pérez-Liñán, Mitchell Seligson, and C. Neal Tate, *Cross-National Research on USAID's Democracy and Governance Programs—Codebook (Phase II)*, available at http://www.pitt.edu/ ~ politics/democracy/democracy.html.

38. We are using the natural logarithm.

39. A first-rate and accessible (for undergraduate students in the social sciences) introduction to graphs, transformations, and data analysis is (if you can find it) is Paul Velleman and David Hoaglin, *The ABC's of EDA: Applications, Basics, and Computing of Exploratory Data Analysis* (Duxbury, Mass.: Duxbury Press, 1981). Another good starting point is Frederick Hartwig and Brian E. Dearing, *Exploratory Data Analysis,* University Paper Series on Quantitative Applications in the Social Sciences, series 16 (Beverly Hills, Calif.: Sage, 1979).

40. Lee Epstein et al., "US Supreme Court Justices Database," 96, 114.

41. The two latest appointees, Elena Kagan and Sonia Sotomayor, are not included for similar reasons.

42. Most introductory texts on regression analysis devote chapters to model diagnostics and the exploration of residuals. One of our favorites is Thomas P. Ryan, *Modern Regression Methods* (New York: Wiley, 1997).

MULTIVARIATE ANALYSIS

PROBABLY ONE OF THE MOST VEXING PROBLEMS facing both political scholars and practitioners is establishing causal relationships. It is no easy matter to make a causal inference such as "The presence of a death penalty deters crime in a state," or "Increasing union strength in a nation will reduce its economic inequality." Both assertions contain causal claims in the words *deters* and *will reduce*. How does one prove arguments like these, which abound in the discourse of politics?

Chapter 6 suggested that the controlled randomized experiment offers a logically sound procedure for establishing causal linkages between variables. The difficulty with experimentation, however, is that it is not often practical or ethical. Researchers then have to rely on nonexperimental methods. One general approach, which is the subject of this chapter, is multivariate analysis. Generally speaking, **multivariate analysis** is a set of techniques for investigating the interrelationships of more than two variables.

BACKGROUND

An obvious first question is, Does adding a third variable to an analysis improve our understanding of the dependent variable? Is there, for example, a reduction in unexplained variation? This question is usually answered by comparing the fits of two models: one without the extra variable (the reduced model) and one with the variable added. Looked at this way, we say that one model is *nested* inside another. Suppose a model has just two variables, and X is used to predict Y. The variables are the set XY. Adding a third variable, Z, produces a larger set (XYZ), which contains the first one. The strategy is to contrast the adequacy of a model containing the full set of variables to one in which one or more variables have been eliminated—in other words to compare the fit of the "full" model to the fit of the "reduced" model.

To what purpose are these comparisons put? If one can identify a connection between, say, X and Y that persists even after other variables (say, W and Z) have been held constant, then there may be a basis for making a causal

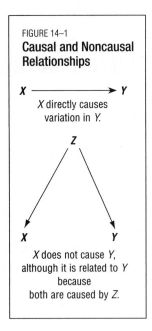

FIGURE 14–1
Causal and Noncausal Relationships

$X \longrightarrow Y$

X directly causes
variation in Y.

Z

X   Y

X does not cause Y,
although it is related to Y
because
both are caused by Z.

inference. We know by now that simply because a factor exhibits a strong relationship with a dependent variable, it does not follow that the former caused the latter. Both the independent and dependent variables might be caused by a third variable, which could create the appearance of a relationship between the first two. Only by eliminating this possibility can a researcher achieve some confidence that a relationship between an independent and a dependent variable is a causal one. Figure 14–1 illustrates the problem of distinguishing possible causal explanations.

The case studies presented in chapter 1 illustrate the problem of making causal inferences. Recall that Ansolabehere, Iyengar, and Simon wondered what effect negative political advertising (so-called attack ads) would have on political participation.[1] They conducted a laboratory experiment that offered convincing evidence about the deleterious or damaging (to voter turnout) effects of exposure to hostile political commercials. But their research has been questioned on several grounds, one of which is that the results cannot be generalized to broader, more "realistic" populations. Whether this criticism is fair or not, it raises the question: Could the causal effects be demonstrated in another way? Multivariate analysis provides an answer.

Take, for instance, the case of cross-national income inequality introduced at various points throughout the book. What explains why some countries have much greater disparities in income and wealth than others? Results developed in the previous chapter show that one indicator of inequality (the so-called Gini coefficient) is related to a measure of labor strength, "union density" or the percentage of workers who belong to organized unions. But is there a direct connection or is it spurious (see figure 14–1)?

To find out, we introduce the notion of "controlling" or holding a variable constant. Simply stated, this means that when measuring the strength and direction of the relationship between an independent and a dependent variable, the impact of other variables is removed or taken into account. In an experiment, the investigator physically manipulates explanatory variables; in nonexperimental, research statistical adjustments are required.

THE LOGIC OF HOLDING A VARIABLE CONSTANT

Suppose you are investigating the connection between an opinion on some issue and party identification. The first box in figure 14–2 represents a *total* or *original*

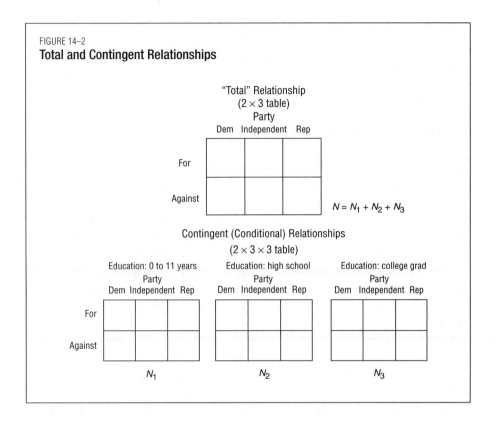

FIGURE 14–2
Total and Contingent Relationships

"Total" Relationship
(2 × 3 table)
Party

$N = N_1 + N_2 + N_3$

Contingent (Conditional) Relationships
(2 × 3 × 3 table)

association for a sample of size N. The box suggests a cross-tabulation table, but it could stand for a single statistic such as a correlation or regression coefficient. This table or statistic assesses the strength and nature of the relation between party and issue *with nothing else taken into account.* But, what if you believed that another variable, say education, affected the original relationship? You could then hold education "constant" or, what is the same, "control" for its effects. How? By looking at the party-issue association for only those subjects with approximately the same levels of education.

In the case of cross-tabulations, it is necessary to create "contingency" or "conditional" tables, one for each level or value of the control variable. We can then obtain a weighted average of whatever statistics are being used to measure the association. Note that this general idea is not confined to categorical variables but extends to quantitative variables as well. The original relationship shows how X and Y are related exclusive of anything else. When controls are introduced, there will be *partial* relationships to examine. As we will see, the original and partial associations can differ substantially, and, if they do, we have a more complicated or nuanced story to tell.

Another way of looking at this concept is to think of the education-party identification-opinion relationship as a full model, while the one with just the original two variables is the reduced one. Does the former add anything to our understanding over and above what we learned from the simpler case? Our goal is to show you how to approach this problem with different kinds of data.

MULTIVARIATE ANALYSIS OF CATEGORICAL DATA

Consider categorical data (nominal or ordinal scales). Suppose that we have hypothesized a relationship between attitudes toward government spending and presidential voting. Our hypothesis is that "the more a person favors a decrease in government spending, the more likely he or she is to vote Republican." Table 14–1 seems to confirm the hypothesis, since 64 percent of those who favor decreased spending voted Republican, whereas only 46 percent of those who favored keeping spending the same or increasing it voted Republican. This difference of 18 percentage points among a sample of 1,000 suggests that a relationship exists between attitudes toward government spending and candidate preferences.

At this point, you might ask, "Is there a causal relationship between opinion and vote (see the upper arrow diagram in figure 14–1), or does another factor, such as socioeconomic status (e.g., family income), create the apparent relationship?" Or, even if you are not interested in causality, the question arises: "Can the explanation of presidential voting be increased by including another variable?" After all, 36 percent of those who favored decreased spending (Democrats) voted contrary to the hypothesis, as did 46 percent of those in favor of maintaining or increasing spending levels (Republicans). Perhaps it would be possible to provide a better explanation for those voters' behavior.

TABLE 14–1

Relationship between Attitudes toward Government Spending and Presidential Vote

Dependent Variable: Presidential Vote	Independent Variable: Attitudes toward Government Spending		(N)
	Decrease spending	Keep spending the same or increase it	
Republican	64%	46%	(555)
Democratic	36%	54%	(445)
Total	100%	100%	
(N)	(550)	(450)	(1,000)

Note: Hypothetical data.

A second independent variable that might affect presidential voting is personal income. People with higher earnings might favor decreased government spending because they feel they gain little from most government programs. Those with higher incomes might also be more likely to vote Republican because they perceive the GOP as favoring government policies that benefit the affluent. By the same token, people having lower incomes might feel both that increased government spending would help them *and* that Democrats generally support their interests. Therefore, income might influence both attitudes toward government spending and presidential voting, thus creating the appearance of a relationship between the two.

To consider the effect of income, we need to bring it explicitly into the analysis and observe the resulting relationship between attitudes and voting. In a **multivariate cross-tabulation,** we control for a third variable by holding it constant. In effect, we **control by grouping;** that is, we group the observations according to their values on the third variable and then observe the original relationship within each of these groups. In our example, each group consists of people with more or less the same income. If a relationship between opinions on spending and voting in these groups remains, it cannot be due to income.

Table 14–2 shows what might happen were we to control for income by grouping respondents into three income levels: high, medium, and low. Notice that it contains three contingency tables: one for each category of income, the control variable. Within each of the categories of income there is now *no* relationship between spending attitudes and presidential voting. Regardless of their attitudes on spending, 80 percent of respondents with high incomes voted Republican, 60 percent with medium incomes voted Republican, and 30 percent with low incomes voted Republican. Once the variation in income was removed by grouping those with similar incomes, the attitude-vote relationship disappeared. Consequently, income is a possible alternative explanation for the variation in presidential voting.

The original relationship, then, was spurious. Remember that a spurious relationship is one in which the association between two variables is caused by a third. Note, however, that these remarks do not mean that there is *no* relationship between spending attitudes and presidential voting, for there is such a relationship, as table 14–1 shows. But this original relationship occurred only because of the variables' relationships with a third factor, income. Thus, spending attitudes cannot be a cause of presidential voting because within income groups, they make no difference whatever. (See the lower arrow diagram in figure 14–1.)

Because we have been using hypothetical data, we can easily illustrate other outcomes. Suppose, for instance, the control variable had absolutely no effect on the relationship between attitudes and vote. The result might look like the outcomes in table 14–3. We now see that the strength and direction of the relationship between attitudes and voting are the same at all levels of income. In this

TABLE 14–2
Spurious Relationship between Attitudes and Presidential Voting When Income Is Controlled

Control Variable:	Independent Variable:		
Income;	Attitudes toward Government Spending		
Dependent Variable: Presidential Vote	Decrease Spending	Keep Spending the Same or Increase It	(*N*)
High income			
Republican	80%	80%	(240)
Democratic	20%	20%	(60)
Total	100%	100%	
(*N*)	(250)	(50)	(300)
Medium income			
Republican	60%	60%	(210)
Democratic	40%	40%	(140)
Total	100%	100%	
(*N*)	(200)	(150)	(350)
Low income			
Republican	30%	30%	(105)
Democratic	70%	70%	(245)
Total	100%	100%	
(*N*)	(100)	(250)	(350)

Note: Hypothetical data.

situation, members of the upper-income group behave just like those in the lower levels. Given these data, we might be tempted to support the argument that attitudes toward government spending are causally related to candidate choice. But, of course, a critic could always say, "But you didn't control for *Z*." That would be a valid statement, provided the skeptic provided a plausible reason why *Z* would have an effect on the original relationship. A randomized controlled experiment, by contrast, theoretically eliminates all alternative explanatory variables at one fell swoop.

These hypothetical data illustrate ideal situations. Consider, then, an actual multivariate cross-tabulation. Political pundits and campaign strategists, for example, are preoccupied with geographical variation in attitudes and voting. They talk of "blue" (Democratic) and "red" (Republican) states to describe typical voting patterns in these areas. Let's investigate regional differences regarding an ongoing "cultural" or social issue, prayer in public schools. To start, we created a purely ad hoc "region" variable by combining respondents in the 2008 General Social Survey into four groups: (1) the "coasts," which includes the Pacific, New England, and mid-Atlantic states; (2) the "industrial" upper Midwestern

TABLE 14–3

Relationship between Attitudes and Presidential Voting after Income Is Controlled

Control Variable:

Income   Independent Variable: Attitudes toward Government Spending

Dependent Variable: Presidential Vote	Decrease Spending	Keep Spending the Same or Increase It	(N)
High income			
Republican	64%	46%	(183)
Democratic	36%	54%	(117)
Total	100%	100%	
(N)	(250)	(50)	(300)
Medium income			
Republican	64%	46%	(197)
Democratic	36%	54%	(153)
Total	100%	100%	
(N)	(200)	(150)	(350)
Low income			
Republican	64%	46%	(179)
Democratic	36%	54%	(171)
Total	100%	100%	
(N)	(100)	(250)	(350)

Note: Hypothetical data.

states; (3) the traditional or deep south; and (4) a conglomeration of south Atlantic and mountain states, which we label simply the "extended Sun Belt." The first two generally support Democrats for president and are thought to be centers of "liberalism." The remaining two are commonly identified with conservative and Republican voting patterns. (Needless to say, there is a lot of heterogeneity in these groupings; we use them merely for illustrative purposes.) Table 14–4 shows how people in different regions think about Supreme Court rulings limiting prayers in public schools. (For simplicity's sake, we have recoded the responses to "yes, favor" and "no, do not favor" prayers in the classroom.) The variation in the percentages saying "no" suggests an effect of region on public opinion. More than half of those on the coasts approve of the Court's decision, while only a quarter of those in the south do. The other regions fall in between. What, if anything, accounts for these differences?

More precisely, is there something about a geographical area that induces people to think one way or another? Or—more likely—do different regions contain different kinds of voters, and do these characteristics, not geography per se, explain variation in opinions? Since the south stands out so much and we are

TABLE 14–4

Total Relationship between Region and School Prayers

Prayers in public schools okay?	Generally Democratic (Blue) States		Generally Republican (Red) States	
	East and West Coast	Industrial North Central	Extended "Sun" Belt	Traditional South
No	53.6%	40.2%	40.3%	24.2%
Yes	46.4%	59.8%	59.7%	75.8%
	100%	100%	100%	100%
	(386)	(275)	(423)	(199)

N = 1283; chi square = 47.9, 3 df; prob = .000; phi = 0.19.

Question: "The United States Supreme Court has ruled that no state or local government may require the reading of the Lord's Prayer or Bible verses in public schools. What are your views on this—do you approve or disapprove of the court ruling?"

Source: James A. Davis, Tom W. Smith, and Peter V. Marsden, *General Social Surveys*, 1972–2008, Roper Center for Public Opinion Research, University of Connecticut/Ann Arbor, MI: Inter-university Consortium for Political and Social Research.

dealing with a religious issue, an obvious candidate variable to add to the mix is some kind of indicator of religiosity. After all, the deep south was familiarly known as the "Bible Belt," and even today it is thought of a stronghold of Christian conservatism. Therefore, let's include "fundamentalism" in the analysis. The GSS survey contains an item, "Fundamentalism/liberalism of respondent's religion," to which responses are coded "fundamentalist," "moderate," and "liberal"; the latter category presumably includes atheists, agnostics, and skeptics as well as religious people who nevertheless do not take sacred texts literally. Table 14–5 shows a multiway table in which the original region-opinion relationship is examined for each of the three levels of fundamentalism.

To make sense of the data, we need to explore each subtable individually and carefully. Look first then at the fundamentalists, table 14–5a. The overwhelming majority of respondents in *each* region favor allowing prayers in schools. The percentages run from 67 to more than 80 percent. There are differences to be sure—the fundamentalists on the "coasts" appear to be a bit more secular than their counterparts elsewhere. Nonetheless, the relationship is rather weak. The same is true for moderates (the middle table), although the proportions saying "no" are somewhat larger. Finally, we see that the region-attitude association is strongest and clearest in the last category, "liberals." Except in the South, a majority of respondents oppose organized prayer reading in public education. But opposition declines as one moves across the table.[3]

TABLE 14–5
Controlled or Contingent or Conditional Relationships

a. Religiosity = fundamentalist

Prayers in public schools	The "Coasts"	Industrial North	Sun Belt	Traditional South
No	32.9%	15.4%	25.2%	20.0%
Yes	67.1%	84.6%	74.8%	80.0%
	100%	100%	100%	100%
	(51)	(64)	(143)	(85)

N = 343; chi square = 5.68, 3 df; prob = .13; phi = 0.13.

b. Religiosity = moderate

Prayers in public schools	The "Coasts"	Industrial North	Sun Belt	Traditional South
No	47.1%	39.9%	41.8%	26.0%
Yes	52.9%	60.1%	58.2%	74.0%
	100%	100%	100%	100%
	(181)	(117)	(125)	(75)

N = 498; chi square = 9.92, 3 df; prob = .02; phi = 0.15.

c. Religiosity = liberal

Prayers in public schools	The "Coasts"	Industrial North	Sun Belt	Traditional South
No	73.0%	59.3%	52.2%	32.6%
Yes	27.0%	40.7%	47.8%	67.4%
	100%	100%	100%	100%
	(132)	(89)	(140)	(34)

N = 395; chi square = 23.06, 3 df; prob = .000; phi = 0.24.

Further insight is achieved by looking at the chi-square statistics in each table and as compared to the overall chi square in table 14–5. They seem to indicate a weak to nil association in the first two levels of fundamentalism and a moderate one in the third table. We see, for instance, that even among non-fundamentalists in the South, there is solid backing for school prayers (67%) but not so on the coasts, where the opposition exceeds 70 percent. So our overall conclusions might be that (1) there are regional differences in attitudes and (2) these differences are partly explained by one's degree of religious commitment.

Using summary statistics such as categorical measures of association helps because we can quickly average them across tables. The overall chi square for table 14–4 is 47.9 with 3 degrees of freedom; the weighted (by number of cases in each subtable, N_i) average of chi squares in table 14-5 is 12.2, again with 3 degrees of freedom. So the "controlled" relationship seems weaker than the total association. The average of the phi coefficients (remember that phi is the square root of the observed chi square divided by the sample size) is a tad smaller than the value in the main table (.17 versus .19).[4]

Admittedly, this sort of analysis requires absorbing a lot of numbers and trying to discern patterns among them. Here are some guidelines, although in a moment we present a more formal procedure. (Figure 14–3 may help.)

- Keep separate in your mind the original, uncontrolled relationship, X-Y, from the conditional or partial relationships. The goal is to see what happens to the former when additional variables are introduced.

- If at each level of the conditioning variable, Z, there are approximately the same kind and degree of connection between X and Y as appear in the original, then Z may not be relevant to the X-Y association.

- Are the controlled relationships on average weaker or smaller than the original? If so, Z may be a (partial) spurious cause of the X-Y relationship, *or* there may be a causal sequence: $X \rightarrow Z \rightarrow Y$. (Controlling for Z in either case reduces or eliminate the X-Y association.)

- Is the relationship between X and Y strong at some levels of Z but not others? If so, there may be statistical **interaction**. Interaction means that the strength, direction, and nature of the X-Y relationship depend on levels of the control variable. At the high end of the Z scale, there may be little or no connection between X and Y, while in the middle there is a negative correlation and there is a modest negative relationship for those cases with low values on Z. If interaction exists, the impact of X on Y depends on another variable and merits careful scrutiny. Such activity is sometimes referred to as "specifying" the relationship.

When dealing with tabular data, it may also help to find averages of summary measures (e.g., gamma), as we did earlier. Still, this kind of analysis is a bit informal and subjective. Social scientists and statisticians have developed rigorous methods for making these kinds of judgments underlaid by straightforward ideas of controlling and interaction. Nonetheless, social scientists are largely moving away from the analysis of multivariate cross-tabulations with percentages and measures of association. A variety of sophisticated and powerful techniques have been developed to describe complex contingency tables with "parsimonious" models.[5] There are two general approaches. Many sociologists, biometricians, demographers, and economists have developed methods designed explicitly to tease out of cross-tabulations as much information as possible.

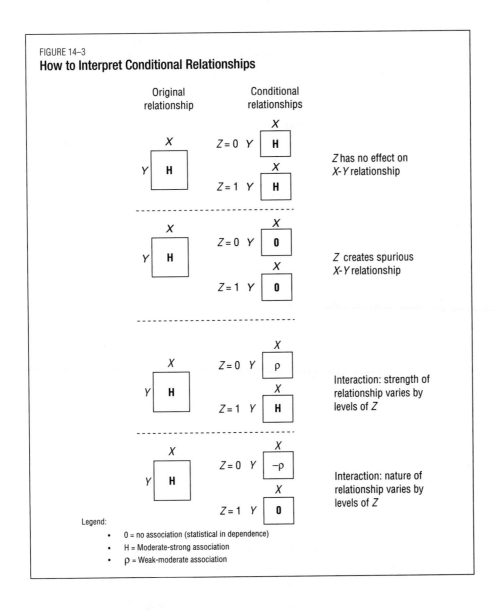

FIGURE 14–3
How to Interpret Conditional Relationships

Legend:
- 0 = no association (statistical in dependence)
- H = Moderate-strong association
- ρ = Weak-moderate association

Another, more widely adopted method in political science and other fields is to apply generalized linear models that include combinations of quantitative and qualitative data.[6] We conclude this section by comparing the analysis of cross-tabulations with the randomized experimental design discussed in chapter 6. The goal of the latter is to see if one factor causes another. By randomly assigning individuals to treatment (experimental) and control groups, the investigator (in theory at least) can scrutinize a relationship between X and Y uncontaminated by other variables, such as Z. In most research settings, however, randomization is simply not possible. Given a hypothesis about voter turnout and social class, for instance, how could a researcher randomly place someone in a particular occupation and then wait to see what effect this placement had on the person's behavior? Therefore, instead of using randomization to get rid of potentially contaminating variables, it is necessary to try to control for them manually. That is, the investigator has to explicitly identify variables (for example, Z) that might be influencing the X-Y relationship, measure them, and then statistically control for them just as we did in table 14–5. In that case, we looked at the association between the variables *within* levels of the third factor. This approach is possible if the control factor is categorical and the total number of cases is large. Other techniques are needed for different circumstances. In the next section, we discuss the cases of one continuous dependent variable and two or more categorical test factors.

LINEAR MODELS

The analysis and interpretation of multidimensional contingency tables like those just presented are complicated because so much information has to be gleaned from so many cell percentages and column totals. Moreover, though we could summarize some aspects of the data with a few coefficients, we did not supply a general method for formulating and testing statistical hypotheses. We now move to a framework and set of tools that overcome those and other problems. More important, this analytic structure extends to mixtures of categorical and numeric data. The result is that we treat a dependent variable as a (linear) function of various combinations of nominal-, ordinal-, and interval-scale independent variables.

Multiple Regression Analysis

When the dependent variable is measured at the interval or ratio level, we usually use **multiple regression analysis** to investigate how its values are affected by two or more independent variables. As noted above and in chapter 13, the aim of regression analysis is to propose and estimate a model (an equation), $Y_i = \beta_0 + \beta_1 X + \varepsilon_i$ that in some sense best describes or summarizes how X and Y are related. Finding the "best" model is called "fitting" the data, and predicted scores are called "fitted values." Recall in addition that a regression coefficient, which lies at the core of the model, tells how much the dependent variable, Y, changes for a one-unit change in the independent variable, X. Regression analysis also allows us to test various statistical hypotheses such as $\beta_1 = 0$, which means that, if true, there is no linear relationship between an independent and a dependent variable. A regression equation moreover may be used to calculate the predicted value of Y for any given value of X. And the residuals or distances between the predicted and observed values of Y lead to a measure (R^2) of how well the equation fits the data.

As the name implies, multiple regression simply extends these procedures to include more than one independent variable. The main difference—and what needs to be stressed—is that a **multiple regression coefficient** indicates how much a one-unit change in an independent variable changes the dependent variable *when all other variables in the model have been held constant or controlled. Control by adjustment* is a form of statistical control in which a mathematical adjustment is made to assess the impact of one or more additional variables. That is, the values of each case are adjusted to take into account the effect of all the other variables rather than by grouping similar cases as was done in contingency table analysis.

The general form of a linear multiple regression equation is

$$Y = \beta_0 + \beta_1 X_1 + \beta_2 X_2 + \ldots + \beta_K X_K + \varepsilon.$$

Let's examine this equation to make sure its terms are understood. In general, it says that the values of a dependent variable, Y, are a *linear* function of (or perhaps caused by) the values of a set of independent variables. The function is linear because the effects of the variables are additive. How the independent variables influence Y depends on the numerical values of the βs.

As in previous chapters, parameters are denoted by lowercase Greek letters. The first beta (β_0) is a **regression constant.**[7] It can be interpreted in many ways, the simplest being that β is the value of Y when all the independent variables have scores or values of zero. (Just substitute zero for each X and note that all the terms except the first drop out, leaving $Y_i = \beta_0 + \varepsilon_i$.)

The other βs indicate how much Y changes for a one-unit change in the independent variables when the other variables are held constant.

ASSUMPTIONS OF LINEAR MODELS

For the estimation, testing, and hence interpretation to make sense, certain conditions have to be met, at least to one degree or another. The assumptions are extensions of those presented in chapter 13.

- Independent observations

- No measurement error in the Xs

- Correct model specification

  - All relevant Xs are included. (Irrelevant independent variables will inflate the prediction error but not mess up the estimators.)

  - The dependent variable is a linear function of the independent variables.

  - A current value of Y is not a function of previous values of Y. Violations of this assumption are likely to be present in time series data.

- Multicolinearity

  - No X is an exact linear function of another X or Xs. For instance, if $X_1 = 2X_2$, the variables are said to be *collinear,* and the estimation process breaks down. If X_i, X_j are highly but not perfectly correlated, the estimates of relevant betas may be suspect.

- Error term, ε

  - The expected value of the errors is 0: $E(\varepsilon_i) = 0$.

  - Constant variance (homoscedasticity): The variation in Y is the same at each level of X.

  - Errors are uncorrelated with any X. That is, linear model analysis assumes that, say, $\rho X_{\varepsilon i} = 0$ where $\rho_{x i \varepsilon i}$ is the correlation of X_i and the error.

  - Errors are mutually independent: The correlation of ε_i with ε_j is zero.

Textbooks are loaded with advice and techniques to check the tenability of these assumptions. It is often possible to take corrective action when data do not seem to meet the requirements, but for the most part we will just take them for granted.

Each β is called a **partial regression coefficient** because it indicates the relationship between a particular X and the Y after all the other independent variables have been "partialed out" or simultaneously controlled. The presence of ε (epsilon), which stands for error, means that Y is not a perfect function of the Xs. In other words, even if we knew the values of every X, we could not completely or fully predict Y; there will be errors. (In the symbols used in chapter 13, we denoted this idea by $Y - \hat{Y}$.) But regression proceeds on the assumption that the errors are random or cancel out and that their average value is zero. Hence, we can rewrite the regression equation as

$$E(Y) = \beta_0 + \beta_1 X_1 + \beta_2 X_2 + \ldots + \beta_K X_K.$$

Read this last equation as "The expected value of Y is a linear (or additive) function of the Xs."

Finally, predicted values of Y (denoted $\hat{Y}$) may be calculated by substituting any values of the various independent variables into the equation. With these predictions in hand, one can also compute residuals. It works this way:

- Predicted values: $\hat{Y}_i = \hat{\beta}_0 + \hat{\beta}_1 X_1 + \ldots + \hat{\beta}_K X_K$
- Residuals: $\hat{\varepsilon}_i = (Y_i - \hat{Y}_i) = Y_i - (\hat{\beta}_0 + \hat{\beta}_1 X_1 + \ldots + \hat{\beta}_K)$

Residuals, which estimate the errors (ε_i) in the model, are an important tool in verifying assumptions and gauging the fit of the model to the data, as we see below.

Interpretation of Parameters

So important are the partial regression coefficients that we should examine their meaning carefully in the context of a couple of specific examples. First, let's briefly return to the problem of inequality. In the previous chapter, we discovered that union membership is negatively correlated with income inequality as measured by the Gini coefficient. Suppose we want to extend the analysis by adding an additional explanatory variable. Since we are interested in how workers are able to influence the distribution of wealth through the mobilization of labor power, a sensible candidate for inclusion is an indicator of "employment protection," which the Organisation for Economic Co-operation and Development (OECD) described as follows:

> Employment protection is described along 21 basic items which can be classified in three main areas: (i) protection of regular workers against individual dismissal; (ii) regulation of temporary norms of employment; and (iii) specific requirements for collective dismissals. The information refers to employment protection provided through legislation and as a result of enforcement processes.[8]

TABLE 14–6
Regression Results

	Simple Regression Gini ~ Union			Multiple Regression Gini ~ Union + Labor		
	Estimate	Standard error	t statistic	Estimate	Standard error	t statistic
Constant	36.44	1.34	27.97***	40.58	2.30	17.62***
Union density	−0.14	0.03	−4.65***	−0.12	0.04	−3.38**
Labor protections	—	—	—	−2.24	0.99	−2.27*
		$R^2 = .39$			$R^2 = .53$	

$N = 21$. * significant at .05, ** significant at .01, *** significant at .001.

Calculations carried out with more significant digits than reported; hence, quotients do not round exactly.

Source: Table 11–1 and Organisation for Economic Co-operation and Development, "OECD Indicators of Employment Protection," accessed March 3, 2011, from http://www.oecd.org/document/11/0,3746,en_2649_37457_42695243_1_1_1_37457,00.html.

Raw data have been converted to a 0–6 scale in which 0 is the lowest or weakest level of protection and higher values indicate more safeguards. Table 14–6 shows what happens when this additional variable is included. (The table, by the way, follows a generally accepted way of summarizing the results.)

The left-hand panel shows the bivariate regression of Gini scores on union density; the right side of the table shows what happens when "labor protections" is added to the equation. There are several points to note.

■ Now that a second independent variable has been added, the estimate of the constant *and* the regression coefficient for union density have changed slightly. That's because the extra variable has been factored in.

■ As assessed by R^2, the fit of the model is greatly improved with the extra variable: "explained variation" increases from 39 percent to 53 percent.

■ The negative signs attached to the coefficients have substantive meaning and support our general hypothesis: the greater working-class organizational and political strength, the *less* unequal the distribution of a nation's wealth.

■ The regression coefficients are measured in units of the dependent variable, but their numerical magnitude reflects the measurement scales of the Xs. Thus, the sizes of the coefficients are *not* directly comparable. Just because the beta for labor protections is −2.24 while the one for unions is −.12 does not necessarily mean that the former is a more important explanatory factor.

■ All of the coefficients in the expanded model are statistically significant. (We describe hypothesis testing shortly.) This suggests that the two independent variables work partly independently to explain variation in Y. Presumably, if one were superfluous in the presence of the other, its coefficient value would be close to nil and would not be significant.

■ In regression analysis, the effect of one independent variable is not simply added to the effect of another independent variable to get the "total" effect on Y, unless their covariation is zero; that is, the independent variables are independent. In this example, union concentration and labor protections are themselves weakly correlated ($r_{union,labor}$ = .19). Regression-computing algorithms automatically adjust for this relationship, and the adjustment affects the magnitude of the coefficients and their standard errors.

Indeed, this last point again takes us to the meaning of regression analysis. The partial regression coefficient for union density, $\hat{\beta}_{Gini \sim union,labor}$ = −.12 means that inequality declines .12 units for every 1 percent increase in union density, *after* the labor protection variable has been held constant. The same is true for labor protection: a 1-unit increase in it brings a 2.24 *decrease* in inequality. And again, since the independent variables have different scales, we have to explore their construction to see what a "one-unit" change means in the real world.

Examining Residuals

We have emphasized that one goal of regression analysis is to make predictions. You may recall from the last chapter that the difference between predicted and observed values is called a *residual*. Although a formal analysis of residuals in the multivariate context can be tricky, a systematic scrutiny of their sizes may reveal some aspect of the data worth exploring further. Table 14–7 contains the predicted and observed Gini scores based on the most acceptable model we have found so far: $\hat{Y}_i$ = 40.58 − 0.12union − 2.24labor. The twelfth case, Japan, has been highlighted because its residual stands out for being (in absolute value) nearly twice as large as any other residual in the table. For whatever reason, this case does not seem to fit the mold, and one wonders what would happen if it were (temporarily) eliminated.

To see what happens, we regress Gini on union density and labor protections for all countries except Japan and compare the results to the original model. Table 14–8 shows the comparison.

As we might have anticipated, removing a case with such a large residual (Japan) greatly improves the apparent fit of the model, especially as measured by R^2 and the increases in significance. *Consequently, from now on we exclude Japan from our analyses.* We would *not* adopt this tactic in real research, except with solid statistical and substantive judgment to back up the decision, but in this chapter we only intend to explain regression and putting the "aberrant" case aside helps simplify the presentation.

So far, we have found a linear model that seems to fit the data. The level of working-class mobilization does seem related to inequality. Hacker and Pierson's

TABLE 14–7

Observed and Predicted Gini Scores and Residuals

Country	Observed Gini	Predicted Gini	Residual $(Y_i - \hat{Y}_i)$
Australia	35.2	34.558	0.642
Austria	29.1	31.095	−1.995
Belgium	33.0	32.205	0.795
Canada	32.6	32.734	−0.134
Denmark	24.7	26.479	−1.779
Finland	26.9	25.160	1.740
France	32.7	34.113	−1.413
Germany	28.3	31.487	−3.187
Greece	34.3	33.672	0.628
Ireland	34.3	33.295	1.005
Italy	36.0	31.543	4.457
Japan	**24.9**	**33.930**	**−9.030**
Luxembourg	30.8	26.217	4.583
The Netherlands	30.9	32.636	−1.736
New Zealand	36.2	34.895	1.305
Norway	25.8	28.005	−2.205
Spain	34.7	32.269	2.431
Sweden	25.0	26.546	−1.546
Switzerland	33.7	33.578	0.122
UK	36.0	34.515	1.485
USA	40.8	36.968	3.832

TABLE 14–8

The Effects of Deleting a Case with a Large Residual

Data set	Estimated model	Fit indicator
Complete data ($N = 21$)	$\hat{Y}_i = 40.58^{***} - 0.12^{**}\text{union} - 2.24^{*}\text{Labor}$	$R^2 = .53$
Japan deleted ($N = 20$)	$\hat{Y}_i = 42.10^{***} - 0.14^{**}\text{union} - 2.48^{*}\text{Labor}$	$R^2 = .73$

*** = prob < .001, ** = prob < .01, * = prob < .05

"Winner-Take-All Politics" article discussed in chapter 1 and elsewhere argues that growth in business power explains increases in inequality in the United States.[9] We do not have evidence to support that particular claim, but we have reason to believe that *in general,* the better able workers can protect and advance their interests, the greater the economic equality in a democracy.

Before getting carried away with this inference, though, we need to remind ourselves that (1) multivariate analysis depends on all sorts of complexities and nuances—only a few of which we have come close to describing—and (b) it also rests on various assumptions being reasonably true. So, for example, the estimates in table 14–8 will be biased if the model is seriously misspecified (i.e., the wrong kind of equation is used), and without a lot of comparative study we really cannot say how appropriate a linear model is for these data. Maybe we should add a multiplicative term like X^2. Or perhaps we have the real causal ordering reversed, and union density should be on the left-hand side of the model's equation. Quite possibly our operational indicators (union density, Gini scores) of the theoretical variables (working-class mobilization, inequality) are badly out of alignment, or, in the words of chapter 5, their "construct validity" may be weak.

And, of course, the same holds for our more fine-grained analysis. Is Japan a special case? Does its outlying status support or undercut the generalization implied by the model? Here again, subject-matter expertise will be required. If anyone can explain why the Japanese labor force structure doesn't predict its level of inequality, it will be area specialists. At this point, we simply encourage you to think about the interplay of data analysis and politics and policy.

Statistical Tests

Now that we have discussed regression coefficients, we can move on to testing hypotheses about them. Remember $\hat{\beta}_k$ s are estimators of population parameters. Just because we have an observed value of 2.24 based on a sample of 21 cases, we cannot yet assert that this value or something close to it represents the true coefficient. Hence, hypothesis testing. A test for statistical significance, remember, requires the researcher to define a parameter(s) of interest; state null and alternative hypotheses; identify an appropriate sample estimator of the unknown parameter and determine its sample distribution under the null hypothesis and for the given sample size, N; establish a critical region for deciding when a sample outcome is unlikely if the null hypothesis is true; obtain the estimator and its standard error to calculate the observed test statistic; compare that against the critical value; decide whether or not to reject the null hypothesis; and interpret the results. (For testing purposes, we assume that the errors are normally distributed.)

There are two very closely related methods for testing statistical hypotheses; tests of individual coefficients and global or overall model tests.

INDIVIDUAL COEFFICIENTS.   It turns out that under the assumptions of the regression model, the sampling distributions of the betas is known and well tabulated. For small samples, we use the t distribution; as the sample grows past 30 or 40, the t distribution increasingly approximates the standard normal. A general practice is to compute t statistics for each coefficient and compare the observed value with a critical t (or z) based on $N - K - 1$ degrees of freedom.[10] The observed t values are calculated, as shown in chapter 12, from the formula

$$t_{observed} = \frac{(\hat{\beta} \quad 0)}{\hat{\sigma}_{\hat{\beta}}} = \frac{\hat{\beta}}{\hat{\sigma}_{\hat{\beta}}},$$

where $\hat{\beta}$ is the estimated coefficient and $\hat{\sigma}_{\hat{\beta}}$ is the estimated standard error or standard deviation of the regression coefficient. Since it is standard practice these days to report standard errors along with the estimates themselves, if you have an estimate and its standard error, you can immediately calculate the observed t. If you also know the sample size, you can check its significance. We use zero in the numerator because in most published research, the null hypothesis is that the population coefficient, β, is zero. But in theory, you could check that a coefficient equals any hypothesized value.

Examine table 14–6. Take the coefficient and standard error for the partial regression of Gini on union while holding labor protections constant: –.14 and .03. Dividing gives an observed t of approximately –4.67. Since the regression is based on 21 cases and there are 2 independent variables in the model, union and labor, the degrees of freedom is $21 - 2 - 1 = 18$. If you look in appendix B at the row for 17 degrees of freedom, you will see that the critical t (two-tailed test) at the .002 level is 3.610, and at the .001 level it is 3.922. Thus, the probability under the null hypothesis of a coefficient this large or larger is somewhere between 1 and 2 in 1,000.

GLOBAL TEST.   A global test assesses the overall model. In particular, the null hypothesis is

$$H_0: \beta_0 = \beta_1 = \beta_2 = \beta_3 = \ldots = \beta_K = 0.$$

That is, the test is of the hypothesis that all the coefficients (that is, the βs) equal zero. What about the rival or alternative hypothesis? For now, it is simply that *at least one* of the coefficients is nonzero in the population, but the particular one(s) is left unspecified. The mechanics of the test are a bit beyond the scope of the book, but we can sketch out the general idea. As in analysis of variance and two-variable regression, we calculate three sums of squares: total, explained (by the regression model), and unexplained or error. When a sum of squares is divided by its appropriate degrees of freedom, it becomes a "mean square," which is an estimator of a population variance (hence, the name "analysis of variance"). Under the null hypothesis that the regression parameters are all zero, the expected (long-run) values of the error and regression mean squares will be equal. If, on the other hand, the null hypothesis does not hold in some respect, the expected mean square for regression will be larger than the corresponding error mean square. This suggests that taking the ratio of the two would provide a way to judge how tenable the null hypothesis is. For given that H_0 is in fact true, then the expected value of this ratio will be 1.0.

The sums of squares are generated by most regression software. The information is usually arranged in the form of an ANOVA table like the ones we visited in the last chapter. Table 14–9 shows the results for the inequality data.

To deconstruct the table, look at the "Source" column. It lists the origins of the "explained" components—the contribution of union and labor—as well as the error and total, and next to them are the sums of squares. The total sum of squares (at the bottom) quantifies the total variation in the dependent variable, and you can see that it consists of three components, one for each of the independent variables and one for the error or residuals. The explained by regression is about 73 percent of the total; this is the meaning of the multiple correlation coefficient shown in the last row. Two variables, union density and labor protection laws, account for more than half of the variation in Gini scores.

R^2 is a descriptive measure that shows us how well the model fits the data. But it is not in and of itself a hypothesis test. So go to the second column: it gives the sum of squares. The third column contains the degrees of freedom associated with each sum of squares. For the regression or explained portion, there is a degree of freedom for each independent variable in the model; for the error, it is N minus the number of parameters including the constant, or $N - K - 1 = 20 - 2 - 1 = 17$ because the model contains a constant and two regression coefficients. The total sum of squares has $N - 1$ degrees of freedom. Notice that sums of squares and degrees of freedom are additive. For example, 191.77 + 65.77 + 93.82 = 351.37 and 2 + 17 = 19.

TABLE 14–9
Global Test

Source	Sum of Squares	df	Mean Square	$F_{Observed}$
Explained				
Union	191.77	1	191.77	34.74***
Labor protection	65.77	1	65.77	12.10***
Union + Labor	257.55	2	128.77	23.33***
Unexplained				
Error (residual)	93.82	17	5.52	
Total	351.37	19	—	

Global $_{F2,17}$ = (257.55/2)/(93.82/17) = 23.33***.

R^2 = 257.55/351.37 = .73.

Critical F with 2 and 17 degrees of freedom: .01 level = 6.11; .001 level = 10.66.

***Significant at .001.

In the fourth column are the mean squares, which, as we said earlier, *independently* estimate the error variance if the null hypothesis is true. If the hypothesis does not hold, then the expected value of the regression mean squares will be larger than the error mean square. The table provides information for testing the coefficients one by one or as a group (a global test). So, for example, we need to compute the mean square errors and take their ratio. In the case of a single variable, such as union, the test statistic has the form

$$F_{obs\,(1,17)} = \frac{\text{(Mean square for union)}}{\text{(Mean square for error)}} = \frac{\left(191.77/1\right)}{\left(93.82/17\right)} = \frac{191.77}{5.52} = 34.74.$$

Under the null hypothesis, this ratio, called the F statistic, has a distribution like other statistics we have come across. As with the t and chi-square distributions, F's distribution is a family, each member of which is defined by the degrees of freedom used in the calculation of the two mean squares. So this statistic can be compared to a critical value obtained from appendix D. To do so, first decide on a level of significance (.05, .01, .001); then determine the "numerator" and "denominator" degrees of freedom. These are simply the quantities used to calculate the mean squares, the former being K, the number of variables in the model, and the latter being $N - K - 1$. With 1 and 17 degrees of freedom, the critical values at the .01 and .001 levels are respectively 8.40 and 15.72. Our observed value, 34.75, greatly exceeds the second, and we conclude that the partial regression coefficient is significant at the .001 level.

Alternatively, we can conduct an overall or global test by combing the regression sums of squares and degrees of freedom, as shown in the "Union + Labor" row. There on the right you will find the observed F for the model as a whole (i.e., Y as a linear function of the two independent variables). It is calculated the same way: find the total sum of squares due to regression, divide by the combined degrees of freedom, and divide that quantity by the error mean square:

$$F_{obs\,(2,17)} = \frac{\text{(Mean square for regression)}}{\text{(Mean square for error)}} = \frac{\left(257.55/2\right)}{5.52} = \frac{128.77}{5.52} = 23.33.$$

What does statistical significance in this context tell us? We have rejected the null hypothesis that *all* the regression coefficients are zero. Naturally that means that one or both independent variables is correlated with inequality even after controlling for the other. Which one(s)? Referring to the tests of the individual coefficients in the table 4–9, we see that both union concentration and labor protections are significant at the .001 level.

If you look in appendix D, you will see that the critical F with 1 and 18 degrees of freedom at the .001 level of significance is 15.38. Our estimate barely misses that standard, so we say the partial regression coefficient is significant at the .01 level. This statement implies that we believe labor union strength does affect the level of inequality even when we factor in another variable, worker protections.

COMPARISON OF NESTED MODELS. The analysis of linear models can be looked at still another way. Suppose we add a third independent variable to the analysis of Gini data and estimate this model:

$$\text{Full:} \quad \hat{Y}_i = \hat{\beta}_0 + \hat{\beta}_1 \text{Union} + \hat{\beta}_2 \text{Labor} + \hat{\beta}_3 \text{Employ}.$$

Employ stands for "employment ratio," which is the proportion of a nation's working-age population actually in the labor force. This contrasts with the previous, two-independent variable model:

$$\text{Reduced:} \quad \hat{Y}_i = \hat{\beta}_0 + \hat{\beta}_1 \text{Union} + \hat{\beta}_2 \text{Labor},$$

which as can be seen is "nested" within the larger one (Full) in the sense that all of its independent variables are a subset of those in Full. (There is no variable in Reduced that is not in the full model.) Since the complete model has more explanatory terms than its cousin, it has at least as much and presumably more explanatory power. The difference will show up in the R^2s and explained regression sum of squares, both of which in the full model will be equal to or greater than in the reduced model. How much greater? We could obtain sums of squares and degrees of freedom from the two models and insert them in an ANOVA table exactly as above. This procedure, however, boils down to an *incremental F-statistic:*

$$F_{K-p,N-K-1} = \frac{\left(SSRegress_{\text{Full}} - SSRegress_{\text{Reduced}}\right)/(K-p)}{SSRegress_{\text{Full}}/(N-k-1)} = \frac{(N-K-1)}{(K-p)} \times \frac{\left(R^2_{\text{Full}} - R^2_{\text{Reduced}}\right)}{\left(1 - R^2_{\text{Full}}\right)}.$$

This quantity has an F distribution with $K - p$ numerator degrees of freedom and $N - K - 1$ degrees of freedom in the denominator, where K and p are the number of independent variables in the full model and reduced models respectively.

Calculating this statistic is straightforward with the appropriate software: obtain R^2 for the full and reduced models and determine how many variables are in each. Then plug them into the formula. By way of illustration, table 14–10 shows the two estimated regression models with their R^2s.

With these numbers in hand, we can assess the improvement in fit obtained from adding employment ratio to the mix: R^2 edges up from .53 to .55. This doesn't look like a big deal. But is it a statistically significant improvement? The test statistic,

$$F_{1,17} = \frac{(N-K-1)}{(K-p)} \frac{\left(R^2_{\text{Full}} - R^2_{\text{Reduced}}\right)}{\left(1 - R^2_{\text{Full}}\right)} = \frac{(20-3-1)}{(3-2)} \frac{(.74-.73)}{(1-.74)} = .310,$$

TABLE 14–10
Full and Reduced Models with R^2

Model	Estimated equation	Number of predictors	R^2
Full	$\hat{Y}_i = 44.36 - 0.13\text{union} - 2.45\text{labor} - 0.03\text{employ.}$	$K = 3$	.55
Reduced	$\hat{Y}_i = 42.09 - 0.14\text{union} - 2.48\text{labor.}$	$p = 2$	.53

$N = 20$, $F_{1,17} = .619$, prob $> .44$

tells us "no, not significant at even the .1 level." (The critical F with 1 and 17 degrees of freedom is 4.45 and the observed F is far less, so it does not fall in the critical region.) Thus, we do not reject the null hypothesis that $\beta_{\text{employ}} = 0$. In simple words, the extra variable adds nothing to the explanation of inequality. This "negative" finding may or may not have practical import. If the employment ratio variable loomed large in discussions of politics and inequality, we would spend time discussing possible reasons for the lack of significance. If, on the other hand, we had added it to the model just to see what would happen, we would probably mention but not dwell on the result.

The current example is trivial because we reduced the full model by just one variable and could have anticipated the finding from the small boost in R^2. But the general strategy of comparing models with an incremental test is quite flexible and handy. We'll see an illustration in the next section, but for now assume we have, say, five demographic variables and two economic indicators in a full model. We might want to evaluate the impact of dropping the first five as a group. The complete model would then have $K = 7$ parameters plus the constant, while the reduced one would have just two coefficients plus the constant. If R^2_{Reduced} is not much less R^2_{Full} and if the F is insignificant, we might conclude that demographic factors are not essential to the analysis.

CONFIDENCE INTERVALS. After identifying significant and/or interesting partial regression coefficients, one can place confidence intervals around the estimated values. To review a confidence interval for a given alpha (level of significance), the equation has this form:

$$\text{Estimator} \pm t_{(1-a)/2}, \hat{\sigma}_{\text{Estimator}},$$

where $t_{(1-\alpha)/2,}$ is the critical value of a test statistic (usually t) at the $(1 - \alpha)/2$ level of significance with the appropriate degrees of freedom, and $\hat{\sigma}_{\text{Estimator}}$ is the standard error of the estimator. The estimator and its standard deviation fall out of the regression analysis, as we have already seen.

TABLE 14–11

99% Confidence Intervals for Inequality Model

Parameter	Estimate	Lower	Upper
Constant	42.09	37.14	47.06
Union	−.14	−.22	−.060
Labor protection	−2.48	−4.566	−.398

Earlier we presented a model that contained two independent variables, union concentration and labor protection. The estimated equation is

$$\hat{Y}_i = 42.09^{***} - 0.14 \text{ union}^{***} - 2.48 \text{ labor}^{**}.$$
$$\quad (1.711) \quad (.026) \quad (0.719)$$

(Note that as usual, the stars indicate the level of significance.) If we want 99 percent intervals for each coefficient, the critical t with 17 degrees of freedom is 2.898. Putting all this in the formula gives, for example, the interval for union:

$$CI_{.99} = -.14 \pm 2.898(.026)$$
$$= -0.22 \text{ and } - 0.06.$$

Table 14–11 summarizes the results.

These confidence intervals agree with the significance shown in the model's equation: none of them includes zero. As we said in chapter 12, confidence limits provide another way of looking at hypothesis testing, so the fact that the limits exclude zero is just another way of saying that the null hypothesis is not accepted.

CATEGORICAL VARIABLES AND LINEAR MODELS

Suppose we have a categorical variable such as region or gender. How can it be entered into a linear model? It turns out to be surprisingly easy because there are various ways of doing so. One method that won't work (at least not usually and not very well) is to treat any numbers assigned as group names as just plain numbers. If region labels are 1, 2, 3, . . . , but are used for convenience, they won't function as numbers in regression analysis. Therefore, we need a different approach.

A common method is dummy variable coding. A **dummy variable** is a hypothetical index that has just *two* values: 0 for the presence (or absence) of a characteristic, group membership, condition and so on and 1 for its absence (or presence). The digits 0 and 1 are more or less arbitrary—we could use 1.5 and 100 to mark the presence and absence of a trait—but 0 and 1 lead to some facile interpretations. Dummy variables—sometimes we use the phrase *indicator variables*—are widely used to convert categorical data into a form suitable for numerical analysis.[11] Here is the general idea: Convert an ordinal or nominal variable, *X,* into a set of dummy variables, one for each category. The dummy variables are created by assigning the value 1 if an observation is a member of that category and 0 otherwise. If a variable has $J = 4$ classes, any individual will get a score of 1 on one of the dummy variables and 0 on the other three.

As always, a concrete example helps. Return once again to judicial decision making. Following journalists and scholars, we advanced the proposition that newly confirmed Supreme Court justices do not (no doubt cannot) banish all political preferences or predispositions from their minds when they take office. Instead, we propose, justices carry those predispositions with them into their deliberations. To test this idea, we compared the justices' liberalism-conservatism indicator on various issues to the party and attitudes of the president and Senate that nominated and confirmed them. Although the universe is quite small (twenty-three justices), we found modest associations between partisanship and their rulings in a number of policy areas. Let's explore the idea more deeply by measuring the impact (if any!) of the justices' family social status when growing up. The data set we have been using—US Supreme Court Justices Database— contains a variable that "indicates the general socioeconomic status of the nominee's family during his or her childhood." The court members are assigned to one of five categories: lower, lower-middle, middle, upper-middle, and upper. Because there are so few cases in the first group, we combined lower and lower-middle for a four-category scheme.

In order to follow what comes later, look at figure 14–4. Here is another boxplot that compares the distribution of economic liberalism scores (Y) within levels of family social status (X). We see that the medians (the solid lines in the boxes) trend downward as we move from lower to upper class. The substantive interpretation is that the lower the category—here the categories have an implicit order—the higher the economic liberalism measure and vice versa. Those justices born and raised in a particular milieu apparently carry their socialization into their adult lives. Needless to say, this conclusion is very tentative since it rests on a tiny sample and unverified assumptions about errors in the model. Still, let's analyze the data more formally, if for no other reason than just to provide a numerical example.

Back to dummy variables. With four socio-economic groups we need four dummy variables, one for each category of status. However, in the ensuing analysis, we have to drop one of the variables in order to make the model estimable. A quick example shows why. Denote the categorical variable Z and its individual category dummy variables as Z_j. Table 14–12 lists four justices and their families' socioeconomic background category. If you spend a little time looking at the table, you can tell that, if you know a person's score on any three variables, you can predict exactly his or her value on the remaining one.

Start with Earl Warren. Once you know his first dummy variable score is 1, a little thought shows that his scores on the other three must be zero. Why? Because a 1 indicates membership in a class and belonging to it automatically

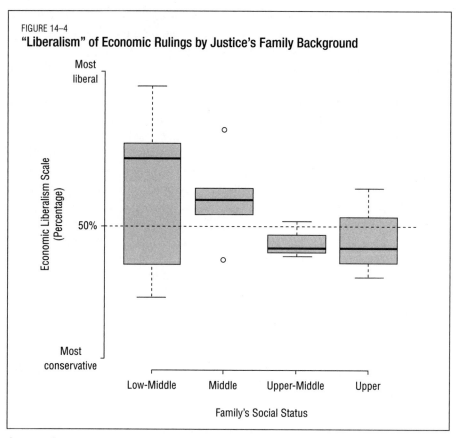

FIGURE 14–4

"Liberalism" of Economic Rulings by Justice's Family Background

Source: Lee Epstein et al., US Supreme Court Justices Database, 2010.

TABLE 14–12

US Supreme Court Justices and Socioeconomic Background

Justice	Status category	Dummy variables (Z_j)			
		$Z_{\text{Low-middle}}$	Z_{Middle}	$Z_{\text{Middle-upper}}$	Z_{Upper}
Earl Warren	Low-middle	1	0	0	0
Byron White	Middle	0	1	0	0
Sandra Day Connor	Upper-middle	0	0	1	0
John Paul Stevens	Upper	0	0	0	1

means he can't be in any of the others. Conversely, if you knew that Warren's scores on the last three are 0, you wouldn't even have to look to know that he gets a 1 on the first variable. In statistical language, $Z_{\text{Low-middle}}$, Z_{Middle}, $Z_{\text{Middle-upper}}$, and Z_{Upper} are perfectly linearly related. As the list of regression requirements stated, this condition is a no-no. A peek under the hood of the computing machinery would show you that there are too many coefficients to estimate given the available information. The way to avoid this so-called multicolinearity is to drop one of the dummy variables from the analysis. The principle is this: *for a variable with J categories, create no more than J − 1 indicator variables.*

Dummy variables are often defined in these terms:

Z_j = 1, if observation is in category j; Z_j = 0 otherwise.

Since there are four statuses, we need $4 - 1 = 3$ dummy variables. We convert status (Z) into three indicator variables as follows:

Middle: Z_2 = 1, if a justice is from middle-class background.
                        = 0, otherwise.
Middle-upper: Z_3 = 1, if a justice is from upper-middle class background.
                        = 0, otherwise.
Upper Z_4 = 1, if a justice is from upper-class background.
                        = 0, otherwise.

There is no Z_1 for low-middle. Instead, it will serve, as we see momentarily, as a reference or base or comparison category against which the effects of X are measured. Any category can serve as the reference point, but always try to pick one with substantive meaning because you'll be saying things like "Compared to justices in the lowest status, the effect of 'moving' to the next higher level is such and such." If you picked a category in the middle of the scale, comparisons might be a tad harder to sort out.

Whatever the choice, these variables are treated as numeric and inserted in the model like any other set of independent variables. To accommodate different kinds of variables, we will for convenience use lowercase lambda (λ) and lowercase delta (δ) to stand for the population partial regression coefficients for dummy variables. And we now denote the constant with alpha (α). These symbols are used for different purposes elsewhere, but the context should make their meaning clear.

The regression model for dummy variables take various forms depending on the kind and number of variables in the model (see table 14–13). Please don't turn away from the equations. They are not as intractable as they seem—we'll discuss the details in a minute.

In the current example, we have just one categorical variable (status) with four levels that we want to utilize as a predictor. In symbolic form the model is

$$\hat{Y}_i = \hat{\alpha} + \hat{\lambda}_2 Z_2 + \hat{\lambda}_3 Z_3 + \hat{\lambda}_4 Z_4,$$

TABLE 14–13

Some Models Using Dummy Variables

Procedure	Variables in model	Model equation	Comment
Single dummy variable regression	One categorical variable (Z) with J classes	$\hat{Y}_i = \hat{\alpha} + \hat{\lambda}_2 Z_2 + \hat{\lambda}_3 Z_3 + \ldots + \hat{\lambda}_J Z_K.$	Equivalent to ANOVA
Two-variable dummy variable regression	Two categorical variables (Z and W) with K and J levels respectively	$\hat{Y}_i = \hat{\alpha} + \hat{\lambda}_2 Z_2 + \hat{\lambda}_3 Z_3 \ldots + \hat{\lambda}_K Z_K + \hat{\delta}_2 W_2 + \hat{\delta}_2 W_3 + \ldots + \hat{\delta}_J W_J.$	Additional categorical variables can be added. Possible alternative to two-way ANOVA.
Analysis of covariance	Both quantitative and categorized variables	$\hat{Y}_i = \hat{\alpha} + \hat{\beta}_2 X_2 + \hat{\lambda}_2 Z_2 + \hat{\lambda}_3 Z_3 + \ldots$	βs across groups are equal.
Analysis of covariance with interaction	Quantitative and categorical variables plus interaction term: $I = XZ$	$\hat{Y}_i = \hat{\alpha} + \hat{\beta}_2 X_2 + \hat{\lambda}_2 Z_2 + \hat{\lambda}_3 Z_3 + \ldots + \hat{\omega}_1 X Z_2 + \hat{\omega}_2 X Z_3$ $= \hat{\alpha} + \hat{\beta}_2 X_2 + \hat{\lambda}_2 Z_2 + \hat{\lambda}_3 Z_3 + \ldots + \hat{\omega}_1 I_1 + \hat{\omega}_2 I_2 \ldots$	βs across groups are *not* equal.

Interaction: $I = XZ.$

α is the constant; λ and δ are regression coefficients for categorical variables Z and W, respectively; β is the regression coefficient for X; and ω is the regression coefficient for the interaction variable, I.

Note: The *first* category is the base or comparison point and is omitted from the models. Any category, however, can serve this purpose. Make the choice as substantively meaningful as possible.

and the estimation turns out to be

$$\hat{Y}_{\text{Liberalism}} = 57.17 - 1.06 \text{Middle} - 11.21 \text{Upper-middle} - 10.47 \text{Upper}.$$

The complete results appear in table 14–14. We'll talk about the statistical tests later; for now, concentrate on the meaning of the coefficients.

In the case of these types of variables, one can apply the standard rote interpretation to the estimated parameters: "a one-unit change in . . ." This is perfectly valid and will make sense if one reflects on what a "one-unit change" in a dummy variable would mean. Thinking abstractly, one could imagine a justice somehow coming from a different social and economic environment. What would the "effect" be? The regression parameter gives the answer. Changing Earl Warren's family status from low-middle to middle would be expected to lead to a 1 percent (1.06) *decrease* in his economic liberalism score.

Or we can write out the equations for each category. Doing so takes advantage of the fact that some coefficients will drop out because if an observation does not belong in a group, its score on the corresponding dummy variables is zero. For instance, look first at only those justices in the comparison category, low-middle. Substituting values for the dummy variables in the equation gives

$$\hat{Y}_{\text{Liberalism}} = 57.17 - 1.06(0) - 11.21(0) - 10.47(0) = 57.17.$$

TABLE 14–14
Supreme Court Decisions by Social Status

Category	Coefficient Estimate	Standard Error	Observed t
Constant = mean of observations for base category	57.173	4.76	12.01***
Middle	−1.06	7.01	−0.15
Middle-upper	−11.21	7.90	−1.39
Upper	−10.47	7.90	−1.33

ANOVA Table:

Source	Sum of Squares	df	Mean Squares	F_{Obs}
Status	535.57	3	178.53	1.1245
Error	2698.90	17	158.76	
Total	3234.47	20		

Critical F with 3 and 17 degrees of freedom = 3.20 at the .05 level.

All these people are in the first category and so have zero values on the middle, middle-upper, and upper dummy variables. This result, 57.16 percent, is the predicted or expected liberalism for those appointees of "humble" origins. (It also equals the mean economic liberalism of the justices with lower- to middle-class origins, as we pointed out when explaining the meaning of the regression constant.) But what about someone from a middle-class family, the next category? Just write out the equation to find out:

$$\hat{Y}_{Middle} = 57.17 - 1.06(1) - 11.21(0) - 10.47(0) = 57.16 + (-1.06) = 56.11.$$

The predicted value has dropped a modest 1.06 percent. We can keep going and derive some meaning from the remaining coefficients by making the appropriate substitutions:

$$\hat{Y}_{Middle-upper} = 57.17 - 1.06(0) - 11.21(1) - 10.47(0) = 57.17 - 11.21 = 45.96.$$

$$\hat{Y}_{Upper} = 57.17 - 1.06(0) - 11.21(0) - 10.47(1) = 57.16 + (-10.47) = 46.70.$$

The mean economic percentage drops a precipitous 11 percent when moving from low-middle to middle-upper and 10.5 percent when moving into the upper status category. We can simply read these effects from the estimates in the table. In the one categorical variable case, the regression constant equals the mean Y for those in the reference or comparison class. The regression coefficient measures the "effect" of moving from one category to the next. For instance, to find the mean liberalism of middle-class justices, just add the regression coefficient to the constant: 57.17 + (−1.06) = 56.11. That is, the consequence of a move from low-middle to middle is a lowering of the average liberalism by about 1 percent. So, in this simple case, the measurement of the "effect" of middle-class status is 1.06 percent.

Does a Model Fit? ANOVA and Dummy Variable Regression

Did you notice that in the previous example, we were effectively comparing one mean with another? As you might recall, that is what analysis of variance does: it tests for differences in group means. And so does regression analysis. There is little surprise in this statement because the starting point of both procedures is the linear model, $E(Y_i) = \alpha + \beta_1 X_1 + \ldots + \lambda_1 Z_1 \ldots$. And both are essentially efforts to see how independent variables explain variation in Y. Consequently, dummy variable regression gives the same results as ANOVA. In fact, regression and analysis of variance are frequently computed with the same methods.

This point becomes clearer when we come to hypothesis tests. For now, look again at table 14–14. The bottom of the table displays the ANOVA analysis. It answers the general question: Does knowledge of a judge's social background help predict the direction and content of his or her rulings on economic disputes? More formally, it compares a full model ($\hat{Y}_i = \alpha + \hat{\lambda}_2 Z_2 + \hat{\lambda}_3 Z_3 + \hat{\lambda}_4 Z_4$) with a reduced model ($\hat{Y}_i = \alpha$). The latter model effectively states that there is no explained variation and so $R^2_{\text{Reduced}} = 0$. Let's use the incremental F-test introduced above. For that we need the following:

- $N = 21$, the sample size (number of justices excluding recent appointments)
- $K = 3$, the number of parameters (*excluding* the constant) in the full model
- $p = 0$, the number of parameters (*excluding* the constant) in reduced model
- $R^2_{\text{Full}} = 535.57/3234.47 = .1656$. (Sums of squares are in table 14–14)
- $R^2_{\text{Reduced}} = 0/3234.47 = 0$.

Inserting these values in the formula gives

$$F_{1,17} = \frac{(N-K-1)}{(K-p)} \frac{\left(R^2_{\text{Full}} - R^2_{\text{Reduced}}\right)}{\left(1 - R^2_{\text{Full}}\right)} = \frac{(21-3-1)}{(3-0)} \frac{(.1656-0)}{(1-.1652)} \approx 1.245,$$

which fails to exceed the critical value at even the .10 level.

The top of the table contains regression results along with the standard errors and t statistics for the individual coefficients. (None of them except the constant reached anything close to significance, which in this context tells us only that the mean Gini score is not likely to be zero.)

Like all statistical analyses, t- and F-tests rest on assumptions about the distribution of the errors. We generally prefer using the incremental test over calculating multiple individual t statistics, but both are widely reported in the literature.

Models with Quantitative and Categorical Variables: Analysis of Covariance (ANCOVA)

There is no reason we cannot simultaneously investigate the effects of both quantitative and categorical variables on a numeric dependent variable. As a matter of fact, doing so often leads to interesting conclusions. Here is a continuation of a previous example, inequality in postindustrial democracies. We are trying to find out what factors explain cross-national variation in inequality. We started with union density, then added labor protection to obtain a model that fits reasonably well. Can it be improved further? Here is where literature review comes to the fore. A survey of books and articles reveals that some scholars believe there is a difference between European and Anglo-American political culture when it comes to attitudes about workers' rights, social insurance, and welfare spending, all of which affect the distribution of wealth. To test this proposition we created a crude indicator:

$$\text{Culture } (Z_2) = 1 \text{ if Anglo-American, } Z_2 = 0 \text{ otherwise.}$$

(The excluded variable is $Z_1 = 1$ if European, 0 otherwise. So our reference category is Europe, and we will gauge the effects on inequality of "changing" from it to Anglo-American.)

The general form of the equation is

$$\hat{Y}_i = \hat{\alpha}_0 + \hat{\beta}_{\text{Union}}\text{Union} + \hat{\lambda}_{\text{Culture}}\text{Culture}.$$

The first coefficient is, of course, the constant, and the second is the partial regression coefficient of inequality on union membership with "culture" held constant. *Note that we are holding type constant, not ignoring or simply excluding it.* The coefficient ($\hat{\beta}_{\text{Culture}}$) shows the effects of "moving" from one culture to another. The estimated equation is

$$\hat{Y}_{\text{Gini}} = 35.92 - .13\text{Union} + 2.85\text{Culture}.$$
$$\quad\quad (1.45) \quad\quad (.03) \quad\quad (1.40)$$

Following standard practice, we present the estimates along with their standard errors. If you divide one into the other, you can obtain observed t statistics to decide which will be statistically significant at a particular alpha level. Keep in mind that due to the small N and the fact that basic assumptions (e.g., normally distributed errors) may not be met, we should take the hypothesis tests with a grain of salt. Besides, we'll come back to them later when describing inference for multiple regression. More important at the moment is nailing down what these numbers mean. Once more, writing out the estimated equation and substituting various values for the independent variable help. First, what happens if there are *no* unions (union = 0) and we are looking at only European countries (culture = 0)? The equation simplifies greatly:

$$\hat{Y}_{Gini} = 35.92 - .13(0) + 2.85(0) = 35.92.$$

This is the mean Gini score for those nations meeting these conditions (union = culture = 0) and appears meaningless because no country is entirely without a labor movement. But it provides a baseline for comparison. If a culture could somehow switch from European to Anglo-American, the effect would be to increase inequality:

$$\hat{Y}_{Gini} = 35.92 - .13(0) + 2.85(1) = 35.92 + 2.85 = 38.77.$$

That is, inequality would increase to 39. (We know there should be an increase because of the plus sign attached to the coefficient.) In words, the Anglo-American nations are a bit more unequal (by this standard) than those on the Continent. But our real objective is to see how the two independent variables work together to achieve their effects. Let's set union density at its mean for this group of countries, 35.51, and again consider the European nations (culture = 0). Substituting these values into the estimated model, we get

$$\hat{Y}_{Gini} = 35.92 - .13(35.51) + 2.85(0) = 35.92 - 4.73 = 31.30.$$

In other words, the predicted Gini score for non-European nations with an average level of unionization is 31.20. How do non-European countries (culture = 1) with the same mean union density stack up? Just plug the data values into the equation:

$$\hat{Y}_{Gini} = 35.92 - .13(35.51) - 2.85(1) = 35.92 - 4.62 - 2.85 = 28.45.$$

We see that inequality increases: Europe has slightly more economic equality than Anglo-American nations do *even when the level of unionization is controlled.* That is, culture adds a bit to our understanding of political economy over and above what social and economic factors supply. (Needless to say, "culture" is a broad-brush attempt to capture complex and nuanced aspects of society, and we employ it mainly for expository reasons.)

We have been following a general method of inserting prespecified and meaningful values into estimation equations. It's a trick that is helpful for understanding the next application of dummy variables to regression analysis.

Interaction

Earlier in the chapter, we introduced a concept that is very important in linear models, interaction. Interaction, as we said then, means that the nature of a relationship between two variables, Y and X, depends on levels of a third variable, Z. The test is: does holding Z constant—that is, measuring the Y-X relationship at each level or value (or interval of values) of Z—affect the relationship between Y and X? Or, to put it another way, looking to see if the relationship between Y and X is different for different values of Z. Testing and measuring interaction effects in the context of linear models are often called the analysis of covariance (ANCOVA). In the simplest case, the one we present here, there is quantitative dependent variable, Y, a quantitative independent variable, X, plus a categorical factor with J categories.

Table 14–5(b) illustrated the idea with categorical variables. Figure 14–5 does the same for interaction between two quantitative variables, X and Y, and one qualitative variable with two levels, Z_1 and Z_2. (For convenience, we denote them as "group 1" and group 2.") The figure contains two panels. The first illustrates "no interaction." It is meant to show a situation in which the effects of X on Y are the same regardless of the value of Z. The regression constants ($\alpha_2 > \alpha_1$)

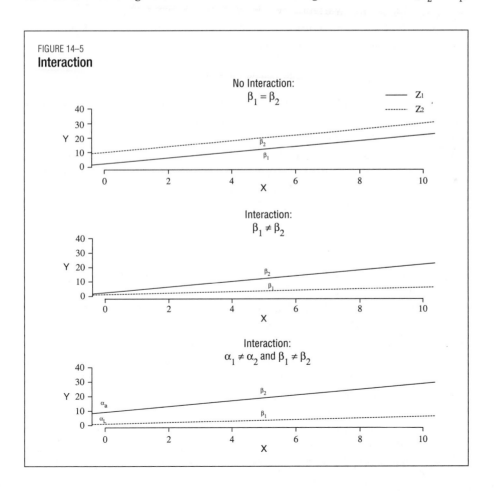

FIGURE 14–5
Interaction

differ so that for a given value of X, observations in group 2 have higher Y values than do those in the first level. But the difference is constant across the range of X. Even more important, the nature of the relationship between Y and X—its strength and direction—are the same in both groups. Thus, X has the same impact on Y no matter what Z is. Not so in the second graph.

Here we see that the two slopes differ: $\beta_2 > \beta_1$. This suggests that for a one-unit change in X, Y increases more in group 2 than group 1. Depending on the context, the difference could have theoretical or substantive importance. Seen another way, note that, although the two regression constants are the same, the difference between the lines is not constant. The third plot is a picture of a situation in which interaction exists ($\beta_2 > \beta_1$) and the intercepts also differ ($\alpha_2 > \alpha_1$). In cases where this condition holds, we might say that there are two separate linear processes at work: one that applies to group 1 and another that applies to group 2.

No real data set will follow exactly these patterns, but plots and regression analysis with dummy variables will indicate when interaction might and might not be present. An interaction "variable" is created from the independent and categorical variables by simple multiplication:

$$\text{interaction: } I = XZ.$$

How do you multiply a categorical variable by anything? You don't. Instead, you multiply X by each dummy variable representing the categories of Z. So if Z has $J = 5$ categories, there will be 4 dummy variables, each of which is multiplied by X to create four interaction variables. So a model with an interaction term looks like this. Consider a Z with two categories, the first of which is treated as the reference point. It appears in the model as Z_2. The interaction is represented by multiplying the two explanatory variables in the equation:

$$\hat{Y}_i = \hat{\alpha} + \hat{\beta}_1 X + \hat{\lambda}_2 Z_2 + \hat{\eta}_1 X Z_2 = \hat{\alpha} + \hat{\beta}_1 X + \hat{\lambda}_2 Z + \hat{\eta}_I I.$$

Important: For various reasons related to the interpretation of parameters, it is usually advisable to retain *all* "parent" variables in the interaction term. (Technically, these are called "hierarchical" models.) Thus, if I consists of XZ, then the two variables should also appear separately in the equation. (For example, don't force a computer to estimate this model: $\hat{Y}_i = \hat{\alpha} + \hat{\eta}_1 I$, where $I = XZ$.)

Another way of looking at interaction is this: the independent variable's influence on Y consists of more than its additive main effect (represented by the " $+ X$" term) but is "supplemented" by an additional multiplicative effect of the form $I = XZ_j$. (The same can be said for Z.)

The interaction component can be confusing until one revisits the substitution method. Pick a set of meaningful values for the independent variables, substitute them into the estimated model, and observe how changes in one factor affect the response variable while the others are held constant. To demonstrate, we extend the previous model by adding an interaction term:

$$\hat{Y}_{\text{Gini}} = 35.43 - .13 \text{ Union} + 8.27 \text{ Culture} - 0.20 \text{ Interaction.}$$
$$(1.42) \quad (.03) \quad (3.63) \quad\quad\quad (.12)$$

The "main" (marginal) effects of unionization and culture are $-.13$ and $+8.27$, respectively. (Note again, moving to Anglo-American culture decreases the Gini score by about 8 points, which means a decrease in inequality.) There is a single interaction term, $-.20$, which is the only new wrinkle. We need to see what it means. The best way for now is to make substitutions as we have been doing. So let's say we want the predicted inequality score for European countries whose union density percentage is 35.51, as we just saw. With $X = 35.51$, $Z_1 = 0$, and $I = 35.51 \times 0 = 0$, the equation reduces to

$$\hat{Y}_{\text{Gini}} = 35.43 - .13(35.51) + 8.27(0) - .20(35.51 \text{ X } 0)$$
$$= 35.43 - 4.62$$
$$= 30.81.$$

Compare this to the prediction for the Anglo-American countries,

$$\hat{Y}_{\text{Gini}} = 35.43 - .13(35.51) + 8.27(1) - .20(35.51 \text{ X } 1)$$
$$= (35.43 + 8.27) - (.13(35.51) - .20(35.51)) \text{ after rearrangement}$$
$$= 43.7 + 35.51(-13 - .20) \text{ factor out } 35.51$$
$$= 31.98.$$

INTERPRETING MODELS WITH DUMMY VARIABLES AND INTERACTION

If dummy variables are coded 0 and 1, one can simplify equations and gain a better understanding of what they mean by replacing Zs with these values and rearranging terms. Consequently, a model for Y with a quantitative variable, X, and a single categorical variable, Z, with $J = 3$ categories looks like this in general:

$$\hat{Y}_i = \hat{\alpha} + \hat{\beta}_X X + \hat{\lambda}_2 Z_2 + \hat{\lambda}_3 Z_3.$$

Z_1 has been omitted, and the first category serves as the reference point. Since the Z's can only be 0 or 1, we can simplify the equation. For members of the reference class ($Z_1 = 1$), Z_2 and Z_3 are both 0, and terms associated with them drop out:

$$\hat{Y}_i = \hat{\alpha} + \hat{\beta}_X X + \hat{\lambda}_2 (0) + \hat{\lambda}_3 (0) = \hat{\alpha} + \hat{\beta}_X X.$$

(Box Continued)

(Box Continued)

This looks like a simple two-variable regression, and indeed it is. But it is restricted to the observations in the base category. Now look what happens when we add the second group for which $Z_2 = 1$ and $Z_1 = Z_3 = 0$. Make the substitutions and rearrange terms:

$$\hat{Y}_i = \hat{\alpha} + \hat{\beta}_X X + \hat{\lambda}_2 (1) + \hat{\lambda}_3 (0)$$
$$= \hat{\alpha} + \hat{\beta}_X X + \hat{\lambda}_2$$
$$= \left(\hat{\alpha} + \hat{\lambda}_2\right) + \hat{\beta}_X X$$
$$= \hat{\alpha}' + \hat{\beta}_X X.$$

This, too, appears to be a linear regression with the same main effect of X but a new regression constant, $\hat{\alpha}'$. As you can see, it consists of two parts, the original constant, $\hat{\alpha}$, and the coefficient for category 2, $\hat{\lambda}_2$. Recalling that the constant can be interpreted as the expected value of Y when X is zero, we see that the regression coefficient for a dummy variable can be interpreted as an "adjustment" (up or down depending on the its sign) to the expected value of the dependent variable.

Deconstruction of an interaction model follows the same logic:

$$\hat{Y}_i = \hat{\alpha} + \hat{\beta}_X X + \hat{\lambda}_2 Z_2 + \hat{\lambda}_3 Z_3 + \hat{\delta}_2 X Z_2 + \hat{\delta}_3 X Z_3.$$

Consider Z_1. Then, $Z_2 = Z_3 = 0$ and $I_2 = X Z_2 = I_3 = X Z_3 = 0$, and simplification follows:

$$\hat{Y}_i = \hat{\alpha} + \hat{\beta}_X X + \hat{\lambda}_2 (0) + \hat{\lambda}_3 (0) + \hat{\delta}_2 X (0) + \hat{\delta}_3 X (0),$$
$$= \hat{\alpha} + \hat{\beta}_X X.$$

Another simple regression equation. And, as you might anticipate, the presence of interaction is going to affect both the regression constant and partial regression coefficient. To see this point, compare the previous equation with what we get when insert $Z_2 = 1$ in the model and Z_1 and Z_3 are both zero. Notice that now $I_2 = X Z_2 = X$:

$$\hat{Y}_i = \hat{\alpha} + \hat{\beta}_X X + \hat{\lambda}_2 (1) + \hat{\lambda}_3 (0) + \hat{\delta}_2 X (1) + \hat{\delta}_3 X (0),$$
$$= \hat{\alpha} + \hat{\beta}_X X + \hat{\lambda}_2 + \hat{\delta}_2 X,$$
$$= \left(\hat{\alpha} + \hat{\lambda}_2\right) + \left(\hat{\beta}_X + \hat{\delta}_2\right) X,$$
$$= \hat{\alpha}' + \hat{\beta}' X.$$

Similarly for the third category, $Z_3 = 1$:

$$\hat{Y}_i = \hat{\alpha} + \hat{\beta}_X X + \hat{\lambda}_2 (0) + \hat{\lambda}_3 (1) + \hat{\delta}_2 X (0) + \hat{\delta}_3 X (1),$$
$$= \hat{\alpha} + \hat{\beta}_X X + \hat{\lambda}_3 + \hat{\delta}_3 X,$$
$$= \left(\hat{\alpha} + \hat{\lambda}_3\right) + \left(\hat{\beta}_X + \hat{\delta}_3\right) X,$$
$$= \hat{\alpha}'' + \hat{\beta}'' X.$$

We have three linear equations for predicting Y from X. But they have differing constants and regression parameters. These differences of course stem from the effects of going from one level of Z to another.

The real meaning and importance of interaction can perhaps be seen here: interaction means that the nature and strength of a linear Y-X relationship as measured by the regression parameters depend on the level of another variable.

Hence, we observe quite a jump in the predicted inequality (given $X = 35.51$) from about 31 to more than 32. There seems to be an added boost over and above that predicted by the main effects of union and culture. If you look back at the previously estimated equation with no interaction, you'll see that the predicted inequality level for Anglo-American with union density equal to the mean was 31.20; adding the interaction element changed it to 31.98.

Remember that the main effect of percent employed was not significant, so in practice we would drop it and any interaction terms based on it. As the hierarchy principle states: no main effect of X, no interaction involving X in the model.

Standardized Regression Coefficients

As discussed in chapter 13, a regression coefficient calculated from standardized variables is called a standardized regression coefficient or, sometimes, a beta weight. Under certain, restricted circumstances, it might indicate the relative importance of each independent variable in explaining the variation in the dependent variable when all other variables are controlled for. Standardizing a variable, you may remember from chapter 13, means subtracting its mean from each individual value and dividing by the standard deviation. The results are frequently called *scaled* variables, a term we use intermittently hereafter. To obtain the standardized regression coefficients, you standardize all the variables, including Y, and then regress the standardized Y on the standardized Xs. It is the same procedure demonstrated in chapter 13, except that now there are more than two variables. A standardized coefficient shows the partial effects of an X on Y in standard deviation units. The larger the absolute value, the greater the effect of a one-standard-deviation change in X on the mean of Y, when controlling for or holding other variables constant. Most software offers the option of calculating unstandardized or standardized coefficients.

Table 14–15 presents a comparison of the regression using standardized and unstandardized variables.

Columns 2 through 7 show alternatively raw scores and scaled values for the Gini, labor, and union in our abbreviated (minus Japan) data set. The standardized or scaled variables are calculated with the raw data with the method introduced in chapter 13. For instance, to convert or transform Y to a standardized score, y, use the formula

$$y_i = \frac{(Y_i - \bar{Y})}{\hat{\sigma}_Y},$$

where $\bar{Y}$ is the mean of Y and $\hat{\sigma}_Y$ is its standard deviation. (In common usage, lowercase letters denote standardized variables.)

The bottom of table 14–15 demonstrates the properties of standardization. Note that the means are zero while the standard deviations are 1.0. In essence,

TABLE 14–15
Raw and Standardized Inequality Data

Country	Gini Index	Scaled Gini Index	Labor Protection	Scaled Labor Protection	Union Density	Scaled Union Density
Australia	35.2	0.732	1.38	−0.946	23.1	−0.594
Austria	29.1	−0.686	2.41	0.407	35.7	0.009
Belgium	33.0	0.221	1.02	−1.418	55.6	0.962
Canada	32.6	0.128	1.91	−0.250	28.2	−0.350
Denmark	24.7	−1.709	2.29	0.250	72.5	1.771
Finland	26.9	−1.198	3.00	1.182	74.8	1.881
France	32.7	0.151	2.63	0.696	8.2	−1.307
Germany	28.3	−0.872	2.97	1.143	23.2	−0.589
Greece	34.3	0.523	2.11	0.013	24.5	−0.527
Ireland	34.3	0.523	1.39	−0.932	36.3	0.038
Italy	36.0	0.919	2.58	0.630	34.0	−0.072
Luxembourg	30.8	−0.291	3.39	1.694	42.3	0.325
The Netherlands	30.9	−0.267	2.23	0.171	22.4	−0.628
New Zealand	36.2	0.965	1.16	−1.235	22.6	−0.618
Norway	25.8	−1.453	2.65	0.722	53.0	0.837
Spain	34.7	0.616	3.11	1.326	16.2	−0.924
Sweden	25.0	−1.639	2.06	−0.053	78.0	2.034
Switzerland	33.7	0.384	1.77	−0.433	17.8	−0.848
UK	36.0	0.919	1.09	−1.326	29.2	−0.302
USA	40.8	2.035	0.85	−1.642	12.6	−1.097
Means	32.05	0	2.1	0	35.51	0
Standard deviations	4.3	1	0.761	1	20.89	20.89

we have converted the original measurement scales (e.g., percentages) to ones that are now (in a statistical sense) comparable. Hence, whereas a one-unit change on the original union density scale means a 1 percent increase or decrease, it now means a one-standard-deviation change. Similarly, labor protections, which are measured on a 1 to 6 scale in the original units, now are measured on a scale in which the basic unit is a standard deviation. (Examine table 14–15 to glean further insights.)

Regression analysis now simply entails using scaled variables instead of raw data. The results of standardized regression will be the same as those of unstandardized regression in these two respects:[12]

- Many measures of fit (e.g., r, R^2) will be the same.

- The results of tests of significance (e.g., t and F statistics, probabilities) will be the same.

But they differ in these two ways:

■ There is no constant in the standardized equation.

■ The numerical values of the standardized regression coefficients will not be the same, but they will have the same sign.

The differences can be seen into the two estimated models from the data in table 14–15 (note the absence of Japan):

Raw (unstandardized): $\hat{Y}_i = 42.10 - .14\text{Union} - 2.28\text{Labor}$, $R^2 = .73$, $F_{2,17} = 23.33$.

Scaled (standardized): $\hat{Y}_i = -.66\text{Union} - .44\text{Labor}$, $R^2 = .73$, $F_{2,17} = 23.33$.

If the results are basically the same, why bother? For one thing, one runs across results based on scaled variates all the time in scholarly literature, and it is advantageous to be familiar with them. In addition, many computer programs routinely report standardized regression coefficients (sometimes called *beta weights* or simply *betas*). More significant, perhaps, the comparability of regression coefficients calculated from standardized data supposedly allows one to assess the "relative" importance of explanatory variables. The coefficient for union concentration in the second equation, –.66, presumably implies it is a slightly better predictor of inequality than is labor protection, the coefficient of which is –.44. This alleged advantage might be reflected in statements such as the following: "All else being equal, a one-unit (one-standard-deviation) increase in unionization gives a .66 unit reduction in Gini scores, while an identical change in labor protection produces only a .44 decline. Since both are measured by the same metric (standard deviations), union density really is a more important explanation."

The seeming comparability of the standardized coefficients tempts some scholars into thinking that the explanatory power of, say, X, can be compared with that of another independent variable, say, Z. It would be easy to conclude, for example, that if b_{YX} is larger in absolute value than b_{YZ}, the former might be a more important or powerful predictor of Y than the latter. (Remember, we are talking about the standardized coefficients, which now presumably have the same measurement scale.) Yet you should be extremely careful about inferring significance from the numerical magnitudes of these coefficients. Such comparisons of the "strength of relationship" are possible only to the extent that *all the original independent variables have a common scale or unit of measurement*. The standardization process just changes the variables to standard deviation scales. It does not change or enhance their substantive interpretation. Also, standardization is affected by the variability in the sample, as can be seen by noting the presence of the standard deviations in the above formula. So if one independent variable exhibits quite of bit of variation while another has hardly any at all, it may be wrong to say the first is a more important explanation than the second, even if its standardized coefficient is larger.[13]

We reemphasize two points. First, transforming variables by standardization just changes their measurement scales. It does not alter their interrelationships. Therefore, tests of significance and measures of fit are the same for both sets of data. This is apparent from the two equal R^2 values (that is, $R^2 = .73$ in both instances). This will always be the case. And the regression constant drops out of the equation when standardized variables are used.

Measuring the Goodness of Fit, R^2

A lot of ink has been spilled over the best way to assess the adequacy of linear models. It is safe to say that no single number will tell us all we need to know. Consequently, political scientists have to reach deeply into their toolbox for devices that show different aspects of the model. Many of these are relatively advanced, however, so we will stick with the much used (and abused) multiple correlation coefficient, R^2, which of course is the explained (by regression) sum of squares divided by the total sum of squares.

R^2 varies from zero to 1. R^2 never decreases as independent variables are added. But just throwing more variables into a model usually will not add to the understanding of variation in Y. Each independent variable added must be carefully considered. Moreover, the number of variables in a model *cannot* exceed the number of data points, and, if they are equal, the model will fit perfectly and R^2 will be 1.0.

ADDING AND SUBTRACTING VARIABLES FROM A MODEL.   This might be a good place to recap. Pierson and Hacker (chapter 1) argued that growing business domination in the United States has partly contributed to rising economic inequality, since the capitalist classes are able to appropriate disproportionate increases in GDP to themselves. Throughout the last several chapters, we have examined the other side of the coin: labor's influence on policy making. Our general hypothesis has been that to the extent that workers can mobilize and press their interests in the political arena, they gain greater shares of national wealth for those in the lower strata. To investigate this idea, we used a comparative, cross-sectional design with aggregate data. The operational or empirical indicators of working-class strength were union density and the degree of labor protections in a country. We found a modest relationship between them and the dependent variable, the Gini index, and the direction of the partial regression coefficients agreed with the hypothesis.

Although this simple linear model seems to fit the reasonably well, it's natural to wonder whether or not it can be improved. It would be tempting to throw additional variables into a regression program in hopes of adding further explanatory power. There are, however, a number of problems.

- Degrees of freedom: If we keep adding variables, we may end up with almost as many explanatory factors as cases. That is, N will be close to K, the number of variables in the equation. In the current situation, we have only twenty nations. Given two independent variables and a constant, the degrees of freedom is $N - K = 20 - 3 = 17$. If K is a large enough proportion of N, R^2 may be misleadingly high. Remember: When adding a variable to an equation, the explained sum of squares and R^2 can only stay the same or increase. To compensate for this fact, it is sometimes advisable to compute an adjusted R^2,

$$R_{adj}^2 = R^2 - \frac{K\left(1 - R^2\right)}{\left(N - K - 1\right)},$$

where N is the number of cases, K the number of variables, and R^2 the unadjusted multiple correlation. The adjustment factor effectively "penalizes" R^2 proportionally as the number of parameters to estimate grows relative to the degrees of freedom. As the proportion grows, the multiple correlation coefficient declines to and below zero. (A negative R^2 is a sure sign that something is wrong.) One bit of advice: Think carefully about which variables you want in the analysis; don't use them all just because they are in a data matrix.

- Multicolinearity: A fact of life in applied multivariate analysis is the intercorrelations among predictors. X, for instance, will normally not be correlated just with Y but also to other variables (e.g., $V, W, Z, \dots$) as well. This multicolinearity creates all sorts of problems, most of which we ignore. But we have to pay attention to standard errors and statistical tests based on them. (More technically, the standard error of a partial regression coefficient for a variable, say X, depends partly on the strength of its correlation with other independent variables in the model. As variables are added and dropped from a model in an attempt to find one with the highest R^2, standard errors may flop around and make hypothesis testing problematic.)

Still, we are faced with the question of how best to build a model. As with so many other topics in data analysis, research on this one is too extensive and advanced to be summarized here. Many, if not most, statistical computer packages

TABLE 14–16
Comparison of Models

Model	Estimated Equation	R^2	Incremental F Statistic	Result of Adding Variable
Union + labor	$\hat{Y}_i = 42.10^{***} - .14\text{Union}^{***} - 2.28\text{Labor}^{**}$ $(1.71) \quad (.03) \qquad (.72)$	.73	–	–
Union + labor + left voting	$\hat{Y}_i = 50.25^{***} - .11\text{Union}^{***} - 2.91\text{Labor}^{***} - .15\text{Left}^{*}$ $(1.71) \quad (.03) \qquad (.72) \qquad (.05)$	.82	$F_{1,16} = 7.93^{*}$	Improvement
Union + labor + left voting + turnout	$\hat{Y}_i = 49.02^{***} - .12\text{Union}^{***} - 3.08\text{Labor}^{***} - .17\text{Left}^{*} + .03\text{Turnout}$ $(1.71) \quad (.03) \qquad (.72) \qquad (.05) \qquad (.04)$	.83	$F_{1,16} = .69$	No improvement

come with procedures that might appear to automate model fitting. We caution, however, that the procedures (one of them is called "stepwise regression") are not as foolproof as they may seem. The old adage "garbage in, garbage out" applies to them as well as to any technique. Instead, we suggest that students begin with their substantive knowledge of the problem and lots of common sense.

Is there anything in our limited data set that might contribute further to our understanding of the politics of inequality? We explore the effects of a new variable, percent for liberal or left-wing parties. This measure is based on the share of votes for the lower legislative house (in the United States, the House of Representatives) garnered by such parties as the Democrats (US), Labour and Liberal (UK), and labor and socialist parties in Europe and elsewhere. If our basic idea is correct, working- and lower-class strength should be approximately proportional to their electoral behavior and have an effect on equality over and above what labor organization and protections predict. We might also surmise that the large turnout in elections would enhance citizen power and, hence, reduce inequality through distributive and redistributive policies.

LOGISTIC REGRESSION

Suppose we want to explain why people in the United States do or do not contribute money to political causes. Is it mostly a matter of public spiritedness or partisan passion? Or do donations depend mostly on economic well-being? As we have suggested many times before, such a study should start from a theory or at least a tentative idea of political participation. We might hypothesize, for example, that demographic factors such as education, age, and income are related to participation: older, well-heeled, college graduate whites will donate more frequently and generously than lower-status individuals do. Alternatively, we could propose that partisanship will trump social and economic factors: strong partisans will be generous no matter what their financial or social situation is. To test this proposition, we could collect measures of these concepts from a survey or poll.

Table 14–17 shows ten cases selected randomly from the United States Citizenship, Involvement, Democracy study that we have previously used for examples. Besides indicators of education, income, age, and so forth it asked respondents if they had donated to a political organization in the last year. Replies are coded 0 for "no" and 1 for "yes," thus creating a binary or dichotomous dependent variable. The questionnaire also contained material from which we constructed a four-category ordinal variable of partisan feelings: nonpartisan, weak, moderate, and strong.

One might wonder how we could use a method like multiple regression to analyze these data, since, strictly speaking, the dependent variable, contributed or not, is not numeric or quantitative. (Earlier we saw that categorical independent variables like partisanship can be coded as dummy variables and entered into regression equations along with quantitative variables.) Indeed, a major problem for the social scientist is to explain variation in dependent variables of this type. Consider, for instance, figure 14–6, which shows the plot of donation ("no" or "yes") by respondents' age.

Incidentally, this figure and subsequent analyses are based on a sample of 150 cases drawn randomly from the complete data file. This sample of a sample is called a "training" data set, and we use it to develop and test models. When one

TABLE 14–17
Citizen Involvement in Democracy Data

Donated	Income	Age	Partisanship	Education
1	5	60	Strong	Post high school
0	7	35	Nonpartisan	High school
0	4	55	Strong	Post high school
0	7	56	Strong	College or more
0	9	57	Moderate	High school
0	8	44	Nonpartisan	High school
0	3	31	Moderate	High school
1	6	64	Strong	Post high school
1	3	35	Strong	High school
0	9	59	Strong	Post high school

Education, originally recorded with eight categories, has been recoded into one with four levels.

Source: Source: Marc Morjé Howard, James L. Gibson, and Dietlind Stolle, "The U.S. Citizenship, Involvement, Democracy Survey," Center for Democracy and Civil Society (CDACS), Georgetown University, 2005.

TABLE 14–18
Marginal Distribution of Political Contributions

Response	Frequency	Proportion
No	116	.77
Yes	34	.23
Total	150	1.0

seems to fit, we can apply it to the larger, "verification" data that remain in the original sample. Using a relatively small N often simplifies one's analysis. For one thing, we do not have to plot more than 1,000 points, which usually leaves a blob of ink on the page. Moreover, even trivial relationships can be statistically significant when N is large.

In any case, we observe two parallel lines of dots that do not tell us much, if anything, about the relationship between contributing and age. One thing we can infer is that there are fewer "yes" than "no" responses. Table 14–18 shows the marginal distribution of this variable.

What to do? We might conceptualize the problem this way. Denote the two outcomes of the dependent variable, Y, as 1 for "yes" and 0 for "no." Each person

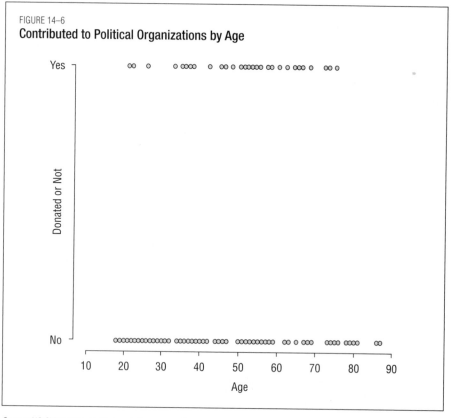

FIGURE 14–6
Contributed to Political Organizations by Age

in the study, in other words, is assigned a score on the dependent variable of 1 or 0, depending on whether or not that person contributed. For a number of reasons, this type of response variable creates problems for ordinary regression analysis. As a consequence, we often do not analyze Y per se but rather some function of it. That is, the dependent variable is not Y with its two values but Y', which is a function of Y.

When confronted binary responses such as "no" and "yes," we can slightly reconceptualize the situation as one of predicting a "no" or "yes" answer. To do so, interpret the expected value of Y as "the probability that Y equals 1" because

$$E(Y) = [1 \times P(Y = 1)] + [0 \times (P = 0)] = P(Y = 1).$$

Note that $P(Y = 1)$ means "the probability that Y equals 1," which in this context is the probability that a person donated. Similarly, $P(Y = 0)$ is defined as the probability of not giving.[14] (Frequently, the generic terms *success* and *failure* are employed to describe these probabilities, as in "The probability of success is P, and the probability of failure is $1 - P = Q$.) As noted before, the expected value of a variable can be thought of roughly as the sum of its possible values times the probabilities of their occurrence.[15]

Therefore, our job is to understand and predict probabilities, not raw scores as in the inequality models. We construct a linear regression model for the probability that Y equals 1, which we will denote simply as P. That is, for an independent variable, our desired model has the general form

$$E(Y) = P = \hat{\beta}_0 + \hat{\beta}_1 X.$$

This is called a **linear probability model,** and it means that the expected value of the binary dependent variable, or what is the same thing the probability that Y equals 1, is a linear function of an independent variable, X. The regression coefficient, the beta, simply indicates how much the predicted probability changes with a one-unit change in an independent variable, given that all the other variables in the model have been held constant.

The idea might be clarified by calculating a linear probability model for the data from the Citizen, Involvement, Democracy study. The result is

$$\hat{Y}_i = .11 + .003\text{Age}.$$

The parameters still have the usual interpretation: when age equals zero, the predicted probability of donating is .10 or 1 in 10.[16] For each one-year increase in age, the probability of making a donation increases .003. So, for example, a 45-year-old person would have a predicted probability of

$$\hat{Y} = .11 + .003(45) = .25.$$

How does this compare to a younger person, say age 20? Make the substitution age = 20: $\hat{Y}$ = .11 + .003(20) = .17. There is not a huge difference, although as expected older people are slightly more willing or able to give than are younger citizens. To make sure that you understand this point, substitute different ages to get the predicted chances of donating.

For further practice we added an additional variable, income. Income is recorded in eleven order categories. Just for the sake of simplicity and explanation, we will take the category numbers literally and treat the variable as interval. (Many analysts would probably prefer to consider income as an "order factor" and represent each level with a dummy variable. We see how this works in a moment.) The addition of income leads to the estimated equation:

$$\hat{Y}_i = -.05 + .003\text{Age} + .032\text{Income}.$$

The "mean" income in the sample is 5.09, while the age mean is 46.08. Putting these numbers in the equation gives the predicted probability of having made a political donation in the last year for a typical American:

$$\hat{Y}_i = -.05 + .003 \times 46.08 + .032 \times 5.09 = .25.$$

This is about the same as the overall proportion of donors in the sample that we reported above. Again, we encourage you to make meaningful substitutions in order to better understand the substantive implications of the coefficients. In fact, you can learn a lot just by noting their signs. The plus signs tell us that as age (income) increases, the propensity to donate also goes up. How much? When income is controlled or held constant, a one-year increase in age "raises" the probability that an individual will give by just .003, apparently not much. But before deciding this increase is inconsequential, try thinking in decades; aging ten years raises the probability about 10 × .003 = .03, again a seemingly minor amount, but don't forget that a probability's maximum is 1.0.

Note one other thing. Suppose we set the independent variables to zero. (Granted it does not make much sense, but mathematically, it is perfectly valid and instructive.) With the independent variables out of the picture, the predicted probability is -.05. But a probability lies between 0 and 1, so the "perfectly valid" method led to an impossible result, a fact that we come to shortly.

Although not all the coefficients are statistically significant by the usual standards,[17] and the typical measure of goodness of fit, R^2 = .05, is quite low, the equation's interpretation is fairly straightforward when seen in this light. Yet, the fact that the dependent variable is a dichotomy and the linear probability model led to a meaningless result (i.e., predicted probability less than zero), it is reasonable to wonder if linear regression is in fact the right technique for analyzing dichotomous dependent variables.

The linear probability model works reasonably well when all predicted values lie between .2 and .8, but statisticians still believe that it should not generally be used. (Here, we should note again, the observed proportions of "no" and "yes" are .77 and .23 respectively.) One reason is that the predicted probabilities can have strange values, since the linear part of the model can assume just about any value from minus to plus infinity but a probability by definition must lie between zero and 1. In addition, the linear probability model violates certain assumptions that are necessary for valid tests of hypotheses. The variance of the error term (ε) in the model, for example, violates the assumptions of homoscedasticity and normal errors, and the results of a test of the hypothesis that a β is zero might be suspect. For these and other reasons, social scientists generally do not use a linear probability model to analyze dichotomous dependent variables.

So what can be done? We certainly do not want to give up because many dichotomies or binary dependent variables or responses are frequently worth investigating. A common solution is to use **logistic regression** analysis that at first blush appears to either have a strange dependent variable *or* an even stranger equation. (You can easily move from one form to another.) The apparent "weirdness" arises because we can either use a nonlinear equation to explain Y (or probability of success) or a linear model to explain a function of Y, so to speak. Table 14–19 lays out the choices. (We explain odds and log odds a little later.)

TABLE 14–19
Modeling Binary Responses

Type of Regression	Form of the Dependent Variable	Form of Model	Model
Linear probability	Probability $Y = 1$	Linear	$\hat{P}_i = \hat{\beta}_0 + \hat{\beta}_1 X$
Logistic	Probability $Y = 1$	Nonlinear	$Prob(Y = 1) = \hat{P}_i = \dfrac{e^{(\hat{\beta}_0 + \hat{\beta}_1 X)}}{1 + e^{(\hat{\beta}_0 + \hat{\beta}_1 X)}}$
	Odds: $Y_i' = \dfrac{p}{(1-p)}$	Nonlinear	$Y_i' = e^{(\hat{\beta}_0 + \hat{\beta}_1 X)}$
	Log odds (logit): $Y_i' = \ln\left(\dfrac{p}{(1-p)}\right)$	Linear	$Y_i' = \hat{\beta}_0 + \hat{\beta}_1 X$

ln = natural logarithm, e = exp = exponential function.

The logistic regression function for two independent variables, X_1 and X_2, and a dichotomous dependent variable, Y, has the form

$$Prob(Y = 1) = \hat{P} = \frac{e^{(\hat{\beta}_0 + \hat{\beta}_1 X_1 + \hat{\beta}_2 X_2)}}{1 + e^{(\hat{\beta}_0 + \hat{\beta}_1 X_1 + \hat{\beta}_2 X_2)}}.$$

This rather mysterious-looking formula can be easily understood simply by looking at some graphs and making a few calculations. First note that e, which is often written *exp*, stands for the exponentiation function. A function can be thought of as a machine: put a number in, and another, usually different number comes out. In this case, since e is a number that equals approximately 2.718218, X enters as the exponent of e and emerges as another number, 2.71828^X. For instance, if X equals 1, then e^1 is (approximately) 2.7182, and if $X = 2$, e^2 is about 7.3891. (Many handheld calculators have an exponentiation key, usually labeled e^X or $exp(X)$. To use it, just enter a number and press the key.) Although this function may seem abstract, it appears frequently in statistics and mathematics and is well known as the inverse function of the natural logarithm; that is, $\log(e^x) = x$. For our purposes it has many useful properties.

Ways of Thinking about Dichotomous Variables

In bivariate and multiple regression analysis the dependent variable (Y) is quantitative or numerical, and one statistical goal is to explain its variation. Because the conceptualization of Y seems so natural, understanding regression coefficients is relatively straightforward. In the case where Y has just two categories (such as 1 and 0), however, there are a couple of ways of setting up and interpreting models. One approach is to examine Y directly by modeling the probability that Y equals 1 or zero. These models have regression-like coefficients for the Xs, but they appear in the exponents of somewhat complicated-looking equations for the probabilities and cannot be understood in the simple "a-one-unit-change-in-X-produces-a . . ." framework of ordinary regression. So understanding the meaning of logistic coefficients is not intuitive.

It is possible, however, to model, not the probability that Y equals 1, but the odds that Y equals 1 as opposed to zero. (The odds that Y equals 1 are not the same as the probability that Y equals 1, as we emphasize later in the chapter.) In this formulation, the odds become a kind of dependent variable, and the analyst's objective is to study what affects it. Furthermore, it is frequently convenient to transform the odds by taking their natural logarithm to get "logits." So logits, too, can be considered as a sort of dependent variable. The use of logits is popular because models for them are linear in the explanatory factors, and a (partial) logistic regression coefficient does have the interpretation that a one-unit change in X is associated with (partial) beta-unit change in the logit or log odds when other Xs have been controlled. The difficulty, of course, is that now the meaning of the dependent variable—a logit—is not obvious. Fortunately, all these formulations are equivalent, and it is possible to move back and forth among them. The first part of this logistic regression section develops and explains models for probabilities, and a latter part looks at models for the log odds.

The logistic function can be interpreted as follows: the probability that Y equals 1 is a nonlinear function of X, as shown in figure 14–7. Curve a shows that as X increases, the probability that Y equals 1 (the probability that a person votes, say) increases. But the amount or rate of the increase is not constant across the different values of X. At the lower end of the scale, a one-unit change in X leads to only a small increase in the probability. For X values near the middle, however, the probability goes up quite sharply. Then, after a while, changes in X again seem to have less and less effect on the probability, since a one-unit change is associated with just small increases.

Depending on the substantive context, this interpretation might make a great deal of sense. Suppose, for instance, that X measures family income and Y is a dichotomous variable that represents ownership or nonownership of a beach house. (That is, $Y = 1$ if a person owns a beach house and 0 otherwise.) Then for people who are already rich (that is, have high incomes), the probability of ownership would not be expected to change much, even if they increased their income considerably. Similarly, people at the lower end of the scale are not likely to buy a vacation cottage even if their income does rise substantially. It is only

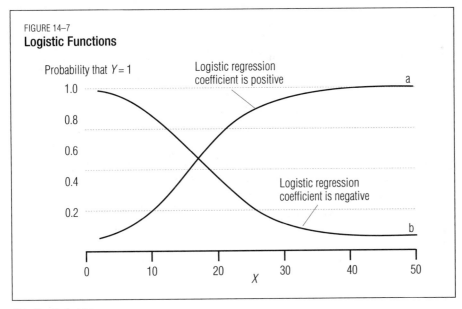

FIGURE 14–7
Logistic Functions

Note: Hypothetical data.

when someone reaches a threshold that a one-unit change might lead to a large change in the probability.

Curve b in figure 14–7 can be interpreted the same way. As X increases, the probability that Y equals 1 decreases, but the amount of decrease depends on the magnitude of the independent variable.

The essence of nonlinear models is that the effects of independent variables are not constant but depend on particular values. So the logistic regression function has a reasonable interpretation. It also meets the objectives mentioned earlier, namely, that predicted values will lie between 0 and 1, which are the minimums and maximums for probabilities, and that the assumptions of hypothesis testing will be met.[18]

Logistic regression can be further understood with a numerical example. Using a procedure to be described shortly, the estimated logistic regression equation for the participation and democracy survey data with donated ("no" or "yes") as the dependent variable and age and income as predictors is

$$\hat{P} = \frac{e^{-2.89 + .02\,\text{Age} + .18\,\text{Income}}}{1 + e^{-2.89 + .02\,\text{Age} + .18\,\text{Income}}}.$$

In this particular equation, $\hat{\beta}_0$ equals -2.89, β_1 equals .02, and β_2 equals .18. These numbers are called **logistic regression coefficients,** which are related to multiple regression coefficients in that they show how the probability of voting changes with changes in the independent variable.

Although an explanation of how the coefficients were calculated goes beyond the scope of this book (and computer programs for doing the work are widely available), we can start to examine their meaning by substituting some values for the independent variables into the equation. Keep in mind, however, that logistic regression coefficients (the βs) are similar to regular regression coefficients: they indicate the effect that a change in a particular independent variable produces when the other independent factors in the model have been held constant. In this sense, they are like partial coefficients of multiple regression because each isolates the impact of a specific X net of all the other Xs in the equation. But remember that a β does not have a simple linear effect on Y for a given change in X. It instead is nonlinear in its consequences. This interpretation becomes clearer as we go on.

Consider a person who reports zero income and age ($X_1 = X_1 = 0$). Then the equation becomes

$$\hat{P} = \frac{e^{-2.89 + .02(0) + .18(0)}}{1 + e^{-2.89 + .02(0) + .18(0)}}$$

$$= \frac{e^{-2.89}}{(1 + e^{-2.89})}$$

$$= .05.$$

This expression means that the estimated probability that a person zero years old and without any income will donate to a political cause is .05, signifying no chance at all. (This probability perhaps makes sense for someone who is not born and has no income; its main value, however, is as a baseline that can be compared with the results for a 70-year-old person in the highest income category (11). (Recall that we are using the category labels as an actual interval variable.) Consider next a white person (X_2 = 1) with the same amount of education (X_1 = 0). The predicted probability of voting is now

$$\hat{P} = \frac{e^{(-2.89+.02(70)+.18(11))}}{1+e^{(-2.89+.02(70)+.18(11))}}$$

$$= \frac{e^{(1.63)}}{1+e^{(2.63)}}$$

$$= .62.$$

Here we see that an individual with these characteristics has a better than 60 percent chance of contributing. Similar substitutions show how different combinations of the independent variables change the probability. Let's fix (hold constant) income at its mean value (5.09) and let age vary from 20 to 90 by 10-year intervals. We can stick those numbers one after another into the estimated model to produce a table of predicted values (see table 14–20).

Using the table, we can see that for a fixed value of income, the probability of a contribution increases with age. (Always pay attention to the sign of the coefficients.) Yes, the table tells us that age is positively related to donating, but what about income? Its coefficient also has a positive sign, so we assume that probabilities will increase as income goes up, for fixed values of age. Another simple table reveals that this is so (see table 14–21).

TABLE 14–20

Effects of Varying Age While Holding Income Constant on Predicted Donations

Income	Age	Predicted Probability of Donation
5.09	20	0.17
5.09	30	0.20
5.09	40	0.24
5.09	50	0.27
5.09	60	0.32
5.09	70	0.36
5.09	80	0.41
5.09	90	0.46

With age set at its median value (45 years), we see that as income increases, so too does the predicted probability. Both results make sense. Older and wealthier people are generally more civic minded than, say, the poor and young, so we would expect them to be more apt to donate. What about the effects of both variables simultaneously? Can they be visualized? Figure 14–8 shows a particularly simple but instructive way to graph these. First look at the x-axis, which is marked off by ages; the Y scale is just the predicted probability of making a political donation. The points (symbols) stand for the predicted probability for cases with specific category combinations of the independent variables.

TABLE 14–21

Effects of Varying Income While Holding Age Constant on Predicted Donation

Income	Age	Predicted Probability of Donating
1	45	0.14
2	45	0.16
3	45	0.19
4	45	0.22
5	45	0.25
6	45	0.29
7	45	0.33
8	45	0.37
9	45	0.41
10	45	0.45
11	45	0.50

To appreciate what the lines and dots mean, consider the following:

■ Since the x-axis is age, the figures suggest that as age increases, so too does the predicted probability.

■ This pattern is true for *all* three levels of income shown (minimum, mean, and maximum).

■ For any particular age, the higher one's income, the higher the probability of donating.

■ The difference in effects of "income" on probability between adjacent income levels is more or less constant across income. (There is no apparent interaction effect.)

To take a quick example look at the left side of the graph where predicted probabilities for the youngest (age = 18) group lie. Notice that as you jump up from one income level to the next, the probability increases. This means income is positively related to the chances of making a political contribution (remember the positive beta?). And this effect is not spurious because of age, for we have held age constant: at each age, the previously described relationship holds. Now, select an income level, say the mean (middle line). Notice that the line slopes slightly upward, indicating a positive relationship: as age increases, the probability of making a contribution also increases slightly. The same is true for the other two income groups. Conclusion: Age, too, positively affects the propensity to give. Finally, take note of the fact that the lines are more or less parallel. In words, this means that the effect of age on donating is the *same* (direction and strength) at all levels of income. Conversely, the income-probability connection shows little or no interaction.

If we wanted to check for possible interaction effects, we could simply add an interaction variable, Z = age × income, estimate its coefficient, and test to see if it differs from zero. We do some of this in a moment.

Estimating the Model's Coefficients

It is natural to wonder how the coefficient estimates are derived, and it would certainly simplify things if we could provide straightforward formulas for calculating them. Unfortunately, there are no such easy equations. Instead, logistic regression analysis is best performed with special computer programs. Logistic regression has become so widely used that the appropriate tools can be found in many statistical program packages such as Stata, MINITAB, R, and SAS. Your instructor or computer consultant can help you find and use these programs. We recommend that if you have a dependent variable with two categories and want to perform regression, ask for a logistic regression program.[19]

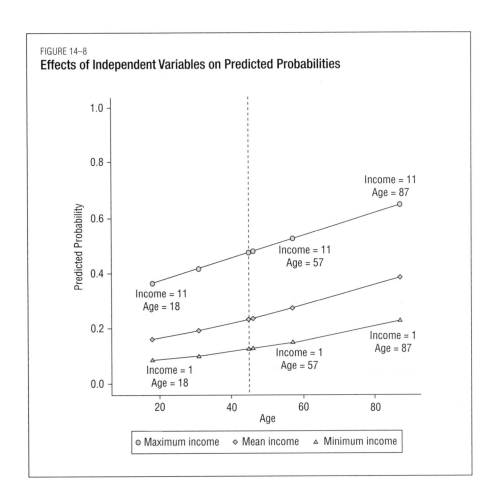

FIGURE 14–8
Effects of Independent Variables on Predicted Probabilities

Although the details are beyond the scope of the book, the method used to estimate unknown coefficients relies on a simple idea: pick those estimates that maximize the likelihood of observing the data that have in fact been observed. In effect, we propose a model that contains certain independent variables and hence unknown coefficients. Associated with the model is a *likelihood function, L.* The parameters in the function *L* give the probability of the observed data. That is, the data points are treated as fixed or constant, and the likelihood is a function of unknown parameters. Using the principles of differential calculus, a numerical algorithm selects values of the parameters that maximize *L.* Logically enough, they are called maximum-likelihood estimators. Therefore, the aim of the behind-the-scenes number crunching is to find those values for the parameters that maximize the probability of obtaining the observed data that we did.

For computational purposes, the logarithm of the likelihood function is calculated to give the *log likelihood function,* or LL. Keep an eye open for it because log likelihood functions, which are somewhat analogous to sums of squares in regression, appear in many model-fitting and testing procedures, as we will see in the next section.

If the estimated coefficients are calculated correctly and certain assumptions are met, they have desirable statistical properties. They are, for instance, unbiased estimators of corresponding population parameters and can be tested for statistical significance.

Measures of Fit

As in the case of simple and multiple regression, researchers want to know how well a proposed model fits the data. The same is true of logistic regression. After estimating a model, we want to know how well it describes or fits the observed data. Unfortunately, there is no universally accepted summary measure like R^2 that describes in an intuitively appealing way the agreement of a model and data. Several measures of goodness of fit exist, although they have to be interpreted cautiously. In fact, considerable disagreement exists about which measure is best, and none of the alternatives has the seemingly straightforward interpretation that the multiple regression coefficient, R^2, has.

With ordinary regression analysis, one way to calculate the fit is to compare predicted and observed values of the dependent variable and measure the number or magnitude of the errors. Alternatively (and equivalently), we can determine what proportion of the variation in Y is statistically explained by the independent variables. In the case of binary dependent variables, there are no precise analogs to total and residual sums of squares.

Logistic regression involves roughly analogous steps, but the procedures are a bit more complicated and cumbersome, so we simply sketch out the general ideas. Our main objective is to provide a working understanding of substantive research articles and computer output.

Most logistic regression software programs routinely report the values of log likelihood functions, *LL*. (They will be negative numbers.) Occasionally, as with the popular program package SPSS, the result given is –2 times the log likelihood, but you can switch back and forth easily by the appropriate multiplication or division. As an example, the log likelihood for the logistic regression of age and income on probability of donating is $LL = -83.506$. This number looks large, but what exactly does it mean? Unfortunately, the number is not terribly informative by itself. But it can be compared with the *LLs* obtained for other models. And these comparisons can be used to gauge the overall fit and test hypotheses about sets of coefficients.

A simple strategy for assessing fit is to contrast the log likelihood of a model with one having only a constant term, LL_0, with a model that contains, say, two independent variables, X_1 and X_2. This log likelihood we denote LL_C, for "current" model. A measure of "improved" fit, the so-called pseudo-R^2, compares the log likelihood from the null model (only an intercept) to the log likelihood from the full model (all covariates included), then, is

$$R^2_{\text{pseudo}} = \frac{LL_0 - LL_C}{LL_0},$$

where LL_0 is the log likelihood for the null or "reduced" model and LL_C is the complete or "full" model. The denominator plays the role of the total sum of squares, while the numerator shows the difference in the fit when independent variables have been added and might be loosely considered the "explained" portion. The "pseudo" in the resulting R-squared indicates that this statistic is not the same as the R^2 of ordinary regression, and it certainly does not represent explained variation. But the basic idea is the same: pseudo-R^2 roughly suggests the relevance of a set of independent variables in understanding the probability that $Y = 1$. Moreover, we make use of log likelihoods (LL) in a moment.[20] For the citizenship example, LL_0 for the model with no independent variables (only a constant term) is –87.60, and LL_C for the model with age and income included is –83.51. Thus, the pseudo R^2 is

$$R^2_{\text{pseudo}} = \frac{\left[(-87.60)-(-83.51)\right]}{-87.60} = \frac{-4.10}{-87.60} = .05.$$

It can be easily calculated because the log likelihoods are routinely reported. This number suggests that the addition of two independent variables did not improve the fit very much. But before rejecting the model, keep in mind that the pseudo R^2 is not an infallible indicator of fit and that others have been proposed.[21] More important, as we have said, many statisticians are wary of giving any "explained variation" interpretation to logistic regression results and don't bother with pseudo-R^2 or its many variants. Perhaps because logistic regression has been incorporated into standard political analysis relatively recently, there is no widely accepted and used list of measures. Some authors provide several indicators, whereas others give few. Thus, when reading articles and papers that use dichotomous dependent variables and logistic regression, you may have to reserve judgment about the evidence in favor of a particular model.[22]

Significance Tests

We return to contrasting nested models as a way to assess both overall models and individual coefficients. But the residual or error sum of squares is replaced by *deviance*, which is usually defined as "minus twice the log likelihood": $D = -2LL$. Think of deviance as being analogous to the residual sum of squares. The objective is to find a combination of explanatory variables that make it as small as possible. One way to see if we are making progress is to compare the deviance of models with and without a particular variable, X. If the difference is "large" as judged by some standard, the term significantly improves the fit and is retained; otherwise, it is dropped. The deviance too frequently tumbles out of logistic regression software, so we do not need to dwell on its computation. Instead, we just use the deviances from various models to evaluate the significance of coefficients. What results resembles, but is not equivalent to, ANOVA tables.

TESTING THE OVERALL MODEL.   To start, we can perform a test analogous to the F-test in multiple regression to investigate the statistical significance of a set of coefficients.[23] This procedure follows the steps in the previous section. Let LL_C be the log likelihood for a current or "complete" model—the one with all the explanatory variables of interest included—and let LL_0 be the log likelihood for the "reduced" model—the one with one or more independent variables eliminated or, as the case arises, the model with no explanatory factors, only a constant. Then the difference between the two likelihoods forms a basis for a test of a test statistic, the likelihood ratio chi square (LRX) with degrees of freedom equal to the difference in the number of parameters in the model:

$$LRX = -2(LL_0 - LL_C).$$

LRX can be recast as the difference in deviances, since $D = -2LL$:

$$LRX = D_0 - D_C,$$

where D_0 and D_C are the deviances for the reduced and full models respectively. For large samples and under the modeling assumptions, LRX has a chi-square distribution with $df = K - p$, where K is the number of independent variables in the full model and p is the number in the reduced equation. This observed statistic tests the null hypothesis that a β or a set of βs is zero. It can be used to test one coefficient at a time, in which case the number of degrees of freedom is 1. A small LRX (that is, near zero) means the "tested" coefficients are not statistically significant and perhaps should not be included, whereas a large one suggests that they may be (statistically) important.

Let's apply the likelihood ratio chi-square test to the problem we have been working on, understanding why people contribute to political causes. So far, our model only contains demographic data (income and age), but we can expand it later. First let's do a global test. The software program we use throughout the book, R, gives us the results in table 14–22.

Here we are testing the null hypothesis that $\beta_{Age} = \beta_{Income} = 0$ against the alternative that at least one population coefficient is not zero. The test statistic turns out to be $LRX = 8.19$, with 2 degrees of freedom. (The degrees of freedom

TABLE 14–22
Likelihood Ratio Chi-Square Test

Model	Parameters in Model	Log Likelihood of Model (LL)	Deviance ($-2 \times LL$)	$LRX = D_0 - D_C$	$df =$ $K - p$	Prob.
Null or intercept only	$\hat{\beta}_0 = -1.03$	−87.60	−175.21	−	−	−
Complete	$\hat{\beta}_0 = -2.89$ $\hat{\beta}_{Age} = -.02;$ $\hat{\beta}_{Income} = .18$	−83.51	−167.01	8.19	2	0.02

$K = 2$, $p = 0$.

for testing nested models is just the difference in degrees of freedom for the models or, what is the same, the number of variables in the full model minus the number in the reduced model. Here it is 2—0 = 2 degrees of freedom.) The critical values for a chi-square statistic at the .05 and .01 levels are 5.99 and 9.21 respectively. The observed LRX lies between them (i.e., 5.99 < LRX = 8.19 < 9.21), so we know it is significant at the .05 level but not at .01. The table shows that the attained probability is actually .02. All this testing means simply that if the null hypothesis of no effects of age and income is true, the probability of the observed result (8.19) (or one even larger) is about 2 in 100.

The overall model with both coefficients is significant, but we don't know if just one or both coefficients contribute to the effect. For that we need a test of the individual parameters (see table 14–23).

The interpretation of the table follows. We are now interested in knowing if a particular partial regression coefficient is zero. First calculate LRX from either the log likelihoods or the deviances. (The choice depends only on what your software

TABLE 14–23
Likelihood Ratio Chi-Square Test of Individual Parameters in the Model

Model	Parameters in Model	Log Likelihood of Model (LL)	Deviance ($-2 \times LL$)	$LRX = D_0 - D_C$	$df =$ $K - p$	Prob.
Null or intercept only	$\hat{\beta}_0 = -1.03.$	−87.60	−175.21	−	−	−
Age	$\hat{\beta}_0 = -1.81;$ $\hat{\beta}_{Age} = .02.$	−86.56	−173.12	2.09	1	.15
Age + Income	$\hat{\beta}_0 = -2.89;$ $\hat{\beta}_{Age} = .02;$ $\hat{\beta}_{Income} = .1.8.$	−83.51	−167.01	8.2	1	0.01

df_0, df_C = degrees of freedom for the reduced and complete models.
$K = 2$, $p = 0$.

Note: These results were calculated with R on weighted data.

provides.) As in the other hypotheses tests, if the observed statistic exceeds the critical chi square at a specified level of significance, we reject the null hypothesis (that is, H_0: $\beta_j = 0$) in favor of the alternative ($\beta_j \neq 0$). The first test ($LRX = 2.08$) is not significant. Normally, we would stop here because including age does not help predict behavior and pick another independent variable. But simply to keep the example going, we next added income to see if it improves the model. We see that the second LRX (6.12) has a low probability (under the null hypothesis that $\beta_{\text{Income}} = 0$), and we conclude that income has a statistically significant impact on willingness to donate.

Wald Tests.   Articles in the scholarly literature frequently report significance tests for the individual coefficients using a different statistic. Recall that a statistical test of significance is a test of a null hypothesis that a population parameter equals some specific value, often zero. In the case of logistic regression, we usually want to test the hypothesis that in the population, a β equals zero. As an example, we might want to test the null proposition that the partial logistic coefficient relating education to income is zero. The form of this kind of test is roughly similar to the others we have described throughout the book: divide an estimated coefficient by its standard error. In this case, if the sample size is large (say, greater than 200), the result gives a statistic, z, which when squared has a chi-square distribution with 1 degree of freedom. That is,

$$z = \left(\frac{\hat{\beta}}{\hat{\sigma}_{\hat{\beta}}} \right),$$

where $\hat{\beta}$ is the estimated coefficient and $\hat{\sigma}_{\hat{\beta}}$ is its estimated standard error. When squared, this quotient, often labeled a "Wald" statistic, can be compared with a chi-square statistic with 1 degree of freedom. The test follows the usual path: establish a critical value under the null hypothesis that a β equals some value, compare the observed z to the critical value, and make a decision. (Recall that critical values for chi square can be found in appendix A.)

Software invariably reports the coefficients and their standard errors and usually the z or Wald statistic as well, so we need not worry about computing them by hand.

We conclude this section by pointing out that the accuracy of the Wald (or z) statistic depends on many factors, such as the sample size. As a result, some statisticians advise using the LRX statistic applied to one coefficient at a time. That is, test a model with K independent variables and, hence, coefficients against one with $K - 1$ parameters. (The former would be the "current" model, the latter the "reduced" model.) If the difference is significant, the variable left out should perhaps be included. Otherwise, we might not reject the hypothesis that its coefficient is zero. But since the z or z^2 appears so frequently, it is important to be aware of its purpose.

An Alternative Interpretation of Logistic Regression Coefficients

We might summarize to this point by saying that logistic regression analysis involves developing and estimating models such that the probability that Y equals 1 (or 0) is a *nonlinear* function of the independent variable(s):

$$P(Y = 1) = \text{Nonlinear function of } X.$$

It is possible, though, to rewrite the logistic regression equation to create a linear relationship between the X's and Y. Doing so provides an alternative way to interpret logistic regression results. Instead of explaining variation in Y with a linear probability model or P with a logistic regression, we can work with odds, which are the probability of one response or value of a variable over the probability of another response or value of a variable, and use them as a dependent variable.

Suppose we sampled a person at random from a group of Americans. We could ask, "What is the probability (P) that this individual made a contribution to a political group or organization in the past year?" or, a related question, "What are the *odds* that this individual gave?" Probability and odds are not the same, for the odds are the ratio of *two* probabilities, the probability of donating compared with the probability of not donating:

$$\text{Odds} = O = \frac{P_{\text{Donate}}}{(1 - P_{\text{Donate}})},$$

where P_{Donate} is the probability of voting.

Some examples will help to illustrate the difference. Suppose the probability that a randomly selected citizen makes a contribution is .2. Then the *odds* of her doing so are $.2/(1 - .2) = .2/.8 = .25$, or, as is commonly said, .25 to 1 or, more commonly, 1 out of 4. The person, in other words, is four times as likely *not* to donate as to make a contribution. As another example, suppose the probability of, say, voting is .8; then the *odds* are $.8/(1 - .8) = .8/.2 = 4$, or about 4 to 1. In this case, the citizen is more likely to vote than not to vote. In both examples, the terms in the denominator of the fraction are just $1 - P$, which is the probability of not voting. (Since probabilities must add to 1—either a person did or did not vote—the probability of not voting is $1 - P$.)[24] It is important not to confuse probabilities and odds; they are related, but not the same.

More generally, consider a variable, Y, that takes just two possible values, 0 and 1. Let P be the probability that $Y = 1$ and $Q = 1 - P$ be the probability that $Y = 0$. Then the odds that Y is 1 as opposed to 0 are

$$O = \frac{P}{(1 - P)} = \frac{P}{Q}.$$

The term O has intuitive appeal, since it accords with common parlance. The odds, O, can vary from zero to infinity. If $O = 1$, then the "chances" that $Y = 1$

TABLE 14–24
Probabilities and Odds

Probabilities	Odds
1.0	∞
.7	2.333
.5	1
.4	0.667
.1	0.111
0	0

Note: Read the odds as "*X* to 1."

or 0 are the same, namely, 1 to 1. If O is greater than 1, the probability that $Y = 1$ is greater than 1/2, and conversely if O is less than 1, the probability is less than 1/2. Table 14–23 shows a few more examples of probabilities and odds in a case in which a random process can lead to just one of two possible outcomes.

Why bother with odds? Take a look at the logistic model. It is really a formula that relates P to some Xs, so we ought to be able to rewrite it by putting 1 in front to obtain $1 - P$. Then we could put the two equations together to get an expression for P over $1 - P$. Here is how. To simplify, let $Z = \beta_0 + \beta_1 X_1 + \beta_2 X_2$. Now an expression for P can be written

$$P = \frac{e^z}{1 + e^z}.$$

In the same fashion, we can write $1 - P$ as

$$1 - P = 1 - \frac{e^z}{1 + e^z}.$$

This latter expression can be simplified to

$$1 - P = \frac{1}{1 + e^z}.$$

Now we can put the two equations for P and $1 - P$ together to obtain an expression for the odds, $O = P/(1 - P)$:

$$O = \frac{P}{(1 - P)} = \frac{\dfrac{e^z}{1 + e^z}}{\dfrac{1}{1 + e^z}}.$$

This expression in turn simplifies to

$$O = e^z.$$

Remember that we let $Z = \beta_0 + \beta_1 X_1 + \beta_2 X_2$, so this expression is really

$$O = e^{\left(\beta_0 + \beta_1 X_1 + \beta_2 X_2\right)}.$$

We have thus found a simple expression for the odds. It is still nonlinear because of the exponentiation, e. But a property of the exponentiation function is that $\log(_e Z) = Z$, where log means the natural logarithm. So we find that the logarithm of the odds—called the log odds, or logit—can be written as a linear function of the explanatory variables:

$$Logit = \log O = \beta_0 + \beta_1 X_1 + \beta_2 X_2.$$

In essence, we have three versions of the dependent variable:

- $Y = P$, a probability (nonlinear model).

- $Y = O$, an odds of "success" (multiplicative model).

- $Y = \log\text{-}O$, a logit or log odds (additive model).

See table 14–19 for an overview of the various ways of writing a logistic regression equation.

Back to the logit for a moment. It can be interpreted in the same terms as multiple linear regression *if we keep in mind that the dependent variable is the logit, or log odds, not Y or probabilities.*

Refer, for instance, to our two-variable model of political contributions. We see that it can be written three ways, all of which lead to the same statistical conclusions. The choice depends on how comfortable one is with interpreting particular forms of the dependent variable.

a. $\hat{Y}_i = \dfrac{e^{-2.89+.02\text{Age}+.18\text{Income}}}{1+e^{-2.89+.02\text{Age}+.18\text{Income}}}$

b. $\hat{Y}_i = \hat{O} = e^{-2.89+.02\text{Age}+.18\text{Income}}$

c. $\hat{Y}_i = \text{Log-}\hat{O} = -2.89+.02\text{Age}+.18\text{Income}$

Again, the easiest way to get a handle on what one of these equations is telling you is to make some substitutions. We could, for example, alter our previous perspective by switching from probabilities to odds. What are the odds of individuals with certain traits making monetary contributions to politics? How are they affected by changes in these characteristics? We look to equation (b). It can be reexpressed as

$$\hat{Y}_i = \hat{O} = e^{-2.89+.02\text{Age}+.19\text{Income}} = e^{-2.89}e^{.02}e^{.18}.$$

This means that the effects of changes in X are *multiplicative*, not additive. A one-unit jump in income produces an exponential change in the odds, $exp(.18) = 1.20$. That is, as income goes up one unit, the odds of making a political contribution *multiply* by 1.20. To get a handle on what this means, it is easiest to compute the estimated odds for several combinations of the independent variable, just as we did before. (As a matter of fact, we could just transform the estimated probabilities in the previous tables.) Suppose we hold age constant at 45 years and let income vary through its range. (Remember, we are treating income as a quantitative variable even though it is in fact an ordinal categorical variable with eleven ordered categories.) Start with someone in the first income group:

$$\hat{O} = e^{-2.89}e^{.02(45)}e^{.18(1)} = e^{-1.81} = .164.$$

The odds of this person donating are 0.16 to 1 or 16 out of 100—not very high. Remember these are odds, not probabilities. Compare these odds with a 45-year-old person one income level up:

$$\hat{O} = e^{-2.89}e^{.02(45)}e^{.18(2)} = e^{-1.63} = .196.$$

The odds have increased slightly, a result consistent with the positive sign on the coefficient for income. Finally, look at a 45-year-old in the highest income level (income = 11):

$$\hat{O} = e^{-2.89}e^{.02(45)}e^{.18(11)} = e^{.01} = .990.$$

We can proceed in this manner to find all the predicted odds for income = 1, . . . ,11 (see table 14–25).

Note two things. First, as income increases, so do the odds of making a donation. At all levels, they are less than 1, which means that no matter what their income people are more likely not to give than to give. Second, the differences in the odds are not constant. Moving from one category to the next sometimes produces a miniscule change in the odds of giving; sometimes, the change is larger. That's why we say the effects of income (and age) are multiplicative, not additive.

TABLE 14–25
Predicted Odds of Political Donation by Income Level

Income Level	Probability of Donating	Odds of Donating	Change in Odds
1	.126	.164	–
2	.147	.196	.032
3	.172	.235	.039
4	.200	.281	.046
5	.231	.336	.055
6	.265	.403	.067
7	.303	.482	.079
8	.343	.577	.095
9	.386	.691	.114
10	.430	.827	.136
11	.476	.990	.163

Change = difference between current odds and odds one level above (e.g., .173—.144 = .029).

Note: Results subject to rounding errors.

(If they were additive, the difference in odds would be constant as we moved from one level to the next.) For instance, the coefficient for income is 0.18; if you obtain its exponent ($exp(.18) \approx 1.20$) and multiply it by the odds at a given income level, you obtain the odds for the next level.

We should stress that these remarks are simply an alternative but equivalent way of interpreting logistic regression coefficients. Moreover, we can move from one view to the other by simply manipulating the results with a pocket calculator. Most computer programs and articles report the coefficients, along with other statistical information. To make sense of them often requires substituting actual data values into the equations and seeing what the probabilities or odds turn out to be.

Probability versus Odds.   Keep the terms straight. A probability is not the same as odds, at least in statistical analysis. A probability refers to the chances of something happening, such as a person donating money to a cause. Odds compare two probabilities, such as the probability of contributing to the probability of not contributing. If N_Y is the number of people out of a sample of N who give, for example, the estimated probability of giving is

$$\hat{P} = \frac{N_Y}{N}.$$

The estimated probability of a "no" is

$$\hat{Q} = 1 - \hat{P} = \frac{N - N_Y}{N}.$$

The estimated odds of observing a "yes" as opposed to a "no," however, are

$$\hat{Q} = \frac{\hat{P}}{\hat{Q}} = \frac{\frac{N_Y}{N}}{\frac{N - N_Y}{N}} = \frac{N_Y}{N - N_Y}.$$

If the probability of donation is .6, then the probability of not is $1 - .6 = .4$, and the corresponding odds are $.6/.4 = 1.5$ or 1.5 to 1.

Logits

Finally, for the sake of completeness, we note that a logistic regression model can also be expressed as a linear function of the variables, but the dependent variable is then the natural logarithm of the odds, a quantity that many practitioners find difficult to grasp in a substantive context. Still, the *log* odds (logit) can be expressed as a linear model in which the coefficients have their usual meaning: holding other independent variables constant, a one-unit increase in X leads to a

$\hat{\beta}_x$ change in the logit. Suppose we fix age at 45 and compare logits of people at income levels 5 and 6 (1 unit apart):

$$\text{Logit}_{\text{Income}=5} = -2.89 + .02(45) + .18(5) = -1.09;$$
$$\text{Logit}_{\text{Income}=6} = -2.89 + .02(45) + .18(6) = -.91;$$
$$\text{Difference} = (-1.09) - (-.91) = -.18 = \beta_{\text{Income}}.$$

Clearly, changing income one place increases or decreases the log odds of donating by .18. But how does one make theoretical or practical sense of a logit? Its lack of a clear meaning leads many analysts to convert the logit to odds by exponentiating.

CONCLUSION

As we have seen, multivariate data analysis helps researchers provide more complete explanations of political phenomena. Observing the relationship between an independent and a dependent variable while controlling for one or more control variables allows researchers to assess more precisely the effect attributable to each independent variable and to accumulate evidence in support of a causal claim. Being able to observe simultaneously the relationship between many independent variables and a dependent variable also helps researchers construct more parsimonious and complete explanations for political phenomena.

Multivariate data analysis techniques control for variables in different ways. Multivariate cross-tabulations control by grouping similar observations; partial correlation and multiple and logistic regression control by adjustment. Both types of procedures have their advantages and limitations. Control by grouping can result in the proliferation of analysis tables, the reduction of the number of cases within categories to a hazardous level, and the elimination of some of the variance in the control variables. Control by adjustment, in contrast, can disguise important aspects of relationships, that is, relationships that are not identical across the range of values observed in the control variables.

Terms Introduced

Control by grouping. A form of statistical control in which observations identical or similar to the control variable are grouped together.

Dummy variable. A hypothetical index that has just two values: 0 for the presence (or absence) of a factor and 1 for its absence (or presence).

Interaction. The strength and direction of a relationship depend on an additional variable or variables.

Linear probability model. Regression model in which a dichotomous variable is treated as the dependent variable.

Logistic regression. A nonlinear regression model that relates a set of explanatory variables to a dichotomous dependent variable.

Logistic regression coefficient. A multiple regression coefficient based on the logistic model.

Multiple regression analysis. A technique for measuring the mathematical relationships between more than one independent variable and a dependent variable while controlling for all other independent variables in the equation.

Multiple regression coefficient. A number that tells how much Y will change for a one-unit change in a particular independent variable, if all the other variables in the model have been held constant.

Multivariate analysis. Data analysis techniques designed to test hypotheses involving more than two variables.

Multivariate cross-tabulation. A procedure by which cross-tabulation is used to control for a third variable.

Partial regression coefficient. A number that indicates how much a dependent variable would change if an independent variable changed one unit and all other variables in the equation or model were held constant.

Regression constant. Value of the dependent variable when all the values of the independent variables in the equation equal zero.

Suggested Readings

Agresti, Alan, and Barbara Finlay. *Statistical Methods for the Social Sciences.* 3rd ed. Saddle River, N.J.: Prentice Hall, 1997.

Anderson, T. W. *Introduction to Multivariate Statistical Analysis.* 3rd ed. New York: Wiley, 2003.

Berk, Richard A. *Regression Analysis: A Constructive Critique.* Thousand Oaks, Calif.: Sage, 2004.

Blalock, Hubert M., Jr. *Causal Inference in Non-Experimental Research.* Chapel Hill: University of North Carolina Press, 1964.

Draper, Norman R., and Harry Smith. *Applied Regression Analysis.* 3rd ed. New York: Wiley, 1998.

Fox, John. *Applied Regression Analysis and Generalized Linear Models.* 2nd ed. Los Angeles: Sage, 2008.

Kaplan, Daniel K. *Statistical Modeling: A Fresh Approach.* S.I.: s.n., 2009.

Long, J. Scott. *Regression Models for Categorical and Limited Dependent Variables.* Thousand Oaks, Calif.: Sage, 1997.

Overall, John. E., and C. James Klett. *Applied Multivariate Analysis.* New York: McGraw-Hill, 1973.

Pampel, Fred C. *Logistic Regression: A Primer.* Quantitative Applications in the Social Sciences 132. Thousand Oaks, Calif.: Sage, 2000.

Notes

1. Stephen D. Ansolabehere, Shanto Iyengar, and Adam Simon, "Replicating Experiments Using Aggregate and Survey Data: The Case of Negative Advertising and Turnout," *American Political Science Review* 93, no. 4 (1999): 901–09.

2. Totals do not add exactly across tables because (1) some observations have missing values on religiosity as well as opinion on prayers in public schools and (2) weighted data were used in the analysis and small rounding errors occur.

3. Notice that lambda in this table is zero. You may recall from the previous chapter that lambda will equal zero whenever the modal marginal category of Y is also the mode in each level of X.

4. There are techniques for "partitioning" a slightly different version of the chi square into components—one for each table—that add up to the total chi square.

5. An excellent introduction is Alan Agresti, *Categorical Data Analysis,* 2nd ed. (New York: Wiley, 2002). Another very useful book is Bayo Lawal, *Categorical Data Analysis with SAS and SPSS Applications* (Mahwah, N.J.: Erlbaum, 2003).

6. The seminal work is Leo A. Goodman (with Clifford C. Clogg), *The Analysis of Cross-Classified Data Having Ordered Categories* (Cambridge, Mass.: Harvard University Press, 1984.)

7. In chapter 13, we also called this term the *intercept* because it has a simple geometric interpretation.

8. OECD Indicators of Employment Protection, retrieved January 10, 2001, from http://www.oecd.org/document/11/0,3746,en_2649_37457_42695243_1_1_1_37457,00.html.

9. Jacob S. Hacker and Paul Pierson, "Winner-Take-All Politics: Public Policy, Political Organization, and the Precipitous Rise of Top Incomes in the United States," *Politics & Society* 38, no. 2 (2010): 152–204.

10. The usual explanation for this formula for degrees of freedom is that to estimate the necessary standard deviations, we "lose" one degree of freedom for each regression coefficient plus one for the constant. A more precise explanation can be found in most statistics texts, such as Alan Agresti and Barbara Finlay, *Statistics for the Social Sciences,* 3rd ed. (Englewood Cliffs, N.J.: Prentice-Hall, 1997).

11. This is not the only way to treat categorical data. Another common procedure is "effect coding" or "deviation coding," which uses scores –1, 0, and 1 as measurement units. See Graeme Hutcheson and Nick Sofroniou, *The Multivariate Social Scientist* (Thousand Oaks, Calif.: Sage, 1999), 85–94.

12. Standardizing or scaling variables forces their means to be zero. In a model with only a constant (no predictors), its estimated value will be the mean of Y. If the mean is zero to start with, the coefficient (α) will reflect that fact.

13. For essentially the same reasons, you might not want to compare standardized regression coefficients based on samples from two different populations. See John Fox, *Applied Regression Analysis, Linear Models, and Related Methods* (Thousand Oaks, Calif.: Sage, 1997), 105–8.

14. If you want to clarify expressions like these, simply replace the variable's symbols and codes with substantive names. Thus, for example, $P(Y = 0)$ can in the present context be read literally as "the probability that 'contributed' equals 'did not contribute.'"

15. More precisely, the expected value of a probability distribution is called the mean of the distribution.

16. Note that these estimates are calculated on the basis of the full sample, not just the data in table 14–17.

17. The t statistics for education and race are 16.043 and 2.391, respectively, both of which are significant at the .05 level.

18. Of course, like any statistical technique, logistic regression analysis assumes certain conditions are true and will not lead to valid inferences if these conditions are not met.

19. Quite a few methods can be used to analyze these kinds of data. A related procedure, called probit analysis, is widely used, and if the data are all categorical, log-linear analysis is available.

20. A good review and proposal for such a measure is Tue Tjur, "Coefficients of Determination in Logistic Regression Models—A New Proposal: The Coefficient of Discrimination," *American Statistician* 63, no. 4 (2009): 366–72.

21. See, for example, J. Scott Long, *Regression Models for Categorical and Limited Dependent Variables* (Thousand Oaks, Calif.: Sage, 1997), 104–13. Note also that some statisticians recommend against using most R^2-type measures in logistic regression work. See, for example, David W. Hosemer and Stanley Lemeshow, *Applied Logistic Regression Analysis* (New York: Wiley, 1989), 148.

22. The same comment applies to any data analysis technique: empirical results have to be interpreted and accepted with caution.

23. Consider, for example, a model that contains two types of variables—one group measuring demographic factors and another measuring attitudes and beliefs. The investigator might want to know if the demographic variables can be dropped without significant loss of information.

24. That is, $P + (1 - P) = 1$.

THE RESEARCH REPORT:

AN ANNOTATED EXAMPLE

IN THE PRECEDING CHAPTERS, we described important stages in the process of conducting a scientific investigation of political phenomena. In this chapter, we discuss the culmination of a research project: writing a research report. A complete and well-written research report that covers each component of the research process will contribute to the researcher's goal of creating transmissible, scientific knowledge.

This chapter examines how three researchers conducted and reported their research. We evaluate how well the authors performed each component of the research process and how adequately they described and explained the choices they made during the investigation. As we conducted this evaluation, we used the following thirteen sets of questions:

1. Do the researchers clearly specify the main research question or problem? What is the "why" question?

2. Have the researchers demonstrated the value and significance of their research question and indicated how their research findings will contribute to scientific knowledge about their topic?

3. Have the researchers reviewed the relevant literature? Is their review organized around key themes related to their research question?

4. Have the researchers proposed clear explanations for the political phenomena that interest them? What types of relationships are hypothesized? Do they discuss any alternative explanations?

5. Are the independent and dependent variables identified? If so, what are they? Have the authors considered any alternative or control variables? If so, identify them. Can you think of any variables that the researchers did not mention?

6. Are the hypotheses empirical, general, and plausible?

7. Are the concepts in the hypotheses clearly defined? Are the operational definitions given for the variables valid and reasonable? What is the level of measurement for each of the variables?

8. What method of data collection is used to make the necessary observations? Are the observations valid and the measures reliable?

9. What is the unit of analysis? Have the researchers made empirical observations about the units of analysis specified in the hypotheses?

10. If a sample is used, what type of sample is it? Does the type of sample seriously affect the conclusions that can be drawn from the research? Do the researchers discuss this?

11. What type of research design is used? Does the research design adequately test the hypothesized relationships?

12. Are the statistics that are used appropriate for the level of measurement of the variables?

13. Are the research findings presented and discussed clearly? Is the basis for deciding whether a hypothesis is supported or refuted clearly specified?

In our annotations, which run alongside the research report, you'll see that we link our assessments to the questions listed above.

ANNOTATED RESEARCH REPORT EXAMPLE

State Intervention and Subjective Well-Being in Advanced Industrial Democracies

by Patrick Flavin, Alexander C. Pacek, and Benjamin Radcliff[*]

The study of the market economy is as old as social science itself. This is hardly surprising given that since the emergence of capitalism, market principles have come to structure economic production and exchange, and thereby to permeate the wider social order through that structuring. Whatever their ultimate judgment on capitalism, from advocates (such as Adam Smith or Milton Friedman) to opponents (e.g., Marx or Bourdieu) to those who are both (say, J. S. Mill or even John Rawls), social theorists widely agree that once introduced, the market ultimately comes to influence the entire social order (for an extensive review, see Lane 1991). Thus, as Heilbroner (1985, 79) puts it, the market is "society's central organizing principle" such that it manifests itself in "all aspects" of society, including those "concerned with material life, justice and the social order, custom and belief."

*PATRICK FLAVIN, ALEXANDER C. PACEK, and BENJAMIN RADCLIFF, "State Intervention and Subjective Well-Being in Advanced Industrial Democracies," *Politics & Policy* 39, No. 2 (2011): 251–269. Published by Wiley Periodicals, Inc. © The Policy Studies Organization. All rights reserved.

QUESTION SET 2: The authors point out that their research taps into a long-standing and prominent "markets versus politics" debate about the extent to which (or as they phrase it: "the *degree* to which") market principles should dominate society. Some argue that political interventions into the market should be minimized because they result in unintended and negative social and economic consequences, while others argue that such interventions are positive and can be "the ultimate guarantor of citizen well-being." They point out that this debate has played an important role in politics and is not just of interest to academics.

While the dominance of market principles has long ceased to be contested, disagreement over the scope and power of the market has been the major political, as well as ideological-ideational, axis of conflict in the modern age. Simply put, the issue is the *degree* to which society should be subordinated to the self-regulating control of the market. The Right, as manifested most explicitly in what has been called by its detractors "market fundamentalism" (Soros 1998), and represented in its more conventional form in the mainstream conservatism of Reagan, Thatcher, and the "Washington Consensus" associated with the International Monetary Fund, argues for the maximum of such subordination. The conventional Left, in the form of Labor and Social Democratic Parties and their associated labor movements, argues for less power to the market through a program of supplementing market outcomes with political interventions that seek to make the state, as much as the market, the ultimate guarantor of citizen well-being.

QUESTION SET 2: Here they point out that other researchers have been investigating the real-life consequences of public policies embodying the two main debate positions. Therefore, one can expect that the research in this article will contribute to our understanding of these consequences.

Recent decades have witnessed the emergence of a social scientific research program aimed at understanding the empirical consequences of these two alternative philosophical approaches to crafting a nation's public policy regime. Literatures have become devoted to determining whether such political "intrusions" into the market achieve their objectives of reducing poverty and inequality, whether they have unintended (and generally deleterious) consequences for economic growth, whether they affect rates of social deviancy (such as violent crime), and whether they are complicit in promoting a variety of social pathologies such as "cultures of dependency," higher divorce rates, and so on.

Of course, in the end we concern ourselves with all of these issues, from divorce to economic growth, because of their presumed impacts on the quality of human life. That is, we presume that such outcomes, through both direct and indirect causal mechanisms, ultimately make people more or less satisfied with their lives. In this article, we attempt to take this fact seriously by focusing our attention not on any of the individual or particular effects of market interventions that in turn are thought to have some effect on quality of life, but instead on quality of life itself. Put another way, rather than considering the presumptive effects of political restraints of the

QUESTION SET 1: The research question in this article is clearly stated here. The researchers plan to investigate the empirical relationship between political control of the market and life satisfaction.

market on intermediary variables that are further presumed to have a potential influence on satisfaction with life, we examine directly the connection between political control of the market and life satisfaction. In particular, we ask whether cross-national differences in market dominance affect the degree to which citizens lead lives that they themselves regard as positive, rewarding, and satisfying.

This article is now possible given the development of a sophisticated literature devoted to studying life satisfaction. With the refinement of the tools necessary to measure, with reasonable reliability and validity, how people subjectively evaluate the quality of their lives, we are now capable of testing theoretically derived hypotheses about the observable factors that tend to affect subjective well-being. In sum, we are capable of measuring subjective quality of life in a rigorous fashion, theorizing about concrete conditions that determine such differences and testing the resulting empirical predictions (for reviews, see Diener and Suh 2000; Frey and Stutzer 2002; Layard 2005). We do so by examining how life satisfaction across the industrial democracies corresponds with different outcomes in the conflict of "politics versus markets." We thus hope to understand how state intervention to "protect" citizens against pure market forces affects the overall quality of human life, using the extent to which people enjoy their lives as the appropriate evaluative metric. To anticipate our findings, we find that life satisfaction varies directly with the extent of such protections, net of economic, social, and cultural factors. We also find that this relationship is constant across different levels of income and different political ideologies, such that the effects of social policy benefit everyone in society, rich and poor, liberal and conservative.[1]

QUESTION SET 11: While the authors do not fully describe their research design here, they indicate that they plan to compare the life satisfaction of citizens of different countries (i.e, a cross-sectional design).

QUESTION SET 1: The authors further explain their research question here. Subjective well-being is the main concept of interest and is the dependent variable.

QUESTION SET 8: While they do not go into detail here, the researchers assert that a reliable and valid measure of subjective well-being exists. They imply that lack of such a measure hampered empirical research on this topic previously.

QUESTION SET 11: The authors rely on existing variation in their key independent variable ("different outcomes in the conflict of 'politics versus markets.'"

QUESTION SET 13: The researchers clearly summarize their findings here. This isn't always done early on in an article, but the summary would have been included in an abstract if there had been one.

---

[1] The intellectual infrastructure for studying subjective well-being is sufficiently developed and familiar as not to require extensive elaboration. A voluminous literature has documented that conventional survey items utilized to measure subjective well-being are reliable and valid (for a discussion, see Myers and Diener 1995). After an exhaustive review, Veenhoven (1996, 4) concludes that any misgivings about measurement "can be discarded." Similarly, the collective evidence strongly endorses the proposition that linguistic or cultural barriers (including social pressures for over-or underreporting self-reported satisfaction) do not meaningfully detract from

The article is organized as follows: we first articulate the basic theoretical debate between "markets versus politics" before turning to an appraisal of the existing evidence on how reliance upon these two mechanisms differentially affects human well-being; we then articulate our research design and discuss the empirical results; and we close with a discussion of the implications of the findings for our appraisal of the markets and the study of life satisfaction.

QUESTION SET 3: This section contains the literature review. Notice that the review is organized around the key dimensions of the debate: "markets versus politics." Later on, they review research in which a variety of dependent variables other than, but related to, overall well-being have been used.

The Logic of State Intervention

It is widely agreed that the most basic and persistent axis of political and ideological conflict in the industrial democracies is that of the nature and extent of public intervention into the market. Within the political economy literature, this conflict is typically described as one of markets versus politics (e.g., Lindblom 1977). As these are also the two fundamental mechanisms through which well-being can be both produced and distributed (Esping-Andersen 1990), they are the natural focus of attention for those seeking to understand how different political outcomes may affect quality of life.

At the most basic level, the issue at hand is whether to leave the generation and allocation of well-being to the "invisible hand" of the capitalist economy, or to make it at least in part subject to the political decisions of voters. Those favoring the latter ultimately do so because, as Lane (1978, 16) puts it, markets are "indifferent to the fate of individuals." Esping-Andersen (1990, 36) summarizes the argument perfectly when he notes that while capitalism certainly has many positive aspects that doubtlessly do contribute to quality of life, in the end "the market becomes to the worker a prison within which it is imperative to behave as a commodity in order to survive." As it is not controversial to suggest that human beings do not enjoy being reduced to

---

our ability to make cross-national comparison (see, e.g., Inglehart 1990; Veenhoven 1996, 1997a, 1997b). Another literature, again conveniently summarized by Veenhoven (2002), convincingly argues for the theoretical appropriateness of subjective measures of quality of life, such as satisfaction, as opposed to purely objective indicators (such as income or other measures of consumption). We do not ignore the fact that recent dissenting opinions call into question the empirical usefulness of contemporary happiness/life-satisfaction research. Wilkinson's (2007) thoughtful piece expounds the position that most happiness surveys do not in fact capture precisely what they intend to in respondents' answers and that better designed surveys will be necessary in the future to justify the often-sweeping claims of happiness scholars. Nonetheless, for now the scholarly consensus is that the survey instruments hold up reasonably well provided one is careful not to attribute explanatory power to them beyond what they represent.

a commodity, it seems equally unremarkable to suggest—*if we accept the metaphor*—that people's lives are likely to be less rewarding and satisfying the more they are subject to the insecurities inherent in the market. Put differently, the more individuals are "decommodified" by social policy, the greater should be their well-being, to the extent that the critics of markets are correct in their socio-analysis of capitalism.

The counterarguments are equally straightforward. Two are especially worthy of note (for a review of others, see Veenhoven 2000, 112–9). The first, most familiar to students of political economy is the conventional one of the "unintended consequences" of the welfare state specifically, and by extension, other interventions in the market designed to protect workers. Such claims are animated by sophisticated (if not universally accepted) economic theory and (equally disputed) empirical evidence. If the defenders of unfettered markets are right, we should observe precisely the opposite relationship: "decommodification" becomes an ideological mask for inefficiency and wastefulness, which will impose itself as costs on the population (by inhibiting economic growth, employment, and wages), so as to lower the general level of happiness. In this view, the state's efforts at redistribution and provision fail because they actually reduce both the "quantity" and the "quality" of well-being, relative to markets. This is principally because they displace the church and the family as sources of emotional support and, more critically, because they encourage "collectivization" with deleterious consequences for individual privacy, freedom, and autonomy.

Another related but logically distinct line of argument, popularized by Murray (1984) and analyzed as a more generalized "ideational" phenomenon dating from the nineteenth century by Hirschman (1991), is what has become known as the "perversity thesis": efforts to ameliorate problems created by the market in turn create "perverse incentives" of a purely moral nature. In this approach, market interventions to insulate individuals from the market are construed as imposing moral costs on society, sometimes expressed in ways that do not lend themselves to ready falsification using conventional economic indicators. Somers and Block (2005), for instance, document the way in which this approach, utilized in both England during the debate over the 1834 "New Poor Law" and in the United States during the Reagan years, was deployed by elites to suggest that

QUESTION SET 4: The authors present competing explanations for the impact of public intervention into the market on individual well-being. One predicts that interventions will result in inefficiencies and wastefulness, which will negatively affect economic growth, employment, and wages, which in turn will lead to lower general happiness among the population. Negative consequences of government intervention are also predicted by those who argue that such interventions, to the extent that they insulate individuals from market incentives, create perverse incentives (e.g., welfare creates an incentive not to work, induces laziness, and degrades welfare recipients) that reduce societal happiness. Others predict that intervention into the market has a positive impact on happiness because it prevents workers from becoming prisoners in the market or behaving like "commodities" in order to survive. The more people are subjected to market insecurities, the less rewarding and satisfied lives they lead.

income maintenance programs induced "laziness" and "degradation" among clients of the welfare state—and, since abstractly, welfare always exists as an option once introduced, for society more generally. As a consequence, again, the greater the level of political intrusion into the market system, the less satisfying life becomes, in this interpretation.

Recent work in political economy offers some insight into this question. Pontusson's (2005) thought-provoking analysis of "social market economies" (SMEs) versus "liberal market economies" (LMEs) during the 1990s and 2000s highlights the differential impact of state intervention. His research suggests that SMEs can simultaneously produce strong employment and economic growth outcomes while avoiding the levels of inequality that haunt the LMEs. Certainly the literature on life satisfaction is replete with evidence for the impact of unemployment (and, to a lesser degree, economic growth) on levels of subjective well-being (Banks and Jackson 1982; Greenberg and Grunberg 1995; Kenny 1999; Oswald 1997; Platt and Kreitman 1985; Veenhoven 1994). While the evidence is more mixed for the impact of income inequality, at least some empirical studies find that increases in inequality exert detrimental effects on life satisfaction (Alesina, DiTella, and MacCulloch 2004; Tomes 1985). Beyond these direct economic consequences, however, Pontusson (2005) observed additional salient distinctions between SMEs and LMEs. Specifically, he noted how SMEs with greater state intervention show higher levels of labor force participation in policy making and security in the labor market. Scholars have, in turn, demonstrated how these situations tend to enhance life satisfaction among those both directly and indirectly affected by them (Cohen and Wills 1985; Erikson 1986; Greenberg and Grunberg 1995; Loscocco and Spitze 1990; Lowe and Northcutt 1988; Radcliff 2005). While subjective well-being *per se* was clearly not the focus of this study, findings serve to illustrate the means by which state intervention might affect subjective well-being nonetheless.

QUESTION SET 2: The authors note that previous research has investigated the impacts of political "intrusions" into the market, with these impacts presumed to have effects on the quality of life, but that previous research has not examined directly the connection between political control of the market and quality of life measured as life satisfaction. Nor has research examining the effects of specific public policies on life satisfaction produced consistent findings.

These abstract arguments can be reduced to an obvious, tangible question: do interventions into the market designed to protect citizens against the insecurity and inequality of the market ultimately contribute to greater or lesser levels of subjective well-being? Surprisingly, scholars have devoted little attention to this question. The very few empirical works that speak of this issue tend to focus on specific aspects or consequences of public policy for life satisfaction and do not reach consensus. For example, DiTella, MacCulloch, and Oswald (2003) find some evidence that more generous unemployment benefits are associated with higher national well-being. A more comprehensive appraisal of welfare policies by Pacek and Radcliff (2008) reaches similar conclusions, finding a strong effect of both indicators of "decommodification" and the "social wage" on life satisfaction. In contrast, Ouweneel (2002) finds a strong negative effect of unemployment benefits on well-being, while Veen hoven (2000) also found, admittedly contrary to his own expectations, no rela tionship between the welfare state and subjective quality of life. In sum, the jury remains out.[2]

Indeed, even if we take the scholars who do find a positive relationship at face value (Pacek and Radcliff 2008), their work may obscure as much as it enlightens. While they frame their analysis as that between politics and markets, they ultimately focus only on the welfare state or on specific aspects of welfare policy. As important as the welfare state is, it is hardly isomorphic to the wider questions of what they call "dependency" on the market. At least two additional issues warrant attention if one is going to consider the general effect of pro- and antimarket public poli cies. One is the size of the state sector, which represents, of course, the total amount of political control over the economy. This variable, more than the size of the welfare state *per se*, has, for obvious reasons, always been considered the most comprehensive way of appraising the degree to which the state is in fact capable of directly organizing "the production and distribution of well-being." The correlation between welfare spending and size of the state sector is actually fairly modest, such that the two remain empirically as well as theoretically quite distinct. If we wish to understand how much "a program of emanci pation from the market" affects well-being, we must consider the extent to which the state has in fact displaced the market by considering what econo mists refer to as the level of "governmental consumption," meaning the share of the economy directly controlled by the political process.

QUESTION SET 2: Here the authors indicate that their research will contribute to understanding of the effect of public policies because they plan to measure government involvement in the market more comprehensively using "size of the state sector." Previous research measured government involvement in the economy simply by measuring welfare spending. Note they correlated measures of the two concepts and did not find a strong correlation which indicates that the two concepts are not measuring the same thing.

---

[2] Ridge, Rice, and Cherry (2009) also question the direction of the causality between welfare state generosity and happiness, suggesting that it may be that individuals with high levels of life satisfaction are more inclined to support an expansive welfare state rather than such a welfare state making people happier. Pacek and Radcliff (2008) test for this possibility *vis-à-vis* the wel fare state but find no evidence in their data (or the literature) to support such a contention. In particular, as they observe, there is strong evidence that conservatives—who would oppose the welfare state—consistently show greater satisfaction than the left-liberal proponents of the welfare state.

QUESTION SET 3: By looking at this footnote, we can see that the authors mention the possibility that the direction of causality between welfare state generosity and happiness is reversed, with individuals with higher levels of life happiness being more willing to support an expansive welfare state. But they note that previous research found no evidence for this hypothesis.

QUESTION SET 5: In this section, the authors outline that the dependent variable is well-being or life satisfaction and the independent variable is the size of the state. Income, education, self-reported health, gender, age, martial and unemployment status, church attendance, religion, and interpersonal trust are included as control variables. This is a good list of other characteristics of individuals that affect happiness, but probably many other factors also affect individual well-being, for example, the health of loved ones (children, parents) and exposure to natural disasters. The authors also include some other country-level measures shown in previous studies to affect subjective well-being and life satisfaction: per capita GDP, unemployment rate, and "individualism" of a country's culture. The researchers do not always state how these control variables will affect the dependent variable. In most cases this is easy to surmise; in others it is an open empirical question.

QUESTION SET 6: The researchers do not actually list their hypotheses, but the relationships they are investigating are empirical and plausible. They are also general in the sense they apply to a general category of people living in industrialized democracies.

QUESTION SET 8: What are the units of analysis? With the mention of national well-being and size of the government sector, one might mistakenly conclude that countries are the units of analysis. However, individuals are the units of analysis. The units of analysis in this study are individuals from fifteen industrial democracies. Empirical observations are made about characteristics of individuals such as their income, education, and health and about countries that provide the context in which individuals live.

QUESTION SET 7: The dependent and independent variables are clearly defined, and the operational definitions appear to be valid and reasonable. Size of the state is measured four different ways, all of which are ratio-level measures. Life satisfaction is measured by asking respondents to place themselves on a scale of 1 to 10. Life satisfaction is treated as an interval- rather than ordinal-level measure as it has ten categories or values. This is a common practice, as ten categories make contingency table analysis unwieldy. With an interval-level dependent variable, multiple regression can be used to analyze the data. Measures for most of the control variables are described clearly, but in order to find out how "individualism" of a country's culture is measured, one would have to look in one of the references.

Data and Method

We measured self-reported life satisfaction using data from the most recent wave of the World Values Survey (WVS; 2005–08) (WVS 2009). Self-reported life satisfaction is measured on a 1–10 scale where respondents are asked, "All things considered, how satisfied are you with your life as a whole these days? Using this card on which 1 means you are 'completely dissatisfied' and 10 means you are 'completely satisfied' where would you put your satisfaction with your life as a whole?" In our data, respondents report assessments of life satisfaction along the entire range (1–10) of the scale, with a mean of 7.48 and a standard deviation of 1.87.

We analyze the relationship between the size of the state and life satisfaction across 15 industrialized democracies (Australia, Canada, Finland, France, Germany, Great Britain, Italy, Japan, the Netherlands, Norway, South Korea, Spain, Sweden, Switzerland, and the United States) using four different measures of the size of the state:

1. a country's tax revenue as a percentage of its gross domestic product (GDP) (OECD 2009b);

2. a government's consumption share of a country's real per capita GDP (Heston, Summers, and Aten 2009);

3. the "social wage" defined as the average gross unemployment benefit replacement rates for two earning levels, three family situations, and three durations of unemployment (OECD 2009a); and

4. a country's social welfare expenditures as a percentage of GDP (OECD 2009b).

We also controlled for a host of other factors that might predict individuals' assessments of how satisfied they are with their lives including income, education, self-reported health, gender, age, marital and unemployment status, church attendance, and interpersonal trust (Myers and Diener 1995; Radcliff 2001, 2005). Measuring and comparing self-reported income across countries is a difficult enterprise because of different monetary units and exchange rates. To address this challenge, the WVS reports a 1–10 scale of incomes on which 1 indicates the "lowest income decile" and 10 the "highest income decile" based upon a respondent's self-reported income and the corresponding income distribution for that respondent's particular country of residence. Education is measured using a nine-category response item that ranges from no formal education to earning a university degree. Self-reported health is measured by asking respondents: "All in all, how would you describe your state of health these days? Would you say it is very good, good, fair, poor, or very poor?" (healthier coded higher).

We included a term for both age and age squared because of our expectation of a curvilinear relationship such that both young and old respondents tend to, on average, be more satisfied with their lives than those who are middle aged.

We also included dummy variables to account for a respondent's gender, marital status, and whether they are employed. We measured church attendance on a 1–7 scale where a higher value indicates more frequent attendance. To further account for religious (and thus, perhaps, cultural) differences across religious denominations, we included dummies for Protestants, Catholics, Muslims, Jews, Hindus, and Buddhists, leaving other confessional groups as the reference category. Finally, we measured interpersonal trust using a dummy variable where the respondent is asked, "[g]enerally speaking, would you say that most people can be trusted or that you need to be very careful in dealing with people?" and coded it 1 if they responded "most people can be trusted" and 0 if they responded "need to be very careful."

QUESTION SET 8: The researchers use survey data from the World Values Survey (WVS) to measure individuals' life satisfaction and other characteristics. They argue that self-reported satisfaction with life, a subjective measure, is the appropriate measure of societal well-being. The authors point out that measuring and comparing self-reported income "is a difficult enterprise" but note that the WVS converts self-reported income into a 1–10 scale corresponding to income deciles in each country.

The authors rely on the written record for measurement of the size of the state—primarily reports from the Organisation for Economic Co-operation and Development (OECD) and data collected by researchers at the University of Pennsylvania and available online.

QUESTION SET 10: The authors do not indicate whether or not they are using a sample. But, since the WVS is a survey of respondents from fifteen industrialized democracies, one would assume that some type of probability sample was conducted. One would have to check the World Values Survey to know what kind of sample was used.

QUESTION SET 10: The researchers use a cross-sectional research design. They do not exercise any control over the independent variable, size of the state, but rather use naturally occurring differences in their four measures of the size of the state. It is not clear that the measures of the independent variables occurred before the dependent variable. The publications from which they obtained their data for size of state are from 2009, although it is not clear from which year(s) the actual data came. The researchers measure the dependent variable, self-reported life satisfaction, from WVS, which was conducted, it appears, between 2005 and 2009. Although one might argue that the values of the independent variables would not vary significantly in a country from year to year, it is possible that sizeable changes in the economy occurred in some countries during the time period under investigation, so the exact timing of the independent and dependent variable measures might be important.

We also controlled for a set of country-level measures that have been shown to affect levels of subjective well-being and life satisfaction in previous studies (e.g., Pacek and Radcliff 2008; Radcliff 2005). These include a county's per capita GDP (in 1,000s of U.S. dollars), unemployment rate, and a measure of the "individualism" of a country's culture (all measures are from 2005).

Since the life satisfaction variable we used as our dependent variable has ten categories and is (roughly) normally distributed, we used ordinary least squares (OLS) in all analyses. Because individual respondents are clustered within countries and experience the same country-level conditions (same GDP, unemployment rate, and others), we reported Huber-White robust standard errors clustered on country (Arceneaux and Nickerson 2009). This procedure yields estimates that are robust to both between-country heteroskedasticity and within-country correlation (i.e., robust to error terms being neither identically distributed nor independent).[3]

QUESTION SET 12: Here the authors indicate that they are using ordinary least squares (multiple regression) to analyze the data. You may have surmised this with the earlier mention of "dummy variables." The authors argue that ordinary least squares is appropriate to use because the dependent variable has ten categories (interval- or ratio-level measure) and is normally distributed—two criteria for the proper use of ordinary least squares.

QUESTION SET 11: The four measures of the main independent variable, size of the state, are ratio-level measures. Where control variables are nominal-level measures, the authors create dummy variables. Multiple regression allows the researchers to control for many factors so that they can look for a causal relationship between size of state and life satisfaction. Their analysis has to take into consideration the fact that individual respondents are clustered within countries.

Results

We begin by assessing whether respondents living in countries with more expansive government intervention into the economy report being more satisfied with their lives. In Table 1, we provide the results of four different models that use identical specifications except for a different measure of the size of the state. The variable we used to measure the size of the state is listed at the top of each column. Looking at the coefficients across the four columns, we find that all four of the size of government coefficients are positively signed and boundedabove zero at traditional levels of statistical significance. Substantively, moving from one standard deviation below the mean to one standard deviation above for any of the four measures leads to

QUESTION SET 13: The authors find that a statistically significant relationship exists between life satisfaction and each of the four different variables measuring size of state. Those results are reported earlier in table 1. The signs of the coefficients for size of state are positive, indicating that life satisfaction increases with size of state even after controlling for many alternative explanations for an individual's satisfaction with life. They also report that the size of the impact of size

---

[3] If we instead use a hierarchical modeling strategy to account for the fact that respondents are clustered within countries, we find substantively similar results to those reported below.

just less than one-quarter of a standard deviation increase on the life satisfaction scale. This predicted that change in life satisfaction is roughly equivalent to the predicted change for moving from not married to married or moving from one standard deviation below the mean on the income scale to one standard deviation above. In short, regardless of the specific measure used, we find that citizens living in countries with a larger and more active government report higher levels of life satisfaction even after accounting for a host of alternative explanations. Moreover, the substantive effect rivals that of other traditional predictors of life satisfaction.

of state is about the same as for other traditional predictors of life satisfaction. As the authors are primarily interested in the relationship between life satisfaction and size of state, they do not comment on the statistically significant relationships between life satisfaction and other factors. One interesting finding of their analysis is that being Muslim is negatively related to life satisfaction at high levels of statistical significance.

So, to reiterate, the authors report (1) a statistically significant and positive relationship between individuals' subjective well-being and size of government and (2) the size of this relationship is about the same as for other traditional predictors of life satisfaction. But, take a look at two other pieces of information contained in the tables reporting the regression results. Note the sample size—over 10,000 individuals. Remember that statistical significance is related to sample size and this is a very large sample indeed. Now take a look at the adjusted R^2 values. These are around .20. This means that only 20 percent of the variation in the life satisfaction of individuals is explained by all of the independent variables, including size of state. This suggests that the multiple regression models are not very powerful predictors of life satisfaction.

TABLE 1
Size of the State and Life Satisfaction

	(1) Tax Revenue	(2) Government Share of GDP	(3) Social Wage	(4) Social Welfare Expenditures
Size of the state	.029**	.043**	.018***	.034**
	[.011]	[.021]	[.006]	[.016]
Income	.072***	.072***	.077***	.072***
	[.014]	[.014]	[.014]	[.015]
Education	−.020*	−.017*	−.014	−.020*
	[.012]	[.013]	[.012]	[.013]
Health	.705***	.708***	.703***	.708***
	[.034]	[.033]	[.033]	[.033]
Female	.059**	.056**	.061**	.057**
	[.038]	[.039]	[.039]	[.040]
Age	−.039***	−.038***	−.040***	−.041***
	[.006]	[.006]	[.007]	[.007]
Age^2	.000***	.000***	.000***	.000***
	[.000]	[.000]	[.000]	[.000]
Married	.400***	.389***	.396***	.404***
	[.043]	[.042]	[.042]	[.043]
Unemployed	−.425***	−.429***	−.385***	−.410***
	[.118]	[.123]	[.116]	[.120]
Church attendance	.041**	.039**	.046***	.037**
	[.016]	[.015]	[.014]	[.017]
Trust in others	.228***	.247***	.229***	.243***
	[.053]	[.054]	[.055]	[.055]
GDP	−.006	−.008	−.007	−.008***
	[.022]	[.026]	[.022]	[.028]
Unemployment rate	−.042*	−.035	−.029	−.064*
	[.029]	[.035]	[.026]	[.044]
Protestant	.018	.060	−.008	.025
	[.102]	[.117]	[.099]	[.105]
Muslim	−.435**	−.406***	−.468***	−.470***
	[.156]	[.144]	[.170]	[.160]
Orthodox	−.059	−.107	−.135	−.026
	[.182]	[.164]	[.173]	[.196]
Hindu	−.531	−.575*	−.521*	−.549*
	[.409]	[.407]	[.376]	[.406]
Buddhist	.142	.008	.185	−.030
	[.163]	[.163]	[.176]	[.164]
Jewish	−.259	−.287	−.316	−.294
	[.273]	[.279]	[.286]	[.287]
Catholic	−.076	−.058	−.171**	−.106
	[.092]	[.096]	[.083]	[.084]
Individualism	.127**	.117**	.134***	.100*
	[.050]	[.060]	[.075]	[.062]
Constant	3.036***	3.225***	3.493***	3.806***
	[.449]	[.538]	[.314]	[.487]
Adjusted R^2	.20	.20	.20	.20
N	10, 405	10, 405	10, 405	10, 405

Notes: Dependent variable: self-reported life satisfaction (1–10). Size of state measure used listed above each column. Cell entries are OLS regression coefficients, country-clustered standard errors below in brackets.

*p < .10; ** p < .05; *** p < .01.

GDP, gross domestic product; OLS, ordinary least squares.

Skeptics of the welfare state might object that while the models reported in Table 1 are correctly specified by including unemployment (at both the individual and aggregate levels), the inclusion of such controls might mask the negative effects of state spending on satisfaction. In other words, by controlling for unemployment, if unemployment is itself affected by the size of the state, we may over-estimate the positive impact of state spending. The obvious solution is to estimate the models when dropping the unemployment variables so as to get a better estimate of the overall effect of the size of the state. We do so (while also dropping, at the suggestion of an anonymous reviewer, marital sta-tus, which is also arguably affected by the generos-ity of the welfare state because of changes in the incentives to marry that follow) and report the results in Table 2. As is apparent, each of the four indicators of the size of the state remains significant and of the expected sign. We conclude, then, that our initial esti-mates do not suffer from the problem in interpretation noted above.

QUESTION SETS 4 AND 13: The authors present several variations from the basic regression models presented in table 1. One of the claims made by those in favor of letting markets operate with minimal government interference is that government interven-tion causes higher levels of unemployment. In the models in table 1, unemployment is included as an independent variable, and, thus, the positive impact of size of state could be overesti-mated. It is also possible that the larger the size of the state, the less incentive there is to marry because people do not need marriage as an institution to protect them financially as much. Therefore, the four regressions are run again leaving out unemployment and marriage variables, with the results reported in table 2. The authors conclude that making these changes does not alter their findings about the relationship between size of state and life satisfaction.

TABLE 2

Confirmatory Results for Indirect Effects of State Spending on Unemployment

	(1) Tax Revenue	(2) Government Share of GDP	(3) Social Wage	(4) Social Welfare Expenditures
Size of the state	.025**	.040**	.018***	.022**
	[.011]	[.023]	[.006]	[.012]
Income	.099***	.099***	.104***	.099***
	[.013]	[.013]	[.013]	[.013]
Education	−.017	−.016	−.014	−.015
	[.018]	[.018]	[.017]	[.018]
Health	.726***	.729***	.723***	.728***
	[.036]	[.035]	[.035]	[.035]
Female	.045	.044	.048	.041
	[.041]	[.041]	[.040]	[.044]
Age	−.021***	−.021***	−.023***	−.022***
	[.005]	[.005]	[.006]	[.005]
Age^2	.000***	.000***	.000***	.000***
	[.000]	[.000]	[.000]	[.000]
Church attendance	.046***	.046***	.053***	.040***
	[.015]	[.015]	[.013]	[.015]
Trust in others	.242***	.256***	.237***	.260***
	[.056]	[.057]	[.058]	[.061]
GDP	−.006	−.010	−.002	−.009
	[.022]	[.025]	[.021]	[.028]

(Continued)

TABLE 2   (CONTINUED)
Confirmatory Results for Indirect Effects of State Spending on Unemployment

	(1) Tax Revenue	(2) Government Share of GDP	(3) Social Wage	(4) Social Welfare Expenditures
Protestant	.038	.072	−.000	.061
	[.116]	[.129]	[.111]	[.112]
Muslim	−.425***	−.405***	−.468***	−.424***
	[.154]	[.149]	[.175]	[.158]
Orthodox	−.008	−.062	−.100	.035
	[.197]	[.187]	[.186]	[.210]
Hindu	−.365	−.414	−.366	−.360
	[.381]	[.374]	[.353]	[.380]
Buddhist	.199	.077	.248*	.059
	[.155]	[.148]	[.179]	[.158]
Jewish	−.246	−.267	−.297	−.284
	[.287]	[.291]	[.300]	[.291]
Catholic	−.080	−.062	−.176**	−.101
	[.104]	[.104]	[.089]	[.092]
Individualism	.097**	.092*	.110**	.072
	[.048]	[.055]	[.046]	[.062]
Unemployed	n/a	n/a	n/a	n/a
Unemployment rate	n/a	n/a	n/a	n/a
Marriage	n/a	n/a	n/a	n/a
Constant	2.283***	2.457***	2.762***	2.886***
	[.465]	[.500]	[.323]	[.447]
Adjusted R^2	.19	.19	.19	.19
N	10, 475	10, 475	10, 475	10, 475

Notes: Dependent variable: self-reported life satisfaction (1–10). Size of state measure used listed above each column. Cell entries are OLS regression coefficients, country-clustered standard errors below in brackets.

*$p < .10$; ** $p < .05$; *** $p < .01$.

GDP, gross domestic product; OLS, ordinary least squares.

QUESTION SETS 4 AND 13: A second variation adds an interaction term between income and size of state. One might expect that wealthier individuals would be least positive about government intervention. Even with this term included in the regression analysis, the relationship between life satisfaction and size of state remains positive and statistically significant, although for two of the measures of size of state, the positive effect of size of state on life satisfaction declines as income increases. Those results are reported in table 3.

Turning to a different point, might the relationship between government intervention into the economy and life satisfaction vary across different groups of citizens? Advocates of a greater role for government often couch their position in terms of meeting the needs of the less fortunate in society. One might surmise, therefore, that the net impact of state intervention in politics on life satisfaction will be greater for lower-status citizens than for their better-off counterparts. We thus ask whether the positive relationship between the size of the state and life satisfaction demonstrated in Table 1 is moderated by income by estimating the same models when adding an interaction term between the size of the state and income. The results are provided in Table 3.

TABLE 3

Effect of State Size on Satisfaction Is Invariant across Income

	(1) Tax Revenue	(2) Government Share of GDP	(3) Social Wage	(4) Social Welfare Expenditures
Size of the state × income	−.004**	−.009**	−.001	.001
	[.002]	[.004]	[.001]	[.004]
Size of the state	.047***	.087**	.024**	.041*
	[.016]	[.033]	[.012]	[.030]
Income	.204***	.214***	.105**	.099
	[.076]	[.074]	[.044]	[.090]
Education	−.019*	−.016	−.013	−.019*
	[.013]	[.013]	[.011]	[.012]
Health	.706***	.709***	.703***	.708***
	[.033]	[.033]	[.033]	[.032]
Female	.061*	.058*	.062*	.057*
	[.039]	[.040]	[.039]	[.040]
Age	−.039***	−.037***	−.040***	−.040**
	[.006]	[.006]	[.007]	[.007]
Age^2	.000***	.000***	.000***	.000***
	[.000]	[.000]	[.000]	[.000]
Married	.411***	.396***	.399***	.406***
	[.040]	[.039]	[.040]	[.038]
Unemployed	−.415***	−.416***	−.379***	−.407***
	[.115]	[.122]	[.113]	[.121]
Church attendance	.040***	.039**	.046***	.037**
	[.016]	[.015]	[.014]	[.016]
Trust in others	.228***	.245***	.229***	.243***
	[.054]	[.055]	[.055]	[.055]
GDP	−.006	−.000	−.006	−.008
	[.021]	[.025]	[.022]	[.028]
Unemployment rate	−.042*	−.035**	−.029	−.065*
	[.029]	[.034]	[.025]	[.043]
Protestant	.009	.058	−.011	.023
	[.098]	[.112]	[.097]	[.102]
Muslim	−.466***	−.441***	−.488***	−.479***
	[.155]	[.144]	[.175]	[.164]
Orthodox	−.081	−.146	−.150	−.030
	[.181]	[.161]	[.174]	[.194]
Hindu	−.544	−.582*	−.542*	−.554*
	[.407]	[.397]	[.368]	[.399]
Buddhist	.146	.002	.187	−.030
	[.160]	[.162]	[.175]	[.165]
Jewish	−.284	−.318	−.328	−.300
	[.259]	[.264]	[.275]	[.279]
Catholic	−.093	−.075	−.180**	−.110*
	[.087]	[.091]	[.084]	[.080]
Individualism	.126***	.115**	.132**	.100*
	[.049]	[.058]	[.050]	[.062]
Constant	2.337***	2.468***	3.328***	3.668***
	[.666]	[.771]	[.434]	[.797]
Adjusted R^2	.20	.21	.21	.21
N	10, 405	10, 405	10, 405	10, 405

Notes: Dependent variable: self-reported life satisfaction (1–10). Size of state measure used listed above each column. Cell entries are OLS regression coefficients, country-clustered standard errors below in brackets.

*p < .10; ** p < .05; *** p < .01.

GDP, gross domestic product; OLS, ordinary least squares.

For two of our indicators (Social Wage and Social Welfare Expenditures), the main effects are positive and significant, while the interactions are completely lacking in significance, suggesting that the positive effect of these factors on satisfaction is not moderated by one's income. For the remaining two indicators (Tax Revenue and Government Share of GDP), the main effects remain correctly signed and significant, but the income interactions are, as well, implying that the positive effects on satisfaction do decline as one's income increases. However, it is essential to note that the interaction terms show that the effect of the size of the state variables on life satisfaction remains positive across the range of the income category, becoming zero only for the top income decile. In sum, two of our four operationalizations of state size suggest an invariant effect across income, while two others suggest only a modest decline as income increases. On balance, we conclude that the positive contribution to human well-being of the size of the state is not dramatically affected by one's level of affluence. In other words, regardless of whether respondents are rich or poor, respondents living in a country with greater state intervention into the economy tend to report higher levels of subjective well-being, controlling for other factors.

A Final Note before Concluding

It is sometimes argued that political ideology can play a role similar to income as an intervening variable between political conditions and satisfaction. For instance, DiTella and MacCulloch (2005) argue that left-leaning and right-leaning individuals process effects on happiness differently. Specifically, the authors find that individuals are happier when the party best representing them is in power regardless of economic conditions. At the same time, unemployment has a greater negative impact on the happiness of left-leaning individuals, while inflation more negatively affects right-leaning individuals. The implication, therefore, is that the combination of politics and economics affects the happiness of individuals differently with respect to their ideological persuasion. Presumably, this might apply to the extent of state intervention, which historically conservatives criticize and liberals applaud.[4]

In light of this, we further test to see if ideology plays a mitigating role in state intervention's effect on subjective well-being by including an interaction between

> **QUESTION SETS 4 AND 13:** Finally, the authors investigate the possible interaction between ideology and size of state: it is predicted that conservatives would be less satisfied as the size of the state increases. The results of these analyses are discussed in the authors' final note but not shown.

---

[4]The variable is measured on a 1–10 scale (higher values indicate greater conservatism) in response to the following question: "In political matters, people talk of 'the left' and 'the right.' How would you place your views on this scale, generally speaking?"

the size of the state and self-reported political ideology, along, of course, with the ideology measure itself. The results suggest no evidence that ideology plays this kind of role *vis-à-vis* the size of the state: in none of the models did we observe the pattern of coefficients this would imply (details not shown). Instead, we find that while the main effects remain significant in three of the four cases (social welfare expenditures being the exception, where it remains of the correct sign but not strictly significant, presumably because of collinearity with the equally insignificant—and incorrectly signed—interaction term), in no case was the interaction term between the size of the state and political ideology correctly signed and statistically different from zero.

To summarize the data analysis, we find a positive relationship between the size of the state and life satisfaction. The magnitude of this relationship is substantively large and mirrors that of income or marriage, and the relationship is not moderated by income or political ideology.

Discussion

The principal empirical conclusions emerging from the analysis are clear: life satisfaction varies directly with four specific measures of state intervention in the economy: tax revenue, government consumption as a share of GDP, the "social wage," and welfare expenditures. Equally important is our second finding that these effects are invariant over income and ideology. Our results therefore suggest that state intervention in the economy positively affects the subjective well-being of society in general, not simply of those that one might reasonably expect to be more affected (e.g., lower-status citizens or more pro-state liberal-left citizens). The existence of a strong relationship between an activist state and human well-being that appears to benefit all in society would seem to be of some consequence in light of the continuing ideological debate about the role of government that manifests itself in contemporary politics.[5]

QUESTION SET 13: The authors summarize their findings as follows:

" . . . we find a positive relationship between the size of the state and life satisfaction. The magnitude of this relationship is substantively large and mirrors that of income or marriage, and the relationship is not moderated by income or political ideology. . . .

Our results therefore suggest that state intervention in the economy positively affects the subjective well-being of society in general, not simply of those that one might reasonably expect to be more affected (e.g., lower-status individuals or more pro-state liberal-left citizens."

Flavin, Pacek, and Radcliff are careful to point out that their findings do not suggest that a market economy approach does not lead to well-being and individual life satisfaction. Rather their analysis suggests that market economies *moderated by government intervention* lead to higher levels of societal well-being. Their findings also suggest that theories about the determinants of individual well-being need to pay attention to the role of macro-level conditions in a society, as well as individual characteristics that traditionally have been the focus of research asking what makes individuals more or less satisfied with their lives.

---

[4] Why do our results differ from Veenhoven's (2000) core result, which showed that change over time in satisfaction was not explained by change over time in the size of the welfare state? Veenhoven takes as his dependent variable the change across the two points of time available when

That said, we would also stress that our findings cannot be construed as suggesting that a market economy is inimical to well-being. On the contrary, it seems certain that capitalist economies are superior producers of well-being than prevailing (or historically prior) nonmarket alternatives (see, e.g., Veenhoven 2000). Thus, the essential point of the analysis is not that the market inhibits well-being, but rather that within the context of a capitalistic economy, state interventions that attempt to redress market deficiencies tend to produce greater levels of human happiness. Our results thus do not indict the market as it affects satisfaction with life, but suggest instead that the quality of human life is best when the inequalities and uncertainties of the market are mitigated by state intervention acting in the interests of workers and citizens. Our results might thus be most easily summarized by suggesting that it is "compassionate capitalism" (or, perhaps, the conventional idea of a mixed economy) that seems most consistent with well-being.

Our findings also have implications for the academic study of subjective well-being. Most obviously, we offer further evidence in support of the disputed contention that governmental policies affect quality of life. More importantly, perhaps, this fact, in turn, has implications for our theoretical understanding of what determines well-being. We would argue that the evidence presented here suggests more than we add another set of variables to the list of those thought to affect quality of life. By demonstrating that public (i.e., democratic) "intrusion" into the market improves life satisfaction, we hope to focus scholarly attention on the basic question of theoretical approaches to modeling the determinants of well-being. The conventional approach in psychology and economics is implicitly, and perhaps unconsciously, to assume that society is composed only of individual persons who happen to vary in their many individual-level characteristics but who remain largely undifferentiated by macro-level conditions aside from (1) the level of affluence and (2) culture. Thus, in the much cited, nearly encyclopedic review of the "Three Decades of Progress" in the study of subjective well-being by Diener and others (1999), these are the only two societal factors

---

he was writing (1981–90) and uses the best available indicator of welfare state effort then available in a time serial fashion (social welfare expenditures). We updated this analysis in two ways. First, we use the widest possible range of time available for every country. For most, this implies the difference between the last (2005) and the first (1981) wave of the WVS. For the handful of countries not represented in both waves, we use the longest time span available (e.g., between the 2005 and 1990 waves). In this way, we maximize the amount of variability in the time dimension. Second, we utilize what is now universally acknowledged to be a better indicator of the welfare state, which is the decommodification measure first proposed by Esping-Andersen (1990). As there is now longitudinal data on decommodification, and as this is, again, widely agreed to be the preferred method of measuring the size or generosity of the welfare state, we utilize the change in this variable (over the same time as the change in satisfaction for each country). The results are consistent with our prior results: regression analysis shows a positive and highly significant relationship between change in decommodification and change in life satisfaction.

discussed. To be sure, more recent work, reviewed previously, has touched upon macro-conditions, but the fact remains that far too little attention has been devoted to theorizing about how sociopolitical conditions determine quality of life. In demonstrating the importance of political outcomes, we highlight the need for richer theories that incorporate such factors.

The present article may also point toward the direction such theorizing might take. By illustrating that welfare spending, labor market regulation, and other political interventions into the economy affect well-being, we also suggest the centrality to human life of the market economy itself. As Lindblom (1977) has persuasively argued, we tend as social theorists to take the market for granted in the sense of considering it to be a fixed characteristic—almost a natural force of nature, akin to gravity. Instead, we need to be cognizant of the fact that the market is a variable in the sense that it varies both in its existence and in its character. There are, as is commonly accepted, different "flavors" of capitalist democracy (see, e.g., Esping-Andersen 1990; Rueschemeyer, Stephens, and Stephens 1992). Variations in the nature of the market system across time and space would appear to be essential elements in any understanding of life satisfaction.

References

Alesina, Alberto, Rafael DiTella, and Robert MacCulloch. 2004. "Inequality and Happiness: Are Europeans and Americans Different?" *Journal of Public Economics* 88 (9–10): 2009–2042.

Arceneaux, Kevin, and David W. Nickerson. 2009. "Modeling Certainty with Clustered Data: A Comparison of Methods." *Political Analysis* 17 (2): 177–190.

Banks, M. H., and P. R. Jackson. 1982. "Unemployment and Risk of Minor Psychiatric Disorder in Young People: Cross-Sectional and Longitudinal Evidence." *Psychological Medicine* 12 (4): 789–798.

Cohen, Sheldon, and Thomas A. Wills. 1985. "Stress, Social Support, and the Buffering Hypothesis." *Psychological Bulletin* 98 (2): 310–357.

Diener, Ed, Marissa Diener, and Carol Diener. 1995. "Factors Predicting the Subjective Well-Being of Nations." *Journal of Personality and Social Psychology* 69 (5): 851–864.

Diener, Ed, and Eunkook M. Suh, eds. 2000. *Culture and Subjective Well-Being.* Cambridge, MA: MIT Press.

Diener, Ed, Eunkook M. Suh, Richard E. Lucas, and Heidi L. Smith. 1999. "Subjective Well-Being: Three Decades of Progress." *Psychological Bulletin* 125 (2): 276–302.

DiTella, Rafael, and Robert J. MacCulloch. 2005. "Partisan Social Happiness." *Review of Economic Studies* 72 (2): 367–393.

DiTella, Rafael, Robert J. MacCulloch, and Andrew J. Oswald. 2003. "The Macroeconomics of Happiness." *Review of Economics and Statistics* 85 (4): 809–827.

Erikson, Kai. 1986. "On Work and Alienation." *American Sociological Review* 51 (1): 1–8.

Esping-Andersen, Gosta. 1990. *The Three Worlds of Welfare Capitalism.* Princeton, NJ: Princeton University Press.

Frey, Bruno, and Alois Stutzer. 2002. *Happiness and Economics.* Princeton, NJ, and Oxford, UK: Princeton University Press.

Greenberg, Edward, and Leon Grunberg. 1995. "Work Alienation and Problem Alcohol Behavior." *Journal of Health and Social Behavior* 36 (1): 83–102.

Heilbroner, Robert. 1985. *The Nature and Logic of Capitalism.* New York: Norton.

Heston, Alan, Robert Summers, and Bettina Aten. 2009. "Penn World Table Version 6.3." *Center for International Comparisons of Production, Income and Prices at the University of Pennsylvania* (August). Accessed on August 5, 2009. Available online at http://pwt.econ.upenn.edu/php_site/pwt_index.php

Hirschman, Albert. 1991. *The Rhetoric of Reaction: Perversity, Futility, Jeopardy.* Cambridge, MA: Harvard University Press.

Inglehart, Ronald. 1990. *Culture Shift in Advanced Industrial Democracies.* Princeton, NJ: Princeton University Press.

Kenny, Charles. 1999. "Does Growth Cause Happiness, or Does Happiness Cause Growth?" *Kyklos* 52 (1): 3–26.

Lane, Robert E. 1978. "Autonomy, Felicity, Futility: The Effects of the Market Economy on Political Personality." *Journal of Politics* 40 (1): 1–24.

———. 1991. *The Market Experience.* Cambridge, UK: Cambridge University Press.

Layard, Richard. 2005. *Happiness: Lessons from a New Science.* London: Allen Lane.

Lindblom, Charles. 1977. *Politics and Markets.* New York: Basic Books.

Loscocco, Karyn, and Glenna Spitze. 1990. "Working Conditions, Social Support, and the Well-Being of Female and Male Factory Workers." *Journal of Health and Social Behavior* 31 (4): 313–327.

Lowe, Graham, and Herbert Northcutt. 1988. "The Impact of Working Conditions, Social Roles, and Personal Characteristics on Gender Differences in Distress." *Work and Occupations* 15 (1): 55–77.

Murray, Charles. 1984. Losing Ground: American Social Policy, 1950–1980. New York: Basic Books.

Myers, David, and Ed Diener. 1995. "Who Is Happy?" *Psychological Science* 6: 10–19.

Organisation for Economic Co-operation and Development (OECD). 2009a. "Benefits and Wages: OECD Indicators." Accessed on August 5, 2009. Available online at http://www.oecd.org/els/social/workincentives

———. 2009b. Revenue Statistics 1965–2008: 2009 Edition. France: OECD.

———. 2011. "OECD. Stat Extracts." Accessed on August 5, 2009. Available online at http://stats.oecd.org/Index.aspx

Oswald, Andrew. 1997. "Happiness and Economic Performance." *Economic Journal* 107 (445): 1815–1831.

Ouweneel, Piet. 2002. "Social Security and Well-Being of the Unemployed in 42 Countries." *Journal of Happiness Studies* 3 (2): 167–197.

Pacek, Alexander, and Benjamin Radcliff. 2008. "Assessing the Welfare State: The Politics of Happiness." *Perspectives on Politics* 6 (2): 267–277.

Platt, S., and N. Kreitman. 1985. "Parasuicide and Unemployment among Men in Edinburgh 1968–1982." *Psychological Medicine* 15: 113–123.

Pontusson, Jonas. 2005. *Inequality and Prosperity: Social Europe vs. Liberal America.* Ithaca, NY: Cornell University Press.

Radcliff, Benjamin. 2001. "Politics, Markets, and Life Satisfaction: The Political Economy of Human Happiness." *American Political Science Review* 95 (4): 939–952.

———. 2005. "Class Organization and Subjective Well-Being: A Cross-National Analysis." *Social Forces* 84 (1): 513–530.

Ridge, Charolette, Tom Rice, and Matthew Cherry. 2009. "The Casual Link between Happiness and Democratic Welfare Regimes." In *Happiness, Economics, and Politics: Towards a Multi-Disciplinary Approach,* edited by Amitava K. Dutt and Benjamin Radcliff. Cheltenham, UK: Edward Elgar. 271–284.

Rueschemeyer, Dietrich, Evelyne Huber Stephens, and John D. Stephens. 1992. *Capitalist Development and Democracy.* Chicago: University of Chicago Press.

Somers, Margaret, and Fred Block. 2005. "From Poverty to Perversity: Ideas, Markets, and Institutions Over 200 Years of Welfare Debate." *American Sociological Review* 70 (2): 260–287.

Soros, George. 1998. *The Crisis of Global Capitalism.* New York: Public Affairs.

Tomes, Nigel. 1985. "Income Distribution, Happiness, and Satisfaction: A Direct Test of the Interdependent Preferences Model." *Journal of Economic Psychology* 7 (4): 425–446.

Triandis, Harry C. 1989. "The Self and Social Behavior in Differing Cultural Contexts." *Psychological Review* 96 (3): 506–520.

Veenhoven, Ruut. 1994. "Is Happiness a Trait?" *Social Indicators Research* 32 (2): 101–160.

———. 1996. "Developments in Satisfaction Research." *Social Indicators Research* 37 (1): 1–46.

———. 1997a. "Advances in Understanding Happiness." *Revue Quebecoise de Psychologie* 18 (2): 29–74.

———. 1997b. "Quality of Life in Individualistic Societies." In *The Gift of Society,* edited by Mart-Jan DeJong and Anton C. Zijderveld. Nijker, the Netherlands: Enzo Press. 149–170.

———. 2000. "Well-Being in the Welfare State: Level Not Higher, Distribution Not More Equitable." *Journal of Comparative Policy Analysis* 2 (1): 91–125.

———. 2002. "Why Social Policy Needs Subjective Indicators." *Social Indicators Research* 58 (1–3): 33–45.

Wilkinson, Will. 2007. "In Pursuit of Happiness Research: Is It Reliable? What Does It Imply for Policy?" *Policy Analysis* 590 (April 11): 1–41.

World Values Survey (WVS). 2009. "WVS 2005–2008 Wave." Accessed on August 5, 2009. Available online at http://www.wvsevsdb.com/wvs/WVSAnalizeStudy.jsp

APPENDIXES

Normal Curve Tail Probabilities. Standard Normal Probability in Right-Hand Tail
(for negative values of z, probabilities are found by symmetry)

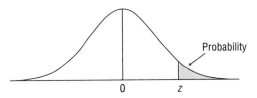

Probability

0   z

	Second Decimal Place of z								
z	.00	.01	.02	.03	.04	.05	.06	.07	.08	.09
0.0	.5000	.4960	.4920	.4880	.4840	.4801	.4761	.4721	.4681	.4641
0.1	.4602	.4562	.4522	.4483	.4443	.4404	.4364	.4325	.4286	.4247
0.2	.4207	.4168	.4129	.4090	.4052	.4013	.3974	.3936	.3897	.3859
0.3	.3821	.3783	.3745	.3707	.3669	.3632	.3594	.3557	.3520	.3483
0.4	.3446	.3409	.3372	.3336	.3300	.3264	.3228	.3192	.3156	.3121
0.5	.3085	.3050	.3015	.2981	.2946	.2912	.2877	.2843	.2810	.2776
0.6	.2743	.2709	.2676	.2643	.2611	.2578	.2546	.2514	.2483	.2451
0.7	.2420	.2389	.2358	.2327	.2296	.2266	.2236	.2206	.2177	.2148
0.8	.2119	.2090	.2061	.2033	.2005	.1977	.1949	.1922	.1894	.1867
0.9	.1841	.1814	.1788	.1762	.1736	.1711	.1685	.1660	.1635	.1611
1.0	.1587	.1562	.1539	.1515	.1492	.1469	.1446	.1423	.1401	.1379
1.1	.1357	.1335	.1314	.1292	.1271	.1251	.1230	.1210	.1190	.1170
1.2	.1151	.1131	.1112	.1093	.1075	.1056	.1038	.1020	.1003	.0985
1.3	.0968	.0951	.0934	.0918	.0901	.0885	.0869	.0853	.0838	.0823
1.4	.0808	.0793	.0778	.0764	.0749	.0735	.0722	.0708	.0694	.0681
1.5	.0668	.0655	.0643	.0630	.0618	.0606	.0594	.0582	.0571	.0559
1.6	.0548	.0537	.0526	.0516	.0505	.0495	.0485	.0475	.0465	.0455
1.7	.0446	.0436	.0427	.0418	.0409	.0401	.0392	.0384	.0375	.0367
1.8	.0359	.0352	.0344	.0336	.0329	.0322	.0314	.0307	.0301	.0294
1.9	.0287	.0281	.0274	.0268	.0262	.0256	.0250	.0244	.0239	.0233
2.0	.0228	.0222	.0217	.0212	.0207	.0202	.0197	.0192	.0188	.0183
2.1	.0179	.0174	.0170	.0166	.0162	.0158	.0154	.0150	.0146	.0143
2.2	.0139	.0136	.0132	.0129	.0125	.0122	.0119	.0116	.0113	.0110
2.3	.0107	.0104	.0102	.0099	.0096	.0094	.0091	.0089	.0087	.0084
2.4	.0082	.0080	.0078	.0075	.0073	.0071	.0069	.0068	.0066	.0064
2.5	.0062	.0060	.0059	.0057	.0055	.0054	.0052	.0051	.0049	.0048
2.6	.0047	.0045	.0044	.0043	.0041	.0040	.0039	.0038	.0037	.0036
2.7	.0035	.0034	.0033	.0032	.0031	.0030	.0029	.0028	.0027	.0026
2.8	.0026	.0025	.0024	.0023	.0023	.0022	.0021	.0021	.0020	.0019
2.9	.0019	.0018	.0017	.0017	.0016	.0016	.0015	.0015	.0014	.0014
3.0	.00135									
3.5	.000233									
4.0	.0000317									
4.5	.00000340									
5.0	.000000287									

Source: R. E. Walpole, *Introduction to Statistics* (New York: Macmillan, 1968). Used with permission.

Critical Values from *t* Distribution

	Alpha Level for One-Tailed Test						
	.05	.025	.01	.005	.0025	.001	.0005
Degree of	Alpha Level for Two-Tailed Test						
Freedom (*df*)	.10	.05	.02	.01	.005	.002	.001
1	6.314	12.706	31.821	63.657	127.32	318.31	636.62
2	2.920	4.303	6.965	9.925	14.089	22.327	31.598
3	2.353	3.182	4.541	5.841	7.453	10.214	12.924
4	2.132	2.776	3.747	4.604	5.598	7.173	8.610
5	2.015	2.571	3.365	4.032	4.773	5.893	6.869
6	1.943	2.447	3.143	3.707	4.317	5.208	5.959
7	1.895	2.365	2.998	3.499	4.029	4.785	5.408
8	1.869	2.306	2.896	3.355	3.833	4.501	5.041
9	1.833	2.262	2.821	3.250	3.690	4.297	4.781
10	1.812	2.228	2.764	3.169	3.581	4.144	4.587
11	1.796	2.201	2.718	3.106	3.497	4.025	4.437
12	1.782	2.179	2.681	3.055	3.428	3.930	4.318
13	1.771	2.160	2.650	3.012	3.372	3.852	4.221
14	1.761	2.145	2.624	2.977	3.326	3.787	4.140
15	1.753	2.131	2.602	2.947	3.286	3.733	4.073
16	1.746	2.120	2.583	2.921	3.252	3.686	4.015
17	1.740	2.110	2.567	2.898	3.222	3.646	3.965
18	1.734	2.101	2.552	2.878	3.197	3.610	3.922
19	1.729	2.093	2.539	2.861	3.174	3.579	3.883
20	1.725	2.086	2.528	2.845	3.153	3.552	3.850
21	1.721	2.080	2.518	2.831	3.135	3.527	3.819
22	1.717	2.074	2.508	2.819	3.119	3.505	3.792
23	1.714	2.069	2.500	2.807	3.104	3.485	3.767
24	1.711	2.064	2.492	2.797	3.091	3.467	3.745
25	1.708	2.060	2.485	2.787	3.078	3.450	3.725
26	1.706	2.056	2.479	2.779	3.067	3.435	3.707
27	1.703	2.052	2.473	2.771	3.057	3.421	3.690
28	1.701	2.048	2.467	2.763	3.047	3.408	3.674
29	1.699	2.045	2.462	2.756	3.038	3.396	3.659
30	1.697	2.042	2.457	2.750	3.030	3.385	3.646
40	1.684	2.021	2.423	2.704	2.971	3.307	3.551
60	1.671	2.000	2.390	2.660	2.915	3.232	3.460
120	1.658	1.980	2.358	2.617	2.860	3.160	3.373
∞	1.645	1.960	2.326	2.576	2.807	3.090	3.291

Source: James V. Couch, *Fundamentals of Statistics for the Behavioral Sciences, Second Edition.* (St. Paul, Minn.: West, 1987), 327. © 1987 Wadsworth, a part of Cengage Learning, Inc. Reproduced by permission. www.cengage.com/permissions

Chi-Squared Distribution Values for Various Right-Tail Probabilities

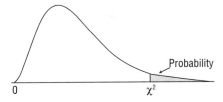

Right-Tail Probability

df	0.250	0.100	0.050	0.025	0.010	0.005	0.001
1	1.32	2.71	3.84	5.02	6.63	7.88	10.83
2	2.77	4.61	5.99	7.38	9.21	10.60	13.82
3	4.11	6.25	7.81	9.35	11.34	12.84	16.27
4	5.39	7.78	9.49	11.14	13.28	14.86	18.47
5	6.63	9.24	11.07	12.83	15.09	16.75	20.52
6	7.84	10.64	12.59	14.45	16.81	18.55	22.46
7	9.04	12.02	14.07	16.01	18.48	20.28	24.32
8	10.22	13.36	15.51	17.53	20.09	21.96	26.12
9	11.39	14.68	16.92	19.02	21.67	23.59	27.88
10	12.55	15.99	18.31	20.48	23.21	25.19	29.59
11	13.70	17.28	19.68	21.92	24.72	26.76	31.26
12	14.85	18.55	21.03	23.34	26.22	28.30	32.91
13	15.98	19.81	22.36	24.74	27.69	29.82	34.53
14	17.12	21.06	23.68	26.12	29.14	31.32	36.12
15	18.25	22.31	25.00	27.49	30.58	32.80	37.70
16	19.37	23.54	26.30	28.85	32.00	34.27	39.25
17	20.49	24.77	27.59	30.19	33.41	35.72	40.79
18	21.60	25.99	28.87	31.53	34.81	37.16	42.31
19	22.72	27.20	30.14	32.85	36.19	38.58	43.82
20	23.83	28.41	31.41	34.17	37.57	40.00	45.32
25	29.34	34.38	37.65	40.65	44.31	46.93	52.62
30	34.80	40.26	43.77	46.98	50.89	53.67	59.70
40	45.62	51.80	55.76	59.34	63.69	66.77	73.40
50	56.33	63.17	67.50	71.42	76.15	79.49	86.66
60	66.98	74.40	79.08	83.30	88.38	91.95	99.61
70	77.58	85.53	90.53	95.02	100.4	104.2	112.3
80	88.13	96.58	101.8	106.6	112.3	116.3	124.8
90	98.65	107.6	113.1	118.1	124.1	128.3	137.2
100	109.1	118.5	124.3	129.6	135.8	140.2	149.5

Source: Alan Agresti and Barbara Finlay, *Statistical Methods for the Social Sciences,* 3rd edition (Upper Saddle River, N.J.: Prentice Hall, 1997) p. 670. Used with permission.

F Distribution

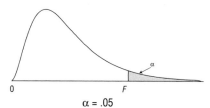

$$\alpha = .05$$

df_2	df_1									
	1	2	3	4	5	6	8	12	24	∞
1	161.4	199.5	215.7	224.6	230.2	234.0	238.9	243.9	249.0	254.3
2	18.51	19.00	19.16	19.25	19.30	19.33	19.37	19.41	19.45	19.50
3	10.13	9.55	9.28	9.12	9.01	8.94	8.84	8.74	8.64	8.53
4	7.71	6.94	6.59	6.39	6.26	6.16	6.04	5.91	5.77	5.63
5	6.61	5.79	5.41	5.19	5.05	4.95	4.82	4.68	4.53	4.36
6	5.99	5.14	4.76	4.53	4.39	4.28	4.15	4.00	3.84	3.67
7	5.59	4.74	4.35	4.12	3.97	3.87	3.73	3.57	3.41	3.23
8	5.32	4.46	4.07	3.84	3.69	3.58	3.44	3.28	3.12	2.93
9	5.12	4.26	3.86	3.63	3.48	3.37	3.23	3.07	2.90	2.71
10	4.96	4.10	3.71	3.48	3.33	3.22	3.07	2.91	2.74	2.54
11	4.84	3.98	3.59	3.36	3.20	3.09	2.95	2.79	2.61	2.40
12	4.75	3.88	3.49	3.26	3.11	3.00	2.85	2.69	2.50	2.30
13	4.67	3.80	3.41	3.18	3.02	2.92	2.77	2.60	2.42	2.21
14	4.60	3.74	3.34	3.11	2.96	2.85	2.70	2.53	2.35	2.13
15	4.54	3.68	3.29	3.06	2.90	2.79	2.64	2.48	2.29	2.07
16	4.49	3.63	3.24	3.01	2.85	2.74	2.59	2.42	2.24	2.01
17	4.45	3.59	3.20	2.96	2.81	2.70	2.55	2.38	2.19	1.96
18	4.41	3.55	3.16	2.93	2.77	2.66	2.51	2.34	2.15	1.92
19	4.38	3.52	3.13	2.90	2.74	2.63	2.48	2.31	2.11	1.88
20	4.35	3.49	3.10	2.87	2.71	2.60	2.45	2.28	2.08	1.84
21	4.32	3.47	3.07	2.84	2.68	2.57	2.42	2.25	2.05	1.81
22	4.30	3.44	3.05	2.82	2.66	2.55	2.40	2.23	2.03	1.78
23	4.28	3.42	3.03	2.80	2.64	2.53	2.38	2.20	2.00	1.76
24	4.26	3.40	3.01	2.78	2.62	2.51	2.36	2.18	1.98	1.73
25	4.24	3.38	2.99	2.76	2.60	2.49	2.34	2.16	1.96	1.71
26	4.22	3.37	2.98	2.74	2.59	2.47	2.32	2.15	1.95	1.69
27	4.21	3.35	2.96	2.73	2.57	2.46	2.30	2.13	1.93	1.67
28	4.20	3.34	2.95	2.71	2.56	2.44	2.29	2.12	1.91	1.65
29	4.18	3.33	2.93	2.70	2.54	2.43	2.28	2.10	1.90	1.64
30	4.17	3.32	2.92	2.69	2.53	2.42	2.27	2.09	1.89	1.62
40	4.08	3.23	2.84	2.61	2.45	2.34	2.18	2.00	1.79	1.51
60	4.00	3.15	2.76	2.52	2.37	2.25	2.10	1.92	1.70	1.39
120	3.92	3.07	2.68	2.45	2.29	2.17	2.02	1.83	1.61	1.25
∞	3.84	2.99	2.60	2.37	2.21	2.09	1.94	1.75	1.52	1.00

Source: From Table V of R. A. Fisher and F. Yates, *Statistical Tables for Biological, Agricultural and Medical Research*, published by Longman Group Ltd., London, 1974. Reprinted by permission of Pearson Education Limited.

$\alpha = .01$

df_2	df_1									
	1	2	3	4	5	6	8	12	24	∞
1	4052	4999	5403	5625	5764	5859	5981	6106	6234	6366
2	98.49	99.01	99.17	99.25	99.30	99.33	99.36	99.42	99.46	99.50
3	34.12	30.18	29.46	28.71	28.24	27.91	27.49	27.05	26.60	26.12
4	21.20	18.00	16.69	15.98	15.52	15.21	14.80	14.37	13.93	13.46
5	16.26	13.27	12.06	11.39	10.97	10.67	10.27	9.89	9.47	9.02
6	13.74	10.92	9.78	9.15	8.75	8.47	8.10	7.72	7.31	6.88
7	12.25	9.55	8.45	7.85	7.46	7.19	6.84	6.47	6.07	5.65
8	11.26	8.65	7.59	7.01	6.63	6.37	6.03	5.67	5.28	4.86
9	10.56	8.02	6.99	6.42	6.06	5.80	5.47	5.11	4.73	4.31
10	10.04	7.56	6.55	5.99	5.64	5.39	5.06	4.71	4.33	3.91
11	9.65	7.20	6.22	5.67	5.32	5.07	4.74	4.40	4.02	3.60
12	9.33	6.93	5.95	5.41	5.06	4.82	4.50	4.16	3.78	3.36
13	9.07	6.70	5.74	5.20	4.86	4.62	4.30	3.96	3.59	3.16
14	8.86	6.51	5.56	5.03	4.69	4.46	4.14	3.80	3.43	3.00
15	8.68	6.36	5.42	4.89	4.56	4.32	4.00	3.67	3.29	2.87
16	8.53	6.23	5.29	4.77	4.44	4.20	3.89	3.55	3.18	2.75
17	8.40	6.11	5.18	4.67	4.34	4.10	3.79	3.45	3.08	2.65
18	8.28	6.01	5.09	4.58	4.25	4.01	3.71	3.37	3.00	2.57
19	8.18	5.93	5.01	4.50	4.17	3.94	3.63	3.30	2.92	2.49
20	8.10	5.85	4.94	4.43	4.10	3.87	3.56	3.23	2.86	2.42
21	8.02	5.78	4.87	4.37	4.04	3.81	3.51	3.17	2.80	2.36
22	7.94	5.72	4.82	4.31	3.99	3.76	3.45	3.12	2.75	2.31
23	7.88	5.66	4.76	4.26	3.94	3.71	3.41	3.07	2.70	2.26
24	7.82	5.61	4.72	4.22	3.90	3.67	3.36	3.03	2.66	2.21
25	7.77	5.57	4.68	4.18	3.86	3.63	3.32	2.99	2.62	2.17
26	7.72	5.53	4.64	4.14	3.82	3.59	3.29	2.96	2.58	2.13
27	7.68	5.49	4.60	4.11	3.78	3.56	3.26	2.93	2.55	2.10
28	7.64	5.45	4.57	4.07	3.75	3.53	3.23	2.90	2.52	2.06
29	7.60	5.42	4.54	4.04	3.73	3.50	3.20	2.87	2.49	2.03
30	7.56	5.39	4.51	4.02	3.70	3.47	3.17	2.84	2.47	2.01
40	7.31	5.18	4.31	3.83	3.51	3.29	2.99	2.66	2.29	1.80
60	7.08	4.98	4.13	3.65	3.34	3.12	2.82	2.50	2.12	1.60
120	6.85	4.79	3.95	3.48	3.17	2.96	2.66	2.34	1.95	1.38
∞	6.64	4.60	3.78	3.32	3.02	2.80	2.51	2.18	1.79	1.00

(Continued)

$\alpha = .001$

df_2	1	2	3	4	df_1 5	6	8	12	24	∞
1	405284	500000	540379	562500	576405	585937	598144	610667	623497	636619
2	998.5	999.0	999.2	999.2	999.3	999.3	999.4	999.4	999.5	999.5
3	167.5	148.5	141.1	137.1	134.6	132.8	130.6	128.3	125.9	123.5
4	74.14	61.25	56.18	53.44	51.71	50.53	49.00	47.41	45.77	44.05
5	47.04	36.61	33.20	31.09	29.75	28.84	27.64	26.42	25.14	23.78
6	35.51	27.00	23.70	21.90	20.81	20.03	19.03	17.99	16.89	15.75
7	29.22	21.69	18.77	17.19	16.21	15.52	14.63	13.71	12.73	11.69
8	25.42	18.49	15.83	14.39	13.49	12.86	12.04	11.19	10.30	9.34
9	22.86	16.39	13.90	12.56	11.71	11.13	10.37	9.57	8.72	7.81
10	21.04	14.91	12.55	11.28	10.48	9.92	9.20	8.45	7.64	6.76
11	19.69	13.81	11.56	10.35	9.58	9.05	8.35	7.63	6.85	6.00
12	18.64	12.97	10.80	9.63	8.89	8.38	7.71	7.00	6.25	5.42
13	17.81	12.31	10.21	9.07	8.35	7.86	7.21	6.52	5.78	4.97
14	17.14	11.78	9.73	8.62	7.92	7.43	6.80	6.13	5.41	4.60
15	16.59	11.34	9.34	8.25	7.57	7.09	6.47	5.81	5.10	4.31
16	16.12	10.97	9.00	7.94	7.27	6.81	6.19	5.55	4.85	4.06
17	15.72	10.66	8.73	7.68	7.02	6.56	5.96	5.32	4.63	3.85
18	15.38	10.39	8.49	7.46	6.81	6.35	5.76	5.13	4.45	3.67
19	15.08	10.16	8.28	7.26	6.61	6.18	5.59	4.97	4.29	3.52
20	14.82	9.95	8.10	7.10	6.46	6.02	5.44	4.82	4.15	3.38
21	14.59	9.77	7.94	6.95	6.32	5.88	5.31	4.70	4.03	3.26
22	14.38	9.61	7.80	6.81	6.19	5.76	5.19	4.58	3.92	3.15
23	14.19	9.47	7.67	6.69	6.08	5.65	5.09	4.48	3.82	3.05
24	14.03	9.34	7.55	6.59	5.98	5.55	4.99	4.39	3.74	2.97
25	13.88	9.22	7.45	6.49	5.88	5.46	4.91	4.31	3.66	2.89
26	13.74	9.12	7.36	6.41	5.80	5.38	4.83	4.24	3.59	2.82
27	13.61	9.02	7.27	6.33	5.73	5.31	4.76	4.17	3.52	2.75
28	13.50	8.93	7.19	6.25	5.66	5.24	4.69	4.11	3.46	2.70
29	13.39	8.85	7.12	6.19	5.59	5.18	4.64	4.05	3.41	2.64
30	13.29	8.77	7.05	6.12	5.53	5.12	4.58	4.00	3.36	2.59
40	12.61	8.25	6.60	5.70	5.13	4.73	4.21	3.64	3.01	2.23
60	11.97	7.76	6.17	5.31	4.76	4.37	3.87	3.31	2.69	1.90
120	11.38	7.31	5.79	4.95	4.42	4.04	3.55	3.02	2.40	1.56
∞	10.83	6.91	5.42	4.62	4.10	3.74	3.27	2.74	2.13	1.00

Glossary

Accretion measures. Measures of phenomena through observation of the accumulation of materials.

Actions. Human behavior done for a reason.

Alternative-form method. A method of calculating reliability by repeating different but equivalent measures at two or more points in time.

Alternative hypothesis. A statement about the value or values of a population parameter. A hypothesis proposed as an alternative to the null hypothesis.

Ambiguous question. A question containing a concept that is not defined clearly.

Analysis of variance. A technique for measuring the relationship between one nominal- or ordinal-level variable and one interval- or ratio-level variable.

Antecedent variable. An independent variable that precedes other independent variables in time.

Applied research. Research designed to produce knowledge useful in altering a real-world condition or situation.

Arrow diagram. A pictorial representation of a researcher's explanatory scheme.

Bar graph. A graphic display of the data in a frequency or percentage distribution.

Branching question. A question that sorts respondents into subgroups and directs these subgroups to different parts of the questionnaire.

Case study design. A comprehensive and in-depth study of a single case or several cases. A nonexperimental design in which the investigator has little control over events.

Central tendency. The most frequent, middle, or central value in a frequency distribution.

Chi-square. A statistic used to test whether a relationship is statistically significant in a crosstabulation table.

Classical randomized experimental design. An experiment with the random assignment of subjects to experimental and control groups with a pretest and posttest for both groups.

Closed-ended question. A question with response alternatives provided.

Cluster sample. A probability sample that is used when no list of elements exists. The sampling frame initially consists of clusters of elements.

Cohort. A group of people who all experience a significant event in roughly the same time frame.

Confidence interval. The range of values into which a population parameter is likely to fall for a given level of confidence.

Confidence level. The degree of belief or probability that an estimated range of values includes or covers the population parameter.

Construct validity. Validity demonstrated for a measure by showing that it is related to the measure of another concept.

Constructionism. An approach to knowledge that asserts humans actually construct—through their social interactions and cultural and historical practices—many of the facts they take for granted as having an independent, objective, or material reality.

Content analysis. A systematic procedure by which records are transformed into quantitative data.

Content validity. Validity demonstrated by ensuring that the full domain of a concept is measured.

Control by grouping. A form of statistical control in which observations identical or similar to the control variable are grouped together.

Control group. A group of subjects that does not receive the experimental treatment or test stimulus.

Convenience sample. A nonprobability sample in which the selection of elements is determined by the researcher's convenience.

Convergent construct validity. Validity demonstrated by showing that the measure of a concept is related to the measure of another, related concept.

Correlation. A statement that the values or states of one thing systematically vary with the values or states of another; an association between two variables.

Correlation coefficient. In regression analysis, a measure of the strength and direction of the linear correlation between two quantitative variables; also called product-moment correlation, Pearson's r, or r.

Correlation matrix. A table showing the relationships among discrete measures.

Covert observation. Observation in which the observer's presence or purpose is kept secret from those being observed.

Critical theory. The philosophical stance that disciplines such as political science should assess society critically and seek to improve it, not merely study it objectively.

Cross-level analysis. The use of data at one level of aggregation to make inferences at another level of aggregation.

Cross-sectional design. A research design in which measurements of independent and dependent variables are taken at the same time; naturally occurring differences in the independent variable are used to create quasi-experimental and quasi-control groups; extraneous factors are controlled for by statistical means.

Cross-tabulation. Also called a cross-classification or contingency table, this array displays the joint frequencies and relative frequencies of two categorical (nominal or ordinal) variables.

Cumulative. Characteristic of scientific knowledge; new substantive findings and research techniques are built upon those of previous studies.

Cumulative proportion. The total proportion of observations at or below a value in a frequency distribution.

Data matrix. An array of rows and columns that stores the values of a set of variables for all the cases in a data set.

Deduction. A process of reasoning from a theory to specific observations.

Degrees of freedom. A measure used in conjunction with chi square and other measures to determine if a relationship is statistically significant.

Demand characteristics. Aspects of the research situation that cause participants to guess the purpose or rationale of the study and adjust their behavior or opinions accordingly.

Dependent variable. The phenomenon thought to be influenced, affected, or caused by some other phenomenon.

Descriptive statistic. A number that, because of its definition and formula, describes certain characteristics or properties of a batch of numbers.

Dichotomous variable. A nominal-level variable having only two categories that for certain analytical purposes can be treated as a quantitative variable.

Difference-of-means test. A technique for measuring the relationship between one nominal- or ordinal-level variable and one interval- or ratio-level variable.

Direct observation. Actual observation of behavior.

Direction of a relationship. An indication of which values of the dependent variable are associated with which values of the independent variable.

Directional hypothesis. A hypothesis that specifies the expected relationship between two or more variables.

Discriminant construct validity. Validity demonstrated by showing that the measure of a concept has a low correlation with the measure of another concept that is thought to be unrelated.

Dispersion. The distribution of data values around the most frequent, middle, or central value.

Disproportionate sample. A stratified sample in which elements sharing a characteristic are underrepresented or overrepresented in the sample.

Double-barreled question. A question that is really two questions in one.

Dummy variable. A hypothetical index that has just two values: 0 for the presence (or absence) of a factor and 1 for its absence (or presence).

Ecological fallacy. The fallacy of deducing a false relationship between the attributes or behavior of individuals based on observing that relationship for groups to which the individuals belong.

Ecological inference. The process of inferring a relationship between characteristics of individuals based on group or aggregate data.

Effect size. How and how much a change in one variable affects another variable, often measured as the difference between one mean and another, often between a treatment group and control group.

Electronic databases. A collection of information (of any type) stored on an electromagnetic medium that can be accessed and examined by certain computer programs.

Element. A particular case or entity about which information is collected; the unit of analysis.

Empirical frequency distribution (*f*). The number of observations per value or category of a variable.

Empirical generalization. A statement that summarizes the relationship between individual facts and that communicates general knowledge.

Empirical research. Research based on actual, "objective" observation of phenomena.

Episodic record. Record that is not part of a regular, ongoing record-keeping enterprise but instead is produced and preserved in a more casual, personal, or accidental manner.

Erosion measures. Measures of phenomena through indirect observation of selective wear of some material.

Estimator. A statistic based on sample observations that is used to estimate the numerical value of an unknown population parameter.

Eta-squared. A measure of association used with the analysis of variance that indicates what proportion of the variance in the dependent variable is explained by the variance in the independent variable.

Ethnography. A type of field study in which the researcher is deeply immersed in the place and lives of the people being studied.

Expected value. The mean or average value of a sample statistic based on repeated samples from a population.

Experiment. Research using a research design in which the researcher controls exposure to the test factor or independent variable, the assignment of subjects to groups, and the measurement of responses.

Experimental effect. Effect, usually measured numerically, of the experimental variable on the dependent variable.

Experimental group. A group of subjects that receives the experimental treatment or test stimulus.

Experimental mortality. A differential loss of subjects from experimental and control groups that affects the equivalency of groups; threat to internal validity.

Explanatory. Characteristic of scientific knowledge; signifying that a conclusion can be derived from a set of general propositions and specific initial considerations; providing a systematic, empirically verified understanding of why a phenomenon occurs as it does.

External validity. The ability to generalize from one set of research findings to other situations.

Face validity. Validity asserted by arguing that a measure corresponds closely to the concept it is designed to measure.

Factor analysis. A statistical technique useful in the construction of multi-item scales to measure abstract concepts.

Falsifiability. A property of a statement or hypothesis such that it can (in principle, at least) be rejected in the face of contravening evidence.

Field experiment. Experimental designs applied in a natural setting.

Field study. Open-ended and wide-ranging (rather than structured) pbservation in a natural setting.

Filter question. A question used to screen respondents so that subsequent questions will be asked only of certain respondents for whom the questions are appropriate.

Focused interview. A semistructured or flexible interview schedule used when interviewing elites.

Formal model. A simplified and abstract representation of reality that can be expressed verbally, mathematically, or in some other symbolic system and that purports to show how variables or parts of a system are interconnected.

Goodman and Kruskal's gamma. A measure of association between ordinal-level variables.

Goodman and Kruskal's lambda. A measure of association between one nominal- or ordinal-level variable and one nominal-level variable.

Guttman scale. A multi-item measure in which respondents are presented with increasingly difficult measures of approval for an attitude.

Histogram. A type of bar graph in which the height and area of the bars are proportional to the frequencies in each category of a categorical variable or intervals of a continuous variable.

Hypothesis. A tentative or provisional or unconfirmed statement that can (in principle) be verified.

Independent variable. The phenomenon thought to influence, affect, or cause some other phenomenon.

Indirect observation. Observation of physical traces of behavior.

Induction. A process of reasoning in which one draws an inference from a set of premises and observations; the premises of an inductive argument support its conclusion but do not prove it.

Informants. Persons who are willing to be interviewed about the activities and behavior of themselves and of the group to which they belong. An informant also helps the researcher engaged in participant observation to interpret group behavior.

Informed consent. Procedures that inform potential research subjects about the proposed research in which they are being asked to participate; the principle that researchers must obtain the freely given consent of human subjects before they participate in a research project.

Institutional review board. Panel to which researchers must submit descriptions of proposed research involving human subjects for the purpose of ethics review.

Interaction. The strength and direction of a relationship depend on an additional variable or variables.

Intercoder reliability. Demonstration that multiple analysts, following the same content analysis procedure, agree and obtain the same measurements.

Interitem association. A test of the extent to which the scores of several items, each thought to measure the same concept, are the same. Results are displayed in a correlation matrix.

Internal validity. The ability to show that manipulation or variation of the independent variable actually causes the dependent variable to change.

Interpretation. Philosophical approach to the study of human behavior that claims that one must understand the way individuals see their world in order to understand truly their behavior or actions; philosophical objection to the empirical approach to political science.

Interquartile range. The middle 50 percent of observations.

Interval measurement. A measure for which a one-unit difference in scores is the same throughout the range of the measure.

Intervening variable. A variable coming between an independent variable and a dependent variable in an explanatory scheme.

Intervention analysis. A nonexperimental time series design in which measurements of a dependent variable are taken both before and after the "introduction" of an independent variable.

Interviewer bias. The interviewer's influence on the respondent's answers; an example of reactivity.

Interviewing. Interviewing respondents in a nonstandardized, individualized manner.

Kendall's tau-*b* and tau-*c*. Measures of association between ordinal-level variables.

Leading question. A question that encourages the respondent to choose a particular response.

Level of measurement. The extent or degree to which the values of variables can be compared and mathematically manipulated.

Likert scale. A multi-item measure in which the items are selected based on their ability to discriminate between those scoring high and those scoring low on the measure.

Linear probability model. Regression model in which a dichotomous variable is treated as the dependent variable.

Literature review. A systematic examination and interpretation of the literature for the purpose of informing further work on a topic.

Logistic regression. A nonlinear regression model that relates a set of explanatory variables to a dichotomous dependent variable.

Logistic regression coefficient. A multiple regression coefficient based on the logistic model.

Mean. The sum of the values of a variable divided by the number of values.

Measurement. The process by which phenomena are observed systematically and represented by scores or numerals.

Measures of association. Statistics that summarize the relationship between two variables.

Median. The category or value above and below which one-half of the observations lie.

Mode. The category with the greatest frequency of observations.

Mokken scale. A type of scaling procedure that assesses the extent to which there is order in the responses of respondents to multiple items. Similar to Guttman scaling.

Multiple-group design. Experimental design with more than one control and experimental group.

Multiple regression analysis. A technique for measuring the mathematical relationships between more than one independent variable and a dependent variable while controlling for all other independent variables in the equation.

Multiple regression coefficient. A number that tells how much Y will change for a one-unit change in a particular independent variable, if all of the other variables in the model have been held constant.

Multivariate analysis. Data analysis techniques designed to test hypotheses involving more than two variables.

Multivariate cross-tabulation. A procedure by which cross-tabulation is used to control for a third variable.

Negative relationship. A relationship in which high values of one variable are associated with low values of another variable.

Negatively skewed. A distribution of values in which fewer observations lie to the left of the middle value and those observations are fairly distant from the mean.

Nominal measurement. A measure for which different scores represent different, but not ordered, categories.

Nonnormative knowledge. Knowledge concerned not with evaluation or prescription but with factual or objective determinations.

Nonprobability sample. A sample for which each element in the total population has an unknown probability of being selected.

Normal distribution. A distribution defined by a mathematical formula and the graph of which has a symmetrical bell shape; in which the mean, the mode, and the median coincide; and in which a fixed proportion of observations lies between the mean and any distance from the mean measured in terms of the standard deviation.

Normative knowledge. Knowledge that is evaluative, value laden, and concerned with prescribing what ought to be.

Null hypothesis. A statement that a population parameter equals a single or specific value; the hypothesis that there is no relationship between two variables in the target population. Often a statement that the difference between two populations is zero.

Open-ended question. A question with no response alternatives provided for the respondent.

Operational definition. The rules by which a concept is measured and scores assigned.

Ordinal measurement. A measure for which the scores represent ordered categories that are not necessarily equidistant from each other.

Overt observation. Observation in which those being observed are informed of the observer's presence and purpose.

Parsimony. The principle that among explanations or theories with equal degrees of confirmation, the simplest—the one based on the fewest assumptions and explanatory factors—is to be preferred; sometimes known as Ockham's razor.

Partial regression coefficient. A number that indicates how much a dependent variable would change if an independent variable changed one unit and all other variables in the equation or model were held constant.

Participant observation. Observation in which the observer becomes a regular participant in the activities of those being observed.

Period effect. An indicator or measure of history effects on a dependent variable during a specified time.

Phi. An association measure that adjusts an observed chi-square statistic by the sample size.

Pie chart. A circular graphic display of a frequency distribution.

Policy evaluation. Objective analysis of economic, political, cultural, or social effects of public policies.

Political science. The application of the methods of acquiring scientific knowledge to the study of political phenomena.

Population. All the cases or observations covered by a hypothesis; all the units of analysis to which a hypothesis applies.

Population parameter. A characteristic or an attribute in a population (not a sample) that can be quantified.

Positive relationship. A relationship in which the values of one variable increase (or decrease) as the values of another variable increase (or decrease); a relationship in which high values of one variable are associated with high values of another variable.

Positively skewed. A distribution of values in which fewer observations lie to the right of the middle value and those observations are fairly distant from the mean.

Posttest design. Research design in which the dependent variable is measured after, but not before, manipulation of the independent variable.

Pretest. Measurement of the dependent variable prior to the administration of the experimental treatment or manipulation of the independent variable.

Primary data. Data recorded and used by the researcher who is making the observations.

Probabilistic explanation. An explanation that does not explain or predict events with 100 percent accuracy.

Probability sample. A sample for which each element in the total population has a known probability of being selected.

Proportionate reduction in error (*PRE*) measure. A measure of association that indicates how much knowledge of the value of the independent variable of a case improves prediction of the dependent variable compared to the prediction of the dependent variable based on no knowledge of the case's value on the independent variable. Examples are Goodman and Kruskal's lambda, Goodman and Kruskal's gamma, eta-squared, and *R*-squared.

Proportionate sample. A probability sample that draws elements from a stratified population at a rate proportional to size of the samples.

Pure, theoretical, or recreational research. Research designed to satisfy one's intellectual curiosity about some phenomenon.

Purposive sample. A nonprobability sample in which a researcher uses discretion in selecting elements for observation.

Push poll. A poll intended not to collect information but to feed respondents (often) false and damaging information about a candidate or cause.

Quasi-experimental design. A research design that includes treatment and control groups to which individuals are not assigned randomly.

Questionnaire design. The physical layout and packaging of a questionnaire.

Question-order effect. The effect on responses of question placement within a questionnaire.

Quota sample. A nonprobability sample in which elements are sampled in proportion to their representation in the population.

Random digit dialing. A procedure used to improve the representativeness of telephone samples by giving both listed and unlisted numbers a chance of selection.

Randomization. The random assignment of subjects to experimental and control groups.

Randomized response technique. A method of obtaining accurate answers to sensitive questions that protects the respondent's privacy.

Range. The distance between the highest and lowest values or the range of categories into which observations fall.

Ratio measurement. A measure for which the scores possess the full mathematical properties of the numbers assigned.

Reactivity. Effect of data collection or measurement on the phenomenon being measured.

Regression analysis. A technique for measuring the relationship between two interval- or ratio-level variables.

Regression coefficient. A statistic that tells how much the dependent variable changes per unit change in the independent variable.

Regression constant. Value of the dependent variable when all of the values of the independent variables in the equation equal zero.

Relationship. The association, dependence, or covariance of the values of one variable with the values of another variable.

Relative frequency. Percentage or proportion of total number of observations in a frequency distribution that have a particular value.

Reliability. The extent to which a measure yields the same results on repeated trials.

Repeated-measurement design. A plan that calls for making more than one measure or observation on a dependent variable at different times over the course of the study.

Research design. A plan specifying how the researcher intends to fulfill the goals of the study; a logical plan for testing hypotheses.

Residuals. Differences between observed values of a dependent variable and those predicted by a specified model (e.g., linear regression).

Resistant measure. A measure of central tendency that is not sensitive to one or a few extreme values in a distribution.

Response quality. The extent to which responses provide accurate and complete information.

Response rate. The proportion of respondents selected for participation in a survey who actually participate.

Response set. The pattern of responding to a series of questions in a similar fashion without careful reading of each question.

R-squared. The proportion of the total variation in a dependent variable explained by an independent variable.

Running record. A written record that is enduring and easily accessed and covers an extensive period.

Sample. A subset of observations or cases drawn from a specified population.

Sample bias. The bias that occurs whenever some elements of a population are systematically excluded from a sample. It is usually due to an incomplete sampling frame or a nonprobability method of selecting elements.

Sample statistic. The estimator of a population characteristic or attribute that is calculated from sample data.

Sample-population congruence. The degree to which sample subjects represent the population from which they are drawn.

Sampling distribution. A theoretical (nonobserved) distribution of sample statistics calculated on samples of size N that, if known, permits the calculation of confidence intervals and the test of statistical hypotheses.

Sampling error. The difference between a sample estimate and a corresponding population parameter that arises because only a portion of a population is observed.

Sampling fraction. The proportion of the population included in a sample.

Sampling frame. The population from which a sample is drawn. Ideally it is the same as the total population of interest to a study.

Sampling interval. The number of elements in a sampling frame divided by the desired sample size.

Sampling unit. The entity listed in a sampling frame. It may be the same as an element, or it may be a group or cluster of elements.

Scatterplot. A graph that plots joint values of an independent variable along one axis (usually the x-axis) and a dependent variable along the other axis (usually the y-axis).

Search engine. A computer program that visits Web pages on the Internet and looks for those containing particular directories or words.

Search term. A word or phrase entered into a computer program (a search engine) that looks through Web pages on the Internet for those that contain the word or phrase.

Secondary data. Data used by a researcher that were not personally collected by that researcher.

Selection bias. Bias due to the assignment of subjects to experimental and control groups according to some criterion and not randomly; threat to internal validity.

Simple random sample. A probability sample in which each element has an equal chance of being selected.

Simulation. A simple representation of a system in order to study its behavior.

Single-sided question. A question in which the respondent is asked to agree or disagree with a single substantive statement.

Small-*N* design. A research design in which the researcher examines one or a few cases of a phenomenon in considerable detail.

Snowball sample. A sample in which respondents are asked to identify additional members of a population.

Social facts. Values and institutions that have a subjective existence in the minds of people living in a particular culture.

Somers' *D*. A measure of association between ordinal-level variables.

Split-halves method. A method of calculating reliability by comparing the results of two equivalent measures made at the same time.

Standard deviation. A measure of dispersion of data points about the mean for interval- and ratio-level data.

Standard error. The standard deviation or measure of variability or dispersion of a sampling distribution.

Standardized regression coefficient. A coefficient that measures the effects of an independent variable on a dependent variable in standard deviation units.

Standardized variable. A rescaled variable obtained by subtracting the mean from each value of the variable and dividing the quotient by the standard deviation.

Statistical independence. A property of two variables where the probability that an observation is in a particular category of one variable and a particular category of the other variable equals the simple or marginal probability of being in those categories.

Statistical inference. The mathematical theory and techniques for making conjectures about the unknown characteristics (parameters) of populations based on samples.

Statistical regression. Change in the dependent variable due to the temporary nature of extreme values; threat to internal validity.

Statistical significance. The probability of making a type I error.

Stratified sample. A probability sample in which elements sharing one or more characteristics are grouped and elements are selected from each group in proportion to the group's representation in the total population.

Stratum. A subgroup of a population that shares one or more characteristics.

Structured observation. Systematic observation and recording of the incidence of specific behaviors.

Summation index. A multi-item measure in which individual scores on a set of items are combined to form a summary measure.

Survey instrument. The schedule of questions to be asked of the respondent.

Systematic sample. A probability sample in which elements are selected from a list at predetermined intervals.

Tautology. A hypothesis in which the independent and dependent variables are identical, making it impossible to disconfirm.

Test stimulus or test factor. The independent variable introduced and controlled by an investigator in order to assess its effects on a response or dependent variable.

Test-retest method. A method of calculating reliability by repeating the same measure at two or more points in time.

Theory. A statement or series of related statements that organize, explain, and predict phenomena.

Time series design. A research design (sometimes called a longitudinal design) featuring multiple measurements of the dependent variable before and after experimental treatment.

Total variation. A numerical measure of the variation in a variable, determined by summing the squared deviation of each observation from the mean.

Transmissible. Characteristic of scientific knowledge; indicates that the methods used in making scientific discoveries are made explicit so that others can analyze and replicate findings.

Trend analysis. Research design that measures a dependent variable at different times and attempts to determine whether the level of the variable is changing and, if it is, why.

Trimmed mean. The mean calculated by excluding a specified proportion of cases from each end of the distribution.

Two-sided question. A question with two substantive alternatives provided for the respondent.

Type I error. Error made by rejecting a null hypothesis when it is true.

Type II error. Error made by failing to reject a null hypothesis when it is not true.

Unit of analysis. The type of actor (individual, group, institution, nation) specified in a researcher's hypothesis.

Unstructured observation. Observation in which all behavior and activities are recorded.

Validity. The correspondence between a measure and the concept it is supposed to measure.

Variance. A measure of dispersion of data points about the mean for interval- and ratio-level data.

Weighting factor. A mathematical factor used to make a disproportionate sample representative.

Written record. Documents, reports, statistics, manuscripts, and other recorded materials available and useful for empirical research.

z score. The number of standard deviations by which a score deviates from the mean score.

Index

Boxes, figures, notes, and tables are indicated with b, f, n, and t following the page number.